THE LETTERS
OF
J. R. ACKERLEY

Edited by
Neville Braybrooke

'We have only a little time to please the living,
but all eternity to love the dead'

Sophocles

'There is no wealth but life'

Ruskin

Duckworth

First published by Gerald Duckworth & Company Ltd 1975

© 1975 letters Nancy West
© 1975 introduction and commentary Neville Braybrooke

ISBN 0 7156 0642 5

Printed in Great Britain
by W & J Mackay Limited, Chatham

The Letters of J. R. Ackerley

J. R. Ackerley in 1960

'definitive edition', not for present action, which is not on the cards, but for your archives. It is how I would have liked the book to appear, and i care Raymond Mortimer sh? be sytised, years hence, when I am under the sod, the book sh? become a 'classic', you now have the full text as originally worked it out — so much better than my falterings — i your hands.

The 'improper' bits — which scarcely merit the term 'improper' — and one or two too dangerous civil-libel bits, which I was also sorry to remove, you will find restored on separate sheets.

Ackerley's handwriting. Extract from a letter to Colin Haycraft in 1962 (Letter 218)

CONTENTS

Contents

Contents

BIBLIOGRAPHY OF FIRST PUBLICATIONS

The Prisoners of War: A Play. London, Chatto & Windus, 1925. Begun 1918. Completed 1925.

Poems by Four Authors. Cambridge, Bowes & Bowes, 1923. Included ten poems by Ackerley. The other poets were Archibald Y. Campbell, Edward Davison and Frank Kendon.

Hindoo Holiday: An Indian Journal. London, Chatto & Windus, 1932. Begun 1923. Completed 1931.

Escapers All: The Personal Narratives of Fifteen Escapers from War-time Prison Camps, 1914–1918. Edited, with an Introduction, by Ackerley. London, The Bodley Head, 1932. Begun 1931. Completed 1932.

My Dog Tulip: Life with an Alsatian. London, Secker & Warburg, 1956. Begun 1954. Completed 1955.

We Think the World of You: A Novel. London, The Bodley Head, 1960. Begun 1948. Completed 1959.

My Father and Myself: A Family Memoir. London, The Bodley Head, 1968. Begun 1932. Completed 1967. Published posthumously.

E. M. Forster: A Portrait. London, Ian McKelvie, 1970. Begun 1967. Completed 1967. Published posthumously.

Micheldever & Other Poems. London, Ian McKelvie, 1972. Edited, with an Introduction, by Francis King. Published posthumously.

INTRODUCTION

I

I met J. R. Ackerley on three occasions, each time with Queenie, his alsatian bitch, and exchanged five letters with him during the last decade of his life. Yet long before I had heard his name, I was an admirer of the Book Chronicle, which he ran in *The Listener*. In the war, I spent many hours in the school library going through back numbers and cutting out the reviews that interested me. (In those days, and until 1958, they were generally unsigned.) I also copied out some of the poems—though this, on my part, was a form of editorial cribbing, since at the time I was running a 'little review' with some school friends, and whenever I saw a poem which pleased me, I would write to the poet and suggest that he should contribute to *The Wind and the Rain*. I remember receiving one such poem, accompanied by a note signed 'Starving and Forgotten John Betjeman'. Others came from Frances Bellerby, Richard Church, Clifford Dyment, James Kirkup, Lilian Bowes Lyon, Hal Summers and Vernon Watkins. Shortly after Ackerley died in 1967, Frances Bellerby wrote to *The Listener* on 22 June: 'He had a kind of personal genius as editor of poetry; and is unforgettable.'

At his death, Ackerley left behind him an autobiography cast in the form of a family memoir. He had completed *My Father and Myself* in March—though there is not a word in it about his literary editorship of *The Listener*. It is characteristic of his modesty and leaves a gap to be filled.

R. S. Lambert, the first Editor of *The Listener* (which had been founded in 1929), regarded Ackerley as 'a catch'. Never before on his staff had he employed somebody 'who had swum in so many different waters'. Ackerley's father might have spoken jestingly of his son's waiter friends and of the members of the Army, the Navy and the Police Force who had sat at his table, but many had good tales to tell and had been persuaded to record them at the BBC, where Ackerley had first been engaged by the Corporation as an assistant producer in the Talks Department in 1928. A number of these talks had later been enthusiastically accepted and reprinted by Lambert.

It went without saying that Ackerley had scores of literary contacts. His play *The Prisoners of War*, which had been tried out at the Three Hundred Club in the summer of 1925, had been transferred to the West End in the autumn. In the BBC Records Office at Savoy Hill in 1928, he was listed as 'a coming playwright', and Arnold Bennett in his journals at this period refers to 'Ackerley the dramatist'.

When Ackerley took up his appointment at *The Listener* in 1935, Lambert had plans for a series of articles built round the eighteenth-century Grand Tour, which would show what a modern traveller would find if he were to follow the same route, and the first letter (20)[1] that Ackerley dictated in the office, on his first day there on 15 April, was an

---

[1] Numbers in brackets refer to Letters to be found in the main text.

invitation to Norman Douglas to contribute. Douglas had been an early admirer of Ackerley's Indian journal *Hindoo Holiday*, which had come out in 1932 and gone into three impressions within three days. 'A book . . . difficult to praise . . . temperately' had been Evelyn Waugh's verdict on 16 April in the *Spectator*.

Ackerley, like his predecessor Janet Adam Smith, was responsible for the literary and art pages of the paper. But the latter provided him with the greater challenge, because although he himself could sketch prettily enough (some of his line drawings had been used in *Hindoo Holiday*), he was 'quite ignorant' of the theory of art and its history. In India, in the early 1920s, he had made a few cursory notes about the sodomitic sculptures in the Gahara temples, but as far as European art was concerned his notebook had remained a blank. So, as soon as he had settled into his new office, he began to teach himself about painting, and modern art in particular. He tried out a number of art critics, attending the same exhibitions as they did and then meticulously going through their manuscripts, checking facts and, now and again, querying an opinion. Yet to find art critics who combined knowledge, intelligence and style was no easy matter: so many had the first two attributes but not the third. In 1939, therefore, he drew up a short list, and would have run it in rotation for ever if Alan Thomas, the second Editor of *The Listener*, had not objected. The list consisted of three names—Sir Kenneth Clark, Roger Hinks and Herbert Read.

In the BBC archives I came across no copies of letters of interest to Roger Hinks, but several to Sir Kenneth Clark—and have included them. Herbert Read's papers have been lodged by his family at the University of Victoria in British Columbia, and among them there are twenty Ackerley letters: I have selected seven. In Sir Kenneth, Ackerley found an admirable adviser ('I wish you would . . . put down . . . some people you think well of as critics of art'), and in Read he found a marvellous standby, who could be called upon to write about poetry, politics or art at a moment's notice. A story current in Broadcasting House in 1936 records a meeting between Lambert and Ackerley in the corridors, which went something like this:

LAMBERT (*looking at his watch*): Half-past three, Joe.
ACKERLEY: I've been out with Herbert Read.
LAMBERT: You seem to be entertaining him rather a lot.
ACKERLEY: He's teaching me about modern art.
LAMBERT: Yes— but is it necessary to lunch him five times a week at the Café Royal?
ACKERLEY: It's not only modern art. It's Korean art, Chinese art, Japanese art and Red Indian art.

Often though, Ackerley had to contend with the Corporation's attitude —'We are not amused.' This was because, in the words of Alan Thomas, he 'was ahead of his times'. Thomas took over as Editor just before the Second World War, and in 1940 Ackerley was rebuked by the new Director-General for printing on 19 December a poem by Sidney Keyes entitled 'Remember Your Lovers'. It contained the word 'lust' (115).

A decade earlier Janet Adam Smith had been summoned by the first Director-General, who had wanted to know why, in a special poetry supplement published on 12 July 1933, there had been so much verse that seemed 'odd', 'uncouth' and 'puzzling'. He had singled out for special comment 'The Witnesses' by W. H. Auden.

In passing, this seems the place to pay tribute to Janet Adam Smith, the first literary editor of *The Listener*. During her six years on the paper, she not only launched many young poets and reviewers, but published articles by Paul Nash, Eric Newton, John Piper and Herbert Read in which the work of then little known painters—among them William Coldstream, Tristram Hillier and Victor Pasmore—was both discussed and illustrated (58). This pioneering tradition which she inaugurated, Ackerley continued; and long after her departure he continued to consult her. In 1938, for example, he was 'badly stuck' for an article on Scottish painting to coincide with the opening of the Empire Exhibition at Glasgow. So, he sent her an urgent note on 24 March, asking if she knew anybody who could 'do it nicely and also objectively'. He ended: 'It is quite illegitimate to bother you with such questions as these, but I feel sure you won't mind . . .' Over the years, there were a good many of these 'botherations' —as he called them.

If in retrospect it is hard to see why Janet Adam Smith should have been catechised about Auden's poem, or why Ackerley should have been rebuked for printing Sidney Keyes's poem, then the catechising and rebuke must be seen in the context of the times. In the early 1930s there was in Broadcasting House a fear of being associated with 'bolshie poetry', and in the early 1940s there was an automatic ban in BBC publications against certain references to sex: 'I have been . . . stopped using a poem containing the word "brothel" . . . [so] I should scarcely therefore be permitted one which contained the words "harlotry" and "randy",' Ackerley wrote to Alex Comfort on 27 January 1941. It must of course be remembered at the same time that Ackerley definitely liked to shock.

In the early 1950s he wanted to publish a poem by James Kirkup about a public urinal. Marjorie Redman, the chief sub-editor on the paper since 1930, struck. Right from the beginning she had been behind Janet Adam Smith in crusading for modern poetry, but this was too much. Let her take up the story:

There the poem was, on the peg, and every female member of the staff was revolted by it. So I reported this to the Editor. He said defensively: 'Joe is a very very good literary editor'. I said: 'Yes. All the same do we want to read about the smell coming out of a women's lavatory?' I then withdrew, remarking as I went that as probably 50 per cent of

Listener readers were female, probably 50 per cent would not care for Kirkup's poem. I never mentioned the matter again to anyone and no one mentioned it to me.

There are two ways to regard Marjorie Redman's protest—as an act of editorial mutiny, or as a stand in the name of good taste. The artist, it can be claimed, is free to express everything—and male and female smells have been described before in poetry and prose.

Ackerley's book *My Dog Tulip*, which he wrote while at *The Listener*, deals with the subject on a canine level. Sub-titled 'Life with an Alsatian', there are scenes in which the author describes her two kinds of urination, distinguishing between when she pees out of necessity and when she does so for social reasons and the marking out of territory. Yet these scenes fill less than four pages out of 158, and form a small but integral part of the whole. In contrast, a weekly journal is made up of contributions from a number of writers, and when a poem is isolated there, it may give a different impression from when it is printed as part of a poet's collection. Anyway, Marjorie Redman's protest was heeded and the Editor bowed to it. 'Yes, Joe Ackerley certainly liked to shock,' she wrote to me on 15 February 1973. Or, as he himself wrote to Stephen Spender (136):

> I think that people *ought* to be upset, and if I had a paper I would upset them all the time; I think that life is so important and, in its workings, so upsetting that nobody should be spared, but that it should [be] rammed down their throats from morning to night. And may those that cannot take it die of it . . .

Ackerley not only liked to upset, but to tease. He loathed censorship of any kind—even a dog's lead he thought a form of censorship—and his criteria remained entirely aesthetic. But sometimes, in the words of Maurice Ashley, the third Editor of *The Listener*, 'he tried to "get away with things" —though acquiesced with the best humour . . . if caught out'.

On 4 November 1959, the day of his 63rd birthday, Ackerley retired from *The Listener*. He had been there for nearly a quarter of a century, and could boast during that period never to have 'cut' a single word without first consulting an author.

'Those splendid business-like briefs' is how Janet Adam Smith recalls the slips which he sent her with review books, after she had left the paper. Sometimes he would begin these briefs: 'Dear Friend'—a habit perhaps acquired during his stay at the court of Chhatarpur whose Maharajah had sent him notes begun in this fashion. Or, often on proofs, Ackerley would scribble a few words of encouragement: John Holloway and Francis King remember how much this meant to them at the beginning of their careers. More established authors at the time never forgot these notes. 'What a pleasure they were to get in his lovely handwriting,' Elizabeth Bowen said to me in 1969. Philip Larkin's first published poem, apart from contributions to his school magazine, was 'Ultimatum', which appeared in *The Listener* on 28 November 1949. The slip accepting it had been initialled 'J.R.A.' 'I have never forgotten receiving it,' he told me. David Wright searched unsuccessfully for some Ackerley letters, dating back to the early 1940s—and wrote:

> He was the 1st editor of a commercially viable paper to publish my poems, & the only one (apart from Howard Moss of *The New Yorker*) to query intelligently the meaning/relevance of particular lines.

It was Ackerley's firm editorial principle, as he once wrote to Herbert Read, that 'no distinction should be made between strangers and friends, and everyone should be treated as Mr Smith'. Certainly his own friends were not immune from having their own books severely criticised by himself, or by his team of critics. He admired Wyndham Lewis, and after the war took him on as an art critic. Twice, in the late 1940s, he wrote to congratulate him on his powerfully phrased articles—once about a Robert Colquhoun exhibition (85), and once on his Edward Wadsworth obituary (95). Yet when Lewis turned in a disappointing review in 1952 of Augustus John's autobiography *Chiaroscuro*, Ackerley was prepared to explain to him the reasons for his disappointment (108). A marked feature of his correspondence is the forthright honesty of his reactions to writers of all generations.

In 1951, when Richard Murphy had his first poem accepted by *The Listener*, he was 23. In January, he had submitted it and in February Ackerley had sent him a number of criticisms: 'And "pelvised"; is there such a word?' (101). Murphy then revised it, re-submitted it, and 'Snow' was published on 27 September. Nine years later, Ackerley wrote to Murphy about another poem:

> You thought [it] finished . . . when you first brought it . . . but it was not . . . It is hardly possible to give too much trouble and thought to the perfecting of any work that one loves: How bitter it is to see the light when one's work is in print and it is too late . . .

That twofold moral he was to expound again and again.

Yet the courtesy and hospitality which he had extended to contributors were not always extended to him. On his retirement from *The Listener*, it was planned that a party should be given at Broadcasting House to bid him farewell and at the same time introduce his successor. The Corporation thought a tea-party would do, and it was only under considerable pressure from the Editor that they agreed to make it a cocktail party (176, 177).

Sometimes, too, when Ackerley reviewed for other papers, he did not receive the same consideration which had marked his own dealings with reviewers. In 1963 the *Sunday Times* sent him *Douchka* by Colette Audry, and asked for 400 words. His notice appeared on 3 November. A few days later he wrote to Donald Windham in New York:

. . . I have just done, with infinite trouble, a review of a dog book for
[the *Sunday Times*], and although it was the exact number of words
and they said it was 'admirable', they have massacred it in their
columns without asking *me* to do the 'cuts' or informing me at all. I do
hate that, don't you, in a signed review, all one's carefully constructed
and balanced sentences ripped to pieces; 25 guineas is no compensation
to my mind . . .

In that fit of righteous indignation, Ackerley perhaps unconsciously
defined his genius as a literary editor. His own prose, he would say, made a
kind of rhythm in his head, and everything sounded discordantly wrong
unless it sounded right. There is a right word for everything in the English
language, and his search for it was unending.

It was this love of precision, coupled with a deep respect for other
men's words, which brought Ackerley the best writers of every generation—
often as unsigned reviewers, even when, like E. M. Forster, Christopher
Isherwood or Edwin Muir, they disapproved of anonymity. Auden, who
was born in 1907, spoke for a whole generation when he said: '*The Listener*
in the 1930s was one of our main outlets . . . ' The fees might be a quarter
of those offered by the serious Sunday newspapers, but such was Ackerley's
charm and reputation that he never seems to have experienced the slightest
difficulty in persuading anyone to write—or even draw for him. On one
occasion, Marie Laurencin sent him a sketch of three of her models, and on
another, Rouault a painting of a clown. He had met neither—but simply
approached them out of the blue; and the fee for an original work that he
had been able to offer in each case had been no more than £10. Only once
did he have to dispute about 'the delicate question of payment', and that
was in 1936 with John Maynard Keynes. The exchange can be found in
Appendix B.

Ackerley told me that the key to being a successful literary editor was
curiosity: 'I read everything in sight—histories of the Ottoman Empire,
instructions on patent medicines, bus-tickets, anything.' W. J. H. Sprott,
one of his oldest friends from his Cambridge days, remarked once that it
was as a result of Ackerley's wide reading that he knew 'exactly which
expert to approach on pretty well any subject'. Sprott was Ackerley's
expert on sociology, and if Ackerley saw an important study of penal
reform announced, he would contact Sprott and then send him everything on the subject which had amassed on the shelves, so that when the
time came for the review to be written, only the most significant books
would be chosen. An incidental advantage of the system, therefore, was
that no book of any worth was passed over—even if it had been out for as
long as half a year.

For fiction, Ackerley used a similar system, only fortnightly, and for
poetry, every other month. When John Lehmann took on a stint of novel
reviewing in 1953, he informed him: '. . . I shall send you everything that
comes, excepting palpable trash' (111). Thus, without fear or favour, a
reviewer was free to select the best novels or books of poems, and those

coming from small presses had just as good a chance of being noticed as those from the old-established firms. Excellence was the one criterion.

Not every publisher appreciated Ackerley's methods. In 1942 Evelyn Waugh's *Put Out More Flags* went unreviewed in *The Listener*, because no copy was sent in by Chapman & Hall. When Ackerley rang up to inquire why, he was told that the publishers had confined their review-list to twenty-five papers, that *The Listener* was not amongst these—though it then had a circulation of 100,000 and Edwin Muir was its fiction critic— and that they did not consider enough of their books had been reviewed in the past (67). So Ackerley took the matter up direct with the author, and Waugh saw that it never happened again.

2

J. R. Ackerley wrote four books, three of which became classics during his lifetime. The fourth, a family memoir called *My Father and Myself*, was published in 1968—a year after his death. From time to time he contributed poems to anthologies and magazines, and the publication of a three-act play in 1925 coincided with its first performance in London.

Siegfried Sassoon, who attended the first production of *The Prisoners of War*, told Lady Ottoline Morrell that it was 'the most powerful . . . and the most impressive play' that he had ever seen; thirty years later its remembered merits became the subject of a correspondence in *The Times*, and in the autumn of 1955 it was revived in the West End. *Hindoo Holiday*, sub-titled 'An Indian Journal', appeared in 1932, and the Aga Khan declared that 'it showed more understanding of India than any other book . . . by an Englishman—including Kipling': he named a race horse after it, and Penguins issued it among their early paperbacks. In 1956 *My Dog Tulip* came out, only to be remaindered before the end of the decade: when it was reprinted in the 1960s, Christopher Isherwood proclaimed it 'one of the greatest masterpieces of animal literature'. The novel *We Think the World of You* was turned down by a dozen firms in England, France and America; yet when it was finally published in 1960, it won the W. H. Smith £1,000 Literary Award: the judges were Elizabeth Bowen, Harold Nicolson and Philip Toynbee.

This is a small output, perhaps, for 'over 50 years of non-stop writing'— but Ackerley was, above all, a perfectionist. Parts of *My Dog Tulip* went through ten draftings, and in Appendix C details are given of five drafts of a poem on which he worked for more than eighteen years. Towards the end of his life, he would frequently devote a whole day to composing a letter (277). 'Compose' is the operative word, because he gave considerable thought and preparation to letter-writing. Seldom did he cross out sentences, and if now and again he dropped a word then this is not surprising when it is remembered that in his later years he might have been several gins up before he settled to his correspondence. On 1 June 1965 he wrote to Francis King:

You would certainly find [my letters] repetitious, if you ever put yourself to the sweat of trying to collect them, for if what seems to me a funny remark crosses my mind when I am writing to anyone, it is sure to get into all my correspondence of that time—perhaps a little improved on the way—so that all my letters of a particular period would be found to be pretty much the same.

It is true that repetitions do occur—but each time they are adapted for the individual to whom they are addressed. Four times, over a period of weeks, he notes that the tadpole of the Common Frog has 640 teeth: once as a pretext to describe a mutual friend who, though toothless, has recently snapped at him (294); twice to recall a session at the dentist (297, 298); and on the last occasion as a device to end a discourse on Zen-Buddhism and thus close on a less mystical note (302). And many of the stories that he related took surprising turns as he developed them.

On 6 November 1966 he wrote to William Plomer about a visit to the fishmonger and of his thoughts on seeing a live eel chopped up for a customer. At Christmas, Sir Kenneth Clark sent him a copy of his Ruskin anthology *Ruskin Today* (1964), drawing his attention to the Ruskin aphorism: 'There is no wealth but life.' Later still, in a letter to David Sylvester (326), Ackerley repeated the eel story, but placed the Ruskin aphorism in a new context by linking it to E. M. Forster's variation on it: 'There is no wealth but *human* life.'

3

On 4 November 1896 Joe Randolph Ackerley was born at Herne Hill. At the turn of the century the family moved to Bowdon in Cheshire, and from there he and his elder brother Peter were later sent to Rossall School in Lancashire.

During his teens, Joe began to write poetry—though he never submitted any to *The Rossallian*. Instead, he published it in *The Wasp*, a magazine of his own invention. One poem in praise of an elder boy nearly led him to being beaten by his housemaster, and would have done so, had he not pleaded that he had imposed a moral on his verses by giving them the title 'Millstones'. Yet no sooner had he left Rossall than he sent in a twelve-stanza poem, which was immediately accepted by the school magazine for their November 1914 issue. 'The Young Adventurers' is about two brothers who set out in an open boat, but whose bravado exceeds their heroism. It was a theme that Joe was to explore further as a dramatist and a poet.

In the trenches on the Western front, and later as a prisoner in Germany and then as an internee in Switzerland, Joe continued to write poetry. An epic running to 124 lines, entitled 'The Everlasting Terror', was completed on the eve of the battle of the Somme: he sent it to *The English Review*, where it was published in November 1916.

During the early months of 1918, in Switzerland, Joe began drafting *The Prisoners of War*. The play is a study of the degeneration of character of five interned officers, four British and one Canadian, who have been quartered for half a year in the same hotel in Mürren and now 'know too much about each other'; the war is drawing towards its finish—and the atmosphere between them is highly explosive.

The central figure, Captain Jim Conrad, is a self-portrait of Captain Joe Ackerley. He is homosexually oriented—though still a virgin. Madame Louis, a flirtatious Swiss widow living nearby, baits him: 'I hear you do not care greatly for the fair sex.'

'The fair sex?' he snaps back. 'Which is that?'

At the 1955 revival, Joe noted that this retort was 'gratefully remembered by elderly homosexuals' who had seen the first production. But he himself was irritated when reviewers and some of his younger friends classified it as a homosexual play. 'The rest [of the characters],' he insisted, 'are entirely normal' (132). This certainty within himself of the heterosexual element in his play is perhaps further brought out by the fact that of the many fan letters which he received, he kept only one—and that was from an unknown woman who wrote: 'Yr. play is sad but ennobling. That beautiful interpretation you give of marriage . . . we shall always remember as one of our "high-lights" in the . . . theatre.' This letter was discovered in Joe's desk after his death, and showed signs of having been constantly read.

In Switzerland, Joe had with him a copy of Plutarch's *Lives*, and in the play there is a scene where Lieutenant Adelby borrows Captain Conrad's copy. Adelby recalls how stirred he was as a boy by the tales of the heroes:

. . . The Theban band! . . . It's a pity we've lost all that, that great hero-worship. Each man used to take his intimate friend to war with him, didn't he? And they'd protect each other. It gave a man something *real* to fight for . . .

Joe's search for such an intimate friend had begun at Rossall, and was to continue until he went up to Cambridge in 1919. There, it gradually became transformed into a search for an Ideal Friend—by which he meant a sexual partner. At Magdalene, he saw many of his contemporaries form successful 'alliances' with men of their own class, and some with those of their own kind but from a lower social level. In this sense he himself never set up house with any partner permanently, and the longest sexual relationship that he sustained—four years—was with a sailor based in Portsmouth.

Yet his capacity for friendship in the wider sense, as this book reveals, was boundless. On the last page of his last diary, he inscribed from the *Antigone* of Sophocles the line: 'We have only a little time to please the living, but all eternity to love the dead.' Two months previously, William Plomer and Jack Sprott had suggested inviting his friends to a party to celebrate his 70th birthday. 'Yes,' he had replied, 'on my 80th birthday

you may do that . . . On this occasion take me out, just the two of you
. . . and Morgan also if he can come . . .' (318).

His friendship with Morgan Forster dated back to 1922—and was to
prove the most momentous in his life. 'Dear Ackerley,' began the first
letter on 26 April:

> I should have met you last week in town but have done so in *The
> London Mercury* instead. I wish it wasn't so hard to praise intelligently.
> Apart from liking your poem ['Ghosts'], what I like in your poem is its
> combination of the reminiscent and the dramatic—I mean that one
> knows about it all in the opening lines, and yet it develops with the
> cleanness and unexpectedness of a play . . . Without drama, a poem's
> a museum, without reminiscence it isn't a poem . . .

At the time, Morgan was 43 and Joe 26; but a year was to pass before they
actually met.

When this happened, Morgan must have been dazzled by the young
man's looks. For he was tall and golden-haired, with finely-cut features;
and if his mouth was thin and rather sternly compressed, it could suddenly
break into an amazingly sweet smile. Joe had been brought up to expect
admiration. His mother doted on her younger son, and referred to him
frequently in his hearing as 'an adonis'. After his brother Peter was killed
just before the Armistice, Joe became the focus of his father's and mother's
attention.

At Cambridge, when he had a fancy to turn from reading Law to English
Literature, no criticism came from his parents. If he got into debt, he had
only to ask and his bills would be paid. When Joe first met Morgan in
January 1923, he had an allowance of £350 a year from his father, most of
which he spent on clothes which were both expensive and theatrical—
'corduroys, cloaks, flowered waistcoats'. The impact that he made on his
fellow undergraduates is illustrated by the remark of one, which he saw fit
to record in a journal some quarter of a century later: 'I wish to God I had
your looks. I'd have a love affair with anyone I wanted.'

In contrast, Morgan had none of Joe's physical advantages. Shorter in
stature, his broad face tapered away into rather a weak chin; he had wispy
hair and a moustache; and in his old cloth cap and shabby raincoat, he
reminded his friend William Plomer of the man who came to wind the
clocks. 'It is awfully difficult,' he confided in Joe, 'for the undistinguished-
looking . . . to think of the problems of the good-looking.' So, when
within two months of their meeting, Morgan was to discover that Joe's
mother was related to the Forsters, he was delighted to have acquired
'such a handsome first cousin'. But 'first cousin' is an exaggeration, for
though indeed they *were* cousins, it was at several removes.

At this period, Joe was finding it increasingly difficult to write: he had
tried his hand, unsuccessfully, at some stories in the manner of Henry
James, and he had been unable to complete more than a few speeches of a
verse play about a fifteenth-century Milanese despot, who had been

assassinated in a cathedral porch for his perversions. Morgan took stock of the situation, and recommended not only a change of scene but a change of country. He told Joe that his friend the Maharajah of Chhatarpur was looking for 'a companion secretary', and suggested that he should apply for the post. He advised him to ask 400 Rs. a month and all found, but to pay his own bearer, so as to keep the man under his thumb.

It was Morgan's habit throughout his life to have 'periodic clear-outs of letters', and during one of these in the late 1950s he threw away most of Joe's. Among the few that survived were two from Chhatarpur (3, 4).

Joe, on the other hand, carefully preserved all Morgan's letters. He would quote the wisdom from them to friends—and copy out extracts: 'I'm sure that if one tries to live only for love one cannot be happy, but perhaps happiness is not your greatest need' (267). Sometimes, he would transcribe a whole letter or, occasionally, lend the original (61).

At the time of receiving Joe's letters from Chhatarpur, Morgan too was full of praise for them and would also read aloud passages to friends, saying that they gave the impression of someone who had lived in the country for years—'not Anglo-Indian years but the years of reality that seldom get lived anywhere and scarcely ever in India'. In March 1924 Joe's father sent on to Morgan a letter of his son's, which described the birth of a princess in the nearby state of Dewas and the subsequent lack of rejoicing that followed because it was a female child. Morgan was so entertained by the account that he arranged (through Sir Theodore Morison) for it to be broadcast on the Newcastle 'Ladies' Hour', in the hope that 'it would make the Newcastle ladies sit up'. Yet when in 1929 Joe approached him about contributing a preface to *Hindoo Holiday*, which was largely based on his letters from India and a journal which he had kept there, Morgan declined. The reasons which he gave were that a good book needed no preface, and that he did not wish to compromise himself over the Maharajah of Chhatarpur ('Chhokrapur' in the book).

These are sound enough reasons. But do they conceal another motive? For Morgan never reviewed *Hindoo Holiday* when it was published in 1932, and his first public reference to it—a brief note—did not appear until twenty-one years later when he published his own letters from India in *The Hill of Devi* (1953). His silence becomes more noticeable if it is remembered that in the same year as *Hindoo Holiday* appeared, he did review Joe's prisoner of war anthology, *Escapers All*, which came out six months later. Why, then, did he keep silent all those years?

It seems now, in the light of the many trails which I have followed up, that Morgan was 'shocked' by *Hindoo Holiday*. It was one thing to enjoy in a letter the 'crafty-ebbing' details of the Maharajah's sexual behaviour (4), but quite another to see them in print. Morgan was a great believer in propriety, and though he was prepared to show his own erotic short stories to close friends such as Lytton Strachey, Forrest Reid or Joe, he never allowed them to be published during his lifetime. When Joe had first shown him the manuscript of *Hindoo Holiday*, then called 'Hindu City', Morgan's mother had been very much on the scene, and he felt that there were some incidents in it in which the author 'had presented [himself] wrongly' and that these would appear 'objectionable' to her. (Mrs Forster did not die until 1945.) Moreover, even if these incidents were to be 'cut', as they were from the first edition and partially from the second revised edition, Morgan still felt that there was dialogue in the book which left no doubt about what the Maharajah had in mind when he spoke of his longing that the Greeks might be reborn in Chhatarpur. In short, 'Joe went too far'.

And Morgan was right about how a parent might react to the book. For at the beginning of 1929 Joe had given his father a copy of the manuscript, having taken the precaution of removing certain passages. Even so, Mr Ackerley had inquired one evening after dinner when they were alone: 'Was the Maharajah a bugger?'

Joe's father had chosen an unfortunate, but for him typical, word. His son was romantic about homosexuality, and bugger was a coarse, rude word, never to be used 'except as a joke'. Joe therefore answered his father in the negative—though no sooner had he spoken than he began to have regrets. He longed for an opportunity to return to the subject, but none was offered and before 1929 had ended his father was dead.

Alfred Roger Ackerley had begun his career as a private in the Guards, and after several abortive attempts as a wine-salesman in the North and as the owner of a pony-farm at Windsor, he became a founder-director of Elder & Fyffes, the Covent Garden fruiterers. 'He was a man of charming personality, beloved by all who came in contact with him,' said the obituary in the *Morning Post*. Joe had come from a home in which neither his sister Nancy nor his brother Peter had been taught the value of money. Now 'this house of cards', as he described it to Morgan (9), came 'tumbling about [his] ears with [his] Dad's death'.

Attached to the will were two letters addressed to Joe, from which he learned that his father had a second family of three daughters living at Barnes. Later, Joe and his sister Nancy were to discover that most of their father's 'business pals' had been let into the secret of this second *ménage*.

After his father's death, Joe, who had been used to saying 'money is nothing'—which Morgan corrected to 'money is *almost* nothing'—found himself considerably less well off. A financial slide began, which he could do nothing to prevent. Meanwhile, Morgan's novels, and in particular *A Passage to India* (1924), were, by the end of the 1920s, bringing in a steady flow of royalties. 'There is no reason why you should ever lack money while I live,' he was to repeat to Joe on a number of occasions, and the role that he took on in Joe's life, as far as money was concerned, was not unlike Roger Ackerley's when he had written to his son at Magdalene: 'Dear Old Lad . . . Drop me a line if you ever find funds running low . . .'

It is the prerogative of a proud father to look for a reflection of himself in his son. With the startling revelations that had come with Roger Ackerley's death—further added to when Joe and Nancy learnt three years later that their parents had not even been married until after the Armistice —Joe became obsessed with the project of trying to discover himself in his father. Extemporising on the facts of Roger Ackerley's early years in the Guards, he wondered whether his father had prowled the Monkey Walk in Hyde Park searching for 'twanks'—which was the word that guardsmen used for regular prowlers like Joe. *My Father and Myself*, begun in the early 1930s, was to take him thirty-five years to complete.

Joe carried out his investigations into his family background with the thoroughness of a private detective, and they were quickly to reveal that his father as a young man had had two protectors—the second of whom was a Count of the Holy Roman Empire—and that each in turn had helped him to purchase his discharge from the Army: from the Royal Horse Guards in 1882, and from the Second Life Guards in 1884. But Joe was never to find any conclusive proof that his father was either a kept man, or that he had had homosexual leanings.

When *My Father and Myself* came out posthumously in 1968, it was acclaimed a masterpiece by the critics. In the 'blurb', the publishers suggested that it belonged to the same category of book as Edmund Gosse's *Father and Son* (1907): but I think it goes back earlier—to Samuel Butler. There is the same questioning of the economics upon which family life depends and the same questioning of Christian morality; and both institutions—marriage and the Church—are found wanting.

Joe was a mosaic writer. Each piece had to be polished and faceted to fit into the whole, and the overall pattern of perfection that he aspired to, he never achieved in his own eyes. He revised endlessly.

When he worked, he did so surrounded with notes scribbled on bits of paper; and when writing letters he would sometimes break off to add another sentence to his notes. Early in his career, Morgan had counselled him: 'Slap your conclusions on the nearest piece of paper, because you won't have time to get to your MS., or if you do you will start reading it carefully, and be done for.'

It was also Joe's habit to store away numerous cuttings from magazines and newspapers, ranging from pictorial supplements about crocodiles on the Zambesi to reports of court cases dealing with homosexual offences. Twenty years were to pass before he made use of the information from a cutting in *The Times* of 30 June 1926, in the last chapter of *My Dog Tulip*: it concerned a beautiful but effeminate boy who had drowned himself in despair on Wimbledon Common (130). In 1942, when there appeared two items in the *News of the World*, concerning twenty men at Abergavenny accused of homosexual practices (three of whom tried to commit suicide during the legal proceedings, and one of whom, aged 19, succeeded), Joe drafted a letter of protest to send to the *Spectator*. Before posting it, he showed it to Morgan. On the whole, Morgan approved—but reminded Joe that a judge had to administer the law: 'Reserve your ammunition for the savagery of the sentence.' Joe accordingly re-worded the letter, and ended it by drawing attention to 'the savage sentences, up to and including ten years' penal servitude, allowed by the law and imposed by the judge . . .' (69).

On a sheet of flimsy writing paper before me now, I have the note which set going the last chapter of *My Father and Myself*. It begins with a phrase taken from one of the letters which Joe found addressed to himself and attached to his father's will:

> 'Kind to my memory'. (End). Kind to your memory—well, why not? I've nothing against you . . . I think you were an excellent father—I only wish I knew what you were really like, and that you knew what I was really like.

I have also in front of me a number of loose-leafed sheets on which he tried out a variety of comments for silencing anyone who criticised Queenie, his alsatian bitch. The most effective and disarming seems to have been: 'I say, please, do not speak so loud. My dog is awfully sensitive.'

Queenie offered Joe what he had never found in his search for a perfect companion—constant, single-hearted devotion. Her main story is recounted in *My Dog Tulip*; but her first eighteen months, and how Joe came to acquire her from a working-class family, is told in *We Think the World of You*.

While I was editing this book, a number of Joe's friends told me that they could not understand how a man who loved poetry and painting, and who had so many friends, could become enamoured of a dog. The truth is that Joe found in Queenie a living work of art. In *My Dog Tulip*, he writes of the dark markings symmetrically dividing up 'her face into zones of pale pastel colours, like . . . a stained-glass window'. In *We Think the World of You*, using almost the identical words, he carries the image a stage further and describes her face 'as the face of a clown, a clown by Rouault'. In 1951 he had written to Sewell Stokes: '. . . she is wonderful to look at. Like a Rouault' (103).

From the moment that Queenie had established herself in Joe's heart, his obsession with sex fell away. Her power was mainly visual. When he went abroad, he would take up his old ways—and some of his escapades with boys, in Greece (186) and in Japan (200), are worthy of a Feydeau farce. But at home, Queenie was the centre of his attention—and proved far more demanding than any wife. Her jealousy of her master's friends was often as great as theirs of her. Nor was she an easy house-guest to entertain—as a letter to Herbert Read illustrates (97).

Once, when she was in season, Joe had put off a visit to Cambridge to see Morgan. 'That *bloody* Queenie,' Morgan had said to Simon Raven. 'How can Joe be such a futile ass?' Another time, in Morgan's flat at Chiswick, Queenie had barked when she had heard the charwoman letting herself in. 'That *bloody* dog,' exclaimed Morgan. Then, seeing her owner's distress, he had pulled himself up: 'Joe, forgive me. It was so *rude*.'

As far as Queenie was concerned, Morgan's second thoughts were generally the best. His first 'puff' for *My Dog Tulip* had been decidedly tepid: 'However much readers like or dislike this book, they will be obliged to agree that it is unlike any other book that they have read' (324). Why was Morgan so lukewarm?

He was not a writer afflicted by jealousy, and when Joe had once talked about Virginia Woolf's comment in her diary for 1923 on the death of Katherine Mansfield—'A rival has been removed,' Morgan had paused for a moment: 'I wonder if I have ever wanted a rival removed?' Then after some thought, he had concluded: 'No, you know, I don't think I ever have.'

It was Morgan's opinion that Joe got away with things in his writings. For when Joe had first shown him the chapter entitled 'Liquids and Solids' in *My Dog Tulip*, which deals with the feeding and defecating habits of dogs, Morgan had said: 'I expect to be disgusted—but it is not a reaction I take seriously.' Chatto & Windus, who had been prepared to accept the book, wanted 'drastic "cuts" ' made in this particular chapter, and Joe, unwilling to remove such 'beastliness' (128), had taken the manuscript away and offered it to Fredric Warburg, who accepted it.

After Secker & Warburg had published the book, Morgan reconsidered his attitude to it, and at the end of 1956, in glowing terms, he gave his reasons in the *Sunday Times* for choosing it as one of the Best Books of the Year (324). 'Thank you, you have opened my eyes,' he said privately to the author.

Joe's novel *We Think the World of You* was begun before *My Dog Tulip*; but for eleven years it underwent constant revisions. In one version, which he sent out in 1955, there is a scene where the narrator goes to bed with an East End charmer called Johnny. Leonard Woolf, who read the manuscript for Chatto & Windus, disliked the scene and accused Joe of 'sexual naïvety'. Fredric Warburg, who also saw the same version, admired the book as a whole—but felt that, since it was so obviously autobiographical, this scene would lead to an immediate prosecution: 'The day after you publish it, the police will be round to arrest you for practising homosexuality.' So, the author withdrew the manuscript, and, 'after months and months of thought', he decided to 'cut' the scene. To his surprise, he found that the 'cut', far from making a gap in the story, tightened the narrative; it helped as well 'to get the emphasis absolutely right', for the objective of the story was to detail, stage by stage, the transference of a middle-aged man's love for a young man to a dog named Evie. Evie, of course, is Queenie.

When the novel opens, Johnny is being held in custody on a charge of house-breaking. To fall for such charmers in life Morgan thought tragic, but he believed that in fiction it was a situation which stood up well.

Early in 1959 Joe re-submitted the manuscript to Secker & Warburg. To Warburg himself, 'the book seemed as good . . . the second time around as the first', and he was keen to accept it; but his partners David Farrer and Roger Senhouse voted against it. Hamish Hamilton also turned it down—though their decision was not unanimous, and Colin Haycraft, who was then working at The Bodley Head and who for many years had been an admirer of Joe's work, wrote to him on 5 June: 'A friend of mine, Richard Brain, at Hamish Hamilton has just told me that to his regret they have declined your novel . . .'

The Bodley Head agreed to take the novel—but, to avoid the possibility of libel, suggested to Joe that he change the London districts in which it was set, and with this end in view he began exploring Victoria Park and Hackney during the latter part of 1959 (177). P. N. Furbank, Forster's appointed biographer, remembers a meeting at the Reform Club, which took place between the three of them on 18 December. Joe had spent all that day wandering around and questioning shopkeepers and passers-by in the Hackney area and at one point had spotted an elderly railway porter coming out of a station, whom he thought might have some valuable memories. 'You've got grey hairs,' he had begun. 'You're the man I want.'

'You use interesting approaches,' had been Morgan's dry comment.

We Think the World of You was published in the autumn of 1960. No Sunday paper or weekly journal gave it a separate notice, nor was it placed top of the fiction columns by the serious Sunday newspapers—or by *The Listener*. Several paperback firms, who saw it during these first few months, turned it down on the grounds that it was 'embarrassing', and no critic chose it among the Best Books of the Year. But in the following May, in *Encounter*, a profound and perceptive review by Stuart Hampshire set people talking about the novel. Sales picked up and at the end of 1961, and despite the fact that it was a 1960 book, three critics chose it for the *Sunday Times* as the Best Book of the Year: Richard Buckle, Raymond Mortimer and Desmond Shawe-Taylor. In 1962 it won the W. H. Smith £1,000 Literary Award (230). Morgan, who had read it several times by now, repeated that many scenes in it were both brilliant and funny—though he felt there was a general scarcity of pleasure (146). It is a criticism which probably stems from the fact that Morgan had never experienced first-hand the pleasure of owning a dog.

4

Morgan casts a long shadow across these *Letters*, and it is perhaps fitting that Joe's last piece of writing should have been 'an 8000-word portrait of E. M. Forster'.

For several years Morgan had suffered a number of strokes—'fallings about' was the way that he chose to describe them afterwards. On each occasion, Joe had been approached by either a Sunday or a weekly paper to prepare an obituary; but he had always refused. It was only in March 1967, when Morgan was 88, that Joe began to wonder what he would say about his 'oldest and closest friend', and that he decided to try and set him down 'before gin and whisky [might] wash all . . . memory . . . away' (330). The piece was completed by the first week in April, and as a check to his memory, Joe occupied himself by going through Morgan's letters to see if the passages which he had quoted by heart were accurate.

It was about this time also that he started negotiations with the University of Texas for the sale of his Forster letters (336). This move he never discussed with his 'oldest and closest friend'. Had he done so, he might have argued that by placing the letters with the University of Texas he was preserving them for posterity. Instead he kept silent, and the reason he did so is because he knew from earlier conversations with Morgan that Morgan did not approve of selling the letters of the living.

The only explanation of Joe's secretive and inexplicable behaviour, I submit, is necessity. He was in need of cash and worried about the future. His pension from the BBC was 'a stingy one', and in November 1966 he had written Morgan a dignified but depressed letter asking him if he would settle a regular income on him (317). Morgan had ignored the request and, in the manner of a jovial Father Christmas, had sent him a fat cheque by return. Morgan thought that Joe sometimes exaggerated his sorrows, and not so long before, when he had subsidised him on a holiday in Greece, he had subsequently warned him: 'If you report you didn't have a varied time . . ., I will produce some postcards to convince you that you did.' Again in 1967, Joe was aware of Morgan's frail health and that he was not a beneficiary in his will 'except for £100' (p. 303n). It must have been tempting therefore to turn his eyes towards another kind of inheritance from Morgan—namely, the letters.

During negotiations with the University of Texas, Joe was worried lest the news might leak out, and one week-end early in the spring of 1967 he told Francis King that he feared that the sale had got to Morgan's ears. Later, this was interpreted as definite fact. Yet this is not borne out by those who were close to Morgan. For at the time he was living in the home of his friends Robert and May Buckingham at Coventry, and had he got wind of the sale he would scarcely have refrained from mentioning it to them. Robert Buckingham wrote to me: 'We only heard about the sale after Joe's death . . . and our first reaction was that Morgan should not hear of it . . .'

A final picture of the two friends is provided by Christopher Isherwood. During May, he visited Morgan in Coventry. Joe was also there staying with the Buckinghams (335), and Isherwood described to me how delighted they were to be together and laughed extravagantly, even at the silliest of their jokes. A young writer who called in was a bit shocked by their frivolity; they were not behaving as befitted their grey hairs. Isherwood added that Joe seemed livelier than he had ever seen him before and in apparently excellent health.

In less than a fortnight, Joe was dead. Early on the morning of 4 June he had died at home in his sleep. Morgan was not told until last thing that night by the Buckinghams, who knew that he had a way of sleeping off bad news. At first, and for several days, Morgan appeared not to have taken in the reality of Joe's death. But on the morning of the funeral, he rallied and remarked at breakfast to the Buckinghams that it was a sad day for all Joe's friends.

Cowes, NEVILLE BRAYBROOKE
5 May 1974

NOTES ON EDITING

I began work on this book in 1969. Four years later I had collected 1,435 letters, and of these I have selected 340 to illustrate the main phases of J. R. Ackerley's life: 336 appear in the body of the text and four in Appendix B. Short extracts from another 72 are incorporated in the footnotes. Inevitably some years have proved leaner than others, but when, as in the 1960s, the choice has been wide, my aim has been to publish those letters which best presented their author's unique genius and reflected his obsession with exact truth. 'For though Truth is eternal,' he once wrote, 'our knowledge of it grows.'

At the outset of my editing, several batches of his papers were handed to me by his sister, Mrs Nancy West: these were invaluable and included newspaper cuttings; uncompleted articles; revisions of poems; draft chapters of *My Dog Tulip*; and notes on loose-leafed sheets—suggesting lines of approach to be adopted in *My Father and Myself*. I have drawn upon all of them in preparing this book.

Practically all Ackerley's friends are represented in this book. But a few gaps were inevitable. The late Professor W. J. H. Sprott discovered that he had kept no letters—'I am rather a letter-destroyer,' he told me. On 12 May 1969 Dame Rebecca West wrote: '. . . one long letter from J.R.A. went up in a house where I had stored some specially interesting papers in Wales in the *blitz* . . .' And when Professor C. Colleer Abbott, the poet and Durham University lecturer, died in 1971, it was found that he had left it in his will that none of his Ackerley correspondence should be released until twenty years had passed.

To keep this collection within bounds has meant being highly selective at times. In the Introduction (part 2) I deal with the main problems. Here I should add that I had to make it a rule that no one recipient should be represented by more than 26 letters. The Index of Recipients shows how the rule worked. Then again there was the matter of balance. In the BBC archives I came across 48 letters that Ackerley had written between 1936 and 1937 in connection with *The Listener* series 'The Artist Speaks'. I selected 7, which traced the series from its inception until its successful appearance (35, 39, 40, 41, 43, 45, 47).

Ackerley was an idiosyncratic speller: sometimes he wrote 'pekinese' (page 8), sometimes 'Pekingese' (page 259); or 'Karachee' in one letter (page 4), and 'Karachi' (page 10) in another. Occasionally he would make up words, such as an 'acquiesce' (page 125), and occasionally he would use obsolete spellings, such as 'motte' for 'mote' (page 139). Often he gave capitals to the seasons of the year—Spring, Summer, Autumn and Winter; I have let these stand: the habit probably originated when he was preparing Spring, Summer, Autumn and Winter Book Supplements for *The Listener*. In all cases, apart from some abbreviations which I have filled out, I have printed his words and punctuation without alteration. His most common abbreviation was the writing of 'i' for 'in': others were 'cd.' for 'could', and 'wd.' for 'would'. Another characteristic of his style was the running on of sentences, using a comma where other writers almost certainly would have used a full-stop. I have left these unchanged. He was sparing too with question-marks. Italics in the text mark his own underlinings—but sometimes present puzzles: for example, the underlining of the o in 'epis*o*dic' (page 81) was no doubt intended in its context to lend the word an extra meaning by way of a pun, since Ackerley enjoyed such punning.

Ackerley nearly always wrote by hand—even when he was a talks producer and literary editor. In these instances it was his habit to date letters in the bottom left-hand corner, after his signature. For the sake of uniformity I have placed all dates at the beginning, but have retained Ackerley's own style of dating—viz. 28/3/39—in order to differentiate letters that he wrote himself from those that he dictated to secretaries, where the dating conformed to ordinary BBC custom—viz. 28 March, 39. Question-marks are used when the exact date of a letter is uncertain, or where I have made a guess as to the month in which it was written—e.g. ?/11 ?/28. An asterisk above a letter's number denotes a postcard—e.g. 121*.

During most of Ackerley's career as a literary editor, the reviews in *The Listener* were unsigned. Certain reviewers have asked that this anonymity should be preserved, and whenever that has been so, I have used in the footnotes the phrase 'the reviewer in question'. Cross-references have been introduced into the footnotes where relevant. In order to keep these within reason, however, an Index of Writings by J.R.A. has been added at the end which lists every writing of his mentioned in the book, and also a General Index by which proper names, if found obscure, can be traced to an explanatory note or context.

Where words appear to be missing, I have added them in square brackets. I have also used square brackets to supply Christian and other names. A short line in square brackets indicates the omission of a name [———] and three dots within square brackets marks a 'cut' [. . .]. 'Cuts' and omissions have only been made in the text where their retention might cause embarrassment to the living. Where dots appear without square brackets, they are Ackerley's—except in the footnotes where they are used to mark editorial omissions.

In the *Letters* there are numerous references to the staff of *The Listener* and other papers—to editors, deputy editors, assistant editors, literary editors and sub-editors. To save therefore introducing yet another editor, I have referred throughout to myself by my surname.

N.B.

ACKNOWLEDGMENTS

My first thanks must go jointly to J. R. Ackerley's sister, Mrs Nancy West, and to his literary executor, Mr Francis King, for the promptness with which they have dealt with the questions which I have put them while editing this book. I should like also to extend a word of general thanks to all those who so generously sent me letters for inclusion.

For personal reminiscences and for much detailed information in preparing the footnotes, I am indebted to the following:

Mrs Mary Albinson; Mr Frank Allen; Professor Warren Anderson; Mr Ian Angus; Miss Renée Ascherson; Mr Don Bachardy; Miss Patricia M. Ball; Mr Clifford Barry; Mr Richard Brain; Professor Quentin Bell; Mrs Frances Bellerby; Dr Angus d'A. Bellairs; Mr Anthony Blond; the late Miss Elizabeth Bowen; Mr Ronald Bottrall; Mr Ronald Bryden; Mrs Anthony Bullock; Mr A. C. Bubb; Mr James Corbett; Mr Adrian Daintrey; Mr David Daley; Mrs Gertrud Dann; Professor Gilles David; Mr Eric de Maré; Miss Kay Dick; Mrs Ruth Dixon; Mr John Donat; Professor Paul Doyle; Dr L. Ega; Mrs T. S. Eliot; Mr David Fairweather; Mr P. S. Falla; Mr David Farmer; Professor Benjamin Farrington; the late Mr Lionel Fielden; Mrs M. S. Fitter, Editor of *Oryx*; Mr C. J. Fox; Mr Philip Lee Fry; Mr P. N. Furbank; Mr D. B. Gardner; Mr David Gascoyne; Mr Norman Gear; Mr John Gibbins; Mr Brian Glanville; Mr Richard Goolden; Mr Robert Greacen; Mr Harman Grisewood; Mr J. P. Green; Mr John Guest; Mr J. C. Hall; Mr P. L. Hedley; Mrs Mary C. Hirth; Mr John Holloway; Mr Bruce Hunter; Mr Christopher Isherwood; Miss Barbara Jones; Mr Carl H. Ketcham; Sir Geoffrey Keynes; Mr Terence Kilmartin; Mr Irving Kristol; Mr J. W. Lambert; Mr Philip Larkin; Dr Stanley A. Leavy; Mrs Wyndham Lewis; Mr William R. Maidment; Mr Derwent May; Mr Ian McKelvie; Dr Margaret Mead; Mr Michael Meyer; Mr James Michie; Mr K. A. Middleton; Mrs Virginia Moody; Mr Edwin Morgan; Mr Raymond Mortimer; Mr Gavin Muir; Miss Luba Mumford; Mrs Mary Middleton Murry; Mr Christopher Neve; Mr Sean O'Fáolain; Mr Timothy O'Keeffe; Mr Charles Osborne; Professor Edmund Papst; Mr David Paul; Mrs Hesketh Pearson; Mr Robert Pocock; Mr Giles Playfair; Mr Anthony Quiney of the Greater London Council; Professor F. Ramu; Mr Simon Raven; Miss Santha Rama Rau; Mr M. A. C. Reavell, Managing Director of Bowes & Bowes, Cambridge; Mr David Rees; Mr Goronwy Rees; Dr Warren Roberts; Mr Brian Rooney; Mr Don Ross; Mr E. Rosenbaum; Professor Joseph S. Schick; Mrs Doris Schiff, President of Fleet Publishing Corporation, New York; Miss M. Sheldon-Williams of the Bodleian Library, Oxford; Miss Akika Shindo of the Japanese Embassy, London; Miss Janet Adam Smith; Miss Constance Babington Smith; Mrs Katherine Sparks; Mrs Diana Spearman; Miss Velda Sprott; Mr Oliver Stallybrass; Mr Derek Stanford; Sir Charles Tennyson; Mr Anthony Thwaite; Mr Ralph T. Topping; Lord Trevelyan; Mr J. C. Trewin; Mrs E. H. Urmston; The Rev Alec R.

Vidler; Mr F. B. Walker; Mr Eric P. White; Mr Robin Whitworth; and Mr David Wright.

I am also indebted to the following libraries for use of letters: King's College, Cambridge (for the letters to E. M. Forster); The University of London (for the letter to Alex Comfort); The University of Victoria, British Columbia (for the letters to Herbert Read); McMaster University, Ontario (for the letter to Bertrand Russell); The University of California (for the letters to Stephen Spender); Cornell University (for the letters to Wyndham Lewis); and The University of Texas (for the letters to Jocelyn Brooke, Richard Church, G. F. Green, Douglas Reed and Hugh Walpole).

For permission to include the letters to Lytton Strachey, I am indebted to the Strachey Trust.

Miss Mary Hodgson, the Chief Archives Officer at the BBC Written Archives Centre, and her staff, greatly assisted me in my researches. They provided me with copies of Letters 12, 13, 14, 17, 18, 20, 21, 22, 23, 24, 25, 28, 30, 31, 32, 33, 34, 35, 38, 39, 40, 41, 43, 44, 45, 46, 47, 51, 52, 53, 54, 55, 56 and 58, and for permission to include them here, grateful acknowledgment is made to the BBC. Miss John Houlgate, the Reference Librarian at Broadcasting House, answered many queries and checked many facts before this book went into proof—and Miss Irene Thornley afterwards.

Mr J. R. Russ, the Sumner Librarian at Rossall School, went through the school magazine—and tracked down an early Ackerley poem (see page xxii).

Mrs Grace Ginnis typed the manuscript—often transcribing from faded originals: no one could have been more painstaking.

Two research grants—one from the Compton Bequest (administered by the Society of Authors) in 1970, and one from the Leverhulme Trust in 1971—enabled me to buy necessary time.

At the proof-stage Mrs John Rosenberg gave the book her expert scrutiny: she has my profound gratitude.

Mr Colin Haycraft, my publisher, has seen the book through the press: it has gained immeasurably from his 'tooth-combing' (see Letter 219).

If, inadvertently, I have omitted above the names of any who have helped me, I apologise. I am aware that there are many people who have worked anonymously for the betterment of this book—notably, in the Reading Room of the British Museum and in the Reference Room of the St Martin's Street Public Library, Leicester Square. My thanks go to them all.

Last here, but in every other sense first, there remains my wife from whose counsels I have benefited at every stage. No editor could have been more fortunate, or had a better or more encouraging collaborator.

5 August 1974   N.B.

GLOSSARY OF NAMES USED IN THE LETTERS

Family

Peter	(brother)
Nancy or Nance	(sister)
Diana or Di	(half-sister)
Sally	(half-sister)
Bunny	(aunt)

Dog

Queenie, Tulip or Evie	(alsatian)

Friends

Bob ⎱ Bucks or Maybobs	Robert Buckingham
May ⎰	May Buckingham
Sandy	Sandy Campbell
Kenneth	Lord Clark
Georges	Georges Duthuit
Goldie	Goldsworthy Lowes Dickinson
Morgan or M.	E. M. Forster
Roy	Roy Fuller
Geoffrey	Geoffrey Gorer
Francis or Frank	Francis King
James or Jim	James Kirkup
Lilian	Lilian Bowes Lyon
Rose	Rose Macaulay
Raymond	Raymond Mortimer
Sonia	Sonia Brownell Orwell
William, S.W.[1] or D.L.B.[2]	William Plomer
Herbert	Sir Herbert Read
Siegfried	Siegfried Sassoon
Edith	Dame Edith Sitwell
Stephen	Stephen Spender
Jack or Sebastian	W. J. H. Sprott
Don	Donald Windham

Editors of The Listener

R. S. Lambert (1929–1939)   Maurice Ashley (1958–1967)
Alan Thomas (1939–1958)

Literary editors

Janet Adam Smith (1929–1935)   Derwent May (1965–   )
J. R. Ackerley (1935–1959)
K. W. Gransden (1959–1963)   *Chief sub-editor*
Anthony Thwaite (1963–1965)   Marjorie Redman (1932–1965)

[1] Sweet William   [2] Dear Little Bird

Part One
PRISONER OF WAR

To his Brother (1895–1918)   5/4/17   1

Dear old Peter
                 just a line to let you know that I am wounded and a prisoner
in Germany—which has successfully killed my War-goose.
     The wound is not bad, but inconvenient, being in the bottom!
Thine
     Joe[1]

---

[1] This note, written in indelible pencil, was posted two days after A., then a Captain in the 8th
East Surrey Regiment, had been wounded at the battle of Cérisy. He was taken 'limping off into
captivity, at bayonet point'—and then sent to a hospital in Hanover. Later he was transferred to
prison camps at Karlsruhe, Heidelberg and Augustbad before being invalided to Switzerland
early in 1918, where he was interned for the rest of the war. A description of the battle was 'cut'
from the first edition of *Hindoo Holiday* (1932), but appears in the second revised edition of 1952.
There the date is given as 3 May, just as May is given as the month of his capture in his anthology,
Escapers All, which is made up of the 'Personal Narratives of Fifteen Escapers from War-time
Prison Camps, 1914–1918' that he first produced for the Talks Department of the BBC in 1931,
and subsequently edited for publication in 1932. But as A. wrote in a memo to Alan Thomas, an
Editor of *The Listener* for whom he worked for nineteen years, 'Memory [is] not my strong point'.
When he came to write his family memoir *My Father and Myself*, published posthumously in 1968,
he had this letter before him and the battle is correctly dated there in Chapter 7: '. . . on April 3, I
had to take *my* men over the top . . . to capture the village of Cérisy . . .'

Part Two
HINDOO HOLIDAY

2 To his Mother (1869–1946)   Bombay to Chhatarpur[1]
                                                         21/12/23

Carissima

        this is a terribly bumpy train, but I'll try and get some news down
for you in the stationary periods!

        I left Bombay—almost penniless—at 12.30 today and, owing to the
courtesy of a railway official (whom I rewarded with one of my last rupees),
managed to get a 2nd class compartment to myself.[2] There isn't much
difference in comfort it seems travelling 1st or 2nd class in India (the difference in price is large, twice the 2nd class fare in fact) except that, in the 1st
class, one isn't thrown so much into contact with the natives. That consideration (put forward by Cook's) didn't weigh with me, of course—indeed I'd
sooner travel with natives than Europeans;[3] but it's nicer still on this
particular journey to be alone. So I have an electric fan and alarm signal all
to myself, also two berths, not to mention a lavatory with a nice aluminium
basin—no paper, soap, or towel; but since I always travel with these things
handy I am not at a loss.

        So, if you want to picture me, I am lying full-length on the seat, my back
propped up against a valise—so nicely packed by Cooper—dressed in one
of my nice new light biscuit coloured suits which, I hope, won't get too dirty.
For I want to look spruce for the dramatic moment of my first introduction
to the Maharajah. Dramatic it will be, of course. He will see to that. Like
most people of his temperament, he has an eye for effect. He won't meet me
in person. The secretary—or prime minister, may be—will do that; and

---

        [1] This letter was written on writing paper provided by Green's Hotel, Bombay, which Forster
had recommended and stayed at on a previous visit. See Letter 3.
        [2] A.'s mother was always interested in details of travel. When a girl her own family had fallen
on hard times and inevitably travelled third class—but only because, as her younger sister,
Bunny, added, there was no fourth.
        [3] It was A.'s habit to write notes and snatches of conversation—even instructions to printers
when he was at *The Listener*—on the backs of envelopes. On one such envelope dating to this period,
he has recorded this snatch: 'You'll never understand the dark and tortuous minds of the natives,
and if you do I shan't like you—it won't be healthy.' The speaker was the wife of an army captain,
and later he incorporated her remark into *Hindoo Holiday*. A. dedicated this 'Indian Journal', as he
sub-titled it, to his mother. Ironically, when it was reviewed on 20 April 1932 in *The Listener*, it
was this notion of 'going native, going Indian' which prompted the reviewer, T. Earle Welby, to
make his one criticism of the book: 'The white woman who warned Mr Ackerley against "going
Indian" may have been a very limited person but was giving him sound enough advice, for the
only *raison d'être* of the white man in India is that he is not Indian.'

2

then, while I am resting and tidying up in my guest-house or lodging, will report to H[is] H[ighness] on my personal appearance. And the report must—will—be satisfactory. Alan Quartermain himself has arrived.[1] I must say—without bias—that this new suit is very becoming; but what it will be like by tomorrow afternoon is another matter. Then, that evening or the following day, I am not sure whether the great man will call on me or I shall be led to him, but I believe the former procedure was adopted in Forster's case, and will probably be the same in mine—he will arrive, heralded by a dark warrior with a spear. I hope he'll play up well to these expectations; but I feel sure he will when he learns from the secretary that Alan Quartermain himself has arrived. But to return. I am stretched very happily on my black Roman cloak[2]—to keep the dust off the seat of my breeches—gazing out over the landscape which so far—(5 p.m.)—has been rather dull—rough, flat, and parched, with here and there a cluster of mud-huts, and a long range of queer, artificial looking mountains in the distance—mostly with little knobs on top as tho' they are wearing topees. Herds of goats watched or neglected by squatting natives; and bright red turbans suddenly vivid against the light fields. It is very hot, so that I have removed my coat. We are halted now in a station. A little boy with a bright yellow pink and blue turban is standing outside near a lady intriguingly veiled in the loveliest japonica veil which reaches to her feet and is held across her face by a coffee coloured arm. And natives in white or khaki pass, selling tangerines, very green bananas, or odd-looking sweets, dispensing water out of beautiful brass jars—their turbans all colours of the rainbow—and large black hawk-like birds swoop down trying to steal the sweets from the trays. In Bombay I was rather dull on the whole, but it had its brighter moments.

The collapse of my chair was, I think, a presage of disaster. At any rate, on the following morning, my two pairs of trousers, which I had sent to be cleaned, were returned to me scorched by an over-heated iron; my watch-strap broke; and—the crowning catastrophe—the nice gold cuff-links with white enamel margins that Dad gave me for a birthday present some three or four years ago were stolen. And paradoxical tho' it may sound I valued them so much, as Dad's gift and for their own intrinsic beauty, that I am glad they are gone. I was never easy with them. When I sent a shirt to the wash I was continually hurrying to the basket to make sure that I had removed the links, and if I then wore a shirt which was not made for links, I never knew quite what to do with them—where to conceal them. But now that they have been stolen I shall not, of course, have these worries any more; and when my other two articles of value have gone in like manner—my tobacco pouch, and the golden fountain-pen of which Nance still persists

---

[1] 'Are there any qualifications?' A. had asked when it was suggested he should go to His Highness in the capacity of an English private secretary and tutor to his son. 'Yes,' came the reply, 'he wants someone like a character named Olaf in *The Wanderer's Necklace* by Rider Haggard.'

[2] Before his departure for India and for some years after his return, A. was much given to parading the London streets in a voluminous black carabinicro's cloak, which he wore cast over one shoulder in the Byronic manner. 'I am often trailed by children shouting rude remarks,' he noted in a diary.

unreasonably in considering herself part owner—I shall not have any worries at all. Really it is a bad principle to have anything at all valuable; its jealous guarding takes years off life. So now I have bought myself a pair of silver links for 1/4, and I do not care whether they are stolen or not. My friend Mr Pollak vanished, to my regret, into obscurity immediately upon landing in Bombay.

He was an amiable old gentleman—Managing Director of the Karachee branch of the celebrated French house of Dreyfus—and I promised him I would be sure to call if ever I found myself in Karachee. But to make up for this the sailor from the *Tevore* did eventually, on the third evening, turn up to dinner.

So he had been expressing his pleasure after all. A coolie brought me a letter from him addressed to:
      'Chiarissimo Signor
        Joe Hackerlay'
which means 'The most illustrious Signor'.

A pleasant letter in Italian expressing his regret that he had been unable to get leave before, but would without fail be with me that evening . . . 'Your sincerely Giorgio———'. A postscript, in English, ran as follows: 'You are a noble-hearted gentleman.' Which referred to a present of 10/- I had given him to send to his Ragusan Mother for whom, with 3 younger brothers and sisters, he was winning bread. Originally well to do, the son of a commandante in the Lloyd Triestino service, his father had died at the age of 45 of angina pectoris, leaving the family almost destitute, and Giorgio had been obliged to leave his study of medicine and Latin and Greek, and become a sailor, in which trade, owing to his father's name, advancement would be quicker. Thus I found him; factotum on the *Tevore*, earning 500 lire a month.

In Bombay also I called on a Mr Camar Tyabji (pronounced, if you can read it, as it is spelt) to whom Forster had given me a letter of introduction.

I took a cab to his private address, a big house surrounded by palms, in the busy centre of Bombay and after hanging about on the porch looking in vain for a bell or knocker, I walked inside—the door was open—and investigated the vestibule. A large sitting-room, with a mosaic floor, full of divans and brass ornaments, lay beyond, and I peered into it thro' various doors and windows from the vestibule, but there was no one to be seen. Then, in a corner of the hall on a dusty shelf, I found a small handbell, which I rang without eliciting any response and then, it being 12.30, nearly lunch-time, continued to ring obstinately until I suddenly perceived, standing just behind me in an attitude which seemed to suggest that he had been there for some time, a native servant clothed in soiled white linen trousers and coat, his feet bare and his teeth and tongue stained red with betel-nut juice. I silently handed him my introductory letter, and he returned with a pencilled note from some invisible inhabitant to the effect that Mr Camar was at his office. But he hadn't returned me my letter, so I sent him back for that, and then there came out a pleasant brown lady, of the Mahommedan sect, a black veil edged with white over her loosely plaited black hair and swathed about her body. A fine white vest trimmed with gold, and dark moroccan slippers on her bare feet completed, with the exception of some pretty jewelry, her attire. She was Camar's mother. She said that she herself was going to call on her son at 2 p.m., and that if I would wait we could go together.

She wished very much to give me lunch—though she had already had hers. And such a funny meal I had in the big sitting-room all by myself—she coming silently in now and then to see if all was well—two fried eggs, some rice with fish-curry-sauce, and a strange sweet called Laddoo—meal, nut, and spice rolled up into balls like round lemons.

And a number of saucers were set round me; one held 3 oranges, another 3 apples, another 3 tangerines and another 3 seed-apples or custard-pears. A small basin held fine white lard instead of butter, there were two glasses of iced water, and bread was piled high on a central plate. It was, she said, the best she could do for me. I was exhausted, and ate heartily to the accompaniment of the hoarse cry of the crows in the palms outside. Later a Mr Tyabji—a cousin—in a black alpaca 'frock coat', white linen trousers and a round astrakhan hat (fez-shaped) came in and kept me company, and then we all drove off to Camar's office in Camar's car and met more Tyabjis there. Never have I seen so many of one family collected together. Camar himself was nice and genial and generous and unattractive; he expressed great regret that I was not remaining longer in Bombay and said I must of course stay with him, instead of in a hotel, when I went thro' on my way back. He arranged to meet me at 4.30 p.m. next day (my last day) and there arrived yet another Tyabji who said that his wife having heard that a friend of Mr Forster's was in Bombay had insisted that I must take tea with her; so off we all went in this Mr Tyabji's car, and had tea with his wife—a lovely Arabian lady arrayed in a bright green satin dress and numerous filmy golden veils.

Afterwards Camar and his relatives drove me about Bombay and shewed me the city from its highest point—Malabar Hill—and pointed out the Tower of Silence round which in sacred gardens the Parsis expose their dead bodies to be devoured by vultures. This is their form of burial.

We saw many vultures on the palms round about—and an aged Parsi gazing at them . . . and I wondered what his thoughts were.

A horrible sinister-looking bird.

Driving back to my hotel, Camar's relative said that if I should like the use of his car after 9 p.m. that evening I might have it; and I, remembering that I was to have Giorgio on my hands, gratefully accepted.

Both of them very nice people, I thought, and very interested in my interest. But I am glad to leave Bombay. It was too hot. I sweated all day and all night, and was so uncomfortable that I carry away only a confused impression of brown bodies and naked limbs, blotches and streaks of bright paint on the foreheads of the Hindoos; airy, transparent nether-garments (like those my Hotel servant wore), very frequent and also useful as handkerchiefs, and of men squatting down in the street against a wall and urinating like women. A somewhat bare impression.

I am wearing my cholera belt now. I only have two, but maybe that's enough, for Norman Douglas[1] told me he never had more than one which he wore night and day for a year.

I'll seal all my letters, beloved, and would like to know if ever the seal is broken.[2]

All my love to you all

Joe

3   To E. M. Forster (1879–1970)   Kothi Palace, Chhatarpur[3]
                                                            23/12/23

My dear Morgan

I began a letter to you in Bombay, but owing to a sailor[4] on my boat the *Tevore*, it was never finished. The voyage was miserably dull, but since I had collected some good copy for a story in Venice[5] this didn't matter to me.

And, as you prophesied, my berth companion was pleasant and dull. Indeed he was so dull that he seemed scarcely human—an American jute-merchant of 60, John Clark by name. I called on Camar Tyabji in Bombay at his private house. Your 'Fort' address was useless, lacking the name of the street 'Bake House Lane'. He was out at his office, but his mother, a nice lady, received me and gave me lunch and took me afterwards in her car to call on Camar with whom she herself had a business appointment. Camar seemed very pleasant, was grieved to hear I was leaving for the centre in two days time and made me promise to give him a long notice before my return and to stay with them—instead of at Green's Hotel, which, I think, must have changed since your time being now as ruinous as the Taj Mahal and, I believe, under the same management.

15 rs. a day they charged me. I met numberless Tyabjis—they grow on every office stool—and they were all very amiable, especially one who had a lovely Arabian wife, who loved you dearly and insisted on her husband bringing me to tea (with Camar) on the following afternoon. I think I got thro' all right, but it was difficult living up to your reputation among them.

After tea this Tyabji took Camar and me out in his car to Malabar Hill (there was no time for Elephanta; I hope to see that returning) and we were all easier and happier, and they laughed long and heartily at nearly everything I said which was surprising but heartening. For the evening they were both engaged—so was I with the *Tevore* sailor—and Mr Tyabji insisted upon placing his car at my disposal, saying that I must certainly see the same view from Malabar Hill at night. So we did. But Bombay was desperately hot—

---

[1] See page 25, note 1.   [2] See last line of P.S. to Letter 3.
[3] Chhatarpur becomes 'Chhokrapur' in *Hindoo Holiday*.
[4] This sailor, with whom A. was later to admit he spent two nights at Green's Hotel, Bombay, had agreed to meet him towards the end of the following year in Turin. When the time for the meeting drew near, A. was in England and vacillated over going. A corrective friend (as A. described him in Chapter 13 of *My Father and Myself*) sent him a reproving shaft: 'You are scared or bored by response.' A. left for Italy. The corrective friend was Forster.
[5] A.'s stories at this period were in his own words 'macabre and in the most clotted manner of Henry James'. None has survived. See Introduction, 3.

indeed the Tyabjis themselves were grumbling—and I was glad to get out of it. Your Rajah friend Dawas was in Bombay, I believe, and Masood[1] was expected to arrive on the following Sat.; but I had already telegraphed the Maharajah the date of my arrival as Sat. (which meant leaving at 12.30 Friday) and had bought a ticket and reserved a seat, so I couldn't well stay. I'd bought some clothes and a hat in Bombay—I didn't trouble about a blazer I'm glad to say: and I had a decent enough journey to Jhansi in a two-berth carriage by myself. At Jhansi a Capt. Stoney I.M.S.[2] met me on behalf of H[is] H[ighness] with a letter from Mrs Stoney asking me to lunch immediately. But I postponed, anxious to get my luggage off my hands. Stoney seemed a pleasant, simple, jovial person. He told me there were 5 other guests at Kothi Palace for Xmas. There are. With him was a black-bearded Mussulman, servant of H[is] H[ighness], bearing a letter from him to say a car would meet me at Harpalpur and that he was looking forward to seeing me. Already, in a letter, I had sent the same message of ardent expectancy from Bombay.

So I sent grateful messages to Mrs Stoney and proceeded with the Mussulman—and a gunner officer, youthful, pleasant and dull, who was going to shoot something somewhere—to Harpalpur. The car, an antique and dingy Belsize, was there in [the] charge of a stout chauffeur, and we all squashed in somehow—a small boy who had suddenly sprung into existence as part of the retinue clinging limpet-like to the splashboard—and drove to the Kothi Palace.

A nice drive—cool and refreshing. I was set down at a small house near the guest house (which is full) which was to be my domain. It consists, as perhaps you know, of two rooms, four tables, a chair, a bed, and a looking-glass. Also there is an outhouse containing a tin bath, a tin basin, a tin W.C. and quantities of ants. It's nice. I like it.

And surrounded by my baggage there I stood. What with one thing and another, the Venetian story, the Tyabjis and the *Tevore* sailor, I hadn't opened the Hindustani book (which is chiefly composed, I now find, of a translation from some poem by Kipling and part of the Lord's Prayer) and I was completely at a loss. The chauffeur, the Mussulman and the small boy all stared awfully at me as though I had been transmogrified—as though, from the person they had with infinite care stored in the car at Harpalpur, I was now utterly and terribly different. I pretended to be unaware of them. I was hungry and tired and I wanted a wash; so I strolled out on to the back verandah and looked into the outhouse, but when I returned they were still there. Then an aged person with a grey beard appeared and added his voice to the general chorus and pointed up to the guest house. Foolishly I thought it was the Palace, and asked if H[is] H[ighness] lived there and was told Yes—by four nods. As a matter of fact they only meant that H[is] H[ighness] was, at the moment there—and then the grey-beard, after profound meditation, pronounced the word 'Ticket'. Of course! My cards!

[1] When Forster's *A Passage to India* came out in the following year, the dedication read: 'To Syed Ross Masood and to the Seventeen Years of Our Friendship.'
[2] Indian Medical Service.

I'd forgotten all about them (printed in Venice) never having possessed any before. I unearthed one, and they all departed satisfied—except the Mussulman who produced a piece of Vinolia soap, a packet of Bronco and some water.

So I removed my coat, collar and tie and was in the middle of a lovely wash when the grey-beard appeared, excitedly, in the door of the outhouse, and remarked that His Highness had come. This was a blow. I had expected a more dramatic introduction than this. I rapidly dried my face and had just time to get a collar and tie on before two shadows fell across the sitting-room threshold and H[is] H[ighness] arrived. I think he must have altered since your time; indeed Mrs Fitzgerald—a venomous woman staying here—wife to an officer—says he has grown visibly more childish since September last. At any rate, you told me he was about 45, but he is really 57 and looks it. Had he teeth in your time? He has none now. He was clad in a round green velvet hat, thickly embroidered with gold; a kind of drab mauve tweed frock-coat with velveteen cuffs and collar of elephant grey, white linen trousers, purple socks of a vivid hue, and dancing pumps. He is now a sufferer from rheumatism (a favourite topic of conversation) and walks *péniblement*, his feet pointing one East, one West, like a decrepit man. But I do not think he is ugly—praps because I dislike misusing the word. If a pekinese is ugly; then also is the Maharajah. But he has a nice expression —childish—rather pathetic; which the secretary, a fat pock-marked man whom you do not know, lacks. The secretary is definitely ugly. He has an ugly look. I cannot remember what H[is] H[ighness]'s first words were. I had told myself to be careful to note them; but with my ears still bubbling with soapsuds I was flustered. At any rate he greeted me pleasantly, and after saying that he had meant personally to meet me on the road but that I had arrived unexpectedly early, he questioned me about his friends. 'I am very anxious for news of my friends. What news have you?'

Alas! I had none. Save of you whom I played for all I was worth, and of Goldsworthy Lowes Dickinson of whom I spoke as though he was a brother. But of Sir Theodore Morison,[1] [R. C.] Trevelyan[2] and [Edward] Arnold[3] I had none—and little enough of Prince Andrew of Russia . . . His Highness's disappointment was obvious; but he summoned up sufficient courage to remark, after an interval: 'At last we are face to face'. He asked then how much money he owed me and I said I hadn't made an acc. yet, and he said he wished to repay me as soon as possible. His secretary to whom I later rendered the acc., frequently expresses a similar anxiety; but I haven't yet had the money. I considered charging up my Bombay hotel bill and my new suits to H[is] H[ighness] but prudently refrained, and charged him

[1] Sir Arthur Cunningham Lothian in *Kingdoms of Yesterday* (1951) writes: '[The Maharaja's] guardian, when he was a boy, had been Sir Theodore Morison.' He also adds: '[The Maharaja] was very fond of the society of individual Englishmen.' In 1923 Sir Theodore was Principal and Vice-Chancellor of the University of Newcastle.

[2] 1872–1951. Poet and translator. Forster's first visit to India in 1912–13 had been in the company of Trevelyan and Lowes Dickinson.

[3] Forster's first two novels *Where Angels Fear to Tread* (1905) and *The Longest Journey* (1907) were originally published by William Blackwood & Sons. But in 1908 Edward Arnold persuaded him to come to his firm (which had been founded in 1890), and there Forster remained for the rest of his life.

only with the extra passage money £25; £5 as being a just return for my passage thro' Italy, and £3.6s.od. my fare from Bombay—calling the whole 500 rs., so as not to confuse the secretary. Since putting in this acc. I haven't made any mention of it, but yesterday morning the sec. spontaneously remarked that he would bring me the money last night or this morning. However, I suppose it will arrive some time if I leave it alone.

H[is] H[ighness] then put me thro' an examination—religion, no. and gender of family, and had I read Hall Caine. Had I read a lot of other books, too; but I hadn't—not any of them. He said I must soon do so and explain them all. Darwin, Huxley, and Marie Corelli. Did I know Rider Haggard? Was I a pragmatist like Mr Forster and Mr Lowes Dickinson? I joined this noble company.

And then about Stoney. Had I liked Stoney? Had we spoken long together? What had we spoken about?

Of course we had spoken about H[is] H[ighness]—the only link between us; but I made evasive reply. But I couldn't help a little smile at this childishness, and H[is] H[ighness] perceiving it, simpered into his sleeve, and changed the subject to 'positivism'. Shortly, however, he meandered back.

When had the Bombay train arrived in Jhansi? And had I been with Stoney all that time? 'O, *all* the time?' and so on. Then I was taken to the guest house by the secretary and shown to the other guests. Three men and two women.

Two of the men are pleasant, a quiet old Gunner Major and a Major in the Med. section; the third man—a naval commander, busy courting the younger of the women—is of no account, and the women are dreadful. They talk the whole time in that bright Anglo-Indian manner, stuffing their sentences with adverbs and florid adjectives—such as 'lethal' and 'septic'.

'Where's my septic hat?' You know the kind of thing.

28/12/23

I must close this rather dull letter. H[is] H[ighness] has been rather more attentive to me lately, but I think he wishes to maintain an attitude of aloofness before the other guests. From him the sec. told me the other day that when I met the P[olitical] A[gent] there was really no need to tell him that I would be receiving a salary here. The P[olitical] A[gent] arrives today—a Major Wilson—detested by H[is] H[ighness]; disliked it seems by everyone else. Perhaps this is a good sign. I got on badly with the crowd here at first. Started off badly, as the elder lady told me later, by not immediately labelling myself—my profession, school, university and business. It was bad of me to leave them guessing. O dear!

I'm glad they're off tomorrow. They spoil things. Xmas Day was devastating. I was obliged to see Mau in their company—also the temples at Khajraho. I haven't called at Nowgong yet—difficulty over cars. H[is] H[ighness] informed me the other day, that he wants me to superintend the guest house where there is much wastage; but since I have no Hindustani this is hardly practicable. My position here doesn't look too easy to me. I don't think I shall want to stay here more than 3 months at the longest—I want to see more of India—but leaving will be hard—especially leaving with my return fare. And I don't suppose the P[olitical] A[gent], already biased v. me, would assist if called upon. Of course everyone here knew about me before I arrived! Do write Morgan. I'll be pleased with a letter.

    Joe

P.S. H[is] H[ighness] during a motor drive with the two Majors yesterday asked me if I had read the works of Edward Carpenter. I said I had. What works? I hurriedly suppressed *The Intermediate Sex* out of consideration for the 2 Majors and produced *Love's Coming of Age*—which, as a matter of fact, I haven't read. H[is] H[ighness] very pleased. Had I liked it? No, I hadn't. Why not[?] Too invertebrate. A veiled smile from H[is] H[ighness]. Please seal your letters. H[is] H[ighness] is so inquisitive.

4 To E. M. Forster (1879–1970)   Chhatarpur
                                                   23/4/24

Dear Morgan

        very many thanks for your last. It was great fun and gave me considerable pleasure in this lifeless period.

It pulls me straight home, in fact—tho' I never had any serious intention to break journey. I haven't accumulated any stability—and I shall once again rush enthusiastically and expectantly home and be sick on the doorstep as usual. But I want to see the [Wembley] Exhibition[1] and see familiar faces and give the Recording Angel some more work to do on the debit side.

Yes—I should like Cairo, I know. Even Port Said exhilarated me, and I made great headway with a hideous and grimy Egyptian child who vended cigarettes at our café table.

He took a great fancy to me—although I only spent one and sixpence on him; offered me his hand when we left; extracted a promise that I would not forget him, and expressed a hope that I would stay some time in Port Said on my return.

Pollak, my companion, spent over £2 on the boy's wares (extortionate prices of course) but got none of these attentions. 'He seemed to like you, that boy,' he observed thoughtfully, as we returned to the ship. An amusing old boy, Pollak: general manager of Dreyfus, Karachi; a Czech, of scurfy and Teutonic appearance. We were the only two people on the boat who held out against evening dress to the bitter end.

'Really!' I used to say to him when he came in to dinner. 'Don't you think you're behaving very badly? Everyone is looking at your suit; and I can't help thinking that a man of your years ought to be showing a young chap like me a better example!' 'I have *broshed* my coat,' he would say with indignation. 'And I do not always do that.'

---

[1] The British Empire Exhibition at Wembley opened on 24 April. Forster had been appointed 'special correspondent for Wembley by *The Nation & Athenaeum*', and on 26 April his one and only dispatch appeared. It ended: 'Millions will spend money there, hundreds will make money there, and a few highbrows will have fun. I belong to the latter class . . .'

It was true. The scurf had disappeared from the collar. He used to come to me for help in English, but never believed anything I told him.

'We will dismount the ship together at Port Said, is it not?' he said one day.

'In English,' I said, 'we don't dismount ships—we disembark.'

But he wouldn't have it.

'In my book,' he retorted, 'it is oderwise.'

What ancient history that seems. I leave here in 18 days (May 11th) and the good ship *Aquileja* sails on the 15th. And I shall be glad to go. It's tiresome now. Gulab Rai, the secretary, has gone off on a well-earned holiday, and I shalln't [*sic*] be seeing him again; his substitute is amiable and stupid; and the Dewan, never very much at one's service, has disappeared completely out of my life. So I'm much alone.* True [His] H[ighness] dribbles along most afternoons to take me for a drive, but he is only a joke now, and usually a chestnut. Besides which I feel that he now looks upon me as a duty which tiresomely deprives him of the company of his new Gods[1] for an hour or two. Finally I suspect him of uneasiness in my company— uneasiness arising from a belief that his servants have betrayed him to me—as indeed they have. I am now informed of everything that takes place in his palace directly after its commission; and it is difficult to keep a straight face before the little man's evasions. Yet he does like me spasmodically.† When the other day he showed me two coloured photos—one of his new God in regalia; the other of his valet in a fig-leaf—and I expressed a genuine admiration for both; he was delighted, gave me the photos (which I will show to you) and said: 'If I give you *land*, will you come out with all your family and live here?' I said dimly that I thought it might be arranged—never quite knowing what to say to these preposterous suggestions.

'How much land will you want?' was the next question; and gazing out over the stony, thorny, unmanageable jungle, I said that if we had enough to sit down on I thought it would do. He nodded pensively. But that kind of conversation no longer sends me headlong to my notebook. One wearies of it and yearns for vigour of mind.

A childish man ('Peter Pan' I called him the other day) full of sudden futile momentary enthusiasms; and, one understands well enough, a man of little appreciation and small intelligence. Yet how they serve him! In all this time I only once heard him spoken of disrespectfully—by Mahadeo, who had cause, having been told by H[is] H[ighness], the evening before, to command his friend Raghunandi, who was also present, to gratify H[is]

---

* Mahadeo and Raghunandi drift in and out all day, of course, but they are more ornamental than companionable, and are quite content to sit with me for hours without giving expression to a solitary thought.

† Also there is a new idea in process of germination—the feeling that he would like to be properly biographed.

Nothing must be omitted. Perhaps I am the man ... So he has begun to reveal to me incidents— chiefly unimpeachable and vaguely mystic—in his past life to illustrate the complexity of his nature, and prepare me, perhaps, for the *worst*.

Read on!

[1] i.e. boys.

H[ighness]'s sexual desires in front of him (Mahadeo).* M[ahadeo] is a constant source of irritation to H[is] H[ighness] because he steadfastly refuses to participate in these affairs; and although H[is] H[ighness] has, I think, long since ceased to feel any passion for M[ahadeo],† he still attempts to break his resistance, annoyed by it as such, or uneasy perhaps at such virtue in a servant.

'He is half-made!' said M[ahadeo] to me.

'What did you do?'

'I said to Raghunandi "Do it". But I touched his foot with mine—also I shook my head. The Maharajah saw me.'

'It is a good thing he saw you,' I said. 'You were a fool to say "Do it". Don't you know your King yet better than that. You must always be honest and plainspoken with him—and if you are a little heroic over it, so much the better. You should have said to him what is true in you, and what he knows to be true in you—"I will love you with all my heart, and I will serve you with loyalty and devotion; but I will never do this work, and I will never tell my friend to do this work." He would have beaten you perhaps, but he would have continued to respect you.'

'Now I understand!' ejaculated M[ahadeo], with quite an amount of vigour, as though he had suddenly perceived the key to a riddle. 'I understand now. Thank you.'‡ He's an intelligent boy, and it is only in the awful presence of the King that his honest wits temporarily desert him. Nor do I wonder. H[is] H[ighness] feeds his personal grievance with any idle wicked accusation that Mahadeo's enemies choose to bring against him—that he steals the guest house furniture; that his friendship with Raghunandi is depraved and evil; that, besides the service to himself, he forces Raghunandi to do sexual service to his (M.'s) widowed sister . . .§ and so on. And H[is] H[ighness] wonders if it is true. To do the little man justice I think he really *is* stupid enough to wonder, and that his persecution of M[ahadeo] is not entirely malicious. But, be that as it may, the result is deplorable: the informers thrive; Raghunandi is one of the richest boys in the State, and Mahadeo one of the poorest without the smallest hope of any advancement, unless he sets aside his scruples and joins the favoured band which his friend Raghunandi so prosperously heads. And there's nothing to be done.

* *Per anum.* The King passive. This was after H.H. had failed to persuade M. to do it himself in front of R.

† If ever he had any. I think it is just the feeling that he had injudiciously exposed himself. *Nescit vox, missa reverti.*[1] I used to extol the rectitude and virtue of M. to H.H. long before I knew that this was one of the little man's chief exasperations. 'He's got rather a fine face too,' I said.

'I've never looked at him closely,' said H.H. with a laugh—which rang very falsely in my memory.

‡ The dreary plan for the forcing and sharing of Mahadeo failed. Raghunandi, who renders, with M.'s knowledge and apparent indifference, constant service of this kind to H.H. *in private*, very spiritedly refused to be put to such shame in front of his friend. He does not *like* doing it at all, but he is so frightened of H.H.'s anger that the very apprehension of it usually brings on nervous prostration.

H.H.'s behaviour needs no comment of course. This sort of thing would be mischievous indeed if it did not merely serve to shew, at any rate to *us*, the essential beauty in the two *boys'* natures.

§ H.H. actually asked me if I knew whether this was true. I told him that if he took the trouble to learn the boy he would know it wasn't, and would then cut out the informer's tongue.

[1] This line comes from Horace's *Ars Poetica* (390), and in full reads: '*Delere licebit quod non ederis: nescit vox missa reverti*' (You can destroy whatever you do not publish: but once published it is out of your hands).

The state is corrupt practically throughout, and the principles of Mahadeo and of anyone else who happens to be troubled by such things have little enough to encourage them. And they do not survive unscathed. I told you once that when first I came out and met R[aghunandi] I suggested that he should kiss me, and he refused. H[is] H[ighness] forbade R[aghunandi] to give further publicity to this incident; but recently Mahadeo informed me that he knew it—which was not a surprise to me, but seemed all very right and proper.

'What did you say when he told you?' I asked.

'I told him he ought to have kissed the sahib if the sahib wanted it.'

'What?' I said scandalised. 'You had no right to advise him like that.* He was absolutely correct to refuse—especially with his experience. You must set him right again on that point.'

It is the power of authority; I think that is the root of it all. They are blindly obedient to it. They prostrate their minds before it (as before all other manifestations of power) whether it proceeds from their parents, their chief, or the conquering European. If M[ahadeo] had not an inherent aversion for such practices as H[is] H[ighness] desires, I have no doubt he would have quietly submitted years ago. He has no real rebellion in him. In his Father's presence he is always ashamed. He never raises his eyes to the old man's face, because of the relationship only; and his Father has the mentality of a sheep, as *his* Father and his Father's Father had before him.

The Banyan tree.[1] I'm weary of it, and want to get back to reason and will power and stout commonsense. To Wembley,[2] in fact. You may have seen in the papers that Marie Corelli is dead. H[is] H[ighness] is broken-hearted. He wants me, with my own hands, to lay a wreath on her grave for him. I said I'd sooner read another of her books. I carried out your instructions. They missed fire. He only remarked that you were a 'wizard.'

Ariverderla

Joe

To Hugh Walpole (1884–1941)   76 Charlotte Street, W.1   5
4/11/25

Dear Mr Walpole

I am very much touched by your response to my play.[3]

---

* For this conversation must have taken place long before M. became a friend of mine.

[1] 'The Dewan, or Prime Minister, himself accompanied us . . . and showed us a fine banyan tree, which, he said, lives for ever, each branch thrusting down a new root into the earth.' See *Hindoo Holiday*, the section dated 29 December.

[2] See page 10, note 1.

[3] This refers to *The Prisoners of War*, which had been produced at the Playhouse in London on 1 September. Earlier, on 5 July, it had been given a Sunday night performance at the Three Hundred Club, founded by Mrs Geoffrey Whitworth in 1924 for presenting 'dramas of distinguished merit . . . likely to appeal in the first instance to a small public'. She had great theatrical flair, and between 1924 and 1931 sponsored new plays by James Elroy Flecker, Richard Hughes and D. H. Lawrence. The producer she chose for A.'s play was Frank Birch—and the cast included Raymond Massey and Robert Harris (Donald Wolfit was the assistant stage manager). This production was subsequently presented at the Playhouse by Nigel Playfair, and the cast was strengthened by the addition of Gordon Harker and Carleton Hobbs. *The Prisoners of War* was published to coincide with its première at the Three Hundred Club and was dedicated by the author to his father.

Many nice encouraging things have been said about it, but nothing has made me so glad as the deep and tender feeling of your pleasure. Morbid, yes; I daresay the ill-attendance was partly due to that infectious word, and the theatre itself in its poverty of outside lighting and desolate, windy situation always reminded me uncomfortably of a tomb, confirming the rumour of disease and death; but I was never sad, except at the exclusion of the pit-purses, and such friendly hands as the one you stretch out to me make everything worth while.

Yours very sincerely

  J. R. Ackerley

Part Three
BBC TALKS PRODUCER

To Lytton Strachey (1880–1932)   The British Broadcasting Corporation, 6
                                  Savoy Hill, W.C.2   13/6/28

Dear Lytton Strachey
                    can you be persuaded to broadcast something for us?
If possible in the near future? Goldie Lowes Dickinson was in just now
and seemed to doubt it from something you'd said on the subject: but I
hope he was mistaken. What do you feel about this? I think you would
probably find it an entertaining experience, and the people here are gay
and pleasant. If you take as kindly as I hope to the suggestion we should
want a quarter of an hour's 'talk' on any subject you like. About 1800–2000
words. I enclose a sort of guide book—but it's really quite simple. I hope I
am remembered.
Yours sincerely
  Joe Ackerley
  (*Talks Dept.*)

To Lytton Strachey (1880–1932)   The British Broadcasting Corporation, 7
                                  Savoy Hill, W.C.2   ?/11?/28

Dear Lytton
            it'll be quite alright if you'll dig and deck up for us one of your
old corpses! I'll write you an *official* letter next week. Miss [Hilda] Matheson[1]
says you are a lazy man—but she wants you at any ~~price cost expense~~—well
anyway at any. I've just had two more sherries at Henekeys so don't
bring this up against me. But *what*—tell us—will you dig up for us, precisely?
I suppose it had better be from *The Nation* [*& Athenaeum*] which isn't read,
cherished, and remembered like your books. Otherwise I'd suggest Beddoes
a little fuller,[2] a little rounder, a little more from behind. But I suppose you
won't. Goldie won't. No one will. But I would if I got paid for it and didn't
want just now to lose my job. In fact Let me know when you're back,
I won't.

[1] Director of Talks (1926–32).
[2] This was a reference to Strachey's essay on Thomas Lovell Beddoes called 'The Last Elizabethan', which had originally been published in the *New Quarterly* (November 1907) and was
subsequently included in his *Books and Characters* (1922).

Lytton, and we'll go to lunch to Genaro's[1] or Fava's or elsewhere.
Yours
   Joe

Come and see Lionel [Fielden][2] one day. He's very nice. And alarming.
Infy-com.[3] And sympathetic.

8 To Lytton Strachey (1880–1932)   The British Broadcasting Corporation,
                                        Savoy Hill, W.C.2 24 September, 29

Dear Lytton,
         I expect you have heard from various sources that I have been
pursuing you all over Bloomsbury lately, and since I have not managed to
run you to earth I expect you guess why I have been pursuing you all over
Bloomsbury lately. We want you to give a talk one evening during the next
two months—or not exactly a talk but a reading in a series which we are
calling something like 'Potted Biographies'[4]—real or imaginary, and to
which Virginia Woolf, Desmond MacCarthy and others are contributing.
    There are no rules to the game of choice—people are choosing just
whatever character—real or imaginary—gives them most fun. I am not
sure what Virginia's choice[5] is, but Desmond is going to write up an
imaginary biography of Dr. Watson, Sherlock Holmes' friend,[6] and someone else[7] is going to do Lord Byron's valet, [William] Fletcher.
    Will you join the group and give us, for instance, the biography of a real
or imaginary minor Victorian? We do hope that you will be attracted by
this idea, and please do not let yourself be influenced against it by any
question of the suitability of your voice.[8] It was, I remember, this which
caused you to refuse an offer which we made some time ago. Voice is really
the least important part of broadcasting and you will find that no strain will
be put upon you. It is just sitting down at a table and reading the manuscript
quietly.

    [1] i.e. Gennaro's in Dean Street.
    [2] Fielden had joined the BBC in 1927 and helped A. 'to get into the Corporation in the follow-
ing year'. But it was an act that he came to regret. He wrote to Braybrooke on 18 March 1971:
'Without that job, Joe would have HAD to write more . . . Over the years I must have had hundreds
of letters from him—and now I have none . . . One phrase does remain with me from a letter written
in deep depression about two years before his death: "Sadly I wake to each unwanted day"'.
From 1930 to 1935 Fielden was Head of the General Talks Department. He died in 1974.
    [3] Inferiority-complex.
    [4] The final title given to the series was 'Miniature Biographies'.
    [5] She chose Beau Brummell. A. was the producer, and her talk was broadcast on 20 November.
It was reprinted in *The Listener* on 27 November.
    [6] Broadcast and produced by A. on 4 December, and reprinted in *The Listener* on 11 December.
    [7] Harold Nicolson, whose talk was produced by A. on 20 November, and reprinted in *The
Listener* on 30 November.
    [8] When Michael Holroyd was working on his two volume critical biography of Lytton Strachey
(published in 1967 and 1968), he quizzed A. about Strachey's one and only audition. But A. was
vague in his replies: Lytton's voice, he seemed to recollect, confronted by a BBC microphone had
wavered, risen, and eventually achieved the sort of pitch that only dogs are meant to hear. So the
whole thing had to be called off. Strachey later wrote to A. to apologise: 'I was filled with such
feelings of guilt and remorse over my behaviour in our broadcasting that I lapsed into what I fear
was a churlish silence. Forgive me.' See Letter 236.

If you let me have your provisional acceptance of this, I will let you know details at once.

Yours sincerely,

Joe Ackerley

To E. M. Forster (1879–1970) The British Broadcasting Corporation, 9
Savoy Hill, W.C.2 3/10/29

D.M.M.[1]

I'm delighted with your Toulon news and look forward to hearing about it soon, with all the rest. It was because I hoped you'd find some happiness there that I suppressed my own gloomy news—also there's too much to put down on paper. This house of cards has indeed come tumbling about my ears with Dad's death, a month ago today. There isn't really—I'd better forewarn you—even a chink of sky to be seen; the wreckage is so overwhelming and complete.[2] There is however, luckily, a certain amount of humour—my Mother, like a character in Tchehof—moving gaily through her heaving, tottering world as though nothing whatever was happening, surrounded by her joblot servants and joblot dogs. She's quite absurd and superb really, and she probably won't read your letter as soon as she sees that it condoles.

Her distaste for the subject of death is greater than anything else, and she's kept throughout entirely out of it all, protecting herself in every kind of way.

I said there wasn't a gleam of light—but of course there is, and has been throughout, Leo[3] and Tom.[4] I can't tell you how helpful, how charming and generous and kind they've been; like lovers to me and mine. I'm sure I don't know how I'd have fared without the unfailing support they've given me.

Gerald [Heard][5] too has been charming, and Harold Monro[6] and Frank Birch.[7] And last but by no means least sweet old Albert.[8] Well Morgan dear I'm glad you're almost back. Indeed indeed I want to talk to you; and I've missed you no end. I may be slipping down to Portsmouth to see Albert this Saturday—unless he elects to come up. I've given him the choice and haven't yet heard. He stayed in Richmond the weekend before last with us all, and I hope he does it again this weekend but I didn't want to fag him.

[1] This probably stands for—'Dearest My Morgan'. Forster at this time used to begin his letters to A.—'Dearest My Joe'.

[2] Attached to his father's will, A. found two letters addressed to himself in which his father confessed that for many years he had been the provider of two households, and that most of his estate had dwindled in educating the three girls of the second liaison and buying for them and their mother a house at Barnes.

[3] 1879–1958. L. E. O. Charlton, Chief Staff Officer, Iraq Command, resigned in protest against the British bombing of unprotected villages in 1925. Three years later he was forcibly retired. He wrote two volumes of autobiography and a number of books for boys. See Chapters 13 and 18 of *My Father and Myself*.

[4] Tom Whichelo—formerly an aircraftsman—lived with Charlton and was referred to by him as his secretary. See note 3 above and Chapter 13 of *My Father and Myself*.

[5] See page 209, note 1.   [6] See Letter 60.   [7] See page 13, note 3.

[8] A sailor from Portsmouth—'simple, normal, inarticulate [and] working-class'—whom A. had met by introduction. Their affair is described in Chapter 12 of *My Father and Myself*. See Introduction, 3.

Will you please thank your Mother very very much for her letter to me. Harry [Daley][1] took me out last night—he thought it would be good for me—to *The Seagull*! and then, when I was very tired at about 11.30 p.m. and on the way to bed at my flat—I met a friend of his, Bob Buckingham,[2] another P.C. and rashly I asked him in and he stayed till 2 a.m.—just talking—at a distance. I enjoyed having him there—but it meant a bad night—and that must be remembered when reading this.

Love dear Morgan

Joe[3]

10   To Lytton Strachey (1880–1932)   The British Broadcasting Corporation,
                                      Savoy Hill, W.C.2   8 October, 29

Dear Lytton,

This Corporation is quite willing to pay you Fifty Guineas for a broadcast talk of twenty minutes[4] in the series of 'Miniature Biographies'. The fee offered is inclusive of publication in *The Listener*,[5] which means that we retain the British Serial rights of publication for ten days; after which, whether we publish or not, you may dispose of your manuscript as you wish.

We have all had our heads together for suggestions to offer you for your biography; but nothing has occurred to us except—for what it is worth—Mr Robert Raikes,[6] of whom we know nothing; but whose statue graced the Embankment Gardens outside this building until recently, when it was removed in a kind of tumbril with a rope round its neck, in a very ignominious fashion.[7] Whether there is anything to be made of this, I must leave to you.

I enjoyed my lunch with you the other day and hope when you're next In Town you'll let me know and lunch with me. Also I know a General of the Air Force[8] (retired at an early age) who is very nice and lives in Esher and would like me to drive you there to supper one evening if you would like to go.[9] He is a friend too of Morgan and Gerald Heard.

Yours

Joe Ackerley[10]

[1] See page 62, note 2.

[2] A.'s sister writes: 'This proves that Joe was the first one to meet Bob Buckingham, altho' Morgan always said that he introduced them to each other.' See page 161, note 1.

[3] This letter was discovered in a drawer of A.'s desk after his death. Presumably Forster must have returned it to him when A. was working on *My Father and Myself*. The letter has been annotated in Forster's hand: 'Dad's death. Ref. to Bob.'

[4] Cf. Letter 11, note 1.

[5] The first issue had appeared on 16 January.

[6] The eighteenth-century English philanthropist and pioneer of the Sunday School Movement.

[7] The removal was only temporary and for cleaning purposes. Afterwards the statue was returned to its original site at the north-east end of Victoria Embankment Gardens, where it had first been unveiled in 1880 and still stands today.

[8] L. E. O. Charlton. See page 17, note 3.

[9] A week later A. wrote: 'Will it do if I call for you at your club at about 6 p.m. tomorrow night? . . . I shall bring my car; so I hope it will be fine, for it's an open two-seater and the hood leaks.'

[10] The last paragraph of this letter was written by hand.

To Lytton Strachey (1880–1932)   The British Broadcasting Corporation,   11
                                 Savoy Hill, W.C.2   30 October, 29

Dear Lytton,
          I sent you a rather wild and tipsy letter the other day;[1] but this is a very sober one.

It is quite all right about your suggestion for broadcasting one of your already published biographical sketches in this series of 'Miniature Biographies', and we would like to know, as soon as you can let us, the subject of your choice. What about Carlyle?[2] The time allotted to you will be twenty minutes, which means about 2,500 words, which may mean that you will have to expand any article you have published in *The Nation* [*& Athenaeum*]? By the way, we are not at all certain how we stand with *The Nation* [*& Athenaeum*] over this; but we believe that the copyright is yours and that it will, therefore, be all right. I am asked to offer you a fee of fifteen guineas, inclusive, if the already published work you choose will be read without any further alterations; but up to twenty-five guineas if you are obliged to do any considerable work upon it to make it suitable to broadcasting requirements. Will you let me know what you think of this, and approximately what sort of date will suit you for broadcasting?

And can you have lunch with me one day next week? I haven't any engagements at all so far I think.
Yours
   Joe[3]

To Hugh Walpole (1884–1941)   The British Broadcasting Corporation,   12
                              Savoy Hill, W.C.2   14 May, 30

Dear Mr Walpole,
          I am so glad that you are giving your talk on 'Enjoying the Opera' tomorrow night, and this is just to confirm the time, which is 9.25 p.m. I have ascertained that the talk will start punctually at 9.25 p.m. and, as it is very important that the next item on the programme should also start punctually at 9.40 p.m., will you please manage to bring your talk to an end with about a minute to spare, i.e.:—at 9.39 p.m. This is rather important and I am sure it will suit you as I know you want to get back to the theatre.

---

[1] No BBC records have survived of the fees paid in 1929, but A.'s offer made earlier in the month of 'Fifty guineas for a broadcast talk of twenty minutes' when compared with the terms offered here probably accounts for his reference to his previous letter (10) as 'a rather wild and tipsy' one.
[2] *The Nation & Athenaeum* had published Strachey's article on Carlyle on 28 January. It would seem moreover that he must have toyed with the idea of broadcasting it—perhaps he answered this letter verbally, because on 4 November A. sent him a telegram reminding him that the script was due by 29 November. Michael Holroyd commented on 25 March 1972: 'I personally believe that "Carlyle" would have been the best suited of all his essays for radio.' But in the event it seems once more that Strachey developed cold feet. There is no record by the BBC of any script ever having been received.
[3] The last paragraph of this letter was written by hand.

Finally, could you let us see the manuscript of your talk? Perhaps if it is finished you would give it to the boy who bears this, for our paper, *The Listener*, is very anxious to see it. I presume you will not mind our publishing it?[1]

Yours sincerely,

J. R. Ackerley

13   To A. G. Macdonell (1895–1941) The British Broadcasting Corporation, Savoy Hill, W.C.2   5 September, 30

Dear Macdonell,

                I hope your dashing career as a broadcaster has not come to an abrupt end, but we have all felt here that there has been a slight progressive deterioration in the manuscripts you have been sending us. You started off gaily enough, but the standard of your first talk has not, in our opinion, been kept up and your later manuscripts have had the air of having been rather 'knocked off'. That is really the truth of the matter. We do not usually tell the truth in this office if we can possibly avoid doing so, but I gather from your letter that my excuse did not take you in.[2] The same criticism applies to your broadcasting manner. This also has grown less, rather than more satisfactory and we thought that the way in which you gave your last talk was far too staccato and clipped. I say 'we' because, of course, I would not dream of laying down my own private opinion in this way; but all the other people here who heard you made the same report, so I presume that there must be something in it. There is truth as well in my previous letter to you.

'The Syllabus' is starting very soon and the 'Silly Season', in which we had more space than we knew what to do with, has practically drawn to an end.

Yours sincerely,

J. R. Ackerley

14   To Hugh Walpole (1884–1941)   The British Broadcasting Corporation, London, W.1   28 July, 32

Dear Hugh,

                I am wondering whether I can interest you in a new series of weekly talks I am trying to get together for the autumn, i.e. from the beginning of October next, under the title of 'To an Unnamed Listener.'

---

[1] Walpole replied: 'I haven't a ms. They always let me do it without one. I do it better so, but of course you can publish it, if someone takes it down as I give it, in *The Listener. I'll be up to time.*'

[2] A. had written on 26 August: 'I am afraid we can't use this talk about the Scotsman. Our new syllabus starts very shortly and leaves us practically no spaces to play with.' Macdonell when replying defended himself against the charge of having 'knocked off' the script, and wrote back to point out that first he had written it as a formal essay, then 'knocked' it about in a second session to give it an impromptu appearance. Subsequently all was ironed out between the two, and Macdonell became a regular broadcaster.

This series will be personal addresses from a named broadcaster to some particular unnamed and probably imaginary listener. The rest of the listening public will be therefore in the position of eavesdroppers on private communications, and may of course, if the particular personal message has a universal application, identify themselves with the person addressed. In any case all messages will, of course, have to have what is called 'human interest.'

To give you some more definite idea of what I mean I have the following proposals on my list. Desmond MacCarthy says he would like to talk 'To a Day Dreamer'; Gerald Heard may ask the medical profession questions in an address 'To a Doctor'; near Armistice Day Henry Williamson may address 'The Unknown Warrior', and George Grossmith is down to speak 'To a Lady who Wants to be a Film Star'. We have also approached Max Beerbohm, Walter de la Mare, Hilaire Belloc, A. P. Herbert, Rosamond Lehmann and others.

As you will see, the series gives endless scope for variety of stuff—serious, humorous, fanciful or in the way of belles-lettres—but we do not want to devote it too much to the lighter kinds of address but hope to have suggestions for messages of a more purposeful and stimulating character. I should be so glad to know what you think of this, and whether anything comes to your mind in connection with it which you would like to broadcast.[1]

Yours sincerely,

J. R. Ackerley

To Brian Hill (1896–)   The British Broadcasting Corporation, 15
London, W.1   9/11/32

Dear Mr Hill

I have a letter about you from Theo Bartholomew[2] who says you would like to work here[3] and also that you and I should meet. I don't know what use I shall be over the first of these propositions; but the latter presents no difficulties from my side.

Would you perhaps care to lunch with me one day? I should be delighted to meet you.

Yours sincerely

Joe Ackerley

---

[1] By return of post Walpole answered that he would like to broadcast a piece addressed 'To a Friend Afraid of Optimism'. A. replied immediately, saying: 'That's splendid.' The series of talks went ahead, but Walpole's name did not appear in the final list of speakers. Walpole liked broadcasting and had told A. on a former occasion to look to him 'whenever the Corporation were hard up for optimists'. He had described himself then as 'optimistic (but only a sort of Nero for Rome; certainly *burning*!) novelist'.

[2] The Assistant Librarian of Cambridge University Library. He died in the following March and was described by *The Times* as 'a great bibliographer'. He was also an authority on Samuel Butler, having been appointed trustee of the literary estate after H. Festing Jones.

[3] Hill had in mind a job on one of the BBC publications.

16   To Brian Hill (1896—   )   The British Broadcasting Corporation,
                                                   London, W.1   22/11/32

Dear Hill
                thanks so much for your letter, and I'm glad to hear you're driving
at the Corporation through other approaches besides myself. I've passed
down your 'autobiography' to Nicolls, who runs our publications, and
perhaps other applications will be made to him by [A. C.] Siepmann[1] etc.
when you pull the other strings.
    I'm afraid I can't come out on Friday evening, and would really prefer
to lunch with you one day if that can be arranged. The fact is that I have
just started on some private work,[2] and since I have to devote 2 or even
3 evenings a week to my Mother I don't get much time left over. That's the
worst of having a job, and no doubt you find the same thing. I heard from
Theo [Bartholomew][3] the other day—cheerful I thought.
Yours sincerely
    Joe Ackerley

17   To Air-Commodore P. F. M. Fellowes (1883–1955)
                        The British Broadcasting Corporation, London W.1
                                                              2 February, 33

Dear Air-Commodore Fellowes,
                                Thank you very much for your letter of
January 27th and the draft of the proposed talk on the Everest Flight. I
think the manuscript is largely very interesting, but from the point of view
of style it is not written in a way very suitable for broadcasting. As you
probably know, the trick of broadcasting is to make people think that you
are not reading a manuscript but talking to them extempore in an easy,
conversational manner, and you will not give this illusion, of course, unless
the script from which you are reading is written in an easy, conversational
manner. Your manuscript has a strong tendency to be more of an article
than a talk—I mean to say it is rather formal and stiff—and I have therefore
taken the liberty of making suggested corrections on it and having it re-
typed for you to see. These, of course, are nothing more than suggestions
for you to work on, and if the changes I have made are repugnant to you,
you can revise them, keeping the main principle in view.[4]
    The other point about it is that we set our faces against advertisement.[5]

    [1] Director of Talks (1932–5).
    [2] The first draft of *My Father and Myself*. See Letter 162, note 3 and pages 224, note 3 and 240,
note 3.
    [3] See page 21, note 2.
    [4] The Air-Commodore agreed to all these corrections and wrote back on 6 February: 'I think
you have improved the talk immensely.' However he wished to retain two sentences that had been
cut. 'The idea of flying over and photographing Mount Everest originated with Colonel P. T.
Etherton and Colonel Stewart Blacker, both well known in central Asian and Himalayan explora-
tion, but it was not until Lady Houston took an interest in the expedition that any definite plans
could be made. She not only provided the funds which enabled the expedition to be carried out,
but she also personally interested herself in the organization and the preparation for the expedition.'
A. replied on 7 February that he 'was quite agreeable to this amplification', and the talk went out
on the evening of 13 February under the title 'The Lady Houston-Mount Everest Flight'.
    [5] See Letter 18.

I am sure you will understand the reasons for this. If we allowed people to advertise everyone else would want to do so, and we should find ourselves doing nothing else. Furthermore, these things have no interest at all for the great majority of listeners. I have therefore also taken out those parts of your manuscript in my re-draft of it, and should be glad to know what you feel about this?

Yours sincerely,

    J. R. Ackerley

To Hugh Ruttledge[1] (1884–1961)   The British Broadcasting Corporation,   18
                              London, W.1   28 August, 33

Dear Mr Ruttledge,

       I think you had better make no reference to the possibility of [F. S.] Smythe[2] broadcasting tomorrow night since there seems to be some doubt of his doing it. At any rate the only news I have is that he feels he must get permission from the Everest Committee, and this permission is not yet forthcoming.

    I like your MS. very much indeed, and am enclosing it herewith. I have no comments to make excepting that we are not allowed to advertise,[3] and if, therefore, 'venesta' is a trade name some such phrase as 'ply wood' should be substituted; and secondly if Mr D. F. Richards is a private contractor his name should be omitted too.

Yours sincerely,

    J. R. Ackerley

To William Plomer (1903–1973)   Maida Vale   19
                                            20/12/34

S.W.[4]

       here is this small sad collection[5] at last—sad in execution and much else, besides their story—for I fear they tell a story. However you will expect them to be personal and old-fashioned, and you will be right. Otherwise I'm afraid you will be disappointed. A certain mysteriousness and coyness in my behaviour over them may have led you to expect all manner of things—but I feel I can hardly claim even impropriety for them— I wish I could. As for the first extraordinary display, which I expect will bore you a lot, perhaps I ought to explain that it never was much more

---

   [1] Ruttledge had been appointed to lead the fourth attempt to climb Everest. Before his team left, he gave a talk which subsequently appeared in *The Listener* on 6 September under the title 'The Latest Attempt on Mount Everest'.

   [2] Smythe, on a previous ascent, was the climber who had reached the greatest altitude unaccompanied. On 13 September a talk of his was published in *The Listener* under the title 'The Highest Lone Climb on Everest'.

   [3] See Letter 17.

   [4] Sweet William.

   [5] A small book in manuscript, containing a number of homosexual love poems. The longest, called 'Notes for a Portrait of a Sailor', runs to 118 lines of a somewhat Whitmanesque nature. Among other poems was one of thirteen rhymed four-line stanzas entitled 'The Jacket', and six sonnets, two of which are unfinished.

than you will find it—roughish notes. There was a great deal more of it which I have destroyed, and it was going to be an epic (whatever an epic may be), but life started to bang me on the head soon after, and it turned, as you will notice, into a kind of aspic.

However it is inexcusable to excuse oneself as well. If I hadn't very much wanted to please you, D.L.B.,[1] I don't suppose they would ever have got spruced up at all; but a pukka sahib always keeps his word, and so here they are, my Xmas card for 1934.

I've kept no copies of them, so you now have the first and only edition of one; but I did tell Morgan that I would give him a copy too, so if you think them worth the bother of recopying will you let me have it back sometime so that I can do one out for him. Apart from him though I imagine you won't want to show them around.

With my love

   Joe

---

[1] Dear Little Bird.

Part Four
LITERARY EDITOR OF *THE LISTENER*

To Norman Douglas (1886–1952)   *The Listener*, Broadcasting House, W.1   20
15 April, 35

My dear Norman,
I expect this letter will be a surprise to you,[1] and I wish
that I could think that it would be a pleasant one. Its main object, however,
is to try to persuade you to do an article for *The Listener*, which, as you
probably don't know, is the British Broadcasting Corporation's journal. I
am the literary editor of it; and my editor R. S. Lambert, who has devised
the series of articles in which it is hoped something from you may be
incorporated, asked me to write you a personal letter when he heard that
we were acquainted.

The series of articles he contemplates are to be published during the
summer months; and his idea is to use the Grand Tour, with which the
aristocratic young Englishman of the 18th and early 19th century used to
complete his education, for purposes of comparison with a modern tour
covering the same route. I believe that the usual route for the Grand Tour
in the 18th century must have been from London to Paris, on to Geneva,
and so through the Alpine passes to Italy; thence across into South Germany
and back through the Low Countries. Lambert's idea is to divide this
journey into five stages,[2] covering the different parts, and to have a separate
writer for each part who would act as a kind of literary courier. Each article
would cover a stage of the Grand Tour and would refer to the descriptions,
comments and adventures of English travellers of the past, such as Beckford,
Byron, etc. The idea would be to compare the sights which they saw and the
conditions of travel in those days with the sights and conditions today.

We wondered whether you would consent to do the Italian part of the
journey for us?[3]

---

[1] Douglas was one of A.'s earliest admirers. In *Late Harvest* (1946) he wrote: '[George Gissing's]
Ionian Sea is a favourite of mine. This book, with its pervading scholarly pensiveness and friendly
outlook, has an aroma of its own and is one of the few which, like Joe Ackerley's *Hindoo Holiday*,
might with advantage have been lengthened to twice its size.'
[2] Subsequently increased to nine, after various editorial discussions between the Editor, A. and
several of the contributors.
[3] Douglas declined. On 21 April he wrote to A.: 'I have dropped writing; shut up the shop—for
the time being at all events. Sick of it!' He also said that the series 'ought to come out in book-form
later on'. Which is what happened. *The Grand Tour*, edited by R. S. Lambert, was published by
Faber in the autumn of that year.

We are also writing to Osbert Sitwell, Mona Wilson, [G. J.] Renier, and Evelyn Waugh, I think.[1]

The length of the article would be not less than 2,000 words; and then we come to the question of fee. I am afraid that you are likely to be far too expensive for us, but I have no knowledge on this point, and can only tell you that the fee we are thinking of offering all round is twelve guineas.

Joe

21 To Edmund Blunden (1896–1974) *The Listener*, Broadcasting House, W.1

13 May, 35

Dear Mr Blunden,

Thank you for your letter of 10th May.[2] I am very pleased that you will do the article; and we shall certainly be collecting the illustrations, but most of them will have to be chosen after we see the text of your article. If any suggestions occur to you for illustrations that you would like us to look out, or lines that we could follow up, I should be very glad to hear of them.

Yours sincerely,

J. R. Ackerley

22 To Sacheverell Sitwell (1897–) *The Listener*, Broadcasting House, W.1

30 May, 35

Dear Mr. Sitwell,

I am writing, as promised on the telephone the other day, to give you details of your contribution to our series of articles on the Grand Tour, which we are very glad you are able to undertake.

With regard to the question raised as to the actual period of the Tour, it may help you to know that the introduction, which is being written by Miss Mona Wilson, covers the origin of the Grand Tour and the routes followed by such great tourists as Sir Philip Sidney, John Evelyn, Horace Walpole, William Beckford and Byron. You could, therefore, I imagine, make your backward comparison with any or all of these people and the period they cover. As we arranged, we want you to cover the Italian journey—Genoa, Florence, Rome and Venice;[3] this we should like you to

---

[1] Of this group, only Mona Wilson agreed to contribute. She wrote the first article, entitled 'The Grand Tour—How It Began', which appeared on 3 July. Other contributors included Douglas Woodruff on 10 July on 'The First Stage—From London to Paris'; Edmund Blunden on 17 July on 'From Paris to Geneva'; Janet Adam Smith on 31 July on 'Switzerland and the Alps'; Richard Pyke on 7 August on 'Italy—Roads, Inns and Travellers'; Sacheverell Sitwell on 14 and 21 August on 'Venice and Florence' and 'Rome and Naples'; and Malcolm Letts on 28 August and 4 September on 'South Germany and the Rhineland' and 'Cologne—the Journey to the Coast'. See Letters 21, 22 and 23.

[2] This was in answer to the Editor's suggestion of 8 May that Blunden might 'contribute the third article, dealing with the journey across France [from Paris to Geneva]'. 'I am better acquainted,' he replied by return of post, 'with the Northern part of the French journey, but will willingly try that Southern section.'

[3] The final division was: 'Italy—Venice and Florence', 'Italy—Rome and Naples'.

divide up into two stages, devoting an article to each, and each article should be about 2000 words in length.

I hope that this is quite clear, and that you will be able to let us have your manuscript by the end of June.[1]

Yours sincerely,

J. R. Ackerley

To Richard Pyke   *The Listener*, Broadcasting House, W.1   23
31 July, 35

Dear Mr Pyke,

I enclose a proof of your Grand Tour article, for which we are very grateful to you.[2] I have taken the liberty of deleting the first two paragraphs and altering the first sentence of the third, to make it follow on a little more smoothly from the previous article; I hope you will not strenuously object. If you have any corrections would you please let us have the proof back by tomorrow afternoon? If you care to ring up, we could send a boy to collect it.

Yours sincerely,

J. R. Ackerley

To Eric Newton (1893–1965)   *The Listener*, Broadcasting House, W.1   24
24 October, 35

Dear Mr. Newton,

I am so glad that you will be able to do an article for me on the New English Art Club's fiftieth anniversary.[3] I had better, perhaps, repeat the instructions I gave to Mrs. Newton, which are that I want a 1,500 word article about the work and significance of the Club in general and the present Exhibition in particular. The article should be in my hands by Monday morning. I am enclosing herewith a booklet which I picked up at the Exhibition, which I have just visited. The show seems to me to be a little dull, but no doubt your article will give it the congratulations and encouragement which I suppose we all like to have on our fiftieth birthday.

The pictures with which I shall probably illustrate your text, and to which you may refer in it if you wish, are:

No. 13 John's 'Head of a Girl'
„ 101 Rothenstein's 'Portrait of a Student'
„ 220 Mary Adshead's 'Cottage Sitting-room'

[1] Sitwell replied on 2 May: 'I am so sorry to keep on bothering you, but your . . . letter did not make it clear that it is, in effect, *two* articles of 2000 words each that you want. This entails a lot of work, and I cannot see how I can undertake it unless a fee of eight guineas applies in each case. I accepted the offer understanding that only one article was under consideration.' It was agreed to pay eight guineas in each case.

[2] 'Italy—Roads, Inns and Travellers.'

[3] It appeared on 6 November. All the illustrations mentioned in this letter by A., save the Nash, were included.

and possibly either:—

No. 8   Paul Nash's 'Landscape' or
„ 123 Jamieson's 'April in a London Garden'.

Yours sincerely,
J. R. Ackerley

25   To Duncan Grant (1885–)   *The Listener*, Broadcasting House, W.1
12 December, 35

Dear Duncan,
I don't know how far you have got with your panels for the *Queen Mary*, but am wondering whether there would be any chance of your giving *The Listener* permission to publish photographs of them as soon as they are ready? We shall, eventually, I hope, be having an art article on the complete decorations of the ship; but it would be nice for us if we could reproduce your panels separately in advance.[1]
Yours sincerely,
J. R. Ackerley

26   To Clifford Dyment (1914–1971)   *The Listener*, Broadcasting House, W.1
?/?/36

Dear Clifford
like a fool I left your letter behind in my flat this morning, but it was next Thursday I think you said you'd be in London. If so I hope you'll lunch with me. I was already engaged with May Lowes Dickinson,[2] that amateur theatrical, but have postponed her now to Friday.
Excuse rush. So glad about the news of your short story and ambition realized. H. Warren[3] has just been 'at' me for not liking his poems. He says that since you like them and I like yours I oughter like his. That gives me a headache. Because you like mine and I like yours ought I to like his? I don't anyway; they make me wynce [*sic*], but what I consider your bad taste in liking mine does not arouse in me the equal bad taste to dislike yours. Now I hope *you* have a headache. I think H.W.'s a bit of a coon.
See you Thursday.
Joe

[1] The three panels were intended for the central lounge—but were turned down by Cunard. Two years later, in November 1937, they were exhibited at Agnew's. M.C., the art critic for *Country Life*, described them on 20 November as 'far too good for the decoration of a luxury liner'. Raymond Mortimer suggested the Tate, since then it would not be necessary to travel first class to New York to see them. In December 1972 Agnew's put them on show again in an exhibition of Twentieth Century British Art and they were bought by a private buyer.
[2] The eldest sister of Goldsworthy Lowes Dickinson. She was thought by some to be rather a poseuse with regard to intellectual matters.
[3] C. Henry Warren, one time Assistant Editor of the *Radio Times* and occasional contributor to *The Listener*, mainly on country topics. He died in 1966.

To Stephen Spender (1909–   )   *The Listener*, Broadcasting House, W.1   27
14/2/36

It's alright, dear Stephen; money is an important matter, and though the English apologise for mentioning it as if it were rather indecent, like shit, this is only part of their general hypocrisy and is not, I hope, shared by me.

I do recall some conversation with you about it; but Heaven knows what and it would have been just like me to have been too optimistic about ten. That I fear would seem to my dear Editor rather excessive, so let us split the difference and call it eight. I have put this *en train*, but the machinery I am told will not deliver the extra two at your door for about a fortnight, if you don't mind waiting that time.

I should take it to your casino and put it on 'rouge' since it was purely incidental that I chose that coloured ink and perhaps it is the blood of the lamb.

I was going to send you a book called *Friendship in Adolescence*[1] to review, but it turns out awful tosh; G. Dimitroff's *Letters [from Prison]*[2] have gone to you instead.

I'm so glad you all go on so well. Weather is better here than you say it is with you—coldish and a clear sky, but we are so bored with this beastly city, William and I, and take no pleasure from it. We went to see the new C. Chaplin film[3] yesterday hoping to be cheered up, but the boredom outweighs the fun.
Love to you all
   Joe

To Clive Bell (1881–1964)   *The Listener*, Broadcasting House, W.1   28
9 March, 36

Dear Clive,
        I found your letter when I came in this morning, and also a telegram from the Cunard people, saying they had made arrangements for you to look over the *Queen Mary* on Wednesday of next week.[4] I had of course already written on the previous Friday asking for facilities for you for the weekend. I did not therefore bother you with this piece of silliness; but have telephoned to their Mr. Derry in Liverpool since, and have told him that you are an extremely busy man and that the weekend alone will suit you. He seemed reluctant to arrange this—merely because it conflicted, I gather, with some of his own arrangements. But I pressed the point, and have arranged things to suit you. Their Mr. Hughes will therefore meet you at the Central Hotel, Liverpool,[5] at 9.30 on Sunday morning—a letter is to be sent to me to confirm this. Mr. Derry said that he hoped you would

---

[1] Correct title—*Friendship-Love in Adolescence* by N. M. Iovetz-Tereschenko.
[2] No review appeared in *The Listener*.   [3] *Modern Times*.   [4] See Letter 25.
[5] 'For Liverpool I propose to read Glasgow,' Bell replied by return, quite correctly. The ship had not yet sailed south.

be able to see all you wanted to see on that day, because he himself wanted to come to London on the Monday. I replied, however, that the job of seeing over the ship would obviously be a long and tiring one, with which he immediately agreed, and that I wanted you to have the option of a second visit on Monday if you needed it. I said I did not see why he should remain in Glasgow for that purpose; that there must be other people who could show you round. He agreed with this and said that you could arrange matters to your liking with their Mr. Hughes. I imagine that we shall be sending you a railway voucher from here to cover your journey.[1]

Now, there are one or two things I think I should pass on to you, although I don't want to make you any more unhappy about the business than no doubt you already are. Mr. Derry is the head of their publicity business, and it is he, perhaps under orders from above, who has been and still is pressing for a view of the manuscript before it is published. He repeated this request to me on the telephone, but I am anxious not to have any dispute with the Company, and said that I was only the Literary Editor and that the question was entirely one for the Editor himself. If they bother you with a similar request you can, of course, make whatever reply you like, but I think it is, perhaps, good policy, if we are to get this thing through with as little trouble as possible, to adopt an evasive attitude. You have, as you know, been given permission by the Corporation to have a completely free hand, but I think it would be as well, nevertheless, to avoid disputes just now. They will be very nice after the article is published. The reason they give for wanting to see this script is that it may contain technical errors, or such mistakes as placing a decoration in the Main Saloon which really belongs to the Galley, or, that since alterations are still in progress, changes may be made after your manuscript has been written. Would you therefore take particular care in making your notes to verify your facts.[2]

I am sorry, but I shan't be able to come with you. I hope, however, that Raymond Mortimer will be able to do so. Although I suppose Sunday and Monday are not days on which the Press is being generally admitted, and you are being given exceptional facilities I do not see why they should not be extended to Raymond too. Is there anything else to be said? You will, of course, make notes, and, if it is easy, secure photographs of any objects with which you would like your article illustrated. In this connection I have already in my possession a large bundle of photographs of the decorations, but they all seem to me quite monstrous, with the exception of the panels of [Edward] Wadsworth and [Algernon] Newton,[3] which are not without prettiness.[4]

Yours sincerely,

Joe

---

[1] The next day A. sent this hasty note: 'Apparently it is without precedent that a railway voucher should be given to anybody who is not a member of the staff; with people like yourself the system is to pay expenses afterwards. I hope this is all right.'

[2] Bell replied: '... rely on me to be conciliatory and evasive and, I hope, precise in my facts.'

[3] After the war, in an undated letter, A. wrote to James Kirkup: 'I sit on my terrace in the fading light and the river, quite motionless in the heat, lies below me like an Algernon Newton.'

[4] The article appeared on 8 April. Its title gives its tenor—'Inside the *Queen Mary*—A Business Man's Dream'. Several artists were praised—among them 'Wadsworth, Cedric Morris, Lambert,

To Clifford Dyment (1914–1971)   *The Listener*, Broadcasting House, W.1   29
                                                                  30/6/36

Dear Clifford
                lovely little poem.[1] Thank you. Accepted with gratitude and
enthusiasm. My secretary is away: she is always ill curse her, and so I have
to write all my letters manually and am therefore in a constant rush. So
excuse a short note. I've just come back from a week's holiday in Dover
which was lovely, and return for 3 weeks in the middle of next month. But
London in between is awful, hot, damp and rackety; it's a marvel how one
keeps one's head at all. Reith probably won't reply himself: but you never
know. I hope he will.[2]
Yours ever
   Joe

To Bernard Shaw (1856–1950)   *The Listener*, Broadcasting House, W.1   30
                                                            25 August, 36

Dear Sir,
        The Listener has just started this week a series of articles called
'Art and the State', which constitutes an international enquiry into the
present condition of modern art at home and abroad, and its relationship
to the various political régimes that have been set up. By art is meant
primarily painting, sculpture and architecture, and the pageantry of
national festivity and public ceremony; but other forms of art, such as
drama, opera, ballet, and so on, are not excluded, if contributors wish to
discuss them. Articles have, therefore, been invited from the most authoritative sources in Russia, Italy, Germany, France and America to explain

---

Skeaping, Vanessa Bell, Connard and Newton'—but the general tone was highly critical: 'To name
the persons who have disfigured this beautiful ship with their titterings in paint, wood, glaze, plastic
and metal, would be invidious, and is, fortunately, unnecessary. Their doings may be compared
with those of the mosaicists—almost all of them—who have defiled the glorious interior of Westminster Cathedral.' Bell bitterly regretted that Duncan Grant, 'the best decorative artist in
England and one of the best England has produced', should have had the panels he designed for
the central lounge refused. 'All competent judges who have seen [these] canvases . . . consider them
masterpieces . . . Frankly, is it proper or seemly that, on a matter of taste, some ignorant business
man should be allowed to overrule the best official and unofficial opinion in England?' A. sent a
copy of the issue to Kenneth Clark, who replied on 13 April: 'Clive's article . . . seems to me
perfectly fair criticism and my wife, who has seen the boat, says that it errs on the side of leniency.
I regret only the expression "business man" used as a term of abuse in the heading and throughout
—I suppose because I am a business man myself; but so after all were the Medici.'

    [1] 'A Christmas Poem', which was published on 4 November. Dyment was first introduced to A.
by Janet Adam Smith, the first literary editor of *The Listener*. 'The meeting was an exciting one,' he
wrote to Braybrooke in 1969, 'as I already admired him as author of *Hindoo Holiday* and liked his
poems—especially one called "The Conjuror on Hammersmith Bridge"—which I had in a volume
called *Poems by Four Authors* published by Bowes & Bowes of Cambridge. I was too nervous to tell
him about this at the time, but wrote to him soon afterwards. He replied: "How amusing that you
should have known me before you met me and saved up that old poem of mine. I don't however
consider myself much of a poet and am a little ashamed of most of the stuff I have published."'
In his last years he was sad to see the kind of poetry in which A. and he excelled—lyrical, reflective
and meticulous in design—go out of fashion. 'He was a perfectionist,' as Robert Greacen summed
up in the obituary columns of *The Times* on 8 June 1971.
    [2] A. had suggested that Dyment should approach Sir John Reith about a job on the BBC. Noth-
ing came of it.

how art is faring in those countries, what is her function and position under their political constitutions, to what extent they influence, help and direct her—in short what is the relationship in theory between art and the politics of these countries, and what are the fruits of these relationships in practice.

N. Milyutin contributes the Russian article, Herr [Hans] Hinkel (with Goebbels' supervision) the German, F. T. Marinetti the Italian, Georges Duthuit the French, and Lewis Mumford has been asked to speak for America; and the article will, of course, be illustrated with reproductions of recent works of art. Mr Maynard Keynes has contributed an introductory article, which I am forwarding under separate cover, and I am writing to ask whether we can persuade you to sum the series up for us? If, as we very much hope, the suggestion appeals to you and you consent to undertake the concluding article, I could send you at once the Russian and French contributions, and the remainder when they reach us in a few days' time. The length of the article I am wanting is about 2000 words, and I should need to have it in my hands by September 21st.

Yours faithfully,
    J. R. Ackerley

This concluding article should of course be a survey of a comment upon the whole series.[1]

31   To Clive Bell (1881–1964)   *The Listener*, Broadcasting House, W.1
                                                        31 August, 36
Dear Clive,
            I am delighted with your letter[2] and send immediately herewith N. Milyutin's Russian article, which comes out on Wednesday.[3] As soon as the printers have got Georges Duthuit's straight, that shall go to you as well. I am so grateful to Miss Jane Bussy[4] for her work on it, and shall write to her immediately. But, in all fairness to Miss Ritchie, it should be noted that she was not quite dotty in her translation of 'biche'—'leaning on hands' being merely a printer's error for 'leaning on hinds'. I am afraid that this peculiar misprint at the beginning put everyone rather more against Miss Ritchie than perhaps she quite deserved, Georges himself writing a furious letter to say God knows she must be crazy to get 'hands' out of 'biche'. Actually her writing was very bad, and all the spelling errors were due to the difficulty the printers found with the text.

When we meet on the third I shall have to consult you over my difficulty with the Italian contribution, and show you the only script I possess—and feel I am likely to possess—which comes from Marinetti. I asked him to

---

[1] Shaw misread the letter, believing that A. was asking for a script for broadcasting—and declined. Before Shaw, A. had originally approached Kenneth Clark, who had agreed to write the summing-up. But sudden pressures of work 'forced him to withdraw', and A. then sent on 30 August an urgent note by hand to Clive Bell, who came to the rescue and contributed the concluding article, which was published on 21 October under the title of the 'Failure of State Art'. See Letters 31, 34 and Appendix B.
[2] In this Bell had agreed to write the summing-up article in the series 'Art and the State', which had begun on 26 August and was due to run until the end of October.
[3] Publication day of *The Listener* was originally Wednesday. On 2 June 1938 it was changed to Thursday.   [4] See Letter 32.

re-write it, but a telegram, after a lapse of three or four weeks, informs me that he is now on his way to Buenos Aires. Ugo Ojetti, for whom I have also been angling and whom, at one moment, I thought I had landed, since we satisfied him over the question of fee and only had to negotiate a date, has now closed up like an oyster and refuses to reply to letters or telegrams. I shall therefore be wanting to know whether you will agree that I shall publish the ridiculous script Marinetti has sent me with equally ridiculous photographs. The German script is now said to be on the way, but, heaven knows, it has been on the way for the last two months.

Yours,
Joe

To Jane-Simone Bussy (1906–1960)   *The Listener*, Broadcasting House,   32
                                                W.1   4 September, 36

Dear Miss Bussy,
        Thank you so much for the corrected proof. Georges now writes very happily, pleased with everything, and only offering a couple of suggestions to complete his satisfaction.

I feel I cannot let you undertake all that work for no remuneration, and have asked our accounts department to send you a guinea as some small expression of gratitude for the kindness of your help. I wonder whether, when a future occasion arises (as no doubt it soon will, for I am keen on Georges's work), you would care to undertake the translation altogether? If so, I should be glad to place it in your charge, and I am sure that Georges, also, would be much relieved.

I should very much like to come to tea with your mother[1] and yourself, and could do so next Monday, September 7th, if that suits you. I am very pleased and interested to hear that your mother helped my book *Hindoo Holiday* into France, for I have often wondered how it got there, and why Gallimard submitted to terms which they absurdly said would ruin them.[2]

Yours sincerely,
J. R. Ackerley

To Paul Nash (1899–1946)   *The Listener*, Broadcasting House, W.1   33
                                                         4 September, 36

Dear Mr Nash,
        There is, as you may know, an exhibition of Inn Signs at the Building Centre on November 2nd, and I am wondering whether

---

[1] Dorothy Bussy, sister of Lytton Strachey and wife of Simon Bussy, the French painter.

[2] The French edition had come out in 1935 under the title *Intermède hindou*. The translator was Marie Mavraud, and there was a Preface by the Aga Khan who, whilst negotiations were on with Gallimard, had written to A. on 11 August 1934 to say that if the publishers were agreeable ('I am very well known in France'), he would be willing to write a short introduction to the 'French translation—in French of course.' He also said: 'I want to read it myself with the passages in question restored. My wife, also, will probably understand it better in French. It is a great pity that in England artists are not allowed to express themselves freely, and their works are often cramped by such prejudices as those of your publisher who urged you to omit certain passages . . . Even in France Gide has been forced—in the 2nd edition of *Si le grain ne meurt*—to drop parts which I always thought were essential in the original edition . . .'

this is the kind of subject that you would like to take as the theme for an art article? We have found between us so much difficulty, so far, in thinking out something suitable and tempting to you, and I wondered whether the above suggestion would interest you. I thought the article might be on design in Inn Signs generally, using the exhibition as a peg. If you like this idea—and it might produce some pretty illustrations—I should like to put it in promptly, in our issue of November 4th, which means that I should like to have the article—from 1500 to 1800 words—in my hands a fortnight before that, which would be October 21st.[1]
Yours sincerely,
J. R. Ackerley

34   To Lewis Mumford (1895–   )   *The Listener*, Broadcasting House, W.1
17 September, 36

Dear Mr. Mumford,
I want to thank you most sincerely for the article you have written for my 'Art and the State' series.[2] I thought it, in fact, one of the most interesting and stimulating of the whole collection, and am more than grateful for your kindness in consenting to do it.

I don't know whether you would like to receive copies of *The Listener* which contain the other articles of the series, but, feeling that it would be only proper since you are taking part in it to let you see what is happening, I am arranging for the whole lot to be sent to you. You will find, I am sure, what pleasant reading the democratic articles make, as against those of the dictatorship countries, but this, no doubt, will not come as a surprise to you.
Yours sincerely,
J. R. Ackerley

35   To Walter Sickert (1860–1942)   *The Listener*, Broadcasting House, W.1
7 December, 36

Dear Sir,
I am encouraged to write to you by Duncan Grant to ask whether you can be persuaded to contribute an article to this paper—*The Listener*—of which I am Literary Editor. I do not know whether you ever see the paper, but, if so, you will know that it contains material on Literature and the Arts independent of what is broadcast, and among other things an independent art article every week.

To vary the ordinary round of topical articles by art critics on Art publications and exhibitions, I am trying to arrange for a series of articles by the artists themselves—French and English—on some personal subject which they may choose, such as the work they are immediately engaged upon, or some particular question which happens to interest them. I am

---

[1] Nash was unable to meet this deadline, but the article appeared a week later on 11 November. It was called 'Signs' and began the issue.
[2] It was published on 7 October.

asking them whether, besides contributing articles, they will consent to do special illustrative sketches for them, or, at any rate, permit me to reproduce as illustrations works of theirs which have not hitherto been exhibited.

So far I have been approaching the French painters and have received acceptances from Rouault, Masson, Marie Laurencin, Dufy and Léger, of whom Rouault, I believe, wishes to write something about Stained Glass Window Design; Léger on the Re-awakening of Mural Art, and Marie Laurencin on some subject connected with Costumes.[1]

I feel I cannot dare to hope that you would consent to do a specially illustrated article, but would it nevertheless be possible for you to write something for me—preferably on the work you are at present engaged upon? I feel that a series of articles of this kind from the artists themselves would have considerable interest and educative value to our readers and I should feel very proud if I were able to include you in it.
Yours faithfully,
J. R. Ackerley

To Fred Urquhart (1912–)   *The Listener*, Broadcasting House, W.1   36
21/12/36

Dear Mr Urquhart
　　　　　　　I think the story you've sent me is a very good story indeed; it is more economic and tighter than the previous two—but I'm almost equally sure that *The Listener* won't take it. However I always 'try it on', and at the moment it's with the Editor, who will no doubt like it and reject it in due course.[2] It calls a spade a spade, which is so badly needed; but as you no doubt realize if you listen to the wireless at all, broadcasting does not consider it can go in for such plain speaking, and its publications are similarly limited. I get what I can into my art and literary pages—*The Listener*'s so called independent side, but apart from the somewhat fruity conversational passages in your story, which I think will also be jibbed at, they would never put up with a story which set out to make army recruiting prospects even worse than, thank God, they are at present. However, it's been a pleasure to read it, and if, as I anticipate, I have to return it soon, I hope you will not be put off trying me again. I'll certainly look out for your [*London*] *Mercury* story; it sounds very much up my street, and glad you liked my play,[3] though personally I think better of a book I wrote (my only

---

[1] In the autumn when planning this series 'The Artist Speaks', A. had written in a memo to the Editor: 'The kind of people I am aiming to get are Picasso, Matisse, Sickert, Braque, Paul Nash, Edward Burra, Duncan Grant, Marie Laurencin, André Masson, Léger, Rouault, Henry Moore, Corbusier, Winifred Nicholson and so on.' Setting his sights high, he found himself far more successful than he 'ever dreamed'. Sickert, though, was not among the contributors, because A.'s letter 'miscarried and never reached him', and the final team included Henry Moore, Fernand Léger, Jack B. Yeats, Marie Laurencin, William Coldstream and Georges Rouault. A special feature of the series was that each article 'was illustrated with recent examples of each artist's painting or sculpture, including one original sketch'. Cf. Letters 39, 40, 41, 43, 45 and 47.
[2] Which is precisely what happened in the following month. The rejection slip was initialled 'J.R.A.'—and read: 'As expected. So sorry.' The story was 'Those Things Pass' and was subsequently published in *The Left Review* (March 1937).
[3] *The Prisoners of War*.

other 'work') called *Hindoo Holiday*. If you haven't got it, I'd be delighted
to send you a copy.
Yours sincerely
J. R. Ackerley

37   To Fred Urquhart (1912–)   *The Listener*, Broadcasting House, W.1
                                                                      19/1/37
Dear Mr Urquhart
                       no, you have still to write a story for me; but at any
rate these, like what else I have seen of your work, convince me that you
are one day going to do so.[1] At present you seem to me to be feeling your
way if I may say so; but in the right direction. There is a great advance
from 'Piano Accompaniment' to 'Fields of Amaranth'; but in my view
you have not yet reached again the high standard of that story. 'Debut'
does not get there (nor, I think, does 'I Fell for a Sailor'); it seems to me
too undigested, inconsequent and too long. Art and life are not the same;
the writer must use the former to present the latter. There seems no reason
why the story should end when it does; and if the whisky was life, art should,
I think, have eliminated it. The seeds of disappointment are already in the
situation, in the young man's character and high ambition; art does not
require the whisky.
   Art should have developed the snob, too, I feel; might he not have been
one of the young men whom your hero first encounters for instance—something anyway to put him out a little more. You must excuse these, probably
impertinent, remarks: they come only from interest. And this is not to say
that one wants stories with a 'smart' turn at the end, a surprise in the tail,
or even a full-stop. But one wants a little more tightness, a little more
economy than you employ. At least that is what I think.
Yours sincerely
J. R. Ackerley

38   To Ariadna Tyrkova Williams   *The Listener*, Broadcasting House, W.1
                                                                26 January, 37
Dear Mrs Williams,
                       I have been very much disappointed by your article
on Pushkin—to such an extent indeed that I have decided to put off
publication of the commemorative article about him until the issue after
next in order to give you the opportunity to re-write it.
   The fault I find with your article is that it seems to me to contain nothing
except the few biographical facts about his life which I think anyone could
have supplied; your general remarks about him, his place in literature, the

   [1] This was to prove true twelve years later, when Urquhart's 'Alicky's Watch' was published
on 11 August 1949. But the letter of acceptance came from the Deputy Editor—then Maurice
Ashley, who wrote on 13 July: 'Would a fee of twelve guineas be agreeable to you?' A. had set the
manuscript aside as 'a possible *Listener* story' before going on holiday in June. When he returned,
he managed to bump the fee up to fifteen guineas.

Russian view of him and the general significance of his work, seem to me to have turned into little more than an uninformative and superlative eulogy which might equally well have been written about any great man. Moreover, I must say that the writing itself is not at all satisfactory and a good deal more work would need to be done on that alone. The effect of the whole is quite the opposite of what you intended. I feel that it will not interest readers in Pushkin in the least and, indeed, your opening pages and final paragraph seem to be almost unreadable.

I know I did not give you much time to do this article, and it is with a view to helping you in this matter that I have decided to postpone publication for a week; if indeed you had told me in the first place that the time was really too short for you I would have given you the extra allowance then, but some writers do things quickly whereas others need time and leisure. Actually I thought at first that by making some alterations in your script I might manage to put it together myself, and as you will see from the enclosed, I have taken that liberty with it—omitted altogether your last page and transferred your opening to the end, not because I particularly want to begin in an autobiographical manner, but because I don't think that readers would persevere beyond your first opening paragraph. On re-reading my revision, however, I cannot feel that it is satisfactory and am, therefore, returning your own script with my revision to you in the hope that you will be able to let me have a better piece of work by next Monday morning.

I think perhaps you should not follow my revision, but rewrite the whole article, illustrating it perhaps with some couplets or quotations from his work. I don't know whether this would be possible, but put it forward as a way in which it may be practicable to enliven your assessment of him.[1]

And now with regard to the book you kindly sent me and the photographs you have indicated, I thought I understood from you on the telephone that there were some self-portraits of Pushkin which were better and more interesting than those already known; but the portrait which you have indicated in the book is one of the best known of all, is it not?—and possibly a rather romantic version of him. The other picture I do not care for at all. Yours sincerely,

J. R. Ackerley

To Marie Laurencin (1885–1957)   *The Listener*, Broadcasting House, W.1   39
le 29 janvier, 37

Chère Madame Laurencin,

Je dois vous faire mes excuses de ne pas vous avoir répondu plus tôt. Maintenant j'ai le plaisir de vous informer que je

---

[1] She re-wrote the article and delivered it by hand on the morning of 1 February with the accompanying note: 'I hope you will be more merciful and I shall have a quick affirmative answer.' A. sent his reply by messenger: '. . . your revised article . . . is enormously improved and quite acceptable.' Later that afternoon he received another note: 'I am very glad that this time I passed.' The article appeared on 10 February under the title 'Russia's Greatest Poet', and was followed by Maurice Baring's translation of Pushkin's poem of 1826, 'The Prophet'.

prendrais volontiers un article de vous ayant pour titre 'Le Modèle' comme vous le proposez. Cet article ne doit pas dépasser 1,500 mots et, comme M. Duthuit vous l'a déjà dit, je vous serais très redevable de vouloir bien me faire quelques esquisses spéciaux qui serviraient d'illustrations. Je pourrais utiliser trois ou quatre.[1]

Veuillez agréer, Madame, mes salutations empressées.

J. R. Ackerley

40   To William Coldstream (1908–   )   *The Listener*, Broadcasting House, W.1

22 April, 37

Dear Mr Coldstream,

I am sorry not to have replied to your letter[2] before but have been rather busy with a Literary Supplement. The title you suggest for your article sounds a good one, if you mean, as I hope, that it will be something in the way of a self-critical explanation of your work.

It will be quite all right for you to have a month to produce your article. I should like to have it if possible by the end of May, and if you make one original sketch I shall be quite satisfied, assuming that the other illustrations will be examples of your hitherto unexhibited work.

Yours sincerely,

J. R. Ackerley

41   To Jack B. Yeats (1871–1957)   *The Listener*, Broadcasting House, W.1

7 May, 37

Dear Mr Yeats,

I am so very pleased with the original sketch[3] you sent me and the photographs of your beautiful paintings: two[4] of these at any rate should come out well enough in *The Listener;* for the others I am more

---

[1] When the article arrived, A. wrote to Vyvyan Holland inviting him to translate it. He added: 'I asked her for an art article but what she has sent me is really more in the nature of an essay or short story. However, since she has also sent me an original sketch to illustrate it, I am reluctant to tell her that her article is not altogether suitable, and am hoping that a good translation may make of it as much as possible.' Holland replied on 15 March: 'The . . . article is a little thin, but her name and sketch should carry it . . . Why she uses a model is a mystery. All her ladies look exactly alike.' The article appeared on 8 September under the title 'My Model'.

[2] In this letter Coldstream had agreed to contribute to the series 'The Artist Speaks' and suggested as a title for his article 'Choosing a Subject'. Later this was changed to 'How I Paint'. The text was accompanied by four illustrations, three of them paintings: 'Giraffes at the Zoo' (1930), and portraits of Miss Anrep (1936) and W. H. Auden (1937). The fourth illustration, specially commissioned for *The Listener*, was a drawing of A.—though no name of the sitter was given in the caption beneath it when the article appeared on 15 September. In the previous month, Coldstream had visited Forster at 26 Brunswick Square with the idea of making a drawing of him for *The Listener*. Sir William told Braybrooke in 1972: 'I do not think I ever finished the drawing and cannot remember whatever happened to it.' But he added: 'I clearly remember drawing Ackerley . . . He was living then near Paddington Station. I was first introduced to him—or at any rate he heard of me—through Auden, whom I had recently painted and who had been a close friend of mine for a number of years. I saw Ackerley on only a few occasions after that—and I have no memories of particular interest beyond the fact that he struck me as an exceptionally nice man and a marvellous conversationalist.'

[3] The sketch was of a boy looking into a forest and seeing an artist at an easel under every tree. It was entitled 'As a child he saw artists under trees . . .'

[4] Five had been submitted, but in the end only one was used—'A Second Visit': it was a new and hitherto unexhibited work.

doubtful. Your article too (a proof of which I enclose) is most interesting, but I do rather feel, as I hinted in an earlier letter, that by giving your description of a painter's life autobiographical form you tend, I think inevitably, to give to the picture a somewhat remoter interest than auto-biography would have held.

I feel, however, that I am here on rather delicate ground, for although I take the impression that the article is autobiographical, I have no grounds for doing so. If it is autobiographical, I should like to say that I perfectly understand this sensitive method of presenting one's own story, but, as I have already said, it loses, to some extent, significance thereby.

I wondered, therefore, whether—assuming that I am correct in suppos-ing that the article is autobiographical—you would consent to say so at the end; some such sentence perhaps as 'You will be wondering whether this friend of mine was not myself. Perhaps he was.' I may, however, be wrong in my original assumption.[1]

Yours sincerely,

J. R. Ackerley

To Fred Urquhart (1912–)   *The Listener*, Broadcasting House, W.1   42
26/6/37

Dear Urquhart

I've only just received your letter, having been away in France for three weeks holiday. So glad [R. F.] Dunnett[2] has been seeing you (I don't remember him, or speaking about you to him; but I suppose I must have) and shall be interested to hear if anything comes of it. They are more go-ahead in the provinces than here.

I haven't come across your Curtis Brown[3] stories yet, but have only had time so far to attend to personal correspondence. I expect they are in my short story file, and I shall look forward to reading them.

I had a very nice time in the South of France and Paris. How much more civilised the French are than ourselves. They do not spend all their time preventing people from enjoying themselves.[4]

Yours sincerely

Joe Ackerley

[1] No fair reader could quarrel with this summing up. The article was called 'A Painter's Life', and when returning the proofs the artist had written on 1 May: 'I dislike the idea of talking about my own paintings for integral reasons, and because I hold myself free to change my ideas, as some hot-necked people change a limp collar at a dance. But you . . . have responsibility for *The Listener*, so I have added something of what you suggest at the end . . .' The addition read: 'Perhaps in describing my friend's life I may, at times, have described my own. But then perhaps it is true that the more we are the same, the more we are different.' The article came out on 1 September.

[2] A Talks Producer in Edinburgh who dealt with short stories.

[3] Curtis Brown was then A.'s literary agent: 'He acts for me, but if he places your stuff abroad he will try and rob you of 20% (10% for his London office, and 10% for whichever of his foreign offices is involved), a practice which seems to me extortionate. He always caves in—with me, anyway; but then, having a regular job besides, I'm in the happy position of not caring whether my things are published abroad or not, because I don't depend on them.'

[4] Later A. was to revise this view. On 14 June 1960 he wrote to Francis King: 'I did have a bit of fun [in Paris] before being run down. If it could be called pleasure any greater than having a shit. The French give pleasure without enjoying it themselves, the Greeks give and enjoy, and one therefore pays them more gladly.'

43 To Georges Rouault (1871–1958)   *The Listener*, Broadcasting House, W.1
6 July, 37

Cher Monsieur Rouault,
Je suis absolument enchanté de la petite peinture que vous m'avez envoyée;[1] elle est d'une beauté et fera le plus grand honneur à mon journal. Mille remerciements également du nouveau manuscrit; je l'envoie, ainsi que vos premiers 'Soliloques', à notre meilleur traducteur de francais,[2] qui, je l'espère, assemblera les deux séries de façon à en faire un article intéressant pour cadrer avec votre peinture.
Croyez bien, je vous prie, à mes meilleurs sentiments.
J. R. Ackerley

44 To V. S. Pritchett (1900–   )   *The Listener*, Broadcasting House, W.1
13 July, 37

Dear Pritchett
I very much enjoyed reading your short story[3] in *Night and Day*—the only decent thing it contained, I thought—and wondered whether you had any other stories by you (up to 2,500 words) you would like to submit to *The Listener*.[4]
I need hardly say that the BBC being what it is, a story as naughty as the one I enjoyed would scarcely be likely to pass the censor here.[5]
Yours sincerely
J. R. Ackerley

45 To Henry Moore (1898–   )   *The Listener*, Broadcasting House, W.1
24 August, 37

Dear Moore,
Your letter was unfortunately kept downstairs for some days with our photographic people, and it has only just come to hand.

[1] A head of a clown, painted specially for *The Listener*, and published on 29 September.
[2] Vyvyan Holland. See Letter 47.
[3] The story was entitled 'Upstairs, Downstairs' and had appeared in the first issue of *Night and Day*—a weekly which had been launched on 1 July and ran until the end of the year. In 1956 when Pritchett reprinted it in his *Collected Stories*, he changed its title to 'Eleven O'Clock'.
[4] Pritchett replied three days later: 'I'm glad you were amused by the *Night and Day* story. I wish the paper would grow up a bit. I've nothing short enough that would do . . . at the moment but I'm hoping to do one or two things in the next fortnight and I shall be glad to send these if they come off.' Subsequently several stories were sent in by his literary agent, but six years elapsed before one was accepted. This appeared on 6 May 1943 and was called 'The Oedipus Complex'. It had originally been broadcast in the Overseas Service.
[5] A. had in his desk at this time a story by John Collier that he wanted to publish. But the Editor would not play. 'He's being awfully irritating,' A. wrote to Fred Urquhart in the following month. 'He made me return a lovely story to John Collier.' This was to be a recurring theme in A.'s letters to contributors. To David Paul he wrote in 1950: 'I was sorry [your story 'Darkness'] . . . don't pass; the copulation scene is too well described—though that is not said. "It's not for us" is the phrase used, as if we were the *Church Times*, and perhaps we are . . .' Cf. Letters 36 and 136.

I quite agree with you about the title 'The Sculptor Speaks', and you are quite right in your supposition as to the reasons for the change. A good deal is being done at present to give *The Listener* a more striking kind of journalistic presentation, and it was thought that your own title was insufficiently attractive. Since the series had already been advertised in *The Listener* under the title of 'The Artist Speaks', I do not think you need have any fear that readers would think that the title given to your article was your own choice, or was meant to convey anything more than a variation of the general designation of the series.[1]

I, too, would have liked more pictures to go in and that they should have been larger, but the length of your script unfortunately made this impossible. Furthermore, as I think I said in a previous letter, the fact that the rest of the photographs you sent me were all works which were already familiar to me and the public generally, made it difficult for me to reproduce them, in view of the publicity I had already given to the fact that the works reproduced would be either original or hitherto unexhibited.[2]

I am arranging for you to have prints of your drawings.
Yours sincerely,
J. R. Ackerley

To William Coldstream (1908–   )   *The Listener*, Broadcasting House, W.1   46
24 August, 37

Dear Coldstream,
         I saw E. M. Forster this weekend, and he says he has no objection to your doing a sketch of him, though he hopes it will not take too long, as he is not a very good sitter. Perhaps you would now like to get into touch with him yourself, to find out when a time can be arranged which will suit you both? I know he is to be in London this Friday and again the following Monday or Tuesday, but expect this will be too early for you and there is, after all, no hurry for a couple of weeks.[3]

His addresses are—
West Hackhurst, Abinger Hammer, Near Dorking,
and 26, Brunswick Square, W.C.1.
He spends most of his time at the former.
Yours sincerely,
J. R. Ackerley

[1] Moore had written on 19 August, the day after the article appeared: 'I was a bit upset by the Epstein title "The Sculptor Speaks". I hope it won't be thought that I gave the article that title— I'd much rather it had been headed with my own—"Notes on Sculpture" . . . But perhaps it's clear to others, from your line or two of introduction immediately after the title, that the heading is *The Listener*'s, not mine; so I am getting touchy unnecessarily.'

[2] There were two illustrations: a photograph of Moore's 'Two Forms, in Hornton Stone' of 1937, and a drawing of shapes and figures presented as an example of the way in which this particular artist generated 'ideas for sculpture'. Moore wrote to Braybrooke on 24 February 1972: 'I had great admiration for Joe and found him very sympathetic and nice to me, a younger person.'

[3] Before Coldstream visited Forster, A. sent a note in advance: 'He is a nice young man and you will like him.' The sittings took place in Brunswick Square, but the drawing was never completed. Cf. page 38, note 2.

47   To Douglas Cooper (1911–)   *The Listener*, Broadcasting House, W.1
9 September, 37

Dear Douglas,
            Without previous enquiry or any warning I am sending you, under this cover, some material which I am very anxious for you to help me with as quickly as possible, for I think you are really the only person who can do for me this very tiresome and, I think, very difficult work.

As you know, in this series of articles from the artists themselves, I invited a contribution from Rouault. I asked him to give me something about his early work in stained glass window design. He sent me, in fact, a series of what he called 'Soliloques', which had practically no bearing whatever on the subject. I then returned to the attack and asked him if he could possibly furnish me with a few more of his 'Soliloques', a little less abstract in nature and more concerned with his own work. He politely consented and sent me an article on Cézanne.

I did not know what to do with these articles and sent them to Vyvyan Holland, asking him whether he would read them for me and tell me (a) which was the better for me to use, or, (b) whether, if both were bad, a kind of mélange could be made out of them with as free a translation as he liked. He replied that he did not see how to combine the two, as they were written in quite different styles; that Rouault appeared to mistake confusion of thought for depth of thought; that however much one tinkered with the 'Soliloques', he thought that nothing readable would emerge; and, that the second article about Cézanne was written in such a strange style and in such odd grammar as to be practically meaningless. He ended by saying that he really thought that both contributions were rubbish.

I therefore thought that the only thing I could do would be to conceal from the general reader the rubbish of this writing by publishing one of the articles—and I chose the 'Soliloques'—in the more decent obscurity of its difficult French; for my main object, as you know, in this series was to publish the original paintings or drawings I was extracting from the contributors—the text seeming to me of supernumerary importance. And of all the original designs I have received, Rouault's is the most beautiful.

My Editor, however, now intervenes and says he will not publish rubbish—even by Rouault, and even in French; that he will not have an article on Rouault to present the special painting, since we have already had one article[1] on him recently, and, that the only way, therefore, in which I can use and publish this special painting by Rouault in my series in *The Listener* is to get somebody who will take the trouble to write an article, the main object of which will be to present to our readers as much of Rouault's thought as is intelligible in these two manuscripts, in a kind of introductory article.

I hope I make the distinction clear, that I do not want so much an article about Rouault as one presenting him and his thoughts, in so far as they can intelligibly be extracted from these manuscripts, to the public. The article

[1] The Editor was confused. What had appeared on 26 May was a page of illustrations devoted to works by Constable, Renoir and Rouault. The text had been confined to captions.

might be, for instance, something in the way of a dialogue between Rouault and another, or it could be a straight article somehow framing the meditations and observations of this important and somewhat mystically-minded French painter.[1] In either of these cases, you see, the article could still fall suitably under the general heading of the series—'The Artist Speaks'.

Now, will you be an angel and do this for me and let me have it back at the latest by Monday morning, September 20? I don't mind how liberally [*sic*] you translate the extracts from Rouault's scripts, nor do I mind how short the article is—it could be anything from 1000 to 1500 words—presenting Rouault, his work and his thoughts to the public. I shall publish with it, the charming original sketch, 'Head of a Clown', and also another of the pictures he has sent me—I expect a rather stained glass window 'Christ'.[2]

Finally, I hope you won't mind me putting this on you without previous enquiry as to whether you are too busy to do it, or not. There is absolutely nobody else who can undertake it, and urgency, desperation and confidence in you, drives me to this very unorthodox course.

Yours,
Joe

P.S. I have sent *Mexico Around Me*[3] down to Groom Place, as you request, but doubt whether you will think it worth notice when you see it.

Encl.: Rouault's two original scripts (which please return carefully);
  A very rough translation I had made of the 'Soliloquies';
  A short rough translation by Vyvyan Holland of passages from both the articles;
  Rouault's final corrected proof.[4]

To Richard Church (1893–1972)   Maida Vale   48
                                                                        ?/12/37

Dear Richard
          I haven't seen your corrections, but these are the cuts I myself suggest for your article on A.E.H.[5] If you are specially anxious to retain the last para. I will do my best to keep it in, but allowing for 10 words per line, you are about a dozen lines over the 800 words, and the quotes add to the length, of course. Will you look at it, and consider the queries I raised on the phone? I don't want to 'claim' Housman unwarrantably

[1] Cooper, under the pseudonym of Douglas Lord, chose the second alternative, and the article was entitled 'The Wisdom of Georges Rouault' and published on 29 September. He had also been responsible for obtaining and translating an earlier article in the series—'Revival of Mural Art' by Fernand Léger, which had been published on 25 August. See page 35, note 1.

[2] 'Christ aux Outrages.'

[3] By Max Miller. Cooper did not review it for *The Listener*.

[4] A. had written to Rouault on 3 August, saying he was having the original article set up in French. A few days later he sent a proof with this note: '. . . il y a . . . un certain nombre de passages obscurs, resultant . . . de l'omission de quelques mots. Je vous serais donc infiniment reconnaissant si vous voulez bien revoir l'épreuve avec le plus grand soin, y faire les corrections nécessaires, quelles soient, et me la renvoyer ensuite.'

[5] This was the lead review for the Christmas Book Supplement on 8 December. The book was *A.E.H.: Some Poems, Some Letters, and a Personal Memoir* by Laurence Housman.

for the homosexuals, but I don't, also, see why facts thought proper by his very correct brother to mention should not be alluded to in any review—even in our respectable *Listener*. If Laurence had wished to hide A.E.'s curious 26-year old friendship with the Venetian gondolier, he could easily have suppressed the letters in which allusions are made to it, and if you, a critic, are to select, for 'revealing' purposes, a friendship with a German governess, begun, I suggest, in boyhood, if not childhood, rather than in youth, and extending over a period of about 60 years, I don't see why you should not add, without comment, and just as another instance of his long friendships, the fact, as it appears, that he seems to have been attached to a Venetian gondolier for 26 years. Will you not then add this small item of information, without any remark, in its appropriate place? I very much dislike the idea that *The Listener*, more than any other paper, should suppress such matters: I do not even insist that they are significant: but they seem to me as interesting and significant as the German governess, since you do, in any case, plunge into that 'mystery'. Don't you agree? The two letters in which the gondolier is mentioned are on pp. 142 and 150–151.

If you disagree with any or all of these alterations, or wish to make any other changes, I bow to your decision.[1]

Yours ever

Joe

49   To Fred Urquhart (1912–   )   The Royal Automobile Club, London, S.W.1   23/6/38

Dear Urquhart

I only got back from abroad a few days ago and found your book[2] waiting for me; I don't know how long it had been there. Thanks very much for sending me a copy, but to be honest—and I must be—I don't really get on with it very well. Nor, to continue honestly, was I altogether surprised, for I've thought for some time past that your work was becoming experimental in the wrong sort of way, and a short story of yours[3] which I read on the boat from Alexandria to Rhodes in the Penguins' *Weekend Book*[4] I thought definitely bad. I don't know how necessary it is for you to publish your writings—that's so often the curse with authors—but I do think you'll damage a reputation which I do agree with [Edwin] Muir is promising

---

[1] But Church agreed with the points that A. had raised and re-phrased the relevant part of his review thus: 'Mr Housman warns the reader against sentimental mystery-mongering about A.E.H.'s celibacy. None of the family knew why he never married. He had several friendships with women, one of them beginning in his boyhood and lasting all his life. This was with a German lady, fifteen years his senior, who corresponded with him until her death at the age of ninety. Another example of his enduring interests appears in his letters, which seems to show that he befriended a gondolier in Venice over a period of twenty-six years.' A fortnight before Church died on 4 March 1972 he wrote to Braybrooke: 'Joe Ackerley never interfered in the articles by his contributors, unless there were flagrant literary mistakes, or outrageous and unfair prejudices involved. He was a catholic and tolerant literary editor, at least as I had dealings with him over some twenty-five years . . . *Hindoo Holiday* is a masterpiece . . . His prose was always immaculate, like his personal good manners, and his capacity for disinterested friendship.'

[2] *Time Will Knit.*

[3] 'The Christ Child.' Cf. Letter 50.

[4] Correct title—*Penguin Parade* (No. 2).

if you don't exercise a more careful judgment—for I've an idea that you know very well when you've done something good and when you haven't. I was glad Muir praised you[1]—your book deserves praise of course, and broadly I agree with his judgment; but I should have smacked you harder and praised you less—tipped the scales a bit more the other way in fact—if I had been in his place. For in spite of all the good points in your book he picks out[2]—and as I say I think his appreciation of them was sound—my own view of the book is that it's exceedingly difficult to read—indeed I shall say flatly that I think it's unreadable, by which I mean that it seems to me to fail completely to pull the reader along. It contains some well observed characterisation, as Muir said; but no real form, no expectation, and to be confronted with two different dialects in one book (one is putting-off enough in my opinion) is too much. Nor does the trick 'knitting' frame pull the thing together;[3] it seems to me only obtrusive and tiresome—all those devices are, I think; one should never notice the frame of a picture at all.

I'm sorry to write such a dashing letter, but it's my opinion for what it's worth: I don't think you've allowed enough time to digest your ideas properly. The impression I get is that you just faked up a makeshift framework and poured the whole mixture in.

Your second letter comes while I am actually writing this—on my way through London. I have 14 (fourteen) weeks holiday, you see, and still have five to go. Expect to visit Glasgow, but probably not Edinburgh—but I'll let you know if I do—though I expect you'll be less pleased to see me after this letter?
Yours sincerely
  Joc Ackerley

To Fred Urquhart (1912–)   33 Marine Parade, Dover   50
                                                      10/7/38
Dear Urquhart
          your letter was very civil and decent and made me ashamed of my own[4] which I had in any case regretted as soon as it was irrevocably in the box—and you are quite right, I was too harsh altogether, and did not do sufficient justice to that fact that your heart is in the right place. But you do not seem to speak sufficiently from it. Instead of that we get too much of what is called 'cleverness'. I think that that is what I mean about your experimenting in the wrong way. Perhaps if I ask you the question

---

1 On 16 June Muir had reviewed Urquhart's novel in *The Listener*, along with *Pathetic Symphony* by Klaus Mann and *Pray for the Wanderer* by Kate O'Brien. Muir had described it as 'a first novel of unusual promise'.
2 'There is a great deal of extraordinarily effective character writing . . .'
3 The novel's title was drawn from Harold Monro:

Time will knit
And multiply the stitches while we look.

The plain stitches are supplied by an American young man of Scottish ancestry who returns to Scotland and meets various relations, while the purl are provided by the elders among his relations —his grandparents and aunts.
4 Cf. Letter 49.

'Why have you gone in for trying to imitate tough American dialogue?' your answer may explain me better than I explain myself. But perhaps it won't, for I didn't find your defence of your book—its 'unreadability' as I called it—very convincing. Surely a 'transcription of life' is not enough? You might as well shove a dictaphone in the sittingroom of your home for a week and publish the result as a novel. It would be a 'transcription of life' certainly; but no one would be bothered to read it. Something more than that is required. Your work reminds me in some ways of that of John Simpson's—or John Hampson as he calls himself—if you look at his books *O Providence, Strip Jack Naked, Family Curse*, and of course *Saturday Night at the Greyhound*, you will see what I mean.

In *Family Curse* he goes in for a trick frame, much as you do with your 'knitting', but to my mind he brings things off and you don't. Possibly it's because he tells a story, and you don't—you don't in the sense that you don't keep the reader in any state of expectation or suspense, which is not to be confused with what you call 'entertainment'; and surely it must be obvious that if you don't offer the reader a carrot or two the poor donkey won't go forward with you. Doesn't E. M. Forster in his *Aspects of the Novel*[1] go into all this? It is a book you should read: it is a very interesting book indeed. As for the 'canons of the art' I really don't know what they are, and I bet you don't either.

Yours ever

  Joe Ackerley

N.B. 'The Christ Child'[2] was nothing—so say I, and so said the Professor of English at Cairo University, an exceedingly cultivated man, far more so than I, for I made him read it on the Alex. to Rhodes boat, and, when I heard his comments, read it myself. I'm sorry, but that is what we both felt, that it was cheap and nothing.

51 To G. F. Green (1911–)   *The Listener*, Broadcasting House, W.1
                                                               ?/8/38

Dear Mr Green

              I have just returned from a three months' holiday, and find your story[3] which seems to have been waiting for a decision for some time. I like it very much, and have recommended it to the Editor who accepts it: a proof is enclosed herewith. It is just possible we may be putting it in immediately, so would you send corrections if any by return. The only doubt in my mind in first reading your story was as to the genuineness of the dialect. Actually I am not familiar with any of our county dialects, and so far as I recall the scene of the story is not specified, but for what such

---

[1] 1927.
[2] Cf. Letter 49.
[3] 'A Summer Night', which was published on 11 August. In the following year, on 27 November, A. wrote to Green: 'It must be over a year since you sent me a very interesting short story . . . I have been disappointed not to get anything from you since . . . I should be very glad to see anything you care to send.' This is a good example of what A. called his 'follow-up tactics'. It usually brought rewards—in this case several more stories over the years from Green.

a remark may be worth it did not bring to my mind a feeling of reality, but seemed more like a kind of mixture, 'abaht' reminding me of the London East End, 'maun' of Masefield in *Nan* and the rest vaguely Lancashire or Yorkshire. I hope this will not seem cavilling—but since the conversation in the story did pull me up and worry me a little I thought it worth mentioning: no doubt you have a definite county in mind, and your phonetic spelling of its dialect [is] beyond reproach.

Yours sincerely

J. R. Ackerley

To T. S. Eliot (1888–1965)　　　*The Listener*, Broadcasting House, W.1　52
30 December, 38

Dear Eliot,

On the 19th January, we are producing the Tenth Anniversary Number, over which a great deal of trouble and enthusiasm is being expended—there is even to be a coloured cover[1]—and I am writing to ask whether you could let me have a poem for it?

You never have sent me anything, excepting poor young men in need of work; do let me have something for this special number.[2]

Yours sincerely,

J. R. Ackerley

To Sir Kenneth Clark (1903–　)　*The Listener*, Broadcasting House, W.1　53
9 January, 39

Dear Clark,

Thanks for your letter. I thought your '100 Details' book[3] very beautiful and reluctantly parted with it to Roger Hinks who is going to do me a glorified book review with illustrations for the Tenth Anniversary Number.[4]

Your Olive Cook has sent me two glossy prints of the Bronzino Masks and Hogarth's 'Cat' as suggested illustrations, but I am not clear whether the suggestion comes from yourself or not. Her letter says that they are the most popular and interesting details, but if popular means that they are being reproduced elsewhere, I should naturally like to choose some others.

[1] By Barnet Freedman.
[2] Eliot temporarily mislaid this letter and wrote to A. to apologise on 23 January 1939. In the meantime, on 10 January, the Director-General of the BBC had repeated the request and asked for a poem: 'Nothing ad hoc or laureate-ish is looked for . . .' Eliot replied to the Director-General on 12 January: 'The simple fact is that I have not written a single poem since my collected volume appeared two years ago, because all the time and energy that I have had to give to poetry has gone to the play which I have just completed. One or two people have asked me to let them print bits out of this play, but I have consistently refused, because I do not feel that any fragment will be intelligible by itself, and I wanted the play to appear whole before it is taken to bits.' The play was *The Family Reunion*, which opened at the Westminster Theatre on 21 March.
[3] *One Hundred Details from Pictures in the National Gallery*, with an Introduction and Notes by Kenneth Clark (1938).
[4] The review did not appear in this issue, but was delayed until 26 January. 'I hope you will like the "100 Details" book,' Sir Kenneth had written to A. on 2 January. 'It is intended primarily as a book of pretty pictures but secondarily as an aid to appreciation. I am annoyed when people treat it solely as a parlour game in which the players have to guess from which pictures the details come.'

Incidentally, she has enclosed a bill with them, which I think must be a mistake. We are not usually expected to pay for reproducing pictures to illustrate book reviews.

Yours sincerely,

J. R. Ackerley

54   To Sir Kenneth Clark (1903–)   17 February, 39

Dear Clark,

As we failed over Henry Moore, I think I must really try you again over Picasso—your reaction to the suggestion was, I feel, more a hesitation than a reply. I think there is no doubt that the show will be a very important one, and I do wish you would do me a column on it—or, indeed, more if you like. Nor am I this time in a hurry, for I understand that it opens to the public on the 1st March, so I should not want the script until that day.

I do hope you will find the time and the inclination to say Yes, for God knows there is no one else to turn to.[1]

Yours sincerely,

J. R. Ackerley

55   To Paul Nash (1899–1946)   *The Listener*, Broadcasting House, W.1
                                              21 November, 39

Dear Nash,

So sorry not to have answered your letter.[2] The trouble is when one does not deal with the illustrative side of articles oneself that correspondence about such articles sometimes falls between two stools. I rather took it for granted that Miss Scott-Johnston herself was keeping in touch with you.

I went down with her myself to the Royal College of Surgeons and we selected one of [Henry] Tonks' Wounded Heads for photographing. We had to be careful as some of them were so horrible that the editor would not have accepted them for publication even if the Director of the College would have allowed us to photograph them, which he said he would not. We have taken one of a study of a head taken with its wound, a badly lacerated mouth and painted again after reconstruction. But even in this the torn mouth is so disgusting that the Editor may jib.[3]

The other picture is of the reconstructed face—a good drawing I think—which still shows the war scars.

[1] Sir Kenneth replied on 20 February: 'Yes, I will try and do something, although God knows it will get me into the most frightful trouble on all sides.' His article 'Recent Paintings by Picasso' appeared on 9 March.

[2] This concerned the illustrations for an article Nash was writing for A. about the Oxford 'Arts Bureau'. See Letter 56.

[3] He did not—and the drawing appeared alongside the same face after it had been reconstructed by plastic surgery. Other illustrations in the issue of 30 November included a 1919 painting of 'A Battery Shelled' by Wyndham Lewis and 'New Arrivals' by Gilbert Spencer, showing a ward in No. 36 Stationary Hospital in Mahemdia, Sinai before the first attack was made on Gaza in April 1917.

We have still no success over 'The Gas Attack'.[1] I have written to Ernst Gombrich of the Warburg Institute to ask if he can help. I do not know from your letter what you can mean by choosing whatever looks interesting from the categories enclosed. What about one of [Eric] Kennington's drawings or paintings, if all else fails?

The article arrived safely and a proof will go to you on Wednesday. I certainly do not care for the James Fitton[2] but I am afraid the shape will do and it is too late, I think, to change it. It will look rather a curious illustration superficially in your war article. However, perhaps readers will think it is Florence Nightingale.

Yours,

J. R. Ackerley

To Paul Nash (1899–1946)   *The Listener*, Broadcasting House, W.1   56
24 November, 39

Dear Nash,

      I am afraid that you will be angry with me, but on reconsideration of the title of your article, we did not like it in your form. We thought the title 'Arts Bureau in Oxford' was an unattractive one to readers, besides being clumsy. We also thought it less suitable than my own title of 'Letter from Oxford', considering the very personal style in which you had written the article. Mindful, however, of your own wishes in this matter and anxious to satisfy them so far as seemed journalistically possible to us in the circumstances, we have decided to keep my original title of 'Letter from Oxford', adding, however, a bold sub-title that the article concerns itself with your Arts Bureau. The whole title will therefore read 'Letter from Oxford. Paul Nash on the New Arts Bureau'.

I hope, therefore, that both honour and expediency are thereby satisfied.[3]

Yours sincerely,

J. R. Ackerley

To Francis Watson (1907–)   *The Listener*, Broadcasting House, W.1   57
8 December, 39

Dear Mr Watson,

        I am so very pleased to hear from you, and although

---

[1] By William Roberts. It had been made for Canadian Records during the First World War.

[2] 'Eve'. This painting was referred to by Nash in a postscript to his article in which he dealt with the Exhibition of Younger British Artists that had just opened at the Ashmolean, Oxford. He wrote: '"Eve" . . . has been selected by the organizers as representing the tone and character of the exhibition.' But privately he had written to A.: 'The . . . lady *is their pick* because what I chose caused a flutter among the dovecotes.'

[3] Nash replied on 4 December: 'I *was* very pleased with the way you presented my article, but a little dashed to receive no complimentary copy!' A. sent a dozen by return of post.

Literary Editor of The Listener

Mr Herbert Read's information appears to have been incorrect,[1] it nevertheless leaves you in the, so far as I am concerned, delightful position of being able to contribute an article to my paper on Indian Art.

I don't quite know how you intend to organise your article, considering you are doing so much, but from the ideas which emerge from your letter, I am sure that you will be sending me something entertaining, topical, and even perhaps educational.[2]

So very interested to hear that you got to Chhatarpur. Yes, it was the place I lived in, but the King is dead, and my friends there scattered, I believe. I wonder what you thought of it.

Yours sincerely,

J. R. Ackerley

58 To John Piper (1903–)   *The Listener*, Broadcasting House, W.1

3 April, 40

Dear Piper,

I wrote to you the other day about one thing and now another occurs to me—to ask whether you would be free and willing to do a column for me on the current art exhibitions in London for next week?[3] I should want the article—600 to 700 words—by Friday morning at the latest.

The exhibitions I have received notification for so far are:

> Cyril J. Ross
> Claude Rogers
> Angela Kinross
> Frances Hodgkins
> John Aldridge
> Colin Colahan

This pre-supposes that you are not doing these exhibitions for *The Spectator*.

Yours sincerely,

J. R. Ackerley

[1] Namely, that Watson was teaching art in an Indian State. He had in fact been living in the household of the Rajah of Aundh in an honorary capacity reorganising and advising on the Rajah's art collection, but by the time A.'s letter reached him he had been recruited to the General Staff, Army Headquarters, for war-service.

[2] Nothing came from him until after the war, when he contributed on 29 November 1945 his first article to *The Listener* on 'What is Indo-English?'

[3] Piper was unable to do this, but contributed the 'Round the Art Exhibitions' piece for 6 June. In it, he reviewed the work of eighteen artists, including Paul Nash, Robert Medley and Graham Sutherland, who had contributed to a show entitled 'England in Wartime' at the Leicester Galleries. He also covered exhibitions at Wildenstein's (Victor Pasmore), and at Tooth's (Matthew Smith, Stanley Spencer, Nadia Benois and Tristram Hillier). Piper's first contribution to *The Listener* had been an article on Duncan Grant which had appeared on 24 June 1931. He told Braybrooke in 1973: 'I had hundreds of letters from Joe—well, dozens anyway—but I fear we were careless in those days, and only this one seems to have survived. In 1933 I remember writing for Janet Adam Smith, who was at that period running *The Listener* art and book pages, two articles on the "Younger English Painters" [22 March and 29 March]. They were illustrated, and showed for the first time in print some then almost totally unknown painters such as Victor Pasmore, William Coldstream, Ceri Richards and Robert Medley. Joe kept this tradition going when he took over two years later.'

To Douglas Reed (1895–   )   *The Listener*, Broadcasting House, W.1   59
                                                      29 April, 40

Dear Mr Reed
                I am very interested in your long letter,[1] but not altogether
informed by it—it is too emotional to be clear—and I think I had better
say to you at once that I really cannot have you appealing to me as a
'Britisher'. It is an appeal to the emotions, and it is most important that the
emotions should be kept firmly out of any discussion of this subject. 'You,
as a Britisher' is the emotional clan call to arms, and I am too old to respond
to it. I am an Englishman, and I love my country and do not wish to live
anywhere else. But if I am asked to say that it is better than any other country
I shall not say so, for I don't believe it. Indeed, like all other countries, I
believe it has faults, and that the sexual suppression we are corresponding
about is one of them, and that it could learn a lot, if it chose, from its neighbours. So I must at once reject the 'Britisher' appeal and also the 'patriotic'
one. I don't believe in patriotism either, and if this war does not knock the
national out of 'democracy' as well as out of socialism, and lead us towards
some international order then I do not believe that any good can come of it.
                So far as I can make your letter out, you are in favour of sexual freedom
so long as it is not exploited. If you had thought that the young people of the
Weimar Republic were exerting their own free will, then, your letter seems
to say, you would have raised no objections? That is to say that you don't
mind stage nudes, strip-teasers, homosexuals, etc. expressing themselves
freely and enjoying themselves? If that is your attitude, I think it is a
humane and reasonable one; but your letter to *The [Daily] Telegraph*[2] did
not strike me as a reasonable or humane letter or seem to carry this meaning,
and I am obliged to regard with some suspicion the anger and emotion in
your letter to me, so perhaps I have not interpreted you aright?
                Although I did not see the Weimar Republic at the height of this business,
I have no doubt that there was a good deal of exploitation going on, but it is a
quite unreal view of life to imagine that no young people (one in a thousand
is your figure) do these things freely or because they like them. A word with
an intelligent psychologist would put you straight over that. Exhibitionism
alone is a very common thing, both in women and in men, and if it were not
so we should have no 'revue' girls for instance. Am I to understand from
you that not only in Germany but all over the world all girls who kick their
legs about on the stage wearing (as they all do) as few clothes as their censors
will permit are White Slaves, frustrated in their ambitions to be doing
higher things? Are Mr Cochran's young ladies white slaves, and the
pitiful scarecrows of our Prince of Wales' Theatre and the admirable nude
ladies of the Folies Bergère, Moulin Rouge, etc.? For the 'moral' distinction

---

[1] See page 119, item 470, in *An Annotated Calendar of the Letters from E. M. Forster to Joe R. Ackerley in the Humanities Research Center, the University of Texas at Austin*, edited by Philip Lee Fry (1974).
[2] April 13. The correspondence was headed 'Sex on the Stage' and sub-titled 'Influences from Abroad'. Reed's letter ended: 'The one thing that National Socialism did, which even its most inveterate enemies, including myself, were unanimous in praising, was to stamp out the revolting conditions which the Weimar Republic allowed to develop in Germany. If, in this of all matters, we allow the Berlin of 1918–1933 to enjoy a second lease of life in London, we shall make our invocation to the cause of Freedom ridiculous and repugnant.'

between the girl who wears as little as the censor officially permits and the girl who wears less is extremely difficult to define, and I must reassert, in spite of your contradiction, that since the object of all these nude or semi-nude entertainments is to arouse the sexual interest of the audience they are therefore a 'matter of sex'. I really cannot accept correction in a definition when I am clearly speaking with exactitude. I went to see the exponent of strip-tease[1] who appeared in this country at the Victoria Palace,[2] and though her performances may have been a slight modification of the Weimar Republic performances—discreeter lights—the spirit was the same, and to regard her sentimentally as a victim would be nonsense. On the contrary she obviously thought she was a Great Artist and the Venus de Milo rolled into one, and has since written to the papers to express her pique that the English public did not take her more seriously.

But to return to your Republic. I don't really see any use in adopting a tone of moral indignation against a country when it falls into the condition that Republic exemplified. The sensible thing is surely to look for the cause of the condition, and, as your letter indicates, the circumstances which offended you there were largely symptomatic of the economic collapse— though no doubt there were attendant reasons, such as those found in the neurosis of anxiety and defeat. Whatever their nationality, when people have no money and no work you will always get a rise in prostitution and procuring and a movement towards the already existing centres of sensation and amusement—cabarets, theatres, bars, locales, brothels, baths and so on. The remedy for this, if it gets out of control, is not persecution; any psychologist will tell you of the dangers of driving things underground, and any intelligent policeman of the inevitable results in his department (blackmail, robbery and violence). The remedy is, quite obviously, an improvement in the economic situation. If Hitler had given Germany 'butter' instead of guns, the overbalance you deplore would automatically have readjusted itself without the application of persecution and purges, for the victims of the economic situation—the people, that is to say, who found the business antipathetic would have been set free to get employment elsewhere. For this reason then I thought it inhumane of you to hold up this unfortunate Republic as an object of disgrace and disgust, and particularly unreasonable to praise the Nazi régime for succeeding it. The ways of peace are surely always better than the ways of war, and even if the former seem to us to be decadent and corrupt, it is comparatively a self-corruption and more easily susceptible of cure than is, for example, the disease which Hitler has introduced in its place and which is ravaging now the whole world. Who would not wish the Weimar Republic, with all its faults, back now? I feel it difficult therefore to understand how you can have praised Hitler publicly for doing away with one set of circumstances in favour of a worse set—the more so since you admit that his motives were dishonest. Furthermore, can you approve of the application of brutality in any circumstances? for the 'purification' of Germany was not effected without great cruelty. *And* injustice—for I take it that the police made no distinction between those

_____
[1] Diane Ray.   [2] In 1937.

who were having some fun and the 'exploiters'; all, so I have heard, were swept away together to punishment and prison.

And is it not invidious to accuse a country for an over-emphasis in these matters which had temporarily got beyond its control, when precisely the same conditions, though in lesser, more normal, degree, are freely and openly to be found, as you must surely know, in every other country in Central Europe (I am speaking, of course, of the pre-Hitler-annexation period)—excepting our own? Paris, Copenhagen, Stockholm, Vienna, Budapest, all provide their stage-nudes, brothels, bars, locales, Turkish Baths, cabarets and the rest of it; and, though I have not been to Italy since Mussolini took it, I was told by some young German chaps on Rhodes in 1938 how much they enjoyed spending their holidays there (luckily for them, for they were allowed practically nowhere else), for there one could still live a comparatively free sex life whereas in Germany the whole subject was surrounded with persecution and fear.

In all these places, then, to my knowledge, in twenty-five years of travel, 'night-life' with its haunts and diversions of all descriptions has gone on, fluctuating in activity according to economic and other circumstances; boring to some, amusing to others, an important part, however small, of the free and spontaneous life of the people. Abhorrent to Britishers? Certainly not. Many that can afford to make a bee line in their holidays to such centres of freedom and gaiety (the Weimar Republic was no exception, in spite of your assertion to the contrary) are only too glad to open up and have a bit of fun for a change, away from a country where, since a man's chest is considered an indecent object, the ban still lingers on trunk bathing-shorts. (G. J. Renier's *The English: Are They Human?*[1] provides an interesting portrait of ourselves.)

Sex and fun. Sex and gaiety. The conjunction of these words, which fall naturally together in the minds of all other Europeans, would never for an instant be permitted by our governors and governesses here where the good old world 'unwholesome' is at once trotted out to join the word 'nudity' (cf. 'Janus' in last week's *Spectator*),[2] where everything is driven underground and there is always someone on the alert to stamp on it the moment the dreadful beast raises its head.

What often interests me is what harm is supposed to come to people by participation in all this business. Excepting that they may well get bored as I usually do myself, I often wonder how it is supposed to affect them. Besides 'unwholesome', we trot out all the usual words of course, 'unclean', 'demoralising', 'undesirable', 'unhealthy', etc. etc. I always want to ask, how do the French and Danes for instance seem to survive the contamination of permitting in their midst all the things which we consider so injurious

[1] 1931.
[2] On 19 April 'Janus' had written in 'A Spectator's Notebook': 'The question is whether, particularly in wartime, it is a wholesome thing to induce growing soldiers in their early twenties, who by the nature of their calling are deprived much more than normally of women's society, to pay their money to see women stripping, or already stripped, on a music-hall stage.' In the course of the same paragraph, there was a reference to Forster's views. 'Mr E. M. Forster, I see, deprecates the pother being made about the business, and says that people who like nude shows should be left to go and see them, and people who, like himself, don't should stay away.' 'Janus' was the pseudonym of the Editor of the *Spectator* (Wilson Harris).

to public health? Are they corruptible, while we are not? The Danes in particular have always seemed to me the most sympathetic people in Europe. Gay, honest, healthy, sport-loving—one could not wish for a more civilised country. Yet, as no doubt you know, there is the minimum of interference in people's lives. Even the pervert is acknowledged and allowed his freedom and locales, instead of being jailed as he is here ('For the colour of his hair', as A. E. Housman put it) to the embarrassment of our more enlightened prison commissioners like Alex. Paterson,[1] who do not know what to do with him when they've got him. The Danes make only two stipulations: there is a strict age limit (I forget what it is) for boys and girls, and people must not misbehave in public. Contravention of either of these rules is heavily punished. Perhaps such a rule as the former answers your views about exploitation? One cannot after all continue to protect people in such matters indefinitely into adult life. Besides, as Milton said 'Banish all objects of lust, shut up all youth into the severest discipline that can be exercised in any hermitage, ye cannot make them chaste that came not thither so'. People have exploited each other since the world began, and will no doubt continue to do so until they can all quote Milton too: and where the passions are concerned they naturally exploit each other most. At present we are privileged to watch the exploitation of pain and death; a spectacle I, personally, find less attractive than the exploitation of 'love'.

I said earlier on that there was no distinction between nudity and strip-tease, but in fact I believe there is a difference, and an important one, for there is something honest about nudity. As for strip-tease, it seemed to me exactly the sort of thing our censors would, and indeed did, pass. It was arch, it was teasing ('Aha, I know what you're thinking!'), it was essentially prudish ('Oh no you don't!'). It was suppression and censorship in action— Miss [*sic*] Grundy herself. It was what Lawrence calls 'The dirty little secret'. No wonder it was approved by a convocation of British clergymen. And no wonder it was received with 'miaows' and 'wisecracks' by the gallery. They recognised it all too well. It was 'the young lady who leads you up the garden and then won't soldier', as the troops put it. I thought it the most pornographic and degraded spectacle I had ever seen, the direct result of the very thing you have advocated—suppression; but I would not dream of interfering with it all the same. Why should one? The working classes who, in spite of the censor, usually have a pretty sane outlook, had already turned it down, and if it answered the dream of some poor inhibited bank clerk, let him have it. It is our fault, not his, if he is inhibited, for it is only by allowing people freedom of knowledge that you will give them freedom of thought, and enable them to sort out what they want and escape from the 'dirty little secret' which, in my view, largely characterises the British attitude towards sex.

Yours sincerely,

J. R. Ackerley[2]

---

[1] 1884–1947. He was knighted in his last year for his services to penal reform.

[2] A. sent Forster a copy of this letter, and Forster replied on 3 May: 'I *like* your letter very much, but regarded as controversy, is it not rather the pot calling the kettle hot?' He also added that he thought it rather emotional in parts.

To H. B. Mallalieu (1914–   )   *The Listener*, Broadcasting House, W.1   60
26/7/40

Dear Mallalieu

I am much gratified at having a poem dedicated to me,[1] but I shall not speak of it now, but next week when I have had the weekend to read it quietly.

I'm glad you liked my own and daresay you are right about 'Enough!' I don't consider myself a poet, and don't really know anything about these things. Ordinarily I tinker at my work endlessly, but am never convinced that it gets any better—or worse. Harold Monro once said to me of a poem I showed him: 'It's alright, except that every word is wrong': I accepted that as a likely verdict on my poetry.

I didn't tinker as much with *Micheldever* as I would have done if we'd been peaceful. The war depresses me too much.

The whole of the second section bored me, but I couldn't work at it any more. The last sections seemed to me to have some virtue, so I let Stephen have it.[2] If it makes a small contribution to the gen. undermining of our plutocratic constitution, I ask for nothing more. It was coarser and slangier at first, and the offending line originally ran

'And parson licked their arse. You'd had enough.'[3]

I didn't want to be told that wouldn't suit the printers, but as I say was too 'off' it to trouble myself much.
Yours sincerely
J. R. Ackerley

To Roger Senhouse[4] (1900–1970)   *The Listener*, Broadcasting House, W.1   61
?/ ?/41

Dear Roger

I am truly horrified you think of reprinting that ghastly poem.[5] Do please suppress. I would much sooner not figure in your vol.[6] at all,

---

[1] 'Letter in Wartime.' Two lines summarise its mood:

Bombs, indifferent to love or hate,
Are aimed finally at the human heart.

In the following year Mallalieu included it in a collection which took for its title the title of this poem.

[2] The poem appeared in *Horizon* (August 1940). The review had been founded in January 1940 by Cyril Connolly, who continued to edit it until it closed in 1950. Until 1941 Stephen Spender was a co-editor, 'and it was largely due to him', Connolly wrote in 1953, 'that we printed such good war poetry . . .' Strictly speaking *Micheldever* is not a war poem—although in Part V the forgotten army of English labourers who revolted against injustice in 1830 is linked with those in 1940 who 'fight' to make a better world free of 'greed and fear'. See Letter 65.

[3] This was changed to: 'And parson toadied after them. Enough!' The version which appeared in *Micheldever & Other Poems*, issued in a limited edition of 350 copies by Ian McKelvie in 1972, followed the *Horizon* text.

[4] Director of Secker & Warburg from 1936 to 1962 and translator of Colette and other French writers.

[5] 'The Portrait of a Mother.' See page 59, note 5.

[6] The anthology which Senhouse had in mind was *Poems in Our Time, 1900–1942*, chosen by Richard Church and M. M. Bozman (1945). Senhouse gave considerable help in the choosing of poems, and A. finally agreed to let his 'Ghosts' (1922) be reprinted 'in a revised and shortened form'.

feeling I am not really 'one of the poets' and have no right there; but if I can't altogether be washed out, could you not substitute this,[1] or is it too long? It's the same sort of date (1922) and really not bad in its [Edgar Allan] Poey way[2]—at least not now that I have tidied it up. Even untidy, it brought me Morgan's friendship (see his letter enclosed—interesting document which *please return*)[3] and is worthier of perpetuation than any of my other early outpourings. I confess I rather like it, and would like it resurrected: it appeared in *The London Mercury*,[4] then in a publication called *The Best of the Year: 1922*[5] (now defunct) and then in a small vol. published by Bowes & Bowes,[6] long since out of print.[7] If it won't do, I will search about for something else, and perhaps send my new thing if I ever finish, but don't think it contains anything extractable.[8]

Love
   Joe

P.S. I am not sure that 'Recollective' (St[anza]s 1 and 22) is right, or whether 'Bringing us grief' would not be better.[9] Stanza 20 might be omitted altogether, perhaps.[10]

62   To Roger Senhouse (1900–70)   [Office and bus][11]
                                                   ?/?41

Dear Roger
      there's also this,[12] extracted from what I'm now doing,[13] but I doubt if you'll want it, or whether really I want you to want it. Since I haven't yet shown it to William, or indeed anyone, and don't know if it's any good or putrid.

[1] 'Ghosts.' In 1967 A. wrote: 'The poem . . . opened . . . a life-time of friendship with E. M. Forster . . .' In the version that A. enclosed with this letter, he tried 'to iron out some of its many and manifest crudities . . .'

[2] Forster had written to A. on 26 April 1922: '. . . Poe brings off the same combination in 'Ulalume'—(so much so that he imposes on his readers a vision that verges on bunkum), and I think indeed that this particular quality must be very near the secret of poetry . . .' See note 3 below.

[3] See Introduction, 3.

[4] April 1922.

[5] Correct title—*The Best Poems of 1922*, selected by Thomas Moult (1922).

[6] *Poems by Four Authors* (1923). See Bibliography.

[7] M. A. C. Reavell, Managing Director of Bowes & Bowes, wrote to Braybrooke on 17 April 1973: 'The book is remembered well by Mr Stanley Smith, who has just retired . . . He recalls that, ironically but perhaps typically, it sold very slowly and had to be reduced in price towards the end of its career—which bears no relation to its merits, I'm sure.'

[8] A. subsequently changed his mind. See Letter 62.

[9] In the end A.'s revisions were more extensive. Stanzas 5 and 10 were heavily re-worked, and stanzas 8, 11, 18 and 22 were omitted.

[10] This stanza was not omitted.

[11] The last two verses of the poem included in this letter 'were tacked on . . . in a hurry, on the bus', A. later told Senhouse. The letter had been begun at *The Listener*.

[12] See notes 8 above and 13 below.

[13] The extract comes from a long poem by A., most of it unpublished, whose overall title is 'Destination D.' It was addressed and dedicated to F.H.—a Welsh guardsman—who was reported 'missing' in Greece, early in the war. He was a pale-faced youth—hence the reference in the opening stanza, 'pale sentinel'. Another section of the poem was offered to the Editor of *The Listener* in late 1942 and rejected. It appeared instead in the *Spectator* on Christmas Day 1942, entitled 'December (To F.H.)'. See Letter 68 and Appendix C.

Destination D.

1

What were you doing there? No one can tell.
What were you striving for, there on the Isthmus,
You and your likes who had nothing to sell,
Only your lives and the pleasures of Priapus?
What did you die for, pale sentinel,
  There on the Isthmus?

2

Nothing for you would come out of it, no;
Wasted the blood as you lost it or spilt it;
Wasted the courage and wasted the woe,
You with your forage caps jauntily tilted,
You with your ribbons and pretty tattoo,
  You the gay kilted.

3

Nothing for you but the toil and the trudge,
The death in the ditch and the medal for valour;
Would you then kill with no personal grudge
The British, the German, the little French sailor,
Grinding them down with your wheels in the sludge,
  Your comrades in squalor?

4

No settlement even to carry away?
No bargain, no blackmail, no future insurance?
All for a handful of coppers a day,
All that dark murder, that pain and endurance?
Will you then always accept and obey?
  Ah, the improvidence!

5

Yours are the weapons, the odds and the game:
If you must use it then, all that munition,
Why not discharge it at those more to blame,
Banker, monopolist, sly politician,
And build if you can on their failure and shame
  A safer condition?

6

Ah, the futility?! Baseless and false
All that you perished for, there on the Isthmus,
There on the Isthmus and everywhere else.
How then recover the truth that has tricked us?
Never by violence, so let us refuse,
  All of us, all of us.

The point of the title is that it was one of the official addresses for the B[ritish] E[xpeditionary] F[orce] to the Middle East in 1940.
Love
  Joe

No more, I promise you.

63 To Desmond Hawkins (1908–)   *The Listener*, Broadcasting House, W.1
?/4/41

Dear Hawkins
                  you must think me very rude not replying to your letter
sooner: the fact is I didn't know what to say.[1]
  But though I don't want to disappoint Z. B[okhari], I think I really
must refuse. You see I'm simply not qualified. I haven't been in India for
15 years, and was only there for 5 months then: I've not attended to it, its
literature and problems, since. Haven't read [George] Orwell, haven't
read [C. A.] Kincaid; and though it's true I did read one of [Maurice]
Collis's books it was about Siam.[2]
  Why don't you get Lionel Fielden to do it, now that he's no longer a
member of our staff?
  Joe Ackerley

64 To James Kirkup (1923–)   *The Listener*, Broadcasting House, W.1
14/7/41

Dear Mr Kirkup
                  yes, I see that you are experimenting in form, and of
course one always loses something in the process, but as with the artists,
you may well emerge at the other end with valuable knowledge to fortify
your poetry when it returns, as I hope it may, to subjectivity. So do not be
discouraged (there is evidence of discouragement in carelessness of typing)
if these experiments seem unsatisfactory to you; these transitional stages
are always disappointing and limited. You are not free at the moment,
but 'Persecution' in this bunch seems to me to show that you are not
wasting your time, and you might do worse than work at it a bit more.
Things improve amazingly the more one tries. It is an interesting surrealist
nightmare poem, but very uneven. Verse 3 has gone typographically
wrong somewhere. V.5 is excellent, V.9 incomprehensible (is it necessary
to the poem?) and the remainder rather feeble. I think you might do

---

[1] At this period Hawkins was editing a series of literary talks on the BBC Indian Service under
the general title 'Turning over a New Leaf'. On 25 February he had invited A. to broadcast on
the theme 'The Englishman Goes East'. Z. A. Bokhari was the Indian Programme Organiser.
Hawkins reviewed regularly for *The Listener* during the 1930s and early 1940s.
  [2] *Siamese White* (1936).

something with it with a little more thought and invention: should be interested to see it again.[1]
Yours sincerely
J. R. Ackerley

To Demetrios Capetanakis (1912–1944)   Putney   65
                                                        19/8/41

Dear Demetrios
             forgive me for not having answered at once. I do not yet fit into my new dwelling. I like to look at it, but cannot sit down.

    I'm so glad the visit was a success, especially since I was rather dismayed to realize that you had made the journey only to see me; I felt I should have explained that I could spend but a few hours in your company. Also I should not have recommended myself as a suitable object for pilgrimage. However it would be wrong to belittle what you esteem so warmly. Only do not praise me too much! I should not know what to do with it.

    When I visit my friend Plomer I will get and send you a copy of the *Horizon* which contains my Elegiac poem.[2] It is overlong, and clumsy and dull in parts;[3] but you may be interested in it because of [Thomas] Gray, and some of it you will like, I think. It is rather doubtfully digested communism.[4] Anyway it is far better than that shameful 'Mother' poem[5] you

---

[1] The poem was never published, but Verse 5, singled out by A., gives a hint of the quality that he discerned in Kirkup's work. Here it is:

> I have smoked
> my finger away
> and tapped the ashes
> into a little tray

This was the first letter that Kirkup received from A. In the previous year when Tambimuttu had published some of his poems in *Poetry* (*London*), William Plomer had read them with enthusiasm and suggested to A. that he should 'drop Kirkup a note asking to see further work'. Kirkup then sent in poems regularly, but it was not until three years later that A. accepted one—'Mortally', which appeared on 18 February 1943.
[2] *Micheldever*. See Letter 60.
[3] To Oscar Collier, one of his American publishers, A. was even more depreciatory on 10 June 1963: '. . . the only contribution I ever made to *Horizon* was a long, somewhat flat-footed poem called *Micheldever*, based upon J.L. and Barbara Hammond's *The Village Labourer* (1760–1832) . . .' See note 4 below.
[4] This needs both amplification and qualification. For the guiding spirit behind A.'s poem was really the same as the spirit behind *The Village Labourer* by the Hammonds (1911)—and is to be found crystallised in their book's epigraph from Lord Acton: '. . . the men who pay wages ought not to be the political masters of those who earn them (because laws should be adapted to those who have the heaviest stake in the country, for whom mis-government means not mortified pride or stinted luxury, but want and pain, and degradation and risk to their own lives and to their children's souls) . . .'
[5] The full title was 'The Portrait of a Mother'. A. had written the poem when an undergraduate at Magdalene. One stanza ran:

> What do you see? That fixed relentless look
> Searing my visage seems to learn from it.
> The face of man is not an open book
>   In which his sins are writ.

Later, he was to comment: 'What my mother, the last person in the world to wear a "fixed relentless look", thought of the poem, I don't remember.' But he himself thought that, if it was put into the hands of a psychiatrist, it would be a proof that however much at Cambridge he had regarded himself 'as free, proud and intellectually unassailable as a homosexual', he was in fact 'profoundly riddled with guilt'. Cf. Letter 61.

praised. Excuse me, but it says that love is guilty; I am very sorry I ever published it.

Let me know when you come to London again.

Joe

66   To Rupert Hart-Davis (1907–   )   *The Listener*, Broadcasting House, W.1
25/3/42

Dear Hart-Davis

I got your address out of William to ask whether you can give me a line on Gerald Kersh who, as no doubt you know, has just produced a book about the rank and file of the Coldstream Guards. Is he still surviving or now ex.? I've been looking at the book, which seems more likely to please the upper than the lower deck so far as I could see in a rather cursory examination; and felt rather interested to know more about him personally.

I suppose you would not care to review the book (*They Die with Their Boots Clean*) for me anonymously? I'd send it along with pleasure if you had the time and inclination: and could even add to it another of much the same ilk, and rather more recent; Michael Joseph's account of his experiences as an officer: forget the title, but it's something about a scabbard. No reason why they should not be combined.[1] But when I told William I would propose this, he said you were too busy he thought. He is very well and fairly censorious as usual. We've just been eating a leaf together at Shearns.

How are you, I wonder. I was surprised to hear that you were so busy: I mean the army generally seems rather desperately not to be: but in view of William's remarks I feel rather guilty about troubling you for a letter, let alone a review.

Yours sincerely

Joe Ackerley

67   To Alex Comfort (1920–   )   *The Listener*, Broadcasting House, W.1
9/7/42

Dear Mr Comfort

I would be much obliged if you would order your publishers to send me a copy of your novel[2] for review, for since we have not yet received one, I assume that none will be forthcoming unless you yourself take steps.[3] The arrival of new books is no longer punctual, as it used to be, but I discovered from Messrs. Chapman & Hall the other day when I

[1] He declined both books. The fact that he was serving in the Coldstream Guards at the time explains why A. offered him the Kersh book. Michael Joseph's account of his experiences as an officer was called *The Sword in the Scabbard*. A. himself reviewed Kersh's book, along with *Bless 'em All* by 'Boomerang', in an unsigned notice on 30 April. Forster wrote to A. on 1 May to say how much he had enjoyed reading him 'on the Guards'. Joseph's book was reviewed on 11 June.
[2] *The Almond Tree*, which had been published on 22 June.
[3] Comfort took steps—and five days later A. wrote to him: 'Thank you v. much for the book. I've sent it up to [Edwin] Muir without further delay.' Muir reviewed it on 13 August, along with Arthur Waley's translation of Wu Ch'êng-ên's sixteenth-century novel, *Monkey*.

rang up to ask for a copy of Evelyn Waugh's novel,[1] that *The Listener* is no longer on their list of journals to which review copies are sent. I understand from them that this list had now been reduced to 25 journals and that *The Listener* was not among them. It emerged from my conversation with them that our exclusion is due to two factors: pique, because we have not reviewed, in their opinion, sufficient of their books, and an apparently genuine belief that our status does not entitle us to a position among the first twenty-five important reviewing journals, [even though] our circulation is now 100,000. It is true we do not review all the books Messrs. Chapman & Hall send us; we do not review all the books any publisher sends us: we review only what would properly be considered as worth-while books, and it is rare indeed for any of those to pass without notice in our columns.

An attack from you on your publishers would be most welcome. I am writing to Waugh too.
Yours sincerely
J. R. Ackerley

To Alan Thomas[2] (1896–1969)   ?/11/42?   68

If nothing better arrives, you may like to consider this as your Xmas poem. It is by me—but do not feel at all embarrassed, for I am not sensitive about such things, so turn it down without compunction if you don't take to it.[3] I cannot judge myself—but do believe it is the only *sort* of Xmas poem that can be written.

It is a year old, so I only produce it *faute de mieux* and out of a desire to satisfy your wishes.
J.R.A.

P.S. I daresay I could improve here and there if you wanted it.

To the Editor of the *Spectator*[4]   Putney, S.W.15   69
November 20, 1942
Sir,
Is it considered that educated thought and scientific progress are not

1 *Put Out More Flags*, which had been published on 16 March.
2 He was the second Editor of *The Listener* (1939–58). 'The best of Editors,' A. addressed him on several occasions. Thomas wrote a number of novels and died on 24 November 1969. When *The Times* published its 10,000th crossword, he contributed an article to mark the event. Characteristically he began it: 'A decachiliad is not to be sneezed at.' When A. died he sent in this tribute to *The Times*, which was published on 13 June 1967: 'In your admirable notice of Joe Ackerley you refer to him as an incomparable editor. He was indeed that. I worked with him on *The Listener* for over 19 years. The going, particularly in the early days of his literary editorship, was not invariably easy, mainly, I think, because in many respects Joe was in advance of his time. The "climate of opinion" 30 years ago, both in the BBC and outside it, was very different from what it is in the 1960s. But the distinction which *The Listener* as a literary journal won for itself and still enjoys, is due in very large measure to Joe Ackerley's influence. As you say, he will not be forgotten either as a friend or writer. Apart from the books you mention he also wrote a remarkable poem entitled *Micheldever* which appeared, I think, in *Horizon* (I asked him a year or two back if he could let me have a copy of it, but he hadn't got one—so like Joe). In addition to his own writing, the back numbers of the journal he served constitute for him a fine memorial.'
3 The poem was 'December'—but the Editor turned it down. Cf. Letter 62. See Appendix C for its history.
4 The letter appeared under the heading 'A Subject for Thought'. Forster had given A. considerable help with its wording. After its publication, letters supporting it were published in the

yet sufficiently advanced to permit ventilation of a subject which, although it may be freely and objectively discussed in psychological, anthropological, biographical works, &c., seems still to be regarded in contemporary life as almost unmentionable anywhere except in the *News of the World*. I refer to homosexuality. During the course of the legal proceedings against twenty men recently concluded at Abergavenny, one youth of nineteen committed suicide on the railway lines, and two others attempted unsuccessfully to do away with themselves by hanging and poison, to avoid the shame of exposure. The reports from which these facts are gathered were published on August 23rd and November 8th in the newspaper referred to above.

It would be interesting to know whether public opinion today regards such suffering as merited, and the savage sentences, up to and including ten years' penal servitude, allowed by the law and imposed by the judge, as the most enlightened method of dealing with this matter.

Yours, &c.,

J. R. Ackerley

---

70   To Demetrios Capetanakis (1912–1944)   *The Listener*, Broadcasting
                                                   House, W.1   9/2/43

Dear Demetrios

            a book here—part of it at any rate—brings you to my mind: *The Heritage of Symbolism*, by C. M. Bowra (Macmillan, 15/-). Bowra attends to Valéry, Rilke, Stefan George, Blok and Yeats. I wondered whether you might feel you could and would review it for this lousy journal? But I cannot afford more than about 600–700 words alas—and the review would be unsigned.[1]

Hope you are well.

Joe

---

71   To Harry Daley[2] (1901–1971)   *The Listener*, Broadcasting House, W.1
                                                            ?/8?/43

Dear Harry

            I enjoyed reading this [short story]—and also laughed at your jokes—but your sailor friend was right not to give it unqualified praise; it is style it mainly suffers from, and irrelevancy, and a rather uneasy relationship between truth and fiction.

Spectator from Athelstan Rendall and Dan Wilson on 27 November; Kenneth Walker on 4 December; and H. L. Philip on 18 December. The correspondence was then closed. See Introduction, 3.

[1] It appeared on 1 April.

[2] Daley joined the Metropolitan Police in 1925, and in the following year when on duty in Covent Garden he recognised A. as the author of *The Prisoners of War* (then running in the West End) and fell into conversation with him. In *My Father and Myself* A. referred to him as 'the intellectual policeman' and quoted from his letters. David Daley, his brother, believes that the short story mentioned in this letter, and in the following one, concerned a petty thief found in an empty house in Wandsworth. He writes: 'I am not sure it was ever published, as Harry practically destroyed all his literary efforts before his death in 1971.'

The amateurishness is in the style. It is jagged and uneasy, too many parentheses, too many commas. It's like travelling in a car with a flat tyre, bump, bump. That's easily cleared up: it's a matter of rearrangement and editing. And you haven't given your dramatic moment its full effect either. The gooseflesh isn't communicated. It's little more than a matter of punctuation, for the stuff's all there.

Irrelevancy: do you want pp. 4 and 5, or most of them? You are telling a story and they hold the action up, and I don't think that they have excuse enough to do so. There are one or two other passages also that might profitably be scrapped.

And I'm dubious about the young men in the bath. Are they truth or fiction? They seem rather dragged in—especially since children so seldom seem to me like their parents—*immediately recognisably* like them, I mean.

But your character and genius lie upon it, and it has much interest. If you like, and have a spare carbon, I'll tamper with it for you with a view to publication. I can't say how it would come out, but I'd try if you liked.[1] My Ed. might be pleased with it.

Joe

To Harry Daley (1901–1971)   *The Listener*, Broadcasting House, W.1   72
9/9/43

Dear Harry

I'm sorry to have been so long with this [short story],[2] and send it back in this—I hope not too—mucky condition; because my revisions are meant only to be suggestions, and you had better see what you think of them before we proceed further. They are my first thoughts on the story anyway, and if you disagree with some, some may seem useful and improving. I'm afraid I may have taken liberties here and there—done more according to my own ideas than was strictly necessary; but take that merely as a sign of interest, for that is all it is. The object of most of the tampering has been (1) to give the sentences balance and (2) to enhance the dramatic effects; but I couldn't defend myself if required to do so on either of these scores, for it is all a matter of 'ear', and your or anyone else's ear may hear the sound of the prose quite differently.

I think it's a v. amusing story, better than I first thought; but I *doubt* if my Editor will take it owing to its being rather near the knuckle in certain parts. I think he may wrinkle his nose, and say it is not *Listener* goods.[3] We'll try it on him anyway if you like; and if he refuses John Lehmann might bite.[4] I take back what I said of the swimming-bath end: that stands alright; but your digression on pp 4–5 will have to come out and be used in some other story or article. Over Bill's grievance, which precedes it, I

1 Daley asked A. to do this. See Letter 72.
2 See Letter 71.
3 This proved to be the case—and none of Daley's stories ever appeared in *The Listener*. Ironically though, in 1929 during the paper's first year of existence, two talks of his about being a policeman (which A. had produced for the Home Service) were reprinted: '"Not a Happy One"?' on 27 March and 'While London Sleeps' on 13 November.
4 For *Penguin New Writing*.

am not sure, and would like to see it in your revised version; it may be relevant enough to the theme.

Joe

73   To Harry Daley (1901–1971)   Putney
                                                                      ?/12?/43

Dear Harry

I think this is a great improvement from a writing point of view on your first ms.; it goes much more smoothly and competently, and that you have enjoyed writing it is obvious: your enjoyment communicates itself to the reader.

But it has less claim to the title of 'Short Story' than your other script. In fact I don't really think it can be said to be a story at all. It is reminiscence, a chapter from your autobiography, and I personally feel it is miscalled, and that 'Deserters' would be a better title and that it would be better recognised on that subject only. The idea with which you start is very amusing, and so are the opening scenes, they should not be lost; but your subsequent deserter episodes are not a natural development of this theme—with its interiors, modes and manners, the way people live. But although there is still something of all this in your first deserter anecdote, it is deserters now, not social life, that 'reminds' you and carries your memory on; you are no longer primarily interested in other people's houses, but in the theme of desertion, and the thread of your title has been lost.

You must have a great deal more, both entertaining and malicious, to say about pretentious and snobby interiors—a subject very little written about and fascinatingly interesting. If I were you, I should expand that theme from the top of p. 4, describing perhaps not merely genteel lives, but coppers' lives generally—Sanders, for instance, with his odd uncomfortable intelligence, and his daughters; Archie Jones with his crisps; and that other nice mounted policeman (what was his name?) whose wife used to follow him about shouting for the rent. I should omit the old boy with bloodshot eyes who doesn't fit and isn't v. interesting, and you have a new chapter at the bottom of the same page entitled 'Soldiers and Deserters'. In fact you will then be doing, what I have always wished you would do, making a book of reminiscences.[1] And I hope there will be a long chapter in it called 'Odds and Sods'. I will help you to write it if you like, and we will get Roger Senhouse[2] to publish it!

Anyway, as it stands, this, though interesting throughout and moving in parts, is too anecdotal and digressive to form a short story or even a unity, and I have not made any marks on it for that reason.

As an *aide-memoire* to the book which I hope may eventually be built, I enclose a few notes that I made about you in the old days. I used to think

---

[1] Daley, after his retirement from the Metropolitan Police, took A.'s advice and wrote 'a book of reminiscences' under the title *This Small Cloud*. Several pages in it are devoted to deserters in war-time London. The manuscript remains unpublished. See Letters 258 and 260.

[2] Director of Secker & Warburg.

your stories too good to be lost and jotted down these few in a notebook: sorry I did not keep it up.

Joe

To Roy Fuller (1912–   )   *The Listener*, Broadcasting House, W.1   74
16/12/43

Dear Fuller
        I was so sorry not to be able to come and meet you at [John] Lehmann's the other day; I admire your poetry very much, and should have liked to have seen you.

And how pleasant now to be receiving offerings from you direct! I have extracted from this batch 'Tchechof'[1] and 'The Coast'.[2] I am often asked for a short poem, and the former will therefore please our make-up people for that reason as it does me for other reasons; between 'The Coast' and 'The Statue' I found it hard to make up my mind, and return the latter with regret, but my Editor would not accept more than two at a time.[3]

I will get them in as soon as I possibly can, but as you know poems are ill-used in journals; space is never made for any particular one; they have to wait until a space into which they will fit falls vacant.

J. R. Ackerley

To Demetrios Capetanakis (1912–1944)   *The Listener*, Broadcasting   75
House, W.1   ?/2?/44

Dear Demetrios
        I'm sorry to hear from William that you're ill, and not one of those enjoyable illness [*sic*], as we first thought, when one lies cosily in bed and reads. Do you like visitors, and may they bring anything in their hands, and if so may I bring what in mine and when? I was fascinated by your article[4] in *N[ew] W[riting] and D[aylight]*;[5] so fascinated indeed that I could not wait another moment to read all the books of his which I have never read, for I only know the four big novels. So I borrowed *Letters from the Underworld* from Elizabeth Bowen with whom I dined last week, and hope to begin it this evening. The air-raids have worried me so much lately that I have found it difficult to concentrate. Most people have been frightened, I think, and I don't suppose it has been at all pleasant for you in hospital. One of my windows was bust, and my pigeon has been looking very careworn and distrait—and quite thin, like a snake.[6]

Well, I hope you will be feeling better, dear Demetrios, by the time you

[1] Published (but as 'Chekhov') on 20 January 1944.   [2] Published on 13 April 1944.
[3] This rule was relaxed after the war.   [4] 'On Dostoevsky.'   [5] Winter 1943-4.
[6] Earlier in the war, A. had written in a poem called 'The New House, 1941':

                                        disregard
                The cobra in the basement, it's a pigeon.
Later, he revised this poem several times and changed these lines to:
                                        disregard
                The snake on that far threshold, it's a pigeon
                Craning for crumbs.
The final title that he gave to the poem (in 1965) was 'After the Blitz, 1941'. Cf. Letters 282 and 297.

get this; and that I may come to see you if you are feeling up to being visited.
Love from
    Joe

76   To Herbert Read (1893–1968)   *The Listener*, Broadcasting House, W.1

                                              ?/11?/44
Dear Herbert
        I am so very pleased and proud to have your new book,[1]
and your love between our names. I am very fond of you, as you know, and
have passed many evenings this week in my own secular and insecure
retreat with your book on my knee, thinking of you and your words. I have
taken much pleasure and thought from them. William told me first of your
new long poem and how impressed he had been by it; and then I saw it,
but only really to touch, in Lilian's house, and now how glad I am to read
and possess it. It is a lovely poem; your best I think, excepting perhaps for
'The Conscript of 1940'; I get far more from it than from the 'Ode', which I
find now a little too narrative, though it contains certain passages, such as
p. 13, which are beautifully done. But 'The World within a War' with its
calmer and deeper thought comes wholly off, strong and sure from its fine
descriptive opening to the end. I also very much like 'The Song for the
Spanish Anarchists', 'Summer Rain', 'Kirkdale', 'The Heart Conscripted'
and 'Bombing Casualties in Spain'—and deeply regret we didn't publish
the last. I do wish you would manage somehow to free yourself from the
clutches of the business men,[2] where you have become so lamentably
buried away; a 'nervous breakdown' is called for, I feel sure.
    Have you read a short story of Rebecca West's called 'The Salt of
the Earth' from her volume *The Harsh Voice*?[3] Morgan put me on to it. It
is a remarkably good story—he thinks one of the world's best. I didn't know
she could do things like that.
    Goodnight, dear Herbert, I must turn in. Let us meet again soon.
Love from
    Joe

77   To Robert Donat[4] (1905–1958)   *The Listener*, Broadcasting House, W.1

                                        22nd January, 1945
Dear Mr Donat,
        I rather gather from Mrs. Howard's recent letter to me

    [1] *World Within a War.*
    [2] In May 1939 Read had joined the publishing firm of Routledge & Kegan Paul. Within a
month he had been made a director.
    [3] 1935. The four stories that make up the volume are described as 'short novels' on the title
page: the other three are 'Life Sentence', 'There Is No Conversation' and 'The Abiding Vision'.
    [4] Between November 1943 and November 1946 Robert Donat ran the Westminster Theatre.
In his search for new plays he employed a number of readers of whom A. was 'the most literate
and prolific'. J. C. Trewin, who wrote Donat's biography (1968), also told Braybrooke: 'His
reports were written in a clear delicate hand, often without erasure, and frequently on BBC paper
headed "PLEASE CIRCULATE QUICKLY TO ALL OCCUPANTS OF ROOM".' Herbert
Read had recommended A. to Donat, and among the dramatists whose works A. read were
H. E. Bates, Clifford Bax, Paul Vincent Carroll, John Drinkwater, Patrick Hamilton, A. P.
Herbert, Margaret Kennedy, Louis MacNeice, Elmer Rice and Peter Ustinov. He advised too on

that you have decided not to continue with this Calderon play[1] after all, but I had already read it and had better therefore record my opinion, while it is fresh in my mind, for your files.

It is a beautiful poem, but quite unsuited to stage production. Indeed, [Edward] Fitzgerald did not make it for the stage, and says so expressly in his introduction. Of the story, only the relationship of Sigismund to King Basilio his father is fully developed, only *their* characters explored; the rest does not come over dramatically, and is vague and questionable even to the reader's eye: the Lady Rosaura who opens the action so mysteriously and heroically, and, assisting in the liberation of Sigismund, seems clearly cast for his eventual bride, turns out to have an apparently quite fortuitous part in the action, her significance is only vaguely indicated, she fades out almost unexplained, and Sigismund proclaims his nuptials with the Princess Estrella, a lady he meets only once and whom we take to be his enemy, for she has reason for resenting his existence, and he says to her: 'Why does this warm hand shoot a cold shudder through me?'—a remark which is never explained. The great Wagnerian scene of the Fortress on the rock would be hard to convey convincingly, and as for the battle for the Crown of Poland, all Fitzgerald says of it is: 'A battle may be supposed to take place. After which—' The long speeches are of inordinate length; and though it is a pity that such lines as:

> 'Oh, those stars,
> Those stars that too far up from human blame
> To clear themselves, or careless of the charge,
> Still bear upon their shining shoulders all
> The guilt men shift upon them!'

should not be spoken, there it is.

Yours sincerely,

J. R. Ackerley

P.S. I have heard again from Mrs Howard since getting this letter typed, and will read the Trend-Birch affair.[2]

To Margaret Howard[3]   The British Broadcasting Corporation,   78
Broadcasting House, W.1   28/5/45

Dear Mrs Howard

this was the only note the play contained. Nevertheless,

---

novels which might make films and interest Donat as either an actor or director—or both. See Letters 78, 79, 80, 81, 82 and 173.

[1] *La Vida es Sueño* by Pedro de la Barca Calderón (1600–1681). The translation that A. was sent was one which had been made by Edward Fitzgerald in 1853. See note 2 below.

[2] On 12 January A. had written to Donat: 'Fitzgerald's *Such Stuff as Dreams Are Made Of* . . . is a poetic version of the original: it is beautiful, . . . but less Calderón than Fitzgerald.' He also then gave details of two more recent translations—one made jointly by J. B. Trend and Frank Birch, which was published in 1925, and one made by H. Carter, which was privately printed by the translator in 1928. A. read the former for Donat in the following week, but it was never put on at the Westminster Theatre.

[3] She was Robert Donat's secretary for a period, and later became General Manager of his company Fanfare Productions when it presented *Much Ado About Nothing* at the Aldwych Theatre in October 1946.

I did ask myself whether Mr Donat would not like me to attempt to provide some words of advice or comfort for his friend: it is the kind of thing I have to do in the BBC. However, this letter did not say so, and you once gave me to understand that Mr Donat did not bother about such things and wanted only the UNVARNISHED TRUTH!

Will you say to him though, that if he would like me at any time to draft out, instead of, or as well as, a report, a letter for him to return with some special rejected script, I will gladly do so. I don't, however, want to get involved with long correspondences with loonies; I have enough of that with the poets, whom I find it wiser, generally speaking, to reject with no comment at all.

J. R. Ackerley

79 To H. K. Ayliff[1] (18??–1949)   17 Star & Garter Mansions, Putney,
                                        S.W.15   13/7/45
Dear Ayliff
            I think you should certainly read Herbert de Hamel's and R. L. Mégroz's *Rossetti* in this pile.[2] Interest has been increasing in the Pre-Raphaelites lately with [William] Gaunt's two books,[3] and their curious story was certain to be dramatised sooner or later. There will be sure to be a public interest in them, as in the Brownings, and—first come, first served. I know nothing of de Hamel, but Mégroz, though not a sound historian, has historical knowledge of the period. The play is not a bad one, and gives the facts and atmosphere with knowledge and justice. It will not disgrace you from a literary point of view, and though I have a number of qualifications to my approval, it is well worth your attention.

(1) I think there are rather too many short scenes, but I see that it is difficult to get across the years—some six or seven pass—without, and since there need be no interval between most of them, perhaps the snippetiness will be less noticeable on the stage than on paper.

(2) Characterisation is disappointing in some important minor characters. Rossetti himself and Miss Siddal are well presented; Fanny Cornforth will pass, though her cockney-ism is sometimes overdone; Emma Brown has her 'respectability' and nothing else; Swinburne and Madox Brown have nothing at all, no substance. This is a pity, for Swinburne, at any rate, was an interesting man. Christina was interesting too, but she has little here but her jealous solicitude for her brother. Ellen Grant is an invention, but in the last two scenes in particular her hollowness becomes apparent.

---

[1] Ayliff for a short period during 1945 was Robert Donat's artistic director at the Westminster Theatre. In March he produced a revival of *Yellow Sands* by Eden and Adelaide Phillpotts and in July *The Cure for Love*, a new play by Walter Greenwood.
[2] A few months later, A. read another play about Rossetti—*We Dig for the Stars* by T. B. Morris. He thought it 'historically convincing . . . but monotonous', and in the course of his report wrote: 'Remorse is one of the most tiresome emotions, and it is the note struck throughout: we therefore soon get bored with Rossetti, his melancholy and his conscience, his dead Beata Beatrix and his chloral.'
[3] *The Pre-Raphaelite Tragedy* (1942) and *The Aesthetic Adventure* (1945).

(3) Another scene which is particularly ill-contrived is that between Fanny and Lizzie in Act I, Sc. 2 pp. 32–33. This conversation is badly handled and led up to, and is quite unconvincing, even given Fanny's forthright manners.

(4) The Pre-Raphaelites took themselves very seriously of course, and much of their creed now seems to us artificial, self-conscious and boring. So do the unhappy tangled relationships in which they involved themselves. A modern audience might well regard the affaire Rossetti-Lizzie as much ado about nothing. Would they laugh at it: such scenes as Act I pp. 20–23, Act II, pp. 14–17, and 22–25? It is difficult to say. It is difficult, in any case, to have much feeling for Lizzie; in reality she was a dead sort of woman, and her interest was mainly clinical or pathological.

The other plays are no good.

J. R. Ackerley

To Robert Donat (1905–1958)   17 Star & Garter Mansions, Putney,   80
                                S.W.15   28/8/45

Dear Mr Donat

            sorry I'm a bit late with this play in which you take a personal interest; I did not open the packet that contained it until this weekend.

A Woman of Worth, by Richard Henry & Arthur Crawford

I'm afraid this play is no use at all; it is naively crude dramatically and in every other way. Its technique, such as it may be said to have, is that of the novel, not the drama: it opens, for instance, with a series of three short scenes (the first could scarcely play for more than 10 minutes), which are duologues on some particular point, and when there is nothing more to be said about it the curtain is brought down to show that that conversation is over anyway, just as one puts an end arbitrarily to chapters in a novel. Moreover, since the authors have really nothing to say, their ideas are soon exhausted; the dialogue is not about anything much, and soon peters out, and then, of course, the curtain has to come down.

The story seems to concern a lady doctor, of distinguished ability (Jean Cunningham), who is so fond of her husband, Bruce, another but *undis*-tinguished doctor, that she always puts her domestic interests before her career wherever they conflict. In spite of the interference of friends ('Woman must not sacrifice herself on the altar of man's mediocrity') and the remarkable follies of Bruce (who has got himself mixed up with a designing nurse named Sue), she adheres unswervingly to her love and faith—at least I suppose so, for there is no reason to read further than pp. 53–54, where Bruce discovers, to his indignation and disgust, that Sue, with whom he has been flirting and arranging a clandestine holiday at a Cheltenham hotel, is expecting him to go so far as to sleep with her ('Good God! You calculating little vixen! So that's your little game . . . What a fool I've been.') This is not only an adult speaking, but an experienced doctor. Why the authors have chosen the medical profession to write about it would be difficult to say, for if they know anything at all about it or about doctors, they do not manage to convince us that they do. To convey a suitable nursing-home atmosphere in Act 2, they suggest that the smell of carbolic should be wafted into the auditorium.

I fear they have no dramatic or literary talent at all: perhaps more important still, they seem to have no knowledge of the world.

J. R. Ackerley

81   To Margaret Howard   The British Broadcasting Corporation,
Broadcasting House, W.1   30/3/46

Dear Mrs Howard
               I was only asked [by Mr Donat][1] to 'dip into' this book *The Robe*,[2] which I have done, so I have not enough of the story for a synopsis, but enough to say that it is about the Roman Empire at the time of Christ, and may be said to be a novel constructed on the New Testament. The hero, the Roman Tribune, Marcellus, is present at Christ's crucifixion, and gradually becomes impressed by stories he hears of Christ's teachings, personality, miracles and increasing influence on contemporary thought, until he is won over to the new faith and goes to his death, by Caligula's orders, head erect and hand-in-hand with his wife Diana, daughter of Gallus, as a martyr. The Robe of the title is the blood-stained robe worn by Christ on the cross.

The main trouble with it as scenario material for Mr Donat is that though the figure of the young Marcellus is suitable, dashing and attractive, the chief 'character' is really Christ, or rather (for He is crucified early on, and might not even 'appear' on the screen at all) the legendary Christ, for the middle part of the book seems to be taken up with reports and eye-witness accounts of his doctrines and activities—the New Testament story, in fact, retold in Mr Lloyd [C.] Douglas's naturalistic-Roman idiom. This is unfortunately heady and wordy: 'Remember' [says Marcellus to his devoted slave and friend Demetrius] 'that I shall be burning with desire to learn that you have not been apprehended. Notify me of your needs. If you are captured, I shall leave no stone unturned to effect your deliverance.' Naomi Mitchison (who would have done the book better), writing the same passage, would have said: 'I shall be awfully anxious about you. Let me know if there's anything you want, and if you're caught I'll do everything in my power to have you set free.'

In fact the book's stodgy. The play, which accompanies it, is no good at all.

J. R. Ackerley

[1] A. also read novels between 1944 and 1946 for Robert Donat with a view to finding suitable parts for him to play on the screen. Among those that he reported on at length as possibilities were *The White Company* by Conan Doyle and *The Man Who Was Thursday* by G. K. Chesterton. He thought that, though the first did not have a star part suitable for Donat, it was 'very filmable' and might interest him as a director. In the case of the second, he thought that 'the novel cried out for film treatment' and that the part of Gabriel Symes the poet was 'right down Mr Donat's street'.

[2] By Lloyd C. Douglas (1943). A 'film of the book' was made by Twentieth Century Fox, directed by Henry Coster, in 1953.

To Margaret Howard   The British Broadcasting Corporation,   82
                            Broadcasting House, W.1   5/4/46

Dear Mrs Howard
                    you asked my opinion [for Mr Donat] of the [Paul
Vincent] Carroll play,¹ which I went to last night. I liked it very much,
and thought it a good play, with reservations—but even with reservations,
far better than anything else almost on the West End boards. The 'funny
man' who supplied the contrast-comedy was the chief fly in my ointment;
far too much of him, and so very unfunny with his reliance for laughs on
the word 'shocking' and his business with the teapot—scarcely one good
line. I thought him a cheap, reach-me-down device from the Sean O'Casey
stock-room; not a live figure at all, but just a sort of hired clown, the tradi-
tional trick for sharpening the drama. Otherwise I was very interested,
though there were occasional jarring notes. I did not believe in Nora—or
whatever her name was—the girl who does not appear—Peter's love; or at
any rate I did not believe in Peter's feeling for her; and the moment when
Francis tells Peter he has fixed matters so that he will find Nora waiting
for him, and Peter goes off hilarious, was very unsatisfactory, I thought, and
struck a quite false note. Also, I did not find the argument on ways of
life—the core of the play—violence v. non-violence—between Francis and
Father Tiffney very clear; I knew what they both meant, of course, but they
did not seem to me to make it sufficiently telling. Muddly rather. The
acting was splendid. I was pleased to have seen it.
    J. R. Ackerley

To Marie Belloc Lowndes (1868–1947) *The Listener*, Broadcasting House,   83
                                     W.1   1/7/46

Dear Mrs Belloc Lowndes
                       thank you very much for your long and most
interesting letter about O[scar] W[ilde].² It was of special interest, since I
was reading the [Hesketh] Pearson *Life*³ (borrowed from Plomer), which
is a really first-rate book; no doubt you have read it by now yourself.
Pearson acknowledges in it some information about O.W. that you gave

---

¹ *The Wise Have Not Spoken*. Later in the year, on 26 October, A. reported on Carroll's *The
White Steed*, which had been sent to Robert Donat. After providing a synopsis of the plot, A. went
on: 'It has . . . a gallery of vivid characters, suspense up to a point, a good deal of humour and a
dash of poetry.' But there were 'weaknesses' which cancelled out 'these virtues', the chief of which
was that no explanation was offered as to why the new village priest was a puritanical killjoy,
no less intent on 'cleaning up' the village than Ireland itself, and determined in the process to turn
his parishioners into a local congregation of moral policemen. A. summed up: 'Psychology has
taught us a lot about such people as [this priest], and that their puritanical zeal in "cleaning up"
the world is due to sexual frustrations or "kinks" in themselves, and that they are usually found in
their private lives to be fearfully indulging the appetites they attempt to starve in others. If [this]
priest were seen to make a furtive pass at . . . his tartish servant girl Meg, we should understand him
better . . .'
² This letter has been lost. See page 72, note 1.
³ See page 72, note 1.

him.[1] What a sad story it is, and I had no idea that Charles Brookfield,[2] who was a friend of my Mother's (who was on the stage in her youth and acted with Tree), had behaved so abominably.[3]

Plomer's operation was done—successfully—on Friday, and he should be out of his nursing home in a fortnight's time. I have sent on your letter to him, for it will interest him as much as it interested me. I know he will be as delighted as I shall be to dine with you when he is up and about again.
Yours sincerely
Joe Ackerley

---

[1] Mrs Hesketh Pearson believes that the information referred to in the late Mrs Belloc Lowndes' letter is that quoted in Chapter 15 of her husband's *Life of Oscar Wilde* (1946). Here is the relevant passage: 'Although they had drifted far apart by the beginning of 1895, Oscar and his wife were still on outwardly affectionate terms. During the period of his prosperity they were to be seen together at the first performance of new plays, and, though she never enjoyed the experience, Constance continued to appear on special occasions in striking clothes of her husband's design. Mrs Belloc Lowndes sends me this: "I remember a private view at the Grosvenor Gallery, which she attended in a green and black suit and hat which recalled coloured engravings of eighteenth-century highwaymen. It made a considerable sensation, for instead of looking at the pictures most of the women present were eagerly asking each other whether they had yet seen Mrs Oscar Wilde." On his side Oscar made a point of attending his wife's weekly receptions: "The drawing-room would be filled Sunday after Sunday with a crowd of interesting and amusing people," continues Mrs Belloc Lowndes, "and to my thinking Oscar was by far the most interesting and amusing of those there. Unlike many men celebrated for their wit, he was just as delightful, and took just as much trouble to entertain and cheer his guests in his own house, as he did in those of other people. To me an agreeable addition to those gatherings was the presence of the two little boys, Cyril and Vyvyan. With regard to their children, the Wildes followed the French habit of having them present when they had visitors, instead of keeping them well out of sight, as was then the English custom. Both boys had pretty manners, the younger possessing some of his mother's charm. I remember better the elder of the two, who was later distinguished for his remarkable ability, and who was killed early in the 1914–18 war, for he used to hang delightedly on his father's words . . ."'

[2] Actor, playwright and in 1912, his last year, Examiner of Plays.

[3] It has been said in many books that Brookfield was responsible for putting the police in touch with the prostitute who declared that Wilde and his associates were ruining her trade. It has also often been said that Brookfield and Charles Hawtrey gave a dinner to celebrate the Marquess of Queensberry's victory in court in 1895. Rupert Croft-Cooke in Chapter 1 of *The Unrecorded Life of Oscar Wilde* (1972) claims that there is 'no truth' in these stories.

Part Five
'MY DOG QUEENIE'

To William Plomer (1903–1973)   Putney   84
                                                  14/10/47

D.L.B.

I rather doubt now whether I shall be able to keep my own date with you on Monday after all. Getting away seems so very complicated, and I don't see how I can avoid *two* journeys to London from Ferring that day, which may well postpone my second journey to an unsuitably late hour. It is Queenie,[1] of course, and her meat. I go off with her and Bunny tomorrow, by car, carrying 10 lbs or 12 lbs of horsemeat which I shall have to buy in the morning. She eats 2 lbs a day, and it is no good buying more than about 5 or 6 days' worth at a time, for it will not keep. I need hardly say that it is unobtainable in a place like Worthing, so it looks to me as though I shall have to run up to London on Monday morning to secure and take back to Nancy a further supply for her to last the first 5 or 6 days of my Italian absence, and then return to London to sleep before going off. I supposed, vaguely, that I might have to do something of this sort, but hadn't thought it out: now that I fix my shrinking eye upon it more bravely, I think the likelihood of my reaching Town finally in time to dine with you is rather slender. The horsemeat butcher has, very kindly, offered to send a consignment down to Sussex to keep doggie going during the last part of my Italian 10 days, for what I cart down on Monday will not last the whole of it. But I have to supply him with the receptacle to send it in, ready labelled. I am off in search of that receptacle today. It should be a small hamper, I suppose, so that some air can get in—difficult to obtain. I thought of asking him to send the two lots, to save me Monday morning's visit, but that would mean *two* receptacles, or that the one should be posted back to him for refilling, which I feel I cannot trust either of my two female relations to do efficiently and safely. It will be safer for me to get the first lot myself, and trust him for the second.

So you see what a bow-wow involves. However, she is my sweetie, and the closer my Italian trip draws the less I enjoy thinking of it, for I am not really happy about her welfare in my absence. If I *can* manage Monday after all, I will so say.

Love

Joe

[1] His alsatian bitch (alias 'Tulip'). She was born in 1945, and when A. acquired her from 'some working class-people, who though fond of her . . ., seldom took her out', she was eighteen months old. She lived 'to the great age of sixteen-and-a-half.'

85 To Wyndham Lewis (1884–1957)   5/11/47

Dear Wyndham Lewis

I am just back from abroad and read at last for the first time your article on Colquhoun,[1] and want to thank you for it. A fascinating article, brilliant and powerful, beautifully phrased. How gratified he must have been—me too. I note again, not for the first time, the absolute first-rateness, the true spark that is struck when the mind's interest is really engaged—what fun it is, in short, when a writer has something he particularly wishes to say—and I hope you will phone me again whenever you have another desire to speak.

J. R. Ackerley

86 To his Sister (1899–)   Putney
                                                              ?/12/48
Dear Nance

I write in haste, and no doubt illegibly, but this is my 5th letter this evening, my first free evening for three days, for I have had to spend many evenings this week in my office in order to do justice both to Queenie and to my *Listener* Xmas Supp. So I have been running back to Putney after lunch, taking Goose Juice[2] out on Wimbledon Common in the afternoon, and returning to my office from 7.0 to 10.0 p.m. But now, thank God, the weekend is here.

I am so very glad you like your new room, and I am glad it is in a place where there is some life and company if you wish it. Your last place was so depressing that this could not help but be a change for the better. I do want to come and see it, but don't know when. It is so very hard to fit everything in—to give Queenie her exercise and meals every day and yet to visit William (still unwell in Notting Hill), Lilian (back in Brompton Sq. and longing to be seen), Siegfried, ill of a duodenal in an Acton Hospital, Edwin and Willa Muir waiting for me to fix a visit to Redcliffe Gardens— Gwen, Markus, Hetty Lowes, Diana, Elizabeth Bowen, Hester Chapman— all wanting to be taken out, I don't know how to do it and also to keep going at my Queenie book[3] and all the rest of it. But one highly important thing has happened—my visit to Mrs Cecil Wright has borne fruit, and a Mrs Muspratt, living in Hampshire, writes to say that she particularly wants an Alsatian bitch to breed on her farm—to supply her with another dog in place of the one, aged 14, who has just died—and that she would like me to bring Queenie along. She would be willing to look after Queenie during whelping and for the following weeks when she is suckling her pups. So I

---

[1] 'Round the Art Exhibitions', which had appeared on 23 October. The article concentrated mainly on Robert Colquhoun, but also mentioned briefly the work of James Wood, and a Welsh Exhibition which included pictures by Ceri Richards, Mervyn Peake, Merlyn Evans and Augustus and Gwen John.

[2] A nickname for Queenie. 'Eat your biscuits, you great goose!' A. would sometimes scold her. Other nicknames were Loony Weenie and Weenie Woony. See A.'s short story called 'A Summer's Evening', published posthumously in the *London Magazine* (October 1969).

[3] *We Think the World of You.*

74

shall take Q. along to exhibit her as soon as I can. I told her (Mrs. M.) that I would renounce claim on all pups—unless you happened to want one and were able then to have it. That would be her recompense for giving Q. a home. She is a keen dogger, and her own (now defunct) Alsatian bitch was a show dog and won prizes—she is interested in such matters. So this is something, as you will realize. I haven't answered her yet, but shall fix to trundle Q. down to Alresford—a 2 hour journey—at the earliest poss. moment, for the weekend. If I could really fix her up for a nice bit of sex and a proper litter next March it would be an immense help to me.

Don't bother to send back my £5 old dear. Instead of that, don't expect any more from me until you are short, then write to say, and I will send. It is good of young P[aul][1] to send—he must have very nice feelings really, though he was dreadfully silent when he was here. I haven't written him yet, but I will—oh God, if one only had a stenographer! But I will.

My Supp. goes on till Dec. 9—publication day. It has only just begun. I haven't thought beyond that yet, but Jack arrives in London on Monday for the day and I lunch with him then. I bet your old lady at 90 is missing you.

Not much of a letter, dear Nance, but I will write again soon.

J

To his Sister (1899–)   Putney 87
                                                              15/12/48

Dearest Nance

       thinking over your problems it occurs to me that unless you are now pursuing something that at all entices you,—if, instead, you are bothered or worried over the whole situation—why not drop the idea of a job altogether and try again for that best of all ideas, an unfurnished cottage. This was always the thing that was admittedly the best answer to everything, and is a better answer than ever now; and we only gave up the search because it seemed such a hopeless one. But the housing problem is getting more hopeful all the time, and I don't really see, if one takes it without desperation, but leisurely, why we should not now, by quiet looking about, light on something that I could afford. I would gladly put down about £1000 to £1500 if you could find something somewhere of that sort of price. But no good thinking in larger terms, for it would have to be furnished too, and my means are limited. I would keep an eye open in the papers for you, too. For I *expect* your S. Downs district is more expensive than others. If you found something of that sort you would then have a *home*, and a place for your son to stay if he came over, and a place for the furniture etc. and, more important than all, a job—for you would take it with the idea of a lodger. This you would have to get, for if I paid out all that money my means of keeping you would be naturally diminished. Once safely there, with no more rent to think of, you would be more happily placed for pursuing your husband over alimony if you still had none and

---

[1] Her son. See Letters 88 and 89.

meant to get it, for if you then had cottage and lodger you would be more independent in your mind. You would want 3 bedrooms at least. I see in *The Times* today that two thatched cottages are for sale near Newmarket for £3000. So why not one, so to speak, for half that? Anyway it would be the most satisfactory solution of all our problems if it could be found, and since you are now—I hope—comfortably placed in your little room and not therefore *urgently* in need of a place, you could take a year to look about if need be.

Excuse haste. What do you think? I will send you another cheque for Xmas.

Love

J

88   To his Sister (1899–)   Putney

16/12/48

Dear Nance

I hope the letter I posted to you yesterday[1] made sense, and did not add any further jar or jangle to your nerves. I daresay it's a bore to start looking again for unfurnished cottages, but I will give you as much help as I can, and now that you are more comfortably settled than you were before—at least I hope so—and the problem is altogether simplified. Don't you think it would be the best thing to give up one's mind completely and undistractedly to the one single idea of finding an unfurnished cottage, with 3 bedrooms, anywhere, at a reasonable figure. Would this not satisfy and settle your life more happily than anything else you or anyone else has suggested, such as financing a 'course' for you in something or other, or buying you a taxi (or sit-down life, which you are anxious not to have)? If we could find some place for you like that at a reasonable sort of figure, and spend a couple of hundred pounds in furnishing it, you would then feel you had something solid beneath you and could put in a lodger who would supply you in rent with at any rate the greater part of your living income. You would have no more bother about rent, would have a place for me or Paul[2] to come and stay, could take the bloody furniture, and even Queenie too betimes, and perhaps other people's dog or dogs for boarding. I feel sure that if something of this sort could only be found—and after all other people find them—it would be the answer to the maiden's prayer. But it won't be easy—no matter—and may oblige you to take train journeys. However, if found, don't you think it would meet your case much better than any odd job you could find?

Love

J

Are you coming up for Xmas?

[1] See Letter 87.
[2] See page 75, note 1.

To his Sister (1899–   )

Well old girl I have got all your letters now, so will begin afresh, for the letter I had started has now been said on the phone—except that my reason for the first postponement was that I'd made a previous date with Joan Evershed and then forgotten all about it. And I could not very well postpone her because it was the first time I'd ever taken her out, in return for many kindnesses, and the purpose of this particular invite was to distract her mind while her husband Raymond was undergoing an operation, on his bottom (fistula).

My cold is better now, though costly in handkerchiefs; it was the same brand as the one I brought down to Worthing before, only rather worse. It is a good brand, for no temperature goes with it; it is simply a sudden catarrh of bronchial and nasal tubes, and I would not have minded coming down to you with it if it had not been for Queenie; she presents various problems as a travelling companion, and one does not welcome problems in that condition. I'm sorry we shan't be together for Xmas, but I will come down soon after. Now that I am sure of your phone number, so unaccountably silent the other evening, I can get you at quick notice. Your idea of my coming in the evening and staying the night is a good one, and I will do that soon. It will probably be a Fri. night, so that I can go straight back to Queenie Sat. morning, or on Sat. night, of course, when I can return to take her out Sun. morn. All other nights would be too bothersome. *You* should be doing the same sort of thing, you know, but you don't seem to have any impulse that way. It is quite a business for me to visit you, with all the manifold pots I have to keep boiling here so to speak; but I do it, and I *like* to do it, and adventurously undertake the transport of Queenie just for a day trip, or sleep without minding on any old bed you are able to find to put under me—but let it be noted that you don't return the compliment, tho' you could more easily do so. Not that I wish to embarrass you, dear Nancy, by suggesting something you may not wish to do; but of course you would be much less lonely if you did it: if I paid a visit to you once in six weeks or so, and you paid a visit to me, even a day one, in six weeks or so, the chunks of time in which you are left entirely on your own would be chopped into shorter—3 week—fragments. I should have thought, too, that the expedition, given a nice day, might not be without interest and attraction, and would certainly 'take you out of yourself'. I could meet you, with Queenie, at Victoria, and we could have the whole day—Saturday?—together, with dinner in London before you return.

The trouble about parking Bunny[1] out, which I have gone into again this Xmas, is that there simply isn't anywhere for her to go—at any rate at

---

[1] Bunny was the younger sister of A.'s mother and outlived her by fifteen years. She married twice, and as a young woman had been a mezzo-soprano of concert-hall and operatic standard. Later, she was reduced to singing in musical comedy and understudying Connie Ediss at the Gaiety Theatre. A. was devoted to her and he would tell friends: 'She is the least conventional member of my unconventional family. She may be infirm—but she makes no demands on me, absolutely none.'

present. The only *possibility* is Ann[1] (Leslie[2] just has no room), and Ann is now a cripple and a pauper, and her flat is the chilliest place I ever was in—and I was only in it on an Autumn day. She hasn't a single gas-fire, you know, in the place, and (when we visited her) no coal fire burning, either because she hadn't the money for coal or because she hadn't the strength to lay and light one. The only way we kept warm was by drinking cups of hot tea. She is no better off now; her leg is still in irons, she has no job, and no lodger (which she spoke of trying to get), and her relatives have abandoned her because she tried to borrow £10 off Ida. I have been giving her a little money since. We have had no news of her since her visit here when I stayed down in Hampshire; but we now know that her state is just as it was, no improvement at all. So since there was no possibility of Bunny going over there—and Bunny is quite amenable to making room, by disappearing, for you to come and spend a day or two with me—we have asked Ann here on Xmas day— which rather selfishly suits me alright, for I can now spend the whole of that day with Queenie at Bob's[3] guzzling turkey, while Bunny and Ann eat up the chicken here. But, you see, Bunny is partially a cripple too. True she is not in irons; but her left hand is almost useless, and the fingers of it always stone cold like a dead person's hand, and cold is particularly painful to it and to her shoulder; so the notion of her staying with Ann in the latter's flat in winter is quite out of the question. What the spring or summer will bring forth remains to be seen. She certainly ought to go there some time or other, for she has left their various bags and objects, and will have to retrieve them some day. But I think it would have been quite cosy and pleasant if you had accepted to stay in one of the hotel rooms next door—though I don't, of course, know whether one was available for I didn't ask; but the management has changed, and the new manageress (whom I've never met, for I don't like the beer so never go in) is a friend, apparently, of Mrs Eton's, so I expect I could have arranged something there through her. And I do *know* that the beds there are jolly good (unless the departing manageress has taken them away with her), for I have slept upon them myself, and they are far superior to Mrs Young's or that other Worthing bed I inhabited—forget its owners' names.

Well, that is that. Now your alimony. My dear, I don't disagree with anything you say. I never disputed your right to it, and daresay that if you are pushed to it you ought to get a lawyer going again, if it can be done without too much expense. I only think (i) it is a frightful labour and bore for which I myself haven't the time to spare and (ii) you won't get much change out of it. It is one thing to have a right, and another thing to get your money. That is why I continue to hope it will come right in a nice gentlemanly manner; that Paul senior *doesn't* mean to ditch you altogether, or that junior will persuade him not to, or get a marvellous job himself so that he will have money to burn, or that conscience etc etc all round will bring about a change of heart—I make silly remarks, I know—but what I

[1] She had been their mother's servant for many years.
[2] Bunny's nephew.
[3] i.e. at Robert and May Buckingham's. See page 161, note 1.

do believe is that if Paul senior *does* mean to abandon you and dodge his liabilities, he can do so many things to make life—financial life—miserable for you, without getting himself into trouble that your life, if dependent upon it, would be appalling. It has been far from satisfactory up to date; yet I think one might truthfully say that since the war began you have had *some* measure of what lawyers call 'good will'. Even with that, it has been one crisis after another. I will conclude in another envelope tomorrow.[1]

To his Sister (1899–   )   Putney   90
                                                          27?/12/48

Dear old Nance
                there is one thing anyway that must be done immediately, and that is to send you this. I am most frightfully concerned to think you have no warm clothes, and beg you to go out as soon as the shops are open again and get yourself whatever you need. It is dreadful to think you have nothing suitable in weather like this, and I need hardly say that I had no notion of it at all, for I knew you had been acquiring a few things, some of which you told me about. However, I ought to have questioned you about it, I see. I'm most awfully sorry about the whole money business and that you should have supposed I would let you down over it. I shall be most upset and vexed, Nance dear, if you haven't got yourself warm things when I come down to see you again this week, whatever evening you suggest, and if this is not enough you must let me know. I can only hope you took no further harm from that journey yesterday, and shall be very worried until I hear from you.
Fond love
    Joe

To D. J. Enright (1920–   )   *The Listener*, Broadcasting House, W.1   91
                                                          22/2/49

Dear Mr Enright
                I am very grateful to you for sending me your book of poems *Season Ticket*. I think they make a very impressive collection, and I am glad to think that some of them appeared in this journal, and hope you will send me some more soon. You may be sure that we should have reviewed the book if it had been published over here;[2] but unfortunately, and particularly now when space is so restricted, the editor is disinclined to review books which our readers are unable to obtain. Is there no chance of one of our publishers taking it? I should have thought that T. S. Eliot (Faber) or Herbert Read (Routledge) would have been interested in your poetry.[3]
Yours sincerely
    J. R. Ackerley

---

[1] This letter has been lost.   [2] It had been published in Alexandria.
[3] Enright sent in this letter as an example of 'Ackerley's kind-heartedness'—and added: 'I ought to have a number of letters . . . but cannot find them. Possibly they were destroyed during one of my many migrations abroad. I remember one in which he doubted the existence of striped

92   To Paul Dehn (1912–   )   Home
                                                                23/2/49

Dear Paul

            when I thanked you for your book[1] I had not opened it, except
at the inscription. I have been reading it this evening. Lovely poems, my
dear. I am really rather surprised, because I had forgotten perhaps, and
perhaps because you have not been sending me such good things lately.
But these are beautiful, really fine, every one of them gives immediate
pleasure and satisfaction—always the right word, the perfect image, and
feeling and sincerity and sweet music. I am much impressed, and cannot
believe I have 'published the best of them' as you so generously say, indeed
it would be hard to point the best. It is a small and very discriminating
selection; that was right. It is a very good book indeed, very moving, and
should win you much praise. I am proud to have it, with your inscription.
Thank you very much. I do not usually read poetry when I have an alternative, but this is something that I like.

      Joe

93   To his Sister (1899–   )   ?/3?/49

. . . forward with you into a better future.[2] All these anxieties and troubles in
your mind will vanish, you know, the moment you are here with Queenie
and me.[3] O how I wish you had been on that train yesterday; I should have
fetched you; today would have been so sweet, instead of what it has been.
Do 'pull yourself together' quickly, dear old Nance, and come down and
look after poor old Joe and Loony Weenie.[4] We are alone here now, like
two sailors on a raft, and greatly in need of succour. There is nothing to
worry about so far as our dear old Bunny is concerned; she knows I want
you with me and that you can be of much greater help to me than she can,
and she is snugly instated with Ann—I took her over there on Sunday—and
registered now in that district. She is a dear old soul, as you know, and only
wants us both to be together and happy; and she herself is in good company
with Ann, for they are very fond of each other; so all that fits nicely, and
the only missing piece now in my jig-saw puzzle is you. It is my plan, when
you come, that we should each of us visit her and Ann on alternate weeks,
to give them a jolly day, taking Queenie with us from time to time to wake
up the Thornton Heath dogs and cats. Dear old Nance, don't let me down

mosquitoes (and therefore the propriety of comparing them to footballers' jerseys), but such
definitely did exist in Thailand.' The poem was called 'Mosquito Smitten with Love'. Four years
later Herbert Read took Enright's 'first U.K. collection' for Routledge & Kegan Paul—*The
Laughing Hyena*.

      [1] *The Day's Alarm*.
      [2] First page(s) of letter lost.
      [3] On 2 January she had attempted to take her life. She writes: 'There is no secret about this.
I was sent to a sort of loony bin near Chichester, where I stayed until the first week of March. Joe
used to visit me whenever he could and finally fetched me home.'
      [4] i.e. Queenie.

now; come soon, and let us make a future together. We can be of such immense service to each other, and to them, and to silly old Queenie. What I would like would be to collect you from your dreary old nursing home this weekend; but I don't properly know how you are. The doctor said you would soon be alright again, but refused to define 'soon'. And though I have phoned him this evening, he is away for the day.

Anyway, old darling, without hastening your electrical treatment, and certainly without upsetting yourself over worthless me, bring me your love and your sweet help soon.
Your fond old
Joe

To John Lehmann (1907–   )   *The Listener*, Broadcasting House, W.1   94
3/5/49

So sorry, dear John, not to have thanked you before for the personal copy of [Gore] Vidal's book.[1] Whoever sent it to me put the note in the back of the book, so I only found it lately. Very pleased to have had the chance to read it, though I can't truthfully say that I thought as well of it as I was glad to see [P. H.] Newby did.[2] I mean I think it is a book that one's reviewer ought to get people to read; it helps, but I couldn't get much interested in it myself. Too much involved, perhaps, in the subject: my top classes of novels that are taboo, so far as my own personal tastes are concerned, are novels about (i) buggers (ii) Indians. They both bore me to *extinction*. But I thought Mr Vidal himself rather a poppet I must say. Would much sooner have spent an hour with him than with his episodic book. But thanks, dear John, all the same.
Joe

To Wyndham Lewis (1884–1957)   *The Listener*, Broadcasting House, W.1   95
29/6/49
Dear Lewis
may I just say how extremely pleased I was with your article on Wadsworth.[3] One gets so bored with the usual obituaries, with crêpe armlets so to speak, which utter only the conventional grave cliché and are models of empty good taste. To read your salty remarks was most refreshing.[4] It was a good instance of what I mean when I say (my journalistic creed)

1 *The City and the Pillar*—a novel published by the firm which John Lehmann ran under his own name from 1946 to 1953.
2 Newby's review of it appeared two days later in *The Listener* on 5 May.
3 'Edward Wadsworth: 1889–1949', which was published on 30 June.
4 'About 1920 I remember Wadsworth taking me . . . on a tour of some Yorkshire cities . . . We arrived on the hill above Halifax . . . We gazed down into its blackened labyrinth . . . "It's like Hell, isn't it?" he said enthusiastically. (To forestall correspondence, it did not seem to me like Hell. But perhaps I am more particular.) A series of small scenes of the black industrial savagery . . . perhaps they were woodcuts, was Wadsworth at his best . . . For he had machinery in his blood and he depicted a machine with as much loving care as another man would lavish upon a cow or a bunch of grapes.'

that criticism unhampered by fear or favour is always the best. No doubt you will smile at that, reflecting upon what you might have said if freedom really existed; but it remains true nevertheless that the closer one can get to speaking one's mind the more readable and interesting one becomes. Yes?

J. R. Ackerley

96   To Herbert Read (1893–1968)   Putney
                                                                    ?/2/50
Dear Herbert
            I've sent the book: do with it as you like.
    The poorness of the weather has occurred to me, but, you are right, I don't notice it a great deal, except when it is perishing, and then only indoors, for my room is draughty and the gas fire temperamental. So far as the outside world is concerned, I have a good pair of gum boots and a serviceable U.S. army mac., and encased in these I take my dog out whatever the weather may be doing to prevent me. Every morning for the last 10 days, sustained by a pot of tea, I have been out on Wimbledon Common with her from 7.30 to 10.30, rambling about the woods. She is on heat, a worrying time, and I have to get her to the comparative safety of these woods before the Putney householders rise from their beds and, opening their front doors, loose their dogs (who all know of Queenie's condition) upon the streets. An eccentric way of life though this may sound to you, I don't mind it—indeed I rather enjoy it. Perhaps I have a Richard Church mind (*vide* his Country Notes) and enjoy beginning my day among squirrels, rabbits and green woodpeckers.

Nutting
by Richard Church

As I went ambling up an Autumn lane
I asked myself, and somehow did not know
How hazel nuts first started. Was it so
In the pre-squirrel period? And once again
Both my back braces' buttons came away
As I stooped down to lace my boot. And then,
Deciding that I'd nutting much to say
I put my pencil by and pottered home again.

Perhaps you would like this for some future Routledge anthology?[1] It is actually by Siegfried Sassoon, C.B.E.[2]

I haven't been to the new I.C.A. premises,[3] though I might. I was on the verge of going to the opening, but feared that [— —] might be there. But it would be jolly to have a drink with you there soon; do ask me. My only

[1] A. was fond of such spoofs—though few have survived.
[2] See note 1 above.
[3] The Institute of Contemporary Arts had opened its new premises this month in Dover Street. In March 1968 they moved to Nash House in the Mall.

art news is that I have taken on Eric Newton to alternate with Wyndham Lewis—and that I have just been playing with [Alexander] Calder's pretty toys.[1]

Have you news of James Kirkup's progress at Leeds? And have you entertained him yet? I hope the flu, which seems to be in your area, has passed you by

Love

  Joe

To Herbert Read (1893–1968)   17 Star & Garter Mansions, Putney,   97
                             S.W.15   10/3/50

Your nice letter, dear Herbert. I would love to come and see you this year, and love, of course, to bring my bitch, but I don't know whether I should impose her on you. She is not used to sheep certainly. She knows now that chickens and horses are not playthings; cows frighten her; sheep I think she has never met. However, I don't anticipate any trouble there, partly because she is highly intelligent and does what I tell her, and partly because she never leaves my side. Indeed, this latter characteristic of hers is rather a bore: at Siegfried's, for instance, although his 250 acres abounded in rabbits and such like attractions and she only had to walk out of the house to be in a canine paradise, I always had to take her for walks, she would never go off on her own, even tho' I was well in sight, trying to read a book under a tree. So I expect I could control her over the sheep alright. But I fear she may defecate in your house the first night, for the excitement of journeys always upsets her stomach. Ordinarily she never goes in the night, but if she should happen to want to here, there is a terrace for her to walk out onto; but on the last two occasions that I have taken her to friends in the country, I fear she has let fly in my bedroom—on the first night; for the rest of the time she was alright. On the first of these occasions it was my fault; she woke me up and did her best, poor girl, to get me to take her into the garden; but hearing the cat mewing there, I mistook her motives and let her down. What happened at Siegfried's later I do not know; I was worn out when I got there and don't know whether she tried to wake me or not.

This worries me rather; it would be alright, of course, if she had access to the garden in the night—or if you could give me a camp bed somewhere on the ground floor or in an outhouse. But otherwise I fear your beautiful house would be in danger during our first night—tho' I must say she is jolly considerate usually in selecting linoleum for her operations, or the oldest and darkest mat.

Well, say what you think, dear Herbert. The journey daunts me a little—old age—but the prospect of seeing you, and *en famille*, and in a county I have never yet visited,[2] all enchants me, and I would like to spend a week; but at the same time I should feel easier in my mind, assuming that you beckoned after the foregoing, to know that there was somewhere in the

---

[1] An American sculptor who works principally in steel wire and sheet aluminium.
[2] Yorkshire.

village that you could shuffle me into in case we turned out to be a bloody nuisance to you or Ludo[1] or sheep or anyone else at Stonegrave Manor.[2] I am tied to Town from March 20 to April 20, and then again from May 23 to the end of June: these are my two Spring and Summer Supplement periods, and the latter, which you will observe to be longer, also includes Queenie's spring oestrum (3 weeks) which just overlaps the second Supplement. After that I am free again until Mid-September, when the first Autumn Supplement begins.

It was nice seeing Georges, wasn't it? And you will have seen that he brought me a new article.[3] It was a little out of date, but less inscrutable than the first. Poor Alan did not take to it wholeheartedly however, but he was luckily indisposed—the pocket flu—at the crucial moment, and I got it past Ashley without trouble and so in. Ah yes—and your little Existentialist etc. book[4]—was it too 'jolly', the review? I expect you will ask me who wrote it, and I expect I shall tell you.[5] Ah yes, again: your *Hogarth* publication;[6] I was sorry about that. I did try to direct it decently, but it all went wrong.

Soon, I hope, you will find an exceedingly improper poem by Henry Reed in *The Listener*.[7]

Love

Joe

98   To Herbert Read (1893–1968)   Putney

?/3/50

Thanks, dear Herbert. Flaubert's *Letters* have gone. So has Richard Aldington.[8] And the Adrian Stokes book *is* a reprint. There really seem to be no books *at all*, and I can't think what I'm going to make my supp. out of. But unforeseen objects may turn up. What a pity you are the purveyor of Gurdjïeff & Ouspensky[9]—what a pity for me, I mean. It is only by publishing such works that one can avoid being asked to review them: I expect that's why you did it. They have put me to much troubled thought. Should the works of the Master be handed over to an apostle, who thinks he understands the sense and sees the Light—or to Professor Sprott, *par exemple*, or near-Professor Hampshire, who giggles even at the title of Gurdjïeff's book? A worrying question—particularly worrying when one of the apostles, raw with sensitivity, is at one's elbow, and one happens to like him. Well,

[1] The name by which Read's second wife Margaret was known among her family and friends.
[2] The Read family home since 1949.
[3] 'The French Symbolists', which had been published the day before on 9 March.
[4] *Existentialism, Marxism and Anarchism*, which had been reviewed on 9 February.
[5] Read did ask him and A. told him—W. J. H. Sprott.
[6] This monograph was by R. B. Beckett and was third in the series entitled 'English Master Painters'. They were published by Read's firm Routledge & Kegan Paul—and largely under his supervision. An unsigned review of *Hogarth* had appeared on 9 February.
[7] 'Movement of Bodies', which was published on 6 April.
[8] *Portrait of a Genius, but . . . The Life of D. H. Lawrence, 1855–1930.* An unsigned notice appeared in *The Listener* on 6 April.
[9] *All and Everything* by G. Gurdjïeff and *In Search of the Miraculous* by P. D. Ouspensky. Both books had been published by Routledge & Kegan Paul, largely due to Read's influence.

they are offered to Kenneth Walker,[1] as you might guess, though he has been commanded to formalize the Message, and not just say how wonderful it all is. I thought of wiring Gerald Heard for an autopsy—also of turning Govind[as V.] Desani, author of *Mr Hatter*[2] onto it—it seemed to me the same language—but I am really very fond of Walker and could not bear to wound him. I wonder what dear Herbert would have done in poor old Joe's shoes.

You will have seen [Benedict] Nicolson's protest at your attack upon another Master.[3] Will you be replying, I wonder.[4] We hope so—tho' no need really: but how could you know that someone else has now fallen, tooth and nail, upon Nicolson? Who, you cry with delight, has taken up the cudgels on your behalf? The answer will deflate you somewhat: Douglas Cooper.[5] You have indeed exploded a bomb, I notice. Hampshire, tho' amused, thinks you have been unfair. I need hardly say that he knows not who 'you' are: I fancy he thinks you are Mr [Geoffrey] Grigson. Which brings us to another matter: it is perfectly true that G. made no mention of you in his article.[6] I was down with 'flu when the piece went in, but did not know anyway the extent of your contribution to the volume—I fancied it was just a kind pat on the back. But are you really telling me that G., whom I have always regarded as a buddy of yours, might have ignored you deliberately? One really never knows where one is: a monastery for me.

Your plan for my visit sounds most agreeable and sensible; tithe-barns are the very thing. And of course I don't ever expect to be looked after or entertained, I am never bored by myself but always afraid of boring others; I like to be sent for, like the doctor or the court fool—then forgotten. Siegfried says to me 'I work all morning and rest in the afternoon, but we shall meet at tea.' That suits me fine—though it would suit me finer if he said 'We shall meet at supper,' for he is so very exhausting. I am going down to him again in June.

Let us think then, dear Herbert, of Friday, May 5 for you; but your plan does not look as simple to me as it does to you. Is not your Fri. afternoon train pretty packed—what class do you travel—and do you expect to eat

---

[1] Walker at this time was writing his *Venture of Ideas*—an account of the teachings of Gurdjieff and Ouspensky—which was published in the following year. But he reviewed neither of their books for *The Listener*. In the end they were offered to J. Middleton Murry whose signed review of them appeared on 20 April under the title 'Cosmoses and Consciousness'.

[2] A 'free-association novel' of 1949.

[3] On 16 March Read had reviewed anonymously Bernard Berenson's *Aesthetics and History*. His tone was severe—and he questioned Berenson's limited view of history, based on Dr Johnson's dictum that 'almost everything that sets us above the savages . . . has come from the shores of the Mediterranean'. He also questioned Berenson's neglect of Chinese, Japanese, Korean and Red Indian culture because they had not 'contributed anything to Hellenism'. The review ended: '. . . his humanism [is] a sham.'

[4] Read replied on 30 March. Here is the last paragraph of his letter: 'Mr Nicolson objects to the tone of my review, but it merely corresponds to the tone of a book which describes Professor Strzygowski as "this Attila of art history", and refers contemptuously to great scholars like Max Dvorak ("another German professor with a Slav name") and August Schmarsow ("yet another German professor with a Slav name")—taunts that ill become one who has recently dropped the Germanic "h" from the middle of his Christian name.' Berenson's early writings had been signed 'Bernhard Berenson'.

[5] A letter in defence of the review appeared from Cooper on 30 March.

[6] 'Courbet to Bonnard', which had appeared on 16 March. This review-article on Maurice Raynal's *A History of Modern Painting* had made no mention of Read's Introduction.

a meal on it? I like (I mean Queenie likes) an emptyish train and a first class carriage and sandwiches in my pocket—if one is running through a major meal time, that is to say. Tell me when next you write when your train leaves and gets in, and its main stops on the way. Very likely I shall arrange to join you at some halfway halt. The animal has little repose, I fear, and I daresay it would be less disturbing for all of us if I broke what will seem to her a pretty endless journey.[1]

Yes, dear Georges . . . is to send me soon a review or article on Malraux,[2] perhaps even bring it, for another 20 guinea visit. I've constituted him my 'Paris Correspondent', and what, theoretically, could be a better choice?— but I fear my editor will jib at last, and I know not how to defend him. That Symbolist[3] thing—'lucid for Georges,' Yes—'a child could understand it' he said to me triumphantly—but I doubt if many readers regard themselves as sufficiently child-like, and indeed and worse still it seemed to me who had to read it a dozen times at least—for elucidating, altering and cutting—to be unrewarding after one had reached the point of understanding—the more one read it the less, except words and repetitions, it seemed to contain.

Love
   Joe

P.S. Fancy not putting Forster's name on our last cover![4] Or Siegfried's, for that matter.[5] Vernon Bartlett, [Henry] Treece and Wyndham Lewis— and the Editor presumably supposes those to be selling names

99   To James Kirkup (1923–)   Putney
                                                     ?/12/50

Thank you, dear Jim, for your card and its very beautiful poem, a very sure success, every word perfect and dropping perfectly into place. Is it on the market?[6] And do, please, thank your parents for their card too: Nancy and I were most pleased and touched to hear from them. We have missed you in London: but the reason is all too easily understood. I have been lecturing Nancy on expenditure, and telling her that such items as frozen peas,

[1] In the end A. decided to postpone the journey. He wrote to James Kirkup on 5 May: 'I felt I really *couldn't* . . . put Queenie on a train for 4 hours with no means of leaving it—except by pulling the communication cord—for the York trains appear to stop nowhere on the way . . .'
[2] On 11 May, under the title 'The Fall of the West', there appeared a review-article by Georges Duthuit of *The Psychology of Art* by André Malraux.
[3] 'The French Symbolists', which had been published on 9 March.
[4] Forster had reviewed *The Cocktail Party* by T. S. Eliot on 23 March. In the play one of the characters becomes a missionary nun and is crucified on an ant-hill. When sending out *The Listener* proof, A. had written across it the suggested title 'A White Lady?' Forster would have none of it. Even though he 'did not care deeply for the work', he felt that Eliot was 'too serious a man to be made the target of cheap jokes'. He insisted that the review should be called—'Mr Eliot's "Comedy" '.
[5] In the same issue there had been two poems by Siegfried Sassoon—'An Asking' and 'At Max Gate'.
[6] The poem was a Christmas one—'The Blessed Received in Paradise', which originally had been published in *Time and Tide* on 4 December 1948. Kirkup writes: 'I copied it out for Joe and Nancy as a Christmas card.'

mushrooms, lettuces etc. which appear at almost every meal are now taboo. Not to mention clothes.

We pass a quiet day, until the late afternoon when we walk Queenie over to the Buckinghams[1] in Shep. Bush to spend the evening with Morgan, the Bucks., and two Americans, husband and wife, whom I like very much. If you had been about I should have commanded your presence. We have a turkey here too, of which you would have partaken—a last-minute turkey, marked up at 65/-, but reduced to 35/- because the butcher has a crush on Nancy. So my females have their uses, tho' I confess to being rather bored with them and the middleclass over-crowded squalor in which they oblige me to live. Bunny has been parked out for the holiday with a friend of hers in Sheen; if anyone had asked me, I would have parked myself out too.

Well, I have seen some friends anyway: William, Rose Macaulay, Henry Reed, Morgan, Blair Nyles and some odds and bobs. This morning I visited Morgan's aunt Rosalie, and sat with the old dear for an hour, Penny the cat having been shuffled into the kitchen out of Queenie's way. Queenie seems well, and ought to be 'in season' but is not. Gentlemen dogs begin to be interested, but the moment continues to be delayed. I thought of mating her again, but wonder if I can face it: I have 3 or 4 suitors to choose from, but *that* is not the difficulty. In a more civilised world there would be lying-in homes for bitches and after-care organisation for the children; but as we know all too well this is not a civilised world.

Well, God bless, dear Jim. A happy and prosperous 1951 to you, death to Gen. MacArthur, Syngman Rhee, Chiang Kai Shek, Winston Churchill, Pres. Truman . . . I leave you to extend the list—and a good-natured free-for-all for everyone else.

Joe

To Wyndham Lewis (1884–1957)   *The Listener*, Broadcasting House, W.1   100
20/1/51

Dear Lewis

you were so wonderfully good in the way you gave me your tragic news[2] on Thursday that you enabled me too to get easily through an interview distressing to us both. When I left your cool presence I felt wretched beyond words. I have not yet had to put up a show of that kind; I only hope that when I do I shall carry it off with something of your courage and dignity.

---

[1] See page 161, note 1.

[2] This news concerned Lewis's approaching blindness—and in April he wrote to A.: 'I am afraid I depressed you by my account of the dark room into which I am going to be locked. But there is an *interval*. May it be long! And we are all going into some even darker room after all: we none of us ever give a thought to that, so why should I anticipate my more limited blackout! . . .' Those memorable sentences caught the imagination, it would seem, for it is worth recording that when in 1969 the preparations for the publication of this book were first announced in the Press, more than seventy people wrote in to draw attention to the letter which Lewis had sent A.—and whose full text is included in *The Letters of Wyndham Lewis*, edited by W. K. Rose (1963).

I told my editor about it next day. He was deeply shocked, and knows, as I do, that *The Listener* will suffer an irreparable loss. He asks me to say that to you, and to express his gratitude for everything that you have done for us. Your articles have been one of the most notable features of our paper, a main source of whatever vitality it has had. But he has some doubts about giving *immediate* publicity to your news; and after talking it over with him I am inclined to think that he is right. The object of publishing the news will be to explain why you have ceased to do criticism for us, and that object will be served best when, a little later on, our readers write in, as write they will, to ask what has happened to you. To make a statement at once, he thinks, would be out of place, since although you have been a constant, you have not been a regular, contributor; and since, moreover, you have been engaged, up to date, in controversy in the paper, the stupid or knowing mind might still connect one with the other, whatever announcement we made. Don't you think there is something in all this, and that we should leave it for a little? Valuable though you have been to us, you could not be at once missed, simply because you have never been a weekly contributor; but in a few weeks' time, when the Lawrence correspondence[1] is forgotten, and when our readers are asking themselves and us why Wyndham Lewis is writing no more, we will tell them the sorry fact. But my editor adds, that if this does not agree with your own wishes, he will do his best to accommodate you in any other way.[2]

I do hope that your trip to Paris will reap some benefit for you.

Joe Ackerley

101 To Richard Murphy (1927–   )   *The Listener*, Broadcasting House, W.1
3/2/51

Thank you for letting me see these poems. I enjoyed reading 'Snow', which has much of interest and feeling in it, but suffers, to my mind, from too many adjectives, especially hyphenated ones. And 'pelvised'; is there such a word? And the 'sentence' beginning 'Like evergreen burned berries' (which I like) bewilders a little. One wonders whether the tense has not

---

[1] A controversy in the correspondence columns of *The Listener* had broken out on 'Art and Nature' in the previous November. On 4 January Lewis had opened one letter with this characteristic blast: 'Mr A. K. Lawrence, R.A., proposes a debate on what is "beautiful". There would be little sense in debating that with an Academician. If the white Lady Godiva which dominated the sculpture gallery at the last Royal Academy exhibition is beautiful, then I do not like beauty. I prefer the ugly, such as we find in Henry Moore's head, reproduced in *The Listener* last November, or let us say Epstein's head of Einstein . . .'

[2] Lewis wrote: 'The editor is perfectly right . . . the statement which I suppose must ultimately be framed must be very carefully worded . . .' The statement took the form of a valedictory article entitled 'The Sea-Mists of the Winter', which was published on 10 May. It ended: 'Were I a dentist, or an attorney, I should probably be weighing the respective advantages of the sleek luminol or the noisy revolver. For there is no such thing as a blind dentist or a blind lawyer. But as a writer, I merely change from pen to dictaphone. If you ask, "And as an *artist* what about that?" I should perhaps answer, "Ah, sir, as to the artist in England! I have often thought that it would solve a great many problems if English painters were born blind." And finally, which is the main reason for this unseemly autobiographical outburst, my articles on contemporary art exhibitions necessarily end, for I can no longer see a picture.'

uncomfortably changed from present to past, whether the verb should be 'races'—and later, 'You see . . .' etc. But I may perhaps have missed your meaning, or some intentional effect.[1]

J. R. Ackerley

To Francis King (1923–   )   17 Star & Garter Mansions, Putney, S.W.15   102
4/2/51

Dear Francis
          it was very nice to hear from you. Such a nice long letter. I was so pleased. The paper-boy (rather handsome, carefully dressed, well-kept long-fingered hands, clean pointed nails, a chain bangle on one wrist: 15? hobbies, woodwork and birds . . . well, well, the best we can do) has just paid a short social visit and carried off your stamps. 'Only connect'. Otherwise I shouldn't have obtruded him. And do forgive this mingy paper. I do hate it, it means such a bundle if one writes a lot—which I don't mean to do just now.

I don't know about your translations[2] either—how could I?—whether you catch what you had to catch, but they provide something which one begins to read over again after reaching the end (one of my tests) so I will take one,[3] for the fun of it. Perhaps you won't get a proof, though I will try to get you one. Other poetry news, gratifying to you: the Milani[4] bludgeoned me with another wadgett of her flimsies, and I must say I was stirred up again by her in reading them and have told her I will give her a try-out. So I will, though on re-reading and trying to choose, I must say it is difficult to pick out a single one which either stands up in its own strength or passes an examination in the common rules of grammar. I rather think that her effect is cumulative, she should be read as she writes, in bulk, and in a rush. However, I have told her I will make her a famous poet, so now I suppose I must.

And you, dear friend? Why no poems from you? I envy you like anything in your tawdry Greek seaside town. At least (and how much that is) an icy rain does not fall on you, as it does on us, day after day, week after week. One wades now, not walks, on Wimbledon Common, in gum boots; the ceilings leak, and a chill blast blows through the flat, giving poor Queenie a cold in her eyes. Fucking country—alas, not even that. Nevertheless, I have so far avoided the influenza and the smallpox, which have been carrying off my fellow countrymen and women in large quantities, in, respectively, the North and Brighton. With which I now close, adding that I see a great great deal of Henry Reed and hardly anything of anyone else. Oh, and

---

[1] This was the first note that Murphy received from A.—and in March he returned 'Snow' in a revised form. 'You have much improved it,' came the reply. 'Only one tiny point: since you have "ribs" in your anatomy of the land in l[ine] 9 ["The ribs of rock, the sloping side and pelvis"], could you not find some more interesting or less repetitive word than "side" in the same line later—"flank" or "groin" are all I think of . . .' The poem was published on 27 September.
[2] From the Greek of G. Th. Vafopoulos.
[3] 'The Elegy of the Brothers', which was published on 5 July.
[4] Ella Milani Comparetti, who wrote under the pseudonym of Alexia Mitchell.

adding of course that I still extract a sort of interest from life (thin, acid) much strengthened and stiffened by such greetings as yours.

Joe

P.S. I much like 'unstitch/my motionless image'[1]—but, on the whole, am more interested in the other poem.

103   To Sewell Stokes (1902–   )   17 Star & Garter Mansions, Putney, S.W.15

5/3/51

Dear Sewell

thanks for your letter and v. kind invite. I should like to come to lunch on Sunday and meet your brother very much, and would like to bring Queenie too for him to see, but that part of the programme is not as easy as all that and will need a little planning. The bus routes aren't suitable (longish journeys are v. uncomfortable for bow-wows, who aren't allowed on the seats, and in any case conductors won't always take her) and I would probably bring her by rail—the Metropolitan from Hammersmith to—where?—Euston Sq.? And I suppose I would have to bring her dinner with me, for she dines at 4.0: no, cancel that sentence, if I said goodbye to you at 3.30 I could get her home in time for a 4.30 meal. You will have had enough of us by then, I expect, for she is unused to visiting and is rather a fidget. And your brother may be rather disappointed, for she is fixated on me, and does not welcome affection from anyone else. Which does not mean that she will bite him, but she may well bark away any unwanted attentions. What do you think? Shall I come alone? Of course she is wonderful to look at. Like a Rouault.[2]

I haven't seen the book you mention, and have a vague idea that G. Gorer asked for it. I must look at my list, which I forgot to do.

Love

Joe

P.S. If I *did* bring her, you wouldn't have to cater for her *at all*. Bones are not allowed![3]

104   To Herbert Read (1893–1968)   *The Listener*, Broadcasting House, W.1

3/4/51

Dear Herbert

there was no time (slowness of printers) to send you a proof of [Ezra] Pound[4] and it has puzzled us a little, and slightly disturbed the

---

[1] The phrase came from the second translation of Vafopoulos, which King had submitted.

[2] A. was to write later in *We Think the World of You*: 'Framed in its soft white ruff, this strange face with its heavily leaded features and the occasional expression of sadness imparted to it by some slight movement of the brows, was the face of a clown, a clown by Rouault' (page 77). See Introduction, 3.

[3] Queenie could not digest hard bone. Inbreeding had deprived her of the powerful gastric juices that she should have had. Bone remained in her stomach or reached her gut almost unchanged. She would scream when she tried to defecate and have to be given an enema. Cf. Letter 195.

[4] An unsigned joint review of *The Letters of Ezra Pound*, edited by D. D. Paige, and an *ABC of Reading* by Ezra Pound.

Editor's peace of mind. He wished it had been a signed review. However, it has gone in without alteration, except for the removal of the word 'monstrous' which I agreed to take out, though it was difficult to tell, from the construction of the sentence, whether the Editor was justified in thinking that it was a comment-word only appropriate to signature. Perhaps it is the 'but' in line 3 of that para. that somehow bothers: should it be 'and'? Anyway one is not clear whether you mean that it was 'monstrous' to shut P. up because of political expediency, or, as seems from what follows (in which you seem hardly to give him a clean bill of mental health), for the other 'part' (some sort of mental instability), or at all. The Editor wanted to change the whole sentence to 'The poet, however, is now detained in a mental hospital, and the reader will undoubtedly scan ... etc.' which would certainly have clarified the passage. But I would not let him, although I too wasn't clear about your meaning.[1] He would have liked to see it go for another reason: libel. I believe it would be libel here to allege that someone had been shut up in a loony bin for political expediency— or so Maurice Ashley[2] thinks—but who would be libelled? The medical authorities? Anyway, as you see, I have had a chatty morning, and you have lost 'monstrous'.

Love
  Joe

To James Kirkup (1923–)   *The Listener*, Broadcasting House, W.1 105
20/5/51

Dear Jim
      thank you for your interesting package this morning.[3] I have not digested it yet, as you may suppose, but will do so after Easter. This is just to send you the third of the Hand & Flower Books.[4] I know what I think about all this and that is I don't wish to pat poor poets on the back just because they are poor poets. I understand and sympathize with the fact that poetry is in a bad state and that I must do what I can to help it to sell; but I don't think it would be doing it any service to boost it indiscriminately. I have to discriminate over everything else; only the best novels and the best other books are sorted from the continual stream of pretentiousness and mediocrity that ripples through the office and (what I am getting at) I am rather disinclined to advertise, even by a mention, these Hand & Flower books if they are just (as looks to me the case) giving some minor poets an undeserved opportunity of getting into print their

---

[1] In the printed version, published on 5 April, the passage read: 'The poet, however, is now detained in a mental hospital. That detention is in part an act of political expediency, but the reader will undoubtedly scan these pages for evidence that may justify such a procedure against such a man of genius. There are, as everyone knows, degrees of mental disturbance, many of which do not merit incarceration. No unprejudiced observer will fail to observe in these Letters a progressive egocentricity, and even the cause of it is not far to seek. A man who sets out (1908) with the idea that "no art ever yet grew by looking into the eyes of the public" is bound to find himself increasingly isolated from the social matrix which ensures "sanity" (which admittedly may be no more than an accepted code of conduct).'

[2] Deputy Editor—later the Editor.

[3] A batch of Kirkup's poems.

[4] *Guitar* by Rob Lyle, published by the Hand & Flower Press.

minor poems which no discerning publisher will take.[1] I expect you will think this severe, but I not only have not the space to be anything else but severe, I also think that it is necessary to try to have or set a standard of value, and that far too much, O far far too much is being written.

Love
  Joe

---

106 To James Kirkup (1923–)   *The Listener*, Broadcasting House, W.1
?/5 ?/51

Dear Jim

     I think this is a really wonderful poem[2]—the best thing you have ever done (though all the poems in your batch showed an immense advance, I thought, and I have taken 3 more, proofs of which will go to you later). Now do give careful thought to this before passing it as perfect. It seems to me much improved by your improvements, excepting perhaps for the introduction, so courteously made, of the extra verse. Though I like it, I'm not sure that it *does* improve, and it gives 'sleeps in' as a line end, while you have 'beats on' as another line end in the next verse. It gets also, the poem, a little messy, I feel in these middle stanzas after Verse 6. Although I took a syllable out of your 'sphygmomanometer' after consultation with Webster's Dictionary, it is still, of course, quite a word, as also is electro-cardiogram, and though you must have them both if you insist,[3] the rest of the verse seems to me to go to pieces beneath their weight. And then, would it not be tidier if you run Verse 7 into Verse 8, somehow like

The pink black lung like a revolted creature heaves

Then, as if by extra fingers, is .ˑ.ˑ.ˑ. neatly. held aside

What do you think? And is 'laid bare' . . . 'yet not revealed' okay?

Love
  J

---

107 To William Roerick (1912–)   17 Star & Garter Mansions,
Putney, S.W.15   8/8/51

Dearest Bill

     I am not really at the address above, but in 'The Rose of Normandy' below my office, drinking a pint of Bass after 4 poached eggs

---

[1] Kirkup thought differently. On 31 May he reviewed anonymously three collections of poems—*The Blessed Pastures* by W. R. Childe, *Farewell, Aggie Weston* by Charles Causley and *A Distant Star* by Charles Higham. The latter two were published by the Hand & Flower Press in the series 'Poems in Pamphlet' (Nos. 1 and 2). Later, A. was to revise his view of the series. In the following year when Hal Summers appeared in it, A. wrote to the reviewer in question: '[Your] review is alright—yes, possibly slightly sketchy; when you pass the proof you might perhaps add a little more critical comment, to Summers for instance, to help him and us. Ignore Francis Brett Young if you don't want to play, and keep the book for your trouble . . .'

[2] 'A Correct Compassion', which was dedicated 'To Mr Philip Allison, after watching him perform a Mitral Stenosis Valvulotomy in the General Infirmary at Leeds'.

[3] In the final version Kirkup took A.'s advice and dropped the words 'cardiogram' and 'sphygmomanometer': the latter (according to Webster's Dictionary) means 'an instrument for measuring blood pressure and esp. arterial blood pressure'. The poem was published on 28 June.

(one broken) and some cheese. I oughtn't to be writing to you, merely because my Biro, never a friendly and personal pen, is coming to the end of its ersatz ink and making splodges; but it was so nice to have your picture of your life at Lost Farm, lovely name, that even if you cannot read and this is another letter to Madan Blanchard,[1] I shall write. It is dinner, incidentally, that I have eaten, not lunch. Such late hours—it is 8.30 p.m.—don't mean that I am busy. Indeed I have spent the afternoon at the cinema with Morgan's wicked undergrad. Simon Raven. But Queenie is on heat, and since it upsets me to see her in that condition, and it upsets her to see me, I am purposely spending my evenings in London until it is over. It is almost over. I know it is cowardly, and I always mean not to be that, but when the time comes I can't face going through with the plans I constantly make to provide her with another husband and more children—she had one litter of eight three years ago—and break all my promises to her and to myself. It entails—I know from experience—four months of anxiety and trouble; two months of pregnancy, and then two months of helping her with the offspring (the second month of which, when their teeth grow and she gets nipped and bored, one has to look after them and wean them oneself, four meals a day), then finding the little creatures not only homes but decent homes, and then, of course, clearing up the mess. Against that I set, to prop myself up, after all only *one* week of worry, the middle of her three weeks of heat, when she is burning to be had. She is awfully good always, deferring always to my opinion and wishes which she never fails to put before her own; but it is a physical thing which Nature imposes upon her and she has no choice but to seek some sort of help. Even if I put out my hand to caress her, her great tail curls like whipcord round her flank and she pushes her backside against me with an appealing look. I do what I can for her in all sorts of ways, excepting the one thing she needs which is a dog. I get up every morning at 6.30, and have her out of the flat, when I have had a cup of tea, at 7.15 to take her up on to Wimbledon Common. And then we ramble about and have adventures among the rabbits for as long as four hours. She loves it, and so do I; the weather is fine, the Common beautiful, the bracken like a green sea, four feet high at least; and with indefatigable energy she pursues the early morning rabbits in it, leaping like a dolphin among the waves. All else is forgotten in the joy of this, and I hope in this way to tire her out so that her condition will worry her less.

Ages have passed—weeks anyway—since I began this letter, and now the scene has changed, like my Biro refill, and 'The Rose of Normandy' has turned into Westgate House, Lewes, Sussex, where I am having a week's holiday. Queenie (who is with me of course) began her heat here on my short visit five weeks ago, and here we are again now that she has recovered. I like it very much. It is such pleasure to be entirely alone with no one to

---

[1] This was a reference to Forster's 'A Letter to Madan Blanchard', which had been published separately as a pamphlet by the Hogarth Press in 1931. Blanchard was a sailor who was shipwrecked in 1783 in the west Pacific, and Forster writes him a letter from the London Library in the belief that it will definitely reach him. The piece was subsequently reprinted in *Two Cheers for Democracy* (1951)—dedicated to Jack Sprott and Roerick (mis-spelt Roerich in the first edition).

please but oneself. I have friends scattered about and can go and see them
if I wish or bring them along to this small furnished flat—Leonard Woolf in
Rodmell, Clive Bell and Duncan Grant at Charleston, Lydia Lopokova
at Tilton, my publisher at Iford,[1] Geoffrey Gorer in Haywards Heath, all
within walking distance or a short journey. And I have brought *Robinson
Crusoe* to read, a perfect holiday book, and there are the great Downs on
three sides, and the sea within walking distance. I have my bathing trunks,
but the weather has given way, rain and wind, so it doesn't look as though
I shall use them. Nothing matters though, for our week. And I am wearing
your lovely blue Homesteader shirt,[2] which I dearly love and always wash
myself.

What news have I for you? Ben[jamin Britten] has been ill with some
infection, and perhaps still is. He answered my letter at last, as he did yours,
and very friendlily. He is thinking now of getting William Plomer to attempt
his libretto,[3] but I doubt if he will persuade him. Morgan, who is in good
health and spirits, hobbled off to Cambridge on Saturday, supported by
Bob, to stay with Francis Bennett.[4] Kenneth Clark was glimpsed, in a silk
hat, from the top of a bus, entering the grounds of Buckingham Palace for
the Garden Party. Very spry did he look.

He wrote to *The Times* to say how deplorable it was that the re-opening
of the Walker Gallery in Liverpool with its Stubbs exhibition had had so
little publicity; so I asked him to give me an article for *The Listener* about it,
but he said he was too busy. But draw not your fine brows together, for I
love and honour him nevertheless.

No more news. We were caught in a downpour on the High Downs
above Offham—pronounced Oafham, perhaps because we were there,
Queenie and I, on such a dubious morning—today, and got pretty wet,
although we sheltered under a thorn bush. Now I have rheumatism in my
left knee, always my 'heel of Achilles'. That is old age. But I found this
feather, which I send you with, to dear Tom also, my love

Joe

How I wish I could be over for the opening night of *Lady Windermere's Fan*.[5]

108 To Wyndham Lewis (1884–1957) *The Listener*, Broadcasting House, W.1

21/3/52

Dear Lewis

I am sorry to have vexed you. No one cares to be called 'petty',
so you push me to the explanation which it was my object to avoid, and

---

[1] I. M. Parsons. See page 104, note 3.

[2] A. also used to wear 'army fatigues' (i.e. denims) sent him by Roerick. Their advantage when
he was working at *The Listener* was that he could carry 'Queenie's dinner in their large leg pockets'.

[3] In 1947 Plomer had written the introduction to a new edition of Herman Melville's *Billy Budd*.
But it was not until 1952 that Benjamin Britten asked Plomer to write his first libretto for him—
namely, for *Gloriana*, which was first performed at Covent Garden Opera House on 8 June 1953.
The libretto for Britten's *Billy Budd* opera was written by E. M. Forster and Eric Crozier, and was
first performed at Covent Garden Opera House on 1 December 1951.

[4] i.e. E. K. Bennett (1887–1958). See Forster's obituary tribute published in the *Caian*
(Michaelmas Term 1958).

[5] Part of a summer stock season in which Roerick was appearing.

which simply is that I was disappointed in your review,[1] I did not think it interesting. It seemed to me that you had written it more with a view to please John than to entertain my readers. Excepting for the amusing remark at the beginning about the kangaroo,[2] it fell very short of my expectations. That these had been high is sufficiently proved, I think, by the facts that I did offer you the leading page and a larger fee than was offered to anyone else in the Supplement.[3] Indeed I thought I had a 'scoop'. But in the event it seemed to me that Homer had nodded, and that other reviews in my possession, Rose Macaulay's among them,[4] to which I gave your place— were to be preferred to yours.

You may accuse me therefore of lack of taste if you wish—that is a charge I could not answer—but I cannot see what 'pettiness' has to do with it. It is my job to make my paper as attractive as I can, without fear or favour,[5] and I cannot but suppose that if our positions had been reversed you would have acted as I did, placed your best wares in the forefront of the shop.

J. R. Ackerley

To Hal Summers (1911–   )   *The Listener*, Broadcasting House, W.1   109
5/5/52

Dear Summers

I should have written before to thank you for the personal copy of your book.[6] I am so pleased to have it. Lovely poems. I am proud to think we published so many of them.

J. R. Ackerley

To G. F. Green (1911–   )   *The Listener*, Broadcasting House, W.1   110
4/12/52

Dear Mr Green

one does not get such a letter as that every day of the week. Besides signing your copy of my book[7] I thought you would like me to complete it for you. It is now whole, as it was originally offered for publication twenty odd years ago. When it was to be reprinted last year I was

---

[1] *Chiaroscuro* by Augustus John, which A. in an earlier letter had recommended to Lewis as 'a kind of scrap-book . . . well written and easy to read and not too long . . . You appear in it both as a plate and in the index'. The review had been published on 20 March.

[2] 'Augustus John is an exceptionally good writer; and upon this reviewers have dilated, with a tendency to compare him with painters who have written books. This is the obvious reaction, it would seem, when a painter takes to the pen: to see a man of that calling engaged in literary composition affects people as if they had surprised a kangaroo, fountain-pen in hand, dashing off a note. The truth is that Augustus John is doubly endowed: he is a born writer, as he is a born painter . . .'

[3] On 14 February A. had written: 'I could give you the whole of the front page—900 to 1000 words—of my Supplement. Signed of course, and a picture. And 25 guineas.'

[4] A review of *Hugh Walpole* by Rupert Hart-Davis.

[5] A. was fond of this phrase. He had already used it to Lewis earlier. See Letter 95.

[6] *Visions of Time*—which was No. 4 in the series 'Poems in Pamphlet', published by the Hand & Flower Press. It was reviewed anonymously in *The Listener* on 3 July, along with *Into Hades* by Andrew Young and *The Sailing Race and Other Poems* by Patric Dickinson.

[7] *Hindoo Holiday*.

given leave to replace all the cuts; but a couple of weeks or so before its date of publication some old Indian civil servant published his memoirs[1] in which he took occasion to expose the identity of my native State. Something of a hullaballoo ensued and both our books were withdrawn, his to have all reference to myself expunged,[2] mine to have deleted this single passage which was somewhat belatedly perceived to be libellous in view of the fact that, although the Maharajah is dead and his State dissolved, his son and wife are still alive. I parted with it with sorrow, for besides being rather amusing in itself, I think, it is the climax of the book and ties the main characters together. But naturally one does not want to get other people or oneself into distress of mind or fortune, unlikely though it was that any such consequence would occur.

I am sorry that I have not read your new book *In The Making*[3] yet, but I am intending to do so soon. As you may or may not know Forster was very pleased with it and wrote to tell me to look out for it. He also ticked off Stephen Spender—Stephen told me—for not having praised it highly enough![4] So you can imagine that I am eager to read it, and I will write to you again when I have.

If you come up this way do come and have dinner with me—or lunch, but dinner is a nicer meal.[5] I should be so pleased. I shall be on leave from Dec. 12 to 29, but probably at home excepting for the Xmas holiday. My home address is 17 Star & Garter Mansions, Putney, London, S.W.15 and my phone number Putney 1656.

And thank you very much again for your wonderful letter.

Joe Ackerley

P.S. The restored passage is on pp. 251–252.[6] I had to fake a little when it was removed and to fill up the space with that entry about the sundial which I had not meant to use but which can stay.

III To John Lehmann (1907–   )   *The Listener*, Broadcasting House, W.1

22/1/53

Dear John

I am very very very very very very pleased. I have just sent you 3 novels of a sort, and have asked Stephen to pass on to you those of

---

[1] *Kingdoms of Yesterday* by Sir Arthur Cunningham Lothian. Cf. Letter 158.

[2] i.e. from Chapter 2: 'Another of the larger States was Chhatarpur, whose Ruler was subsequently the hero of that curious and somewhat cruel book, *Hindu* [*sic*] *Holiday*, by Ackerley.'

[3] A novel about childhood.

[4] On 30 October Spender had reviewed Green's novel in *The Listener*, along with *Recollections of a Journey* by R. C. Hutchinson, *The Financial Expert* by R. K. Narayan and *A Cry of Children* by John Horne Burns. He had described it as 'a beautifully written, beautifully planned, intensely imagined book . . .'

[5] 'I deliberately avoided this,' Green wrote to Braybrooke on 3 March 1972. 'I met him only once at a party . . . just after he had published my story. I had an immense admiration for him and a deep sympathy with his writing, extending also to his poetry (I remember reading his poem *Micheldever* with great excitement when Spender received it for publication in *Horizon*). Because of this I was afraid that at a meeting I would disappoint him. A strange understanding seemed to have been established in the few letters we exchanged. I didn't want this to be changed. That was why I was fearful of meeting him.'

[6] See Appendix D.

the collection he has which he has not dealt with and which he thinks you should see.[1] And, from now on, I shall send you everything that comes in, excepting palpable trash. But I find publishers rather unreliable, and it not infrequently happens that they omit to send me their books. If therefore you notice at any time a novel reviewed elsewhere which you have not had and want, please let me know at once and I will always obtain it for you. Length? I mostly refrain from giving my reviewers lengths, because they almost always turn out wrong. Length seems to have only a nodding acquaintance with the number of words, presumably because some reviewers use much longer words than others. So I do to them, poor chaps, what I do to you herewith: provide a specimen page, and leave the problem to them. Things to be noted about this specimen page are (i) that if you do four main novels, as Stephen has done here,[2] this text is maximum length. That's to say that my turn review above *has* to have not less than a 12 line turn (4 lines per col.) if the page is to look presentable.[3] If, however, you did three main novels, or even two, and wanted a maximum text, you could have another 3 or 4 lines per col. On the other hand, you need never fill the page so full as Stephen has filled it. You can always write less if you want to, and I shall fill the page up with a larger turn. I hope that's clear. If you wrote more, for four novels, than Stephen has written here, I should have to cut you. (ii) Stephen has done four main novels here. You should not do less than two or more than five. If you have other novels which hardly deserve elaborate analysis and comment yet deserve mention, there is always that useful device (which Stephen seems not to have used here) of the final para. of 'Also Recommended':[4] into which you can stuff, with a few words of comment, anything you like.

I like to have copy in on the Wed. or Thurs. preceding the week of publication. So for the 19th, I should like your script on the 11th or 12th. You will be announced on Jan. 29th.

What else? Oh yes, what is likely to be the date of your last shot? You said something about going away, but I forget when.

Well, dear John, any other queries will be answered to the best of my ability, and I look forward with the utmost interest and pleasure to your term of office.

Love

Joe

[1] See Letter 112.
[2] A. sent the page from the issue of 15 January. On it, Spender had reviewed four novels—*Invisible Man* by Ralph Ellison, *The Producer* by Richard Brooks, *The Witch-Diggers* by Jessamyn West and *The Courting of Susie Brown* by Erskine Caldwell.
[3] Fiction reviews during A.'s editorship never began at the top of the page, but began an inch or so down with the heading 'New Novels' set in bold type and the titles, authors and publishers of the three to five selected novels running across the page. It was a feature in *The Listener*'s make-up that distinguished it from the other weeklies and is still remembered with nostalgia by many. 'What an excitement it was to find oneself reviewed in that fortnightly column,' Fred Urquhart told Braybrooke.
[4] This 'device' was dropped after A.'s departure from *The Listener* in November 1959. But he revived it during his temporary return in September 1965. See Letter 285.

112 To Stephen Spender (1909–)   *The Listener*, Broadcasting House, W.1
22/1/53

Dear Stephen

John Lehmann is agreeable to jump into your shoes, and since he is agreeable to do so at once, that, I think, is the best arrangement. This script of yours, then, that I am expecting shall be your last: he will begin on Feb. 19. Could you therefore, dear friend, pass on to him, or to me for him, every novel you have which you will not be dealing with yourself and which you think he ought to see. This sounds awfully tiresome for you, so if it would suit you better I would send along a messenger to collect the parcel (if you could make it up) and take it straight on to him.

It was jolly decent of you to offer to do me yet another article, with all the unsettling and important things you have on hand. I was very touched. It's been awfully nice to work with you, dear Stephen, and we are all sorry you conclude so soon. You've done me proud, in every way; interesting, readable, reliable and some amusing articles—what more could a lit. ed. want? Yes he could want punctuality also, and has had that too. You are good. And you are sweet.

And I am your grateful and loving friend

Joe

113 To Roy Fuller (1912–)   *The Listener*, Broadcasting House, W.1
9/9/53

Dear Roy

I'm glad to see they have got John's poem in this week.[1] I did not write to him about them because it seemed difficult to steer a course between the schoolmaster and papa's friend, neither of which I felt would be proper. The schoolmaster in me wondered whether it was fair on a young poet to take his first poem: might it not be a flash in the pan, and might I not raise his hopes in the beginning only to dash them forever after to the ground and so send him into a despond, and from a despond into a decline, and from a decline into Fleet Street or the BBC? And papa's friend could fall into far too many errors of tone. So I thought it best to respond formally to his own sensitive formality.

Though too early to say, the poem of his I took seemed to me to show a narrative gift, which he should develop. It was his own poem, in his own voice. The cat poem was skilful too, but it was in your voice, and he must use his own.

I think your review is very good, and the last thing I should ever believe of you is that your judgment could be influenced by pique or anything else.

Love

Joe

[1] September 10. The poem was called 'Circe' and was signed J. L. Fuller. The poet now writes under the name of John Fuller.

To the Editor of *The Times*[1]

17 Star & Garter Mansions,   114
Putney, S.W.15
Oct. 17, 1953

Sir,

The 'banger' i.e., the Mighty Atom, the Mighty Midget, the Little Demon, the Smasher, the Boy Scout Rowser, &c.—has not this small 1½d. firework ('Light blue touch paper. Throw away at once. Must not be held in the hand.') lately received some kind of a commercial push? It is now available for sale early in September and does, according to the noise, a roaring trade until the New Year, and I feel sure that it is only during the last three years that my own district has been so relentlessly afflicted over so extended a period. Life is thereby made exceedingly tiresome for a number of people, especially the middle-aged, who feel that they have had quite enough bangs in their lives, and also for many dog, cat, and bird owners.

The mischief value of the 'banger' is clear; since its function is simply to make a loud bang, it is naturally less fun to startle oneself than to startle someone else, and that is the use to which it is largely put by the local hobgoblins among whom it finds the keenest sale. And the police, as clearly, cannot control it; while one is reading one of their prominently displayed notices announcing that it is an offence to explode fireworks in the street and another offence to sell them to children under 13, children who at any rate appear to be under 13 are exploding them in the streets all round. One can pick up the expended cartridges as one walks. But even the animals, at whom the 'banger' is often thrown (one has been cast at my own dog), might be persuaded to take all this in good part if it did not go on for so long.

Your columns often refer to that percentage of road accidents said to be caused by dogs; may not the 'banger' be a contributory factor? My own dog, who has normally an exemplary road sense and requires no lead, becomes so demoralized from September onwards that she is liable to fly home in a panic across all the main roads. Even on the lead she is not safe, for she has sometimes wrenched herself free when the sudden explosion occurs. Apart from one's dislike to see one's animal frightened, it becomes a real problem to know where to exercise her in safety; the 'bangers' are ubiquitous. That her nervousness is far from exceptional many other animal owners will certainly testify. Cannot the sale of these troublesome objects be strictly confined to that historic day—call it a week—of the year when we all expect to be blown up?

Yours faithfully,

J. R. Ackerley

---

1 The letter appeared under the heading 'Fireworks'. A. was not pleased, and in a notebook he later wrote: 'I sent a complaining letter to *The Times* and entitled it 'Bangers'; it was published, but some interfering official, unable to let well alone, changed the title to 'Fireworks', so that the letter missed its point [which was to distinguish between the 'banger' and fireworks such as the 'catherine wheel', with the result] that other correspondents reproached me for being an old fogey and spoil-sport.' On 24 October one had written: 'I have been told about the letters you have had about small boys letting off fireworks. I am 10 years old and this news makes me mad. Were the people who wrote to you born grown up, and did they honestly never let fireworks off before Guy Fawkes night? Anyway we small boys are not small for ever. Goodbye—Stephen Chamier.'

115 To Stephen Spender (1909–   )   *The Listener*, Broadcasting House, W.1

3/12/53

Dear Stephen

I am sorry about your poem; I did not think that you would mind much whether it was in or not; I would have left it in if I had realized that its exclusion would disappoint you as well as myself.[1] The trouble in arranging the two pages they allotted me was that the 25 years of *The Listener* were shared between two Lit. Eds, Janet[2] and me, and since I naturally remembered and had a more special feeling for the poems I had got and published than the poems that she had got and published, I decided, to start with, that there were four poems I particularly wanted to include: [Edwin] Muir's 'The Combat', Henry Reed's 'Map of Verona', Edith's 'Bagatelle' and a poem by Lilian Bowes Lyon.[3] Having got those fixed, I read back through all the poems published in the last 25 years, Janet's and my own, and—what a job!—made a list of what I would like in, including you, Dylan Thomas, William Plomer, Cecil [Day Lewis] and [Sidney] Keyes. But I couldn't manage in the space, for I had only about ¾ of a page left. So I fitted up what looked like an exact fit and which included you and Dylan and Keyes—shedding a tear over my loss of William, who never gets any publicity as a poet. But alas I had fitted it all up too tightly for the Editor's taste; also he wanted the dates of publication of the poems to go in beneath the signature, which wasted more space still, so that in the end I found that I must throw out not only Keyes, but either you or Dylan too. Dylan having just died, I gave him the space,[4] and then found myself with about 2 inches to fill, so I had to go through all the blessed poems again to find some tiny fill-up to complete the pages.[5] Actually I was almost more sorry to reject Keyes[6] than anyone else because it was the poem which I was rapped over the knuckles by the Director-General for publishing—indecency!—and I thought it would be a sort of beautiful revenge to republish it. However, it isn't really an awfully good poem.

So that's how it happened, not enough space—there are only *six*[7] poems in; an error in make-up; and my initial mistake, I fear, in starting off on the wrong foot with 3 poems that were rather long. After lunch with you I thought I would tear the whole thing up and start again, but it has already

[1] This refers to the Twenty-Fifth Anniversary Number of *The Listener*, which was published on 14 January 1954.
[2] Janet Adam Smith, who was the paper's first literary editor from 16 January 1929 to 12 April 1935.
[3] 'Rhyme to a Lamb.'
[4] 'Poem in October.'
[5] A. chose 'January', a seven-line poem by R. S. Thomas.
[6] His poem 'Remember Your Lovers' had been published on 19 December 1940. The offending verse was:

> When you woke grave-chilled at midnight
> To pace the pavement of your bitter dream
> We brought you back to bed and brought you home
> From the dark antechamber of desire
> Into our lust as warm as candle-flame.
> Young men who lie in carven beds of death
> Remember your lovers who gave you more than dreams.

[7] In the end there were seven poems, the seventh being W. H. Auden's 'Sonnet', beginning: 'Wandering lost upon the mountains of our choice . . .'

gone down to the printers, and all permissions etc. have been obtained, and it seemed too difficult. Then I asked the Editor if there was room in the rest of the anniversary part for an extra poem or two; but there is not.

There are no articles about poets or poems—nothing specially written, I mean. The Supplement contains nothing but re-published talks and republished poems and a story by E[lizabeth] Bowen. I don't know what the talks are that have been disinterred for republication, but I don't suppose you are alluded to in any of them. I expect they are mostly things by G. B. Shaw and H. G. Wells and things of that sort.

I'm so sorry it went that way.

Love

Joe

To Bertrand Russell (1872–1970)   *The Listener*, Broadcasting House, W.1   116

9/2/54

Dear Mr Russell

if you are now well enough, as we hope, to take on any work, would you consent to review a book for my Spring Book Number (March 11)? The book I have in mind is *Military Organization and Society*, by Stanislaw Andrzejewski (R[outledge] & K[egan] P[aul] 21/-). Perhaps, if you do not know it, you would like to look at it and see if it interests you? I should want a signed review of 800 words by March 3.[1]

J. R. Ackerley

Lit. Ed.

To Donald Windham (1920–   )   17 Star & Garter Mansions,   117

Putney, S.W.15   3/5/54

Dear Don

it was lovely to hear from you and be praised by you.[2] I was so pleased. But sorry your own literary projects do not go better. You are a perfectionist, very sympathetic to me in these times of slipshoddery and reportage, but often more rewarding intellectually than financially. Do put Chap. 2 of your novel[3] aside for a time and have a go at some other section or at something else; the subconscious does a lot of work for one when consciousness fails, I find, and suddenly everything that one sought after in vain is handed up, at the oddest moments, by the chef within. I do hope your play[4] will come along, too. It is a medium you should be interesting in: I wonder what it is about.

---

[1] Russell was not well enough—and instead Bertrand de Jouvenel reviewed the book in a signed notice on 11 March under the title 'Arms and the Man'.

[2] Windham had written in April to congratulate A. on his piece 'My Dog, Tulip', which had appeared in March in *Encounter*.

[3] *The Hero Continues* (1960). The chapter mentioned was discarded.

[4] A dramatisation of Windham's story 'The Starless Air'. It had been tried out in the previous year in Houston, Texas. The director was Tennessee Williams.

I have just taught myself to type—two fingers—and clatter away quite rapidly now on the office typewriters in my spare time, transferring a novelette[1] I wrote a few years ago from ink to type. It is fun, like composing an opera. I chant as I go, much to the surprise of people in the adjoining rooms. I don't know whether the result will be a success yet—I never know what I do—but the idea is good anyway. It is Tulip again—an expansion of the few paras. in my story that referred to her early life.[2] Homosexuality and bestiality mixed, and largely recorded in dialogue: the figure of Freud suspended gleefully above.[3]
Very best wishes
Joe Ackerley

118   To Francis King (1923–   )   17 Star & Garter Mansions, Putney, S.W.15
15/7/54
Dear Francis
            I feel I owe you a letter, a number of letters perhaps, for such as you have had from me have been only scraps, but I have been so deeply— well, perhaps that is too pretentious a word—pertinaciously engaged in finishing off my novelette[4] that I have neglected much else. It will be finished once and for all by the end of August: practically all of it has now been tapped out with two fingers on a hired typewriter, and when it has been cleaned up I will have it read to see if it is rubbish. For alas, I do not know. I thought it no good a couple of years ago when I first wrote it,[5] although even then I had devoted much time and loving care to it; but the encourage- ment I received over my little *Encounter*[6] piece swelled my head sufficiently to make me think that perhaps I was cleverer than I supposed, so I dug it out and have now spent upon it another long period of loving care. And yet if it is written off as worthless, by whomever I show it to, I shan't really mind, it has given me a lot of self-indulgent pleasure to write, and I shall be pleased to have brought something to completion: these two reflections will outweigh the sad thought that I have used up so much of my time to no purpose. It is autobiographical of course; I have no creative ability: and the heroine is a dog who becomes substitute love for a boy, and through whose senses the homosexual part of the book is described. Terribly, terribly Freudian. Sometimes I think it the most absurd tosh, and sometimes, at my favourite passages, tears drip from my eyes onto the hired typewriter and rust it up.
            I never wrote you more about your own book,[7] the notices of which, generally, must have disappointed you rather, I fear. My own reviewer[8]

---

[1] *We Think the World of You.*
[2] See page 127, note 1.
[3] Later in the year, in November, A. wrote to Herbert Read: 'The gleeful figure of Freud is, of course, purposely suspended above the plot and the narrator.'
[4] *We Think the World of You.*
[5] Not strictly accurate. A. began the novel towards the end of 1948, but laid it aside in the following year. In 1952 he again began work on it and completed this draft in August 1954. Several more revised drafts were to follow.
[6] 'My Dog, Tulip' (March 1954).
[7] *The Dark Glasses.*
[8] Idris Parry—whose notice had appeared on 8 July.

seemed to me better than most, I thought, though I did not think his criticism of the age of your hero amounted to anything. I myself thought it a solider though slighter book than any you have done; the characters, perhaps because they were fewer than usual, seemed to me to emerge more sharply and with greater emotional force, standing out so real and dark against the brilliant landscape. And yet it disappointed me in a way, perhaps merely because I did not want it to end the way it did, though frustration and jealousy are my themes too. Also, it wasn't very easy to care for, or even be interested in, your Patrick, if that was his name.

Will you be in Athens in early October, and would you care to see me then? I really could and would manage that. My novelette will be finished, my bitch off heat, and my Autumn Book Number over: between October 8th and 30th I could—indeed I shall—go some place or another—get away for a fortnight, and would even commit myself to an expensive aeroplane and indulge in another overdraft.

Tell me what your own plans—and feelings—are.

Love

Joe

Old [Richard] Murphy has been and is now in Paris. I selected, from his bundle of poems, the shortest I could find, and then found I'd published it before!

To Dame Edith Sitwell (1887–1964)   *The Listener*, Broadcasting House,   119
                                              W.1   20/7/54

Dear Dame Edith

thank you so much. I shall be truly delighted to lunch on the 6th and look forward with the greatest pleasure to seeing you again.[1] Will you seat me somewhere on your right hand side (I am not suggesting the most privileged position, but somewhere upon that side) because my right ear has been shutting up shop for some time and no longer hears as it should. But my left ear hears even when it shouldn't. So sorry to be a nuisance. I will try to stay on to tea, but shall not know until the day what I can do. Thank you all the same for offering me such a wonderful extension of happiness.

Yours sincerely

Joe Ackerley

To Roy Fuller (1912–)   *The Listener*, Broadcasting House, W.1 120
                                                   9/8/54

Dear Roy

you are a pet! I am deeply touched and flattered and amused.

---

[1] These luncheons became a fairly regular event in A.'s life. After one he reported to Geoffrey Gorer: 'Gollancz said to me at Edith's luncheon that he couldn't sell a single book, however good. Why then are more and more books being published? They come in at the rate of 25 to 30 a day . . .'

A charming quatrain.[1] I shall have it inscribed upon my tombstone. Thank you, dear friend; and now I carry the very neat, pretty, precious book home through the rain to read on the bus.
Love from
   Joe

121* To May Buckingham[2] (1908–   )   Athens
                                                                    17/10/54

London was cold when we left. Geneva was cold and cloudy. Milan was cold. Venice provided Georges Duthuit and sunshine during the day, but was cold in the evening. The Adriatic was cold and squally and the boat late, grubby, full of unattractive people. But after Brindisi we found what we were seeking, blue skies, calm seas, warm sun. We bathe daily and see the sights and watch the Greek sailors dancing in the taverns of an evening. It is heavenly.
Love
   Joe

122 To I. M. Parsons[3] (1906–   )   *The Listener*, Broadcasting House, W.1
                                                                     25/1/55
Dear Ian
            I see clearly now, after struggling along for a bit, that I shall grow no more 'Tulips' in my garden. The subject has begun to bore me; the oddments I thought I could finish no longer seem worth it, and two people to whom I have shown the fragment of what I thought the most hopeful agree that it don't come up to scratch.
      All that remains therefore is the single *Encounter* piece. Do you want it, as a small separate publication and, if so, could you bring it out this year and in what shape?[4]
      Joe

      [1] This was the dedicatory verse to A. that prefaced Fuller's book of poems *Counterparts* (1952). Here it is:

> Your standards are not wrong:
> Poems should be defendable, like prose;
> Like blood unclotted; even like a nose,
> Not half an inch too long

      [2] See page 161, note 1.
      [3] Partner and later Director of Chatto & Windus since 1930. Now Chairman. Publishers of A.'s *The Prisoners of War* and *Hindoo Holiday*.
      [4] A. did not wait for a reply. Two days later he left at Chatto & Windus three sections of the future book *My Dog Tulip*: 'My Dog, Tulip', the article which had appeared in *Encounter*, and 'two further instalments related to it—"Liquids and Solids" and "Trial and Error" '. He had originally submitted the article to *Encounter* under the title of 'The Two Tulips' and thought a reversion to this 'might be best in the book'.

To I. M. Parsons (1906–)   17 Star & Garter Mansions, Putney, S.W.15   123
27/1/55

Dear Ian

perhaps you had better see these[1] before making up your mind. They are not up to the standard of 'My Dog, Tulip', but Geoffrey Gorer thinks them easily good enough to go with it and urges me to show them. The sexual one[2] intended to ramble on, but it also stands fairly neatly by itself, and perhaps the 3 pieces could make a trio in a book if you liked them. Although they are 'funny', I will add that they are very good observation on dogs, much better than that chap Konrad Lorenz, and the findings about the anal glands, which are my own deduction, have not been written up anywhere so far as I know. They are supported by the views of Harrison Matthews, director of the Zoo, and also by the Professor of Zoology in Nottingham.[3] So do not read them as nonsense.

If you think they can be done as a trio, I don't want to ramble on any further at present with the sexual piece,[4] for 3 or 4 reasons: (i) I am bored (ii) I am broke, but totally, and can't hang on to make a larger book (iii) I think that in such animal books, brevity is necessary. So let me know what you and Leonard [Woolf] think. I leave these by hand because I have no other copies.

Joe

To I M. Parsons (1906–)   *The Listener*, Broadcasting House, W.1   124
7/2/55

Dear Ian

I don't know how you and your examiners are getting on with my tripe, but I have hacked out a further instalment of the sex chapter since then, and send it along, with the opening of the third part, in case you are at all interested. The third part[5] would go on to describe the birth of the litter and its subsequent fate. A concluding part would make such general observations on the sex-life of dogs as I have gathered in my 8 or 9 years among them.[6] I thought I would send you this new chapter so that you could see that the ms. has a rather more serious purpose than the first instalment may have led you to expect. I think it all a bore myself, but am no judge, I thought 'My Dog, Tulip' when it appeared in *Encounter* a bore too, but so many respectable persons thought otherwise that it may not have been. Much of this—and what you have—is slackly written, due to boredom; but if it seemed worth encouraging, and I were encouraged, I

---

[1] See note 4 opposite.
[2] 'Trial and Error.'
[3] E. J. W. Barrington.
[4] But within ten days A. had 'hacked out a further instalment of the sex chapter'. See Letter 124.
[5] In the final manuscript Part 3 became Chapter 4—'The Fruits of Labour'—and dealt with Tulip's pregnancy.
[6] In the final manuscript these observations were worked into an Appendix. See page 111, note 4.

daresay I could pull it together and finish it off. I'm also perfectly willing to excise anything that may be thought too offensive or silly. And of course to verify—so far as that is possible—any doubtful statements. I've no feelings about any of it—except that I would like it to make some money for me!

Love

   Joe

125   To Sewell Stokes (1902–   )   *The Listener*, Broadcasting House, W.1

26/3/55

Dear Sewell

            why ever didn't I think of you? So stupid of me! But alas I didn't and have sent the book off[1]—with the book about prostitutes[2]—to (between ourselves) Jack Sprott of Nott. Good hands; but yours would have been more suitable. I had the book so long, too—read it, skippingly, myself: I wish you had asked earlier. It seemed to me, on the whole, a rather nasty book . . . Silly and nasty. The opening chapters, about his arrest, are really too much—protestations of absolute innocence, of not being 'queer' at all, of having been 'framed': a wicked miscarriage of justice. This initial insincerity with its consequent violent attack upon justice naturally colours and infects the rest of the book, for it has to be maintained throughout—and that is a pity, for he has some interesting things to say about the Scrubs and Brixton, as soon as he is in them, and about the chaps he meets there. He is nice about the screws, gives them a good name. But the strident note of accusation and victimisation goes on, not that he minds 'queers', he wouldn't even have minded being one except that he isn't, some of the best people have been queers (all the old gang are trotted out once more, Shakespeare, Tchaikovsky etc), and although he himself is innocent, the rest of us are all guilty too of something or other and should be in the Scrubs as well, if justice was done—so he reflects, looking out of the van window, as he is driven from the Scrubs to Brixton, at the passers-by, all so despicable-looking, and Heaven knows what they are up to, with their brollies and despatch cases, or what undiscovered guilty secret they conceal beneath their hypocritical exteriors . . . I was very glad that I was no friend of his to be dragged in by name, as some notable people are, into the silly tirade. Not that he has not some interesting, and no doubt useful, observations on prison life to make, as I say, and I hope that Jack will give him his due; but considering the whole tone of the book with its embittered assault on almost all authority, I fear it will be ineffectual.

Love from

   Joe

[1] *The Verdict of You All* by Rupert Croft-Cooke. The book is concerned with the author's imprisonment for nine months in Wormwood Scrubs and Brixton Prisons. No review of it appeared by Sprott.
[2] *Women of the Streets*, edited by C. H. Rolph. Sprott's unsigned notice appeared on 21 April.

To Hilary Corke (1921–) Putney 126
?/4?/55

Dear Hilary
        although I can't add extras to the booklet of mine you have,[1]
could I ask you to look at another,[2] which is connected with it? It is in
typescript, but not tediously long, about 50,000 words. I think it may never
be published—libel once more—so since I have all time—all my own time—
before me I am seeking other people's views to help me improve it, so far as I
am able. I should greatly value yours. Personally I think it more interesting
than the thing that is to appear, but writers seldom know what they do. I
fancy you may have a reason for thinking it less interesting, being more
bored by it, for it has a homosexual colour, but I hope you may regard that,
as I do, as subsidiary, a mere thread in a large pattern. My fidgit [*sic*] about
it is that it may have too great an air of reality, so that it will be regarded
not as a work of art but as a naively contrived piece of autobiography.
Why I should worry about that I am not sure, except that some of the
people who have read it tell me I ought to, that the first person approach
is an artistic mistake, that it needs some sort of other presentation, a dis-
guise.[3] It may be true, I don't know. The quality I believe it does have is
readability, and if that is so it seems to me more important than anything
else and that to tinker about with it between fiction and fact would be a
foolish and perhaps spoiling expenditure of time. You are a clever boy and
I would listen to your verdict with the greatest attention and follow your
advice if I could. If you could take it into Finborough Road[4] therefore,
please do let me send it.
    Joe

To Fredric Warburg[5] (1898–) 17 Star & Garter Mansions, 127
Putney, S.W.15 2/5/55
Dear Warburg
        thank you for your letter. I hope your trip to the U.S. was
both pleasurable and profitable. I will leave a ms. upon you this week or
next at Secker & Warburg—unfinished by some dozen pages, I'm afraid,
but at least there is enough for you to make up your mind. It is three
essays on an Alsatian dog: 'The Two Tulips' (the name I originally gave to
the *Encounter* piece and to which I should like to revert), 'Liquids and Solids',
and 'Trial and Error'. The collection, if acceptable, could be called *My
Dog Tulip*. Chatto & Windus have already made an offer for it,[6] but I do
not think they really want it. Their letter will go with the ms. Their terms
seem to me mean and they desire ruthless excisions. You will see their
pencillings on the typescript, which I fear is a bit scruffy. They may have

---

[1] *My Dog Tulip.*
[2] *We Think the World of You.*
[3] Later this year Stephen Spender suggested that the central character might be a probation
officer. See Letter 136.
[4] Corke's flat at this period in Earls Court.
[5] Managing Director of Secker & Warburg from 1936 to 1971. Now President
[6] See Letter 128.

some right upon their side—I was and am always willing to listen to reasonable advice—but it seemed to me that their strictures completely distorted my picture. I make no claims for that, except that it is a true portrait of a dog, the only true portrait, I think ever written. Excepting for 'Feeding', which I also meant to discuss but haven't got down to, it describes all those problems in a dog's life that are of the first importance to all dog-owners, but are never permitted to be discussed. The final pages, which are not yet ready, are mainly an indictment of the human race for fathering upon their dogs their own sense of sin. Although it makes a joke or two, it is, *in toto*, a serious ms. and I hope it may be read as such. Whether it is an interesting or desirable one is quite another matter, and you will let me know as soon as you can.[1]

Yours

Joe Ackerley

128　To I. M. Parsons (1906–　)　　　*The Listener*, Broadcasting House, W.1

1/6/55

Dear Ian

I left your letter over because I couldn't make up my mind how to reply to it. Although I don't set much literary value on my book,[2] I was perturbed by the drastic cuts you wanted because they seemed to destroy the 'beastliness' which I wished to restore to the life of beasts. You might well be right, I know, but I did not like it. Nor, really, did I like your terms, if only because, being already £100 overdrawn in my bank they would not have enabled me to take the holiday this year that I need. In fact altogether I took the fancy that you weren't really keen on the book, and thought I must look round to see if I could not improve my prospects elsewhere. So this letter, I'm afraid, is to say that, with all regrets to an old friend, I've given the thing to Secker & Warburg, who are agreeable to publish it *in toto* (if the printers will print it) and are sending me on a holiday to boot.

Yours ever

Joe

129　To Fredric Warburg (1898–　)　　　*The Listener*, Broadcasting House, W.1

26/8/55

Dear Warburg

I have got into a state of worry over *My Dog Tulip*. I go on messing away at the end section, but without any real interest, and I begin seriously to wonder whether the book would not be better without it. My feeling now is that it should end on Wimbledon Common. 'Soon it will be over . . . Soon it will be too late' when the animal's breath is caught on the cinder track, and that the rest[3] should be scrapped. What do you think?

---

[1] Before May was out, Warburg had made A. an offer, which included an advance of £200 and a promise of 'as few "cuts" as possible'.

[2] *My Dog Tulip*.

[3] These pages became the Appendix in the final version.

It would still have 5 parts, and would end impressively. Indeed, I am quite vain about Part 1 and Part 5, I think they have a perfection. I am pleased with Part 2 also; it is less well organised, but stands up and has an excellent long final sequence. Parts 3 and 4, alas, are narrative and therefore more pretentious, but they run along all right and contain some amusement and interest. Part 5 is first rate, a kind of poem, and I now feel that the sensible course would be to end the book there, without going on into more and more dog sex. If a play has a good first and last act, critics come away thinking it a good play, even though the middle acts may not have been up to standard. The great thing is not to bore people, especially at the finish, and that is what I fear I shall do if I go on. Would it matter to your plans if the book were a few thousand words shorter?[1] I thought that I would try to finish the conclusion nevertheless and that we could then keep it in hand for, perhaps, a later 'edition with new material', if the book should happen to be a success and earn such treatment.

How much longer may I hang on to the typescript?

Joe Ackerley

To Geoffrey Gorer (1905–)　　　　　　　　　　　　Putney　130
　　　　　　　　　　　　　　　　　　　　　　　　　?/9?/55

Dear G.G.

I thought I had lost this [cutting from *The Times*],[2] but find I have not. It may interest you. 25, even 30, years old? (I omitted to inscribe the date, though doubtless I could discover it if I wished) it made a strong mark upon my young crusading homosexual mind and, one day, I thought, I will do something for young Holland,[3] though possibly he was an odious boy. So you see he is, like all the rest, part of the true furniture of Wimbledon Common, and at first I gave him a more extended biography. But now I doubt if he fits. He is a bit of self-indulgent redundancy. I only wanted to amuse myself by building an ivory tower for Tulip and him and then demolishing it and, apart from the question of good taste (would pain be caused to his relatives by having him thus recorded?), I think I have enough already to pull my tower about my ears. I am fond of the chapter myself and tend to blot (school term) when I read it, but I know that authors are not good judges of what they do, so I am prepared for you to be hard on it.

---

[1] See Letter 131, in which A., with the publishers' help (Warburg and his readers) and also that of Geoffrey Gorer, decided on the final shape of *My Dog Tulip*.

[2] See note 3 below.

[3] In the last chapter of *My Dog Tulip* A. wrote: 'And young Holland, where did he die? Where is the swamp into which he drove his face? Lost, lost, the inconsiderable, anguished deed in the blind hurry of time. The perfect boy face downwards in a swamp . . . The doctor who performed the autopsy remarked that the muscles and limbs were absolutely perfect, he had never seen a better developed boy in his life, nor, when he split open the skull, such deep grey matter. Ah, perfect but imperfect boy, brilliant at work, bored by games, traits of effeminacy were noticed in you, you were vain of your appearance and addicted to the use of scent. Everyone, it seemed, wished you different from what you were, so you came here at last and pushed your face into a swamp, and that was the end of you, perfect but imperfect boy . . .*' That asterisk, which is repeated at the bottom of the page and gives there the source and date of young Holland's death— '*The Times*: 30 June 1926'—, profoundly moved Forster. He told the author that he 'had never seen an asterisk used so before'.

Put this poor little cutting in your pocket and bring it to me when you come.[1]
Love

J

131   To Fredric Warburg (1898–   )   17 Star & Garter Mansions,
                                            Putney, S.W.15   ?/9?/55

Dear Warburg
                here is this thing, as promised. I'm not satisfied with it,
but at any rate I now have a copy and can go on playing with one or two
passages that worry me which you are negotiating with your printer. It is
tidier than it was and better written in places; I'm sorry the ms. is parti-
coloured. The end still worries me, I feel it ought to stop before it stops.
Not that I myself mind going on: but this is an intellectual book, dogs are
an intellectual bore, generally speaking they are a bore to me, and the question is whether I do not over-try the patience of the reader. In a few days
I shall send it to Geoffrey Gorer, who will tell me. He has already read
Parts 1., 2., and 3.; I want him now to read the rest. He is an enthusiast
over what he has read (he is a dog man as well as a sort of scientist), he will
give me good advice. So will you, I am sure. Could you lunch with me one
day next week, after Tuesday? I should like to talk to you about it and to
have your views. As you will see, I have extended it to six parts. It seemed to
me that 'The Turn of the Screw' chapter should stand on its own. The thing
that bothers me most is what follows. It has some virtues, but what about its
vices?
        Now, your points and other points:[2]

[Chap.] 1   I've removed the snapshots.[3] I don't suppose you meant to use
            them, and I felt they might outrage the printer. But you can
            have them back if you want.

Chap. 2   I've removed 'of the lower orders'.
            For 'mess' I've substituted 'hash'.
            For 'Christ's' I've put 'God's'—but you can have 'Heaven's'
            if you prefer.
            I've left 'Shitsy-witsy' in. It amused Gorer, and does not seem
            awfully dashing. The word 'shit' appears in my *Hindoo Holiday*
            book, in a much more startling context. 'You eat shit.'

Chap. 3   (I'm sorry not to have had time to re-type this chapter, but at
            any rate you will see clearer what changes I have made.) I have

---

[1] When the book was accepted for publication in America in 1965, A. again had doubts about
this section. But on his publishers' advice there (which was the same as Gorer's had been), he
decided not to 'cut' the passages about young Holland. See Letter 275.
[2] This referred to a list of 'cuts' and changes, suggested by the publishers. They were fairly
minor—and A. agreed to most of them. Notes 1 and 3 opposite elaborate on two of the more
interesting ones.
[3] These were undoubtedly intended to shock. They showed Tulip 'micturating, crapping, and
conversing with other dogs'.

taken out most of the passage on p. 5, but left a hint in. Is that too much? Naturally I don't want a libel, and had better reveal the facts: the episode of course is generally true. I have faked name and address. The incident of the box of matches is pure invention. The incident of the cap in the garden is fact. And, so far as I know, the man is still alive. I killed him off in my footnote for fun. Is it a libel to say that people are dead when they aren't? Though I cling a little to fun, I will go on revising and omitting if you think it is necessary. I think I've met you over your other comments in this chapter.

Chap. 4   I think I've done all you want here—and also removed the phrase 'by his penis' to suit the printer.

Chap. 5.   All as you wished, excepting that I've retained the footnote.[1] It is meant seriously and is interesting. My vet, who is inclined to think that dogs and bitches may well suffer in their psychology from enforced chastity was much interested when I quoted [Kenneth] Walker's statement about human beings. Incidentally, I now understand that you yourselves are the publishers of Walker's book *Marriage*—revised under a new title. Could you send me a copy of the new edition? I rather want to check up. I've been talking to old Walker about it.

Part 4.   I've done all you want.[2]

I've added some bits you'd better look at: a para. in 'Liquids and Solids', p. 12, a passage in 'Turn of the Screw', p. 8, and various footnotes. I attach [R. C. G.] Hancock's permission to quote, and since his letter contained an interesting piece of information,[3] I have used that also as a footnote in Part 6: *Inconclusion*.[4] I have taken my own vet out to lunch and pumped him, and you will be pleased to hear that he is in the fullest agreement with all my guesses about the anal glands—a subject that has never been aired before, so you have a scoop. The reason why dogs smell each other's arses and sniff at turds in the street is *not* because they are interested in canine faeces *per se*, but because the glandular discharge provides him with information. I don't now think that I have made any rash remarks. But I am still less than satisfied with the end and one or two other small passages, and shall go on tinkering while you try it out on your printer.

[1] This footnote quoted Walker's remark: 'There is no evidence that physical harm results from sexual continence. If any injury is inflicted by chastity, it is not on the body but on the mind.' A. then went on to ask: 'Does this statement have any application to the lower animals?'
[2] In the final manuscript Part 4 became Chapter 6—'The Turn of the Screw'.
[3] This information concerned the use of irradiated chlorophyll, which given in tablet form destroys a bitch's sexual odour and renders her unattractive to the male. The late Major Hancock, a distinguished veterinary surgeon and writer about dogs, when passing this information on to A., wrote: 'Soon there will be no natural history of the bitch for us authors to depend on!'
[4] A. wrote later in the year to Warburg: '*Inconclusion*—please discard.' In its place he substituted an Appendix with some general observations on the sex-life of dogs. Ten years later when *My Dog Tulip* was published in America, one New York reviewer, in the *Bulletin* on 15 June, described the book as 'a sort of sex and the single girl dog effort'.

I enclose a press photo, which someone asked for. Finally: the same person who asked for the photo, asked for names of people who might be interested in the book. I didn't fill in that section then, because I couldn't think but the following names might be put forward: Edith Sitwell, Geoffrey Gorer, Wystan Auden, Kenneth Walker—they are all lovers of dogs and friends of mine.

Joe Ackerley

P.S. I am terribly sorry to find that I did not retype Chap. 3. Does it matter. Possibly someone in your office could tap it quickly out (I am far from quick). If so, could I have a copy?

132   To Stephen Spender (1909–)   Putney
                                                                        ?/10?/55

Thank you, dear Stephen. Your letter interested me very much. The trouble with my play, I think, is that I misnamed it in the beginning. It should never have been called *The Prisoners of War* but *The Interned*. I had the title changed when it was done on the air,[1] but felt I should not tamper with it for stage revival. When the play was first done, 30 years ago, a few critics voiced an understandable surprise to find not barbed wire and bayonets, but comparative luxury. A title like *The Interned* would have prepared them for that, or should have, and for the introduction into the plot of characters extraneous to the central action. In fact the whole set was authentic, and when Conrad voices the opinion that he is unhappier, more unsettled, as an internee than he was in German hands he is voicing what was, in fact, the general truth. Character had already begun to disintegrate in German hands—some of the chaps had been in Kriegsgefangenen-Lagers[2] for years—and comfort, when they got it, was unacceptable to them. They felt that they should not be enjoying it; the life-and-death struggle was still going on on the Western front; they all wished to go back into it to 'do their bit'; they could no longer escape; they felt ashamed, cowards. The place offered rest and happiness; they could accept neither; the jealousies and bickerings were endless. That was the background. As for homosexuality. I'm sorry you thought that there were 'one or two' homosexual characters. If that were so it would certainly be a fault, but it was not intended, and production is always at pains (and managed at The Irving, I thought) to emphasise the normality of the Rickman-Tetford set-up. There is only one homosexual character, Conrad himself.[3] The rest are entirely normal. And although Tetford regards Rickman as *his* pal, the notion of their going to

---

[1] On 3 May 1953 on the Third Programme. There were two 'repeats' on 8 May and 20 June. The producer was Wilfrid Grantham.
[2] Prisoner of war camps.
[3] A. wrote in Chapter 12 of *My Father and Myself*: 'Captain Conrad (myself of course) is asked . . . why he is so fond of Lieutenant Grayle. He replies, "I don't know. He's clean. Fills gaps . . ." ("Fills gaps" I longed to eradicate [this . . . when my] play was . . . in print; I saw that Freud had got away with more than I intended) . . .'

bed together ought to be as unthinkable to the audience as I meant it to be to them. I thought I would explain these matters to prevent misconception. If I had had more of a hand in the production[1] (which had a lot to be said for it anyway) the relationships would, I think, have been less ambiguous. Love

Joe

To Hilary Corke (1921–)　　*The Listener*, Broadcasting House, W.1　133
24/10/55

Dear Hilary

　　　　your poems, your letter. I adore the former, especially the serio-comic ones and do hope the Ed. won't regard them as too frivolous for this stuffy paper. I've asked him to accept both and one of the serious ones, about the phallic tongue.[2]

Your letter: I think I am slightly worried by very rude reviews, at any rate when the author is an undistinguished sheep. It is my tender heart: I feel that I myself, in such a position, would never be able to put my nose into the Common Room again. Sticking pins in the famous or established does not bother me. I'm not sure that I do not have an extra opinion also, which is that reviewers should not derive palpable pleasure out of inflicting chastisement. Ulterior motive, personal spite, is then thought by the reader to have crept in. 'This hurts me more than it hurts you' should, I incline to think, be the note. But apart from that we don't mind aggrieved letters—so long, of course, as we are convinced of our reviewer's rightness, objectiveness and good taste, as we are of yours. Many others—some half dozen (not to be printed)—have leapt to Mr [J. D.] Jump's[3] defence—not names that have ever been heard of, like Prof. [L. C.] Knights.

　　Joe

[1] The producer was Jack McNaughton. The run lasted from 5 October to 16 November, and the next day A. wrote to Richard Murphy: 'I see no prospect of it being revived again for another 30 years . . . I wished I had insisted on producing it myself; it is rather agony to see one's meaning distorted and one's effects lost. If by any chance it does get another theatre I shall muscle in. However people praised it as it was: Stuart Hampshire, Stephen, some others. It wasn't so bad, but could have been infinitely better.'

[2] This was called 'See in the Trees the Bright Birds Sing!' and was published in the following year on 5 April. It ran to five verses. Here are the relevant last two:

> Now I have three tongues in my mouth:
> The evil tongue that only spoke
> To analyse the way it moves;
> The indifferent tongue that spoke the truth
> (Approximately) in the dark
> And yearned towards the known and proved;
>
> And that good tongue too often still
> That made the song and prayed the prayer,
> That stood upright to praise her charms
> And penetrate the loosened will
> With its own muscular desire.
> But better dumb within her arms.

[3] The author of a study of *Matthew Arnold* in the Longmans 'Men and Books' series. *The Listener* review, unsigned, had appeared on 13 October.

134 To Fredric Warburg (1898–   )   Putney
                                                              ?/11?/55

Dear Fredric
             what about this?[1] I want the thing to be firmly planted (as
it is) upon inexperience and personal adventure—I don't want anyone to
have an opportunity of saying 'Bloody cheek! Telling us how to treat our
dogs when we know far more about them than he does.' I think people may
learn a good deal about dogs from the book, but I think it best that they
should not be asked to expect to be taught. Alter as you wish—on these
lines—I've only roughed it out. Much of your own admirable draft remains.
   Joe Ackerley

I've again read my tail-piece and think it fairly well balanced. But do as
you think.

135 To Hilary Corke (1921–   )   *The Listener*, Broadcasting House, W.1
                                                              ?/11?/55

Dear Hilary
             I've been away on a week's holiday, so couldn't write you about
your review of Herbert's book[2] before. I'm awfully sorry, but I can't
publish it, so if you want to try to place the review or go for the book elsewhere you're at liberty to do so.[3] The fact that H. is an old friend of mine
does not place him beyond criticism, by any means, and he has often been
taken to task in my paper on the Art side;[4] but the tone of your review is not
a tone I can use to him, or could wish to use. I expect the book is just as bad
as you say, but he has written some much better poems in the past, many of
which have I published, and that, I think, is the kind of thing that should
have been said when the present vol. was regretfully written off as a disappointment. I take pains always, as you know, not to be 'kind' to my
friends, and go to trouble to obtain objective reviews of their works; but
there is a step from not being kind to being actually cruel which I cannot
take. So I would prefer not to review the book at all. So sorry.
   Joe

136 To Stephen Spender (1909–   )   ?/12?/55

Dear Stephen
             I tap to you on my typewriter, which I hardly ever use for
such personal purposes. I was much pleased that you liked my little booklet.[5]

---

   [1] The 'blurb' for the first edition of *My Dog Tulip*, which ended with this warning: '*My Dog
Tulip* is unique, because it is the only book that examines the oldest friend of mankind as though
it were a new species. Fathers and mothers, therefore, should not present it to their children without
a previous careful reading themselves. For here at last is the truth about dogs and bitches, not a
pretty picture sentimentalised but a down-to-earth study, a book likely to offend those who care
more for themselves than their dogs.'
   [2] *Moon's Farm* by Herbert Read.
   [3] Corke did neither.
   [4] For instance, see Letter 98.
   [5] *We Think the World of You.*

Stuart [Hampshire] (who was also encouraging about it) said: 'Stephen would like this.' So I am glad you do. And he saw it in a more unfinished form; the amusing ball-game with the dog was not there,[1] I had removed it in a non-contributive form, then suddenly saw how it ought to go and what good use could be made of it. I am terribly pleased with your comments; they saw right into it, especially your remark about an 'adult fairy story'— so gratifyingly perceptive to an author who had played with the idea of calling it that himself.[2] But I don't think I can now adopt your other suggestions. It might have been better if I had thought of the probation-officer relationship;[3] to make such a change now would be too fundamental. Probation officers, presumably, can get into prisons without much difficulty to visit their charges; I would have to think up an almost entirely different plot. I can't do that. And, frankly, I don't want to lessen the impact of the sexual relationship. I think it decent and non-obscene as it is; I am not anxious to spare the feelings of the philistines. I have too much of it in my own paper—'It will upset people'—Mr [John] Bratby's lavatory seats, the nudes of [Paul] Delvaux, James Kirkup's poems about W.C.s,[4] Windham's homosexual stories. To speak the truth, I think that people *ought* to be upset, and if I had a paper I would upset them all the time; I think that life is so important and, in its workings, so upsetting that nobody should be spared, but that it should [be] rammed down their throats from morning to night. And may those that cannot take it die of it; it is what we want. Away, away with the obstructionists that clog our lives. Let us be liberated and free in our minds. Pardon me! My typewriter runs away with me! Nevertheless I would not alter a word of my homosexual passages; I do not think that they are pornographic, I should disapprove of that; I believe they are exact and necessary and real. So send it back, for I cannot alter anything; indeed, I would underline the passages if I could see a chance, and I fancy that they are what people actually want, something free and natural and uncomplicated by guilt and psychology—I am only sorry that I cannot end the book happily, I should have liked to have done that.

I think you may be right about the insufficient symbolism of the dog. I have tried to turn her into a symbol wherever I saw the chance,[5] but I have always felt that she remained unassimilated in the middle parts, pretty though they may be. Alterations there will not be so difficult to manage. But I'm sure the little book is all right. I have a feeling about it. I don't often have a feeling about what I write, but I believe in this. It has a kind of structural perfection, like an eighteenth-century cabinet, everything sliding nicely and full of secret drawers. I wish it were coming out instead of my bitty book[6]—though I suppose that is not too bad. At any rate it has the essay that you published,[7] and another on sexual frustration—'The Turn of the Screw', which is played upon the organ and which I think I have brought off. That might make you cry; and another essay called 'Journey's

---

[1] Pages 74–6. See page 274, note 4.
[2] Encouraged by Spender's remark, A. in the following year began to refer to his 'novelette' as an 'Adult Fairy Story'. Later, he slightly altered the phrase. See Letter 152.
[3] Cf. page 107, note 3.   [4] See Introduction, 1.   [5] See page 136, note 6.
[6] *My Dog Tulip*.   [7] 'My Dog, Tulip' in *Encounter* (March 1954).

End' might make you laugh; and if you can make people cry and laugh in a short, or even a long, book, I suppose you haven't done so badly. So send or give me my little poppet back; I don't think I can do anything more to it, but I would like to have a last look.

Love dear Stephen from

Joe

137 To Lucian Freud (1922–)   Corsham

?/12/55

Dear Lucian

so glad you rang up and that I shall be seeing you on Tuesday. I will be back at my flat by 3.0., so you can be sure of finding me there from then on. In case you don't know the building it is now quite conspicuous. As you pass over Putney Bridge it smacks you in the eye immediately upon the Putney side, alongside the water. It cries 'Courage' from its walls, upon which also a cock crows.[1] The entrance to the 'Mansions' part of the building is just beyond the entrance to the pub-hotel, both on the Lower Richmond Road. My flat, No 17, is at the very top. A self-operating lift raises you to the third floor; then you have to walk up another short flight of stairs to me.

I hope Queenie will not baffle you. Her invariable behaviour towards visitors will have advantages, I hope, as well as disadvantages. She will expostulate when you enter my sitting-room, in which she lives and sleeps, and will then place herself on the divan bed, on the other side of the room from the window (north light) to guard her biscuits which it is her habit to collect there. If you are content to sit by the window and draw her she will present a fairly steady picture, I think, staring watchfully at you. But if you are a mover about, I'm afraid she will be noisy. It is her ineducable way. But she does not bite people—at least she has never done so in ten years;[2] she only speaks her mind, rather deafeningly, I fear.

I have to be back in London, Piccadilly area, at 6.30. But my sister would look after you if you wanted to stay on and, indeed, the dog always behaves much better when I am absent.[3]

Yours ever

Joe Ackerley

[1] The trade mark of Courage's ales.

[2] On the one occasion that Queenie bit her master's hand, it was by mistake; she mistook it for a rotten apple which they both were trying to grab simultaneously. 'One of her canines sank into my thumb-joint to the bone,' A. wrote after the event—and subsequently incorporated a further description of the event in *My Dog Tulip*: 'Alsatians have a bad reputation; they are said to bite the hand that feeds them . . . When I held my thumb-joint [where Queenie's canines had sunk to the bone] under the tap . . . I could see the sinews exposed. We all make mistakes and she was dreadfully sorry. She rolled over on the grass with all her legs in the air; and later on, when she saw the bandage on my hand, she put herself in the corner, the darkest corner of the bedroom, and stayed there for the rest of the afternoon. One can't do more than that.'

[3] Freud made one attempt to draw the dog, but 'her behaviour was so unsettling' that nothing came of it. Earlier, A. had offered Secker & Warburg some drawings he himself had made of Queenie. (When *Hindoo Holiday* had first come out, *The Times* in its review of 19 April 1932, had referred to the author as 'a deft illustrator'.) The drawings of Queenie, though, were turned down on the grounds that they were not 'strong enough'. The first edition of *My Dog Tulip* had a letterpress dust-jacket.

To Hilary Corke (1921–) *The Listener*, Broadcasting House, W.1 138
?/?/56

Dear Hilary

no, the distinction simply is—and that not *always* so urgently—
between *very good* books, which are being widely noticed and praised—and
the rest. I daresay you yourself can draw that distinction among whatever
falls to you as well as I. My own personal editorial problem is to have always
on hand some review of the nearest approach to a first-rate *new* publication
(first-rate in a general, not a specialist sense) to start my chronicle off with.
Window dressing, dear. So week by week I look at my bundle and wonder
'What shall I start off *next* week with?' There seems to be nothing; so then
I scan the dispatch book and observe that Mr Corke, good and obliging
Mr Corke, has had in his possession for long enough to read and write about
it one of the 'hits' of the month. Hence my occasional p.c.s
Joe

To Sewell Stokes (1902–) 17 Star & Garter Mansions, Putney, S.W.15 139
?/3/56

Dear Sewell

you are a dear good boy to send me your book.[1] It beguiled a
journey to Nottingham last weekend.[2] When it sparkles, in dialogue and
description, it is amusing, and some of the characters—Lady B.S., Miss
Grimble are in your best vein, well-observed and caricatured, and entertaining. If I had to review the book, I should say that you were too cagey,
or too dawdly, with your plot. I am at present at page 100. Doubtless,
plots—in the old-fashioned sense, the story, what is going to happen next—
are less necessary to novels than they used to be, but personally I like them,
and if novels do not have them it is more difficult for them to become that
kind of novel of which it is said that one 'can't put it down', and, perhaps
unfortunately, your book gives from the start the delightful expectation of
having a *strong* plot: what in the world may not happen when your horrid
young man bursts upon the vicarage and its jumble sales! But after this
intriguing spurt of energy, your characters pursue so leisurely a course that,
by page 100, your cards are still all up your sleeve and, excepting that you
are amusing yourself by poking fun at the Church, I have no real clue to
what you are driving at. True there is a 'situation' between Viola and Lindsay, who are seen not to be making a go of holy matrimony (I fear you have
not noticed how often you explain this rather commonplace relationship
to your readers) and Ivan is seen to be drifting idly into their affairs, but

[1] Stokes' novel, *A Clown in Clover*.
[2] On a previous journey to Nottingham, A. had read Stokes' novel, *Rarely Pure* (1952)—and
written to him (again on the train): 'To invent one bizarre and funny character, like Apthorpe in
Evelyn Waugh's [*Men at Arms*], is a notable feat; to provide a whole galaxy of them, funny and
alive, is a Dickensian gift . . . One small matter, however, I shall take you to task over, is a tendency
you have to seek extra laughs . . . by tormenting the natural flow of your otherwise admirable
dialogue. "Who?" I asked, "is Ronald?" "Have you, Mr Stokes," she said, "a moment to spare?"
"And what story," I said, "does one tell?" I don't think there is any good case for splitting un-
punctuated sentences like that, and since your dialogue is very amusing in itself, it does not need
such false stresses.'

this seems small reward for the expectations aroused by your opening scenes. Ivan. I fancy that he is my trouble, and possibly yours. Charm is difficult to convey in literature, and though he is said to have it, it comes not over to me. On the contrary, as is commonly the case with all the people one has ever met who think and talk exclusively about themselves, he becomes a bore. His rather odious character (as it seems to me) would not matter if one did not have to take him seriously, but as a kind of Reginald or Clovis amusing himself with practical jokes to while away his boredom in the vicarage, which was what I thought to be his function, but there are indications now that he may emerge as a hero, a *deus ex machina*, and he does not seem to me to have been cast for that role. Well, for heaven's sake, you cry, read on do, instead of shooting off your mouth! and so I shall and take back, I daresay, everything I've said. And certainly, if I do not feel myself yet to be entangled in the intricacies of plot, I look forward to meeting again those stray intriguing figures Miss Grimble, Lady B.S., and the two spinsters and the dog-lover who have not yet emerged from hearsay.

Love from

Joe

P.S. Viola seems to me your most solid character, convincingly real and always interesting in her quiet way.

140* To Alan Thomas (1896–1969) and others   St. Thos.[1]
17/4/56

Dear Alan, Elizabeth, Joan, Kathleen, Marjorie, Molly and Pat (alphabetical order)[2]

what a sweet thought and delightful surprise. Although I have been mobile for some days, there is nowhere to go, and so I was flat on my back as usual, reading a book and wondering if the day would ever end. Excepting for prison, where I have not yet been, there can hardly be a longer day than one spent in hospital. So what a jolly surprise to see a familiar face, out of visiting hours, and to have your beautiful flowers and news of you all. My drooping spirits are now upright. My ear gets unplugged on Thursday, and I may be sent out at the weekend, either less deaf, as deaf, or more deaf than when I went in. I will send you further news. Meanwhile I am very well.

Love and thanks to you all.

Joe

141* To Stephen Spender (1909–   )   St. Thos. Edward Ward
19/4/56

And again, dear S. What a love you are. Your Tulips stand upon the medicine chest against the view, cleverly arranged by the well-known female

[1] A. was in St. Thomas' Hospital, Lambeth, awaiting an operation on his right ear. See Letter 119.
[2] The Editor and other colleagues on *The Listener*.

touch (a nurse). I have just had my ear and leg shaved. A piece of thigh skin is to be grafted inside the ear after excavation. It is fidgetty [*sic*] waiting, one feels lonely and rather solemn. Don't ask for an article for *Encounter* on the subject. I am told that I shall probably be able to get up and walk rather dizzily about after 2 days. Well, I daresay it is all preferable to turning into a deaf old fogey—if the surgeon is as clever as he believes. A visit would be lovely—after Monday, I should say. A phone call to sister might save an abortive journey.

Best love

Joe

To Stephen Spender (1909–) St Thomas' Hospital 142
20/4/56

Well, all's done, my lord, and I'm feeling very well this morning—drugged of course. Whether the operation was a success I shan't know for 5 or 6 days when my ear is unplugged, but there are indications that it will be. Skin was not after all removed from the inside of my thigh to graft into the ear, although the surgeon, Mr Bateman, told his students when I first interviewed him that a grafting of skin was usually necessary, since it was practically impossible to chip the bone out of the ear without tearing away the skin there too. However, he seems to have lunched with the Vice-President of the Hospital (who is a friend of mine) before attending to me, so he may have taken extra care. His care, however, did not prevent me from almost passing out. I daresay my heart is not in the first flush of youth, at any rate I did not come out of the anaesthetic and various injections for 8 hours, turned an unbecoming citron colour and caused considerable alarm and despond. Four nurses and three doctors collected round my bed, which they tipped up to send the blood back to my heart, imploring me to speak. It must have been a curious sight, but I did not see it. Operated on at half-past one, I had no recollection of anything until 5.30 this morning. I daresay that in a person like myself who has no very passionate grip upon life, the soul is liable to try to slip away when it finds a chance. My only sub-conscious memory of those 15 hours is that something very unpleasant was happening to my penis. I must ask the doctors about this. I felt I screamed and struggled as though it were being cut off. Yet why should I mind? I seldom use it, except to pee. The sensation occurred twice—whether in the operating theatre or later I can't tell, it was the only sensation that escaped from the pain.

Has anyone ever done a ballet about a theatre in a great hospital? It would be a wonderful theme. The larger underground chamber with its curtained cubicles where operations are in progress, a huge lamp concentrating its curious dark-bright beam upon the table in each, shadows between. Strange shadows here and there, and the chief surgeon and the anaesthetist, masked and green-clad dancing from one to another. In the centre, as in the arena of a tent-circus, an open space with the shaft of a pillar, against which students or physicians gather, leaning gossiping in negligent attitudes, dressed in green linen jackets and tightish green trousers, like figures in a Picasso, or making up their notes. Suddenly out of the shadows the great man, the surgeon, appears as he appeared to me, unrecognisable except by his extraordinary air of calm, self-assurance and authority. 'Well?' he said. 'Who are you?' I asked, though only for confirmation of what I already knew. 'Bateman' he replied—but he might equally have replied, this tiny, erect, charming, cold, Napoleon of the surgical knife: 'I am he who holds your fate in his hands.' He disappeared into the shadows, some mysterious hand put a needle into my arm, and with the memory of green linen trousers tightly stretched over the bottom of a student in front who was leaning his elbow on a table, I passed out of consciousness and almost out of this not-altogether-uninteresting world.

I am *much* too well now to be visited, I fancy, so don't put yourself out.

J

I have a new ear-drum.

143   To Hilary Corke (1921–   )   *The Listener*, Broadcasting House, W.1

24?/7/56

Dear Hilary

delightful little packet and most acceptable—except (b) 'the more important letter', which the Editor thinks doesn't really make a sufficiently important point.[1] Your letter to me gave much pleasure, but I must correct (my fault) a mistaken impression. The noble firm of Secker & Warburg were very good about 'indecency', they required practically no changes,[2] whereas Chatto & Windus, to whom *Tulip* first went, wanted absolutely everything anatomical out. I was quite shocked by their squeamishness, and hurried off to Seckers. No, the fiddling deletions were necessary, I fear, libel: I make speculative fun, for instance, of the Blandishes' sexual lives to account for his optimism over canine behaviour, and a different kind of fun of the Plums. Also the disposition of the puppies, the description

---

[1] On 5 July Hesketh Pearson in a talk reprinted on 'H. G. Wells and Frank Harris' had in passing referred to Wells as 'a lesser Dickens' and Shaw as 'a greater Voltaire'. The latter remark set a correspondence going in *The Listener*. In the following week Denis Browne wrote in to protest, and compared the two writers under the headings of *literature; intellectual honesty; charity and courage; practical sense;* and *sex*. With regard to the latter he wrote: 'Voltaire had the bawdy straightforward humour of Montaigne or Chaucer. I am not alone in finding Shaw's love-letters even more nauseating than those of Swift and Ruskin, who also "touched the hem of Nature's shift, felt faint . . ."' A week later E. R. Tigg took up the question of sex: 'Well, which of the two had a wife anyway?' The letter from Corke (which the Editor never published because he thought it did not make 'a sufficiently important point') did, however, make the point that it was 'well known that Mrs Shaw (a woman of over forty at the time, incidentally) [had] stipulated in advance that the marriage was never to be consummated.' A. thoroughly appreciated the point—and told Corke so in a subsequent letter (now, regrettably, lost).

[2] In September Fredric Warburg wrote to A. to tell him that they were sending 'the ms. of *Tulip*' to their legal adviser. He added: '. . . don't take this too seriously, but it is a precaution perhaps worth taking in view of the unique character of your book.' The legal adviser was Thurston Hogarth, and with the manuscript went a letter from Warburg asking whether it would 'have a tendency to deprave or corrupt those dogs into whose paws it might fall and whose minds might be open to such immoral influences . . .' Hogarth replied promptly: 'What are you worrying about? Dogs can't read, hence no section of the public is open to corruption.' See *All Authors Are Equal* by Fredric Warburg (1973). See page 308, note 4.

of their fates, had to be re-written with greater care. That's all. But every-
thing seemed to get flabbier and feebler in the process of 'toning down', and
I became bored.
Love
   Joe

To Fredric Warburg (1898–)   *The Listener*, Broadcasting House, W.1 144
                                                       15/8/56
Dear Fred
        I'm glad you're pleased about the book.[1] I myself was surprised
by the respect with which it has been received. This, I am told, results
from my having a 'reputation', which I knew I had, though not so firm and
widespread. It's a pity that sales and praise do not always go hand in hand.
    I'm away in Germany for a fortnight from about August 29. Otherwise
in London and at your disposal.
   Joe

I wonder if you have seen more reviews than I have, or vice versa: my short
list is *Listener, Punch*,[2] *New Statesman, News Chronicle, Times, Observer, Sunday
Times, Truth.*

To Fredric Warburg (1898–)   17 Star & Garter Mansions, 145
                                         Putney, S.W.15   ?/9?/56
Dear Fred
        has your traveller tried Putney with my booklet? I always feel
a little hipped never to have seen a single copy of it in Smiths in our High
Street into which I constantly go. Yet (i) I understand that Smiths send in
orders for the book* (ii) our Putney branch is the sort of shop that gives up
a window to the display of certain books. Surely mine is a Putney book?
'*Read about the Putney dogs*' is the kind of thing I always hope to see as I pass,
the window stuffed with copies of *My Dog Tulip*. But when I asked once the
shop had never heard of it. 'But it's about my own dog' I said, for she is
always in and out and a celebrity in Putney, even without the book.
'Really?' said the lady. 'Then I must ask about that.' But nothing has
happened. I don't believe the shop has ever had a single copy.
    And the dog papers, recommended by Major Hancock in the letters
which you keep. Did they ever get review copies? Ought one not to try
to get at doggy people who do not study the reviews of intellectuals?
    Just an idea.
Love
   Joe

* I have seen it on railway stations too.

---

[1] *My Dog Tulip*, which had been published on 16 July.   [2] See page 259, note 3.

146 To Francis King (1923-   ) 17 Star & Garter Mansions, Putney, S.W.15
14/10/56

Dear Francis

you are now in the air—very nice blue air too—and ringing
still in my ears is your valedictory remark about coming to see you in Alex.
Do invite me when you are there and settled in,[1] if the accommodation
includes a spare room, or to a hotel if it does not. I would greatly like to see
the place again, especially with you in it. Not the hottest month; I did that
last time and rather suffered, and now I quite forget what the month was,
for it was more than twenty years ago. My host lived in Cairo, so I saw
more of that than Alex., and Alex. is doubtless cooler than Cairo and gives
more holiday scope. You know my sort of BBC routine life: I have Book
Supplements always at the end of March and in mid-June, so that I am
free to roam only in April and the first week of May, or from mid-June
throughout the summer up to and including the first week of September.
Then I get into further difficulties which leave me with only about the last
three weeks of October to play with. So, if within these limits there is a
chance to ask me, do.

Meanwhile, I hope your problems will be solved for you in a satisfactory
way, or will solve themselves. Possibly they will not seem so teasing and
distressing when your feet are back upon Athenian soil. I do hope they will
not drive you any further towards drugs, psychologists or hypnotists.[2]
Your *Firewalkers*[3] seemed to me to show a far greater command of yourself,
both as a person and a writer, than any of your earlier works. Morgan
Forster has read it, but I fear with some of the same sort of dissatisfaction
that he displayed with my own novelette—'not enough pleasure' was his
comment on that.[4] In you too, he finds 'slight pleasure' and 'very few
thrills.' 'Some of it tender and amusing, but I couldn't get interested in
either of the main characters or always remember which was which. I
think too it is a mistake to have a narrator for a louche story; he is in
danger of having no adventures himself and coming out as a prig. But I
am glad to have read it and that it has been written.'

[1] This never happened because the Suez episode intervened and, after it was over, King was
recalled from his Egyptian posting by the British Council.
[2] King had consulted a psychiatrist at the Tavistock Clinic, London. He was treated neither by
hypnosis nor by drugs—though A. would persist in referring to his 'treatment by hypnosis'. In his
later years, A. himself deliberated whether to have such treatment, believing it might cure his heavy
drinking and increasing melancholia. See Letter 221.
[3] Written under the pseudonym of Frank Cauldwell. Seán O'Faoláin ended his review in
The Listener on 18 October: 'It may be a collector's item; it is now common knowledge that the
author's name is not Cauldwell.' The novel had been published on 13 August. O'Faoláin, an
occasional reviewer for A., remembers with pleasure his 'briefs' to contributors: 'Those notes with
books ("Dear Friend . . .").' 'A noble, unworldly man,' he told Braybrooke.
[4] In a letter A. wrote to Richard Murphy on 30 September 1954, Forster's views on *We Think
the World of You* are recounted at greater length: 'He seems to like my novel. At least he found
some nice things to say about it. But I could not quite make out what his feelings were. He thought
it needed "cutting" here and there—so I suppose he was rather bored here and there. He could
hardly be expected to feel whole-hearted enthusiasm for a book largely about a dog. And he thought
it did not contain enough "pleasure"—enough for his "lustful and self-indulgent" mind.' Later,
when it was eventually accepted and proofs were imminent, A. wrote to Colin Haycraft at The
Bodley Head on 3 May 1960: 'If . . . I disappeared . . . it may be worth saying that I would like
1. E. M. Forster or 2. Henry Reed (in that order) to be asked to pass them for me.'

These comments are not very agreeable,[1] and I'm not sure that he would be pleased with me for passing them on, but thought they would interest you. His comments on my own work—which he saw only in a very early version, interested me, though I didn't agree with them.

It was lovely to see you, dear Francis.
Love from
    Joe

To Francis King (1923–   )   Putney 147
                                                           18/10/56
Dear Francis
            further—as they say—to my last letter.[2] It is indeed true that I should *not* have passed on to you Forster's remarks about your book, for he has taken them back. When I saw him last night he said that in view of the conflict between us, he had read your book all over again and 'liked it very much better'. This was nice for you (for it seems quite a personal compliment to have one's work read *twice* by him) and for him, for he did not like to be in conflict, not only with me but—with another friend of his, Francis Bennett of Caius,[3] who had also told him he had enjoyed it, especially because of the tenderer, more compassionate view it expressed of weak, unhappy humanity. So now we are all pleased and I hope you are too; the only dissatisfaction I have, in noticing my restored, inscribed copy again, is in observing that Osbert Lancaster, in his otherwise good cover, did not put on the piano an *objet d'art* of Theo's which is one of the amusements of your story.[4] I see that it could not have been put there quite realistically; but if *I* had been making your cover I would have seen to its being there and that the initiated would have identified it with a giggle. Well, I always go pretty well all out myself and like to see it in others; Morgan, who never goes all out, except in private, has less of a leg to stand on when he says that your work, and mine, doesn't have enough 'pleasure'.
Love, dear F.
    Joe

To Hilary Corke (1921–   )   *The Listener*, Broadcasting House, W.1 148
                                                           ?/11/56
Dear Hilary
            how you keep me up to the various marks! You are quite the Watch Committee, and that is what a friend and contributor ought to be, so I am pleased and feel you deserve a serious letter.[5]

---

[1] Shortly afterwards Forster revised considerably his views on *The Firewalkers*. See Letter 147.
[2] Letter 146.
[3] See page 94, note 4.
[4] A pottery phallus from which Colonel Grecos, the chief character, pours milk for his guests' tea.
[5] Corke in his letter to A. had raised seven points. Here A. deals with (2), (3), (5) and (7). Corke cannot remember what (1), (4) and (6) concerned.

(3). re [G. H.] Vallins, yes I noticed the report of his death in *The Times* (2 Nov.), and send you your piece about him so that you yourself may make any change you think fit.[1] I wish you would cut it too, you are such a fertile boy, it is terrible. (2). One cannot drop a seed in your garden but a positive fount of flowers or nettles instantly arrives. Pretty flowers, blistering nettles, and if I were the *T.L.S.*[2] I should be delighted, but just look at my slummy space! If you were the only one who took advantage of it it wouldn't be so bad, but unfortunately a high percentage of other reviewers, in every other subject, also think their subjects and their books of much greater importance than any other subjects or books—and I have more than fifty reviews, in the result, all of about this length and longer, going back to March and April of this year—and not a hope in hell of using them.

(5) & (7). I see your point about Bunyan and Browne.[3] People get careless, I fear. It is the same reviewer with whom Dr Redpath[4] is disputing. The reviewer got both books because they concerned Donne, upon whom he has written a monograph himself.

Yes, you shall follow [Ronald] Bryden, but I am v. pleased with him at the moment and may extend his run for longer than usual, especially since he is new to London journalism[5] and in need of shelter. I seldom read novels, but had read [William] Golding's latest[6] with great interest and admiration. Sean [O'Faoláin] found it unreadable (and sold it, so I had to buy another copy in order to try it on Bryden); [John] Davenport said it was 'too deep for him'; but Bryden's review is a perfect piece of criticism, complete mastery and every word sensitive and exact. I am greatly impressed.

Finally, dear Hilary, with regret but firmness (space, space, nothing else), I return [Elizabeth] Hann.[7] If I am to get in yards of Vallins and Churchill,[8] and yards and yards from other people, in praise of their various subjects— *no one*, except W. Plomer[9] and Forster, seems able to condense—I simply can't wreak vengeance on tripe.

Love from
Joe

[1] Corke revised his review of Vallins' *The Pattern of English*—but it never appeared.

[2] *Times Literary Supplement*.

[3] In a review of *A Guide to English Literature: from Donne to Marvel*, edited by Boris Ford, the anonymous critic in *The Listener* on 22 November had regretted that not more space had been given to Bunyan's prose. He had remarked that there was an essay on the prose of Donne and Sir Thomas Browne, but that Bunyan was 'a more important writer than the latter of these'. Corke regarded such a balancing of Bunyan against Browne as 'meaningless'. Originally he had planned to register his protest in the form of a letter to the Editor. On second thoughts he just sent a private note to A.

[4] The editor of a recent edition of *The Songs and Sonnets of John Donne*.

[5] Forster had been particularly pleased with Bryden's review of his *Marianne Thornton* in the *Cambridge Review* on 12 May, and had given A. a copy of it telling him that here was 'a possible reviewer for the future'. Bryden began reviewing for *The Listener* on 14 June.

[6] *Pincher Martin*.

[7] Her life of Gertrude Bell, *Daughter of the Desert*, had come out in the autumn. Corke's review was put into proof but never published.

[8] *The Poetical Works of Charles Churchill*, which Corke reviewed in an unsigned notice on 3 January 1957.

[9] In early 1953 A. had written to Richard Murphy: 'I am thinking of starting a Disciplinary School for Journalists, the prime lesson of which will be to teach them to be concise without being dull. William Plomer who skilfully extracts from books . . . shall be my head teacher.'

P.S. It lodged a little in my conscience that I let you get away with opinions about Sir Eden [*sic*] and Suez with which in fact I totally disagree. Or not that I let you get away, for you have a right to get away with whatever you think, but that I allowed you through an apparent acquiesce [*sic*] to suppose I agreed. I think Sir Eden should be hanged from the nearest lamp-post, or stuffed into a strait-jacket, for surely he is mad—but I only write this to you. I wouldn't say it—now or then—for it would get us into an argument, and Georges Duthuit has taught me never to argue about politics, people only lose their tempers. Also, of course, I am unfit to argue, being ignorant of the subject. But my every instinct tells me that a terrible blunder has been made. So I put that down, and now have forgotten all about it.[1]

To Hilary Corke (1921–   )   *The Listener*, Broadcasting House, W.1   149
                                              ?/11/56

It fits as well as it reads.[2] Thank you so much. Yes, I enjoyed my evening with you immensely. It was smashing.
     Joe

Forgetfulness occurs over returning your original ms. because it is a thing not usually done. Moreover it would be officially frowned on, unless you will kindly return it to us with your corrected proof. The reason is that we are none of us infallible, you yourself might possibly fail to notice some error, worse still, the printers might make some muddle on press day, as they occasionally do—drop the type or something—and if we did not have your ms. to refer to we should be in the cart.
     So, if you *must* have it back for corrections, you also must not fail to return it with your corrected proof.
     Joe

[1] The conversation between A. and Corke about Suez took place over dinner. Corke supported Eden's 'invasion' on the basis that though it might have been badly or even wickedly done, the Franco-British action to get the canal away from Nasser was the lesser of two evils. Corke found few of his own friends and colleagues supported him, and being therefore emotionally and politically isolated, he feels in retrospect, he may have expressed his pro-Eden views with more than necessary force. He comments: 'Joe, who was always one to love people more than even his fiercest political convictions, glided away from the subject. He didn't trust himself not to quarrel, and we had never quarrelled, nor were to. The postscript to this letter says a great deal about two sides of him: one, his great sweetness in personal relations, and two, his refusal to compromise in matters of intellectual honesty. He had to balance these things against one another, and here is a beautifully concise example of how he did it.'
[2] *The Prose of Rupert Brooke*, edited by Christopher Hassall, which Corke reviewed in a signed notice on 6 December. It ended: 'The word "selected" appears neither on the cover nor on the title-page. And when we read in the blurb that "the entertaining and instructive pages of this selection omit nothing of his work in prose which would repay study", the kindest word that springs to mind (and even this is a curious one to use in connection with so old and respectable a firm as Messrs. Sidgwick & Jackson) is "impudence". Rupert Brooke himself would no doubt have had no hesitation in using a harsher.' It is worth adding here that as a literary editor A. never expected reviewers to soft-pedal towards publishers, however 'respectable'.

150   To Stephen Spender (1909–   )   *The Listener*, Broadcasting House, W.1
                                                                    30/11/56
Dear Stephen
             no sooner do I write to accept your party than I hear that
my dear friend Georges Duthuit, son-in-law to Matisse, will probably be
in London and I think I must keep myself free for him. Like you, he is one
of my favourite men.
    How wicked you were to run away so soon from Gallery One! I brought
my enchanting ½ sister[1] to meet you and she, and I, were most disappointed.
Charming and attractive, she has already swept William Plomer off his
feet, also David Sylvester. We were so vexed to find no one but Ernest
Thesiger.[2]
Love
    J

151   To Stephen Spender (1909–   )   *The Listener*, Broadcasting House, W.1
                                                                     4/12/56
Dear Stephen
             I never thanked you for your kindness and sweetness over
my fable,[3] lugging it all over the U.S. and pushing it in here and there.
It was wonderful of you and I am a skab and a skunk not to have said so
before. Rheumatics, a heavy cold and a Book Supplement (now going to
bed) have swept even the common courtesies, let along undying love, out
of my addled head. Your Iowa chap[4] has written, wanting to see the story
again, so I have asked McC. [of Harcourt Brace][5] to post it on. The former
remarked that he had only a rather hazy notion of it since you had got him
out of bed at 2 o'clock in the morning and forced him to read it before 6.0.
What a ruthless man you are!
Blessings upon you
    Joe

Your man Allen Tate gets a nice [signed] review from Sir Herbert in the
Xmas No. which comes out on Thursday.[6]

152   To Donald Windham (1920–   )   17 Star & Garter Mansions,
                                          Putney, S.W.15   6/12/56
Dear Don
             I was so pleased to hear from you. Indeed I did ought to have
written to you again. Is it really a year? Tut tut! I am terribly sorry. No,
it wasn't the booklet you have read, but a rather longer and—I think—much
better one, called *We Think the World of You*. Tulip is in it also, but under a
different name. It is really an expansion of the brief para. in the first of the

---

[1] Diana Petre.   [2] Actor (1879–1961).   [3] *We Think the World of You.*
[4] Harry Duncan of the Cummington Press.   [5] See Letter 152.
[6] In the issue of 6 December Tate's *The Man of Letters in the Modern World* was paired in Herbert
Read's review with *Critical Approaches to Literature* by David Daiches.

Tulip essays where I said that she had had a bad upbringing,[1] and it is largely in dialogue. It is a kind of fable: I call it an Adult Fairy Story.[2] It is much more down your street, and my own, and I meant to send it, but then I started re-writing part of it and mucked up one of my only two typescripts so badly that I had only one left to show to publishers. It is now in your country with a man named Harry Duncan of the Cummington Press, Iowa. Stephen Spender, who seems to like it, showed it to him, and he is said to have enjoyed it and is now considering whether he will set it up. Do you think that is a good idea? The trouble with it is that it is ineradicably libellous—criminal libel—and can't possibly be published here, and I doubt if I could get it off onto any ordinary U.S. publisher either: McCallum of Harcourt Brace rejected it, he said it would get him into too much trouble. He said that if I would consent to remove certain passages he might risk it, but I didn't want to, so now, at my request, he has sent it off to Duncan in Iowa upon whom my last hopes are now pinned. It is not at all indecent, but contains a homosexual relationship. If Duncan rejects it I will ask him to send the typescript to you.

I am so pleased you liked the *Tulip* booklet and wonder how you got hold of it. So far we have failed to get any U.S. publisher to take it; it has been seen and rejected by Harper's, Knopf, Farrar Straus, Harcourt Brace, Random House, Macmillan, Viking, Putnam and Bobbs-Merrill. I am wondering whether to try it on New Directions. I could produce a considerably longer version, with an expanded end, many more footnotes, quite amusing and with some excisions which my publishers have thought libellous restored. I was rather half-hearted in putting it out here and made it as short as I could—writing about a dog I was so afraid of being a bore. But if it isn't a bore I can make it longer, am indeed doing so with a view to U.S. publication if I can get it off on anyone; the sales here have been disappointing, in spite of a good press, and I would like to make some more money out of it. But it never did interest me as much as the Fairy Story down in Iowa.

'The Turn of the Screw' chapter was difficult to do, and may have been too emotional and serious. I was only trying to give an impression of the passage of time and the frustrations of life generally and the vulnerability of ivory towers. In an expanded version I would quote the whole of *The Times'* report (1926) of the boy's suicide on the Common, and that might make the point a bit clearer.[3]

I was pleased to hear from you.

Joe

---

[1] 'She had originally belonged to some working-class people who, though fond of her in their way, seldom took her out. She was too excitable, and too valuable, to be allowed off the lead; on it she pulled. For nearly a year she never left their house at all, but spent her time, mostly alone, for they were at work all day, in a tiny back-yard . . .' It was from such a life that A. rescued her when she was eighteen months old.

[2] In the following year A. began to think 'the phrase "An Adult Fairy Story" open to misconstruction', and when the novel was finally accepted in 1959, and he was asked to prepare a 'blurb' by The Bodley Head, he settled for the phrase 'a fairy story for adults'.

[3] This contrasts sharply with A.'s earlier and later held views that perhaps it would be best if the section were 'cut' about young Holland's suicide. See Letters 130 and 275.

153 To Patricia Murphy (1928–   )   17 Star & Garter Mansions,
                                          Putney, S.W.15   21/12/56

Dear Patricia
          I am delighted with my card from Emily.[1] She is clearly
going to inherit all the parental intellect and turn it towards Art. In time
she will be carving those boulders in your woods and give you the statuary
for your grounds that Richard desired. The card—if she really did it—shows
great promise—more than Minou Drouet in the world of letters, of whom
Cocteau is said to have remarked: '*All* children of nine can write admirable
poetry—except Minou Drouet.'[2]
          I am spending Xmas at home, worn out, in the midst of a cellar of drink,
much of which has been bestowed upon us by our wealthy relatives. It will
be nice to booze and sleep and occasionally scribble for four consecutive
days, and not have to catch the 30 bus. I hope your own Xmas will be as
peaceful and pleasant. If Ireland, like England, has been immobilised by
Sir Eden, as I suppose it has, you will probably not be able to visit or be
visited. Except, perhaps, by that excellent Diana Tomkin[3] who buys my
works in large quantities and writes me such appreciative and perceptive
notes about them. It is such a relief *not* to be taken seriously, and too few
people have done that. It was sadly noticeable in the otherwise favourable
reviews that *Tulip* received—and which did not help at all to sell her—that
scarcely anyone said that the book made them laugh. Perhaps that was my
fault for having tried to make them cry as well; however Miss Tomkin,
bless her, was not taken in by that. Now she writes me a very nice note indeed
about *Hindoo Holiday*. Will you please thank her for it.
          I seem to have been lunching and dining out every day for weeks, which
means late nights, and since I have also got my shoulder rheumatism back
that means early wakings. There have been other interruptions to slumber
too, for the weather has been windy and Queenie does not like the world to
rattle and creak and groan and comes over two or three times a night to
wake me up and ask me what it means. Dogs are dreadfully haunted.
Otherwise she is well and has mistaken the rather mild, humid weather we
have been having for Spring, so that she has started to shed her coat,
tiresome girl, a wardrobe change she does not usually make until late
February.
          Bunny and Nancy are well, though rather cross. Xmas often makes
people cross, I find, and the more festive they try to be the more liable they
are to irritation and anger. I have just read an interesting book about Nero,[4]
who must have been the Rudolph Valentino (in 'The Sheik') of his day,
and with whom Mark Anthony [*sic*] and perhaps Agrippa too, was clearly
madly in love. Now I am reading about *Reptiles*,[5] which I also find fascinating. Did you know that snakes have no external ear or ear drum? Entrancing

          [1] Patricia and Richard Murphy's daughter. She was seven months old at the time.
          [2] A child prodigy. Earlier in the year the publication of her *First Poems* (*Arbre, Mon Ami*), at
the age of 9, had aroused considerable controversy—both in France and England.
          [3] Mrs Diana Tomkin, a friend of the Murphys, was A.'s 'first Dublin fan'. His letters to her
have not survived.
          [4] A slip. For 'Nero' read 'Herod'.
          [5] By Angus d'A. Bellairs—published in the following year.

fact! How delightful science is, as I was telling Miss Tomkin. All that stuff about snake charmers making their snakes sway to music is now seen to be utter balls, *for the snakes can't hear.* Balls too that celebrated story of Conan Doyle's called *The Speckled Band* in which the wicked Doctor pipes his poisonous snake through a ventilator above poor Enid's (*was* her name Enid?)[1] bed. Even Sherlock Holmes, with his wonderful powers of mind, didn't see through that one, and sent the poor Doctor to the gallows, or wherever he went, when he was clearly quite innocent for he simply couldn't have done the wicked act he was convicted of doing. Ah science! How beautiful you are!

Well, best love to you both

    Joe

To Francis King (1923–)   Putney 154
16/1/57

Dear Francis

        lovely long letter, and how I laughed at Veloudios' Xmas Tree.[2] *So* characteristic: it would indeed have been a delicious item for your book. But if you had merely thought of him in connection with an Xmas tree, I'm sure you would infallibly have decorated it for him just in that way.

My own book[3] has been accepted with enthusiasm by the Cummington Press, Iowa. It is to be an edition limited to 300 copies, 15$ a copy, illustrated if I approve of the illustrations they submit. I am pleased—though I see it would be better if it were a commercial publication. But that, they hope will follow. I forget if I told you that it is a pretty smart press, the sort of Nonesuch of the U.S. and has already done writers like Wallace Stevens, Allen Tate and so on. So the item should be decently gotten up. I don't suppose, in so tiny and expensive an edition, that I shall be given many spare copies to bestow upon friends: in fact I am rather inclined to ask for only three—two for myself (one to keep and one to lend) and one for Stephen who got it placed for me.

I long to come out to you, Francis dear, and will see if I can. April perhaps? My main snag at the moment is poverty— and this Iowa press asks me to waive all claim to an advance since they are rather skint themselves. However, perhaps something will turn up to retrieve my fortunes. I'm afraid nothing more can be expected from *Tulip.* Dear Morgan's nice push (I fancy it was the only new book he read last year, so it wasn't too difficult for him to call it the best) was a bit belated;[4] it isn't expected to affect the sluggish sales.

[1] No. Her name was Helen Stonor.
[2] Colonel A. Veloudios on whom King based Colonel Grecos in *The Firewalkers*. Instead of the usual star, he had devised (with the help of an electrician friend) a flashing phallus to put on the top of his Christmas tree. Cf. Letter 147.
[3] *We Think the World of You.*
[4] Forster had chosen it for the Books of the Year feature (Part I) in the *Sunday Times* on 23 December 1956. Cf. Letter 324.

Wintry weather here, bitter and beastly. I've just sent my Travel Book Number to press and am taking the day off. Rheumatism in my right hand; the back of it blew up suddenly last weekend, so that it looked like someone else's hand—Mme Montpensier's perhaps.[1] I must take it to [Dr] Patrick [Woodcock] tomorrow. I had no idea what your Egyptian illness had been, so your letter now puts me wise. Indeed, yes, the food problem in Greece for anyone not allowed grease must be formidable.

Delighted to hear about your new book,[2] d.f.,—I look forward to it muchly[3]—comedy? tragedy?—well, soon we shall see. I haven't read *Every Eye*,[4] but I will. My own miscellaneous reading has been *Herod the Great*[5] (interesting: obviously he was frequently in bed with Mark Anthony [*sic*]), P. G. Wodehouse (once you begin it's hard to stop, yet not stopping means going on almost for ever, so I have stopped), *The Nude*,[6] and a book called *Reptiles*,[7] which contains just what it says. From this I gleaned the information that snakes have no external ears. They cannot therefore hear, except sounds transmitted through the ground and the walls of the body. So that Indian nonsense of making snakes 'dance to the music' is all my eye and Betty M., they sway merrily in imitation of the swaying of the piper's body. Also dear Sherlock Holmes is exposed as not half so clever as he thought, for the wicked Doctor who piped a snake through a ventilator onto poor Enid's[8] bed in *The Speckled Band* couldn't possibly have done any such thing: so Holmes now looks rather an ass—and thus doth science expose our ignorance if we are not careful.

With love, dear Francis, and my prayers that you and Dino have now made it up.

Joe

---

155   To the Editor of *The Times*[9]   17 Star and Garter Mansions,
                                                            Putney, S.W.15
                                                            Oct. 2, 1957

Sir,
        If the Warden of All Souls, whose letter you printed on September 30,

[1] A. loved visiting the Palace at Versailles and may have had in mind Jean Nocret's 'Allegory of the Royal Family', painted in 1670, in which Madame de Montpensier (called La Grande Mademoiselle) appears as Diana. She is shown to have rather puffy hands.
[2] *The Man on the Rock*, a novel published later in 1957.
[3] A. developed a sudden, passing craze for this word. 'Muchly (school word)', he had remarked to Geoffrey Gorer in the previous autumn.
[4] A novel by Isobel English published in 1956.
[5] *The Life and Times of Herod the Great* by Stewart Perowne (1956).
[6] By Kenneth Clark.
[7] See page 128, note 5.
[8] See page 129, note 1.
[9] The letter appeared under the heading 'Cruelty to Animals'. On 10 September an old gentleman of sixty-six was reading a newspaper in the park one Sunday, it was reported, when a puppy, out of its owner's control, jumped upon him and made a nuisance of itself. The old gentleman lost his temper and kicked out at the animal and hurt it; further, according to witnesses for the prosecution, he stamped on it with his left foot. He was sent to prison for six weeks. John Sparrow, the Warden of All Souls, noticed in the same issue of *The Times* a report of a motorist who had been found guilty of dangerous driving which had caused damage to property and injury to a person, and who had only been sent to prison for four weeks. 'But then,' he pointed out, 'his victim was not a puppy—only a woman with a perambulator.' A.'s letter was intended as something 'of a jolly leg-

sat reading his newspaper in the park and my puppy ran up to him and dirtied his clothes I should be deeply apologetic and, were civilized exchanges possible, would make what amends as I could, such as offering to pay for his suit to be cleaned. If, however, he trampled upon my puppy I would fell him to the ground and trample upon him—that is to say, if the law was not prepared to trample upon him for me.

(i) Might not a larger number of such regrettable incidents occur if cruelty to animals were removed, as he suggests, out of the jurisdiction of the criminal law into the sphere of private morals?

(ii) Might not the harshness of my reaction in the event, considered in relation with the all too common magisterial harshness he deplores, have the effect of persuading the Warden, in his minority and prostrate position, that there must be something about dogs that he has missed?
Yours faithfully,
J. R. Ackerley

To Richard Murphy (1927–)   *The Listener*, Broadcasting House, W.1 156
12/12/57

Richard dear
I think it is time I gave you detailed instructions anent the Travel Book Number—or have I done so already? At any rate, to inform or repeat: I want 800 words by Jan. 6. You have a number of books—I forget how many—and *I don't want them reviewed*. The object of the Number is to interest holiday-makers in various countries, at home and abroad, those countries for which relevant literature (guide and travel books) has been published (or, rather, has reached *The Listener*) this year. (The last time, for instance, no book was published about Wales, so Wales did not get a look-in: this time there are a couple, so Wales will get a col.). It follows, therefore, that another object of the Number is to publicize as many worthy guide and travel books about various countries as possible. This pleases the book trade. But they don't have to be reviewed. There is not enough space for that. So what I am looking for from you is a piece about Ireland, revealing its charms to the intelligent traveller—criticism is permitted, so long as it doesn't bulk so large as to overshadow charm: clearly one doesn't want a travel article about a country which advises no one to visit it. If the books help you—enter your ideas, or guide them, in any way—they can be referred to; if you don't use them *inside* your text for passing reference I can always list them in an italics note beneath your piece. You can be as jolly and amusing as you like. All the better to raise a smile: to be serious about Ireland would be to present a far from welcoming picture, I fear.

pull', and in a note to Geoffrey Gorer he explained how he had sent it to a mutual friend of both his and Sparrow's to see if he thought it amusing, and this friend, without telling anybody, had posted it off. When A. first saw it in print he was horrified. Then he consoled himself. 'One must stand up for the dog-wogs,' he wrote in a diary.

Your job is, in short, to make Ireland attractive on the whole: do it in your own characteristic way.[1]
Love

J

157 To John Wickens (1934–   )   17 Star & Garter Mansions, Putney,
                                          S.W.15   7/1/58
Dear Mr Wickens

I am very pleased with your letter of course. To have been positively stalked for six years by a 'fan', no author could wish for pleasanter New Year tidings than that. But alas I can't help you, except to say that I will keep my eye open for a copy of the play for you and send it if I find it.[2] It was already a rarity when it was revived about four years ago[3] at a small theatre, The Irving, off Leicester Square, and the second-hand bookshops were then ransacked, and to some purpose, for a few stray copies were discovered, which of course the cast needed. That ransacking doubtless cleared the central London shops of whatever copies they happened to have; it could now re-appear on their shelves only by chance; it might, however, be discovered in some place like Brighton or Reading or elsewhere, where second-hand shops are to be found. The trouble with the play was that it was never a success with the public,[4] and never went into more than one smallish edition, if I remember rightly (1925), and half that edition was paper-backed so that it could hardly be expected to survive so many years. I possess only one copy myself, a marked one, with which I dare not part in case, by some unlikely chance, the play was staged again. It would be a pity not to be able to offer a would-be producer any copy at all and that production should fail for want of the play. But if I come across another copy in my potterings among books I will certainly remember you. In fact it is a

[1] 'The Charm of Eire' appeared on 16 January 1958. A. chose the title.
[2] A. did eventually find a second-hand copy of his play *The Prisoners of War*—but decided when next writing to Wickens to lend his own in the meantime. 'I will say one word before it falls into your hands,' he wrote on 24 January. 'It was misnamed, it should have been called *The Interned*. Some of the critics expected to see barbed wire . . . and could not understand why men so comfortably and securely situated should have been so unhappy. In fact the play is not really about war, but about a few individuals and the effects of frustration and idleness upon their minds. One of the critics who truly saw what was happening was Hugh Walpole . . .' Cf. Letters 5 and 132.
[3] Three years in fact.
[4] On 14 September 1955 Sir Gyles Isham had written to *The Times* to suggest that in view of the dearth of new plays some distinguished failures from the past might be revived. He cited Nigel Playfair's successful revival in 1924 of Congreve's *The Way of the World* at the Lyric Theatre, Hammersmith. On 23 September Giles Playfair took up the argument and remarked that his father's production of Congreve was 'the very first production of this classic to profit the management as well as please the public'. He also added that he believed that there were a number of masterpieces produced before their time which might be lost for ever 'if no one had the courage to resuscitate them'. He gave two examples within living memory—Karel Capek's *The Insect Play* (which his father had first produced at the Regent Theatre in 1923) and A.'s *The Prisoners of War* (which he had given its first public run at the Playhouse in 1925). The correspondence was headed 'Successful Failures', and when A.'s play was revived in the following month on 6 October the anonymous Dramatic Critic in *The Times* reminded his readers of the phrase. A. had written the play when he was interned in 1918 in Switzerland, recast it at home before he went up to Cambridge in 1919, and then let it lie in a drawer for six years, having been told by several managements that it was 'unproducible'. But during that six years he did do 'a little tinkering' on the script, from time to time. See Introduction, 3.

rather immature work—I wrote it when I was 21[1]—and there is much in it I should like to be able to change, especially the third act, but it would not be possible to recapture the emotional feelings of so long ago.

I'm glad you like *Hindoo Holiday* and have got hold of the revised edition. I managed to put back into it the bits that the publishers thought it advisable to omit when it was first published. It is therefore fuller and more amusing, and the grammar[2] is tidier too.

Have you come across my recent book *My Dog Tulip?* Perhaps you would not like it; it is a very different cup of tea, but I think it is not a bad little book and nicely written. Since you are interested in my work perhaps I shall not seem egotistic to add that a novelette of mine called *We Think the World of You* is supposed to be appearing, in a month or two, in the United States. It could not appear here owing to libel, and even in the States is being published by a small private press, The Cummington, in Iowa City, in a limited edition of 300 copies. I fear it will be rather expensive, about 15 dollars. This book is more in the genre of *Hindoo Holiday* than my play. But maybe it never will appear. The publishers never write to me or answer my letters, they are so amateurish and unbusinesslike, and I hear that their printing press fell over some months ago and fractured itself in sundry places. However, I continue to hope that, in spite of all difficulties and disasters, they are forging, or at least creeping, ahead and that the booklet will one day appear.

Yours sincerely

J. R. Ackerley

To John Wickens (1934–   )   *The Listener*, Broadcasting House, W.1   158
                                                                28/2/58

Dear Mr Wickens

what a lovely present, but it was too generous. I felt sorry to have named a liquor that caused you to spend so much, and would not have done so if I had thought you would go to such extravagance. But I am very touched and grateful, for no one has ever rewarded me for my work before, let alone on so lavish a scale. I wonder whether, as some small return, you would care to have the one short passage in *Hindoo Holiday* that never got in. I will tell you what happened. When the book was first published in 1932, Chatto & Windus advised, indeed insisted on, certain omissions which they thought either damaging to myself or libellous to others. When the book was to be reprinted in 1951, I asked if I could put them back, for I had always thought the book lame and incomplete without them. Moreover, in the intervening years, that is to say since 1923–24 which was the period of my visit to India, the Maharajah had died and his State been dissolved into the new India. Also I had always carefully faked names and dates so that no one knew which my State had been; there seemed no reason why the book should not now be put out in its original form, and the publishers agreed. By a curious and unfortunate coincidence,

[1] A. was 22.   [2] See Letter 260.

however, at the very moment that the review copies of my revised edition were being sent out in 1951, another book, by an Indian Civil Servant, appeared,[1] published by Murray's, in which the identity of my Native State was exposed.[2] The author of this book, whose name I now forget,[3] had also known my Maharajah, and referred to him, to me, to *Hindoo Holiday* and to the actual State. In the course of my job as Literary Editor I happened to notice this myself, for the review copy of his book came into my office with my own, and although I was uncertain what importance attached to this coincidence, if any, I thought I should inform my publishers. They took, in fact, the gravest view of it, on account of a single passage in *Hindoo Holiday* which, if anonymity failed, might still be libellous. They therefore withdrew my book, recalling all review copies, and deleted the passage (I had to supply something else to fill the gap; it was the entry about the sun dial, I think), and they consulted with Murray's, who withdrew *their* book too and deleted all reference to me! However, I managed to retain my own Review copy of my book, so unless Chatto & Windus also have preserved a copy or two of that edition as it was before the deletion was made, the copy I possess is the only printed copy of the complete book in existence.

I send you therefore the deleted passage on separate pages,[4] and you can stick it in your own copy if you like it. It may be that you won't, that you prefer implication (if you feel it is already implied) to explication, or that, having got used to the book as it stands, you may resist additions or alterations; in that case you can always destroy it; but it was, in fact, part of the original ms. and, in my view, the crux of the book. The libel was thought to lie in the proposition that, although the King was dead, his son might still be living and pensioned off for the loss of his State, and that if therefore it was alleged that he was not only *not* the King's son but the son of a low-caste Indian, he might stand to lose his pension as well as his caste. Remote beyond belief, but publishers here dislike the smallest risks. If you have, as I believe, the 1951[5] half-guinea edition, the entry is an extension of the conversation on page 251.

Well, to change a subject that has occupied too much of too many of my letters, I was of course disturbed by yours. Life in your country[6] must be very distressing to a sensitive mind; we are far from being unaware over

---

[1] *Kingdoms of Yesterday* (1951).

[2] A. had called the State of Chhatarpur 'Chhokrapur'. But as he wrote in the Preface, dated March 1952, to the second revised edition of *Hindoo Holiday*: 'The State of Chhokrapur, if indeed it ever existed, has dissolved away in the new map of India.' In the next year when Forster published *The Hill of Devi*, a book made up largely of letters he sent home from India to his mother and to other relatives between 1912 and 1913, and in 1921, he took it for granted in his commentary that everybody now knew that A.'s 'Maharajah of Chhokrapur' was a straight portrait of the Maharajah of Chhatarpur—whom they had both regarded with a mixture of ridicule and genuine affection. Forster ended one section: 'At Chhatarpur . . . delightful tableaux and dances were staged for the benefit of its exotic Maharajah: Lowes Dickinson has described them in his *Appearances*, and J. R. Ackerley in his *Hindu [sic] Holiday*.' See Benita Parry's *Delusions and Discoveries: Studies on India in the British Imagination 1880–1930* (1972). Cf. Letter 110.

[3] Sir Arthur Cunningham Lothian.

[4] See Appendix D.

[5] 1952 in fact.

[6] South Africa.

here of what sympathetic onlookers like yourself must have to endure. Your story about the Indian boy alone was enough. I doubt if I could suffer it myself, any more than I find it now possible to suffer the sight of the treatment of domestic animals—dogs, cats, donkeys—in many European countries, which otherwise I love. It infects my pleasure to see them so neglected or ill-treated in countries like Greece, Spain, Italy; there is so much from which one has to avert one's eyes—for there is really nothing one can do—that I often feel I cannot revisit these lovely places any more. Allowing that human beings are more important than animals, your country would send me off my head. One of my oldest friends, incidentally, is native to it and is involved in its affairs still: William Plomer. Perhaps you know him—doubtless you know of him, for his African books at least (*The Child of Queen Victoria*,[1] *I Speak of Africa*,[2] *Cecil Rhodes*[3] and *Double Lives*[4]) are surely in your library. He was born in, or near, Pretoria and now lives on the Sussex coast. You may even have met him or heard him speak lately, for he was not long ago over with you on a tour at the invitation of one of your universities. His literature varies in quality, I think, but it is always intelligent and humane. His second volume of memoirs is just published— *At Home*—and if you come across it and consult the index you will find a reference or two to myself,[5] including some reminiscences which I am afraid have been improved upon in their telling.

I was pleased to have the news of yourself you sent me and to know that the pains of your life are not unmixed with happiness. And it is better to live among books than many other things. My own office in *The Listener* frequently has the appearance of a library when the publishing seasons are at their height and the review books stream in. My floor is covered with them at the moment, though they are only rejects, books too abstruse, or technical, or boshy, to be reviewed, and awaiting the second-hand dealer to come and cart them away.

Well this seems a long letter, and it is high time I brought it to a close.

Thank you once again for your lavish gift.

Yours sincerely

Joe Ackerley

To William Plomer (1903–1973)   Putney   159
                                                  8/3/58

D.L.B.

I meant to write you some days ago to thank you for the nice book[6]—that is to say to thank you *after* reading it, for I had already thanked you before—but fussification over the Book Number disarrayed my life and thoughts. I've read you twice, dear William, with pleasure, it is a book of rather loose strands which one gathers together with a firmer grip and greater profit on the repeat; also perhaps too diverting a personal curiosity might dilate the eye of those fortunate enough to find themselves in the

---

[1] Short stories (1933).   [2] Short stories (1927).   [3] 1933.   [4] 1943.
[5] See page 136, note 1.   [6] *At Home*

index, and a calmer, more objective view can be taken when that curiosity
has been satisfied. I was most touched and fortified by your character
sketch of myself,[1] flattered indeed to have my natural attainments increased
at one point by the additional gift of your own quick wit, a conversational
quality I fear I never possessed. But it was all the jollier to be William
Ackerley or Joe Plomer, a delicious blend, instead of always one's own
dull self. And throughout it was, of course, the most fascinating, curious,
nostalgic experience to re-tread with you the paths of the past, such paths,
that is to say, as we trod together, and if one was sometimes disappointed
that you did not linger a little longer here and there, that was positive greed,
so much had one to be thankful for already in the remembrance of things
past. The book has many amusing moments—the girl on the beach is
delightfully brought off— and some trenchant observations on life—that
it leaves behind the feeling of being on the whole rather a sad book is
something I do not trace to its source. Maurice Cranston, so far as I recollect
his [*Listener*] review, took the same impression;[2] you will see his review on
Thursday[3] and will derive from it, I am sure, complete satisfaction.
Best love, dear William
   Joe

160 To John Wickens (1934–)   *The Listener*, Broadcasting House, W.1

12/3/58

Dear Mr Wickens
                I think you are being over-sensitive about something. I
honestly don't know to what letter you refer, for I have had none from you
that could conceivably be called 'smug'. If you're referring to the letter
about yourself, the only possible complaint I could make about that is that
the information was perhaps a little slight. So if there was a 'smug' letter,
you will be glad to hear that it never reached my hands.

I'm glad the play[4] arrived safely and did not disappoint. No hurry to
return it, and for heaven's sake don't waste money on registration, I never
do that. I will not forget your wish to possess a copy if I come across one.[5]

What can I tell you about Tulip. She lives, and is nearly 13, and her
real name will make you smile, for it is Queenie, but it was not I who
christened her, for she belonged in the first place to some working-class
people, from whom I bought her—and that, indeed, is the theme of my
novelette *We Think the World of You*, in which she appears under yet another
name, Evie, eternal woman.[6] I have no further news [on the American

---

[1] 'Elegant to the point of dandyism, and fine featured, he had . . . the gentleness of manner that
sometimes goes with strong convictions, independence and pugnacity. The mixture of directness
and vagueness in his manner made me nervous of being a bore.'

[2] Cranston wrote: '. . . the tone of this second volume [of autobiography] is a shade more
autumnal and melancholy than the first [i.e. *Double Lives*], and it is sometimes, like its author,
désorienté; but it is a book of exceptional distinction, written in a style which is at once delicate and
vigorous, and with a wonderfully true and sympathetic feeling for people and things and places . . .'

[3] March 13.

[4] *The Prisoners of War*.

[5] Cf. page 138, note 1.

[6] 'She is Eve, the prototype, Shaw's tigress . . .' A. wrote in the following year. See page 150,
note 3.

front] of that book, and no reply to an enquiry I made six weeks ago. Some further disaster has occurred, I expect; the Press[1] may have fallen down again and broken its neck, or perhaps the man who ran and worked it has died; since he appeared to do it single-handed, there is no one I know of who would inform me of his death. It was supposed to be published by last Xmas, and, considering everything, I have now given up expecting anything to happen.

So glad the missing fragment from *Hindoo Holiday*[2] gave pleasure. It does pull the book together, I think, but it could not be published until everyone concerned is dead.

All good wishes

Joe Ackerley

To Richard Murphy (1927–)　　*The Listener*, Broadcasting House, W.1　161
　　　　　　　　　　　　　　　　　　　　　　　　　　21/5/58

Dear Richard

I must say there is no lack of incident in your lives. 'Never a dull moment if you know the Murphys.' But I should have thought you took too dark a view of your father-in-law's illness. Surely the lip is not so sensitive as all that—'long, painful and horrible death' with 'years of agony' —and is not a cancer there as easily cleared up by radium treatment as it is on the tongue (my father had it), or indeed on any other external part of the body. I remember well my father, during dinner one evening, putting out his tongue at the doctor, who was a family friend and often dined with us, and saying 'What ought I to do about that?' There was a large bluish patch on the tongue, which he'd never mentioned before, though I expect he guessed what it was, for *his* father had had and eventually died of it, operation after operation, in pre-radium days. The doctor gave it a brief glance and said 'Better come round to my place for a few days, old boy' (he had a Hydro next door), 'we'll soon clear it up for you with a spot of radium.' And so it was.[3] So I should investigate your old man's illness a bit more carefully if I were you: ill-tempered he may be, but is he really an urgent case for a visit, on *health* reasons, at least?

You have improved your poem, no doubt, though is 'laughing' (penultimate line) the right word?[4] I've always rather disliked seeing human attributes conferred on animal or vegetable life. Wouldn't 'growing' be enough?

I look forward v. much to seeing you on Sunday.

Love

J

[1] i.e. Cummington Press, Iowa.
[2] See Letters 110, 158 and Appendix D.
[3] When A. came to relate this incident in Chapter 13 of *My Father and Myself*, he added how his father had once said to him: 'You know, it's a funny thing but my old dad had cancer of the tongue and I thought him an old man. In fact he was about the same age as I am. And now *I* have cancer of the tongue and I don't feel old at all.' A. then added: 'I too thought my father an old man; he was the same age as I am as I write this book [i.e. in the sixties] and, although I have not yet had cancer of the tongue, I don't feel old either.'
[4] Murphy writes: 'Sorry, I can't trace this reference.'

162 To John Wickens (1934–)   17 Star and Garter Mansions, Putney,
S.W.15   9/6/58

Dear Mr Wickens
                    I should have written you before to reassure you of the
safe return of my *Prisoners of War*. Indeed I did start a letter to you a few
days after its arrival, but for one reason and another I never got to finishing
it. I have also to thank you for a long interesting letter that announced the
book's return. I'm glad the play pleased you and will continue to keep an
eye open for another copy of it when I find myself in second-hand shops,[1]
but at present we are rather immobilised by a general bus strike which makes
it more difficult and fatiguing than usual to get about. Trains are still available, of course, and now I have to use them, which I seldom did before, but
they can't always take you where you want to go, without entailing considerable walks as well, and since all the other erstwhile bussers are also
forced to use them, they are positively crammed and no pleasure to travel
on. Private car-owners took some pity upon the carless in the beginning
(the bus strike has now been on for three weeks), but charitable impulses
soon get tired and bored and I notice now as I walk over Putney Bridge from
our railway station that many of the unfortunate people, who live perhaps
in Roehampton Village (which has no station) two miles away, thumb for
lifts in vain, from cars which often contain no one but the driver.

I daresay you are right about *At Home*.[2] I certainly did not think it as
good as *Double Lives* which was also a work of art, I mean it had a kind of
unity about it, it made a book, whereas the former is more a collection of
reminiscences. But Plomer is a far more sophisticated man than myself
and could not write with my pen any more than I could write with his. I did
start off an autobiography[3] many years ago, but a well-directed bomb,
falling near the flat I then lived in, interrupted it and I never took it up
again. It would not have been any good, for various reasons, chief among
them being that my memory is bad and that practically nothing of interest
has happened to me in the last 30 years—for I could not write about so
boring an experience as working for the BBC. So nothing will come of that,
and indeed I may be said to have written my autobiography already—as
much of my life, that is, as seemed worth recording—for everything I have
published is rooted in experience. The thing the Cummington Press has
failed to bring out[4] could be regarded as a further instalment, though
transmuted into fiction. I do feel rather sorry that that has flopped, for I
can only assume now that it has. Later on, when I have retired from work,
I shall try to get it printed elsewhere, but I'm afraid that Pretoria would not

---

[1] Eight months later A. found a second-hand copy of *The Prisoners of War*—and posted it off.
Subsequently he remarked to Wickens: 'I have still not got over my astonishment at spotting it, in
one *coup d'oeil*, being in the middle of a vast quantity of other grubby books in the pavement
bookcases of the largest second-hand shop in the Charing Cross Road. The orange colour caught
my eye, and surely it cannot be me, I thought, and pulled it out and it was!'
[2] See Letter 158.
[3] *My Father and Myself.*
[4] *We Think the World of You.*

be a likely place. Paris, perhaps, or Rome, where people like Jean Genet and Henry Miller manage to get into print.

All good wishes

Joe Ackerley

To John Wickens (1934–   )   17 Star & Garter Mansions, Putney, 163
                                  S.W.15   31/7/58

Dear Mr Wickens

it was wonderfully kind of you to go sending me another lot of booze, and I don't pretend not to be pleased to receive it, but also dismayed; it is really too extravagant and can have only one end—you in the bankruptcy courts, I in an inebriates' home! Thank you very much nevertheless. Hedges & Butler did not manage to be quite 'on time', they rang me up to explain your instructions and to say it would be difficult to carry them out and did I mind; and although I did not altogether follow what was meant, for how could I know of this touching anniversary?[1] I *could* not mind, for in fact I was just rushing off on a week's holiday. So the regretful wrecker of your charming plan was not H. & B. but I. However, it made an exciting end to the holiday to find your letter and the bottles waiting. I rambled about Herefordshire and S.E. Wales with an old friend of mine, now the Professor of Psychology at Nottingham,[2] in his car. It is the kind of expedition I enjoy, and since our tastes are much the same, it was great fun. Herefordshire is probably the most beautiful county in England, the Wye valley in particular, quite unspoiled, and a continuous vista of ravishing views; with the *Good Food Guide* in our hands, we stayed in a different hotel every night and visited every church, castle, abbey, motte[3] and country house open-to-the-public that deserved visiting. We went up into the Black Mountains—they are really green—and even visited the coal-mining areas of Merthyr Tidville and the Ebbw Valley; the weather, being English, was partly good and partly bad, but bad weather matters less to the motorist than to the hiker, and I have been both. The country was not altogether new to me, but I had been a hiker on previous visits[4] and there were many little remote churches—Norman or Tudor—which I had never seen and now saw; so it was really quite as exciting as touring France or Italy. Do you ever get away on holiday, and where do you go?

I forget if I told you that I was on the verge of retirement. Another

[1] Wickens told Braybrooke: 'I can't now remember what the "anniversary" was, except that it was an excuse for sending some booze to an author whose writing had given me so much pleasure.'

[2] W. J. H. Sprott.

[3] This is an obsolete spelling of the word 'mote', which means (according to the Oxford English Dictionary): '(1) a mound, hill, especially as the seat of a camp, roman type city, castle, fort . . . or (2) a barrow, tumulus.' A. used it on a number of occasions.

[4] After one such visit, during the Second World War, A. had jotted down the first paragraph for a travel article: 'My Hereford guide book says of Weobley: "Elizabethan England is prescribed in miniature by Weobley. The town is full of old black and white buildings . . . There is no incongruous building to mar the effect." All this, I found, was quite true; even the dog who was sunning itself on a wall of the fourteenth-century Red Lion Hotel was a very clean white terrier with black markings. "Observe," it seemed to be saying as it reclined complacently on the wall, "I, too, strike no discordant note. I am perfectly in period . . ."' The article was never completed and was found in the manuscript of *My Dog Tulip*.

six months or so and I shall be 'at leisure'.[1] I don't get much of that state at present. When I do, I shall really put my mind to getting my *novella*[2] published somewhere or other, perhaps in Paris, and you will be the first on the list for a complimentary copy. If I can't get it published I will get it professionally typed (the present two copies are in my own inexpert typing and much scratched about), as many copies as can be done and will send you one. But I am much too busy and occupied at the moment to give thought to any of these projects.

I am sorry you are so upset by what is happening in S[outh] A[frica] just now and I'm all too sure that it must be gloomy in the extreme, but our own press does not carry much news about it at present and, reading as I do *The Times*, I find it very difficult to make out what is going on. In this country, since the war, an extraordinary change of scene has occurred. Blackamoors everywhere, on the buses, railways, in restaurants, on the streets. Negroes, Indians, Africans, every sort, it is something quite new. So far as I have yet seen they are not allowed to *drive* buses, but they (male and female) conduct them on every line, do it capably and give greater satisfaction and pleasure than the whites. They are very reserved, hard to get to know them, though friendly and good-natured up to the point of intimacy. There is scarcely any voice against them; when one pipes up (see the cuttings enclosed) it meets with little sympathy. How far all this extends beyond London I don't know, for I haven't the experience of provincial cities, but here, at any rate, black labour has secured a strong and sympathetic footing, and in the general view, the colour bar has quite disappeared. What I myself am astounded at is the *competence* of the coloured boys, and girls. They seem to know all the answers—fares, geography, etc— as though they had been conducting London buses all their lives; half the questions that are put to them by ignorant provincial travellers I could not answer myself, but they seem to have learnt everything and have an impressive dignity in all their responses. The whites, in my opinion, like them very much and, I would even go so far as to say, prefer them to the white conductors—they are more polite and considerate. I long to get to know some of them, but there is a kind of reserve, a guardedness, about them . . .
Yours
    Joe Ackerley

164 To Francis King (1923–   )   *The Listener*, Broadcasting House, W.1
                                                                  10/10/58
Dear Francis
                so nice to hear from you and I was pleased to have a story[3] from you to read, though I hadn't read far before a belief crept over me that I'd read it before, though long ago. Could that be possible? I've put it in front of Ashley, but think it won't do. Too gloomy, too long, and, I

---

[1] When it came to it, A. did not retire at the beginning of 1959, but stayed on at the request of Maurice Ashley, the new Editor, until 3 November.
[2] *We Think the World of You.*
[3] 'The Way Out.' King re-wrote and shortened the story on the basis of A.'s criticisms, and included it in his collection *So Hurt and Humiliated* (1959).

think, too long in itself. It is scarcely a developing situation; excepting for the man's illness and the death of the child, and 24 pages seems too many for goading the latter to that. Adrian himself, though elaborately presented, strikes the same note in his first remarks as he does in his last, sub-hysterical, so one gets a bit bored by him in between. I think really it would be 'advantaged' by being cut, and that you would have no difficulty in doing so; I see that there is some point in the drip upon the stone, wearing it away, but he calls his son a girl far too often. So I expect it will home back to Helsinki,[1] dear Francis: meanwhile you must sit down in your delightful happy household and finish for me the one about the alcoholic. I had a few words with an Irishwoman yesterday, which I will give you for your notebook. It was in my local Putney pub, 'The Bull and Star', and I had Queenie my dog with me. This woman (whom I'd not seen before, and turned out to be the char) spoke to Queenie as we were going in to get some lunch.

'What's her name?' she asked. I told her.

'Come Queenie, come' she called. Queenie never speaks to strangers and looked the other way.

I said, 'It's no good. She loves no one but me.'

'Then she's just like me,' said this person. 'I have a husband and two daughters, but I love the lady best.'

'Lady? What lady?' I asked, mystified.

'The Mother of God. I love her best!'

I have no news. It rains *every* day. Hilary Corke, with whom I stayed in Surrey last weekend, has been trying in vain for a month to mow his lawn. This weekend I go to Cambridge.

Love

Joe

To Geoffrey Gorer (1905–   )   Train 165
                                                                 1/11/58

Thanks for your note, dear G.G. Yes, Rose's death did come as a shock.[2] As [Philip] Hope-Wallace said, one did, for some reason, think of her as indestructible: her mummified appearance, perhaps. She died, like Francis Bennett[3] last month, of a coronary thrombosis—woke up at 7.0 with a pain in chest, dead at 8.0. She would have hated a long illness. Best of women, I shall miss her.[4] Am just entering Nottingham station for a weekend with Jack.

Love

J

[1] On a previous occasion A. had written to King: 'Would the Finnish gloom oppress me, I wonder; I am fond of the crepuscular, of mists and fogs; they suit my gloomy-romantic nature.' And on another occasion he had written: 'I hope T[erence] C[ooper]'s visit has cheered you up. Your letter is proof enough how much you are in need of that. Helsinki! A well-deserved name.'

[2] When Forster had heard the news on 30 October, he had written to A.: 'I should like to vanish that way myself...'   [3] See page 94, note 4.

[4] Rose Macaulay was one of A.'s regular reviewers, and in the first decade of *The Listener*'s life, A. often helped the Editor (R. S. Lambert) organise series of articles. One such series in 1938 was called 'I Became an Author'. Rose Macaulay was approached on 17 June, but by return of

166 To Stephen Spender (1909–   )   *The Listener*, Broadcasting House, W.1

26/11/58

Dear Stephen

I adored your party yesterday and thought that you and Natasha and the children managed it all (and what a job it must be) with consummate skill, charm and tact. It is impossible to imagine any other house in which one could be more sweetly and happily entertained. Because you are one of my favourite men it upsets me that you should fall out with Morgan,[1] whom I also love. I think it is perhaps important to say that he does not behave in the somewhat scratchy way in which he does sometimes behave—taking his friends to task—out of any feeling of self-importance, but always on matters of personal, or social, or intellectual relations. He gets upset, and when he is upset he says so. He told me e.g. the other day that it had taken him many years to get over the behaviour of Dame Fanny Farrer to him and his mother over West Hackhurst[2] and that it was only quite lately that he had been able to think or speak of it without agitation. I have been called to order myself a number of times, but I never mind it;[3] indeed I have been glad of it, for I know I don't think enough about other people and I have been glad of help from someone who thinks of nothing else. Morgan puts in his rebuke—it is the rarest thing for anyone to do, in my experience, but surely valuable—he does have an insight, and usually he is right. And of course he is kind. He has a formidable memory, it is true, but he is loyal and just, and when he likes, as I'm sure he likes you, his depressions don't last long. He is a far greater man than T. S. Eliot, and if he came to your house you would never say about him, when you ushered him out, as you said about Eliot 'It was like entertaining royalty.' And you would have had a much more interesting evening, to boot. Don't worry about your scrimmage with him on the Piazza de San Marco.[4] You have done your best to recover the situation, and he cannot be thinking of it still. Since then you have organised [K. W.] Gransden[5] to him and he liked him

post declined the commission because she 'was too busy with other work'. She ended her letter: 'Might I add that the fee of £12. 12s. you propose is, in my case, larger than is necessary. For an article of 1500 words in the other weeklies I should never get more than £5. 0s. 0d. I only mention this in case you are under a misapprehension; some writers, no doubt, get more . . .'

[1] See note 4 below.

[2] A property dispute 'involving [Forster's] eviction from his Surrey home' after his mother's death. See A.'s posthumous obituary article on Forster published under the title of 'Morgan' in the *Observer* on 14 June 1970.

[3] For instance, on 17 June 1938 Forster had been invited by Paul Bloomfield (who was standing in for A. as literary editor) to contribute to the series, 'I Became an Author'. Bloomfield wrote: 'This letter would be being written to you by Ackerley, only as you know he is away on leave; I am doing his work . . .' Three days later Forster replied: 'I'm afraid I don't feel inclined to contribute to the series which you and Ackerley are organising; to my mind, that type of article is better suited to an evening paper than to a literary one.' Cf. page 86, note 4.

[4] Spender (in a letter to K. W. Gransden, dated 17 February 1973,) writes: 'I remember nothing about the Piazza de San Marco. Oh yes, I do. Writing this brings it back to me. Morgan was with Rose Macaulay, just saying goodbye to her, we thought, and we asked Rose to take coffee with us at a café. We could not possibly have meant to take her away from him but he took it as this—and it was quite awful.'

[5] Gransden succeeded A. as literary editor of *The Listener* in November 1959. In 1962 he published a study of *E. M. Forster* in Oliver & Boyd's 'Writers and Critics' series—a volume greatly admired by its subject himself. Spender had arranged that Gransden should write this particular volume.

and did what he could—he is old and often tired—to be helpful. And he knows very well that *I* like you, that I love you indeed. So don't fret about it, go on asking him to do things for you, ask him to your parties or to dinner or lunch, as though nothing had happened, and think of him in a sensitive way, as who can do better than you.

When you have time to get down to my 'purified' booklet,[1] and if you pass it on to someone new to it, remove the letter to you (which gives the old edition away) and the lawyers' letters: it would be better, from a libel point of view, for a fresh mind to approach it without prejudice.
Love, and to darling Natasha
   Joe

To Geoffrey Gorer (1905–)   Putney 167
                                                    7/12/58

Dear G. G.
      I meant to write about this review[2] before but have been too stunned by work and botherations to get down to it. Now I have taken a week's holiday before starting on a Travel Book Number (Jan. 15) and shall sit on my arse (no one else's)in Putney and try to work off a few personal left-overs. Before I left, only a 'rough' of your review had arrived, so I enclose that. I had it set up entire—and am v. grateful to you for doing it— but, unless I have missed something in Jack's book in his references to China —and I have looked at them over again without enlightenment as to your objections—I think it would certainly be offensive to put in your last discrediting paras.—and, indeed, unjust. If you have some specific reason— some point I've missed—for charging him with credulity, I think you should state it specifically, and not just dub him a sap and leave it at that. In fact everything that Jack says is amply substantiated by C. P. Fitzgerald in his new book *Flood Tide in China*[3] which I've just read, and Fitzgerald surely has some claim to serious attention, an intimate personal knowledge of China, both pre- and post-revolution. Jack mentions the various groups of people he came upon 'discussing', and says elsewhere 'one gets the impression that men and women hardly stop attending meetings.' Fitzgerald (who went back to China and journeyed through it 2 years ago with a cultural delegation from Australia) says '. . . the first, the dominant, and the incessant technique of Communist rule (in China) was not violence, but talk; talk, talk, unending talks. "Kai hui", to hold, or attend, a meeting became the duty of every citizen . . . the inescapable obligation to talk and to be talked to . . . not to obey unthinkingly, but to explain themselves, to listen to reasons, to study doctrines . . .' Jack has his story of the office boy (p. 195).[4] Fitzgerald says: ' "We invite your criticism," every organisation in China

---

[1] A revised version of *We Think the World of You*.
[2] Of *Human Groups* by W. J. H. Sprott (1958).
[3] Published in the following year.
[4] 'A case was reported of a meeting in an office. The manager took the chair and said with all humility that he could find nothing to blame in his recent conduct, whereupon an office boy rose up and told him that he had behaved bureaucratically, telling them nothing about what was happening and so on. The manager got a little hot, and admitted his offences . . .'

today unfailingly makes this claim, and expects that it will be met. This book is therefore a response to such an invitation.' And later: 'No adverse views, no doubts, no contrary opinions can be published; criticism of "Why?" is not possible; of *how* the work is being done, it is welcomed and publicized. Criticism is another essential part of the system. Public opinion, silent on the great issues which are not contested in the national Press, may be voiced on the methods employed, through the innumerable meetings and study groups which every citizen attends, and also aired in the correspondence columns of the newspapers . . . Execution of the policy is open to the criticism of any citizen of goodwill who makes his point at a meeting or by a letter.' Everything that Jack says (p. 127) about group participation[1]—it is indeed the whole and only point of his reference to China—is amply substantiated in Fitzgerald on almost every page: e.g. 'There are in fact good reasons for accepting the ideas and exhortations which the regime unremittingly puts forward. The campaign to clear up the filth of cities and villages, to enforce hygiene, to eliminate flies and rats, carried out with a vast apparatus of publicity, met with a whole-hearted response. China is now a clean country, by any standards. Many virulent diseases have been stamped out . . . everyone knows that so striking a change could only have been accomplished by the co-operation of millions, and that this was won by persuasion, publicity and constant exhortation.' And that, in fact, is Jack's whole thesis that 'when people feel they are participating they are more prepared to put themselves out than is the case when they feel they are simply being ordered about by "them"'—and that output and efficiency are likely to improve. He does not say that he *likes* the system, nor does Fitzgerald ('Prostitution, free love, adultery, unnatural vice, these are no longer merely sins, they are crimes, punishable with terms of imprisonment') —it must indeed be ghastly—he only says that if people in the national group have some sense of participation in a great enterprise greater efficiency may result—and that might be said to be proven. If you could organise the citizens of Haywards Heath into a nice Chinese group, my dear boy, you might get rid of those sparrows you so deeply detest: that really is the point of Jack's argument.

You know, instead of discrediting Jack, as he was discredited years ago when he returned from China—one of the first delegations to get in under the new dispensation—by being disallowed by J. Norris to broadcast about the Chinese prison he had seen, he deserves considerable praise for having been perfectly right about the Communist system in China all along. What he saw and believed was *not* shop-window dressing, it was all perfectly and appallingly true, it fits convincingly into the overall picture Fitzgerald paints: 'Repentance and remorse; sincere conversion, redemption through

[1] '. . . If it be true that when people feel they are participating they are more prepared to put themselves out than is the case when they feel they are simply being ordered about by "them", then if there are no oppositional issues to arouse interest, something else must be found. One of the "something elses" is, of course, the arousal of propaganda and by the devices we have been discussing to produce strong unified public opinion. To put the best face on it we may say that in so far as it works it gives people some sense of participating in a great enterprise, it may provide a certain sense of security by the virtual abolition of choice, it is certainly likely to improve output and efficiency. Dur prejudices against Communist countries ought not to blind us to these advantages . . .'

work for the People; even Chiang Kai Shek himself, so one was assured, could return to China in peace, and perhaps to some office, if he really manifested these signs of grace.' It was that same old Norris who urged me to read Fitzgerald and get it reviewed;[1] an excellent book, said he. You should read it yourself—if you don't feel you've done so already! Indeed, I'm most awfully sorry to have put so much of it on to you so boringly; naturally Jack could never resent criticism, nor would I ever attempt to muzzle it, but I hope you may agree that in this instance you have not been just in calling him gullible and irresponsible—for that is what your last par. amounts to.[2] You might say that Fitzgerald was gullible too, and so on, and so on, that attitude of mind becomes prejudice at last; he himself alludes to it in describing the impression made upon him in meeting again some of his academic and intellectual friends known under the old regime; had they all been subjected to ghastly brain-washings and had their spirits broken, or were they all consummate actors, which he'd never suspected before? He had only the evidence of his senses, he says, and 'on the basis of this evidence it must be said that tokens of broken spirits, abject submission, fear and anxiety were not encountered.'

I never mentioned Edith's poem. What could it have been? She has already sent me one—which one felt one had read before, it seemed so very like so many of her others—and I've taken it.[3] But I'm delighted if I'm to get *two*.[4]

Love

J

To Brian Hill (1896–   )   *The Listener*, Broadcasting House, W.1 168*

23/12/58

Thank you very much indeed for your personal and inscribed copy of *Eight Poems*.[5] I am most pleased and proud to possess it.

J. R. Ackerley

To William Roerick (1912–   ) and Thomas Coley (1913–   )   Putney 169

25/1/59

Dear Bill, dear Tom

I knew you weren't well, either of you, but you fought your germs so valiantly that you concealed the *persistent* fact and seemed generally to have the upper hand. What a wretched thing for you both—and that it continues; wretcheder for you than for us who were only occasionally

---

[1] When A. wrote this letter, he had already sent the book to W. J. H. Sprott, who reviewed it on 19 February 1959.

[2] These references were 'cut' by Gorer in his revised review, which appeared on 25 December 1958. In the last paragraph, he wrote: 'Probably no specialist would altogether agree with Professor Sprott's preferences and emphases.'

[3] 'La Bella Bona Rosa', which appeared on 1 January 1959.

[4] The second was 'The Yellow Girl', which appeared on 29 January 1959.

[5] This was a privately printed volume. During the past decade, A. had published a number of Hill's translations of Rimbaud, Verlaine, Gautier and Gérard de Nerval.

frustrated of the company we so seldom have, so deeply love. I knew I should not have come back with you to your hotel after that play—it was clear then that you were both pretty well dished—and I was sorry afterwards that I had allowed your sweetness to cajole me; if you had both had a long good night then at the beginning—that extra hour I took away—it might have made a difference to your thereafter. But as you yourselves so constantly showed, there are stronger influences than the ills of the flesh—even when those ills are someone else's. But how maddening one's body can be, trying to wreck one's pleasure and happiness at their most precious moments; and though you did not allow that, it is a sorry thought that you scarcely even felt, all that time, quite up to the mark. Poor dear Edith [Oliver][1] caved in too towards the end, though she also preserved her fighting spirit; her visit to Coventry[2] to see Morgan for his 8oth birthday celebrations, did her in; in all her life, she said, she had never been so cold for so long, and when I took her to my club for lunch on her return she was running a temperature, I think. I felt really concerned about her and advised her to give the project up; but she has, like you, a triumphant spirit, and come she would. She flew off the following day, I don't know in what shape. Bill [Reed] too (he was with us that day) was under the weather (*how* it gets blamed for everything!). I haven't seen him since. He rang to offer me a spare seat for *My Fair Lady*, but for that very evening, and I already had an engagement. Whether he's gone off yet to Greece I don't know. I liked him very much—that slow, caressing voice—and did notice that whatever I said seemed to amuse him, so that I got to feel I had an entertainment value far greater than I supposed.

Reaction has set in since you all left—the doldrums I think they're called —languor and silence: no one writes to anyone any more (excepting transatlantic sighs like this), no effort is made by anyone to see anyone else. The picture is of everyone slumped dully in their chairs, in London, in Cambridge, in Coventry—well, I can't speak for the last. I had in Norfolk much the sort of weekend poor Edith had with the Maybobs, the most piercing cold, but, tougher than she, took no harm from it. The cats (Jack's sister has five) had sharpened their claws upon two out of the four hot-water bottles available, and I had forgotten to pack my own, so I pretended I never used such things. But oh the cold! They have central heating, but of the most central kind which, like poor Aunt Bunny's heart, is unable to force its warmth to the extremities; the sitting-room, fortified with a fire, was comfortable, the bedrooms bitter, I longed for a hot-water bottle, or even a cat, and lacking both, solved the hideous problem by stripping off the icy sheets and sleeping between blankets. Edith should have thought of that in Coventry.

Nancy rang up on the Saturday night to say that Queenie had been taken ill, so I returned to Putney next day, the day you flew, instead of going on with Jack to Nottingham for Sunday night. She had had a stroke, my sweet creature—not the sort of stroke usually associated with dogs, but

---

[1] 'Off Broadway' reviewer for the *New Yorker*.
[2] Forster was in Coventry, staying with the Buckinghams.

a cerebral hemorrhage (so diagnosed the vet when I had her examined next day, though I myself—it was plain enough—had guessed it already). She could hardly walk for two days—no sense of balance or co-ordination of movement, semi-paralysis of the hinders; she kept bumping into the furniture and, when she tried to shake herself, fell over completely. Her face looked so odd too, her eyes unfocusing and a constant twitch in one eyebrow. She has got over it now, no visible after-effects, and the vet says there is no reason to expect a recurrence. But she is not to chase rabbits any more; her blood pressure is too high. While with him, I asked him to examine her eyes, in which the loving light has been getting less bright, and he said 'Yes, the retina of both has atrophied.' He called them 'clinically most interesting.' How can people speak against dogs? This charming creature has held my household amiably together for twelve years, with her intelligence, her gaiety, and the concentration of her affectionate thought. A sheepdog she, and we have been her human flock. Her work has been well done. Vanish she must, in time, but we shall not fall apart now.

I have just finished reading *Lolita*—after signing a letter to *The Times*[1] to pave the way for its publication here. I did enjoy it very much—a clever, amusing and painful book,[2] I thought, though the sails, it seemed to me, were sometimes really too slyly rigged. Legerdemain. But, to vary the metaphor, the tightrope the author walked was certainly perilous and one could hardly blame him for using a carefully loaded pole. However, too many efforts were made, I thought, to calm and silence the apoplectic reader, and when Humbert-Humbert in the end turns out not to be a nymphet-maniac after all but a comparatively respectable and dependable husband, desiring only a Darby-and-Joan end with his dear Lolita, I felt that he had forfeited both character and interest, and that Nabokov had really gone too far in his anxiety to sweeten the pill.

Will you thank dearest Tom for his letters. Oh dear, to think that it is all over, that you have been and gone, the flags all taken down and put back with the moth balls.

Well, get well and let us write.

Joe

To Roy Fuller (1912–)   17 Star & Garter Mansions, Putney   170
                                          ?/3/59

Roy dear

    I meant to write you earlier about your *Ruined Boys*,[3] but have been struck down by this 1959 flu a week ago, and shake it off I do not. I thought the book had everything (except, perhaps, drama, in a sense of suspense to which it lays no claim as it meanders along) and must be the best book

---

[1] The letter had appeared two days previously on 23 January. The other signatories were Walter Allen, A. Alvarez, Isaiah Berlin, C. M. Bowra, Storm Jameson, Frank Kermode, Allen Lane, Margaret Lane, Rosamond Lehmann, Compton Mackenzie, Iris Murdoch, William Plomer, V. S. Pritchett, Alan Pryce-Jones, Peter Quennell, Herbert Read, Stephen Spender, Philip Toynbee, Bernard Wall and Angus Wilson.

[2] In a note written to Roy Fuller on the same day, A. described the novel as 'a moral tale'.

[3] Fuller's recent novel.

you have done. You always have something serious to say about life, as well as your poet's eye, your delightful sense of humour, and that direct and uncompromising critical vision of yours, and here everything comes in, as well as your sympathetic understanding of the human species. I thought it a remarkable feat of imagination, memory, both so firm and yet so light, so terribly real and convincing—the boys, the masters, everyone—the ghastly school, and that extraordinary overshadowing central figure, for whom (it is part of your delicacy) one could not help feeling a certain reluctant respect. It's a very funny book; at times a very touching one: the relationships, pleasant and beastly, are all of interest, and since everyone has a personality and significance of some sort, we are never bored to meet anyone again. One tiny note of deprecation I will sound: I think you go in slightly too much for what I can only think of calling a kind of Proustian simile. Often apt, telling, or amusing, one begins to notice it as your book proceeds.

This damn flu. First I treated myself with Disprin (our doctor's advice), then his partner (to whom I usually go) said . . . Anadin was the thing, but that since the enemy had now got a hold on me (they had had 48 hours to entrench and consolidate their position) I should have a really powerful drug to dislodge them. So during the last week I have eaten 20 capsules of Acromycin (if I spell it correctly), and in the ensuing struggle for the mastery of this fleshly castle, the enemy invaders have certainly been routed, but my poor temperature, which, after all, was mine and for which I had a kind of affection, has been so buffeted about and demoralised, that it has now sunk with a pitiable stricken look upon its sad quicksilver face, into so remote a sub-normal region that I really doubt if it will ever be able to rise again. Perhaps even worse I have almost totally lost my voice. Loss of voice (laryngitis) is said to be a feature of the 1959 flu—and a most welcome one; anything that can stop the human race shooting off its mouth, if only for a few days, would be of inestimable value. But personally I have some doubt about the connection between my loss of voice and flu. However, we shall see, and meanwhile I have been away from work for 10 days and shall not be back till Monday, if then.

Love

J

171 To Geoffrey Gorer (1905–)   *The Listener*, Broadcasting House, W.1

6/3/59

Dear G. G.

it seems that you have been paid twice for the same review *I was a Savage*,[1] once £5-10-0 on Oct. 30 in advance of publication; again £5-5-0 on Jan. 29.[2] Doubtless you did not notice this among all the cheques that must flow into Sunte House[3] day by day—or you may have thought it a

[1] By Prince Modupe.
[2] The day on which the review appeared.
[3] Gorer's home in Haywards Heath.

present for a good little boy. However, it was caused by illness in the office and a temporary sec. working for the editor (this possibly also accounts for the 5/- discrepancy: she couldn't count.)

Well, the editor thinks justice should be done; which is not that you should keep both sums but that the second should be subtracted from your latest review.

Your loving
  Shylock

To the Editor of *The Times*[1]   17 Star and Garter Mansions,   172
                                          Putney, S.W.15
                                           Mar. 13, 1959.

Sir,
  So, as one feared directly this mischievous correspondence began, the unfortunate bear is to suffer wholesale persecution and death in order to satisfy, for a little longer, a perfectly dispensable human want.

Yours, &c.,
  J. R. Ackerley

To Sir Herbert Read (1893–1968)   as from B.B.C.   173
                                                 2/4/59

Dear Herbert
  I don't think I told you that I have had my final notice to quit from the B.B.C. I am to go on Nov. 3, [the eve of] my 63rd birthday: that was a 3-year extension from the official retiring age, 60. My pension will be inadequate, so I shall have to look about for something else, and since you once put me in the way of a useful job, with the late Robert Donat, I hoped you would again keep me in mind in case anything else came to your ears. I expect it would have to do with literature, I don't know much about anything else: I might be of use to a publisher or to some other journal. Everyone says 'You must write', but (i) how can you write when you have nothing to say? and (ii) I made £200 out of *My Dog Tulip*, and the publishers are talking now of remaindering the 2000 surplus from the 5000 printed. I want something more rewarding than that.

  If I don't get work I am thinking of taking a trip to Japan. James Kirkup is in Sendai, Francis King in Kyoto, and both invite me. Jim says I could lecture the Japs and get some organisation—B[ritish] C[ouncil]—to pay my journey, and though I've never lectured, I suppose I could, though it

---

1 The letter appeared under the heading 'Bedraggled Bearskins'. On 4 March a correspondent had written in to deplore the bedraggled condition of bearskins worn by the Brigade of Guards. Two days later another thought that the cause might be that the willow-frames had been sat on and bent out of position. Why not substitute something less ugly and expensive, suggested a third. A woman reader then joined in and asked if bearskin could not be made out 'of nylon like our modern teddy bears?' The last comment in the correspondence came from A. After reading A.'s letter in *The Times*, Forster wrote to him on the same day: '. . . what a detestable planet this one is becoming . . .'

would be on some dotty subject like dogs or The Rights of Beasts.[1] But he may be talking through his hat. At any rate, I see I shall have to have some alternative to squatting in my flat all day with an aged dog, an aged aunt, and a sister.

I've just had that novelette of mine[2] you once read (improved since then) returned by The Olympia Press, Paris. Not nearly dirty enough, says M[aurice] Girodias (who writes a very intelligent letter), and far too English.[3]

Let us meet soon, dear Herbert.

Love

   Joe

174 To William Roerick (1912–)   17 Star & Garter Mansions, Putney,
                                             S.W.15   27/6/59

Dearest Bill

          your letter arrives in the middle of a thunderstorm, for we too have been having that rare English thing, warm sunshine, a beautiful June, and though I am sure I am not as brown as you I am browner than I was. The air needed cooling as our earth needed rain, I love storms and this is a good one.

But although the sun has shone I have had a bad June. I was all set to go off to Italy a month ago—plane reservation, foreign currency, bag half-packed—when Queenie developed a septic womb for the third time. I felt I should postpone my holiday, and a good thing I did, the antibiotics that had worked before worked no longer, she blew up and had to have an emergency hysterectomy. Sweet creature, how terrible to lose her womb. And, ill luck, my own excellent veterinary surgeon was away abroad on some conference; I had to take whatever I could get in 12 hours, an unknown man. A dingy little surgery, in Ealing, a grubby little kennel maid who took Queenie from me as though she were a parcel; I never saw the surgeon until afterwards. Of course she was old, 14, to have such a shocking thing done to her; even so I fear the job was ill-performed. He left infection in the stump of the womb and we have not got rid of it yet. She had become habituated to penicillin, it lost its power to cope; for over a fortnight she has

---

[1] See page 214, note 3.

[2] *We Think the World of You.*

[3] Two months later on 2 June A. wrote to John Wickens: 'The Olympia Press rejected my novelette in its unexpurgated form as far too mild and tame for their public, and Secker & Warburg have rejected it in its purified form as embarrassingly sentimental. Hamish Hamilton is now considering it, but I expect nothing from that quarter. In fact I have come to the conclusion that it is an unsaleable book in any form.' A. was partly right in his surmise. For on the same day as he was writing to Wickens, Hamish Hamilton was writing to A. to reject the novel: 'Three of us have read WE THINK THE WORLD OF YOU and I'm sorry to say that we've reluctantly decided against it.' He then went on to quote from one of the reports: '. . . [The narrator's] pathos too soon turns to futility and one finds oneself sympathising first with Johnny's relations for being bored by him and then with the unfortunate dog for being put on such a pedestal . . .' A. marked this passage in the letter and wrote beside it in the margin: '. . . And why is Evie "unfortunate"? She (with Megan and Margaret) is the most formidable character in the book and gets her way in the end. She is Eve, the prototype, Shaw's tigress . . . This duffer has missed . . . [the] point.'

been on terramycin—the last antibiotic resort—one tablet every six hours punctually (at 2/6 a tablet!)—and last weekend it seemed that that would not cope either and that she would have to be reopened and the seat of infection cut away. But now it looks as though her temperature, which has been rocketting about in the most upsetting way, is stabilising itself towards normal at last. And her appetite is returning. That was another misery, to get her, when she was fit for solids, to eat, for she was already in a toxic condition when the operation was performed and woefully thin. Every delicacy —rows of plates containing chicken, fish, veal sweetbreads, rabbit—was put down daily to tempt her, she would turn away from them all. I have already spent upon her most of my holiday money, the poor old creature, but I shall go off nevertheless next month to Italy, bankrupt though I may be, if I feel I can safely leave her. It is so lovely to see her whom I carried in my arms, near death the surgeon thought, back to my flat a month ago, picking up at last, barking at the neighbours as was her wont, and the hair growing again on her shaven side. During this period I have seen more films than I normally see in a year, for if you have to administer pills to a sick animal punctually every six hours, how do you space them out to get a reasonable amount of rest yourself? I chose 6.0 a.m., midday, 6 p.m., midnight. But how does one keep awake until midnight, on insufficient sleep the night before and (despondency) more gin and wine than is good for you? The cinema has been a great blessing, I have seen a lot of interesting films and have passed away unwanted time most agreeably.

How nice to think of you and dear Gerald [Heard] meeting and talking about me. If he reappears give him from me love which was ever fond and remaineth that still and tell him (it may interest him to hear the same again) that if I do get to Italy at last, I go to stay with Lionel Fielden in Pisa. Morgan, May and Bob are touring that country in a car—back this weekend; there was some prospect of my joining up with them at some point, but Queenie put a decisive end to all that. No more now, dear Bill. I enclose a *Listener* review[1] I wrote lately of a murder trial in case it should please you. Morgan thought well of it.[2]

Love

   Joe

[1] Of *The Trial of August Sangret*, edited by Macdonald Critchley, which appeared on 28 May. Sangret, a French-Canadian of Indian blood, was tried for the murder of his girl, a camp-follower. Both were Catholics—and their friendship lasted two months. She slept in shacks he constructed for her out of leaves, branches and his army rain-cape. He would slip out of barracks after roll-call and bring her provisions. Once they spent several nights in a derelict cricket pavilion. Then one day she fainted in the street, was pretty sure she was going to have 'a wee one', and was taken to hospital. A.'s detailed examination of the trial (and some of his other reviews such as *The Murder of Lord Errol* by Rupert Furneaux which appeared in *The Listener* on 22 June 1961) show what a formidable counsel he could have been. At Cambridge, in fact, A. had for a short time taken up the study of Law with a notion of becoming a barrister: 'I was interested in the criminal side of it.' The review also shows his talent for recognising the poetry in the prose of everyday statement— and singling it out. Here is a passage he quoted from the girl: '. . . they [the nurses] were horrified when they heard how we had been living, just as if that makes any difference. Gosh, I was never ill when you looked after me, I was happy anyway. I will never regret what we have done, we have had some good laughs, and tears too. (Oh! burning wood, the loveliest smell in the world) . . . I am so used to talking to you, and then listening to you groaning to yourself because I would not sleep. When I turned over I missed you putting your arms round me, I never thought it would be so lonely . . .'

[2] So did Roy Fuller, who also wrote to A. to congratulate him on it.

175 To Francis King (1923–   )   17 Star & Garter Mansions, Putney, S.W. 15
20/8/59

Dear Francis

did you write last, or did I? At any rate it seems moons since I had news of you. I have just returned from a 3-week holiday in Italy to an unimpeded view of the end of my *Listener* chapter: I shall be out in the first week of November. As you probably know, Ken Gransden[1] steps into my shoes. I am looking about for other work—writing to publishers—but before I engage myself in anything else (which I do hope I shall manage to do), I am wondering whether I could not pay a visit to you, and to Jim, for two or three months. But how are you, dear Francis, are you liking Kyoto any better, are you going to stick it? I have written to Jim by the same post, same sort of questions. Though he has been enthusiastic up to date, that may have cooled: you may both be hurriedly packing your bags at the moment to return to dear old England. But if you are not, and if you would welcome me, give me a tip or two. How to come, cheaply—and *when*? From November 4th onwards I shall be free—but are these seasons to be avoided? To be recommended? I have no need to rush, but could rush if our winter with you is a favourable time. Jim, in one of his last letters, thinks I could persuade some official body to invite me to lecture—and therefore, of course, that I should prepare a lecture. This I would be perfectly willing to attempt, though I have never lectured anyone but myself in my life and do not seem to have a subject—except animals, homosexuality, and (I suppose) the trials of a Literary Editor. I have not much confidence in being original, interesting, entertaining, stimulating, or anything else. But I am old enough to try. Otherwise I would make shift to come out at my own expense. I would really like to come, if fingers beckon.

Here we are having an extraordinary summer, weeks, months, of perfect weather. *You* have not come off so well, I seem to remember: typhoons, inundations? I do hope you are not hating every minute of it.

My own life goes on (how life *does* go on) much as usual. The advances in medicine, are they not of very dubious benefit? My aged aunt (91 next week) who has long out-lived her pleasures is 'feeling the heat': my sister has a questionable lung, momentarily alarming to the doctors (X-Ray photos, loss of weight), but it is all in process of being cured: Queenie, (ah, there I suffer) has had her womb out, an emergency operation four months ago, aged 14, but after weeks of anxiety has made a spectacular recovery and has taken on a new lease of life. So my poor pension must still contrive to meet all these expenses. Where, and in what order, among the four of us ageing creatures, will death, so long staved off, eventually place his darts? But I am more cheerful at the moment, and look to hear from you.
Much love
Joe

[1] See page 142, note 5.

To Sonia Brownell Orwell   *The Listener*, Broadcasting House, W.1   176

Dear Sonia   ?/10/59

      I think of you often, though you are not to know that and it is high time you did. For instance, I have been along to that pet shop in Fulham Broadway and goldfish cost 1/- if they are small, 10/6 if they are large (mortality must surely be extremely high, poor dears, or rate of growth abnormally slow). The manager claimed that these figures were a quarter of those charged by Harrods. Of that you may know and it may be a case of all is not gold that glitters! However, this is to think more of Michael[1] than of you, so another instance: it is, or was, possible that my long, long chapter on the above magazine should close with a cocktail party at the end of this month, and we got so far as to draft a list of guests on which you and Michael figured among all my other dear friends. But the party may not now take place, for I behaved in an ungentlemanly manner over it—though the Corporation behaved worse. Having assembled my list of guests I learnt that the authorities had been most reluctant to grant me a cocktail party—a *tea* party would do, said they—and that my Editor had had the greatest difficulty in pushing it through. This vexed me, and I announced that considering how meanly they were treating me all round I would sooner have the price of the gin than the gin. So there may be no party after all, I never wanted one anyway and now want one less,[2] for I am in what's called a 'temper'.

      Dear Sonia, this is by the bye and of no consequence; I have wanted to write to you through all the fidget and fuss of clearing up and clearing out and settling another in; I can hardly wait for the day of my release. Yet the curious thing is that this strange, silent, beautiful and changeless weather seems to hold all the happiness of my summer preserved and enclosed, as under a glass; I think of Tollard Royal as though it were yesterday.[3] However, darkness is now upon us with the turned-back clock, and already the urchins of this district are exploding their November squibs. Fortunately my dear old Queenie cannot hear them, even when they go bang right under my window, for she is infinitely deafer than her master. Once upon a time they terrified her[4] and she had to conceal herself in the W.C. I have seen Stephen Spender for a moment, walking with Sidney Nolan—we were all converging upon the Keith Vaughan gouaches at the Leicester Galleries; and Morgan Forster says that though he can and does think of 'goodness' he cannot think of 'wickedness,' though doubtless it exists; you may remember we discussed it over the corn-cobs and the chicken.

      Well, I hope you and Michael are in the pink, dear Sonia, and Larmer[5] too, though that is hardly a suitable colour for him. I love to think of your lives as moving forwards with the smoothness and tranquillity of the swans that are now gliding beneath my window. I myself cannot hope to be in anything but a dither for another month.

Yours affectionately

   Joe

[1] M. A. Pitt-Rivers, her second husband, from whom she was divorced in 1965.
[2] But the party which A. hoped would be 'off' took place on 29 October. See Letter 177.
[3] A reference to A.'s earlier stay in the Wiltshire home of M. A. Pitt-Rivers at Tollard Royal.
[4] See Letter 114.   [5] M. A. Pitt-Rivers' labrador.

177 To Sonia Brownell Orwell   17 Star & Garter Mansions, Putney, S.W.15
?/10/59

Dear Sonia

so pleased to hear from you. I'm glad you like getting letters yourselves, for I'm afraid your rural peace is to be disturbed by one from my Editor soon: that wretched party of mine, which I thought and hoped to be 'off', is to take place after all it seems. For heaven's sake don't come—I mean no *exertion*—it will be of a *dullness*; though if it so happens that either or both of you are to be up in *any* case, then do drop in for a drink, it would be lovely to see you.[1] Although the ostensible point of it is to give me a send-off—from a paper on which I have rested too long and for which I have never had any great regard—it has (for me) a more stomachable purpose, which is to introduce my successor to my contributors. Ken Gransden[2] is a nice young fellow.

I too was in London on Election night,[3] with Geoffrey Gorer. We traipsed about a bit, not for long. It was a great disaster,[4] but one which, without being a politician, I expected, and could see no grounds for hope the other way. For that reason I did not sacrifice the life of my aged aunt by forcing her to the polls. It would have been the death of her for sure. Hitherto she has been a staunch Conservative, but this time she fell quite in love with the face of Mr [Dick] Taverne (Labour), and I could have persuaded her to vote for him, and killed her in the process, if it had seemed worth while.

Heigh-ho, how bored I am. I cannot fix my feeble mind upon anything at present, and have nothing in my head but a cold, caught I know not how or where. The Bodley Head says it will publish my novelette[5]—Queenie's childhood and adolescent days—if I suppress the name of her breed and shift her early residential area from Walthamstow to Hackney, no great distance.[6] I ought to go to Hackney (unknown territory) and inspect Victoria Park and see if it will fit my topographical 'fictional' necessities—but I seem unable to fix my thoughts on anything. Also I have been chastened and warned by reading William Golding's *Free Fall*. There's squalor for you, with the pants down and another unmentionable object constantly up . . .; the kind of book about which true friends say 'I shouldn't publish it if I were you.' That has been said to me too (Leonard Woolf et cet.),[7] and I confess now to being a little shaken, Mr Golding (unreadable) has shot me in the eye.[8]

---

[1] Two days after the party was over, A. wrote: 'I thought afterwards that it was uncivil of me not to have included Larmer in my invitation . . . I could then have taken Queenie along too, and it would have been a wag-tail as well as a cocktail party.'

[2] See page 142, note 5.   [3] October 8.

[4] There had been a Conservative victory, with a majority of 85. A. had always been a supporter of the Labour Party. 'I am a bolshevist,' he declared in *Hindoo Holiday*.

[5] *We Think the World of You*.

[6] The suggestion came from Brian Glanville—then literary adviser to The Bodley Head.

[7] Woolf had read *We Think the World of You* for Chatto & Windus and turned it down on grounds of being 'criminally libellous'. He had further personally advised A. against publication on grounds that the novel suffered from 'sexual naïvety'.

[8] In a later undated letter to Sonia Orwell, A. returns again to Golding: 'I wonder if you have looked, since your first reading, into *Lord of the Flies*. What it had, and what has diminished since, and what I thought supremely lacking in *Free Fall*, was poetry: it has passages in it—the arrival of the parachuted monster into Eden, the tide carrying away the dead boy's body—I have read them over and over again, his total strength and feeling went into all these, they are of a beauty he has never surpassed and now does not reach at all. I hope he may again . . .'

Yes, dear Sonia, and thank you, I long to come to K[ing] J[ohn]'s house[1] again, and *shall* come, make no doubt of it, but I think I must force myself to Hackney first when I have leisure and (more difficult) guts, and clear up some other oddments that need and never get attention. Have you a decisive mind? I think perhaps Michael has; I wish I had; I have a vacillating mind veering with any wind that blows, it is quite exhausting. I simply can't make up my mind about anything. I remember my Maharajah in India said the same thing: '*How* does one make a decision? *How* does one make up one's mind?' A sad cry, and my own.

Well, my love to you both and to Larmer. I am sorry he is getting stiff in his joints, I think he is too young for that. Medical science is advancing as fast for dogs as it is for us; soon, I believe, dogs (whatever breed they may be) will have a far longer expectation of life than they had in the dark ages—which are within living memory: some 70 years ago, dogs and cats were never vetted at all, only horses, cows and sheep. Since then the search-light has been turned upon our pets, the old scene has changed and continues to change. I see no reason why, in future, dog-longevity should not be as good as, or better than, present cats', 20–30 years, and the cats' longevity increasing also:[2] the scientific interest in these creatures is quite new, it has made differences and could make greater ones. If you ever want a good professional opinion on Larmer, you could not do better, I believe, than go to Mr Singleton, Woodrow & Singleton, in Pont St. I think he is the cleverest vet in the world (always excepting Gordon Knight) and a lovely man to boot. Young, serious, thoughtful, attentive, and clever—no silly jokes: that's what I like. I have a very high regard for him—and indeed, to my delight, the B.B.C. got onto him somehow—he must have been recommended—and made him do a talk recently (Network Three) on animal surgery. If Larmer is ever a cause for anxiety, drive him up to Brian Singleton. I'm sure you would never regret it.

Love to all three of you

Joe

To Marjorie Redman[3] (1907–)   *The Listener*, Broadcasting House, W.1   178
28/10/59

Marjorie dear

I am awfully grieved to hear that you will not be at my

[1] At Tollard Royal. See page 153, note 3.

[2] The longevity figures for cats quoted by A. are not the exaggerations which they may seem at first sight. In the previous year, a female tabby had hit the headlines when she died at the age of 34. But A.'s hopes for 'dog-longevity' have not yet been realised. The greatest age so far recorded for a dog is 27¼—a record held by a black labrador (which died in 1963) owned by a Lincolnshire gamekeeper on the Revesby Estate.

[3] In 1930 she joined *The Listener* as secretary to the Editor. Two years later she transferred to the editorial staff and became chief sub-editor. She was the only member of the paper who was there during all A.'s twenty-four years on it. She has two particular memories of him: 'When he had lately come to the office [in 1935], I remember him sitting on my desk and removing all the petals from a vase of roses to pin all over his tie. And I remember him in the war, wearing an extraordinary little beret and going out at lunch-time to buy horse-meat for his dog. He carried it in a haversack, in which he also carried poems which he took home to read: I have often had to send blood-stained poems to the printers, and used to wonder if he returned rejected ones to authors in a like state.' A. began a note to Richard Murphy in 1954: 'I'm sorry the poem has got a little gory: horse meat, not circumcision . . .'

[*Listener* farewell] party tomorrow—worse, that I shan't see you at all before I take myself off. I went into your room to give you this—the last ex libris I ever shall give you—and Elizabeth [Arnold] told me the upsetting news:[1] upsetting for both of us, I am sure, for that which depresses us both is a personal misfortune for you, I understand. I really am awfully sad and depressed that you won't be with me tomorrow, not that I look forward to the party in the least, for how can one look forward to a funeral party? and that, after all, is its category—'a melancholy occasion,' as Maurice Cranston termed it; so I dislike the idea of it intensely, the more so because I have a personal distaste for the limelight, even in the role of a corpse, and I did indeed tell Maurice Ashley that I hated the idea and would far sooner have a quiet matey drink, at Henekys or somewhere, with my departmental friends; but he forced me into it—he said it would be useful to Ken [Gransden] to meet my friends and contributors—and I saw there was something in that—not much—for he would have met them all in other ways, and indeed I myself have never met a great many of them. But you and I, dear Marjorie, are the oldest pillars of the magazine, and I shall miss your support tomorrow. However, you will not be absent from my heart and I will trot in one of these days to say to you the affectionate parting words that at present remain unspoken. I do hope your troubles will get satisfactorily mended.

Yours ever

Joe

---

[1] Marjorie Redman's sister was to have an operation shortly. See Letter 179.

Part Six
RETIREMENT

To Marjorie Redman (1907–   )   Putney 179
                                                        6/11/59

Dear Marjorie
            it was very nice to hear from you again and I'm only late in
answering because a number of other letters came to express regret at my
demise[1] and I had to make suitable responses. It must be added too that I
haven't been quite so dead as I make out, for I have since been to two other
parties running, one for the Guinness Poetry Prize Award at Londonderry
House, and one to meet M. 'Lolita' Nabokov at the Ritz.

I'm sorry about your own news, dear Marjorie, and hope that the operation on your sister has been satisfactorily performed. Medical science is
wonderfully good now and the anxieties we all used to suffer from are largely
removed. So I do hope your news is good and that, it all being now over, the
remainder of your very distressing holiday will have been happier and
brightened by rejoicing.

Our party was very pleasant after all— or so I am told. It is always difficult for the host to enjoy himself or to have much of a view, he is too much
on the go. I hardly had any conversation with anyone, some new-comer was
sure to pluck my sleeve the moment I started, and then, of course, I got
tiddly, as one always does. I did my best to think of everyone and to get
Roger [Cary][2] and Ken [Gransden][3] to think of them too, so that lonely old
people didn't stand about with no one to talk to, but actually, as I say, I have
no notion of how it went—only that people have said they enjoyed it. Our
star guests did not come—Edith Sitwell and K[enneth] Clark—sudden
colds were alleged—and Leslie Hartley[4] turned up the following evening,
having mistaken the day. But lots of nice people came, including Arthur
Waley (no word with him either, just 'Hullo'), and there was plenty of
booze, and some floral decorations left over from an official luncheon the
day before. I did miss you when I had time to miss anything—the girls lifted
their glasses to me and you were not among them—but when I come into the
office one day, perhaps you will come along to Henekys and have a drink
with me.

[1] i.e. A.'s departure from *The Listener*.
[2] Deputy Editor.
[3] New literary editor who had taken over in November.
[4] L. P. Hartley (1895–1973).

How am I? I don't know. Depressed really and in a muddle. But that is less important than how are you, and yours.

Joe

180　To William Plomer (1903–1973)　　17 Star & Garter Mansions, Putney,
　　　　　　　　　　　　　　　　　　S.W.15　　　　　　　　6/11/59
D.L.B.

　　　you are the sweetest of all. Your charming thought of me touched me deeply and made me feel quite weepy; only you could have thought of such a thing, my darling William. The treasure I have gained in life, and all that makes it worth living, is a love of you, Morgan, and Jack—and my dog's love.

　　I find it difficult to advise you about the Poetry Panel.[1] The reward was not insubstantial when I did it, 50 guineas; I found it rather a chore, at any rate at first. I found it rather a chore simply because I find poetry difficult to comprehend; all my life I have never read it, excepting the weekly submissions to *The Listener*; away from my office desk I have seldom picked up a volume of verse to read for pleasure (unless books by my friends) and have *never* had to review poetry. Therefore, although I managed to read, digest, and judge the occasional short poem received for *The Listener*, I found the Collection, the volume, rather tough going. My mind was apt to wander very soon and did not 'take in', I kept having to start reading poem after poem all over again. However this was a personal disability, I am sure; Roy and Patric Dickinson, who are more accustomed to reading and reviewing the stuff, were not so afflicted—though they seldom agreed in their judgments; I should have thought that you too could take it in your stride. Apart from getting through the quarterly submissions (I forget how many books we had during the year: 40 to 50 in all, I should think) and trying to reach a personal decision, the rest was easy and pleasant, one met or corresponded, argued a bit and finally agreed. I confess to having got rather lazy over it. Patric Dickinson is a determined and forceful character—nice, I think—and was always most decisive in his views; Roy and I, starting out also with what we believed to be sane views, tended to be overborne by his when in conflict. Roy took more convincing than I did—he too is a tough character—but at least once he was forced to change his mind. All this suited me as time went on; diffident by nature, I found it simpler to leave the contest to these clever, oh far cleverer, little game cocks, and to throw in my own vote with theirs. Towards the end of the session I was doing on the books a far more perfunctory job than I had done in the beginning. I don't know who your

---

[1] A. served on the panel of the Poetry Book Society during the last quarter of 1957. His 'poetry reports' (as he called them) were brief and to the point. Here is one that he sent to Roy Fuller: 'The Irishman—[Thomas] Kinsella his name—is the chap who interests me most, though, while he engages my interest, he often evades my understanding . . . I thought he showed taste and enterprise in his metrical shapes, and had something to say (when I could follow him) out of a troubled mind.' In 1958 Kinsella's *Baggot Street Deserta* was made by A., Patric Dickinson and Roy Fuller the Spring Choice of the Poetry Book Society.

companions are to be, but if you don't want to be the game cock yourself and spy one among them, you won't find the choice too hard. I may add that about 90% of the stuff we were given to read was poor, if not downright bad; but that didn't help much, because Eric White[1] *hopes* that however poor the quarterly collection, both a Choice and a Recommend will be made—life is awkward for him otherwise. So although Roy started off, in our first quarter, by announcing pugnaciously '*None* of these books shall be chosen or recommended except over my dead body,' he was soon dislodged (by Patric and Mr White) from that high moral but inconvenient position. Yes, really, it was all quite fun—but only because Roy and Patric were so amusing to work with.

I am entangled in the National Insurance Acts—trying to draw the dole —which is also instructive, though not so amusing. I think an article to *The N[ew] S[tatesman]* will have to be concocted.[2]
Much love and thanks, dearest W.

J

To John Wickens (1934–)   17 Star & Garter Mansions, Putney, 181
                                   S.W.15   8/11/59

Dear Wickens
            I hope you are well. It is sometime since I heard from you. Perhaps you never received my answer to your last friendly letter—some three or four months ago. Since then I have become a retired man, last week in fact. I think I told you that I was on the verge of it, and the axe fell last week, in the disguise of a cocktail party which saw me off. I can't say I looked forward to the party very much—I prefer to be guest rather than host, and alive rather than a corpse—it was, after all a sort of funeral party, a 'melancholy occasion' as some guests termed it,[3] for it was to see me off, after nearly 25 years with *The Listener*. But it was nice after all, practically all my friends turned up to say goodbye, excepting Edith Sitwell and Sir Kenneth Clark (who both got flu), and E. M. Forster, who was so displeased at my being discarded that he refused to come. L. P. Hartley mistook the evening and turned up for the party the following day.

So now I am sitting on my bum at home and wondering what to do. I don't seem to have anything I want to write, at any rate at present, so I am looking for more work to do with some publishing house. At the moment Methuens seem to be taking an interest in me.[4] The Bodley Head have accepted that novelette[5] of mine, now expurgated, if I will make a few other changes, which will not be hard to do and which I must attend to soon. The American Viking Press have carried my only copy of the *un*expurgated copy

---

[1] Secretary of the Poetry Book Society from 1954 to 1971.
[2] See page 161, note 3.
[3] i.e. Maurice Cranston.
[4] See page 162, note 1.
[5] *We Think the World of You.*

back to New York to consider it.[1] I suppose it *may* come out somewhere after all. If it does, I will send you a copy at once. But you will be disappointed— as I now feel.

No other news. I went to a party last week to meet M. Vladimir (*Lolita*) Nabokov, a very lively man. Did you read his *Lolita*? I don't suppose it would be allowed to sully the soil on which you stand.[2] It *may* not be allowed to sully ours; it came out only yesterday and the public hangman may slip in. An amusing—and a serious—book, I thought, prodigiously clever; I enjoyed it a lot.

And how are you?

Joe Ackerley

182 To John Wickens (1934–   )   17 Star & Garter Mansions, Putney,
                                       S.W.15   11/11/59

Dear Mr Wickens
                your letter came soon after I had posted mine.[3] Strange coincidence. And now I forget what I said to you. However, at the risk of repetition, I am now retired and much poorer than I was. But it is not un- pleasant to lie about for a bit with nothing to do except review an occasional book. I have also written a tiny poem about my dog, which *The Listener* is to publish.[4] I expect I shall get bored in time and must look for some new job, to occupy my mind and supplement a small pension.

I doubt if you will much enjoy the Casement Diaries, they are not really rewarding and, pity is, Casement himself was such a bore. I'm sure that if one had known him and however much one might have admired his work for humanity, and even known of his sexual proclivities—one wouldn't have wanted to dine with him more than once a year.[5] *Lolita*, though about a girl, is more fun; I enjoyed that very much.

The Bodley Head seem certain of publishing my novel[6] if I will make a few more quite trivial changes in it. This I shall set myself to do next week. If and when it comes out I will send you a copy—and perhaps restore the page 'as it was'[7]—though you will be disappointed.

All good wishes

Joe Ackerley

P.S. America! A nice change for you. Your sister, I suppose. How long will you be there?

---

[1] Viking Press rejected it. They had first published *Hindoo Holiday* in 1932 and subsequently re-issued it in a 'reprint series' in 1941. But A. fought for his terms. Early in 1941 Viking had offered A.'s English publishers 'a royalty of 10% on each copy sold, of which 50 per cent [would] be paid to the author.' A. insisted on a 75 per cent share—or no deal. Viking cabled back: 'We very much dislike giving one author a better arrangement than we give the others.' A. replied by pointing out that Viking had let *Hindoo Holiday* go out of print and that the rights had reverted to him. On 10 March Viking cabled their acceptance of A.'s terms.

[2] Pretoria, South Africa.   [3] Letter 181.

[4] 'Ditty', which was published on 17 December.

[5] On another occasion A. wrote to Sewell Stokes: 'I am interested in Casement and have read everything I have come across. There was a bad Irish book not long ago . . . which tried to make out he wasn't . . .' A. probably had in mind *The Life and Times of Roger Casement* by H. O. Mackey (1954).   [6] *We Think the World of You.*   [7] See page 190, note 3 and Appendix F.

To Robert Buckingham[1] (1904–   )   17 Star & Garter Mansions, Putney,   183
                                                                  S.W.15   25/11/59

Dear Bob

I am so sorry to hear from Morgan that you are unwell. Before he left he said you were having your neuralgia back, now that it is rheumatism and that you are thought to have a weakness in the spine. The spine, of course, does set up all manner of aches and pains when it gets disordered; I do hope the doctors will soon find out the trouble with yours and prop it, and you, up in your usual stalwart and comfortable erectness. Send me a little line about yourself if you feel equal to such a task; now that I am retired and flat-bound I like to have a nice lot of letters falling daily into my letter-box.[2]

I am cheerful and well and shall remain so while things remain as they are. Which can't be for long. But at present it is cosy, everyone is as happy and healthy as can be expected in our various old ages, and, as in wars, a sort of zeal is felt for Home Defence. Reductions have been made in such dull, unnecessary things as chars and food, in order that the things that really matter, such as cigarettes and drink, may be left undisturbed, and Nancy, after a moment's panic, has got a job. It hasn't started yet (Nov. 30) and can't last long—her employer is 93—but Nancy is taking it seriously—almost too seriously—for she is searching for an alarm clock which will not have too loud a tick to disturb her sleep, but will have a loud enough orgasm to wake her at 7.0 for duty, 10 minutes off, at 9.30 a.m.

As for me, I work from morning to night, writing rubbish of all sorts, articles on The Dole, on Training Dogs, on overheard conversations;[3] book reviews, even poems. But how nice it is not to go to that effing office. Every day is exactly the same. I have to go to London when invited—and I do get invited once or twice a week.

---

[1] Robert Buckingham and his wife May between 1946 and 1970 often had Forster to stay with them in their home at Coventry. Harry Daley first introduced A. to Buckingham in October 1929: both were members of the Metropolitan Police Force. On 20 February 1930 A. produced 'On the 9.20', a discussion between Forster and Buckingham about their different callings: it was No. 7 in the radio series 'Conversations in the Train'. Buckingham wrote to Braybrooke on 22 January 1973: 'My special memory of Joe, and my wife agrees, was his absolute constancy as a friend . . . During Morgan's last years when he was almost blind, Joe shared with me the task of dealing with his letters which meant that either he or I had to be in Cambridge at least two days a week. When Morgan was ill, as he was frequently, and unable to remain at King's, he always came to us and then Joe came here for days on end reading to him, writing letters for him and helping in any way he could. Yes, Joe was a true friend, generous and loving—and we still miss him.'

[2] Letters should be distinguished here from manuscripts. When making his final revisions on the manuscript of *My Dog Tulip*, A. had written to warn Fredric Warburg: 'The ms. [should be posted to the BBC], because the subject of it is all too likely to tear [it] to pieces . . . [if it] falls through the letter-box of my flat.'

[3] A. did complete an article on 'The Dole'—and it was accepted for *Encounter* by Stephen Spender. On 9 December Spender wrote: 'Here is the piece for two or three more screws to be inserted.' A. returned it a few days later—and wrote: 'Here you are . . . I do hope it is not the sort of article it would better not to publish—not just on one's own account but pro bono publico: my Labour Office is attended by the oddest people—smart, with brief cases,—all mingled with dolly blackamoors and drawing the dole—I should not like to blow any sort of gaffe (no, Partridge, *gaf*) . . . No, don't make a sad story or a National Issue of me—though I myself vainly suggested that the B.B.C. might give me a nice fat long-service cheque; if there is any plaguing to be done, I can do it myself.' The article went into proof but was never published.

I do hope you will soon be well, dear Bob. News of yourself would be ever so welcome. And news of May too.

To you both, dear creatures, my fondest love

    Joe

184 To Francis King (1923–) 17 Star & Garter Mansions, Putney, S.W.15

                                                        9/1/60

Dear Francis

          I have owed you a letter for a very long time, four months perhaps. I had a nice Xmas card from you too. I didn't write because I thought that after our interchange whatever I said next ought to be decisive and since leaving the B.B.C. I have felt too inert to make decisions. I have now been retired for two months, and a good deal of that time has been occupied in settling my affairs. I chose after all not to buy an annuity with the whole of my B.B.C. capital (nearly £10,000 counting the so-called Security Pay of a year's salary), but to keep a third of it as capital in my own hands. I think I've fixed things up fairly sensibly. With the barrel scraped I shall have an annual income of about £1300 from annuities, investments, and the dole (which I am drawing) for 5 years, subject to income tax; thereafter, when my Security Pay, which I'm taking in 5 yearly instalments, falls out I shall drop by £380 a year—but, after all, anything may happen in 5 years. Besides this, a contributing interest to it, I have £2,500 in safe investments ('blue chips' in my Bank's phraseology), and have also managed to keep in my current account some £800, upon which I am living at present until annuities start to function properly. This is all not too bad. The days of taking friends and contributors out for expensive meals are over, but living quietly, as I have been doing, the sum should suffice, at any rate until 1965; I have made a few extra pounds reviewing etc.; my sister has got herself a small job, enough to pay her own rent, and in fact money, at present, is not one of my worries. True, I would like to double the sum, and have made it known in the publishing world that I am free for work—literary adviser—if required: but although Anthony Blond nibbled rather eagerly at me for a moment, the news, so far, has aroused little interest.[1] I am delighted to be free of *The Listener* and have such a horror-feeling for it now that I have not darkened its doors since I left: in fact I ought to be feeling some of the joys of uncontrolled enfranchisement, but I am not; I feel instead inert and depressed. I'm afraid that my dog is at the bottom of it all, the fact that she has got so old, 14½, she puts me in a dilemma. It is a dilemma that I ought to be able to face and solve, I know (in the nature of things she will have to die

---

[1] Blond writes: 'I knew Joe slightly, and liked him a lot.' Nothing, though, came of the plan that A. should act as an adviser for his firm. Nor did anything come of the subsequent plan that he should act as an adviser for Methuen. From time to time A. read for The Bodley Head 'when the subject seemed up [his] street'. James Michie, one of the directors, recalls: '[On one occasion I sent him] a biography of Pino Orioli, Norman Douglas's friend. Joe's report was extravagantly funny and salacious and was, as I remember, kept locked out of sight of the, in those days, shockable secretaries.' In 1966 A was approached about 'reading and advising' for the Fleet Publishing Corporation in New York and did report on one book for them—a Tennyson bibliography. See Letter 307.

fairly soon), and perhaps I soon shall make this sensible choice, but to come out to you, of which, now that the year has turned, I think more and more, will be like saying goodbye to her forever, and her constant devotion to me makes that a hard decision to take. Hitherto I have done nothing, partly for the reasons above, partly because I am rather sensitive to cold and thought that, in any case, I would make no move until the Spring, March/April. And now that the year has turned I say to myself almost daily that I must go to a travel agency to investigate ways and means: I hope I may acquire the sense and guts to do so soon. If I can toughen myself, I've decided that flying will be too great a strain on my pocket, and that I should investigate boats—John Morris[1] told me some weeks ago that there is a very comfortable Japanese line, freighters that take passengers, even that is rather expensive, I believe, but not so dear as the air. Do you know anything about them? I believe it's a five-week voyage. Your distance is, of course, the halting snag. It is so far, I mean, that if I set out to you I should set out without the idea of return, and I believe that I should not want to return when I got there. That is why leave-taking here (my ancient aunt too) would be quite a thing to do, a totally different matter from going to Greece or Italy, or to Moscow for the £92 eight-day tourist jet-flight. All that seems simple, but Japan is like for-ever. One good thing is that I know from experience that I scarcely think of my old dog when I am away from her. The great power she exerts is visual.[2]

This letter is awfully unsatisfactory. It may be followed by a better one. But as well as all else I feel quite empty-headed as though, in sixty-odd years, nothing I had ever read, or seen, or felt, or thought, had found lodgment in my head. To write is quite beyond me. I can just manage to tackle a review book in a dim sort of way,[3] and am going to Oxford next week to see the dramatisation[4] of Morgan's *Passage to India* and do a broad-cast comment on it afterwards.[5] But I lack self-confidence and I fear I may muff it.[6]

However, we had a nice Xmas, masses of booze and turkey. May 1960 bring us together.
Love, dear F.
Joe

To K. W. Gransden[7] (1925–   )   Putney 185
                                             28/3/60

Dear Ken
       I meant to write to you before. I can't get through Bjerre['s] *Kala-hari*[8] and wonder if you would like it back, for dear Geoffrey perhaps? I *think*

---

[1] Author of various travel books, including *Traveller from Tokyo* (1946), and the Controller of the Third Programme of the BBC from 1952 to 1958.
[2] See page 311, note 1.
[3] See Letter 185.
[4] By Santha Rama Rau. See page 170, note 2.
[5] This occurred on 19 January.
[6] In the event all went well: 'I enjoyed doing it and was pleased to find myself not in the least nervous . . .', A. wrote subsequently to King.
[7] A.'s successor at *The Listener*.
[8] *Kalahari* by Jens Jacobsen Bjerre, translated by Estrid Bannister (1960).

the man's a bore—he starts boringly anyway, devoting his first chapter to a potted history of anthropology to show that the Bushmen are the oldest link in the Darwinian chain towards first men and apes—and the rest of the book is about the Kalahari Bushmen. My real trouble is that primitive tribes, with all their silly superstitions and mumbo-jumbo, bore me to tears—so I oughtn't to have taken the book, but you did press me. When you think of me again, try to find me a book on civilised tribes—the English, the American—and *their* silly superstitions and mumbo-jumbo; they, at least, can read what is written about them and their blushes are visible. Autobiographies, memoirs, books like that *Dinlock*[1] book I did for you. That was fun. Animals too, of course, but I find myself becoming—it's hard not to become—serious and angry about them. A few humans would be a pleasant change.

I am nursing a bad arm from vaccination (Far East, shall I ever reach it?) I hope all goes well with you. I read a lot of your paper with pleasure. It has become far more interesting since my tired mind was removed from it. [Hal] Summers was much more interesting about his cat[2] than I was about my dog.[3] I liked his poem very much. *All* your poems I like. And [William] Golding[4] was a treat.

Would you like to lunch with me one day at the Royal College [of Art]? I have become quite a habitué.

Joe

186 To Francis King (1923–)   Athens
                                                                    21/6/60

Dearest Francis
                I am flying out of Athens tomorrow, returning to Marseille and Provence, thence home. Another letter before I go. I've enjoyed myself here, though in a baffled and frustrated way: my true misfortune was that *you* are not here. I left notes on Brian de Jongh and Peter Sheldon; the latter never answered though I believe he is here; the former phoned and, after a lot of Greek muddles—the Palladion Hotel where I was staying had my name down wrong—contacted me and took me to dine on the Plaka. He took a lot of trouble over me, but alas I saw him only that once—and at that once we were not alone, E. Gathorne-Hardy and an adenoidal dull young American (name forgotten) were in the party. I asked de Jongh back, and fixed it, but further muddles occurred, English this time, he had to cancel and I never saw him more. As you say, he is a nice man and I would have welcomed a little private conversation with him. For I was there alone, my own American friends had gone off to Mykonos; moreover, Gathorne-Hardy disappeared into Samos, Peter Mayne, who was here, vanished

----

[1] *Weekend in Dinlock* by Clancy Sigal, which A. had reviewed for *The Listener* on 28 January. He summed up the book as a cross 'between fiction and social survey [about] a composite Yorkshire mining village [called] "Dinlock"'.

[2] 'My Old Cat', which had been published in *The Listener* on 24 March.

[3] 'Ditty', which had been published in *The Listener* on 17 December 1959.

[4] 'The Ladder and the Tree'—a chapter of autobiography, which had been published in *The Listener* on 24 March.

somewhere else, and although Henry Reed suddenly materialised later from England and kept me a couple of days company, he knew no more of Athens than I did.

[—] both saved and destroyed my life—at least I think so. I had just begun an affair with a boy of 16, and [—] told me that there was a law against tampering with the under-aged. Of this, I had no inkling, and the news unnerved me. The hotel had regarded the boy, when I had taken him in that day, with what I thought too deep an interest; nevertheless I had got him to my room and we had both had an enjoyable time for a couple of hours. He was a street boy (from Piraeus)—as with Lolita, he did the picking-up, one of a group of naughty boys who operate round the Rex cinema in Venizelos; but he had a nice, affectionate nature, was gay, considerate, active, not grasping and exceedingly prettily made, and, by the sun, coloured. I meant to keep on with him throughout my stay, and had a date with him for the next day—but [—]'s remark unnerved me. [—] had also said: 'Don't enter *with* the boy'—but I *had*: since I could speak no Greek, he no English, it would have been hard to concoct any other plan, my phrase-book does not help.

I should now provide an elaborate description of the set-up of the Palladion Hotel, which is, as perhaps you remember, on Venizelos, down by Omonia. Enough to say that sometimes, too rarely, at the reception desk a girl or two functioned: sometimes the manager and an older more authoritative sort of man whom I took to be the proprietor were added. In fact, usually there seemed far *too* many people about, to welcome one and get one into the lift. I must add that everyone was, and continued to be, extremely friendly to me—most attentive—and the 'proprietor' kept saying that he hoped I found staying there 'just like home'—in spite of my rejoinder (which I don't suppose he understood) that it was from 'home' that I was attempting to escape. At any rate, so far as I recall, when I slipped in with my boy, only the two women were functioning.

Anyway, I was unnerved; I did not keep my appointment with the boy the next day, though he did, I saw him from across the road, smartly dressed in a provocative way, arsing about with the other boys who haunted the 'Rex'. Sorry though I was, I decided to avoid him in future. (I saw him some days later, very gay and naughty, no heartbreak!)

Four days later, as Henry Reed and I were returning from lunch at Vassily's (Henry was in the Alpha Hotel), another boy offered himself, also very pretty. He too could speak no English, but managed to convey that he was a Turkish tourist from Ankara—a story which I have subsequent reason to disbelieve. He was a little older than boy No. 1, either 17 or 18, smartly dressed in a cheap way. Henry soon made himself scarce, I conveyed to the boy that I lived in a hotel down the road, he said he would like to go in with me, and in we went. A *bad* moment? *Everyone* was in the foyer, proprietor, manager, two female receptionists, and two of the positively hideous pages the hotel seemed to have thought it wiser to select. Much polite fussification, 'how do you do?' to me, lift pressed for me, nervous conversation from me, everyone most civil, the manager himself rode us up to my floor, more nervous conversation from me. The boy and I entered my room. My dear, we had not been there *two* minutes before the phone rang. I picked it up—muffled, muddled voices, excited tones—then it emerged that it was a call for the boy in my room. Perplexedly, I handed the phone to him. More excited conversation—of which I understood not a word, but certainly heated, the sort of 'so what!' tone, then he put the receiver down, said 'The Police!' in an agitated way, added 'give me 3 drachmas,' I gave 5, grabbed his little hold-all, and positively fled.

What was it all about? What did he want 3 drachmas for? Who *on earth* had known he was in my room? Would he return? Well, I could write a lot more about it—speculation etc.—but I won't. He didn't return. I questioned the manager, very friendly, no change. 'Someone phoned saying he had seen a young boy enter the hotel in company with an Englishman. He wished to speak to the boy. Of course, I had to put him through!'

Well, there seem to me three possibilities only: (the boy himself *must* have been innocent, for he reaped nothing from it but 5 drachmas); (i) a jealous discarded friend of the boy's had seen our pick-up and dished us, (ii) the police had seen us, and dished us, (iii) the proprietor himself, pretending to be a policeman, had dished us. I think the first rather fanciful and reject it. Which of the other two was right I haven't a clue, but it didn't matter, they had the *same* effect—I simply *couldn't* afterwards, take *anyone* else into the hotel *at all*. Whoever was watching me, I was a watched, or at least noticed man, either the proprietor had discreetly informed [on] me (he was as nice as pie afterwards) that he wasn't going to have things like that in his hotel, or the police had seen and phoned (scouting round afterwards I observed that the kiosk exactly opposite the entrance to the hotel had a phone). So although I have felt as sexy as the devil I have simply had to give everything up since: I incline to adolescents, as you know, and they incline towards me. But I don't think I would dare to take even an adult in—a sailor, for example. So my Athens life has been ruined. And how I have wished you were here! I've thought of changing my hotel—but to what? [— —] told me he lived in a louche hotel—a sort of brothel—wonderfully cheap, on the Plaka, and I think I found it in his absence. I have visited a dozen hotels observing the set-up, managerial faces, asking for prices, but I didn't move. I have only two or three more days here anyway—and how, after all, should I know whether a hotel that admitted whatever *he* liked without bother (does he like the brutal?) would also admit what *I* like, the very young, against the law, without bother? And it is so terribly hot, one really does want a shower in one's room: so does one's boy, and how nice it is to see him taking a shower. Perhaps I should have moved to the Grande Bretagne where, I am told, anything may happen, and indeed it is the middling, family hotel, like the Palladion, which is the difficulty. One wants one so poor and tiny that there are no public rooms for entertaining friends, or one with public rooms so many and so vast that no one can keep track of one's activities.

Dearest Francis, perhaps next year, or the next, you and I could rent an apartment in Athens for the spring. How delicious that would be. I do think the Athenians most attractive and wonderfully endowed. Last time I came I was not in the humour, not awake, I am wide awake now.

Anyway (i) how could I get away from [—], who was determined not to get away from me? and (ii) too much time was spent among tattered English and American queens in Zonar's and in those tiresome tavernas (not visited at all this trip) which cater only for those who like he-men and Tarzans! I don't think you ever took me to a Secondary or even Public School or Borstal. My tastes, I now realise, lie in that direction.

Best love
    Joe

P.S. I am glad to go, yet sorry. I have missed a lot, I know, so much is going on. Yet how hard it is to get on without a common language (not just love itself, there I don't at all mind not being able to communicate a thought, but in the arranging, situating and defending of love). Besides getting one-self into trouble, it would be terrible to involve young boys in one's follies—ready though they do seem to be involved. [—] says there is an animus against the whole thing. I have no means of knowing, and don't want to end up in a Greek gaol (better than English—gayer, I mean—though they may well be) or to land nice little boys there either.

But, I have a second string, with details of which I will not burden an already over-long letter. If he materialises, my lonely week here will be improved though not an intelligible word shall we be able to exchange.

Dear Francis, you cannot write to me here, but you can write to me in Putney. To come out in the autumn to you will mean ordinary London suits I suppose. Plus an overcoat.

Best love
    Joe

To J. B. Blackley[1] (1925–　)　　Hotel Arts et Leman, Rue Mazagran, 187
　　　　　　　　　　　　　　　　Marseille　　　　　　　　　　27/6/60
Dear Mr Blackley
　　　　　　　the Athens proof [of *We Think the World of You*] never came, although I waited until first post Wednesday morning. I also paid a useless visit of enquiry to the main post office. However this proof was await-ing me here when I got in on Thursday and I return it now with my correc-tions. I hope they are clear. *Please* get the sectionalisation of the book right, it is important; some of the sections pp. 46, 66, 120 have got stuck together. I'm sorry to have removed a few lines on the first page;[2] I got bored with that sentence; will it not look all right if you start that page on a lower level, instead of bringing lines back? I have dealt with all Mrs Cohn's queries and

---

[1] Chief Editor at The Bodley Head.
[2] The lines removed occur in the first paragraph and are those in italics: 'Johnny wept when I was taken down to visit him. It was a thing I had never seen him do before, *and although, if I had thought about it, I would have said it was a thing he might easily do, I would have added that it was not a thing he would wish me to see.* I sat down beside him on the hard bench and took his hand in mine.'

objections.[1] Please thank her. Millie's little mistakes in English must remain: 'passionate' for 'compassionate', 'except' for 'accept', etc. With regard to her first query,[2] I think it can stand—at any rate I find it hard to alter. It refers neither to Evie nor Frank, but to Megan. Frank's thought is: First I am shoved out by Megan, now I am left out of my true consideration by Johnny. He bothers about *her* convenience, not about mine.

I expect I shall be back in London within a week.

J. R. Ackerley

188 To Laura Cohn[3]   Hotel Arts et Leman, Rue Mazagran,
                                      Marseille (B. du R.)   28/6/60

Dear Mrs Cohn

I sent off my corrected proof [of *We Think the World of You*] from here by air-mail yesterday morning, and should perhaps say so under separate cover, so I send this to you. I did not reply to your letter of June 14 before because the Athens proof, for which I waited until the first post of June 22, never came. Naturally therefore I could not set to work earlier, and if there has been a troublesome delay it is not my fault. Registration to the Eastern Mediterranean should always be avoided when the object sent is urgent and valueless.

I have dealt on the Marseille proof, which awaited me here, with all the points your reader raised and which you kindly indicated in your letter. Something was certainly left out on p. 115, but I don't think it was an omission on my typescript, to which your reader could have referred. The mistake most worrying to me, because it might pass unnoticed, was the adherence together of several of the sections, which are all separated off to indicate lapse of time and make for bewilderment if they cohere.

On one of the last pages, before the Margaret business, where Johnny and Evie 'make love' to each other, I removed a sentence—'it was what he was good at'—the question of the judiciousness of which has teased me for some time.[4] If it is thought unnecessary to have altered it, it can be stetted. Instead, in order to balance the sentence and save the printers re-running the whole para., I think I put in 'as if by some instinct', and that may be thought a somewhat banal substitute: I find it difficult to think out here. If it is disliked, but some change desired, 'without hesitation' could be used instead; it is innocuous and would keep the rhythmic balance of the sentence.

I shall be here long enough to receive a reply from you if you have anything more to say.

Joe Ackerley

[1] See Letter 188.
[2] The query had read: 'Page 10, lines 7/8: "First to be pushed out by her; now, it seemed, to be left out by him; it was insufferable." This does not seem to fit in sensibly here. [Does] . . . it refer to Evie or Frank?'
[3] Editor at The Bodley Head.
[4] See Appendix F for A.'s final decision about how this sentence (on page 141 of his novel) was to run.

To Laura Cohn Putney 189
11/7/60

Dear Mrs Cohn

    I returned today from France—delayed by a street accident in Paris—knocked down by a car—which sent me to hospital for four days. No bones broken, I am glad to say, but I am a bit cut about and rather groggy. All is well with this letter of yours except point 2.[1] It is *singular* forecast, not plural. If you can change, please do.[2] First Tom says 'Will she go with you? They're one-man dogs, they are'—meaning that Evie belongs to *them* and won't go with Frank. That is his *first* forecast. But it turns out to be balls. She goes with Frank—of course, he is the only person who offers her her heart's desire, a walk. Then Tom sees that she *is* going with Frank after all—that, in a way, she has rejected himself and Millie—so he makes his second forecast 'She'll get away if she can. Keep a tight hold.' This (as Frank thinks) hardly fits in with the first forecast—and in fact does not fit, Evie is already in process of choosing Frank as her one man and has no intention of 'getting away' from him at all. There are the two forecasts only, both wrong, and the word therefore is singular.

    J.R.A.

Your jacket amuses me.[3]

To Francis King (1923–) 17 Star & Garter Mansions, Putney, S.W.15 190
August Bank Holiday,
torrential rain 1960

Dearest Francis

    I have neglected you, but with some small excuse. I returned home from Paris on July 11th—after 4 days in the French hospital and a couple more days resting in my hotel and being expensively fed by the Duthuits—and went to my doctor here next day to consult him over the stitches which were still in my head. I mentioned to him that I ached a good deal round the back of my neck—it had bothered me a lot during the last days in Paris—and thought I must have strained or torn the muscles in my tumble. He at once sent me to hospital to have the neck X-rayed, and it was found that I had in fact broken it, that is to say fractured several little bones. The French, so charming and superficial, had X-rayed only my skull—perhaps fortunately, for if they had done the neck too, I might perhaps be there still, at 5 guineas a day. Here I am being treated for nothing, and draw sickness benefit as well. The breakages are not very serious, I understand, but for the last three weeks I have had to wear a high stiff collar contraption to keep my chin up and my neck still, and this, which I am still wearing makes letter-writing rather a problem. Also I have felt sleepy and tired, but no pain. I am having radiant heat and massage too, three times a week. But it is all

---

[1] Point 2 had read: 'Page 32, line 5: your correction, "other forecasts". I have put this in the plural but was not absolutely sure of your writing.'
[2] In the 1960 first edition the word remains in the plural. This has been corrected in the 1962 second impression. See Appendix F.
[3] By Derrick Greaves.

getting better now, and after another eight days of this tiresome collar[1] I am expecting to be able to leave it off and get my discharge. I have been mobile throughout, but have not made much use of my mobility—a couple of local cinemas, one or two meals in London; it has been more convenient to lie on my bed all day and read. But as soon as I am passed fit—tomorrow week the specialist says—I shall start planning an autumn visit to you. My recent journey, though it ended in the Paris mud, has given me a taste for travel.

Your letter about the Athens business—it amused and rather saddened me—came safely back from Marseille and now I have another from you since. You are now going to be heavily visited by your autumn trio: will you have room for me too? I am most eager to come, and should be able to manage by the beginning of September. Is that what you call Autumn in Japan and would it suit? Or would you prefer me to come later? I am not sure when your summer ends, and don't want to burden my bag with both hot and cold weather suitings. One of the reasons I did not come on to you from Athens— a thought that entered my head—was that I had only the thinnest of wardrobes. Now, I suppose, ordinary English suits will be needed: plus an overcoat? Would I be able—all staying well at home as it now is—to remain on with you into the winter (I dislike cold much less than damp heat). And another thing: would you advise me to bring a return air-ticket, or a single one? I'm not sure whether to take the Polar route or the hoppy one (B.O.A.C.) which I suppose you took. I must say I like Air France, but the latter might be more amusing. The first thing dear Morgan did when I met him on my return from Paris was to press another £200 into my hand (five-pound notes in an envelope). Shrieking with laughter he told me that he was making £5000 a year out of the dramatisation of *A Passage to India*,[2] doing excellent business still at the Comedy. And I have brought nearly £100 in travellers cheques back from my recent excursions. So I am well prepared for anything.

My book is not the thing about my father, which I shan't complete, but the novel[3] about Queenie and her first working-class owners. I don't think anyone will like it, though some of the dialogue is amusing—it's mostly in dialogue and I would be glad to be out of England when it appears (in September).[4] It was written some 5 or 6 years ago and has been castrated since to suit the Law: I am no longer interested in it—much more interested in *your* new book.[5] At any rate I hope we are both better than *Martin Chuzzlewit*, which I have just read—with the utmost nausea—for the first time. I have also tried Rabelais—curiosity—and put him with Chuzzlewit in the wastepaper basket.

Give me a suitable plan, dear F., and I will stick to it.

Love

Joe

---

[1] A. wrote in the same month to Donald Windham: 'I look in this collar like something between a Congo belle and a Regency beau.'

[2] The dramatisation was by Santha Rama Rau. The first performance had been at the Playhouse, Oxford, on 19 January 1960. Later in the year it had a successful run in London at the Comedy Theatre, followed by a shorter run in New York in 1962.

[3] *We Think the World of You.*   [4] Publication day was 27 September.

[5] *The Custom House*, which was published in the following year.

To Colin Haycraft[1] (1929–)   17 Star & Garter Mansions, Putney, 191
                                  S.W.15   3/9/60

Dear Haycraft

the parcel of books arrived from Higham[2] this week. On reflection I think I won't bother to return them to you but post them off myself. I find I have some large envelopes here, into which they can be slipped.

I have read it again myself. It is most accurately set up, and I do congratulate you and all concerned. I noticed only the omission of one quotation mark and a place where the first letter of one word had got stuck to the end of the previous one.[3] Neither matters at all. But the libel aspects continue to bother me, I must say, in spite of my surface falsifications (the unalterable situations vis-à-vis the dog, Johnny's imprisonment, the rows: all so close to reality), and I wish I could have thought of more things to do to make it safer. Two gratuitous insults to Megan would have been better omitted, I now see and wish someone had thought to draw my attention to them: the sentence about her being unwashed on p. 96,[4] and the business about her clapping her hand to her mouth on p. 99,[5] which my sister seems to recall the original actually did before she got false teeth.[6] I daresay, however, it is a common gesture with anyone who has a dental defect. The trouble with the book of course is that it was written so long ago and is so familiar to me, through continual re-draftings, that it had become set in my mind, no longer as reality but as a work of fiction.

I shall be seeing Francis in Tokyo soon. Shall I give him messages from you?

Yours sincerely

Joe Ackerley

---

[1] Publicity Manager, later Editor, at The Bodley Head. Now Chairman and Managing Director of Duckworth and the publisher of this book. See Introduction, 3.

[2] David Higham Associates, the literary agents.

[3] Both misprints were corrected in the second impression (1962) of *We Think the World of You*.

[4] 'And did she ever have a bath, I wondered, looking at her bare legs.' See Appendix F for revised text.

[5] 'Megan gave a single shrill squeal and clapped her hand over her mouth, as she always did when she laughed to conceal the fact that her front teeth were badly decayed.' When A. came to revise the text for the paperback edition in 1962, he decided to leave in this comment unaltered. Nor is there any mention of cutting this passage in the 'definitive edition' which he prepared for Haycraft at the same time. See Appendix F.

[6] Two years later when staying in New York with Sandy Campbell, A. inscribed his host's copy of *We Think the World of You* with this note: 'One of my amusements when I planned this book was to prove in tranquillity that a certain woman whom I had not liked, here called Megan, was a bitch. Other and more interesting aspects of the story arrived as it went along, but that little exercise remained, and it amused me . . . to dress Megan up in Evie's "costume", to the former's disadvantage . . .' This 'dressing up' occurs on pages 110–11: 'Then I noticed her appearance. She was all dolled up, her face thick with slap. She was wearing a two-piece costume, a black tunic and light grey skirt, so unsuitable to her compassionate grounds [i.e. she was pregnant] that she could only have put it on purposely, to accentuate them . . . Over her head was draped a scarf with "Into Battle" printed round its borders; tanks, planes and soldiers crawled on her black hair, and the long barrel of a howitzer pointed down her forehead into her left eye.' This contrasts pointedly with A.'s description of Evie earlier in the novel on pages 43–4, where he writes: 'The dark device in the midst of her light grey forehead was more sharply defined, I noticed. It was diamond-shaped. It was a black diamond and it had the appearance of being suspended there by a fine dark thread, no more than a pencil line, which ran back from it right over the top of her pale poll . . .'

Part Seven
A VISIT TO JAPAN

192 To Leslie and Doll Payne[1]   17 Star & Garter Mansions, Putney, S.W.15
9/9/60

Dear Les and Doll

I am flying to Japan on Wednesday next. I haven't told Nancy the exact date yet, though she knows I plan to go and has accepted it very sweetly. I shall tell her on Saturday—Bunny perhaps later. I dislike uprooting myself again very much, and it will be a wrench to leave my three girls. But I have the means and think I ought to go. Nancy in particular will be awfully bored while I'm away; it would be an act of kindness if one or other of you could pop in from time to time (no need to phone and fix) when convenient, to say hullo. I shall be leaving her lots of money (someone else has paid for my trip)[2] so she will be well off for that—but that is not the thing that matters. She will be lonely.

Japan is a long way away. I shall reach it from Paris in 17 hours by rapid jet, but letters take about 4 days. I shall therefore be rather cut off: Nancy will not be able to put questions to me about Bunny's health or Queenie's health, she will have to make decisions on her own. I am sorry to leave the sweet old girl with such responsibility, and I am sure it would be a great comfort to her if she knew that she could trot round to you for advice or help. How long do I mean to stay away? I haven't a clue. I have a Japanese visa for 90 days—and am told I could prolong it if I wished. I have two friends[3] there to put me up and take me about. I may hate it, I may like it; I may want to return for Xmas, I may want to go on into the Spring. It is a madly expensive journey (nearly £500), and if I like it there and get interested I expect I shall resist attempts to bring me back to Putney, unless I am obliged. The trouble with my life is that everyone about me is so old that the Last Trump might sound anywhere at any moment—it might sound at any moment for me too. But once there—and if I like it—I don't expect I shall return for Last Trumps.

---

[1] Leslie Payne was the nephew of Aunt Bunny and her first husband Ronald Payne.
[2] A. had written to Francis King on 23 January: '. . . sweet old Morgan, so anxious for me to get away to Japan, has presented me with the whole fare, so now, like Mr Eisenhower, I can come for a weekend.'
[3] Francis King and James Kirkup.

Do look in on Bunny and Nancy when you have a moment. I would be so grateful.

Love to you both

   Joe

To his Sister (1899–   )   Heathrow[1] 193
                                                          13/9/60

Darling Nance

             just off to bed, but I must just send you a few lines to say how sad I was to leave you this evening. It was so calm and peaceful sitting on the balcony with you this afternoon drinking tea and talking quietly of this and that—and I had been feeling so wretched.

   You are the nicest girl in the world and I love you better than anyone (except Queenie, of course. You know she must come first!). I will write you a proper letter from the plane.

   Take care of yourself dear Nance and the two poor invalids.[2]

Your loving old

   Joe[3]

To E. M. Forster (1879–1970)   c/o Francis King, Kyoto 194
                                                          21/9/60

Dearest Morgan

             this time a week ago I started on my journey and am only just beginning to be all of a piece. My body preceded my mind, and that only began to catch up when I got into a train in Tokyo for this place. Of Tokyo itself I have the most confused recollections, the outstanding one (after that long tedious journey in which Time got all mixed up and the sun never sank so that one moved from afternoon in Paris to afternoon in Alaska without passing through night, and there was scarcely ever a view, except suddenly and with astonishing clarity the white wilderness of ice and snow of the Pole) being dear Jim Kirkup's face at Tokyo airport, shouting 'Joe!' After that it was endless taxi drives through endless streets, stewing heat that drenched me in sweat day and night, dinner (I reached Tokyo at 6 p.m.) with Francis's friend Cyril Eland (who arranged my hotel and met me there) at his house, visits to louche 'boys' bars afterwards until after midnight, lunch with Ronald Bottrall[4] . . . next day and almost immediately after-

   [1] On the day before A. left for Japan, he and his sister took rooms at a hotel close to the airport, since his plane was due to leave in the early hours of the next morning. She writes: 'We spent the whole day together and Joe bought oysters as a parting treat for me. We ate them for lunch and I brought mine back soon after! I suppose I was feeling too emotional to digest them. I was so sad to think of him going so far away—and probably for six months. But after that we sat on the balcony and I knew he was upset and nervous at the thought of the long plane journey (he hated planes) and at leaving me and Queenie and Bunny for so long, so I tried to be calm, altho' I didn't feel it and when he left he said I had been very good for him—so I was pleased.'
   [2] i.e. Queenie and Aunt Bunny.
   [3] His sister writes: 'I tore up the original of this note in a rage one day!—then the next day I was sorry and wrote it down again, because I loved it. I had been carrying it around so long in my handbag and read it so often to cheer myself up that I knew it by heart.'
   [4] Poet. From 1959 he had been Representative of the British Council in Japan and Cultural Attaché to H.M. Embassy, Tokyo.

wards a visit to the Kabuki theatre (5 p.m. to 11 p.m.) with Eland's Japanese girl secretary (awfully nice), an entertainment arranged by him and which I found exceedingly tedious. You will notice that Jim seems left out of all this; and so the poor darling was, excepting for the Eland dinner to which he got invited, for he was not expected in Tokyo . . . He had said in a letter that he would come to meet me, but I hadn't expected him, for I had at once replied that I must go to Francis first (all my arrangements having been with him), yet he did come (how happy I was to see him, drenched in sweat) and was wanting to take me over Tokyo for two days and then back with him to Sendai; but when he found me helplessly entangled in all Francis's arrangements he returned sadly to Sendai next morning. I was awfully upset by all that and could not sleep at all that night and decided to follow Jim to Sendai after all, but there were too many problems (letting him know, letting Francis know, getting on a train: all trains are crammed, one has to book) and no one to help me, for Eland had vanished . . . You must understand the geography: Francis is 7 to 8 hours from Tokyo by express, Jim 5 to 6 in exactly the opposite direction, a day's journey (very expensive—everything here is expensive—and I have only £80 in travellers' cheques, my left-over from Greece and Marseille) with a change at Tokyo in between. So it is not a matter of popping, shuttling between the two. Now that I am here (I was two nights only in Tokyo) I think I must stay, perhaps until the end of October (Francis can have me indefinitely) and then go to Jim for the rest of my time. But I must think and also ask my bank if they will allow me more travellers' allowance before the financial year closes.

Kyoto was hotter even than Tokyo, but is cooler now. Francis met my train with his car, whipped me off to his large comfortable office-house (4 dogs, 2 cats, 3 Japanese servants, sliding doors, wire and net windows, shoes off on the threshold), then on to a party, most of his 'gay' English and American friends and their 'gay' Jap. boys—high-balls until 1 a.m. I was dropping with fatigue after no sleep and the air and train journeys, but I never say no. Where have we not been since (Francis is the kindest and most assiduous host) . . . the Kokedera or Moss Temple, the Silver Pavilion, Nijo Castle, the Pure Water Temple, the Heian Shrine, Mount Higashiyama and Mount Rocco for the views, not to mention a judo demonstration by students of the university, a conversazione with High School boys and girls, including a tea-ceremony and, yesterday, a drive (2 hours) to Kobe (squalid landscape), where he had to teach and where we dined with a friend. Jap. students pop into the house to chat all the time. My impressions? Oh confusion, confusion, will clarity ever emerge? The size, the distance, the antheap—all so daunting. Though in Kyoto, I suppose we are five miles from the centre, if there is one: endless innumerable streets, crammed with shops and cafés, crammed with people, all gaily glittering with coloured lights at night, I never know where I am—could never get there again. We go from 'gay' bar to 'gay' bar of an evening, tiny bar-rooms containing 'gay' boys, sometimes in kimonos. 1 small bedroom at the back to which you can take one if you fancy him. 25/- about the lowest tariff. Not really my cup of saké, not to mention my pocket. Bad breath, I am told, no circumcision. Good

torsos, no legs. One sees an occasional handsome face, the Simian look pre-
dominates. There is so much Westernisation I hardly feel myself to be in the
East, as I did in India. There is much still to see, and so far it has all been
whirling about in cars. Soon I must take to my feet, exhausting though it
will be. It is the only way to see anything. Jim will be duller than all this so
far as 'sights' are concerned—but to me unversed in Jap. history and culture,
the 'sights' (temples, etc.) already begin to look much the same.
Fond love, darling Morgan
    Joe

To E. M. Forster (1879–1970)   c/o Francis King, Kyoto 195
                                                  6/10/60
Dearest Morgan
            your letter—six days en route—has just arrived. So pleased
to hear from you. No news of Bob and Rob must be good news. My own
Putney news is perfectly satisfactory, and a pleasant letter from my bank
manager appears to herald the approach of another £100 shortly. If it
doesn't materialize I expect Jim will oblige with a loan. He says he has
'heaps' of money, in the spiders' webs. Francis does not like lending or
borrowing money (he has said so as a general statement) perhaps because he
lends so much to the wrong sort of boy and never gets it back. I expect he
would lend me some if I were forced to ask, but, if need be, I will ask Jim
instead who seems to have no reluctances.

My last letter to you was a trifle scandalous.[1] I hope it comes to hand
safely. After writing it I thought it would be wiser not to post it. Then I
posted it—the Frank in my nature coming out. I posted it myself so that it
should have the best opportunity of not being read by someone else. If one is
not scandalous it is difficult to write at all. The weather is a safe subject, and
I will mention it for a moment. The hot humid atmosphere in which I
arrived must have been the fag-end of summer; within a week it was finished
and now it is like an English summer, sometimes sunny and warm, often
raining as at the moment (Japan is said to be the wettest country in the
world). In the evenings an autumnal chill arrives, one needs a coat. Ando-
san, Francis's friend and a professional guide, now sports a waistcoat. It is
full-moon time, important here, for it gives the Japanese something to think
of: they sit about and look at it, or its reflection in water, on one special day
(last Tuesday), after that they pay no further attention to it. They also become emotional about cherry-blossom and the maple leaves when they turn
red. Poor things, they haven't much pleasure in their lives.

                                                  7/10/60
It has rained steadily for two days, so we have all been house-bound and
got rather irritable. It might almost be said to have rained cats and dogs,
for they got irritable too, and all four dogs set on the Siamese cat in the passage yesterday, and gave the poor thing an awful mauling. It fled away and

[1] Letter 194.

stayed out till this morning. And the largest dog was sick in the drawing-room this morning and brought up quantities of bone on Francis's *tatami*,[1] and when I told him it was a mistake to give dogs bones[2] (self-evident, I should have thought), he asked me please not to interfere. Scratchy, you see. I fear I have outstayed my welcome. Also there is cook trouble. The woman has left (ill-health), and her successor, an old boy named Mr Suzuki, has given notice after two days, unnerved by the dogs and cats. I am leaving on Wednesday morning, a night in Tokyo with a man named Geoffrey Penny, then the second half of the journey next day to Jim. I meant to leave some things behind here with a view to returning, but think now that it would be wiser to take everything. I have now been to Osaka, to the Slave Market ('The New Friend,'[3] it was called) but won't write about that. This is a letter from Japan—in case in reading it you have forgotten where I am. So sorry. But for some reason I seem not to be impressionable, though I have seen 40 temples, gardens, monasteries and pavilions, and there are plenty more. Jim says sweepingly that all the famous gardens here are 'fakes' except one, and that Kyoto is the 'crummiest and smoothest and stupidest' of places. These remarks have not pleased Francis nor the Japanese professors to whom Kyoto is the Florence of Japan and Sendai a dull provincial town. At any rate I shall get more to drink there, for Jim likes to tipple and Francis doesn't.

Fond love
   Joe

196 To his Sister (1899–)   as from 33 Kozenji-dori, Sendai
                                               11/10/60

Dearest Nance
        I am off to [Jim's] above address tomorrow morning. Thought I would get this letter in to you before I go, though I haven't much in my head to say. I will write to you from Sendai as soon as I can to tell you how it compares with Francis's establishment. It is a small town, less exhausting, I expect and hope, than this one;[4] I am also hoping that life there will be more restful too. Francis begs me to return here, and I dare say I shall. He is a very kind man and an excellent host; I've done an immense amount of sightseeing at his petrol expense since I've been here. We had a delightful mountain picnic on Sunday, and a friend of his, a boy named Ando-san cooked us a Japanese meal called *suki-yaki* under the persimmon trees. 'San' means Mr. or Mrs. If you were here you would be addressed as West-san; I am Ackerley-san. Everyone is constantly addressed in that way, even domestics and schoolboys. The cook is Suzuki-san (Mr Suzuki), the house-boy Katsumi-san (Mr Katsumi). Other Japanese customs: before entering any house, even this one, you take off your shoes and put on slippers. This has no religious significance, as in India; it is simply to keep the house

---

[1] Rush matting. See Letter 196.
[2] A. was thinking of his own experiences with Queenie. See Letter 103.
[3] A bar-brothel, specialising in boys.
[4] Kyoto.

clean. Japanese rooms are floored with springy rush matting, called *tatami*, difficult to cleanse [*sic*] if dirty. When you eat in a Japanese restaurant or drink in any bar, you are first of all handed a hot damp cloth with which you wipe your hands. The Japanese are great washers and bathers . . . I have been to a Japanese bath; it is a communal affair,[1] everyone, men and boys, sit all together in a large sunken tiled bath of hot water in the centre of the bath-house, after they have soaped and washed themselves at little taps at intervals round the walls. The Japanese have very pretty skins, primrose coloured. Francis doesn't go in for this form of bathing, he is self-conscious about exposing his body and prefers to bath at home in privacy; but Jim adores it, I believe, so in Sendai I expect to spend a lot of time stewing in Japanese baths. I must take care not to catch cold, for it will be colder in the North.

Oh dear, how are you all? I do worry from time to time and wish I were not so far away. But your letters so far have been so comforting. Dear Bunny, dear Queenie, dear you, I think of you much of the time, but there are some 12 hours difference in time between us, so when I think of you at about 5 o'clock in the afternoon, I can't say 'Nancy is now feeding Queenie', because in England it would be about 5 o'clock in the morning and you would all be fast asleep—or so I hope. It has been nice weather these last three days, sunny and warm, not too hot, and a lot more temples and their pretty gardens and charmingly painted servants have been visited. I am very well and the tummy works most of the time, but I get tired and like my afternoon nap.

Fondest love, darling Nance
 Joe

P.S. The bank has sent me more money, so I am okay. Hope you received the two cheques I sent last week.

To Francis King (1923–)   Chez K[irkup], Sendai 197
                                            21/10/60

Dear Francis
        your letter has just arrived. How glad I am, I feared my own to you was still on the way and that you had already classed me among those other ungrateful guests of yours who take all your lavish hospitality and never bother to send a word when they leave. So although it is neither Monday, Tuesday, or Wednesday, love sits me down in my chair to reply to you at once.

Jim Kirkup is a very nice chap and I get along with him well, but there is no escaping the fact that life here is somewhat monotonous. The trouble really is that one meets scarcely anyone. Professors never come as they come to you (and indeed they hardly could, for Jim keeps no servants, seldom eats in . . .); nor are we asked to them; and students don't come either—unless they have bed in view. I have been here over a week and one student only has called in

---

[1] See page 179, note 3.

that time: I caught merely a glimpse of him as he was bowed out of the bedroom. There is another 'steady', a boy in an Insurance office, very nice and nervous of whom I have seen a little. I am told I may see as much of him as I liked, but annual accountancy has kept his nose to the grindstone all the week. There is another student who talks thick and fluent American, hardly seems a Japanese at all, is thought not to be gay—but no one, self included, cares for him enough to find out. As is the way of things, *he* is all eagerness to take me around, and I am all eagerness to avoid him. Finally, a sort of 'cinema' boy, who comes at 10.0 every Sunday morning and was cast into my arms last Sunday. Not a word of English of course. So social life—so far, at any rate—is somewhat thin; I am either on my own or in Jim's company when he is not busy lecturing, reading, or writing poetry; I live largely in my bedroom unless I prowl the streets. This depresses me a bit—not lack of sex, I am not bothered by that—but how does one ever get to know and understand the Japanese unless one meets them?—and this would be an excellent place to know them in, it is about the right size. I speak to students sometimes in the streets, they have scarcely any English at all. Cinemas are said to be highly rewarding (most of J.'s friends have been met in those), so I go to them a lot, without reward. Agreeable companionship of any sort, so long as it was articulate, would make all the difference—but excepting for the brassy Americanised boy, whose grating voice positively jars, there seems no one. Still, I am not easily bored and get pleasure from strolling and looking about—and, one never knows, some blessing may fall. The people are awfully nice here, no doubt of that, very friendly, and much better-looking, I think, than in Kyoto, it is a pleasure to look at them. The sun is shining once more, so I must go forth to look at them again.

I am so glad your new cook suits you. What a relief for you. And I was so pleased with news of all my friends. I have sent cards to Ando-san and Fukushima, via you, and will send one to Katsumi soon. How I do look forward to seeing you all, and the dog-wogs and kitty-cats again.

A cable arrived for me at 7.0 a.m. on Wednesday. Poor Jim, who had gone to bed at 2.0. had to open the door for it and brought it up. I was perfectly petrified. Nancy must be dying I thought, or Queenie, or my aged aunt. But it was merely from my agent to say that two U.S. publishers had offered for my book[1] and which would I choose. Since one, Obolensky, offered a 1500 dollars advance and the other, Knopf, half that, I did not find the choice hard.[2]

Will write again.

Much love, dear F.

Joe

---

[1] *We Think the World of You.*

[2] It proved a disastrous choice. On 11 January 1962 A. wrote to Sandy Campbell: 'The U.S. edition of my novel is a perfect disgrace and has quite upset me. It seems to have been set up from an uncorrected proof—and no proof was sent to me. Can you imagine such muddle and stupidity? In the result it is packed with errors of all sorts, things the very opposite of what I wrote have got into it, and my careful sectionalising of the story has been disregarded so that the rather dramatic little tale has lost much of its drama. I am maddened by it, as who wouldn't be, and have written to complain.'

To E. M. Forster (1879–1970)

Dearest Morgan

I have not written to you for some time. As soon as I got to Tokyo, in a deluge of rain a week ago I began to feel perfectly happy here in Japan, really for the first time. I don't know why, perhaps not being with Europeans but on my own for a change: unfair to Jim, who is a dear. The Y.M.C.A. is a splendid hostel, hideously ugly outside, like a railway station within. But comfortable and cheap (14/- a night compared with the 38/- I paid here in a 'cheap' hotel I was stuffed in when I first came) and a constant *va et vient* of people of all nationality, but mostly Japanese and mostly young. It was my birthday two days later[1] and I was given the nicest present in the world. At 9.30 p.m. The time mattered because it brought it all about. I was sitting in my bedroom concocting an article for *The Listener* (they've asked me)—Impressions of Japan[2]—and you may be surprised to hear,—giving it and the Japanese the highest praise—, when I found my watch had stopped. There was a clock in the passage near the communal wash-house and I went to look. And a young man came out of the wash-house at that moment and gave me a backward look as he went to his room. The whole thing came out of the blue and took place in a trice. He left his door ajar for me to follow. He is a Japanese. His name is Saito. Since then he has been to my room. Once again from the wash-house (one has to wait and hang about, anything but embarrass) 'I will come to your room in a few minutes.' He was going to have a bath after his day's work. He is a business-man, somewhere between 25 and 30, a salesman in a brewery (how romantic!), to me very beautiful. He came in fresh and spotless linen, smelling of scent. So affectionate. So kind. He has been in America for a bit and can speak English. Of course I knew it would happen. The question was where. I thought it might happen in Sendai, but it didn't. It is a country where it must happen; age does not matter and the Japanese are so charming and uninhibited and curious, and so affectionate. It has made a great difference to my outlook—everything is all right now, I know—and so the question is whether and when I go to Kyoto. I like Francis, he is kind too, but I don't think I can bear the Europeans and Americans any longer. They put a rubbishy note on everything.[3] They are here too, I go out with them from time to time—round the bars and the cinemas (the 'feelies', you get 'felt' as

[1] November 4.
[2] The article was never finished. Two years later A. wrote to Roy Fuller on 17 August 1962: 'You may be sure I would oblige you if I could with something for the L[ondon] M[agazine], but I am an emptied and a washed-up vessel . . . Japan came to nothing much; I kept an industrious day-to-day notebook, but it yielded little in the end (Quentin Crewe, Kirkup and many others have done it all—the tourist's first impressions—since), one article only, for *The Listener*, most of which I swotted up from books on Buddhism after my return.' The article was a study of Kobo the Great Teacher who was born in A.D. 774, was a priest, and founded a Buddhist sect called Shingon, which is one of the most flourishing sects in modern Japan. It claims about seven million adherents and some twelve thousand temples belong to it. 'Kobo Daishi' appeared in *The Listener* on 31 August 1961.
[3] After the Second World War, the American authorities made an attempt to stop communal nude bathing. An attempt was also made to clamp down on prostitution, both male and female. Neither succeeded. The Japanese have bitter memories of this period.

you stand in the back of the crowd). It is all 'cute little numbers'[1] and the size of things. They seem not interested in anything but constant change. It is so dull and so expensive. I am pleased with my Saito, and grateful to him. I am all right with him, I know. I don't want to go to Francis—I don't want to come back to England—there is nothing for me there in Putney—excepting my darling Queenie. I do think of her. She has been so very sweet to me. But Nancy—yes I think of her too—would be so upset if I left her too long. I see all that. But for me, excepting to watch my dog die, there is nothing at all. I must decide whether to stay on here near Saito, if it works out all right (I think it will) or make a change. I am tired of changes, and there will be nothing for me in Kyoto except temples, the slaves of Osaka[2] and the cheapness of staying in someone else's house. The latter is rather important for I have £80 only in travellers' cheques left. Sorry to scratch out so much of this letter.[3] I drank too much whisky last night and became a bore myself. Dearest Morgan, I am so pleased to see the result of the Lawrence[4] case, though I have not seen a full report, I have had no letters for a week: they are in Kyoto, I expect, where I myself intended to be by now. I do hope all is better with you and yours; I am thinking of Rob. The weather here is very beautiful at present; yesterday I was in Shinjuku Park, so charming, looking at an exhibition of chrysanthemums, large and little; tonight I go to the Kabuki theatre. Write again soon.
Love
　Joe

199　To Donald Windham (1920–　)　17 Higashi-Tsuta-hachi, Kitashirakawa, Sakyo-ku, Kyoto, Japan[5]　14/11/60
Dear Don
　　　　I have your card from Denmark today. It has been a long time on the road, from there to England, thence to the above address (to which I shortly return), thence to Tokyo, where I have spent the last fortnight. For yes, indeed, I am in Japan. I have had 2 weeks in Kyoto, the great cultural centre, looking at temples, shrines and Zen gardens, another 3 weeks in another University town, Sendai, in the north, looking mostly at bar-boys; here I know not what I look at, myself principally, I think. Sometimes I wonder what I'm doing and getting out of it all. It is attractive and depressing and confusing. My mind spins. Millions of people with a sort of basic face, Simian and charming—I keep seeing in perfect strangers people I have met a few days before—and the rest of the scene resolves itself at times into a

---

[1] On 3 October A. had sent Forster a photograph of himself taken with two 'cute little numbers'.
[2] Male prostitutes.
[3] Four lines have been heavily scored through.
[4] On 20 October Penguin Books had been charged at the Old Bailey 'of publishing an obscene article, to wit, a book entitled *Lady Chatterley's Lover* by D. H. Lawrence'. On 2 November the jury returned a verdict of Not Guilty. Forster had been one of the witnesses for the defence: 'I had an easy time in the witness-box, was not cross-examined, only made my cold worse and even that is better now.'
[5] In Japan A. used Francis King's Kyoto address as a forwarding one. When he wrote this letter he had been in Tokyo since 1 November, staying at the Y.M.C.A. See Letter 198.

muddle of tiny bars, wooden dolls, *pachinko* saloons (a pin-table game, thousands of them, crammed with people), baseball and judo, mass-produced Buddhas, great and small, non-stop and ubiquitous T.V., radio, or gramophone noises, scintillating coloured lights, heads of black-uniformed students and schoolboys, soya sauce, smiles and conversational misunderstandings. All Japanese are taught English, and perhaps because they are taught mainly by Japanese or Americans they can seldom speak it and scarcely ever understand it. 'Queerness' here is called 'gayness', there are 'gay' bars to which the 'gay' go, and there are brothels in which they can be bought (1000 yen, an English pound), and there are slave markets, where, for the same sum, the normal, in return for board and lodging while they search about for work, have to consent to 'gaiety'. You describe your personal tastes to the proprietor, samples are paraded, and you take your choice or go elsewhere. This delight is obtainable in only one city that I know of, Osaka, about an hour's train journey from Kyoto. The 'gay' set off thither in the evening, for organised 'gaiety' begins nowhere until 9.0–10.0 p.m.; it is like going from London to Brighton after dinner for half-an-hour's pleasure.

I am to return to London for Xmas. Will you still be there, I wonder. My actual date is not yet fixed, nor my route (I am thinking of dropping off at Hongkong and perhaps Bangkok and Teheran). I don't much want to re-turn—except of course to see my friends . . . Nor really do I want to stay.

Much love to you and Sandy.

Joe

To Francis King (1923–)   Y.M.C.A., Tokyo 200
                                                                   15/11/60
Dearest F.
              a packet of letters came today. Thanks a lot. They were of no great interest, but I was glad to know that my home life was proceeding without calamity. I have bought my ticket for Kyoto and shall be with you on Thursday (THURSDAY) evening. Can't be bothered with Limited Expresses, so shall come on the 10.0 a.m. train as before, which reaches Kyoto soon after 6.0–6.20 to be precise. Don't bother to fetch me; I will take a hansom. If your dinner is still at 6.30 I shall be late for it, I fear.

Mr. Right continues wrong, but fortunately compensation offered itself last night. More of a Miss than a Mr. Right, and only right in the circum-stances. Dear me, what a place this Y.M.C.A. is. Miss Right has been here only 4 days—she said—and I bowed to her as she fluttered through the en-trance hall this morning. She bowed back. Soon afterwards, as she passed the desk where stood a respectable middle-aged European of my floor beside whom I have often shared and exchanged a few polite words, she gave his bottom a little dig—he turned and smiled—and it was instantly given away that he had had her before me. I was not observed observing this little scene.

Much looking forward to seeing you.

Joe

201 To E. M. Forster (1879–1970)   Y.M.C.A., Tokyo
                                                                          16/11/60

Dearest Morgan

the last letter I wrote to you was over-confident.[1] My romance came to a quick death and I am off to Kyoto tomorrow morning
early, for the last lap of my stay here. I wrote unguardedly to William too:
perhaps you could tell him that my letter to him, instead of anticipating a
future, marked a full-stop. The chap never came near me again, and only
with the utmost trouble and difficulty did I manage to have even a word
with him. The answer to it all I can't supply. Francis, to whom I wrote, supplies one, which may be right. He generalises all the time about the Japanese,
their sexual feelings and so on, and I think it may be true that they are a race
about whom one may generalise. Well, never mind. I have been two weeks
here today, and the first week was wonderful, the second wretched. Fortunately however, when I was at my lowest, a kind providence put compensation in my way—again in the useful wash-house. Nothing like so glamorous,
but it served me well, it comforted. The compensation also vanished afterwards for ever: it may indeed be best to live in a fairy-tale world (as Jim
seems to think) in which good fairies are not desired to do more than wave
their wands over one once and then disappear. The trouble with Saito was
that I had started to fall in love with him—if gradualness can happen in that
sorry business—and how difficult it is to behave sensibly in such a situation.
I fear I may have tangled matters, but shall never know the truth. He left
today with a formal bow to some apartment he had found, I don't know
where, I don't even know his full name. But I comfort myself with the reflection that if it *had* progressed as I once hoped, I should have been in an
awful fix, for what is the good of having a lover in Tokyo, unless one can stay
on for ever. I hope I may manage to forget about it in Kyoto in the brothels
of Osaka. You will be pleased to hear that someone else bore my heart up
and tranquilised my mind during the past week—and that was you. For I
bought a copy (50 yen, about 1/-) of *Howards End* here in a second-hand book
store, the Penguin, and read it while I waited in vain. It was a great pleasure
to have your mind in the room, and a great help. I haven't heard from you
for a long time. I do want to know how Rob is and how you are. I expect to
remain in Kyoto for about a month, then to fly home, perhaps visiting
[Edmund] Blunden (Hong Kong) and Kenneth Harrison on the way.
Fondest love
  Joe

202 To E. M. Forster (1879–1970)   Daimyooin Temple, Koyasan
                                                                           1/12/60

Dearest Morgan

I have your letter, forwarded from Kyoto. So pleased with
your news generally. I am most happy here on this mountain-top, and Saito
no longer troubles my heart or head. Also the way of enlightenment and re-

---
[1] Letter 198.

covery offered, and I took it ... I applied ... to the Y.M.C.A. for his address: 'A kind gentleman of the name of Saito, Room 214, who had been good enough to lend me a guide book and had forgotten to return and who[se] card I had unfortunately lost.' They sent his new Tokyo address to me at once, and before leaving Kyoto I wrote to him, a very careful letter on Francis's advice, though I did not feel careful: Francis said the Japanese are alarmed by emotion, which they themselves are able to control. I have not yet had a reply, perhaps I never shall, though it was a letter difficult for Japanese good manners and politeness to ignore. If I get no answer, the matter that has bothered me will be clarified: I shall know that it was not a stupid misunderstanding but my emotion alarmed him. He was the most prudent and nervous of all the people I have met.

But he has gone out of my mind now. Japan is a fickle place, and I understand better now why the Americans and Europeans are never satisfied and want to have everyone they see. The boys are charming, ready-smilers,[1] cheerful, curious if not actually sophisticated, and extremely good-looking if one likes, as I do, the face which varies between Buddha and the monkey. Certain features—hair, slitty eyes, tiny nose, apricot skins—are so common, that one is able to get confused: I worried, after my first encounter with Saito ... whether I should recognise him again, and kept thinking I saw him in other people. I did instantly recognise him at last, but it serves to show. We have missed something, dear Morgan, by not coming here earlier. You would love it. Especially here. Everyone seems so friendly, gentle, happy, and kind. My little priest sings to himself all the time—any songs—'Jingle-bell'—and is always smiling and laughing. He has not much to laugh about, not a penny, doubtful prospects, ill-fed, one shabby student's suit: 'Priest' means little, by the way; though an ordained priest (ordained last Nov.) and a believer and student of Buddhism, he can take any other job that offers. The benefit of priesthood is that he can stay and board rent-free in any temple in return for services (cleaning the house and grounds) which in certain months, when the pilgrims come in hordes, are very arduous. And it is a life which gives him the opportunity to study—English and Buddhism. But he is so ill-fed, I cannot sit down to my own tasty meals (I pay £1 a day for the room and 3 meals) without sharing them with him. So I myself get pretty hungry. He is a sturdy boy, the Buddha face, infinitely sweet and very clever: he speaks English better than most people I have met and can read and write the Chinese script. He wants to live with me always. The weather is so cold—we have had falls of snow—we venture out only for short periods, to see a temple or a garden, or to sit talking to his professors in their rooms or in the University Commonroom: he is also a student of it and attends lectures there for a few hours each day as well as looking after the temple and me. The rest of the day we are always together in my room, lying side by side in bed, under the quilt under which, at the foot of the bed, the charcoal burns

[1] In the following year on 16 March in *The Listener*, A., in a review of various books about Japan, took Quentin Crewe to task for saying that the Japanese 'smiled little'. 'To me,' he wrote, 'they seemed always on the smile and the laugh, and I believe it is more consonant with their national character, as we know it, that they should be so, in spite of the hardships of their life.'

in a pit: it warms our feet. The room has no furniture, excepting a low table, never used, a vase of chrysanthemums, and large bronze bowl, in which also charcoal burns and keeps a bronze kettle always simmering for tea (green tea). I wear Japanese clothes, provided by the temple—and it is all pleasure and happiness and no pain excepting for the cold and stomach inclined to recoil against being constantly folded up against my knees from sitting always on the floor. I am given meat as [a] concession to my Western tastes, the rest is hard to identify—seaweed I recognise, lotus root, turnip, sweet potato and bean meal. Rice, of course, is the staple thing; and practically all little Kinoshita is provided with. I have been here 5 days, and shall stay another 5. I would like to be here in the spring. I don't want to go and am wondering whether I can disappoint Nancy and not return till after Xmas. She is getting scared of staying in the flat alone[1]—a nice future prospect for me! I could go to Kinoshita's home in Okayama with him at the end of December if I remained: he has a vacation then. My bank is sending me another £100, for I am almost at the end of my last. Hard to know what to do. Nancy can't be having a very cheerful time. I drink no alcohol excepting saké hot—which Kinoshita and I sip at night over an evening meal. In the late evenings other young priests come in (*they* have had no heat until today Dec. 1) and sit with us with their feet too under the quilt. They speak no English, nor does the Master of the Temple: it is [the] Shingon sect. Oh dear, why did we not discover Japan before we were so old!?
Love darling
　Joe

203　To E. M. Forster (1879–1970)　　　　　　c/o Francis King, Kyoto
14/12/60
Dearest Morgan
　　　　　　then you shall have a briefer letter, since you groan at long ones, and this must wish you, May, Bob, Rob, and the little ones a very happy Xmas and, maybe, serve as a birthday letter too. Rob sent me the most lively and amusing and gratifying letter; in case I fail to answer it from here, will you tell him that I was perfectly delighted with it both on account of what it said and how it said it, as also it communicated a feeling of health and vitality that I have long wished for him. I have decided to let everyone down and not return till mid-January. I have nearly £100 left in cheques and think I should be an ass not to spend it here or on the way home. My eleven days in the cold-fingers (the toes keep warm) monastery gave me a great deal of pleasure; the Rev. Jisho (Kinoshita's priestly name) came to spend a night here last Saturday, and I am going back to Koyasan on Dec. 22 (Francis will be going to Tokyo that day on a short hol.) for a couple more days. Kinoshita will then be starting a vacation himself and is going to take me with him for a week, I know not whither but believe to some hot-spring

---

[1] In November Aunt Bunny had gone into hospital.

spa on the Inland Sea. It will be nice for me for I am fond of him and it is much more fun travelling about with the Japanese than with Westerners. I expect we shall be staying in more temples—he has access to the lot. Then I come back here again, by the end of the year. On Jan. 4 I have booked myself off to Hongkong from Osaka by air and hope that Edmund Blunden will still be there, out of term, to fix me up. I have written to him. I could stay 4 days, or split them up between Hongkong and Bangkok, where also I have a contact who said he would put me up. After that I aim to drop off in Teheran if Kenneth [Harrison] will be there and available out of term. I have written to him too. By that time I expect I shall be broke, for my week with the Rev. Jisho will cost me his keep as well as my own, and shall not be able to halt again until I reach London. I don't think I shall be home later than Jan. 15, perhaps earlier. Nancy, who has been writing woebegone letters, now writes cheerfully. Her own health is better. Bunny goes on well in hospital and there is no indication yet that the doctors intend to clear her out and if so where (Nancy is frightened of having her back and I am not surprised, but if she can stay where she is until my return I don't mind having charge of her),[1] Queenie's sphincter muscle is weakening, poor old pet, and she has started to relieve herself in the most unusual and inconvenient places, but I shan't mind that either and she is otherwise well. I went to a good concert last night, the Israel Philharmonic, in the Kyoto Kaikan, a grander building than our Festival Hall, and am now off with Ando-san to see the Golden Temple of Kinkakinji. Your news always interests and pleases, though I don't refer to it, supposing that you would prefer my own. But conjunctivitis should be glanced at: there is a saint here who cures eye-complaints (Trevor-Roper[2] says he spreads them) and I will consider whether to rub his eyes, as the peasants do, on your account. I note that this brief letter has swollen, but there shall be no spiders and mice in the margins:[3] it shall end here.

With fond love to you all

Joe

To E. M. Forster (1879–1970)   [Daimyooin Temple,] Koyasan 204
22/12/60

Dearest Morgan

here we are again, and this carries my loving birthday greetings. A letter from Jack, and a letter from Nancy, arrived in Kyoto just before I left yesterday, the former very brisk and lively, the latter rather

---

[1] True to plan, A. was home by 15 January 1961 and did not learn of Aunt Bunny's death until then. He had given no forwarding address to anyone when he left Japan on 4 January, and had 'stopped off' in Bangkok and Tehran. He wrote to Francis King: 'Old Aunt Bunny died on Jan. 3rd, the day before I left you . . . She was very old, poor darling . . . and it was time she went . . .' She was 92.

[2] Patrick Trevor-Roper, the ophthalmic surgeon.

[3] A. frequently wrote in the margins of letters—especially in the case of air letters—so as to cram in as much as possible. Forster would refer to these additions as 'spiders' and 'mice'.

wistful. However, things seem much the same at home, and will stay the same I hope (no further anxieties, I mean) until I return in about 3 weeks' time. Bunny is still in hospital, unaware that she has had a serious illness, and blaming poor Nancy for putting and keeping her there, though she is far safer and better off where she is, fussed over by nurses, doctors and patients, properly fed, bathed, tidied up and kept off the brandy, than she was at home. But I don't like to think of her feeling herself discarded and if the doctors are agreeable I will have her back when I return. Certainly Nancy can't look after her single-handed.

Francis, with gall-bladder trouble, went off to Tokyo by car yesterday with his friend, interpreter and general factotum, Fukushima, and I have travelled back to this priestly dump. But only for two nights. Tomorrow morning Kinoshita will be free of his temple duties (he is at present brushing spiders off the roofs and ceilings—'What are those little things that make a net?' 'Spiders, dear'—with an immensely long brush or broom with bamboo leaves instead of bristles and feathers) and we go off early to Okayama, a town called Kurashiki, pronounced Kraski, where he lives, and where I am to be shown some sights and perhaps the family and shall mess about with him for a week. I hope it may be fun and worth the disappointment I have caused in Putney by not turning up for Xmas—an occasion always grumbled at when I am there. 'What on earth am I to do if Sally[1] sends the customary turkey?' cries poor Nancy. I see it is rather a lot for one lone female and a dog. Well, no turkey for me; Xmas does not signify in Buddhism, though England and America have imported it into Japan, where also it had no place, and the shops are stuffed with Xmas rubbish while carols stream from the wireless. Francis will be in the midst of it in Tokyo, staying with the Bottralls,[2] but I hope it may pass me by. I return to Kyoto on the 30th at latest, I don't know what will happen to me then except that I must make homeward tracks soon. I have my ticket for Hong Kong (the 4th), Teheran (the 12th), but hitherto no word from either Edmund Blunden or Kenneth Harrison. As you have said, I am not much of a Far Eastern traveller and have no desire to halt in either of those places unless a friendly face can welcome me, so if there is still no word when I reach Kyoto, I shall have to revise my journey and perhaps fly straight home. There is a third person I have written to in Bangkok, a fearful bore but better than nothing and he did say 'Come and stay' when I met him, but hospitality is often regretted when there has been time for reflection and the fumes of alcohol have faded away. Still, out of three feelers I ought to have some response.

It is jolly cold here, though less cold than on my previous visit. Most of the snow has vanished and economy has set in: commons are shorter than they were, fish has taken the place of meat, and coffee has been knocked off altogether. It was always a luxury, Nescafé at 10/- a tin. It has now gone up to 11/- and I am told I can no longer have it. I don't mind, excepting that Japanese green tea has an extraordinary effect on the bladder, about every

---

[1] A.'s half-sister, who became Duchess of [——] in 1963.
[2] Ronald Bottrall, recalling A.'s stay in Japan, wrote to Braybrooke on 10 August 1971: 'A delightful man who always carried a fan.'

half hour one pees a pint to every cup one drinks, a nuisance when one composes oneself for sleep.

Well, darling Morgan, my best and fondest love. I hear that the *P[assage] to I[ndia]* may soon end in London. Sad, but it has had a jolly good run. Love to May, Bob and Robin if with you

Joe

Part Eight
REVIEWING JAPAN

205 To Francis King (1923–   )

Bangkok
9/1/61

Dearest Francis

I have been here since the 5th. Make a firm resolution never to come. The temperature was 90° when I arrived, in two sweaters and three vests from the cold of Tokyo; and this is the Siamese winter. Naturally, I fell ill at once, diarrhoea and sudden vomiting, and [—] has been most awfully kind I must say, giving up his bed to me in his air-conditioned room; but even for his sake, don't come.

The heat is stunning and humid, the place is a network of mostly stagnant waterways, all breeding mosquitoes galore, the terrain is perfectly flat in all directions, a low skyline, no higher than the length of palms, and banana and rain-trees that hem one in. Moving away from dear Japan towards India, all the disagreeable features of that latter country, as I remember it, begin here: the muddy complexion (often diddy-daddied), the muddy eye, laziness, stupidity, dishonesty, betel-chewing, dirt and filthy smells, bad and unhygienic food, no hot water, prickly heat, rampant rabies, and wretched mangy dogs, hairless and emaciated, whom no one will kill, and no one will feed. You would *detest* it, my dear. It is true that certain features deserve praise: the rice is better and better cooked than that sticky white pulp the Japanese are so fond of, and flowers everywhere are of a tropical beauty, and (though I do not praise it, for I don't care, but I know you do) the male human figure is somewhat larger and better built than you find in Japan. Also (unverified: I couldn't even raise a finger, let alone anything else, to investigate in this boiling, sweating atmosphere), sex is said to be easily obtained. The large, lazy conceited dunderhead whom [—] has kindly delegated to show me about might please you with his biceps, but only enrages me with his ignorance and lumpishness, and all this ambition to improve one's English when it's perfectly plain that one is quite unfitted for any job in which English could be of the least advantage. The noodle prostrates himself three times, head to ground, in front of every Buddha he sees, thinks he's a Moslem perhaps. And 'You're welcome' he says to everything. 'Do you mind paying the taxi?' 'You're welcome.' 'Well, home at last.' 'You're welcome.' 'God! It's hot.' 'You're welcome.' I am now so nervous of hearing that phrase that even if it were 20° cooler, I could not unbutton his flies.

One or two of the temples here are worth a look at in their baroque way, mostly they are tawdry,—gold, glass and porcelain—and dilapidated, and since they are mostly built of brick and stucco, their decay is far from impressive. Dirty, white-washed pillars. In Wat Po today a young bitch was dying in one of the courtyards. She was quite young, I could see her teeth, she had some filthy disease, bloody pustules and orange swellings all over her legs and stomach. Lying in the full sun she could not get up, and uttered piercing and heart-rending cries whenever she tried. People everywhere, a soft-drink café where they lounged, a monk was addressing some children ten yards away. Her screams were audible all over the temple precincts, no one gave her the least help, people just skirted round her. I bought her an ice-cream which she feebly lapped, and tried to locate a vet later but even the vets won't put animals out of their misery: against their religion. The temple contains a Buddha, 50 yards away, 'reclining' on his elbow. Wretched piece of nonsense.

Well, I hope I shan't leave my bones here too. I must say I feel much diminished and can hardly wait to get on to Tehran on Thursday. Even England seems a refuge. How in the world could [—] have pretended that this was nicer than Japan. Perhaps he feels differently now, for he was visited by the police yesterday. When I walked in I thought he was holding one of your conversation classes, such masses of shoes in his porch—but they were police shoes. A van was waiting outside to convey him to the Police Station. He was suspected of nefarious activities in the antique line and of being a receiver of stolen goods. I wonder if he is. His protests of innocence have been so vehement and prolonged. This happened yesterday and I really assure you that it has formed a single topic of conversation since, we eat and drink it, he has been on the phone about it all evening to all his friends. Sleeping pill last night. I must say his house is perfectly crammed with Buddhas (what on earth can he want with them all?) and it was perfectly crammed with policemen too, far from polite. He managed to avoid the van. Ah well, come Thursday, 'You're welcome.'
Love to you and Ando-san
    Joe

To John Wickens (1934–   )   17 Star & Garter Mansions, Putney,   206
                                S.W.15   17/1/61

Dear Mr Wickens
            I returned on Sunday after four months in Japan to find your letter of Dec. 13. I'm sorry that your American visit was rather disappointing, though I can imagine that it might be; I have never myself felt any inclination to go. Japan, on the other hand, was perfectly enchanting, I have never liked a people or a country so much, and was delighted and fascinated by all I saw. Sorry indeed to be back in this all too solid and complacent country.
    Yes, I was rather a mess that day you called; but soon afterwards my neck

and skin healed, more or less, and I popped into a plane the moment the doctors discharged me.[1] I took the Polar Route, seventeen hours from Paris to Tokyo by Boeing jet, and returned the Far Eastern route, stopping off at Bangkok and Teheran, neither of which did I greatly like. But by then my heart was already bestowed upon the Japanese, so I had nothing much to offer to the Siamese or the Persians. My Bodley Head book[2] came out during my absence; it got fairly good notices on the whole, but I doubt if it has sold. I have not yet had a statement from the publishers. You say very nice things about me and my work, and naturally I am pleased, but I find it hard to see myself in the hallowed light in which you view me. I doubt if I shall ever be able to supply you with an 'unpurged' copy of my novel, for I believe that the only version I ever had, a typescript, has been lost by my agent, and my wincing mind is unlikely to remind me of what I first wrote,[3] particularly now when all that is the shuffled-off past and my head is now full of other and better things. But first of all you had better read the published version: you may think its implications sufficient and that no more is needed. It's very kind of you to want to send me another present and I am very grateful to you. Let it be gin as usual. Charming though the Japanese are, their national tipple, Saké, is a very poor brew: I drank it all the time I was there, but it was an undeniable pleasure to meet gin once more when I had left their pretty shores. My sister, also pleased with your message, looks blank when I put your question to her, then says 'Ask him to send whatever he thinks I will like.' But since your acquaintance with her is so slight, you can hardly be expected to judge her tastes. However, that is all I was able to get out of her. It was fun meeting you after our correspondence, and I'm glad you found the courage to beard the lion in his den. A poor sort of lion he turned out to be that day, collared like his dog[4]—but I hope you found him tame enough, so that if ever you revisit this island you will have no qualms about calling upon him again.

Yours sincerely

Joe Ackerley

207 To Francis King (1923–   )   17 Star & Garter Mansions, Putney, S.W.15
20/2/61

Dear Francis

I am sending off a parcel to you today, a pullover for Ando-san. I hope it may arrive all right: I expect I shall send it ordinary parcel post to

---

[1] A reference to June 1960 when A. was knocked down 'in the Boulevard St. Germain, in the pouring rain', and taken by ambulance to a hospital in Paris where he had to remain for four days: 'Breakages . . . not very serious . . . but I had to wear a high stiff collar contraption to keep my chin up and my neck still . . .' See Letters 189 and 190.

[2] *We Think the World of You.* See page 170, note 4.

[3] The lost typescript was found, and A. wrote to Stephen Spender on 19 August: 'You have been so kind to me over [*We Think the World of You*] . . . I will copy out the lost bits for you on small sheets of paper so that you can slip them into your copy as alternative readings . . . Whether they are good riddance or bad riddance I don't really know.' In the following year A. did the same thing for Colin Haycraft. See Letter 218 and Appendix F.

[4] See note 1 above.

save expense, but I will see what air-mail costs. If it goes parcel-post, I suppose it won't arrive for six or seven weeks, and you will be entering the summer when pullovers are no longer wanted. Anyway, give it to the dear chap for me when it does come, and please send me his address, which I seem not to have. I would like to write to him. I have had a card from Kinoshita, who is busy with his Goma ceremony—playing with fire I call it, I've written letters to a couple of other chaps I liked, to Okamoto and to the young airforce boy who travelled with Kinoshita and myself up to Kurashiki. But I hardly expect replies unless they come by sea; it would make quite a hole in the boys' pockets to correspond with England by air-mail. Send me also David [Kidd]'s address, I think of him often and I may have some questions on Buddhism to put. I'm sorry to hear of his loss, and gain;[1] a ghost in this flat would be quite a treat instead of the more substantial forms of plumbers, painters and carpenters which have haunted me for the last ten days. Hardly possible to work—not that I want to—and as for poor Queenie, she is almost out of the few wits she has left. So far *her* room, which is also mine, has been left undisturbed except as a repository for lumber from the rest of the flat, but soon we shall both have to move out of it. Oh dear, how old she is, and how touching in her old age, carefully choosing the smoothest bits of road to cross by because gravel and roughness hurt her old paws and make her stumble as she totters along. I keep thinking of her death and what life in this flat, however spruce it may be, will be without her. I think it will be unendurable and I am already planning to make and save money for a return to Japan in the Spring of 1962—if *I* survive. *The Listener* has just sent me some books on Japan to review, a new Donald Keene[2]—if it is new, I seem to have seen most of its illustrations before, travel books by Messrs Quentin Crewe[3] and Esler Denning,[4] and a comic Japanese novel called *Hizakurige* or *Shank's Mare*, by Ikku Jippensha over which I yawn off my head.[5] Every joke—ha-ha-ha—falls as flat as a cowpat: I think I shall say that in my review? Do you know about this novel? Tuttle Inc. have produced it, in great style and at great expense, with appendix notes which all refer to the wrong pages.

Dear Francis, how bored I am, I cannot find words to describe my boredom—indeed I don't think I can even find words to finish this letter space. Everyone in England seems hibernating, my diary is practically empty of engagements, films and plays are putrid, all my money is dribbling away in paint and whitewash, there is nothing to do but drink and sleep, which is

---

[1] Kidd, an American writer and antiquarian living in Japan, had recently moved house. The 'gain' was an even more beautiful house than his first, but the 'loss' was a ghost who had haunted the first and played at night his *o-koto* (a kind of harp).

[2] *Living Japan*, which A. reviewed on 16 March.

[3] *A Curse of Blossom*, which A. reviewed on 16 March.

[4] *Japan*, in Benn's 'Nations of the World' series, which A. reviewed on 18 May.

[5] This novel belongs to the close of the Tokugawa Shogunate, that period of 250 years when Japan isolated herself from the rest of the world. Jippensha (1765–1831) intended that his novel should be a comic guide-book describing the adventures and misadventures of two irrepressible clowns, in their ramblings about the Tokaido, one of the highways connecting Edo (now Tokyo), the capital of the Shogunate, with Kyoto, the seat of the Emperor. In Japan, the book has always been greatly enjoyed and loved. But to Western eyes, A. suggested in his review on 16 March, 'its humour may seem rather childish, tedious and flat, related though it is with great gusto and constantly applauded by the Ha-ha-has and Ho-ho-hos of the irrepressible clowns.'

about all I do do—and dream of 'New Friends' and 'G-Strings'.[1] Would I
were back with you, dear. I try to write, but I feel I know nothing. I am
astounded at the impatience and arrogance of people who trot off to some
foreign country for a few weeks or months and then write a book about it.
Even Mr. Quentin Crewe, after a year in Japan, seems at a loss. 'Ahead, in
the distance,' he begins, 'rose huge blankets of solid cloud wallowing up to
meet us as we gradually lost height: we humped down through the swirls of
mist, and broke through to see below us the coast-line of Japan'. 'Solid
cloud' indeed! That would be a nice problem for air travel. Other writers
start even further back and tell us how they packed and what they took, so
anxious are they not to get too soon to the subject of their book. If you see
Ando-san, ask him this conundrum: what is the difference, if any, between
Ukemochi-no-Kami (said by Sir George Sansom to be the food goddess with
the shrine at Ise), Toyonki-Omikami (said by the *Japan Guide Book*[2] to be the
food goddess with the shrine at Ise), and Uga-no Mitama (said, also by the
Japan Guide Book, to be the Goddess of Rice and Food at Inari). Sir George
complicates matters even further by suggesting that Inari actually is
Ukemochi-no-Kami. You could also put this question to one of your
classes.

Delighted to hear that Jolly Jack Tar has turned up again. I felt sure he
would. Marry Nakatani's mother of course: you could never have a nicer
son and you know how obedient Japanese children are to their parents. Oh
yes, and by the bye, when you come home would it be possible to bring the
negatives of those photos of me feeding the Nara deer to lend to me? They
may be of publicity use one day.

Love from

Joe

208 To Francis King (1923–   )   17 Star & Garter Mansions, Putney, S.W.15
?/3?/61

Dear Francis

so pleased to have your letter, but how distressing about
the puppy,[3] it must have been the most appalling experience for you, you
hadn't told me about it before. It has certainly saved you from having
5 dogs, but I expect you had got attached to the little creature. I find
myself now more upset by the bad behaviour of animals to each other
than the bad behaviour of humans to each other, we are more used to that,
and indeed I do think that generally speaking animals get on better together than people manage to do. Food, love, of course they were trying
subjects, but I never had any canine difficulties of a serious sort there myself. Don't have any more akita dogs anyway, they are always said to be
particularly stupid. I have had an extremely nice letter from Fukuda-san,

---

[1] Bar-brothels in Osaka, specialising in boys.
[2] Published by the Japanese Tourist Board.
[3] An akita puppy had been killed by its father, when it attempted to steal some food from the
older dog's bowl. King, while waiting for the vet, wondered if he himself ought to give it the *coup
de grâce*.

telling me of the same disaster: it came yesterday and I will answer it soon; it is the most rewarding letter I have so far had from a Japanese, closely connected and giving lots of news, infinitely more capable and thoughtful than Kinoshita's letters or the one I've had from Norio, the air-force boy I met on a train. I'm awfully glad your Jolly Jack Tar has been back and given pleasure: do tell me about David and his prejudices, I find myself slightly mystified, I know he dislikes students, and I know he does not wish to be personally entangled with anyone, but does he actually dislike the Japanese in a general way? You sometimes speak of his reactions, in a way that I don't quite follow. I have finished reading Quentin Crewe's book[1] now and have given it a favourable notice. It has many merits—indeed I might say too many—for he has covered all the ground I thought of covering myself. What little was left—Koyasan—has been covered by an American lady named Eliza[beth] Gray Vining.[2] Indeed there is nothing left to write about, it seems to me. All the burning questions you and I and others in Kyoto talked of together—have the Japanese logical minds, individuality, a heart, a head?—all have been attended to by Mr Crewe in a lively and energetic manner: Geisha houses and Japanese inns, he has missed little. And, though exasperated, like you, he comes out friendly and civilised, it is really, on the whole, a pretty good book. I think Sir Esler Denning[3] is good too, though it is largely politics, of which I know nothing, though I have undertaken to review it.[4] He seems a clever and decent sort of man: he was British Ambassador, as doubtless you know, in Tokyo from '53[5] to '57. But he is strongly anti-Communist—or at least darkly suspicious of all the Communist moves—and thinks that Japan would be dotty to sever herself from America, remain unarmed and hope for peaceful co-existence in the Pacific. I do hate that attitude. The whole world is crazy with mutual suspicions, but I think it is time that *someone* took a risk, disarmed, and saw what happened, and I hope Japan's pacifist feelings will prevail. After all, there still are masses of nuclear weapons in the hands of others which can be used upon Japan if her neutrality aspirations got her, and everyone else into trouble. But I do think this risk worth taking. If you want to read him, his important chapters are the last two.[6]

My flat is finished but I cannot shake off my cold, not ill but seedy and bored. Excepting for reviewing I don't want to write—the less so now that I can see that all has already been said. I go occasionally to plays and films, but without great pleasure. Last night I went with Stuart Hampshire to a play called *The Connection*,[7] about the drug traffic in America, in which a

---

[1] *A Curse of Blossom*, which A. had reviewed for *The Listener* on 16 March, along with *Shank's Mare* by Ikku Jippensha, *Hiroshige* by Walter Exner and *Living Japan* by Donald Keene. Cf. Letter 207.

[2] In *Return to Japan* (1961).

[3] *Japan* in Benn's 'Nations of the World' series.

[4] On 18 May A. reviewed it for *The Listener* with Elizabeth Gray Vining's book and Herschel Webb's *An Introduction to Japan*. See note 2 above.

[5] 1952 in fact.

[6] 'Japan's Post-War International Relations' (Chapter 16) and 'Japan's Place in the Post-War World' (Chapter 17).

[7] By Jack Gelber.

boil on a man's neck is squeezed out on the stage, letting us off nothing. The sufferer had complained about his boil and how much it hurt him up to the moment it was squeezed—but I have had quite enough boils and cysts in my neck and life to know that they do *not* hurt at the time when they can be broken, they only itch; it is in the earlier stages, when they cannot be squeezed, that they hurt. How bored one is with such ignorantly sensational plays; the present slap-dash drama is destroying the old, in which care, thought, and discipline were required.[1] Oh a dull life, dear Francis, and no 'New Friends'[2] to repair to. Have you now your Spring? How I wish I were there with you.

Love

Joe

209 To Francis King (1923–   )   17 Star & Garter Mansions, Putney, S.W.15

5/4/61

Dear Francis

between reviewing a book about a Parisian cheetah for *The Listener*[3] and reverting to my Buddhist studies, I am having a letter-writing day. Shirotani has been attended to (I have had a five-page letter from him of such charm that Forster—much referred to in it, for Shirotani has been captivated by his writings—has also sent him a personal line), and James Kirkup (weeping in Bath, to which he returned, over the Pole, earlier than intended, his mother's precarious health having collapsed. It seems he will not now be returning to Japan, too far away from the sick bed. Who took his Sendai place do you know? Close bracket). Now you, dear, and afterwards Kinoshita, who says he has been ill 'with pains in his back'. I wonder if David put them there while they were conversing on Buddhism.

I'm sorry about your accident,[4] but I see you have not read your Ruth Benedict. Clearly the policeman was repaying an *on*,[5] tangled with *giri*[6] or *gimu*;[7] possibly the *on* was a *chu*.[8] No, but frankly, Frank, have you read her *The Chrysanthemum and the Sword*?[9] I have been deeply absorbed in it, and if it is right about Japanese character (is it? I have put this question to Shirotani

---

[1] A. wrote on another occasion to Geoffrey Gorer: 'The current critics are far from reliable, but then who has better taste than oneself?'

[2] See page 192, note 1.

[3] *Our Friend Yambo* by André Mercier, which was published on 4 May. In the middle of A.'s review, there occurs this characteristic passage: 'Out of affection for . . . his owners, [Yambo the cheetah] does his best to return their love and become the domesticated pet they wish him to become. Like the chimpanzee he succeeds almost too well, for "[his] new behaviour and his amorous airs when he looked at my wife were strange and disturbing. Naturally as a college-boy is in love with his school-teacher's wife, in other words without hope but not without passion." Hope or no hope it is thought advisable to have the whip always handy on the coverlet of the bed. An unenterprising amateur with a mere Alsatian dog may be permitted at least to think that with a little less teasing, a little less apprehension, a little less threatening, M. Mercier, who prides himself as an animal tamer, might get along with his cheetah in greater comfort.'

[4] A motor accident. A drunken Japanese had ridden his motorcycle straight into the back of King's stationary car. A policeman who happened to be on the scene mysteriously then decided that King's driver was at fault.

[5] An obligation passively incurred. See note 6 below.

[6] Acceptance of the fact that the repayment of an obligation can never be more than partial.

[7] A debt which must be paid with mathematical equivalence to the favour received.

[8] Duty to the Emperor and/or Japanese law.

[9] 1947.

also. The woman never set foot in Japan, I understand),[1] I don't see how any foreigner can hope to get on in Japan unless he has read it. I believe she was replied to [in] some other book:[2] I must get hold of it. I'm glad you are seeing a lot of Nakatani, Fukuda and Ando (you must give me the last named's address, by the bye; you said he was going to write to me, but he hasn't, so I would like to write to him, even if I had his initial, it would do and I could put a letter through you, but putting just 'Ando-san' on an envelope looks so odd), I wish some nice young men called on me. Actually a rather handsome boy—blue eyes, blue jeans—has appeared on the Putney streets and smiles at me when we meet. Hitherto I have not been able to return it, for, not expecting dalliance in this dull place I have got into the lazy habit of going out without my denture, and to reply with a toothless grin might ruin whatever chances there may be. So I've been wearing my teeth lately, and naturally, the boy has not appeared to see them. But I feel quite cheerful. Cuthbert Worsley[3] last week took occasion to say loudly on 'The Critics' that *My Dog Tulip* was the best dog book that had ever been written—so perhaps my remainder will now sell like hot turds ('pure findings': see [Henry] Mayhew)[4]—and I have also had a cheque from America for nearly £500. I shall hoard it all up and blue it on another Japanese journey next Spring. My sister has been quite seriously ill for a month with pleurisy and pneumonia, but is now recovering, so I have been . . . doing a Florence Nightingale . . . I myself, now that, like Kinoshita, though without [—]'s painful help, I have done my article on Buddhism,[5] have nothing more to write: that clever Mr. [Quentin] Crewe has done it all in his book.[6]

Forster was here this Easter, paying a call, tripped on my doorstep and fell flat on his face. He was awfully badly shaken, I'm afraid, and may have injured a wrist, possibly broken it. I put him to bed for a bit and then he was driven back to Cambridge. I haven't yet heard how he does.

Love

Joe

To Donald Windham (1920–)   Putney 210
    21/4/61

Dear Don

Japanese paper, too thin I fear, and the question, which this letter may answer, is whether it is not better employed in the W.C.—unless it is too thin even for that. I enjoyed your rambling news. Morgan seems better. He returned to King's from hospital on Wednesday, and says 'I am

---

[1] Correct. She writes in Chapter I: 'The fact that [when I was writing this book] our two nations [i.e. America and Japan] were at war meant . . . that I had to forego the most important technique of the cultural anthropologist: a field trip.'

[2] *Without the Chrysanthemum and the Sword: a Study of Youth in Post-War Japan* by Jean Stoetzel (1955).

[3] T. C. Worsley.

[4] 'The pure-finders meet with a ready market for all the dogs' dung they are able to collect . . .' See section entitled 'Of the "Pure"-Finders' in *London Labour and the London Poor* (1851).

[5] 'Kobo Daishi'. On 19 August A. wrote to Stephen Spender: 'My Buddhist article . . . contains my usual ingredients I fear, boys and dogs, but I think it is rather fun.' See page 179, note 2.

[6] *A Curse of Blossom* (1961).

told to keep quiet, and willing to.' I thought he said he had written to Sandy about the article.[1] Perhaps he just meant to and forgot. He wasn't sure what he thought of it at first, inclined rather to dislike himself as such a 'sweet old gentleman', but when I said I liked it he was consoled and came round to like it too. My sister is somewhat better, but still mostly bed-ridden and 'on my hands'. Life is rather dull. The days go hurrying by, and sometimes I sadly hear their little pattering, ticking feet and think of them disappearing into history with nothing in their hands but a yawn. However, *The Listener* has taken my article on Buddhism[2]—it is rather fun, I think—and I have demanded 50 guineas for it, but doubt if I shall get it.[3] But now that Stuart Hampshire has praised my novelette in such high terms in the May *Encounter*,[4] maybe people will stand in awe of me and give me what I ask. Yes, I got your letter about it, thank you dear Don, also the negatives, thank you again: I've done nothing with them yet, but have them safe, I believe, and will return them to you one day. If Truman Capote was a good guy like you, he would send me word direct, for roundabout praise is never so rewarding.

How lucky you are to be among all those attractive boys.[5] The English are so ugly, so odious, and so dirty. I was grumbling the other day to a Professor [Charles] Boxer, a Far Eastern expert here, about American meddling in Japan,[6] and he said 'The Japanese should consider themselves lucky not to have been occupied by the English. Americans are more easy-going than the English and will roll into bed with anyone. But the English would soon have cleaned all the sex out of the country and interfered in every sort of gaiety and licence.' I don't know how true this is, but it certainly found a sympathetic ear, and is true about the English in India.

Well, I must dash. A dentist. He has my denture and must give it back. Not that I particularly want it here. In Japan I kept it always in my mouth in order to be able to flash back a smile at all the smiling boys.[7] Here no one smiles at anything or anyone, so I usually keep it in my pocket, since it is a bit uncomfortable to wear.

Love to both
   Joe

211 To Sandy Campbell (1922–)   Putney

                                                          27/7/61

Dear Sandy

       I couldn't answer any of your questions, though I expect I knew the answers once upon a time, so I referred them all to Morgan for you and

[1] See Letter 211, in which A. deals with questions about Forster raised by Sandy Campbell. Campbell's article entitled 'Mr Forster of King's' appeared in *Mademoiselle* (June 1964).
[2] 'Kobo Daishi.' See page 179, note 2.
[3] A. was right: he received 'only twenty-five guineas'.
[4] The review was printed under the title 'Truth in Fiction', and proved to be a 'breakthrough' review. Only after it had appeared (Colin Haycraft told Braybrooke) did people really begin to talk about A.'s novel. Hampshire ended his notice: 'It remains to be enjoyed, and will be enjoyed, wherever style, as exactness and a just sense of form in telling a story, is looked for in a novel. This is an eccentric and strange episode of the conversion of love. But a very particular case is turned into a general truth by the art of fiction.' See Introduction, 3.
[5] Windham was in Rome.   [6] See page 179, note 3.   [7] Cf. Letter 209.

have his reply today. His aunt was Laura Mary Forster (always referred to as Aunt Laura), his uncle was John Jebb Forster (where do you get your John *T.* Forster from? I find no reference to him in *Marianne Thornton*), and the ms. of *A Passage to India* sold for £6,500. I think that is all you wanted to know.

Your new address sounds good to someone who knows not N[ew] Y[ork]. But the 'trucking area'[1] should provide Don with interest for pen and eye. If he has joined you by now, give him my love.

I have been much upset here by an illness of my dog, a growth in the mouth, which may turn out to be her last illness. She is very old, as you know, 16¼ and that makes parting from her all the more difficult, for she has largely ruled my life and emotions for all that time. It is late for me too to devise a new shape to my life and habit is v. strong, but I suppose that somehow that will have to be done. I don't think she is in pain, yet, but it is a large growth and inconveniences her, and I'm afraid it may grow larger. Not malignant, the vet thinks. So I have been mostly flat-bound for the last 2 months, doing for her such services as I can.

Good of you to send my book[2] to your friend. I hope it pleases her. I'm incapable of doing anything at present—an occasional review has been ground out—but I read a good deal and try to extract such diversionary pleasures from life as offer.

Love from
  Joe

Morgan is v. well, has just gone off for a few days Welsh motoring with a chap he likes.

---

[1] A depot area for large trucks and lorries, downtown in New York, near the Hudson River. Rough rather than residential.
[2] *My Dog Tulip.*

Part Nine
'MY SADDEST DAY'

212 To James Kirkup (1923–   )   Putney
                                                                  28/10/61

Dear Jim

I have decided about Queenie. She is to have her quietus tomorrow, if the vet can manage.[1] I wanted it done today, but the vet is away
at a dog show in Beckenham and won't be home till late. She is to ring me in
the morning. Now that I have taken the decision I feel quite calm; it will
be a great relief not to have to see her in her present state any more. She has
dwindled and dwindled away and is as gaunt as Don Quixote; when I
carried her out onto the terrace this morning and watched her trying to
defecate and collapsing into her own drips of excreta, her hind legs being
too weak to support her, I realized with absolute conviction (the thing I have
hitherto lacked) that the end of the journey had come. The sense of pity has
come, the pity of seeing her so helpless and abject; it is at last utterly clear
that life is a humiliation and a burden to her; it is now easy to take it away.
I shall miss her, as you may suppose, and until I do not have her I shall not
know how much, but I think I shall be all right, the relief of no longer having
to fight this so sad, so disappointing losing battle will be greater than the
grief, I hope.

I posted a letter to you yesterday and your sweet cards came this morning.
I am so pleased that you have read my novelette[2] and liked it. I spent many
years writing it, many years ago, and was satisfied with it in the end, it did
everything I wanted it to do. Based as it is on experiences, it is inevitable that
my friends should read it as autobiography; but as pattern and plot took
charge it became for me an objective work and the narrator an objective
character. One of my friends said to me 'I would have enjoyed it if it had
been written by someone else, but you made yourself out so *nasty*. I couldn't
bear it.' The remark amused me; I saw that I had made of Frank[3] a success.
Personally I regard him as one of the best comic characters in fiction, and
whenever I read the book myself almost everything he says and does, all his
futile and absurd efforts to communicate, his thwarted schemes, his im-
potent rages, his wild surmises, make me giggle. I wrote it as a funny book,
above all, a kind of Charlie Chaplin, an irritable, frustrated figure, perfectly

---

[1] The vet could not manage this, so Queenie's 'quietus' was postponed by a day until 30
October. See Letter 213.   [2] *We Think the World of You.*   [3] i.e. the narrator of the novel.

determined to have his way and coming nothing but croppers all along the line—in the end 'Left with the dorg' as Christopher Isherwood laughingly remarked. Though I injected into it the utmost seriousness, heat, and drama, I intended it to be read above all as comedy, wry if you like, and I was particularly pleased with the passage where Frank keeps treading on the carrot in his flat,[1] the canine equivalent of those human romances when it is the lingering perfume of the beloved lady which reminds the forlorn hero of what he has lost.

Nancy's card tells me you are wandering [around the jungles of Malaysia] for a few days. How I envy you, dear Jim, how I wish you envied yourself. But I do hope and believe that if your new world is not to your liking at the moment, it will improve, with a little patience. *Think* how fortunate you are, darling, not to be sitting in Putney with a dying dog, or in Bath with a blind mother, or in England at all! Think, oh think, and tell yourself that, though you are not in Japan, you are still a fortunate boy.

I am addressing my letters now to the Majestic, partly because I have lost your University [of Malaysia] address, partly to save you the dismal prospect of calling at that horrid place.

Fond love

    Joe

To Geoffrey Gorer (1905–)   Putney 213
                                                       30/10/61

Dearest G.G.

              thank you for your card. I am so glad you had a pleasant time. I visited [the] Lascaux caves some years ago.

I am having my darling Queenie destroyed today, you will be sorry to hear. I realized at last that we could not recover her and that it was not fair to take her further on her downward slope. So I brought my courage to the sticking point at last. She is lying on my bed, fast asleep and looking so beautiful. She has had 4 Soneryls, a heavy dose, and soon I shall carry her insensible to the vet for her quietus. She should have been done by now, for my appointment was for a quarter to three, half-an-hour ago, but although I followed the vet's instruction and gave her her dope at half-past one, it had not worked by half-past two, so I made a later appointment, for I don't want Queenie to know anything that is happening to her. Would that she could die in her present deep sleep. I hope I am not going to be awfully upset. These last months have put a great strain upon me. But I think I shall manage. It is probable, though not certain, that I may bring Nancy to Brighton for a week—on Thursday, I can't leave earlier, for I have to go to the Labour Exchange that morning. I suppose you haven't remembered the name of that Kemp Town hotel you mentioned; if you have and could supply its phone number it would help me. And you said we might visit you if we came. That would be a great help and pleasure too.

Love

    Joe

[1] Pages 89–90.

214 To E. M. Forster (1879–1970)   17 Star & Garter Mansions, Putney,
                                          S.W.15   31/10/61

Darling Morgan

　　　　　　　my sweet Queenie died yesterday I must tell you. It had become clear that I could neither recover her nor take her further, she had become so pitifully helpless and wasted. The only pleasure in life left her was looking at me, and her many physical disabilities had become a burden and humiliation to her. The vet was sweetly good and kind. Lying comfortably on my bed, Queenie was given a tranquilising injection which put her, in ten minutes, into a profound sleep. I carried her in my arms to the vet's car and she was driven off to receive her final quietus in the surgery. I didn't go with her, the vet said there was no point since the animal would not recover consciousness, so I was spared that extra misery. She never knew what happened to her, the pretty creature.[1]

　　　Now I must get used to living without her after nearly 15 years.[2] But I am glad that she is dead in so far as it had become pitiful to see her at last unable to get up without help, unable to eat or drink except what I fed into her mouth. But I expect I shall feel lonely, it was such a long friendship and she made it with her faithful love the happiest time of my life.

　　　Nance has been awfully good and sweet throughout—not very well herself. I offered her a week away somewhere, but she does not want to go, at any rate not yet. We have been considering the question of her future loneliness, for she will now be entirely alone in the flat whenever I go away, which will not be very nice for her. I am going away this weekend, to stay with Raymond in Long Crichel. She has asked whether she can have a little dog for company, some tiny creature like a dachshund, and although I am reluctant to have another animal in the place, it would provide a solution for her. I have told her that if she does have a dog, it must be hers and her responsibility, sleep in her room, her companion not mine. But so far we have decided nothing. She is thinking not so much of mere weekends, but of when I go away again abroad.

　　　I am dining with my half-sister Sally [——] tonight and going to some musical with her.

Much love

　　Joe

---

[1] After A.'s death, this short poem was found among his papers:

> Pretty lady, pray forgive,
> I took your loving life away
> I could not bear to see you live
> Self-soiled and old, so sickly thin
> I let the needle enter in
> Pretending it was play.

Pencilled on the same sheet were the words: 'Forgive it me that I did kill thee.'

[2] In the following May Forster read *Themes in Greek and Latin Epitaphs* by Richmond Lattimore (1962). One Greek epitaph he copied out—and specially translated for A.: 'Do not, I beseech, laugh because this is a dog's grave.'

To Donald Windham (1920–)   17 Star & Garter Mansions, Putney, 215
                                S.W.15   9/11/61

Dear Don

I am a bit slow in answering but have been very unhappy for many weeks, indeed for nearly three months. My darling old dog got ill, she was $16\frac{1}{2}$, and try as I might I could not save her. For over three weeks she could not eat or drink of her own accord and I spoon-fed her with everything, baby foods and slops, and carried her about, for she could not get up unaided and could hardly walk. And she got so thin, it was pitiful; and so humiliated, peeing and defecating in her bed. Night after night I lay awake in case she wanted me, for a drink, or to turn over to a more comfortable position, a thing she could not do for herself, and the thought that I would have to kill her soon, made me feel quite sick. But I had to do it in the end; it became plain at last that I could not recover her, that she was in great discomfort, and that it was unfair to take her further on her downward path. Her only pleasure left in life was to lie and look at me, and her beautiful eyes haunt me still, although it is over a week since she died, and will haunt me for ever. At least I am happy to say she died without knowing anything about it; she was given a strong tranquilising injection here which put her into a profound sleep, I carried her in my arms to the vet's car and laid her insensible in it, and she was given her final quietus in the surgery without regaining consciousness. October 30, the saddest day of my life. I shall never stop missing her, no human being has ever meant so much to me as she meant and I will say for her epitaph that the many years she gave me of her unswerving love were the happiest years of my life.

However, one has to go on somehow to one's own end and to make the best of that interval, and Morgan Forster today has given me something to look forward to, which I think may come off though it is not, of course, yet fixed. His *Passage to India* play is to be produced in N[ew] Y[ork] in January. I said 'What fun it would be to see it there!' and he cried 'I will send you!' He asked me if I would go, as his representative, perhaps for the first night; I said I would love to do so. So he is to write to Santha Rama Rau[1] to express this wish, for me to go instead of himself, which he does not want to do, though he is being pressed; so I think it very likely that I may be coming to New York, for the first time, about the middle of January, for about a week. Oh, dear Don, what fun that will be. I do hope it may come off. I have met Miss Rau and we got on very well together. Among possible substitutes for Morgan, I don't think she would be displeased to have me. But all this has happened only today and I will let you know about developments. I don't see how it can go wrong, acts of God excepted, for I want to come and Morgan wants to put me there. He will certainly not come himself.

Well, love to you, and to Sandy, and how pleased I am to hear about your Roman novel.[2] I am really longing to see you again.

Joe

---

[1] See page 170, note 2.
[2] *Two People*, which was published in 1966.

216 To Francis King (1923–   )   17 Star & Garter Mansions, Putney, S.W.15

6/12/61

My dear Francis

if you mean that you have written to me since your return
to Japan I'm sure I've never had it, though I have heard (not lately) from
Fukushima, Ando and Fukuda—and fairly regularly from Kinoshita. Indeed, I have been wondering about you, so far as I can manage to think
about anything but Queenie, who died some five weeks ago, on Oct. 30th.
I have been very unhappy ever since. If she had only died a natural death
perhaps I should not have felt it all quite so much, but I was obliged to hasten
her end. For over five weeks she was unable to lap, I had to spoon-feed her
with everything, even water. She began to waste away, the bones of her
little bottom stuck out and she could not get up or even lie down without
help, and often in the night I would change her position for her when she got
uncomfortable. I lifted her about everywhere, for she could scarcely walk;
if I left her for a moment, she would fall down and not be able to regain her
feet. She had no pleasure left in life at all, except only to lie and look at me.
I prayed she would die in her sleep, but she didn't: twice I summoned the
vet to destroy her and reprieved her for another few days; at last I could bear
the pitiful sight of her no more and let the needle go in. It is difficult, in this
room that we shared, not to think about her all the time, fifteen years, and
they were the happiest in my life; she provided for it a background of secure,
unalterable devotion, which my nature needed: how I am to get on without
it I do not know. I don't so much mind being *in* the room as entering it, or
indeed entering the flat at all; perhaps the heart of emptiness is a little less
cold than the approaches.

Nevertheless, I have managed to work a little, an old family history[1] a
bomb interrupted twenty years ago[2] which I raked out, I have distracted my
mind a little with that; and Morgan Forster is doing something nice for me,
he is sending me to New York in late January to 'represent' him at the production of *A Passage to India* there. So sweet and kind of him, I shall enjoy
that if I can reach the date (not yet fixed) and it may make a lot of difference
to my present lack of interest in living. I can make no plans, except just the
getting there when I know the date; but I shall nevertheless prepare myself
for any contingency that may occur in a new world, any impulse, any
revivement, so that I shall feel free to do whatever a possibly delivered mind
suggests. I have friends in California, I could fly to them, I could fly to
Japan, I suppose, I could fly to Jim, I could certainly fly home. But 'home'
now, where is that? Anyway, I will see what happens when I get to New
York . . .

Oh yes, I hear from [——] constantly, and try to make sense of what I
hear. He regards himself, from time to time, as a persecuted man, the English, of course, slighting him, gossiping about him, black-balling him from
[their clubs]. At the same time he manages to enjoy himself with the indigen-
ous population . . . What I never hear about, and don't know about, is work,

[1] *My Father and Myself.*
[2] In 1941 A. had been 'bombed' out of his flat in Maida Vale. See his poem 'After the Blitz,
1941', published posthumously in *Micheldever & Other Poems* (1972).

his job . . . Sex on every page; but does he do any helpful work? I must say that, in my own small experience and with the one known exception of yourself, the poor boys in the Far East, often longing to learn, don't seem to get better educated in any skills outside of the bed, if in that. However, I shall go to see him somehow, somewhere, if I can, for, although I think he is perfectly dotty, the Fairy Queen of our time, distributing out of his cornucopia of blessings only his own semen and a large quantity of his own poems, I rather like him.

I'm sorry about your health[1]—what went wrong with you to require such examinations?—and about the news of Ernest[2] (I had no idea he had a name). It is all that latter, together with my memories of the past, that make me feel I cannot stand another beast, not ever. Queenie was my darling friend, but when I think back over the fifteen years of our life, oh dear what hell much of it was: I feel I could never face it again, the responsibility and anxiety of it all. Far better to be dead.

Love from
   Joe

---

[1] A Japanese doctor suspected tuberculosis—wrongly.
[2] A puppy that was killed. See Letter 208.

Part Ten
PASSAGE TO AMERICA

217 To Donald Windham (1920–)   17 Star & Garter Mansions, Putney,
                                  S.W.15   9/12/61

Dear Don

I am rather late in answering. Perhaps you have left your hotel by now—oh no, I see, I had forgotten, I can get at you through the American Express [in Rome]. But I have not very much to say, excepting that I think of you from time to time with affection. Xmas draws in upon us—sometimes life seems to have been nothing but a series of blank pages punctuated by Xmas rejoicings. But let this, having started off on the wrong foot, be a Xmas greeting. My sister and I will stay here, eating the usual turkey sent by the same rich friend, which neither of us really wants. However, there will be plenty of booze too, a good soporific. Indeed what should we do without plenty of strong liquor? I can't imagine an endurable life without it—or, often, an endurable life with it, for that matter. Morgan is not sympathetic towards it, as you doubtless know, and although I enjoyed my two-night visit to him lately in Cambridge I regretted not having had the forethought to take a flask of whisky with me. Fortunately I had some Nembutal to put me out. I fiddle about on this and that, read, trot into cinemas and buy myself lots of tickets for theatres and operas. My wallet at present contains tickets for Ben[jamin Britten]'s *Midsummer Night's Dream*, Tchaikovsky's *Queen of Spades*, *The Cherry Orchard* (Gielgud and Peggy Ashcroft), C. P. Snow's *The Affair* and a film, Ulanova in *The Sleeping Beauty*. It is all rather a pumped-up interest in something in which I suppose one ought to try to take an interest, something we attempt to make the best of and is called Life. Leonard Woolf's autobiographies[1] suit my somewhat sombre thought. He too seems to have seen through it all, and himself. My American plans are no further advanced, I can't do much until I hear from Santha Rama Rau (what names people have, putting one to so much extra trouble) the date of the N[ew] Y[ork] opening [of her dramatised version of *A Passage to India*]. But anyway I needn't go to that. Any time later will do, I suppose it will run a bit, I shall go when I feel inclined. 'Inclined', what a word! At

---

[1] A. was referring to the first two volumes—*Sowing, 1880–1904* (1960) and *Growing, 1904–11* (1961). Woolf subsequently wrote three more—*Beginning Again, 1911–18* (1964), *Downhill All the Way, 1919–39* (1967) and *The Journey Not the Arrival Matters, 1939–69* (1969). The last was published posthumously.

any rate, whenever I do go I shall pack a bag for ever. I can't imagine having a homing instinct again. Nor, unfortunately, can I imagine a new life. However, America is said to be stimulating, perhaps it will stimulate me, new beliefs and interests in the human species may be born in me (most unlikely) and new beliefs in myself (more unlikely still). At any rate I shall pack a goodbye-to-England bag and see what happens to me under the Statue of Liberty. Maybe I shall fly on to Japan again (a dire mistake ever to revisit scenes one has recently liked), or to James Kirkup in Malay. Would that I had the slightest desire to do either, or to remain where I am: Uncle Sam may re-invigorate my tired, bored and cynical mind. There do seem to be two rules in life, to try to do the best for oneself and never to upset one's friends. I'm not sure that I'm being awfully careful about the second of these, and think perhaps it is time this letter ended.
Love from
    Joe

To Colin Haycraft (1929–   )   17 Star & Garter Mansions, Putney, S.W.15   218
8/1/62
Dear Colin
        going through the text[1] for you and for Ace Books[2] as well, it occurred to me to do something else, to restore it for you, as my publisher, to its original state—original, that is to say, excepting for the fiddlings I so inadequately did for you against civil libel, small alterations which can remain. But besides the civil libel there was an obscene one, as you know, the removal of which I regret; but Chatto & Windus and Secker & Warburg were so down on it that I took it out and never thought to restore it for The Bodley Head. Wish I had now, I wonder what you would have said; after all, if you thought the book, with alterations, safe enough in civil libel, would it not also have been safe in any other sort of libel? At any rate, I send it to you now in what I believe is called a 'definitive edition', not for present action, which is not on the cards, but for your archives.[3] It is how I would have liked the book to appear, and in case Raymond Mortimer[4] should be right and, years hence, when I am under the sod, the book should become a 'classic', you now have the full text as I originally worked it out—so much better than my fakings—in your hands.

The 'improper' bits—which scarcely merit the term 'improper'—and one or two too dangerous civil-libel bits, which I was also sorry to remove, you will find restored on separate sheets.

The corrections for Ace Books are in the text. With a few alterations and

[1] The Bodley Head first edition of *We Think the World of You*.
[2] Paperback publishers. Later they became Four Square Books and under this imprint issued A.'s novel in 1963.
[3] See page 190, note 3 and Appendix F.
[4] In the Books of the Year feature in the *Sunday Times* on 24 December 1961, Mortimer had chosen A.'s book: '*We Think the World of You* by J. R. Ackerley appears to me a miniature masterpiece that will become a classic.' Another critic who singled out A.'s novel in the same feature was Richard Buckle: '*We Think the World of You* by J. R. Ackerley gave me the most pleasure, being a sad, funny, true and original study of love—that subject we are more interested in at some times than others.' Desmond Shawe-Taylor also chose it. See page 231, note 1.

additions, they comprise the small amount of change I hope Ace Books may accept. If they don't, they don't. I expect you will see the point of them without the need for elucidation. The charge against Megan (p. 96) of physical uncleanliness[1] ought to have come out earlier; it may be unwise to remove it now for a more popular paperback-admission of guilt? I don't know, and don't much care: I leave it all to you.[2]

But shall I see a proof? If Ace Books are setting the thing up afresh it would seem advisable, for they can make a hundred more mistakes elsewhere while noting those in your edition we point out.

It was nice to see you, as always.

Joe

219   To Colin Haycraft (1929–   )   Putney
                                                                  22/1/62
Dear Colin

a fidgetting matter (though you did use the word 'tooth-comb') but on page 57 line 12 of my booklet,[3] should not the word be '*re*pressed'? Or are they precisely the same? I am far from being Fowler, who anyway doesn't help. But I have been reading psychology, in which 'repression' is the constant word, and correcting my U.S. edition at intervals to take to America, and, coming across 'suppressed', the alternative, perhaps better, popped into my mind.[4] Sorry, but you did say a 'tooth-comb'.

Joe

If *you* notice anything, for Heaven's sake say!

EDITOR'S NOTE

A Passage to India *had its first night in New York on 31 January. Ackerley was not present. He decided not to leave England until 1 March—and during this period sent practically no letters. 'I fell into such a despondent state of mind that every effort seemed too much,' he told Geoffrey Gorer. It was the delayed, but to be expected, reaction to Queenie's death. Even when he reached New York, where he spent eighteen days (four with Sandy Campbell and a fortnight at the Irving Hotel), his despondency continued, and he wrote in a notebook: 'I carry it always—this desolation in the heart.' One morning he set aside for 'a pilgrimage': it was to see Sargent's painting 'The Lady with a Rose', which is in the Metropolitan Museum of Art. The portrait is of Louise Burckhardt, whom Roger Ackerley had married in 1889. (She died of some tubercular trouble three years later.) In the evenings, Ackerley saw old friends and met new ones—among them W. H. Auden, Paul Cadmus, Margaret French, Chester Kalman, Edith Oliver, Carl van Vechten, Keith de Vries, Monroe Wheeler and Edmund Wilson. He remarked: 'To be boozed up at night is good; to wake in the morning renewed sorrow.' While he was in New York, Santha Rama Rau was away on a lecture*

---

[1] See Letter 191.
[2] It remained in.
[3] *We Think the World of You.*
[4] In the end, at Haycraft's suggestion, A. left the word 'suppressed' unaltered.

tour, but she had arranged for him to have seats 'for Morgan's play whenever [he] should want them'—and on 5 March he took his nephew Paul West and his wife. On 18 March, Ackerley flew to Los Angeles for three weeks to stay with Dr Noel Voges and his wife. 'Perhaps California,' he wrote, 'will do something for me.'

To Sandy Campbell (1922–)   2499 Corinth, Los Angeles 64, Cal. 220
22/3/62

My dear Sandy

my third, no fourth, day in Los Angeles, and high time I wrote to you. It is interesting to see how one's friends live, the addresses to which one constantly writes, and this address turns out to be a small, wooden, ramshackle, untidy detached house standing in a garden to which all the adjectives I have just used can also be applied. Very pleasant and go-as-you please. My host and his wife charming. Their son (aged 10) I find . . . demanding and receiving too much attention, but then, unlike Don, I am not sympathetic to children,[1] I suspect them of the adulthood they take so long to attain. The garden contains a pet duck and hen (both unpettable), a number of bee-hives, an avocado tree heavy with fruit, an orange and a lemon tree, wisteria, camellias. Everything is in a state of what one of Sean O'Casey's characters calls 'chassis', meaning 'chaos'. And my mind is in a state of chassis too. The city, I am told, is some 60 miles across, how does one get about in such a place, or visit one's friends, or even shop? And Bill Roerick, my chief hope and standby, is away on tour until May. My host and hostess are at work all day in their respective universities; one leaves at 7.0 a.m., the other at about 8.0 a.m. The child . . . also leaves for school at 8.30. The general return hour is round about 5.0. However for the rest of this week I am to be propped up. Yesterday Gerald Heard called, surprisingly with Kenneth Clark who is lecturing here, and took me off with them to lunch and to see the performing whales and seals in Marine land. The whales were charming and so clever; the seals clever too but repulsively vulgarized, Disney jokes. At midday today Chris Wood calls to see me, tonight Gerald comes again to take me off to dine with him quietly. Tomorrow Isherwood and Don [Bachardy][2] will call and run me about. I hear

[1] Two years later A. returned to this theme in greater detail in the opening paragraph of his article 'I Am a Beast', published in *Orient/West* (March-April 1964): 'I dislike children . . . I didn't mean to begin with that remark. I'm afraid it may pain the Japanese, who are fond of them, or at any rate compassionate towards them, but it slipped out. Shall I modify it and say that Japanese children are the best in the world—well anyway the prettiest? Yes, I will allow that. English children are seldom pretty and often odious, and as for American children the less said about them the better . . . James Kirkup put his finger on an illuminating difference between the Western and Japanese child character in the matter of snow balling, considered by us as a permissible healthy childish sport, by the Japanese as unthinkable bad manners. Nevertheless, by and large, I dislike children. Children seem to me incomprehensible, like inebriates. They inhabit a world of their own which I cannot enter, and the scenery and props of which when I look in soon bore me, it is so restless, senseless, and noisy. Moreover, they go on being children for such an awfully long time. Will they *never* grow up? . . . Then they grow up and become adults, and that is worse than ever . . .'

[2] Bachardy had spent the previous year in London and drawn A. in the summer. He writes: 'I did four drawings of Joe, all in one afternoon [at his Putney flat] . . . Queenie was still alive, though very sick, and in the room with us while we worked. Her illness may have made her irritable, but I suspected her cranky behaviour was due to jealousy of me. How could she understand why Joe should sit still in strict attention in front of me . . .' Cf. Letter 116.

that Chris Wood is going to San Francisco for the weekend, and I am wondering whether I can tack myself on to him, but he is an odd fellow, set in his own private ways. I don't think I shall last here long. I have not been asked to lecture, thank heaven, though I have been asked to take part in a discussion on 'Integrity in Writing', from which I have recoiled. Why do people think that I am clever and have the answers to things when in fact I have nothing in my head at all. As soon as I know where BOAC is and someone will take me there—one has to be taken everywhere—I shall investigate the possibility of using my return ticket from N[ew] Y[ork] to England for a direct flight home over the pole. If I can't manage that and return via N.Y. I will let you know.

I owe to you, dear Sandy, all the abundant pleasure and happiness I received in New York,[1] for it all derived through you, and never shall I forget your kindness to me. If I do not return through N.Y., may we meet again, with dear Don, soon and elsewhere.
Much love
    Joe

221 To Francis King (1923–   )   2499 Corinth, Los Angeles 64, California
                                                            29/3/62
Dear Francis
            before I forget it, if Jim Kirkup is in your orbit will you thank him for his letter to me to Putney, forwarded to N[ew] Y[ork], and say that the only reason I have not answered is that I felt I could not trust the rather vague address in Japan he provided, especially after so much time had elapsed before his letter came into my hand. He is somewhere about Japan now.

I have neglected you too, but you press upon me today because I went yesterday with my host to the State College in San Fernando Valley, some 15 to 20 miles distant, where he teaches the Russian language and literature, and spent the whole day with him. A splendid Campus, upon which American dollars have been spent regardless and in their millions, as they are upon all educational establishments here, and whenever he was busy with his lectures he popped me into the huge college library until he was free. Browsing among the periodicals I found you twice, in *The Cornhill*, an absorbing account of two Japanese boys,[2] so amusing and enlightened, and an equally absorbing article on Lafcadio Hearn,[3] beautifully written. I hope you will add some more pieces to these and make a book of them, they put me straight back into Japan, where I am sorry I am not, instead of here. Not

[1] A fortnight earlier, A. had written to Sandy Campbell: 'Your capital city much impresses me, it has a weird startling beauty . . . The weather deserves less praise, for it is snowing. I must out into it however, and examine the Japanese objects in the Metropolitan [Museum of Art] and feed some of the friendly sparrows in the park.'
[2] 'Dog and Bird' (Winter 1961/2). Cf. Letter 261.
[3] 'One Is a Wanderer' (Autumn 1961).

that I dislike the Americans, who are polite, considerate and good-mannered, but what a muddle of a place. I am told it is 60 miles across and well it may be. There is little public transport, it is impossible to get about unless one has a car. Most Americans have more than one and dash about at 65 miles an hour on the intricate network of 'free-ways', as they are called, which criss-cross the sprawling city, in fly-overs and fly-unders, in every direction: an endless and constant stream of flashing metal boxes. Not that there is anything to see if you *could* get about, except the deserts, hills and mountains round (very beautiful some of it, but perhaps 100 miles distant), the ocean, and one's friends. These, including my host and hostess, have been very kind to me and taken me about as much as they can (the Voges work in their jobs—she is a biologist in the University, studying tape-worms—from 8.0 a.m. to 5.0 p.m., sleep badly and are usually worn out); the others are Gerald Heard, Christopher Isherwood and his friend Don Bachardy, Christopher Wood. But everyone is at a distance from everyone else—10 to 15 miles separate one from all these—so I have to rely upon them coming to fetch me. It is no longer the Englishman whose home is his castle, it is the Californian: everyone has to have a bungalow of his own with a garden, hence the great sprawl of this incoherent place—and apparently 2000 new immigrants arrive every day, so new building goes on all the time. And in spite of power and the dollar, a nervous race, air-raid shelter in N[ew] Y[ork], an air-raid rehearsal at the huge University yesterday, a high rate of suicide—disturbed minds. The students, boys and girls, look awfully childish and dull, with their smooth, small pink faces, and are indeed said to be dull by their teachers: 'unmotivated' is the fashionable word. However, thank heaven for Gerald Heard, so gay, mischievous, sage-like and learned, pouring forth a spate of fascinating ideas. He is a tantric Buddhist, believes in the continuance of the spirit[1] and in mescalin (which I shall try), is fond of champagne, and thinks that all children from the age of seven should have their sphincters penetrated and loosened to dispel anxiety and nervous tension. He is wonderful company, so affectionate too, well worth crossing America to see. I came here chiefly to see him. In England I got into a state of melancholia and made the effort to get to the U.S., as an escape, Morgan having offered me the trip, as he offered me the trip to Japan. I am a bit better now, and am flying to San Francisco on Saturday for the weekend. Soon afterwards, cash having got low, I suppose I shall return home. But oh dear me, I wish I were in Japan instead. How are you, dear Francis? And how are all my friends? If I neglect you, it is not because I don't love you but because I have taken so deep a dislike for myself. Send me a line do and thanks for those articles, which truly helped to restore my drooping spirits. Much love
   Joe

---

[1] Early in their friendship, Heard had written to A.: 'The evidence that the consciousness goes on after the body is shelled off is too strong to be rejected.' It was a letter A. kept for many years. Cf. Letter 233.

222 To Francis King (1923–)   2499 Corinth, Los Angeles 64, California
30/3/62

Dearest Francis

no sooner had I popped a letter[1] to you into the local mail-box than one from you arrived. It brought such freshness into this absurd displeasing city that I answer it at once, so you will not again upbraid me for neglect after two letters in one day. I am writing in a café near my address, an all-night café to which my insomniac host sometimes repairs in the middle of the night to read and write over a cup of coffee. It is 3.30 p.m. I had lunch here too, fried eggs and bacon, a small pad of potato (10/-). A haircut costs £1, so I have not had one for a month. Almost everything is absurdly expensive, and university lecturers' fees are less than the gardeners' who mow the lawns. Don't ever come here. I bussed up to the ocean, your Pacific, this morning and mouched along St. Monica Boulevard. Dogs are not allowed on any green place, nor even upon the sands of the vast sea-shore. Don't ever come here. A long rack on the Boulevard offered free pamphlets and literature, in different receptacles, from no less than 14 varieties of the Christian Church. Don't ever come here. On the bus ride back an old woman stumbled—the bus had started with a jerk—and fell on her knees to the floor. The driver stopped, asked her if she wanted a doctor or ambulance (she seemed not at all hurt and refused), then distributed to all the other passengers, there were 10 of us, pencils and small cards which we had to fill up with a description of what had happened together with our names and addresses. The bus remained stationary for 15 minutes while all this took place. Litigation here is constant. Everyone sues everyone else, the corporations and the city, on the slightest pretext. Don't ever come here. How boring it is. It has nothing to offer but its permanent fine weather.

My depression comes from Queenie's death. Perhaps I oughtn't to have stayed so long in the room we occupied for so many years. I found I could do nothing but brood over my loss and the rather bungled manner of her death;[2] I came away to escape my thoughts, but alas brought them with me. And cheer and distractions are certainly not here. I rather dread returning, but my cash is almost finished, and anyway running away, I see, does not help. I must think what to do—perhaps move out of Putney into the country and adopt more pets. I am happier, I find, with animals, than with people. To be old, on the shelf, half deaf, written out, fucked out—there isn't much left. Curtains would be welcome, but they don't fall when we desire them. Gerald Heard thinks the same, he says, so does my friend Jack Sprott of Nottingham. It is nice to have company in sombre thoughts. I am awfully glad you met and liked Jim. You describe him perceptively. Yes, he is a touching, dear fellow. Do let him know about me if you know where he is. I am pleased too with your news of yourself and your new companion. I wondered myself whether Jim might not be disappointed with Japan. Paradise should never be revisited; and it was indeed a happy surprise to hear that the author of *The Custom House*[3] felt able to rise in Japan's defence. Nice

---

[1] Letter 221.   [2] See Letters 212, 213, 214, 215 and 216.   [3] King's novel of 1961.

words about my own book[1] too, little pleasure though I get from thinking of it now. Morgan's play[2] was pretty good, excepting for Eric Portman as Fielding, and seems to be a success.
Best love, dear Francis
   Joe

[1] *We Think the World of You.*
[2] The dramatisation of *A Passage to India.*

Part Eleven
BIRDS, BEASTS AND LAURELS

223 To Donald Windham (1920–)   Putney
                                                                    21/6/62
Dear Don

 I have neglected you and Sandy. I have neglected everyone. I have at least a latter-day reason—a six-weeks one—for I too find difficulty in writing, though not the same difficulties as yours. I can't sit down. That is to say I *can* sit down but then have to get up again at once. The sciatic nerve at the back of my left leg has gone wrong and all down that leg is pain, often unendurable, and the foot itself has become numb. After six weeks of it, since it didn't go away as one always hopes pain will, I took the drastic step of visiting my doctor, who thought something might be pressing on the nerve—prostate? diseased kidney?—so I was overhauled in hospital this week—fingers up my bottom, a novelty, since I've never been able to take anything else[1]—but no cause was found. So I am where I was. Fortunately I can lie and stand without discomfort and am writing this letter standing up. But cinemas, theatres, and 'masterpieces' are out of the question, for no drug so far has alleviated it—I spend most of my time reading on my back. Perhaps depression is the cause, for I have long felt at a total loss—*The Bridge of St. Luis Rey*[2]—and seldom go to bed at night without hoping I shall not wake up in the morning. However, even one's own rational wishes are never granted, and I certainly did not pray for a pain in my leg.

 Oh, I've been back for ages—at least it seems ages. I was only 3 weeks in Los Angeles, flew straight home (London—anything—is better than that nightmare lesson of our civilisation) and have been hereabouts ever since, going through old letters and papers and casting everything with disgust into the wastepaper basket. To look back into the past—as you enjoy to do and do so well—is abhorrent to me. I am so pleased about your new story,[3] but libel once risked, becomes a great anxiety—or so I have found it—so take that into consideration. I am still always fearing a letter from some in-

---

[1] Not strictly accurate. In Chapter 12 of *My Father and Myself* A. wrote: 'I . . . weathered a dose of anal clap without much fuss (anal, yes; I *assured* the young Grenadier that I was quite impenetrable, but he begged so hard to be allowed at any rate to try).'
 [2] A reference to Thornton Wilder's 1927 novel, in which five travellers in 1714 set out to cross the famous San Luis bridge, woven of osier by the Incas more than a century before, and unknowingly meet their death when it collapses beneath them.
 [3] 'Myopia'—a story which was to form one of the chapters of *Emblems of Conduct* (1963), Windham's autobiography. Cf. Letters 238 and 255.

jured party over my novelette[1]—indeed increasingly, for it is soon to enter the paper-backs.

The depths to which I have sunk will become apparent to you when I say that I am now largely occupied with a fledgling sparrow.[2] I found it on the pavement outside when I was dashing off to meet Morgan; it had fallen 50 or 60 feet from its nest at the top of the building. A few wing-feathers, otherwise bald. It had injured a foot. I took it upstairs and fed it, almost hourly, on brown bread and milk out of a pen nib. Surprisingly it survived—for I am now told that of all birds the sparrow is the most difficult to fostermother successfully. 'You are lucky' people say. It lives in a sort of pen on the floor of my room, barricaded in with large books, such as that bad Oxford Atlas, and I have now had it for a fortnight. It has everything a sparrow requires that I can think of, not insects and worms no, but seed, breadcrumbs, brown bread and milk (its favourite food), water (never touched), an earthy dust-bath (very popular), some sliced grape. No caviare. It has grown up, is able to perch in spite of its crippled foot and can now not merely hop onto the low perches I have provided but fly from perch to perch. It is a horrid, tatty, ungrateful little bird and snarls at me and pecks me quite hard whenever I pick it up, which sometimes I have to do when changing its shitbespattered newspapers. Tomorrow or Saturday I shall set it free.[3] How interesting to know its future life, but I never shall.
Fond love to you and Sandy
   Joe

To William Plomer (1903–1973)   Putney 224
                                                 28?/6/62
D.L.B.

        it seems a long time since we met. Can we have another little Victorian evening? I now have a 'poor leg', sciatica: have you any advice? I remember you had a spinal upset, but my spine has been X-rayed and is far too calcified to crack: 'Older than yourself' said the doctor at St Stephen's hospital, where I am now having a course of physio-therapy. It was thought that something might be pressing on the nerve—prostate or diseased kidney, I am in the age-group for the first, and the second, well it and its partner might reasonably complain of the alcoholic douches I have subjected it to for many years. Having a thorough examination exonerates both. I am comfortable horizontal or erect; sitting down is the trouble, though I now have pills to ease me; the whole of the back of the left leg is affected, down to the foot, which feels numb.

     Tell Charles I am foster-mothering a sparrow. I found it on the pavements outside the flats three weeks ago. It must have fallen 60 feet from its nest and had injured one claw. It had a few wing feathers but was otherwise mostly

---

[1] *We Think the World of You.*
[2] See Letters 224, 225, 226, 227 and 229.
[3] But A. changed his mind and kept Cassidy (as he called the sparrow) until 30 August. See Letter 229.

bald and pink. What does one do? Tread on it deliberately? Pass by? Render first aid? I brought it up to the flat and it has lived in my room ever since. I introduced bread and milk to its little gaping beak with a pen nib for some ten days, and it throve. I am now told that it is quite a triumph to rear a fledgling sparrow; our pet-shop people have often tried but never managed. This little beast has flourished, it can now feed itself, can perch (in spite of a crippled foot) and make low flights (*No*, dear, I am *not* working up to another book!) It is a dirty, tatty, unrewarding little beast, entirely ungrateful but used now to my presence in the room. We chirp at each other. It has a playground by my book-case on the floor, a dish of water to splash about in, an earthy dust-bath in a flower pot, various seeds, ants' eggs (6d a packet) and bread-crumbs. It lives among the books, hopping from shelf to shelf and shits on them all. *Howards End* seems to be its favourite book for resting (and shitting) on, and I think Mrs Wilcox[1] would have approved of that. When it (I think it is a girl)[2] can fly better I shall gradually introduce it to my terrace and the outside world; if it can't gain a living it can always come back and find food. It is an odd little imp, by no means a pal, but it has been interesting to watch its slow development from a lop-sided baby who could scarcely hop and I am pleased to have kept its life going. It would be interesting to know its future in the great world, but I expect nothing personal of it.

I forget how far back you go in 19th century history. Do you happen to know the name of the man—an M.P., I think—who somewhere about the middle of the century (post-Paine) invented the phrase 'Rights of Beasts' and tried—I think twice—to push a Bill through Parliament to protect them?[3] I had his name but have lost it. He was a cranky fellow and made quite a fuss about it all. Not [Jeremy] Bentham.

Love

Joe

225 To Sonia Brownell Orwell   17 Star & Garter Mansions, Putney, S.W.15
?/7?/62

Thank you, dear Sonia. But Geoffrey says I am *not* to have Cortisone, it is bad for the heart. I would sooner have a bad heart than a bad leg, but he is

---

[1] Forster wrote in Chapter II of his novel: '. . . Howards End was a house; they could not know that to Mrs Wilcox it had been a spirit, for which she sought a spiritual heir.' When she dies, her husband and sons regard it merely as bricks and mortar—a valuable piece of real estate. Mrs Wilcox doubtless would have so vehemently disapproved of this, that she would have been glad to see her 'Holy of Holies' shat upon. A. when writing this letter may have had in mind those unconscious connections between faeces and money, which Freud wrote about in *Anxiety and Instinctual Life* (1933). A. had read this some years before with care.

[2] This supposition A. never verified, and subsequently he referred to Cassidy as 'he', 'she' and 'it'. See Letters 225, 226 and 229.

[3] Richard Martin (1754–1834), nicknamed 'Humanity Martin' by George IV, became MP for Galway in 1801. In 1822 he succeeded in carrying into law 'the first modern enactment in Great Britain for protecting the rights of animals'. He was one of the founders in 1824 of the RSPCA. He laboured strenuously to abolish death for forgery, was a superb duellist and brought in a bill to allow counsel to prisoners charged with capital crimes. See 'Ode to Richard Martin, Esquire, M.P. for Galway' by Thomas Hood (1824).

so categorical. He says I must lie flat on my back for days, only getting up for No. 1, it is the only cure he says; but my specialist has prescribed physiotherapy, which means 3 visits to a Fulham hospital a week and tells me to do exercises 3 times a day, lying on my stomach. It is difficult to suit both of them. Am I getting better? I have also knocked off gin—can you believe it? but it was not difficult, for I discovered in myself a disinclination for it. I am certainly no companion for you at the moment.

So I lie about on back or stomach and watch my sparrow, who has a fourth-floor apartment in my bookshelf, on the works of Forster and Gide. I took him out onto my terrace on Saturday for a change of scene, thinking it safe, since he can rise only about 2 or 3 feet in the air, but the foolish bird got through the balusters of my balustrade and fluttered down 60 feet into the road below. I couldn't very well leave him there with his weak wings and inexperience of life, but it took me two hours to locate him among the other sparrows, the parked cars and pedestrians, and another hour to catch him. He took refuge in 'The Duke's Head' across the road, and had to be hunted from bar to bar. He is only a shrimp of a bird, but how he pecked me, the little brute, when I at last collared him. Now he is safely, and apparently happily, back on *Howards End*, but all this did not improve my sciatica.

This begs no answer. I will write you again in a day or two . . .
Love
Joe

To Francis King (1923–) 17 Star & Garter Mansions, Putney, S.W.15 226
27/7/62
Dearest Francis
            I have neglected you, but only because I have been bedridden for a month. It must have been since I last wrote you that my condition worsened, instead of being unable to sit comfortably, I could not stand or walk without the leg filling with pain, sitting or lying was then a relief. Well, one doesn't want to go on about ailments, and it has got better at last, though still it hangs about—but I pity your poor mother and I hope I shall not have recurrences and be a martyr to it for ever. 'A little disc trouble' the orthopaedic man blythely [*sic*] called it, having done nothing whatever for me except to shine some infra-red rays on my pelvis three times a week. Geoffrey Gorer guessed the cause and knew the cure, being a life-long sufferer himself for years: 'What's your mattress like?' Perfectly true, though quite comfortable the springs had 'given' in many places. 'Get a new firm one and lie on it flat on your back and don't get up for any reason, excepting to shit, until you are better.' So I bought a horsehair mattress and a wooden board to go underneath it, and for the last 3 weeks have more or less followed his advice,—I mean less, for there could hardly be 'more'. For I have cheated—a pillow under the head (not allowed), but Veganin having masked the pain I was not uncomfortable, and how can one read properly

with an unsupported head? I have re-read and much enjoyed, after a lapse of 30 odd years, almost the whole of Proust.[1] You might think that all this— the one and only remedy, said Gorer, apart from operations or osteopathy (for which I am too old)—might also be the first concern of one's medical adviser. But not at all. It was I who, just after my examination and dismissal, turned back and said to the orthopaedic specialist 'Is a firm bed important?' 'Very important,' said he. But if I hadn't asked I should have left him without knowing—hospital conditions here now are the limit— crowds of patients, endless hanging about, perfunctory attention when at last seen (unless one is practically dying, when one becomes of interest). Your sister Elizabeth asked me to a party last week, but alas I was too crippled to go.

I hear from Jim that he has settled into a small expensive flat in Tokyo. I was surprised, as from his previous letter he seemed disenchanted by Japan and the Japanese. I hope he will stay there now and find something to do. What is all this he tells me about Ando-san disappearing. I am quite homesick for Japan myself. If Morgan will prop me up for it financially, may I come and stay with you in the Autumn, Sept. or Oct.? So sorry for your news of Geoffrey Penny: a good thing he is resilient.

Did I tell you I had a sparrow?[2] I found it, a fledgling, in the road below some 6 weeks ago, with a crippled foot (like me) and managed to revive and bring it up. Now it lives in my room with me, freely, and has made itself quite at home. It sleeps in my bookshelf, on the works of Morgan and André Gide, and has got so used to me that it hops about all over me as I lie. Not only hops. I think it is a girl, but I call it Cassidy. I don't really care for it in the least, but, having saved its absurd life, have a feeling of responsibility towards it. It is tiny, a midget, half the size of any ordinary sparrow—lack of protein, perhaps, but I have been too ill to go out in search of spiders and insects. I don't think it will ever be able, like Elsa,[3] to re-enter wild life, though I wish it would. It can perch, in spite of its injury.

---

[1] But within a few days A. had changed his mind, and to Roy Fuller he wrote: 'I decided to re-read Proust, whom in fact I never finished 35 years ago when the translation was incomplete; and although I have now reached the last volume, it was a mistaken choice, for he is an exasperating writer when one is in pain. I confess to frequent skippings of many of those maddening parentheses embedded in sentences of which the beginning is already lost to mind and the end nowhere in sight; so, returning to where I started from (dear me! have I caught his style?), your book in which I note that you tease him, was a boon, and a blessing, an excitement in itself and a relief from him.' Earlier in the year Fuller's *Collected Poems 1936–61* had come out, and in one of the shorter ones called 'On Spalding's *Handbook to Proust*', he had 'teased' the French novelist. The opening line ran: 'Like life the novel's just too long to grasp . . .'

[2] A. had written on 10 June to King: 'A sparrow is at present sharing my room with me, I found it on the pavement . . . It must have fallen quite 60 feet from its nest. For some 10 days I fed it on brown bread and milk out of a pen nib . . . It lives in a sort of playground I have made for it on the floor, and spends most of its time there or among the books on the shelves, shitting on them all. *Howards End* appears to be its favourite . . .' Cf. Letter 224.

[3] The lioness made famous by Joy Adamson in her books *Born Free* (1960) and *Living Free* (1961). A. had reviewed the latter for *The Listener* on 5 October 1961. One passage had gone down particularly well with the book trade: '. . . Mr William Collins, Elsa's publisher, to whom she takes, clever girl, in a big way, goes to bed with him twice, almost swallowing his face, and nibbles his ear. For these excesses nervous Mrs Adamson beats her, which seems a pity, for how is Elsa to know that publishers are unaccustomed to being lionized and that if authors are grateful for their royalties they do not normally express their gratitude in this way?'

I agree absolutely about Isherwood's book.[1] I hear he has now started on another. And what you *you* doing, dear F., and how are you?
Love
    Joe

To Donald Windham (1920–)   17 Star & Garter Mansions, Putney, 227
                                    S.W.15   2/9/62

Dear Don
            nice to hear from you and of the adventure in the bookshop. Since I understand that the poor little book[2] was never advertised or reviewed at all, I wonder by what strange concatenation of circumstances the anonymous purchaser was led to it. I have reason to believe that my sales, at any rate here, possibly in the U.S. too, may receive a boost in a few weeks time.[3]

Now what can I tell you, dear Don? If your own news was thin, mine seems non-existent. I met two Americans here the other day who knew you both: Irving Drutman and Michael de Lisio: rather jolly, I thought. I have had 6 days in Edinburgh, roped in to the Writers Conference—part of the festival—and met more of your compatriots: Mary McCarthy (whom I liked), Henry Miller, William Burroughs and Norman Mailer. The Conference was rather undignified and I did not open my beak.[4] I too am reading Wilde's letters.[5] 'Renter' is still in common use here:[6] it really means a male prostitute. Funny you should not have known that, while I had never heard of 'muggers'! What foreigners we are to each other! Another American . . . is staying here and Morgan lent him your last book of stories,[7] which he is enjoying. He came visiting me last week and drove my sparrow out of my room into the great world. This was meant to be helpful, ridding us of an incumbrance, but it has upset me, not knowing what has happened to the creature. It went in fright so does not return and very likely has not survived the unknown world of cats and cars and the fight for life. I was planning to disengage myself gradually and gently, so that the bird might remember this as a home from home. I have been looking about for it in the surrounding gardens and trees, but am handicapped by not knowing in which direction[8]

---

[1] *Down There on a Visit* (1962). A. had written earlier in the year to Geoffrey Gorer: 'Isherwood's [novel] . . . has considerable power; it particularly interested me because I saw something of my present self in Paul . . .' But A. was mistaken, for Isherwood wrote to Braybrooke on 11 July 1973: '. . . my character Paul wasn't in any respect intended as a portrait of Joe . . .'
[2] The American edition of *We Think the World of You*, which had been published in December 1961. See page 178, note 2.
[3] By the forthcoming W. H. Smith £1,000 Literary Award for 1962. See Letter 232.
[4] See Letter 229.
[5] When A. had finished them, he wrote to Georges Duthuit: 'Oscar Wilde must have been one of the kindest of men; he is one of the few people I should have liked to know.'
[6] At the trial of Oscar Wilde in 1895, when one of Wilde's letters to Lord Alfred Douglas, dated March 1893, was read out in court, the phrase here italicised 'I would sooner *be blackmailed by every renter in London* than have you bitter . . .' was omitted. See *The Letters of Oscar Wilde*, edited by Rupert Hart-Davis (1962).
[7] *The Warm Country* (1960) to which E. M. Forster had contributed an Introduction.
[8] A. must have suffered a lapse of memory, for a week later he remembered exactly in which 'direction' the bird had flown off. See Letter 229.

it flew. Morgan is well, off soon to France for a fortnight. I myself am still not well, though better I suppose. The sciatica has left me with a deadish leg and foot, though most of the pain has now gone. I am still undergoing physiotherapy. But my spirits are gloomy and tired: perhaps they caused the sciatica. I don't know if *Quaint Honor*[1] is still to be had: I have no copy myself or would send it. It is an excellent play.

Bless you and love to Sandy also

Joe

228 To E. M. Forster (1879–1970)   Putney

8/9/62

Darling Morgan

all is over, I hear from Bob tonight; Robin[2] died quite peacefully at about 7 p.m., May with him. Well, he had endured, and so uncomplaining, long enough that wretched fatal illness of raised and shattered hopes. I am glad it has reached its inescapable, exhausting end; glad too that he was able to get pleasure out of bits of it (I think of Weymouth), pleasure made possible by your darling self. How malevolent fate sometimes seems (I think of Sylvia),[3] picking on people and crushing them down, blow upon blow. Thank heaven she has the children, as well as her great courage. Poor Bob and May: was it for this the clay grew tall[?][4] But they too have the children.

So glad you get off on the 14th, if you still can. It sounds a pleasant easy round of visits. Nancy and I could not manage Weymouth, the hotel was fully booked right into October; I didn't know or want any other hotel, and don't know whether we shall go as late as that. But Jim Kirkup flew home from Tokyo yesterday to join his old blind mother in Bath; he wants to see me there, so I am thinking of taking Nancy there instead. I am waiting to hear from him.

Fondest love

Joe

[1] By Roger Gellert. A. had reviewed it for *The Listener* on 26 February 1959. He began the notice: 'In the present state of our society in which the right of the law to interfere in people's sexual relations is being disputed, it is important that works such as this should be read. So rapid has been the advance in knowledge and understanding of sexual psychology, that "homosexuality", a word which twenty years ago respectable newspapers would have refused to print, has become a headline topic for public discussion, and there is now a widely held opinion that, so long as youth is protected and public decency preserved, a man's private life should be allowed to be his own affair and no one else's. In recommending "that homosexual behaviour between consenting adults in private be no longer a criminal offence," the Wolfenden Report fixed adulthood, "for the purposes of the proposed change," at twenty-one. Mr Gellert's play, which was performed at the Art Theatre last year, is about the young whom the Report seeks to protect, boys of fifteen to eighteen at a public school, and however "immature" the Report may consider them to be, they are presented here as perfectly in command of their senses and situations and as little likely to be grateful for legislation on their behalf as they are for their housemaster's pi-jaw—or "set piece", as he calls it—with which the play opens.'

[2] Robert Morgan Buckingham, the only son of Robert and May Buckingham. He had been born in 1933 and was known among his family and friends as Robin or Rob.

[3] Robin's wife.

[4] The phrase comes from Wilfrid Owen's poem 'Futility' (1917).

To William Plomer (1903–1973)   Putney 229
                                                          9/9/62
D.L.B.

        so pleased to have your nice long letter. Robin Buckingham died yesterday evening,[1] peacefully, May with him. Bob phoned me soon after.

        I have been trying to take Nancy away for a week or two for a change, but the hotel at Weymouth I like and hoped to return to is full right to October. Too late, I think, for the English seaside then; but Jim Kirkup flew from Tokyo yesterday to stay with his old blind mother in Bath until she dies, he wants me to go along there, so it may be that, quite soon, I shall take Nancy there instead. Neither of us has ever seen Bath. All this leads to my saying that I had better not make a plan for Rustington at the moment: I shall be hearing from Jim quite soon. But if you have a spare dinner time in London that would be nice. My leg is not totally free from pain, perhaps it never will be or lose the numbness of the foot. I still go 3 times a week to hospital for physio-therapy. Don't think it does the slightest good.

        Cassidy[2] has gone. An American friend, . . . thinking to be helpful and knowing of my problem over the bird, drove it out of my room when my back was turned. It flew onto the terrace and away—10 days ago. It was a stupid piece of interference, for it only added extra sadness to my already sad mind. I wanted to return the bird to its normal life and was having difficulties, for it had accustomed itself to my room and myself and did not want to leave—for doors and windows left open it showed no curiosity. But I had a plan, of gradually enticing it into the dining-room by moving its food and drink towards my door, then through it, and, when it had grown used to entering the dining-room, of leaving the terrace door open so that it could see other sparrows hopping about outside and join them if it wished. In this way, I hoped, it might become more enterprising, have some fun outside and return here whenever it was hungry or frightened. I should have liked that. But my American defeated me, the little bird flew off in fright and has never returned, and although I have hunted the neighbourhood ever since and enticed and inspected the swarms of sparrows who live in the trees and gardens round about I have never seen it. I would easily identify it by its crippled foot, unusual smallness, and the white feathers on its back. I was in time to see it fly off—it went into the garden of the Constitutional Club, on the other side of 'The Duke's Head', where there are two cats. I am much afraid that catastrophe soon overtook it, and although I was not deeply attached to the little creature and it remained always wary of me—it made use of the warmth of my body, nestling against my ribs or my legs as I lay on my bed, but would never let me touch it—I had saved its life and had a feeling of responsibility for its future. I was surprised that an intelligent and elderly man . . . should not have learnt what is surely one of the most serious lessons of life, which is never to interfere in other people's affairs, however noble one's intentions, unless one's opinion or help is desired.

        The [Writers] Conference in Edinburgh[3] had pleasant moments, I liked

---

[1] See Letter 228.   [2] See Letter 224.   [3] See Letter 227.

Mary Macarthy [*sic*] and also liked Henry Miller who talked about practically nothing else but indecent *graffiti*—not in public but at the various parties and receptions; I also liked the Glenconners, with whom I dined. But the whole business rather worried me, for although Sonia had said I needn't do a thing, only go, I felt I *ought* to say something—and was asked by Stephen and Angus [Wilson] to do so—but being well advanced in softening of the brain I found myself with no mind left.

Rebecca West remarked that there should have been *two* conferences, one for those who wanted to talk about the novel, and one for those who wanted to discuss homosexuality. This was soon after the Dutch delegate had got up and announced: 'I am a homosexual.'
Fondest love, d.l.b.
  Joe

230 To William Plomer (1903–1973)   Putney
                                                                         11/10/62
  Darling William
              I am so sorry about Charles and his operation, though relieved to hear that it is not of an alarming nature. But even the slightest operation is upsetting: do give him my love and tell him how sympathetic I feel. I am not awfully well myself, nothing specific and caused I daresay by the fact that I find so little happiness now in life; it has become for me indeed a great bore and will never again be anything else. Odd to feel like this almost on the eve of having £1000 given to me (yes, that is my surprise), but so it is: I shouldn't be telling you, for it is not to be announced until the party on the 16th, but I have won the W. H. Smith Award.[1] I thought at first that your fairy form must be lurking behind this choice, for I knew you had been judging, but learnt later that Harold [Nicolson], Eliz[abeth] Bowen and Philip Toynbee had selected me. Well, of course it is nice to have £1000, though one has to suffer an ordeal to get it,[2] but I have no interest to expend it on now—excepting perhaps booze. Yes, I trotted Nancy down to Bath and kept her there for nine days...Jim Kirkup was there...and came along to us most evenings. Charming fellow. We made excursions during the days, to Longleat, Wells and Glastonbury, Clifton and Cheddar, so that we saw the countryside etc. And for a week the weather was fine as now; then it started to rain, Nancy's shoes were found not to be watertight (both pairs); also she had had for many months a loose lens in her spectacles, 'secured', against my advice, with sellotape, which fell out and smashed in the Bath Museum when she was peering at a hideous German clock; so, disabled at both ends, she had to be brought home. Well, it was pleasant enough.

  [1] A. himself thought the award should have gone to Richard Hughes for *The Fox in the Attic* (1961).
  [2] Forster had written to A. earlier in the month: '... you can't expect to get all that money from a commercial firm without hopping through a hoop...' He also wrote 'a J.R.A. comic acceptance speech, [ending]: "Your generous cheque (for which once more I thank you) will cover all incidental expenses, and I accept it in the spirit in which it was no doubt given: an advance payment for lust." ' See note 4 opposite.

No, it is news to me that I appear in Rose's letters—unless it *is* the reference, already published, to our visit to Billy Graham.[1] I have not been approached about anything—but I don't mind. Glad your labours on that diary[2] are coming to a point: do let us meet soon.

Fond love, as ever

Joe

To Marjorie Redman (1907-   )   Putney   231
                                                                 24/10/62

Thank you, dear Marjorie, for your nice letter. Yes, of course, when I thought of it I realized that you could not very well come to my party on [*The Listener*'s] press day. What a pity. If it had occurred to me earlier—and I knew about it all two months ago[3]—I would have asked [W. H.] Smiths for a different day. However, I don't suppose I should have seen much of you: I saw hardly anything of anyone, but was instantly plucked away; it is really no fun being Principal Boy and I was glad when it was all over, and a nervous wreck the following day.

Sciatica seems to have gone, but has left me with a numbness in foot and leg. It is rather disagreeable but doesn't affect mobility; I expect to have it for 'keeps'.

Well, dear Marjorie, I will look in to see you all one day. I doubt if I shall get back to Japan, though I said so for want of anything else to say,[4] but energy and enterprise now are not among my most noticeable characteristics.

Love to you all

Joe

1 This *was* the reference. Plomer had reviewed for *The Listener* on 25 October *Last Letters to a Friend from Rose Macaulay 1952–58*, edited by Constance Babington Smith. In one of these letters dated 'May Day, 54', Rose Macaulay had written to her cousin, Father Hamilton Johnson, an Anglican priest, about how she and A. had gone to hear Billy Graham, the American Evangelist, at Harringay: '. . . we sat under him, in a packed stadium full of thousands of people, while he addressed us on the 7th Commandment, to which he gave the exclusive name of "immorality" (the breaking of it, that is). He was very fervent, preaching with great gesture and power, very crude and simple, even illiterate (in phrasing and thought, not in accent). Of course it was *not* what Joe Ackerley or I could stomach. But the packed thousands did, and *hundreds* afterwards walked up to be "saved"—a very impressive crowd . . . All very strange. God certainly does move in a mysterious way, His wonders to perform. I think he really *is* converting many people to a Christian life; he is a Baptist . . . Joe Ackerley came out murmuring "Dreadful creature!" I tried not to feel this, because I think he is sincere, though melodramatic.' The next day at the office when Marjorie Redman had asked A. what he thought about the meeting, A. had replied: 'The fellow's a fascist! If I hadn't shut my eyes when he told us all to, some of his young men would have thrown me out.'
2 Plomer was editing the diary (1932–61) of Richard Rumbold, which was published posthumously in 1964 as *A Message in Code*.
3 See Letter 227.
4 In preparation for the W. H. Smith party on 16 October A. had written three speeches. When it came to it, he delivered 'the briefest and dullest'. Forster had advised him: 'Stick to dullness and avoid the Press.' Fredric Warburg, who was present, believes it must have been one of the shortest speeches ever given on such an occasion: 'Thank you for the £1,000—I shall take myself off to Japan with it—couldn't afford to go there otherwise—I've always wanted to return.' See Warburg's *All Authors Are Equal* (1793). See note 2 opposite.

232 To Donald Windham (1920–)   Putney
                                                                          2/12/62

Dear Don

many thanks. I was asked—by [W. H.] Smiths—not to spread the news of my good fortune—I was told about it two months before the event—because they wanted to announce it then, at the party, as a surprise, they thought it would make a greater 'impact'. On whom? on what?—I haven't a clue. Anyway, I did manage to hold my tongue to some extent, telling only Morgan, Gorer, Jack Sprott and my sister, the people I see most of.[1] It was a quite unnecessary self-discipline, for I found that all sorts of unlikely people knew of it long before the presentation—so I might just as well have come clean with you.[2] It is jolly to have a thousand quid, free of income tax, but I must say I found the hoops I had to go through for it rather unnerving: indeed I was almost a hospital case by the Great Day and even contemplated escaping to the Continent and leaving a proxy to collect the dough. But I stuck it out. Smiths (quite decent in their business-like way) were hoping I would bring my old dog Queenie with me on the platform at the Savoy Hotel where the presentation, by [...] Lord Longford,[3] was made, and were depressed to hear that she was dead. Various other thoughts flitted through their heads—perhaps another alsatian could be found to take her place?—well, blown out photographs of her on the stage?[4]—so sad for me, and besides she was one of the main pointers to the libel inherent in the book. I got out of all that, but I didn't enjoy it, and the thought of having to make a speech upset me, though I believe I managed all right in the end.[5] I'm glad it's all over; I doubt if it had much effect upon sales, but I suppose one shouldn't expect more after a gift of £1000.

So pleased to have your letter and news, dear. I am a bit drunk tonight (not unusual, so rather incoherent perhaps); but I loved your letter with news of your writings, Sandy's job, and the divine name 'Paul [Cadmus]',[6] messenger of my luck. Please give that sweet fellow my love, and do hope he liked Jack Sprott who so much liked him. I think of him, Paul, often with a very particular affection.

Morgan is all right, excepting that he tumbles about now more than he did. He knows it and said to me lately that he was afraid he had become a tumbler, he couldn't prevent it. But his latest sprained ankle is getting better. Yes, he or the printers leave an 'e' out of my name in *Marianne Thornton* (1956),[7] but I've often thought that the final 'e' was quite unnecessary.[8]

---

1 Also several others including Francis King, Sonia Orwell and William Plomer.
2 See Letter 227.
3 The event was described in *The Times* on 17 October: 'The fourth W. H. Smith & Son annual literary award was presented at the Savoy Hotel last night to Mr J. R. Ackerley ... Speaking in front of a miniature stage set representing a typical scene in the part of London in which the novel is set, Lord Longford, who made the presentation, described the book as a "delicate, beautifully written tale by one of our most distinguished men of letters".' See *All Authors Are Equal* by Fredric Warburg (1973).
4 A. had written to Roy Fuller just before the event: 'The idea that I could have a naked boy instead of a dog beside me on the platform seemed not to occur to them.'
5 See page 221, note 4.   6 Cadmus had told Windham of A.'s award.   7 i.e. 'Ackerly'.
8 In America, Coward McCann left out the same 'e' on the bindings and copyright page of the first copies off the press of *My Father and Myself* (1969).

I am just coming to the end of what I hope may be the final draft of my memoir[1]—if 'memoir' it can be called, for I can recollect practically nothing about my past—of my father and myself. I think I have now got outside of it all, so that I can view his life (what little I knew of it) and my own (what little I understand of that) objectively. It is a failure book—we were both failures —but contains, I think, a certain amount of legitimate amusement. I think that in its feeble, apologetic way (for I have to keep saying 'I don't know') it just manages to stand up. And it has enabled *me* to go on doing that. I have been pissing on it, off and on, for thirty years. Shall I crumble up when I have put 'finish' to it? It would seem to be the Thornton Wilder moment.[2]
Much love, dear Don

Joe

To Francis King (1923–)   Putney 233
                                                                                          25/2/63

Dearest Francis
                such flattery is irresistible; I did not know I was a letter-writer, though I know I write letters. But are you any longer in my *milieu*, for I am now related to a Duchess? My half-sister, Sally [——], became Duchess of [——] last week, and I'm not sure that she would like me to correspond with Tom, Dick, and Harry. You will see that my writing is not as firm as it was, but that has another cause—drink. The monotony of old-age life, how is one to endure it? My mother took to the bottle, I am my mother's son,[3] and God bless the [W. H.] Smith Award for enabling me to be careless of expense. This morning as I lay in my bath I noticed with surprise some bruises and abrasions on my carcase and wondered how on earth I had sustained them. Then I vaguely recollected that in bending down to remove my shoes the previous night before going to bed, I had fallen forward on my face among various articles of furniture. And after only three tots of whisky: abstemious. Considering how many whiskies I used to drink with you on our nightly round of the gay bars of Kyoto, I found that surprising. But of course, our Scotch is stronger than Japanese whisky. However, I seem fairly well, a bit rough in the bronchials.

Yes, James is back in Tokyo, and intends to stay there for at least a year. I didn't see him before he went; I suppose he made a sudden dash. No job yet—he hopes to find one; but the magazine *Orient/West*[4] may provide a little pocket-money. I have had a couple of cards from him: he is now lodging with a Japanese family. I think he is fairly flush, pro tem: the [Friedrich]

---

[1] *My Father and Myself.*
[2] Cf. Letter 223.
[3] In *My Father and Myself*, A. wrote in Chapter II: 'I was more my mother's son than my father's . . .' In some notes made for the same book but never used in the final text, he also wrote: 'My father did not come of a refined family: the culture, such as it was, was on my mother's side.'
[4] A bi-monthly which had been founded in Tokyo in 1958. Its aim was to publish articles by famous scholars on literary, social and historical subjects connected with the Far East (mainly Japan), as well as poetry, short stories, translations and book reviews. James Kirkup had been appointed literary editor and at his suggestion A. contributed two articles—but only one appeared: 'I Am a Beast'.

Dürrenmatt play[1] (successful), his new Malayan book advance,[2] some translations, the sale of his Malayan car; but his expenses in England (his mother) must be pretty heavy; how long he can last remains to be seen . . .

What else have I to tell you? Precious little, since little happens. Every now and then I turn, with revulsion, to the family memoir[3] I have been picking at and recoiling from for some 30 years. It will never be any use. Edwin Muir says in his autobiography *The Story and the Fable*[4] (such a good book) 'I realised that I must live over again the years which I had lived wrongly, and that everyone should live his life twice, for the first attempt is always blind.' That is what I do, and the occupation is not pleasant; if I feel wiser for it, which I doubt, I also feel the sadder. Gerald Heard believes that the soul does not, cannot, leave the body after death until it has lived its life inside the dissolving body all over again.[5] To have to go through that hoop twice, during life, and after death, is devastating. Our saints certainly do not let us off. You are still too young to think about such matters!

I have had a couple of nights in Cambridge with Morgan and expect to see him in London tomorrow. He is well, but not as sure-footed as he used to be. You may know that we have had—still endure—the worst and coldest winter of the century. Almost all heating failed; even paraffin was a job to find, transport could not get about. For three or four weeks I went to bed in my clothes, between blankets, it seemed sheer lunacy to take off one's warm things and put on pyjamas. The poor birds have been absolutely frantic, and how stupid people are about them, throwing out their stale bread into the ice and snow, but in slices or hunks, not troubling to crumble it, so that the famished creatures have not been able to break and eat it. Much of my time has been spent in crumbling stuff for them wherever I find it.

I go to cinemas a good deal, the local ones let me in as an old-age pensioner for 9d if I go before 4.0 p.m. and also provide hearing aids free of charge (sort of telephones plugged into the seat) if the sound track is bad. I have seen dear Cliff Richard's new film[6] twice, though, as a film, once is more than enough. Evenings I get stuck to the telly. Not much of a life, you see, with little use left for mind and body. In September I go to Greece for a few weeks with Jack Sprott and his sister: no other plans at present. I have just been to lunch with Villiers David who asked for news of you.
Much love
   Joe

234 To Geoffrey Gorer (1905–)   Putney
                                                                 21/3/63
My dear G.G.

        for some reason I knew your news before opening the envelope. I am deeply grieved, dear G.G. She was a sweet-natured lady and

---

[1] *The Physicists.*
[2] i.e. for *Tropic Temper: A Malayan Memoir*, which was published towards the end of the year.
[3] *My Father and Myself.*   [4] 1940.   [5] Cf. Letter 221.   [6] *The Young Ones.*

your faithful friend and you will miss her sadly.[1] I never speak of Queenie now who died 18 months ago (what is the good) but I think of her every day, her death and the manner of it destroyed me also, and I am nothing now but an old soak, keeping up some sort of appearance for the sake of my friends. How wretched for you to have a sick thumb too, though you speak lightly of it; excepting for a persistent tonsilitis, which makes smoking a curse, I seem to get along without physical liability. Well, I won't turn to other things—if there are any others—I am thinking of Meg, and how good and affectionate she was to you, and even to me, and this shall be her letter. Love from
   Joe

To John Lehmann (1907–)   Putney 235
                                         26/3/63
Dear John
      it was such a nice party, beautifully arranged, I enjoyed it very much. I liked Mrs Sansom,[2] who managed to get into my bad ear, and although I was a bit at sea with Ghika[3] I like him too. Your niece[4] I thought as pretty as a picture (I can't fix the painter she reminded me of) and perfectly charming. I joined the Club[5] before I left, perhaps unwisely but out of enthusiasm for you and your delicious hospitality: if one takes a friend in at 6.30 or so for a quiet chat, would one ever get a seat in so small a room? But it is amusing to have these little pop-ins, and I hope for the best—if I can remember that I now belong.

I had hardly any conversation with you, dear John: come and have lunch with me at my club, the Royal College of Art, this week or next. Give me a ring when you are free; I have too few engagements. And I do hope your dog has recovered: so sweet of you to go through our hoop when you were worried. How well I understand all that terrible anxiety.
Love from
   Joe

To Michael Holroyd (1935–)   17 Star & Garter Mansions, Putney, 236
                        S.W.15   7/6/63
Dear Mr Holroyd
      I can be of little use to you, I fear. Though I knew Lytton [Strachey] I did not see much of him and if I stayed twice at Ham Spray House I did not visit him more often than that. Moreover I am afflicted by an extremely bad memory. The biographer of Arnold Bennett[6] wrote me a similar letter to yours some years ago—my recollections of Bennett—and I

---

[1] Meg, his yellow labrador.
[2] Ruth Sansom, wife of William Sansom the novelist.
[3] The Greek painter.
[4] Mollie—the wife of the Hon. Hugo Philips (Rosamond Lehmann's son).
[5] Le Petit Club Français, off St. James's Street.
[6] Reginald Pound.

replied that I had never met him. In fact I had, at the Herberts'[1] house in Hammersmith, for the meeting is mentioned in his *Journals*[2] so you see how little I can be relied upon. The only anecdote of Lytton I recall is second-hand, the hoary old story of his pacifism in the War: when asked about what he would do if he saw a Hun raping his sister, he replied in his squeaky voice 'I would try to get in between.' Whether this story is true I don't know; it has an authentic sound. My files contain only two letters from him, his first invitation to Ham Spray (1925) (I am in doubt if I ever went again) and a later letter, which the mice seem to have got at, written to me to Savoy Hill (I joined the B.B.C. in 1928) apologizing for something that took place at an audition we gave him. 'I was filled with such feelings of guilt and remorse over my behaviour in our broadcasting that I lapsed into what I fear was a churlish silence. —— me.' The mice have eaten the penultimate word, which I suppose to have been 'forgive' or 'excuse'.[3] (The rest of the letter, which quips about my private life, I am using in a family memoir I am writing, so I cannot let you have it.)[4] What happened at the B.B.C. of course I don't recollect; I fancy that his voice was useless to us, but my then colleague may remember if you care to write to him: Lionel Fielden, Massa Macinaia, Nr. LUCCA, Italy. The mice have also had most of the date of this letter: Jan. 1st, 1930?[5]

J. R. Ackerley

237   To David Sylvester (1924–   )   Putney
                                                                        14/7/63
Dear David

          I was much interested in your *questionnaire* of Francis Bacon in today's *S[unday] T[imes]*. It shed much light. There is one question, however, I wished you had put but did not. What is his *emotional* state of mind when he paints? For I suppose his paintings are not just a matter of technical problems to be overcome; his own despairing psychology is deeply involved. Are practically all his pictures—'Crucifixion' and all—self-portraits *au fond*? Though he may not know it. Does he attack his canvasses in a mood of (drugged and drunken?) self-hatred or self-pity? Does he strew them with deformed, whimpering creatures, blood and entrails out of pity or hatred for creation or out of self-hatred? Does he weep as he paints, or snarl as he spatters his canvases with maculae? The question may not be important, but it interests me as a writer, for I think writers (it certainly applies to me)

---

[1] A. P. Herbert and his wife.
[2] 'We dined at the Herberts': Mark Gertler, Pitman and wife and Ackerley the playwright. One or two people came in afterwards, including the Wilenskis.' This passage occurs in *The Journals of Arnold Bennett*, vol. 3, in the entry for 29 June 1927.
[3] It was 'forgive'. See page 16, note 8.
[4] In the end A. did not use the rest of this letter in *My Father and Myself*, but only its ending (in Chapter 13):
                              'With best regards to
                              The Army
                              The Navy
                              and The Police Force.'
[5] A more likely date would be towards the end of 1928. See Letter 8.

live often in a state of emotional overflow as they work, tears (perhaps maudlin), self-hugs of delight, grins of satisfied hatred: these pleasures are partly psychological, partly artistic and the exact right phrase or word [produces] the inalterably perfect passage. But about painters I do not know; is their excitement *purely* artistic, or is it also emotional? Francis seems to me pre-eminently the painter to whom such questions could be applied.

Hitherto I have never quite known what my reactions were to his pictures (art apart), except, of course, fascination (horrid word) and astonishment. But whether these terrible images were intended to make one shudder, weep, or even laugh at the tragi-comic plight of humanity I have not quite known. In front of his present exhibition I felt inclined to cry, especially with the 'Portrait of P.L.'[1] Is this an interesting matter? Francis, of course, will not understand his own psychology, any more than I understand mine, but when he paints (as I believe out of it) what is he telling himself and us? That we are deformed and hideous worms, that he is the great worm of the world, or that we are all the most pitiable creatures on the face of the earth?

Nancy and I have not forgotten you. We have been waiting for a decent day so that you could sit out on my terrace. The flat otherwise is so tiny and claustrophobic. Since we saw you not a single suitable day has occurred. But to have you here, and the darling, charming and beautiful Pamela is truly our dearest wish.

Love

Joe

Excuse scrawl.

To Donald Windham (1920–   )   17 Star & Garter Mansions, Putney, 238
                                 S.W.15   17/7/63

Thank you, dear Don. A most delightful morning's mail brought me you and a letter from William Plomer. 'Myopia'[2] is of absorbing interest, one of the best things you have done, beautifully composed and controlled, as round and firm as a crystal illuminated by its own internal and refracted light. I *almost* wish I were still Lit. Ed. of *The Listener*, I would have been so proud, with your consent, to publish it. It connects with my own thought, about myself and my life, in various ways and about my family memoir,[3] one's own abdication (I am among your uncles and aunts) and the failure of communication in adolescence, indeed into adult life. I shall send it along to Morgan, who, indeed, said to me not long ago 'We have all deteriorated.'

I'm sorry that Rupert [Hart-Davis] has given you up. It is true that your last book[4] is often to be seen as a remainder in our second-hand bookshops,

---

[1] A portrait painted in 1962 in memory of Peter Lacey.
[2] A chapter from his autobiography *Emblems of Conduct* (1963). Cf. Letter 223.
[3] *My Father and Myself*.
[4] *The Warm Country* (1960).

but so are the books of other good writers, including my own. Why not try The Bodley Head, who published my last? They were nice to work with, though I think they need to be argued with over terms. No, I don't like the title you propose for your Roman novel either; it is too much like a film title —indeed, isn't there a film called *Suddenly Last Summer*, or something similar[?] However, you will rightly take no notice of me but go your own way.[1]

I feel very aimless and dreary most of the time; if it weren't for alcohol I wouldn't get through. I know it's wrong to have so little attachment to life, but it is a psychological thing, nothing to be done about it. Fragments of pleasure are sometimes found in the ashes, but they are rare. The main interest I get is from animals. I paid my first visit yesterday to Whipsnade, our great zoo park in Bedfordshire, 600 acres of it where the animals live under more or less natural conditions. I particularly wanted to see Kaseh the tigress with her two six-week old cubs, and there she was, superb creature, stretched out on the grass in the sunshine beneath a tree in the glade in which she lives, lazily keeping an eye on her children who were asleep in each other's arms in a large open straw-strewn shed some distance away. I had the pleasure of seeing her rise to her feet and go over to visit them to see how they did. She licked them both awake and they came stumbling after her like kittens to the edge of the platform where they fell asleep again, while she returned to her couch on the grass. Lots of the other animals were also of absorbing interest (the Kangaroos, the Beavers, the Gibbons), only the people didn't do, especially the shrieking children and the silly giggling schoolgirls, feeding the animals they were asked not to feed (they become sick and unhappy on a wrong diet) and teasing those who were trying to sleep. I dislike the human race more and more. The place itself is wonderfully beautiful (did you ever visit it, I wonder), some eight hundred feet up on the Chiltern Hills, Dunstable Downs, with spectacular views; if only our weather would improve, the wind drop and the rain cease I would go and fix myself in Dunstable for a week and explore the zoo more thoroughly and some of the fine country houses thereabouts which are open to the public. But at present it is very unwise to venture out without an umbrella.

My sister and I are just off to listen to William Plomer reading his poetry at the Royal Court Theatre. It is Festival of Poetry week. Morgan has been silent for some days, but I believe he is all right.

Much love to you, dear Don and to dear Sandy

Joe

P.S. Someone here is trying to turn my novelette[2] into a 'Pop' musical![3]

---

[1] Windham had thought of calling his Roman novel *And Suddenly It's Evening*, based on Quasimodo's poem '*Ed e Subito Sera*'. But on A.'s advice he decided against this and chose instead *Two People*.

[2] *We Think the World of You.*

[3] Nothing came of this during A.'s life. The adapter in question was Ingaret van der Post, who told Braybrooke in 1974: 'I have someone in television who is interested in the idea . . .' See Letter 241.

To James Kirkup (1923–   )   17 Star & Garter Mansions, Putney, S.W.15   239
19/7/63

My darling Jim
I am not *at all* surprised by Mr [Maurice] Schneps' opinion. I wondered what you could be up to, stocking your mag.[1] with odds and ends from previous publications; *The Listener* too would never have permitted that—doubtless a reason why, in the long course of years, I got so worn out, having no assistant and only my own poor mind to rely upon in finding material which had always to be fresh and original. Killing work for one head, and in the end it killed me. You may be sure that if I can devise anything for you I will, for I love you and would like to help you adorn your mag., but the last two years have not invigorated my thought. However I am thinking of taking myself up into Bedfordshire soon for a few days to stay, perhaps in Dunstable, within easy reach of Whipsnade Zoo which I visited this week for the first time and take the interest to explore more thoroughly. If some little piece on animals, including my memory of the Matsushima tigress,[2] came out of that I would submit it to you. No, dear, I cannot write about Goldie Dickinson, though oddly enough I am reading about him in Morgan's biography,[3] which I have not looked at for many years: a beautiful book. *Appearances*[4] by him I never read. He (Goldie) was in love with me when I was a young man and I had to disengage myself from an emotional relationship I did not want. He managed to sublimate it, as he sublimated all his unreciprocated passions.[5] I have not thought of him or it for a great many years, preferring not to I suppose, until lately in my family memoir[6] I have been trying to examine and explain a psychology, my own, which was never able to be generous in such matters and which, although I could not and cannot help it, has been no pleasure to try to discern.

I have written to Francis who asks me to go out now and return with him on his P. & O. But, as you know, I am at present engaged to spend the last two or three weeks of September in Greece with the Sprotts. The plan wobbles a bit at the moment, for Jack's health is not good and is under medical survey. However, I hope all will be well. If we go, and Greece props up my failing mind to greater enterprise than it at present possesses, I might come on to you and your welcoming friends. A sweeter and warmer invitation than yours could not be imagined.
Love as ever
Joe

[1] Schneps was the Editor of *Orient/West*, Kirkup the literary editor. Kirkup had wanted to include an article by A. which had appeared elsewhere, but Schneps had made it his rule only to publish new work. See page 223, note 4.
[2] Within two days, A. began drafting an article: '. . . When I looked over the fence in Matsushima I found myself staring into the eyes of a tigress. She was so close that if my arm had been three times its actual length I could have touched her. She was a young tigress, I judged, large, radiantly beautiful. Standing in her cage she gazed up at me. I gazed down at her. Then, with a slow, voluptuous movement, she rose up on her hind legs, stretched herself to her full height to the top of the cage, which her head almost touched, clasped the bars with her fore-paws and, resting her chin upon them, looked down into my eyes. For some moments we remained thus, then I returned the way that I had come . . .'   [3] *Goldsworthy Lowes Dickinson* (1934).   [4] 1914.
[5] See *The Autobiography of G. Lowes Dickinson*, edited by Sir Dennis Proctor (1973).
[6] *My Father and Myself*.

240 To Georges Duthuit (1891–)   Putney
                                                                     22/7/63

Dearest Georges

now that I have posted my letter to you and read again
yours, I think I have been rather stupid. It was to my father's secret[1] (which
you know all about, of course) that you were referring, and not to secrets
of your own? It was your phrase about 'rending one's heart' that confused
me. I don't think my father suffered from his secret[2] much, if at all. I don't
see him as a worried man, tossing about on a sleepless bed. In fact I think
he was a naturally secretive man; there are many other instances in his life.
But I am sorry that he could not tell me until after his death, in letters. I
believe it was largely my own fault. I did not think of him enough, in fact
scarcely at all, and it is difficult to speak confidentially to sons who have
never attended to you or taken you seriously. No confidence had ever
passed between us, there was no channel for such a thing. However, if you
too have a secret, you can tell it to me and I will tell you whether you can tell
it to your son . . .

I am going up to Dunstable for a few days soon to stay alone in a hotel.
It is in Bedfordshire. I want to be near Whipsnade Zoo to finish my philo-
sophical article 'I Am a Beast'.[3] I want to see Kaseh again.[4] Do you know
about her. She is a tigress and has just given birth to two cubs. She is radiantly beautiful. I saw her last week. She was reclining on the grass under a
tree in her large sunken glade, keeping watch upon her children who were
asleep in each other's arms in a kind of open Nativity shed some distance
away. I was privileged to see her rise to her feet and go over to inspect her
children to reassure herself that they were well. She licked them awake and
rolled them over with her great paw. Then she returned to her couch on the
grass. I have bad memories of the Rome zoo. I remember people throwing
gravel at a lion because he was asleep. They had paid to see him and
thought it their due that he should wake up and roar. The human race does
not come out well in my article.

Joe

241 To Desmond Shawe-Taylor (1907–)   17 Star & Garter Mansions,
                                             Putney, S.W.15   31/7/63

Dear Desmond

you made some very gratifying remarks about my novelette

---

[1] i.e. Roger Ackerley's 'secret orchard' and 'double life'. See Letter 9 and Introduction, 3.
[2] Earlier A. had written to Duthuit on 12 January: '[My] memoir of my father and myself . . .
is a sort of examination of his life and character, and of my own, to try and understand why we
had so little confidence in each other, friendly though we were, and did not share each other's
secrets. He led a double life, as you know, and so did I, and many people were let into the secret
of his life—excepting me.' See Letter 306 and Introduction, 3.
[3] See Index of Writings by J.R.A. for full list of references to this article.
[4] See Letter 238.

some eighteen months ago;[1] have you the time to make a remark or two about the enclosed letters?[2] They speak for themselves—indeed the worry I feel about bothering you is that the second letter speaks far too much; but perhaps the first page of it, before Mr [——] and his typewriter become erratic, may give you some clue to his mind and capabilities. I myself am at sea in his world of 'pop' music and 7/4 and 4/4 times. He wrote out of the blue, with touching enthusiasm, and I said 'Certainly, have a shot.' Since then he has called. A youngish man: I didn't make much of him and believe he has not yet made any sort of mark, except upon the mind of Lionel Bart, who is said (by Mr [——]) to think highly of him. The first of the two letters intrigued and amused me and seemed on the spot; the second, too, has some grasp, I think, but rather shirks the all-important question of how the dog is to be presented. If you could spare the time, dear Desmond, to give me your impressions I would be most awfully grateful.
Love from
   Joe

To Desmond Shawe-Taylor (1907–)   17 Star & Garter Mansions,   242
                                     Putney, S.W.15   8/8/63

Thank you, dear Desmond, a wise and delightful letter. I don't really worry about 'reputations' or anything like that, but simply have a feeling that I shan't be able to judge, when called upon to do so, what the young man has done, when and if he does it.[3] However, perhaps I shall; I like Cliff Richard and Tommy Steele (though Mr [——] doesn't), and feel that if he could get Cliff to play the part of Johnny, or even of Evie, my fortune might be made.

Who do you think put the idea of writing to you into my mind? Villiers David. He seems to think the world of you and claims a fairly solid acquaintance. Have you heard of him? I have got to know him well, since Kyoto, and we have become fast (be careful how you interpret that word) friends.

If all goes well (my sister's health has started to loom as a problem) I go to Athens with Jack and Velda Sprott on Sept. 8, night flight. Our seats are booked. We propose to take one of CHAT'S bus tours—the Five Day Archaeological Tour, which seems to take in most things, then to fly for another 5 days to Crete and Rhodes. The Sprotts return to England on the 23rd. I hope to stay on for another fortnight at least—indeed if Cliff Richard undertook the part of Johnny I daresay I would stay there for the rest of the

---

[1] This had been in the Books of the Year feature in the *Sunday Times* on 24 December 1961, where Shawe-Taylor had written: 'Two novels have given me special pleasure: J. R. Ackerley's *We Think the World of You*, a study of moral fecklessness and irresponsibility which contrives to be at once very funny and hopelessly sad; and Ivy Compton-Burnett's *The Mighty and their Fall*.' Here too is perhaps the place to put on record Dame Ivy's comment, made six years later, when she read A.'s family memoir *My Father and Myself*: 'It would have been nearer the truth if he had called it "Myself—and my Father".' Cf. page 205, note 4.
[2] These letters were concerned with turning *We Think the World of You* into a 'pop' musical. Cf. Letter 238.
[3] The 'young man', who wanted to write the music for a 'pop' version of *We Think the World of You*. See Letter 241.

year—so if anything could be arranged with you it would be very pleasant for me. On the other hand, would I be a good companion to you? I am more than half deaf, and sexually effete, I fear. It is just possible that Greece might stiffen me up, it could not unstuff my ears.

Well, there you are, and thanks for your letter and
Love from
    Joe

243 To Desmond Shawe-Taylor (1907–)   17 Star & Garter Mansions,
                                             Putney, S.W.15   ?/9/63

Dear Desmond
                sorry to have missed your phone call. My sister in hospital (she is all right), and I have been staying with Villiers David in his flat, which is more fun than my own. No further news about the Greek trip, nor I think is there likely to be until I reach Greece, for then only shall I know how I am likely to feel when deserted by Jack and his sister on Sept. 23. If I feel that I should burst into tears at being left on my own among the savage Greeks I shall probably return with them. On the other hand, pending your arrival, I might meet someone else willing to put up with me for a time. I do think I need someone to carry me about like a parcel—a light parcel, for there is nothing in it.
Love from
    Joe

244 To James Kirkup (1923–)   Putney
                                                          25/11/63

Dearest Jim
                but I sent you my little article[1]—as far as it had got, about ten pages—nearly a fortnight ago. It must have gone astray—what a nuisance. 4/6 it cost me, and I remember taking care in writing your address. It was in a long air-mail envelope. If you haven't got it and can't trace it, I *could* do it for you again, but it would be a second labour of love and do I love you twice? Yes, I do. Your little balls[2] get through safely to me; I am sorry that my balls[3] didn't get through to you.

How sickening about your 'Kirkup-tells-all' book.[4] Do resist cuts if you can. I wonder if The Bodley Head would take it. Or who is the publisher who is taking a risk over *Fanny Hill*?[5] I doubt if even *you* could have gone much

[1] 'I Am a Beast.'
[2] Japanese folk-art objects which are the equivalent of English witchballs.
[3] First ten pages of 'I Am a Beast'. See note 1 above.
[4] A volume of autobiography.
[5] In 1963 Mayflower Books reissued a new edition of John Cleland's *Fanny Hill: Memoirs of a Woman of Pleasure* (1749), unabridged. The publishers were prosecuted in the following year and issued an abridged edition.

further than that. Have you read it, by the way? You should. It is extremely exciting—erotically—or so I found it when I read it in Morgan's rooms in Cambridge some months ago, although the copulations are all hetero. Morgan thinks that the pleasure we both derived from it is due to the fact that the organ upon which the most careful description is always lavished is the male organ.[1] I wish I had an organ still, even a female one; yet what would I do with it here if I had? Francis is here, already sorry for himself. He has rented a flat for a year, somewhere in Kensington. I took him to lunch at the Royal Coll[ege of Art] last Friday and Morgan, whom he had not met before, joined us.[2] Francis was very nice and they got on well together. Not so Morgan and [———— ————] who came in by appointment for a quarter of an hour before lunch. He had asked Morgan to autograph his collection of Morgan's books; Morgan hates that kind of thing but had not liked to refuse so eminent a writer. So [————], fat and prosperous looking, appeared at the club by arrangement, carrying a satchel of some dozen books, and Morgan toddled off with him into a side room—and, after quite a long time, toddled back looking very vexed. It seems that [————] had not been satisfied with autographs, he had demanded inscriptions ('To [———— ————] from E. M. Forster'). Morgan complied, but thought him an awful cad, and stood him the smallest and cheapest drink available. All this was going on at about the time that the shot rang out in Dallas.[3]

Ram Gopal[4] is seeing my agent today about the option on *Hindoo Holiday* and is sending his car round to fetch me to lunch with him on Wednesday. He adores champagne, an excellent thing in a friend. I only wish he didn't talk so much; my head spins. He thinks that mankind must be cleansed in the fire: the next nuclear war he thinks inevitable. He also feels that anyone cruel to an animal should be put to torture or death. This, of course, is more agreeable to me, though I have never gone so far as he goes. With all this he is a 'joy-injector', like you.[5] I try sometimes to imagine how you and he would get on together—that is to say when I am not wondering how he and I are going to get on together. I have never written a scenario. Is it easy? . . . How noisy the world is, and would be even noisier if our ears were able to detect the shrill ultrasonic cries of bats, mice and shrews.

Love, darling Jim, as ever

Joe

[1] In the previous May Forster had written to A. to tell him that he had just read *Liber Amoris* by Hazlitt (1823). He remarked in passing: '. . . what an unusual little book—second rate but sincere, and if you put bootboy for housemaid poignant.'

[2] Forster and A. were both honorary members of the Club.

[3] On 22 November President John F. Kennedy had been assassinated at Dallas, Texas. David Rees, who was on the staff of the *Spectator* at the time, recalls how that night, when he was dining with Goronwy Rees and his wife, the other guest present was A., whose immediate reaction to the shooting was not so much one of horror as concern for his American investments. 'I suppose they'll drop,' he said sadly.

[4] Indian dancer.

[5] Kirkup writes: 'I used to urge Joe to come and stay with me again in Japan for another "joy injection", which was how I looked upon life in Japan.' Similarly, Gopal would urge A. to come to India.

245 To Francis King (1923–   )   17 Star & Garter Mansions, Putney, S.W.15

27/11/63

Dear Francis

what a ghastly cutting![1] It has quite ruined my morning.

Come and lunch at my club again whenever it suits you (*not* Tuesdays, Thursdays, or weekends). It could be convenient for you while you are moving in, would be a pleasure to me, and is wonderfully cheap. Morgan liked you very much, he said. I saw that you were a success, interesting and restful, a rare combination. But what a *funny* lunch! I didn't realise how vexed he was with [——] for demanding inscriptions instead of autographs.[2] He gave him a small drink on purpose (so I should not have stood him another, but didn't twig), and his remarks to me to be the one to 'lead the way' to lunch were really suggesting that I should do so at once, he wanted to be rid of [——] as fast as possible. Afterwards he called him a 'literary cad'. But over all this my antennae were not functioning properly, I fear. And I suppose that it was at about this time that the shot rang out in Dallas.

Phone me whenever you like, dear Francis.

Joe

P.S. Morgan commented happily upon your Larry too: 'The warm Mediterranean smile, how unmistakeable and pleasant it is!'

246 To James Kirkup (1923–   )   Putney

31/11/63

I loved your letter and Takuso-Dick's P.C. I wonder why he thinks so highly of me now when he came not near me in Sendai. I am reading a little book called *My Kingdom for a Donkey*[3] by Doris Rybot. Someone gave it to me to read because I fell so deeply in love with the ubiquitous little donkeys in Greece. It is surprisingly good, sensitive and not silly. She treats animals in the right way, allowing them to develop their personalities to the full, and gets the best out of even a hen. I think perhaps I was stupid not to move into the country after Queenie's death (two years ago yesterday). I might have had a little Jersey and whatever else came along. I am far more interested in animals now than I am in people. I feel closer to them. It is, in a way, what the article I tried to write for you was about.[4] And for that very reason I find myself disturbed by the thought of further involvements in animal lives. I wish I had started all that when I was younger, instead of running about all the time after boys.[5] Now I feel too old, also frightened. I don't think

---

[1] It concerned two police 'agents provocateurs', dressed outrageously, who had been the recipients of advances from a baker, father of five, in a Hastings public lavatory.

[2] Cf. Letter 244.

[3] 1963.

[4] 'I Am a Beast.'

[5] On 28 September A. had written to Georges Duthuit: '[——] is an elderly, bald-headed man in his sixties. He is still wildly and imprudently preoccupied with sex, which I have given up or, perhaps I should say, which has given up me. I can't complain of this, of course; doubtless he is in

anyone should attempt to gain possession of an animal heart unless they feel as sure as mortality can feel that they will never fail it. To get the confidence of any animal and then let it down seems to me almost the worst crime anyone can commit, human relationships matter less, people understand people, suffer though they may; animals understand nothing, only loss.

Your Mr [——] seems to have been rather a snake in the grass—except that I am fond of snakes. You will have noticed how arrogant human beings are in having made use of the animals for almost all their terms of contempt, disgust, or abuse. I wonder if one could inject enough scorn into the word 'human'—'You human!'—to make it sound insulting. I'm afraid one would only get a complacent smile. Has Mr [——] put you off poisonous S. America?[1] ...

To Richard Murphy (1927–)   17 Star & Garter Mansions, Putney, 247
                                 S.W.15   2/12/63
Dear Richard

I've enjoyed this poem[2] very much. It's not merely the best poem you've ever written, it's a very fine poem in its own right. I don't always get on with your poetry, as you know. The things you write about interest me too little and your own interest in them doesn't always reach me. Technical accomplishment is always there; here it comes to full flower; the poem, packed with thought, image, feeling, moves effortlessly along, on its dignified nostalgic line, unerringly selecting the right word and the most inspired and exact near-rhyme. *The Sunday Times*[3] should be proud to have it. It is a highly dramatic poem about something of the most urgent and deepest importance, and through all its great, yet concealed, skills, feeling flowed and brought tears to my eyes. I do congratulate you. You must certainly go and read in America; before you do so, write a poem for me. While you are in S[outh] A[frica], inform yourself about the wild animals and write me a poem about them.[4] If you have the feeling, no one is better equipped than you. The feeling I want was put into words by Walt Whitman when he wrote 'I think I could turn and live with animals ... They

---

the right and we should try to keep, until the grave receives us, every appetite for pleasure with which we embarked upon the Great Adventure of Life. But I confess to finding it slightly distasteful to see an oldish man so hotly and incontinently pursuing the young ... I am glad that I am no longer inflamed by such desires; while he runs after his *ignis fatuus*, I, like some aged spinster, go about feeding the stray dogs and cats. I have a little box in which I store for them ... bits of meat ...' A. himself was 66 at the time.

[1] The rest of this letter has been lost.
[2] 'The God Who Eats Corn.'
[3] Though they bought it, they never printed it. Subsequently it was published in *The Listener* on 6 August 1964.
[4] Murphy's visit to Rhodesia, where his parents were living at the time, was cut short, and there was no time to visit a game reserve. 'So I never wrote the poem Joe wanted about the wild animals of Africa,' he told Braybrooke. 'But I have some notes for a poem about Joe, which I hope to finish some day ...'

bring me tokens of myself . . . they manifest them plainly in their possession.'[1]
It is a lost thought of the deepest profundity, I believe; I am glad to think
that I reached it myself, through Queenie, before ever I saw the Whitman
quotation, but the article which I have been trying to write for almost a year,
called 'I Am a Beast' somehow fails me in its end. If ever I finish it I will
send it to you to S.A.

Thank you very much.

Love from

Joe

248 To James Kirkup (1923–   )   Putney
                                                              4/12/63

Dearest Jim

so it did arrive after all![2] And what are you setting it up for?
may I ask. Don't tell me that *Orient/West* means to publish it?[3] In that case I
must finish it, I have some notes, and will try to do so tomorrow instead of
fiddling about with one of [Ram] Gopal's film scripts which he wants me to
re-write for him[4]—I sent him so critical a report of it. I must say I prefer
revising other people's work to inventing my own, and am really rather
bright at it, though I says it as shouldn't. Reverting to my own piece, I suppose you don't happen to remember whether the animal in Balzac's story
was a panther.[5] It was one of the great felines, but I'm not sure which. '[A]
Passion in the Desert' was the English name of the story,[6] and Lord Wavell
included it in his anthology of animal stories.[7] My library hasn't got it, and
I shall have to check up somewhere unless you happen to remember.

I have just had 3 stitches taken out of my scalp. So strange, I had a sort of
black-out in my room late on Thursday night. Not drink, I think my intake
is always the same, but there had been a long wrangle with Nancy, a re-

---

[1] A. was quoting from memory—and was not quite word perfect. The verb in the last line is
not 'manifest' but 'evince'. The passage comes from stanza 32 of the 'Song of Myself':

> I think I could turn and live with animals, they're so placid and self-contain'd,
> I stand and look at them and long and long.

> They do not sweat and whine about their condition,
> They do not lie awake in the dark and weep for their sins,
> They do not make me sick discussing their duty to God,
> Not one is dissatisfied, not one is demented with the mania of owning things,
> Not one kneels to another, nor to his kind that lived thousands of years ago,
> Not one is respectable or unhappy over the whole earth.

> So they show their relations to me and I accept them,
> They bring me tokens of myself, they evince them plainly in their possession . . .

[2] First ten pages of 'I Am a Beast'. See Letter 244.
[3] The article was published in the March–April 1964 issue.
[4] Indian dancer. See Letter 244.
[5] Correct. See note 6 below.
[6] *Une Passion dans le Désert* (1830).
[7] Lord Wavell never edited any anthology of animal stories. A. must have been thinking of
another collection—possibly of *A Treasury of Animal Stories*, edited by E. L. Mally (1946), which
included Balzac's story. A.'s confusion may have sprung from the fact that Lord Wavell was
sometimes referred to as 'Wavell of the Desert', because of the part which he had played in 1941
in routing the Italian armies in the Libyan desert. Lord Wavell, however, did compile an anthology
of poetry—*Other Men's Flowers* (1944), which included a section on 'The Call of Wild'. In this there
were references to lions and leopards but none to panthers or Balzac.

current one which always upsets me, accusations against our char for (Nancy alleges) using her cosmetics and wearing and stretching her shoes. As if it mattered! What worries me is that she may drive the char—a nice woman, even if naughty—into giving notice again (she's done it once and I had to placate her), putting me to the trouble of finding another. *Anyway*, no sooner had I left Nancy than she heard a dull thud (almost midnight) and found me stretched pale, senseless and bleeding on my back in my room. Falling, I had struck the back of my head on my bookcase and was concussed. Poor girl, what a shock she must have had! a salutary one, I hope. As for me, I remember nothing about it, only how peaceful and comfortable the world seemed for a change (I've now been twice concussed and found both occasions quite delicious); some poor doctor was wrenched from her bed, a woman, and came and stitched me up as I lay on the floor. Nancy says I conversed with her quite rationally; I don't remember her in the least. Nor do I recall a thing about my stretcher-and-ambulance journey to hospital, to which she sent me. I have a vague recollection of an asiatic medical face bending over me there, and of saying 'are you Japanese?' He said 'Chinese'. I said 'I'm sorry'—but he quite understood me and rather unkindly remarked 'Yes, you've got me out of bed.' What they did to me there I've no idea. I simply felt wonderfully comfortable and happy. Nor do I remember the journey home at about 4.0 a.m. in a taxi they provided. I remember nothing, but woke up next morning at 11.0 a.m. feeling quite well and, covering my bandage and bloody scalp with a knitted skull cap, took Nancy and the Goronwy Rees's to lunch at my club, which I had arranged to do. Isn't that a nice story? Four or five times in my life I have been upon the outskirts of the Valley of the Shadow—once, indeed, almost in it, when I nearly died of Spanish grippe at the end of the first World War—and the experience has *never* been unpleasant. Death deserves a welcome, just for the kindness which Life is not too quick to bestow.

I am now off to celebrate Sir Herbert Read's 70th birthday at a dinner in London. He was a staunch friend of mine for many years, though I haven't seen him since my retirement. I like him and wonder what he adds up to in all his voluminous writings: not much, I fancy. But then I haven't read them all.

Another nice letter from you this morning (5/12/63) but no time to answer. Nor time to finish that article today.[1] And I am going off for the weekend (Nottin ham and Norwich). But I promise to send the end of it early next week.

Fondest love

Joe

P.S. How inattentive not to get the title of your book right: *The Times* 5/12/63.[2]

Stop-press. Look, dear, I have done it[3] for you, after all, this afternoon, well

---

[1] 'I Am a Beast.'

[2] Kirkup's book was called *Tropic Temper. The Times* reviewer had referred to it as '*Tropic Cancer.*'

[3] i.e. the second half of 'I Am a Beast'.

or badly I don't know. *Do* criticize! I only hope I have resumed where I left off. Can't quite remember.

249 To Stephen Spender (1909–)   17 Star & Garter Mansions, Putney,
S.W.15   5/12/63

Darling Stephen

    I am terribly sorry about today. I had quite forgotten that I had invited my sister to come with me to a local film, *The Informers*, and she, poor dame, suffers from disappointments. The crack on the head I received last week may have deranged my few remaining senses.[1] Can you lunch with me at my clublet, the R.C.A.,[2] on Dec. 11, 13, or 16? It was so nice seeing you and dearest Natasha, that warmest-hearted of all lovely girls, at poor old Herbert's.[3] How nice he is. Do you think he adds up to as much as is claimed for him? Anyway, he is all that matters, a dear. I *do* want to see you again. Not on the phone this weekend, shall be trailing round Nottingham and Norfolk examining Jack Sprott's abandoned affairs; he is in Ghana, lucky boy.

Best love

    Joe

250 To Paul Cadmus (1904–) 17 Star & Garter Mansions, Putney, S.W.15
3/1/64

Dear Paul

    your card has just come and I spring to attention, a thing I seldom do now, having left off attending to the human race. But to hear from you!— that is a very different matter. I have been studying your card—now over a glass of sherry—on and off ever since it fell through my letter-box some hours ago, and I suppose it may be true, if you have been hearing saddening things about me, that I haven't for some time been feeling any more festive than the figures by the Master MZ[4] appear to be, though the Cup-Bearer of course is ever welcome. But I am no invalid, Paul dear, and manage to squeeze some mild pleasure from life every now and then, such as the month in Greece I had in September—one has to go abroad to do it. What happens to you, I wonder, I think of you, you know, and that delicious meal you gave me on March 8, 1962, and those two boys—what were their names? Michael and Nicki, have they danced their way to fame and fortune? and the flashing figure of Jacques d'Amboise[5] to whom they led me?

    I have been occupying myself lately, at his request, with the domestic

---

[1] See Letter 248.

[2] Royal College of Art.

[3] At the dinner held the previous evening to celebrate Sir Herbert Read's seventieth birthday. Cf. Letter 248.

[4] An early German engraver who was born about 1477. He was one of Dürer's first pupils. The initials stand for Matthäus Zasinger.

[5] A leading dancer of the New York City Ballet Company.

affairs of our friend Jack Sprott, who went off to Ghana and that Nkrumah at the end of October for 4 months, leaving behind him in Nottingham, where he lives, two sad hearts, his servant-friend of long standing and his marmalade cat.[1] It is the latter who really touches my own heart, and I go up to keep him company whenever I can. A neutered male, but female in appearance and character, he lives all alone in the cold, empty house in Nottingham, visited by the man-servant for a couple of hours every day—perfunctory visits to put his food down. He is so timid that he never leaves the house and has no cat-friends. I know that cats are not very *busy* creatures, but I keep wondering what a cat does with itself all alone in a cold and empty house for 22 hours out of the 24. He lavishes upon me whenever I appear a grateful affection so extravagant that I can hardly put him off my lap upon which he always lies; though I know little about cats it has become for me a sort of romance to journey up to this uncomfortable house in the Midlands with some tit-bits in my bag to meet this cat's crowning happiness for a night or two. The human heart—but I will not go on with that, I am dangerous on the subject.

I have a letter from Don also to answer: may I, for when next you see him, kill (in that unsuitable phrase) two birds with one stone? The part of his letter that worries me is his notion that because Morgan has not written to him for so long, he must have *offended* Morgan. Nothing could be further from the truth. Morgan had a birthday the day before yesterday. How old is he? I never remember: 85, 86?[2] Anyway he is a very old man. Don must try to remember this. Morgan is tired and muddly. Even I, who have been his friend for 40 years, get little from him now, scraps of ricketty writing. It is silly for Don—whom everyone loves—to have a feeling of persecution. If he wrote a letter which stung Morgan in the right place—I can give no recipe, but it would be somewhere in the middle—he might strike a spark. Otherwise he will never hear at all. Tell him this, dear Paul. And tell him I will write to him when his book comes.

My really best love
    Joe

To Richard Murphy (1927–)   Putney 251
                                                              14/1/64

Thank you, dear Richard. A letter deserves a letter, so a letter you shall have, and a letter also to Auden when you need it. I wondered what had happened to your [*Sunday Times*] poem,[3] which should not have been ousted by [Peter] Ustinov, though I daresay the Pope may be thought by

---

[1] In an appreciation published in *The Listener* on 15 June 1967, ten days after A.'s death, W. J. H. Sprott wrote: 'His concern for the animal kingdom mounted. He foresaw the day when cats and dogs would be eliminated in the interest of hygiene while other creatures were being destroyed in the interest of what is known as "progress" ... When I was teaching in Ghana he came from time to time to stay in Nottingham because he thought my yellow cat would be lonely while I was away.'
[2] 85.
[3] See Letter 247.

some to have a prior claim. Well, it's an ill wind . . . and you've been able to polish;[1] as for me I'm in a fury with Kirkup who tells me in a careless and evasive postscript that I'm not to get a proof of my Beastly article after all.[2] Moreover, that his Editor, who never liked it, is correcting the proofs. What does one say to such people? In all my 25 years as Lit Ed. of *The Listener*, a weekly paper, not a monthly like Kirkup's, and therefore more rushed, I never published a signed article by anyone without sending a proof. I would have considered it the greatest impertinence to do otherwise. But Americans (Kirkup's Editor is an American) think they can do as they like and cheerfully re-write one's articles if they believe they can improve upon them or dislike what the author says. Oh beware of America when you get there! You cannot be too much on your guard! The world is ruled from there, in the American imagination, and everything the world contains. And they stop at nothing. However, my chief grievance is against Kirkup, and I have shot a few searing bolts into his bottom—in so far as one can send searing bolts into the bottom of anyone in so distant a country as Japan. I fear they cool as they pass over the North Pole. I wrote the article entirely for him, at his request, to help him in his new Literary-Editorship of *Orient/West*; I had such trouble with it that I thought I could not finish it, and sent it at last in two parts; proofs were requested and promised, and now I don't even know if the two parts fit. What would *you* have thought of such behaviour, dear Richard, if it had happened to be your poem, which you have been allowed to polish to your heart's content? So I am in a perfectly helpless rage.

Ram Gopal too has been a total loss. Having bestowed kisses upon me and Nancy at our lunch with him in mid-December and invited us both to spend Xmas Day with him, he vanished. I have already written to remind him of this engagement and to say that for re-writing his [scenario] I wanted £20 a week. No reply. We had to demolish the Duchess of [——]'s 18 lb turkey on Xmas Day with the help of Mr Pink, the porter. What a bore the unfortunate bird was, nothing seemed to make any impression on it. Eventually we boiled it all down into soup, sick of cold turkey, minced turkey, and turkey omelettes. Sorry, too, for the turkey itself, robbed of its life to spread such boredom. Then, about a fortnight ago, when I was out, Ram's secretary phoned to wish us a happy new year and to say that Ram was in Paris but would be home that weekend and would ring us. Not a sound since, and of course I've done nothing about his scenario, not having had his acceptance of my moderate terms. Instead I have been trying to finish that family memoir[3] which I have been trying to finish for the last 30 years. Every horror of an English winter has been, and still is, our lot and my chest and bronchials are in a sorry state. However, I have derived con-

---

[1] Early in 1959 A. had written to Murphy about another poem: 'It improves all the time: I hope you are giving to that fact, which you yourself will admit, its full significance: you thought the poem finished and perfect when you first brought it to me, but it was not. The moral is twofold: it is hardly possible to give too much trouble and thought to the perfecting of any work that one loves: How bitter it is to see the light when one's work is in print and it is too late.' The poem in question was 'The Woman of the House', which appeared in *The Listener* on 23 April and was read by the author on the Third Programme on 17 May.

[2] 'I Am a Beast'. Kirkup had second thoughts and sent proofs in the end.

[3] *My Father and Myself*.

siderable pleasure from reading *Gulliver's Travels* for the first time in my life. It is a joy to find a few hitherto neglected classics in store for one's old age; in this particular case one appreciates it more when one has had the experience of living. What a savage book, even more appropriate to our own times than to Swift's; it is very much my own view of the world. Your brother Chris phoned some ten days ago (I had sent him particulars of my [financial] affairs) at about 8 p.m., in the middle of Perry Mason or Maigret,[1] to discuss stocks and shares with me. Can you imagine? I find them hard enough to understand on paper when I am sober; I had to tell him that after three double gins and ½ bottle of wine I wouldn't know whether he was talking or singing. So he is to contact me when he returns from holiday.
Much love
  Joe

To James Kirkup (1923–) Putney 252
                             18/1/64

Dear Jim
      you are now the best of boys once again, the boat rocks no longer, we may rest on our oars and have a quiet chat, for the storm has passed. Indeed, it had passed before your letter came and I was experiencing some *faint* regret at having cast a spanner into your works. But then I reflected that, after all, as Lit. Ed. of *The Listener* I would never have dreamed of publishing a signed contribution without sending its author a proof,[2] and would have considered myself as richly deserving such spiky protests as I sent to you had I ever done such a thing. I have a pleasant unruffled note from Mr [Maurice] Schneps[3] this morning and am glad that I gave no offence in my letter to him (if he ever got it, the box number I used may have been out of date), or, at any rate, that he has taken none. You see, dear, I rather incline to share his doubts about my article—doubts all the more unresolvable since I do not have a complete copy of it and can't remember what I wrote; and praise never registers with me; I think that my intellect (if I can any longer call it that) is a sort of permanent invalid, perhaps a *malade imaginaire*, one of those patients who actually prefer to be always discussing their symptoms with the doctor or anyone else they can button-hole, and are affronted to be told how well they are looking, or that there is nothing wrong with them at all. Well, enough about all that; I am glad to hear from Mr Schneps that the magazine is not to end in March after all, and from William Plomer, with whom I lunched this week, that he has reviewed your poems in it. He asked me why you had renounced poetry and I told him that it had all got into *Tropic Temper*[4] and that he should read it. Poor [——] drifts homeward,

[1] A. wrote to William Plomer on 5 August: 'I have just discovered through a fault in judgment, I have not read half of Simenon's novels, always preferring Maigret to the "serious" ones. So I am reading him almost non-stop, and still have some 30 novels to find. I believe you are one of those who, like Morgan, see nothing in him. I think that some day you should have another shot: *Aunt Jeanne, The Train, The Widower, The Murderer* would be a good start.'
[2] A. was referring to his article 'I Am a Beast'. See Letter 251.
[3] See page 229, note 1.
[4] Published in the previous year.

somewhere between Hong Kok and Bang Kong, more and more deflated and now dejected by bad news of his London domestic scene. It was naughty of him to stand you up on his last evening (is that not part and parcel of the gay, capricious life of dear Japan which you extol? I much prefer Daniel's way of treating everyone quite selfishly for one's own pleasure). He will become more serious and dependable when English standards impose themselves again; but he seems to deserve to get into your novel for that alone, we shall both enjoy to identify him in it. Can't you squeeze me in too? No one ever bothers to caricature me and it is the very lesson I have always wanted to learn, the kind of figure one cuts. Indeed, I have been lamenting it in my family memoir, the difficulty of knowing what impression one makes upon others.[1] I am getting along now to the end of that—and about time too, for it has been lying about half-baked for a good thirty years, and I don't think I have a lot of time left. It is quite a good joke; whether it is the truth is a different matter. I have just had a wonderful experience. What do you think? I have read one of our great classics for the first time. *Gulliver's Travels* (1724).[2] It is *my* book, and I am glad that I have neglected it hitherto, it is a book to which a mature mind and personal experience have to be brought, and I think it must be more applicable to the present day than to the day on which Swift wrote it. Do you ever lecture upon it? Japan enters, as you doubtless know.

I didn't say that my publishers were sending me to Japan in April [for the Tokyo Book Exhibition], I said only that I had applied. Not a sound yet from anyone. I will let you know if there ever is.

Fond love

Joe

253 To James Kirkup (1925–)   Putney
                                                              4/2/64

Dearest Jim

thanks for your pretty p.c. It was stupid of me to forget *These Horned Islands*[3] and *Gulliver's Travels*. As soon as you prompted my memory I recalled it, and have since looked it up. It was also a pleasure to look into your book again. Nothing much happens here, but we have been fortunate, these last few weeks, to have a mild winter. Not much rain, sunshine, cool air but not too cold. Really rather a pretty January. You will not enjoy your return of course, except to see your mother, but a 2-month torture is not long and I will slip down to Bath to see you. No word yet about the Tokyo

---

[1] In some notes made while working on *My Father and Myself*, A. wrote: 'E. M. Forster once said to me that it was difficult for him . . . to see the viewpoint of the goodlooking; it is even more difficult for the goodlooking themselves to regard this quality of theirs with detachment.' Later, in the same set of notes he returned to this subject: 'If E. M. Forster cannot put himself in the shoes of the handsome, how can the handsome tell of the effect of his handsomeness upon E. M. Forster?' See Introduction, 3.

[2] Two years after A.'s experience with Swift, A. had another 'wonderful experience', when for the first time he read Mrs Gaskell's *Wives and Daughters* (1866). He wrote to Geoffrey Gorer on 8 August 1966: 'So delightful in old age to discover a "top" classic one has not read before.'

[3] Kirkup's own book of 1962, sub-titled 'A Journal of Japan'.

Book Exhibition, except a hand-out to say that the organisers were about to deliberate.[1] I am glad [Maurice] Schneps got my proof.[2] There was a ghastly error in it which, perhaps, would not have been noticed, the word 'understand' instead of 'instruct' in Galley 2, Col. 2, line 13.[3] If that had slipped through it would have rendered all the Zen paragraphs entirely incomprehensible. Since then a friend of mine here has pointed out a [few] obscurities but they are slight and I shan't attempt to bother you with them at this date. So glad your mag. has found another backer and that William's review pleases. I have been seeing a lot of plays, chiefly because an old Cambridge friend of mine, C. Colleer Abbott[4] (did you ever meet him?) having planned for himself a riotous visit to London from Durham where he lives, and bought seats for all the best plays, difficult to get into, suddenly had a stroke and sent all the tickets to me. A mild stroke, he recovers, and tonight I start on the 3-part cycle of *The Wars of the Roses* at the Aldwych (Shakespeare's Henry VI *et seq.* done up afresh) which takes me back there tomorrow for matinée and evening performance. I have lately seen dear old Morgan (now 85) and on Thursday dine with Desmond S[hawe]-T[aylor] and perhaps spend the weekend with Jack in Nottingham. All that pleases me and stocks my empty life. And I have written an article about Queenie 'snarling', which I referred to in your piece,[5] for a man named Neville Braybrooke who is editing a book of autobiographical essays called *Authors and their Animals*.[6] I am happier about it than I was about the thing I did for you. I wonder how negotiations over your own book develop. No further news dear.

Fond love as ever
Joe

To Neville Braybrooke (1923–   )   Putney 254
                                                      4/2/64
Dear Braybrooke
                you might also answer these questions when you write again:[7] What actual length of article were you thinking of?

[1] A. heard nothing more from the organizers.
[2] Of 'I Am a Beast'.
[3] The galley had read: 'When [my Alsatian bitch] was young I attempted to understand her in the ways of the world.'
[4] 1889–1971. Poet and editor of the letters of George Darley, Gerard Manley Hopkins, Robert Bridges, Gordon Bottomley and Paul Nash. Abbott left it in his will that A.'s letters to him were not to be published before 1991.
[5] '. . . My bitch used to snarl at me every day, baring her dazzling white teeth, the most amusing of her many faces . . .' See note 7 below.
[6] See Letter 254.
[7] In January Braybrooke had invited A. to contribute to a collection of autobiographical essays to be called *Authors and Their Animals*. When A. sent the above letter, he had already written a piece for it about Queenie 'snarling'. But the book never got off the ground and A. never posted the article. Attempts to find it amongst his papers have failed—though some notes found in a folder (mostly in dialogue) give perhaps some indication of what the article was about: '"Well, I didn't like that, the dog was all right, only young, and friendly with me . . . so I said 'You don't 'ave to ['ave the dog destroyed]. I'll take 'im off of you if you're going to do that', and [the butcher] said 'Okay, you can 'ave 'im for ten bob'. 'Ten bob!' I says, 'I thought you was throwing 'im away?' 'Oh, all right,' says 'e, 'make it five and you've got a bargain' . . . I paid 'im 'is five bob, and when I went down to fetch the dog that evening, d'you know what? 'e growled at me! 'E was sitting

Does it have to be absolutely fresh material? For instance, I have an article called 'I Am a Beast' coming out in March in an American-Japanese mag. called *Orient/West*,[1] practically unknown in this country. I could lend you a proof of it to read if you like. 'Tulip' enters it, but she might be said to be wearing a kimono.

What exactly is your book about? Is it an autobiographical compilation? Yours

J. R. Ackerley

And who is your publisher?

255 To Donald Windham (1920–   )   Putney

14/2/64

Dear Don

yes, I got your book,[2] thanks awfully, and should have written before, it is a pleasure to have it, it is beautifully produced and I'm delighted to know that you are getting swell reviews. Amusing about your Atlanta relatives and their silences. I saw Morgan last week and he told me he had written you at last; we went to a theatre together, *The Wings of the Dove*, but suffering both of us from deafness did not hear a lot of it, sit though we did in the third row of the stalls. Most of the cast are women: a sex in the theatre unrewarding to deaf men. Gene Baro is over here and I see him from time to time and try to sell him the works of friends of mine for his U.S. British-Writing anthology. He would like something from Morgan, but I doubt if Morgan will play; I am attempting to bring them together soon, not without misgivings.

Not much happens to me, dear Don, that's really why I get idle about writing, how to take up a pen when one's mind is empty of all but gratitude, which does not fill an air-letter. News, news—from where in my dull pedestrian life can I drag news? Oh yes, there is one thing, some English queer, a top-drawer fellow, who went to jug for interfering with the boys in a youth-hostel he ran, has written a play, autobiographical, which he longs to have published before his release (next Jan., I believe). With much difficulty a publisher . . . was found who reluctantly agreed to publish if the play was rid of libel and 'unfairness' to any living character. The author's solicitors have been on to me, through a mutual friend, to pronounce judgment and make any necessary alterations. I agreed (curiosity) to read the thing, sent

there with a bone and 'e looked up and growled at me! Well, I wasn't going to 'ave that, not after all I'd done for 'im, paid five bob for 'im and saved 'is life, and it was me what give 'im the bone an' all. So d'you know what I done? . . . I went straight in and sloshed 'im in the jaw! I didn't 'alf make 'is teeth rattle! And that was the only bit of bother I ever 'ad with 'im. 'E'd do anything for me after that. 'E understood what I'd done for 'im, see, and 'e was sorry for what 'e done to me. Gratitude, that's what it was. 'E was meek as milk."

'Tulip growls at me every day, but I never slosh her in the jaw. Why should I deprive myself of the pleasure of seeing one of the most amusing faces in her repertoire? . . .' See page 243, note 5.

[1] See page 223, note 4.
[2] *Emblems of Conduct*, Windham's autobiography, which had been published in America in 1963.

in a tough report ('Exhibitionism, militant self-pity, and lack of all knowledge of the theatre') and refused to touch it. But they have come back at me 'Oh please reconsider. Publication means so much to poor Mr X. We are sure you would wish to help him.' Can you imagine? Such an appeal to me, who have never met Mr X., have no ambition to meet him, have lost all interest in the doings of the human race, and am practically a pauper to boot. I replied that for a fee of five hundred guineas I would try to do a little superficial surgery. 'Oh thank you, so kind. We will have to consult our client.' I do hope I don't get left with [the] troublesome thing after all, and now wish I'd asked for a thousand guineas. I thought guineas sounded better than pounds because doctors always require guineas.

    Well bless you and thank you.

And love to you and Sandy

    Joe

Part Twelve
AUTOBIOGRAPHY

256 To David Higham[1] (1895–)   Putney
                                                                    19/2/64
Dear David

          the book[2] has been sailing along fairly well (150 pp., half type, half ms.); a rather troublesome chapter lies ahead, but the end is in sight and I should have it completed in a few weeks. I mean as a first draft. Then it will need typing, to which I do not look forward with my two fingers, rusty at that, but it is too scandalous to hand over to anyone else. Then it will need further research—memory does not serve and I haven't so far bothered to get dates, etc. right so far as my own part in it is concerned. Then it will need the scrutiny of another particular mind (who may not wish to give it)[3] to verify the truth of that part which is *not* my own—all this merely in the interests of Truth. And then I expect it will have to live in a drawer for a good many years.

          I am quite sure of the impossibility of its *complete* publication at present; I am uncertain of the advisability—perhaps I mean propriety—of its incomplete publication ever. That is to say I wonder whether the whole truth, so far as it can be known, about any*one* is fit for general consumption, or, more important still, acceptable to others. The answer, it seems to me, might be: 'Well, thank you very much, you have certainly been extremely frank, but why should you suppose we wanted to *know* all this about you?' You may have noticed lately in the papers that a man tried twice to board an underground train stark naked. He was wrapped in a blanket and hustled away: he wasn't *wanted*. I am inclined to believe that that would be the answer also to my book. If it has a saving grace it is that I have played for laughs. It is, to me, very funny—but a sense of humour, you know, is one of the least infectious things in the world.

          When I have got a bit further, perhaps you will come and lunch with me at that inconvenient club of mine, the Royal College of Art? It would be nice to see you again.

          Joe

---

[1] A. had appointed Higham his literary agent in November 1959.
[2] *My Father and Myself.*
[3] i.e. his half-sister Diana Petre. See Letter 306.

To David Higham (1895–)　　　17 Star & Garter Mansions, Putney,　257
　　　　　　　　　　　　　　　　　S.W.15　　　　　　　　　　19/6/64

Dear David

　　　no, I haven't been attending, the thing[1] is still in the messy, semi-typed state in which it has lain for the last year or so. You will think me a hopeless fellow and you will be right. The fact is that the point when I got bogged down was one which showed me all too plainly that I could no longer remember the chronology of my own life in the 'twenties and 'thirties (exactly when I went into my various rooms or flats, how many years I stayed, when I moved, etc) and that my only chance to get at these necessary details was to read through several thousand letters which are lying about in my bureau, most without (post-marked) envelopes, often undated in themselves—a jigsaw puzzle I shrink from undertaking. But I have been reading (sporadically) the memoir to a friend[2] with whom I stay from time to time, and if his reaction to it is encouraging, from the publication point of view, I may make another spurt. It remains far too messy to send about: only I can find my way through it. Smoking has been bothering me too; I smoke too much and my bronchials and digestion go wrong; there is only one thing to do, drastically to reduce it, which I have been doing and thereby improving my health—thereby also putting myself in a state of fidget so that I cannot even write a letter (I am smoking now), let alone a book. So I have spent my cigarette-less time (no fags till mid-day drink time, no fags thereafter until the evening gins) bird-watching on the river: a mallard foolishly brought her brood of nine down here some months ago, perhaps supposing it to be a pond, and her vicissitudes (human interference, jealous swans, the speed-boats, rats, the rising and falling tides, oil on the water, thunder-storms) have had all my attention ever since. She is a valiant bird and clever, and has discovered now the safest places to rest (when the tide is out), to float (when the tide is high), between here and Wandsworth, crossing and re-crossing the stream according to her plan. Her brood has gradually got reduced to four, but those I think will now survive, unless boys with catapults get them. I know exactly where to find her now at any time of the day, and sometimes mount guard over her.

　　　Such has been my life—and here is a letter to make up for no script.

　　　Joe

To Harry Daley (1901–71)　　　　　　　　　　　　　　　Putney　258
　　　　　　　　　　　　　　　　　　　　　　　　　　　19/8/64

Dear Harry

　　　this book[3] of yours certainly ought to be published, it is full of interesting material, but to an outsider like myself the tasks confronting you in the way of making it suitable for publication seem so formidable that I wonder if you will have the patience to undertake them—that is to say if you

---

[1] *My Father and Myself.*
[2] Geoffrey Gorer. See Letter 266.
[3] *This Small Cloud.* See Letter 73.

want to publish. (I am sorry about my writing this morning, sometimes my pen won't obey me).[1] I thought of offering to help you myself, but as I went on, saw that I could not, I should not know where to begin. It is in need of cutting for its own sake, it has a tendency to ramble and repeat, and the Vine-Beak St. section is far too long and has a surfeit of whores. In fact it all wants tightening up. But such operations, I fear, would amount to a mere nibbling at a bulk which, I suppose, from the publisher's point of view, will have to be almost halved. And then of course the libel. The book reeks of it, and unless you happen to know that the many people who come in for denunciation, contempt or derision are dead, I imagine they will have to be altogether eliminated from your story, unless you and a publisher would be satisfied with the kind of faking and disguising, so boring to do, which I had to perform upon my own book for the same reason.[2] I doubt whether in your case such tinkerings would suffice. Of one thing however I do feel certain: you have material enough and to spare here to make a full and interesting book without attempting to include your sea-faring adventures. Indeed, from what I remember of your accounts of those, they are rich enough to make a second volume as bulky as this one and should not be curtailed.

I hesitate to offer criticisms, and indeed it is difficult to do so, for we all write differently, and this book is very much YOU and should not, perhaps cannot, be anyone else. Nevertheless, I think it would be stronger if you could manage to reduce the amount of personal comment, whether affectionate or accusatory. It is enough, in my opinion, to describe your various characters and their actions, which you are perfectly able to do, and leave comment to the reader; but you are too much at his elbow with an extra adjective or two at the least to slip in for a guidance he doesn't need. I took ~~very~~ few notes as I read and cannot produce instances, except (too trivial) [Sir Oswald] Mosley, who can hardly appear on your stage without having such adjectives as 'odious' or 'loathsome' attached to him. After your excellently described scene in the Albert Hall, the reader can supply these adjectives for himself. Adjectives (though it is not only a matter of adjectives), good or bad, should be used sparingly, I believe, they often weaken what they are meant to strengthen. Beware the adverb 'very'; more often than not it is an idle, layabout, parasitic little beast, who does no work at all; it creeps into my own writing and when I find it dozing there I always turf it out. Is a good man any worse than a very good man, or a bad man better than a very bad man?*

The things in your book that stick in my mind particularly are the moving description of the death of your father, the long and hilarious Blanche episode in the Vine-Beak St. section, and almost the whole of the Wandsworth section, even though a slight note of sentimentality creeps in.

You write in an easy flowing style, and though the writing is by no means free from peculiarities in grammar, syntax and construction, perhaps they

* You may notice, on page 2 of this letter, that I have already scratched out the word 'very' where it managed to insert itself, the stupid little thing, in front of 'few'. [See line 27 above.]

[1] There had been two crossings out in the first sentence—a rare occurrence in A.'s letters.
[2] *We Think the World of You.*

don't greatly matter; if you turned on the style of Gibbon you would no longer be YOU. I started to pencil in a few notes and suggestions, because Raymond told me he had also done so; then I remembered that I was not Raymond and did not have your permission. In any case, why not leave all that until the book has been shortened? They are easily erased. I will say, however, that you seem rather addicted to the split infinitive, and unhappily there is a case for its occasional use. Nevertheless it is not common usage and personally I can never see a split infinitive without wincing. A word you use a good deal is 'presume'. I think it should mostly be 'assume', but the matter is tricky. Is not the difference between 'presume' and 'assume' that with the former you have a few facts to go on, with the latter none? 'Suppose' is a simpler word; one can hardly go wrong with that.

One other tiny point that interested me, you refer—quite often I think—to people you are fond of as 'clean and wholesome'. Are such words allowed? I thought they belonged exclusively to the language of those persons—reformers, head-masters, scout-masters etc.—who wish to stamp out vice (which includes you and me) and generally disinfect the country.

Geoffrey Gorer, whom I saw yesterday, is curious to read your book. He is professionally interested. As a sociologist he thinks it should contain 'important material'. I was, of course, non-committal—feeling that perhaps you would not care for the book to be regarded in so bleak a light.

Love from
   Joe

To Arthur Waley (1889–1966)   17 Star & Garter Mansions, Putney, 259
                                          S.W.15   4/9/64
Dear Arthur
       I'm afraid I shan't be able to come to your party. I am so very sorry, it is a real grief to me. I go off on Tuesday next with Jack (Sebastian) and Velda Sprott (his sister) to Italy, and shall not be back until after the 26th. I have wanted to see you again ever since the Sonia Orwell party. My halting trouble in social life is that I have got so deaf. My right ear does not function at all, and though my left is still serviceable for a *tête-à-tête*, I fear it deteriorates, at any rate it seems worse on some days than on others, and it is such a bore to be always saying 'What?' At any rate I am very sorry not to be able to say a 'What?' or two to you and Alison on the 26th. Pray give her my best remembrances.
Yours affectionately
   Joe Ackerley

To Harry Daley (1901–71)   Putney 260
                                                      1/10/64
Dear Harry
       I got back only last night, to find your letter of the 9th. The touring journey—very pleasant—did not permit the forwarding of letters.

Of course you are quite right about your book,[1] it should be written in your own personal style and no one else's and I'm sure you will bring it off without help. It was, in fact, I think, rather impertinent of me to fiddle with it; excuse it as the mentality of someone who has spent 25 years as a literary editor and has got into the habit of tinkering with other people's scripts.[2] So ingrained has the habit got that my eye even rearranges sentences in published books as I read them. And the funny part is that I'm not sure of myself. A few years ago I was taken down a number of pegs by my friend Henry Reed. My *Hindoo Holiday* book was going into its new unexpurgated edition, and he said to me 'I hope you'll take the opportunity of correcting its grammar.' Surprised, I said 'What's wrong with its grammar?' He said 'I'll show you, if you like.' And did. I was astounded, and mortified. He took a lot of trouble and pointed out errors on almost every page. In fact he cleaned the book up for me, for I saw that all his strictures (he was a schoolmaster for some years) were right. So you see that, in your case, I am hardly to be depended on!

I'll pop down and see you again soon.

Love
Joe

P.S. In an earlier note you asked whether publishing extracts from a book affected its chances of publication as a whole. I think not, at any rate it is often done. If the extracts are entertaining they whet the appetite of both the public and the publishers.

261 To Francis King (1923–) 17 Star & Garter Mansions, Putney, S.W.15
11/10/64

Dear King-san

your short stories[3] arrived yesterday and I have devoured them in one swoop, interrupting my study of the Gospel of St Mark to do so. This evening I am taking them up to Villiers David so that he too may have the pleasure I have had—though on second thoughts perhaps I won't, he is a buyer of books and should buy your volume. It is excellent, dear Francis, each story absorbing from its first page. All are written with skill and craft, ('L'Acte Gratuit' is an outstanding example of the art of story-telling), you have a mastery in this form, the stories are subtle and sometimes beautiful ('Festival of the Dead'), and the characters, Japanese and European, are real and therefore interesting. Indeed you have done something quite remarkable, you have not merely explained the Japanese to us, but made them tick, in a sympathetic, human way ('A Corner of a Foreign Field')—that sentence is not well put, but you will understand what I mean. 'The Crack'

---

[1] *This Small Cloud.* See Letter 258.
[2] On 24 August. A. had written to Daley: 'In my own pencillings I have put brackets round a few paras. or sentences (throughout my long years as a Lit. Ed. I was never able to learn how to write the delete sign, &. is the best I can do) which seemed to me removable.'
[3] *The Japanese Umbrella & Other Stories.*

and 'Dog and Bird' (a good little story)[1] I had already read elsewhere; the rest were all new to me. Besides those I have already mentioned, I particularly liked 'The Japanese Umbrella' and 'Sentimental Education'. It is too late now to speak of the way the stories are arranged, but I wonder whether it was wise—from a sales point of view—to kick off with the two most macabre stories, for that is far from being the character of the collection. There are lots of squeamish people about—though you may say there are a lot of ghouls also. Anyway, I would have preferred to see the volume begin with a story like 'A Corner of a Foreign Field', both amusing and profound, before coming upon the horrors. However, it may well be a matter of taste, in which, in this cruel world I, longing for pleasure and happy endings, may be out of date.

I have been in Italy for three weeks, and I hear you have been in Greece. Perhaps you are still there. Come and bring Kunio[2] to lunch when you are back.[3] I think I am a trifle brighter than I was, which is not saying much. On Morgan's advice I have been attacking our local Parliamentary candidates on the subject of the Wolfenden Report.[4] Before I cast my vote, will they let me know whether they will support it in Parliament or not. A tiresome, but good, question, don't you think? No replies yet. The Gospel of St Mark ought to be explained, it is the question of the character of Christ—old hat, perhaps. But when you come to look into him, was he not a thoroughly nasty man? How can one excuse the barren fig-tree, or the Gadarene swine, or the (to St Peter) 'Get thee behind me, Satan'? If you attend, it is awfully hard to like him.[5]

Your cover is a success. I am writing to [John] Guest[6] to thank him for sending me the book, which I hope may get its due, the highest honours.
Love
  Joe

To Francis King (1923–   )   Putney 262
                                                             19/10/64
Dear Francis
            Friday is perfect: come as early as you both can and like, Kunio's joint will be ready at 8.0. If you care to, before you go, you can come down with me to the pub below for a 'night-cap'; there you will see, and meet, one of the young men upon whom I have wasted, I fear, a certain

---

[1] Cf. Letter 221.
[2] The brother of a student who had been King's chauffeur in Kyoto. The boy came to England to work in King's house, while studying English.
[3] On another occasion A. sent King a postcard: 'You and Kunio can both visit us here whenever it should be convenient to you, lunch, tea, dinner or anything else, not that there is anything else except breakfast.'
[4] See A.'s review (for his general attitude to the Wolfenden Report) of *Quaint Honor*, a play by Roger Gellert, in *The Listener* on 26 February 1959. See page 218, note 1.
[5] Previously A. had written to King: 'I am another Leonard Woolf. I cannot understand religiosity, though I try. I can never see it as anything but fear ...' He felt sympathy, too, for Forster's criticism of the New Testament expressed in *The Hill of Devi* (1953): 'The canonical gospels do not record that Christ laughed or played: Can a man be perfect if he never laughs or plays?'
[6] Guest was the literary adviser to Longmans from 1949 to 1972.

amount of senile emotion (now in check). If caution was ever important, I went too fast; we are quite friendly still, but I fancy that now a game of skittles—rather than pocket-billiards—is as far as we shall ever get. No matter; I never managed to be considerate in matters of sex and I daresay it is better that I should not start again. I doubt if it is a subject in which one gains wisdom if one has never had any. The other chap is hardly on my map either, though for different reasons: a married man, a business man, with many leisure hobbies,—painting, fishing, night-schools, girls—he is unlikely to add me to the list, though I think he likes me and might pop in if I called him up. However, (this *does* sound as though wisdom had been gained) I *would* prefer him to pop in *without* being summoned.

I am awfully sorry about Raymond. His enthusiasm about your stories will not now get into print, I suppose, if ever that was on the cards; however, I do believe that no one could read your book[1] without being entertained and deeply impressed.

I don't know what to say about your Cretan. Can't you 'afford' to collect foreign boys like postage stamps? If so, gum him up and to hell with it. A heavy cold afflicts me, which I hope will have gone by the time I see you. I have been weekending in the Kenneth Clark's British Castle[2]—a super pleasure and not the cause of my cold.
Much love
  Joe

263 To Lady Clark   17 Star & Garter Mansions, Putney, S.W.15
                                                            22/10/64
Dearest Jane
              this is no bread-and-butter letter but a love letter, for when I think of my weekend with you both I think of it with love. Everything was heavenly, excepting myself, whom I would not have brought with me had I known that a small roughness in the throat would turn into a hacking cough and shake the Castle[3] to its foundations. Indeed, colds are prominent among the bores we were trying to define; never welcome they always seem to settle and even spread themselves: I do hope mine didn't. It prevents me at present from going to see Natasha [Spender], who phoned me earlier in the week and is now visible. She spoke well—or at any rate lightly—of herself, but Stephen's inexplicit account of her (I lunched with him today) is not happy. I certainly can't risk taking her the germs I fear I scattered over Saltwood.

Dear Jane, you were so sweet to me and I wanted to ask if I might bring away the flowers you cut for my bedroom. I changed their water both mornings and the stock in particular had so many buds to come, but I remembered them too late.

I do hope your Italian trip provided more pleasure than was expected

---

[1] *The Japanese Umbrella & Other Stories.* See Letter 261.
[2] Saltwood Castle, Hythe.
[3] See note 2 above.

of it, and that you were never physically uplifted nor spiritually brought low.

Much love to you both

   Joe

To Oscar Collier[1] (1924–)   17 Star & Garter Mansions, Putney, 264
                                     S.W.15   25/10/64

Dear Mr Collier

              a personal note on top of the rest. I hope you will not be thinking that I have behaved unfriendly or unfairly to you in this matter. Authors generally are not businessmen, we leave the decipherment of our contracts to our agents. The only part of a contract I understand is what Royalties I get and the size of the advance. As you know I was dissatisfied with the former of these and myself got them improved, against Mr [——]'s advice which (by and large) was to make the best of a bad bargain. This peeved me a little; after all your letter of Oct. 6 had called the contract a 'modest offer' which he would 'probably seek to improve' and (I have had your explanatory letter since). I expect my agents to do all that for me. What else are they paid for? I thought, therefore, that the printed part of the contract—Greek to me—had better be examined to see what other 'modesties' it contained if any and asked the Society of Authors to look it over for me. The Society exists to safeguard our Authors' rights; it is also highly sympathetic to the rights of publishers (I was put in the wrong by them years ago in an argument with Secker & Warburg). You may be sure that I gave them the most honest account of the sad history of my book and of your work for and claims upon it. The situation was perfectly understood by them. Mr [——] will show you their findings, upon which I must now take my stand. I'm afraid they will be unacceptable to you and Fleet, which grieves me; but perhaps, later on, when you are more firmly seated in your new saddle and have made, I hope, a fortune for Fleet, you will again whistle to *My Dog Tulip*.[2]

Yours sincerely

   Joe Ackerley

To Paul Cadmus (1904–) 17 Star & Garter Mansions, Putney, S.W.15 265
                                              17/12/64

Such a nice long letter from you, dear Paul, and full of helpful information, which I have passed on to Mr Oscar Collier. But having missed his Spring list (dispute over my contract) I have not lately heard from him, nor has the promised revised contract come. I am supposed now to be in his Summer list, but Summer may not come either, it may depend upon how many

---

[1] Assistant to the President of Fleet Publishing Corporation. Later, from 1966 to 1967, he was President.

[2] Fleet Publishing Corporation accepted these 'findings' and brought out *My Dog Tulip* in 1965.

buttercups and other golden flowers bloom in the Spring. I have put another friend on to you and hope he may get in touch. Alan Tagg his name, theatrical designer his profession. He comes to N[ew] Y[ork] soon, can't remember when, to 'set' a play on Broadway. Don't know him as well as Jack Sprott, but I like him. He is very talented, I believe; he did the décor for *Peter Grimes*, is a close friend and colleague of Cecil Beaton's. Modest, charming, pale, slightly haggard [. . .]; he speaks so low that I, with my deaf ear, have almost to sit in his lap to catch what he says. I think you will like him, or I would not have given him your precious name. I am wondering whether he might not be the chap to 'set' *Howards End*, which is expected to be produced in Cambridge next year, and have written to the dramatist[1] to suggest him.[2] Darling old Morgan has not been very well, as how can one be very well at the age of 86,[3] and was in hospital for a few days in mid-November. He was found wandering about the Buttery regions of King's in his pyjamas in the small hours of the morning, aphasic and incoherent. It was thought at first to be a slight stroke, but there was no physical disability, and no treatment, so it was then called a 'spasm'. I saw him in hosp. and he was as gay and lively as he always is, though not as clear as usual in his mind. Now again he is not awfully well, though there is nothing, except old age, to diagnose. I spent the day with him in Cambridge on Tuesday, and go down again tomorrow for the day. He is well looked after—almost *too* well, for he doesn't like being fussed over, though kindness is always a happiness to him—and goes to spend Xmas with Ben Britten in Aldeburgh, or so we hope, for he is eagerly looking forward to it. Then he goes to Lord Sandwich for a few days. I hope all will go off as he desires. The trouble—apart from his age and natural disabilities—is that this is our most foggy time of year. He wanted to be in London today, but fog and ice are everywhere; he had to cancel, and a good thing, no weather for old gents, or young ones like you and me, to be bumbling about in. If this gets to you in time, dearest Paul, a Happy Xmas. If it doesn't may the New Year preserve and prosper you in that beloved and admired image which resides in the heart.

Your affectionate
    Joe

266 To Geoffrey Gorer (1905–)   17 Star & Garter Mansions, Putney,
                                         S.W.15   ?/1 ?/65
Dear G.G.

    I am so glad you will look at this thing for me.[4] You gave me such

---

[1] Lance Sieveking. See page 288, note 4.
[2] Nothing came of this. The 'sets' for the Cambridge production were designed by Michael Clarke, those for the subsequent London production by Dacre Punt.
[3] He was 85. Cf. Letter 250.
[4] This refers to Gorer's agreement to read part of the manuscripts of *My Father and Myself* (i.e. Chapters 12 and 13 as they appeared in the first draft). Later, after A.'s half-sister Diana had 'passed' the manuscript in its entirety in May 1966, A. sent it to Gorer to 'criticize, read and evaluate'. Gorer read it and, as he had done with Chapters 12 and 13, recommended substantial

valuable help with my dog book.[1] I am expecting that you will find lots of faults with this, and I shall welcome whatever you have to say. If it interests you enough to bother, do pencil in comments, as lightly as possible, in the margins. It is short, but it is also too long; I hope you understand that it is not meant to be a *thorough* case-history, it has to fit in with a wider scheme, it is a race-through and, in the scheme, the really only important part of it is my dealings with the Guards. It is one that all connects up with my father's life; the rest is self-indulgence.

Morgan sometimes says to me: 'Never apologise.' I am never perfectly sure what that means,[2] but I hope that none of this reads like self-apology. It is not meant to be that, but a detached examination of myself. As you say, that is extremely difficult to pull off; although I have thought about it a lot, I still regard it as a rough draft, and expect I have misinterpreted such evidence as I have put in and left out the really important things that don't want to reach my conscious mind. I'm sure you will know all the answers and I hope you will give them. I also hope it may amuse you a little.
Love
    Joe

P.S. You can send or bring it as you wish; we meet on the 13th, and to have it back then would suit me and save the botheration of a letter. So sorry I didn't change my typewriter ribbon earlier, most of it is rather faint.

To Sonia Brownell Orwell   17 Star & Garter Mansions, Putney, S.W.15   267
13/1/65

Darling Sonia
            indeed I got the New Year bottles, about 10 days ago, and what a glorious surprise they were—also, as you rightly surmise, something

---

'cutting'—to which the author agreed. In July A. wrote: 'Doing your bidding rather breaks my heart, all those wholesale cuts and lost jokes, but I am sure you are right.' Again in March 1967, he wrote to Gorer: 'The cuts . . . I am sure are artistically right.' And the book itself carries an acknowledgement of A.'s debt to Gorer: 'When I had completed this so-called memoir . . . a friend of mine who read it for me said I had fallen into the error of self-indulgence . . . Having started to examine my sexual psychology . . . I became so interested in it that I worked it out to the end. My friend criticized this and I agreed with him; the book is *not* an autobiography, its intention is narrower and is stated in the title and the text, it is no more than an investigation of the relationship between my father and myself and should be confined as strictly as possible to that theme . . . But what was I to do with the excisions? The book had been a considerable sweat to write and they merited, I thought, a better fate than the waste-paper basket . . . For the interest therefore of psychologists . . . I have preserved these discarded pages in the appendix.'

[1] *My Dog Tulip.*
[2] P. N. Furbank, Forster's appointed biographer, writes: 'It was another principle of Forster's never to listen to apologies or explanations; and when he made up his mind against anyone, fairly or unfairly, he was most unlikely to change it.' See Furbank's article on 'The Personality of E. M. Forster' in *Encounter* (November 1970), in which he discusses A.'s posthumous *Observer* obituary of Forster, subsequently printed in full as *E. M. Forster: A Portrait* (1970).

of a puzzle. For had I not already received from you a large gift of booze. True, this earlier gift from you had been in conjunction with *Art and Literature*,[1] but I assumed that you had been the instigator. Gift No 2 was preceded by a charming letter from Michael to say that he hoped some bottles would come and that if they did they were from him and you in conjunction. They came later in the day. Well, of course I felt pretty sure that you must be the presiding deity, for why in the world should dear Michael remember me on his own? I never see or hear from the boy from one year's end to another, whereas you and I are life-long buddies. However he had heralded and dispatched the gift, so I wrote him a letter, which I hoped might amuse him, to thank you both and, I'm afraid, just as a joke, gave away the fact that I had already had a delicious present from you, though in another conjunction. Does it matter, dear? I do hope not. In my role of comedian I was trying to think up things to amuse him.

Bless your sweet heart, how kind you are and I am sorry you are not happier. But I know nothing about happiness, though I get pleasure from time to time, and you, dear Sonia, contribute to that. Many years ago, some forty years ago, Morgan Forster, trying to guide me through some miserable love affair, wrote to me 'But happiness may not be your deepest need'.[2] It was an impressive remark, especially from a man who can't read Freud and generally dislikes what is called 'Psychology'.[3] More recently, indeed quite recently, he said to me 'You don't want to be happy'—not so good, but adding up. He himself is a happy man, he has cultivated his garden. For many of us, at any rate for me, that has not been possible, but why? is an unanswerable question. It was a part-purpose of that Memoir[4] I fiddled with, a bit of which I sent you,[5] to see myself objectively, but no one can do more than scratch away a little at the top-soil. I have never been happy, I believe, nor ever can be, I was not equipped to be that, though what my 'deepest need' was and is I do not know. These are things I never say, but I can say them to you who understand so well. If one has failed to cultivate a garden and wakes every morning with a groan to find oneself confronted with another unwanted day, one can at least keep up a cheerful public face, and that I endeavour to do. And of course, as you say, and as you and others devise, nice things do happen to me; were it not for one's friends life would be past bearing indeed.

---

[1] In No. 2 (Summer 1964) there appeared 'Boom Ravine', an account of A.'s experiences and capture during the First World War. Later, with a few minor alterations, it became Chapter 7 in *My Father and Myself*.

[2] In Chapter 12 of *My Father and Myself* A. quoted several sentences from the letter giving this advice. Forster is referred to anonymously as 'a close friend', and the complete sentence reads: 'I'm sure that if one tries to live only for love one cannot be happy, but perhaps happiness is not your deepest need.'

[3] Forster was always suspicious of both psychological and symbolic criticism. He once told A. that he thought modern critics had read more symbolism into his novels than 'existed' there. When Patrick Wilkinson, Vice-Provost of King's College, asked him if he had heard Frank Kermode's Third Programme talk on 'Mr E. M. Forster as a Symbolist' (reprinted in *The Listener* on 2 January 1958), he had replied: 'Yes, wasn't he clever thinking of all that.' See script of BBC obituary programme on E. M. Forster, which was broadcast in the Third Programme on 29 June 1970.

[4] *My Father and Myself*.

[5] See note 1 above.

I am just off to the Old Vic, to see Edith Evans in *Hay Fever*, so you see I entertain myself nevertheless.

Much love, dear Sonia, and many thanks

Joe

To E. M. Forster (1879–1970)   Putney 268
                                                                      1/2/65

Dearest Morgan

I have sent you separately Don Windham's new Roman novel *Two People*. Though in typescript form[1] it is not difficult to read and I think you will like it, even if the 'two people' don't interest you deeply and the story seems a little lacking in development. In his covering letter Don says: 'I had a terrible time finishing the book—a moral block about it— which I think you must be familiar with and will understand. Times have changed since Morgan wrote *Maurice*[2] (and publishing since you wrote *We Think the World of You*, I dare say), but my relatives haven't. And yet I think I finally managed to write just what I wanted to as if they didn't exist, and hope I am right to have done so.' He has done well, I think; the episode is so pretty, fresh, natural and unimportant that it might easily set his relatives packing for Rome. I wonder why he calls it *Two People*;[3] it is really about Rome. Well, I hope it will keep you warm this cold weather in front of your fire. It leaves a pleasanter taste in the mouth than the cutting I enclose from our local Boro' News; Putney is sadder than Rome. It is rare for such reports to enter our paper; more typical items of news are as follows (from last Friday's issue): 'Mabel Kennedy, 15, of Hayward Gardens, Ashburton Estate, Putney Heath, accidentally walked into a lamp-post in Wandsworth High Street on Thursday last week. She was treated in hospital for a bruised eye.'

It was lovely to hear your voice yesterday, and sweet Bob's. What pleasure lies ahead of us, if some distance ahead. However, it is a scientific age and, as Bob remarked, Time has learnt to fly. It has been rather grounded here lately, but we had a jolly surprise visit from Forester and his brother Albert (a chauffeur), who stood us double whiskies in the pub below. Gerald [——]'s[4] operation revealed nothing that can't be cured, so there is much rejoicing, except among the foxes of Cheshire.

Much love, darling Morgan

Joe

[1] It was published in 1966. See note 3 below.

[2] Forster had written the first draft of this novel between 1913 and 1914. He revised it in 1919 and in 1932, and more drastically between 1959 and 1960. The book is concerned with homosexuality, and, at the author's wish, was not published until after his death. It appeared in 1971.

[3] See A.'s letter (238) to Windham in which he criticised the original title—*And Suddenly It's Evening*. Windham chose instead *Two People*—a title which could mean either 'Two Individuals' or 'Two Nations'. 'The inspiration of the novel lies exactly in this ambiguity,' Mario Soldati wrote later in *Il Giorno* on 15 July 1965.

[4] A.'s brother-in-law.

269 To Frederick Laws (1911–) 17 Star & Garter Mansions, Putney,
  S.W.15 10/2/65

Dear Laws
    I daresay I could do a little for you in your E. M. Forster pro-
gramme if you wanted it. It would be tiny, a couple of hundred words, and
confined to his help to me on *The Listener*.[1] It would simply say that he was,
in the 30s and 40s, the supreme reviewer, for whom any Lit. Ed. would have
given his head; that he did unsigned reviews for me, although he disapproved of anonymity, and so on.
    I know nothing more about the 'different Indias' than what I put in
Hindoo Holiday—haven't thought of that country since—and I shouldn't
imagine that Forster could now say much more than he has put into *A
Passage to India* and *The Hill of Devi*.
Yours sincerely
  J. R. Ackerley

P.S. A question Forster would have asked when he was working for the
Corporation: How much would I get paid?[2]

270 To James Kirkup (1923–) Putney
  21/2/65

Dearest Jim
    I have instantly written to Mrs [Rena] Clayphan to welcome
her to come for the [Maurice] Feild portrait [of you][3] whenever she likes
and told her we will give her a meal here if it should suit her. I am sorry
about you. You have, fortunately for yourself, forgotten what England is like
and the numbing effect it has upon the spirit, especially in winter. I have
often started to write to you, but it is one thing to begin a letter, another
matter to finish it. The darkness soon descends, and the fumes of alcohol rise
to meet it. Nothing else rises ever. But your card is another spur and I must
manage to complete the letter while the mood remains. What are you up to,
dear, in Osaka? And what is 'Perfect English Publicity'?[4] Correcting 'sand
witches' on Japanese menus? A real need. Is it an enterprise invented by you,
financed perhaps by Mrs Clayphan—or by those Japanese industrialists
with whom you flirted in that amusing and amazing book you sent me?
Have you left Tokyo? Lethargic though I have become, I long to know all—

    [1] See Appendix E.
    [2] It is true Forster would have asked this question, but it was A. in fact who had first taught
him to ask it: 'In the early days of Morgan's fame I recommended him always to reply to *The
Listener* or any other journalistic proposal: "How much will you pay me?"' Laws has pencilled at
the bottom of A.'s letter: '10 gns—15?'
    [3] This portrait had been painted by Feild when Kirkup taught at the Downs School, Colwall
—and had hung in A.'s bed sitting-room in his flat since then.
    [4] Perfect English Publicity was an ill-fated publicity service that Kirkup founded with some
Japanese friends and Maximilien van Dongen, a Dutch photographer, with the aim of 'improving
the English in Japanese advertising'. They also brought out, under the imprint of P.E.P. Publications, two volumes of Kirkup's essays about Japan, her industries and folk-art.

and am indeed, through my lethargy, a greater sufferer than you, for I have deprived myself (as I said to Francis some time ago) of the most amusing letters that have ever been written. He has now left London for Brighton, with his Japanese servant, Siamese cat, and Pekingese dog, so I have temporarily lost sight of him; but he told me that, as literary adviser to Weidenfeld & Nicolson, he had read your travel book, removed from Collins, and also recommended some shortening and cutting. What has happened since? Francis is not a person to cut for prudery, you may be sure, so I hope that whatever his advice was, met with your approval. It now occurs to me that perhaps I shouldn't be telling you this, so pray regard it as confidential if it comes to you as a surprise. Francis may be anonymous in that publishing firm, which I believe to be somewhat slow in movement—so you may not even have heard from them yet. But I hope you have and that the book is under way, for I want to read it. A friend of his, and mine, lives in Osaka. Perhaps you have enough friends of your own (but in case you should care to call, his name is Norikasu Fukushima, 280 Kaminoshima, Amagasaki). He is an extremely plain, one could almost say ugly, queer Japanese, exceedingly good-natured, obliging and kind, and speaks excellent English. I believe he now teaches it. Francis thought more highly of him than of any other Japanese he met, and I liked him too, so give him my love if you happen to see him. We called him 'Fukey'. It was a misfortune for the good boy, and for us, that he was so very unattractive. I think his health—kidneys, perhaps —was not good either.[1] I paint a rather gloomy picture, but he is a really nice and helpful chap.

I don't think I have much news of self—not much anyway to raise that smile or laugh which it is the polite social thing to do. Villiers is away in Bangkok, so I am specially lonely, since I have been living more in his strange, dramatic life than in my featureless own. I seldom set pen to paper, even, as you say, for letters, though I do like getting them, Kirkup-san, so though you may question my health (mental), do not question my heart. No, never. My *Tulip* book is, at last, to come out in the States this year, so though the cards are stacked against it selling, I hope for money, which, like you, I begin to need.[2] (Money tends to become so terribly *fluid*). The trouble with the book is that it falls between two stools: the dog-lover, who does not want to take his dog seriously, and the intellectual, who doesn't want to take dogs at all.[3] It is addressed to both of them, and irritates or disgusts the former, and fails to attract the latter (dogs!), though he would enjoy it if he looked, for I have a high opinion of it. Morgan keeps fairly well—I stayed

---

[1] Fukushima died in his early thirties, during a visit to England.

[2] On a previous occasion A. wrote to Roy Fuller: 'Money, the next most important thing to friendship.'

[3] A. seldom bothered to keep reviews of his books, but one of *My Dog Tulip* which had particularly pleased him was R.G.G.P.'s [Richard Price's] in *Punch*, which had appeared on 18 July 1956. A. had 'gone to the Putney Public Library to copy it out'—and it was found amongst his papers after his death. The notice ended: 'This is the first highbrow dog-book ever written, highbrow not in the sense of relating the keeping of a dog to general theory, but of striking the note of the solemn highbrow joke that is essentially serious. It will, one hopes, infuriate the stupid dog-lover. It may make non-owners queasy by its scatological and gynaecological detail, for it is, among other things, a beautiful plea for the understanding of the sexual nature of bitches. It will be as indestructible as Mr Ackerley's *Hindoo Holiday*.'

two nights with him in Cambridge this week and read over again all his un-published erotic stories,[1] which gave me—that now rare thing—a lustful feeling. He occasionally deplores that no one else writes such things, because he would like to read them.[2] Why don't you oblige? too busy trying to make money, as we all are, no doubt. Though not wealthy, he has always had private means;[3] one may doodle on those. Still, other writers also have private means and do not doodle or rudele for our pleasure.

No more, dearest Jim—at least, I can't remember any more. As my life passes it vanishes, as in a kind of following fog, and is never seen again. This is the story of
Your loving
    Joe

271 To Geoffrey Gorer (1905–)   Train to Nottingham
                                                                          27/2/65
Dear G.G.
            O.K., it shall be done.[4] The death of Laurel[5] saddened me more than the deaths of Edith, Eliot, or Churchill. Have you seen *It's a mad, mad, mad World*? Rather long (3 hours) but very lively, amusing slap-stick comedy-situations more than people. I saw it yesterday in Putney and much enjoyed it. It still hangs somewhere about the West End, I believe.

Off for a weekend with Jack. Will send you chapter 13 when I return.[6]
    Joe

272 To James Kirkup (1923–) 17 Star & Garter Mansions, Putney, S.W.15
                                                                          16/3/65
Dearest Jim
            you see I am now becoming quite a good correspondent—better than you, in fact, for pretty though your post-cards are, they are rather short of news. However I am pleased with the present one, pleased with your

[1] Twice during his life Forster carried out a burning of his erotic stories. An entry in his diary dated 8 April 1922 reads: 'Have this moment burnt my indecent writings or as many as the fire will take. Not a moral repentance, but a belief that they clogged me artistically.' Then, early in the 1960s, A. was chosen by Forster to read through his stories and destroy those which he did not think good enough to merit posthumous publication. Those that survived were included in *The Life to Come*, edited by Oliver Stallybrass (1972).
[2] Forster believed that the cultivation of erotic thoughts could help in times of stress. He disapproved of the Christian doctrine of vicarious suffering. See P. N. Furbank's article on 'The Personality of E. M. Forster' in *Encounter* (November 1970), in which he discusses A.'s posthumous *Observer* obituary of Forster, subsequently printed in full as *E. M. Forster: A Portrait* (1970).
[3] In 1904 Forster had inherited £8000. 'This sum alone made a literary career possible,' he told A. on one occasion. See *The Literary Life* by Peter Deane and Robert Phelps (1968).
[4] A reference to buying seats for the National Film Theatre.
[5] Stan Laurel, of the Laurel and Hardy film partnership.
[6] Gorer advised on chapters of *My Father and Myself* as they were completed. Cf. Letter 266.

poem,[1] pleased about your prize[2] (why didn't you collect it yourself?), and pleased with the dish-wipe, if that is what it is intended for. So now that you have another letter and a large sum of money, buy an air-mail stamp and send poor old Joe (who is not feeling very well today) a larger account of your life and your comings (and goings). Are you now a permanent decoration to the fortunate city of Osaka? Has Tokyo's tiara lost one of its brightest jewels? Were you expelled from that city? (I am still wondering why you didn't collect your prize in glamorous person.)[3] Are you now what's called 'in business'? Have you an office and are you the Boss? And why Osaka? You see how little I know.

I am having a Japanese day here today, for the British Council (forgive me for mentioning it) has bidden me to a cocktail party to honour Yukio Mishima.[4] I don't know how they thought of me; perhaps Francis King (now living in Brighton) put my name forward. I liked the only book of Mishima's I've read—a queer one—and from his photos he looks an attractive man. Tomorrow I transfer myself to Villiers' St James's Park flat for three nights to keep Anna, his pussy-cat company. He is in Hong-Kong. It is rather fun for me having a London house as well as a country one (Putney), and of course it is cheaper to drink someone else's gin and whisky than to drink one's own. Jack Sprott and his sister—perhaps Nancy too—are to dine with me there on Thursday and go on to a play. Feeling that the dear dark angel is close at hand, I am pushing on with my Family Memoir[5] so as not to leave it in rags and tatters. It is terribly sad and rather funny. And what are *you* hatching, sweet Jim? Oh yes, of course, I remember, the same sort of egg upon which I sit.[6]

Spring seems to have arrived and my little sycamore—a dried-up looking old brown stick only last week—now has tiny green swellings on it. I am moved, and rather envious; *I* have no swellings to greet the spring.
Much love, darling Jim
   Joe

To Lady Clark   17 Star & Garter Mansions, Putney, S.W.15 273
                                     29/4/65
Dearest Jane
          how sweet and kind you are, how dreamy your castle![7] I'm afraid I wasn't very helpful to you in some of our conversations, especially

---

[1] *Japan Marine*, a sequence of poems by James Kirkup.
[2] This sequence of poems was awarded First Prize in the Japanese P.E.N. Club International Literary Competition, held to coincide with the Japanese Olympics in 1964.
[3] Kirkup writes: 'I did not collect the prize myself in Tokyo because it had been agreed between the Japanese organizers of the competition and myself that as I was officially *persona non grata* with the British Council, and as their Representative in Japan was to present the prize, I should absent myself from the proceedings.'
[4] Japanese novelist (1925–70).
[5] *My Father and Myself.*
[6] A volume of autobiography.
[7] Saltwood Castle, Hythe.

the one in the train; I wanted to be helpful, but how difficult it is to be helpful to others—out of the heart, I mean, which has only love to offer. The mind can offer other things, philosophy, but I have no mind; such sustenance as I myself draw from life I draw from friendship only. Perhaps we shall talk about it again another day. You wanted Jack (Sebastian) Sprott's address. It is:

Professor W. J. H. Sprott
116 Portland Road
Nottingham

Do invite him along. Though he carries his learning lightly he is one of the wisest of men in all those antiseptic subjects of which I know too little (psychology, philosophy), you might find a chat with him interesting, and K. could tackle him on the subject of the death penalty, he is an expert in criminology.

Bless you, dear Jane, you made Morgan and me so wonderfully comfortable and happy. I'm sorry to hear that the Raymond luncheon was far from being up to Saltwood scratch. It heaped coals of fire on Morgan's head (am I mixing my metaphors?), for he was cock-a-hoop over the government's measures against expense accounts—until he tasted the fruits of their victory.

I hope you enjoyed Paris.

Much love to you both

Joe

274 To Oscar Collier (1924–) 17 Star & Garter Mansions, Putney,
S.W.15 4/5/65

Dear Mr Collier

I have anticipated your wishes, as you will know by now, and put myself to some trouble without being asked. I too want *My Dog Tulip* to sell and will bark at anyone you name. Unfortunately it was not reviewed here by the grandee reviewers, lesser fry took it on. I don't know what Elizabeth Bowen thought of it, but I will ask her;[1] she was one of the judges who awarded me the W. H. Smith award of £1000 for my novel in 1962. Harold Nicolson is no longer approachable, the poor old chap is quite ga-ga. Wystan Auden[2] liked it very much, and is a dog man; he is also resident in America, you know. I gave his name some time ago to you or Mr Seligmann. I gave also the names of other fans of mine for you to consider approaching: Christopher Isherwood, Tennessee Williams, Truman Capote, Lionel Trilling, Melvin J. Laski (present American co-editor of *Encounter* with Stephen Spender), and Irving Kristol, who preceded him,

[1] She sent A. this 'puff' to forward to his American publishers: 'This is such a book as has never been written before. Nobody who reads it will forget it. It carries, like all else J. R. Ackerley does, the stamp of his unique vision and particular genius.'

[2] No 'puff' appeared from Auden on the dust-jacket of *My Dog Tulip*, but subsequently he included two extracts from it in his commonplace book *A Certain World* (1971).

now in the States.[1] I wonder whether Rosamond Lehmann would be of any use to you; I will write to her on the chance;[2] she adored the book. Yes, I know Alan Pryce-Jones; but whether he read it or would praise the book I haven't a notion. Some people hated it, you know, such as Edith Sitwell. Cyril Connolly liked it but was slightly disgusted. It might be worth while for you to phone a novelist of yours and old friend of mine, Donald Windham, 3 E. 80th St. N.Y.21; though not suitable for the jacket, he might give you a tip or two about U.S. writers who like me; I have done him much service in my time; a new novel of his[3] has either just appeared or is just about to appear. Isherwood's address is 145 Adelaide Drive, Santa Monica, Cal. Tell me what else you want and I will bark my head off. But I hope you won't ask me for photos for I haven't any.[4]

Yours sincerely
Joe Ackerley

To Oscar Collier 17 Star & Garter Mansions, Putney, S.W.15 275
26/5/65

Dear Mr Collier
          I returned your proofs [of *My Dog Tulip*] to you today, air mail of course. They were wonderfully clean, I read them twice, but found few mistakes. It is true nevertheless that authors are not the best proof-readers; over-familiar with the text, their eyes are liable to skate blindly over their own well-known sentences; I found almost as many things to correct in my second reading as in my first, so your own proof-readers may easily find things I have missed. I saw you had altered 'lift' to 'elevator' here and there but not throughout, so I have completed, I hope, that variation, assuming you to desire it.[5] At two points I hesitated over making cuts; in the end I made neither; but *you* can make them if you like. You said in one letter that it was a pity that Tulip should die. You may be right. If you prefer her not to die, you can take out the last sentence of the book, letting it end with the word 'successful'.[6] The other thing I brooded over was the paragraph about

---

[1] The publishers were successful with Isherwood and Kristol. Isherwood's 'puff' was printed on the front of the dust-jacket: 'This is one of the greatest masterpieces of animal literature, and Mr Ackerley achieves it by writing about his Tulip simply and shockingly as a dog.' Kristol's 'puff' appeared on the back: '*My Dog Tulip* is a little gem. It is a book about a dog—but it is also a book about love and death, their triumph and defeat. It is poignant, memorable, and—incredibly enough—very amusing.'

[2] She sent A. this 'puff' to forward to his American publishers: 'I have just re-read *My Dog Tulip*. I had half-forgotten what a flawless minor masterpiece it is, and it dealt me a series of fresh shocks of pleasure and disturbance! It is the only "dog book" I know to record a human-canine love in terms of *absolute* equality between the protagonists.'

[3] *Two People*, which was published in 1966. Cf. Letter 268.

[4] Later that year, *Time* magazine sent a photographer to A.'s flat in Putney: 'Some hundred photos were taken of me—and not used.' But a review of *My Dog Tulip* did appear on 8 October, which the author thought 'as fair as fair could be'—excepting for the reference to him as 'Bachelor Ackerley'. 'Why that upper case B?' he wrote to Donald Windham. 'Was it a jibe, a sneer or a typographical error?'

[5] 'Lorry' had also been changed to 'truck'.

[6] Collier decided not to make this 'cut'—and the American edition ends: 'Whatever blunders I may have admitted in my management of this animal's life, she lived to the great age of sixteen-and-a-half.' The subsequent Bodley Head (1965) and Penguin (1971) editions of the book end with this sentence and, like the American Fleet (1965) edition, restore a certain amount of material 'cut' from the first edition of 1956.

'young Holland' at the end of 'The Turn of the Screw'. I wonder if it should continue into your American edition. It adds nothing (we have had two suicides already) and may seem rather perplexing to your readers. Does it stick in your gullet? If so, cut it out—and of course the footnote reference to *The Times*. The passage would then run from 'The place must be full of ghosts . . .' to (new par.) 'The cold night mists are still dissolving from the naked grove.' It is an easy cut and I leave it to your judgment. It may be that the last par. in that chapter would tack on better if 'young Holland' and his footnote were removed.[1]

I hope you received *Hindoo Holiday* and that all goes well with you and Fleet.
Yours sincerely
J. R. Ackerley

276 To William Plomer (1903–1973)   Putney
                                                                     28/5/65
Dearest William
                        a more exciting, and more rewarding, present I never had; I have already devoured it and am ½-way through a second reading.[2] I note that Mr [Hilary] Corke thinks me right to ignore the Introduction.[3] Anyway Introductions should always be Postscripts, or at any rate come to at last, for one does not wish to know the opinions of others until one has found one's own. Perhaps I will attend to loquacious Laurens [van der Post] (what a contrast always to your own disciplined and economical prose!) in the end. I thought the photo of you very touching because characteristic— the large hands twiddling some little thing, a leaf, a straw—a bus ticket.

I wonder how you settled upon the name Turbott Wolfe.[4] Tell me one day. I see that you could not have called it anything so ordinary and earthy as Tom Jones, but your own choice goes to a quite bizarre extreme. Perhaps that is what you wanted. I only wonder whether my co-Public Library users will do what I want them to do, pick out a book with so enigmatic a title as to seem neither fish, fowl, man, nor good red riding hood.

It is a highly charged, very powerful book. After it had got going, somewhere about p. 90, I couldn't stop reading. I think it is in the writing as much as in anything else: the excellent characterisation, the spare, unwasteful dialogue, the fine choice of words, and the African scene itself which you evoke in your short tense sentences with the vividness of the best Russian writers, all fuse into something beautiful for all its horror, a kind of passionate poetry. The horse's tail blown sideways by the breeze, the bird's claw printed in the mud, the light in the water-butt, the climbing sheep, the

---

[1] Collier decided not to make these 'cuts'. See pages 109, note 3 and 110, note 1.
[2] Plomer's novel, *Turbott Wolfe*, which was originally published in 1926. In 1965 a new edition appeared, with an Introduction by Laurens van der Post.
[3] Corke had reviewed it the day before in *The Listener*: 'Stunningly over-introduced by the very serious Mr van der Post (skip this), *Turbott Wolfe* is definitely a classic for the shelves.'
[4] Plomer told Braybrooke: 'I think the name just came into my head. I wanted it to be unusual. I can't at all account for "Turbott". The idea of a lone wolf may possibly have suggested "Wolfe", but so may the name of Edward Wolfe, the only professional painter I then knew.'

rocking chair—these are the kind of things I think of in the dream and haunt of your electric emotional atmosphere.

Thank you, dear William

Love from

Joe

To James Kirkup (1923–   )   Putney 277
                                                             29/5/65

Darling Jim

you see that, when thought dead, I resurrect myself, like some-one else[1] we have heard of. The mood takes me, my eyes brighten, blood flows into the word 'Jim' which is written on my heart, I seize my pen and lo and behold! a letter gets written at last—at least I hope so. Pickled and bottled, I drowse over letters now; to write one takes a whole day; this dull cold day is yours; our Rena must wait for another, do give her my love when you write and tell her she is not forgotten, her day will come. She swept in upon us some weeks ago, a Juno or Athene among women, kept us enter-tained for three hours with her sparkling vivacity, and swept off with your portrait which has left a blank on my wall.[2] You have a wonderful friend there, honest, good-natured, warm-hearted, courageous and devoted. Her understanding is large, as also are her sympathies. But I am no match for her; her energies, her *joie de vivre*, enfeeble an already abdicated mind, she anwers all letters instantly and at length, and doesn't seem to mind that my weak, quavering replies are seldom heard.

I have, actually and strangely, been somewhat occupied lately, correcting proofs of *My Dog Tulip* for America, and looking after old Morgan who had a severe stroke a month ago. It paralysed him on one side and threw him into convulsions; his number, it was thought, was up. This happened in Coven-try, when he was staying with his friends the Buckinghams. He has made a remarkable recovery. I have been up twice to spend some days with him in their house, the paralysis has vanished and he is now restored, excepting that his sight, speech, and calligraphy have suffered to some extent. When last I went up I took your prize poem[3] with me and read it to him in the small, pretty garden, full of the most delightful blackbird song. He kept exclaiming 'My! what a wonderful vocabulary!' (yours, not the blackbirds') 'What a beautiful choice of words!' and asked me specially to thank you for having given him so much pleasure.[4]

He is being returned to Cambridge this weekend, and thereafter, if all goes well, I am to act as a part-time secretary to him, spending a couple of days a week in King's to help him with his correspondence. Meanwhile, I

[1] Forster—see second paragraph of letter. See Letter 278.
[2] See Letter 270.
[3] See Letter 272.
[4] Throughout his life, Forster wrote to people whenever what they did 'moved or pleased' him. A., in helping him with his correspondence, often wrote such letters on his behalf during the latter years. Forster believed in giving praise where praise was due, and feared that too little was given compared 'with the readiness to find fault'. A. followed Forster's practice. For instance, see Letter 299.

have about finished my Family Memoir,[1] the last book I shall ever write,[2] and am busy tearing and tidying up the remainder of my life, the mass of rubbish this room contains, so that my executor (Francis King) will not be put to too much trouble.[3] He lives pleasantly, I think happily, in Brighton, where I stayed a weekend with him not long ago. If his life is not as full as he could wish, he extracts from it much interest and amusement. Jack Sprott is well and sends his love. [——] is not very well; his winter tour of the Far East (Japan was not taken in) was not the usual success he was expecting, he returned with an upset stomach and an upset mind. Literature instead of painting is now his ambition, a new novel; the struggle is constant, the success, I fear, is small.

Well I have written you a letter—even a love-letter—darling Jim. Reply in kind and in kindness.

Joe

278 To Sir Herbert Read (1893–1968)   17 Star & Garter Mansions, Putney, S.W.15   17/7/65

Dear Herbert

it was such a pleasure to see you again—twice indeed did Fortune turn her wheel for me—and I meant to say this sooner, but Morgan's tired and unpredictable health and his correspondence, which takes me to Cambridge two days every week as a help-meet or -mate, rather dislocates my thought and time. He had another slight stroke that night after we saw you—if 'stroke' it can be called that muddles up one's speech and makes one feel sick; a doctor had to be summoned—a most excellent man as it turned out—who kept him in bed for 24 hours and would have kept him there longer had he been able to prevail against Morgan's determination to do what he wants to do. So the day after, I removed him from Chiswick to Cambridge, the hard way since he desired it, by train to King's Cross, train thence, bus from the station to the Town Centre. The doctor had recommended a car the whole way! Morgan is a thrifty man. He gives his money lavishly to friends who need it—I have had thousands of pounds from him since my retirement,[4] and he has propped many other friends up too— 'Aren't I lucky to have so much money?' he says—but he won't spend a penny on himself if he can help it.[5] A saintly man. He was unwell again when I left him last Wednesday afternoon, sick and tired, and he recovered as he

---

[1] *My Father and Myself.*

[2] A. never did write another book—though he had plans for one. See page 310, note 4.

[3] A. had written to King on 21 May: '. . . tidying up my own life as well as Morgan's I think I should appoint an executor for my will (a thing I have not hitherto done) and wondered whether I might not name you. My estate is not large, nor my affairs complicated . . . You are . . . the person I would most like to name.' King agreed to be his executor by return of post.

[4] See Letters 190, 192, 216, 221, 226 and 317.

[5] It was common knowledge among Forster's friends that in 1949 he had turned down a knighthood on the grounds that it would send up his bills. He had written to A. at the time (2 December): 'Yesterday I was offered a knighthood, and ever since refusing it have been wondering whether to have been called Sir Edward Forster or Sir Morgan Forster.' In 1953, he had received a C.H., and in 1968, two years before his death, he was awarded an O.M.

seems always to do (can these mental disturbances be strokes? they are becoming frequent and he enjoys himself between them), we sat in the garden of Clare College, in about the only burst of sunshine we have had this summer. A Peacock butterfly settled on my knee, and he said 'How right that it should prefer your knee to mine,' a charming remark, but the cause was different, my trousers were of much lighter colour than his. I go to him again on Tuesday and to see *Howards End*,[1] which has such an unlikely plot that I fear it must be a failure, especially because the casting is poor; I saw a rehearsal of it yesterday.

There is some possibility that I return to *The Listener* in September; they are in a jam, the new char (Anthony Thwaite) clearing out and no newer char yet appointed; I have been asked if I will tide them over by bringing along my bucket and broom for a month or two and, although I am now out of touch with current reviewers, I have said yes: the monetary offer is so good.[2] But nothing is settled yet.

You asked me to York, dear Herbert. I have never been so far north since I visited you with Jack Sprott, and supposed York to be in the Hebrides. Now I realize that it's no distance at all. Do ask me again, when you have a spare moment.

Love from
  Joe

To Sir Herbert Read (1893–1968)   17 Star & Garter Mansions, Putney, 279
                                    S.W.15   8/8/65

Dear Herbert
              I'm a bit late in answering, but not very. I'm sorry you've lost your zest for life, and hope you may regain it. Once lost, can it be regained? The mind is so dark one doesn't know what it's up to, what efforts it can make or wishes to make. In some people, it seems, no effort is needed; the spirit, though momentarily dashed from time to time perhaps, accepts all and zestfully rides on. Is this something one is born with, or can it be acquired (philosophy)? If it can be acquired, perhaps it can be lost. It has its degrees also, I suppose. I doubt if I know what it is, this appetite, this forward-looking spirit that buoys people up. I see it about and think it wonderful, and incomprehensible. It was missed out of me, I think, when I was made, as, looking about, it seems to have been missed out of some of my friends, such as [—— ——] and [—— ——]. Can we be seen as leaping from the womb with a shout of joy, armed against fate? Not that I pity myself; 'what you've never 'ad you never miss'; I simply notice that I have no drive, and if I have lost it, I doubt if it was ever much to lose. These reflections arise partly from the fact that I have lately been trying to psycho-analyse myself in a Family Memoir[3] I have written; but can one do it? I think one can only scratch the surface.

[1] At the Arts Theatre, Cambridge. See page 288, note 4.
[2] A. was offered £10 a day.
[3] *My Father and Myself.*

Morgan goes zestfully on. (Wonderful! Incomprehensible!) He is being driven up to London today by a friend to spend a few days at his Chiswick flat, eager for amusement and the society of his London friends. Whether I shall be seeing him I don't yet know. He has had a good deal of me lately, and I have sometimes wondered whether the company of the zestless (however bright the face they put on) may not seem insufficient to the zestful. The man who drives him up and stays with him is crammed with zest . . .

No news from the B.B.C., so I expect they have found some other solution to their difficulties.[1] I hope so.

Yes, I met Piers[2] in Morgan's rooms and thought him a charmer. The Becketts I think I do not know. Rupert [Hart-Davis] I do; he is good for a deaf ear with his booming voice: *there's* zest for you, whether you want it or not. Fox-hunters No. I have one in the shape of a brother-in-law who, when asked some years ago by his wife what he would like for a birthday present, said 'A tie-pin made out of the penis-bone of a fox, for my cravat.' A fox-hunter herself, she was nevertheless rather shaken, but I believe she got it for him in the end.

Much love, dear Herbert

Joe

---

[1] Finding a temporary literary editor. See Letter 278.
[2] Piers Paul—Read's second son by his second marriage.

Part Thirteen
A MONTH AT *THE LISTENER*

To Jocelyn Brooke (1909–1966) *The Listener*, Broadcasting House, W.1 280
7/9/65

Dear Mr Brooke
I am posting books to you every day, which may be better than the ones you have had, so it would be better not to assess word-allowances until you are obliged to start your article. Naturally if P[amela] Hansford Johnson's book is still then outstanding, you will give her pride of place and such wordage as you think she deserves.[1] You say nothing about the Iris Murdoch novel,[2] which rather worries me. It worries me because I don't know whether it has arrived or not. Could you give me its title, if you know. At present I can't tell whether it has gone to [Hilary] Corke or not. Someone should look at it, I'm sure you'll agree. I'm trying to get used to Anthony Thwaite's[3] muddle, which is quite different from my own muddle of seven years ago—which I perfectly understood!
Yes, Sept. 22 is your D-day.
J. R. Ackerley

To Sewell Stokes (1902–) *The Listener*, Broadcasting House, W.1 281
7?/9/65

Thank you, dear friend, herewith and herewith and my word, how jolly good and amusing and beautifully written your own book is.[4] It is all a book should be, and has helped more than anything else to get me through my first week of cigarette renunciation.
But you mock me, I fancy, over your dog couplet.[5] It is not unfaithfulness

---

[1] On 30 September Brooke gave her *Cork Street, Next to the Hatters* pride of place: 'There must be many reviewers . . . who, on unpacking their current bunch, heave a sigh of relief at finding it includes a new novel by Pamela Hansford Johnson . . . She is invariably competent, often very funny, and always entertaining.' The other novels he reviewed were *P. S. Wilkinson* by C. D. B. Bryan, *Passion Flowers in Business* by Rosalind Erskine, *One of the Founders* by P. H. Newby and *A Vision of Battlements* by Anthony Burgess.
[2] *The Red and the Green*—which Brooke subsequently reviewed on 28 October. See page 272, note 1.
[3] Previous literary editor from 1963 to 1965.
[4] *Our Dear Delinquents* (1965). The book is mainly concerned with Borstals and detention centres.
[7] This remains a mystery. Stokes told Braybrooke: 'I have never written a dog couplet in my life!'

in hounds, but death, that is the worm i' the flower: their day is too brief. One should love a tortoise; faithful and everlasting.[1]
Love
J

---

282   To Francis King (1923–   )   Putney
                                                                 16/9/65
Dearest Francis
              I am so happy to have your novel,[2] with its dedication and beautiful Latin compliment to me.[3] I am deeply touched. I've started to read the book, on the 30 Bus on my way home, and am *absorbed*. A well-contrived, suspenseful story with (so far) only a few characters, all interesting —your books have sometimes had too many. There is something of the detective story about it, a popular *genre* to which I myself often turn, without much gain, the motives for murder being usually so unoriginal. I am writing this at page 25—I will write to you again when I have finished. My present view is that it is an excellent selling book. I have avoided reading your blurb. That shall be left to the end. Your doggery is just what the dog-wogs need.[4] They will clap their paws.

Could you bother to read the enclosed?[5] It is by me, 25 years old; *The Listener* needs poems and I dug it out of a drawer. And can't make up my mind about it. Does it read like a fake? Is it obscure? Is it awfully old-fashioned? Would you advise for or against? In short, is it worth publishing? I rather dislike publishing anything, never feeling confident of merit. Of course, one often has an affection for what one writes—but that is a very different matter. Tell me what you think.
Love
   Joe

---

283 To Hilary Corke (1921–   )   *The Listener*, Broadcasting House, W.1
                                                                 29/9/65
Dear Hilary
              an interesting and amusing piece,[6] but since you are so critical, I think we should not add taunts, so I have taken one out. And besides

---

[1] A. was reading Byron's *Letters* at this time. Perhaps part of one to the Hon. Augusta Leigh, dated 9 September 1811, had stuck in his mind: '. . . for my part (since I lost my Newfoundland dog), I like nobody except his successor a Dutch Mastiff and three land Tortoises brought with me from Greece.'

[2] *The Last of the Pleasure Gardens*. See Letter 285, note 2.

[3] *Omnia praeclara tam difficilia quam rara* (All distinction is as difficult as it is rare).

[4] There are many admirable observations in the novel about the upbringing of dogs. A. in this letter was referring to Part I.

[5] 'After the Blitz, 1941'. See page 65, note 6.

[6] A review of *The Penguin English Dictionary*, compiled by G. N. Garmonsway with Jacqueline Simpson. This review appeared in *The Listener* on 7 October and, in the course of it, Corke wrote: 'Its pronunciations are appalling. The compiler seems to have confused a dictionary (which cannot avoid making certain value-judgments as between alternatives, since part of its function is to be referred to as an arbiter, a standard, not of pedantry, but of current 'correctness') with a sociological

showing that the book is not up to much, the further step of actually advising readers not to buy it goes too far—so I have eliminated your last sentence.[1]

Joe

Correct carefully, with so many odd words.

To Oscar Collier (1924–) Putney 284
29/9/65

Dear Mr Collier
                a single copy of *Tulip* (I hope some more may follow) has now reached me. I am very upset to see that William PLOMER's name has been mis-spelled POLMER on the dust-jacket.[2] This is surely a piece of carelessness, since the quotation and signature occurred in print on the cover of my English edition, which you have. Perhaps his name is not known in America; here he is a prominent writer, well-known as novelist and poet, and as librettist to Benjamin Britten. He is also one of my oldest friends. This mistake saddens me.
                Otherwise the book, in its interior, looks excellent, and the array of 'puffs' on the jacket ought to sell any book—though they don't seem to.[3] I wish I had sent you my own drawing of Tulip for your cover—I didn't think of it. Though a back view, it is more sensitive and more revealing of 'My Dog Tulip' than Mrs [Gladys Emerson] Cook's crude drawing of a male Alsatian.[4]
                Well, all good luck to you—and to
                J. R. Ackerley

To Jocelyn Brooke (1909–1966)   *The Listener*, Broadcasting House, W.1 285
29/9/65

Dear Brooke
                that sounds excellent. In my young days on this paper, the time of Edwin Muir, we used to get rid of commendable though unimportant

---

report on vulgar speech-habits. Not even an alternative is offered to such horrors as *naycher* and *proseejer*, and goodness knows in that case why we are spared *chewn* (what one plays, you know) and *chewzdi* and *jewrayshon*. Why, if we must say *egzakt*, are we still allowed *eksaserbayt*? And have you, dear reader, ever spent a night upon licey straw and lotus-blossoms in one of those primitive hostelries deep in hairy Ainu country, a *paan(g)syon(g)*? Oh but no, wait a minute, it appears to be in France! It is a *po(ng)syaw(ng)*. Then we veer wildly from these imperative vulgarities to impossible pedantries such as *wenzdi/wednzdi*, or *indewr*, which for my money is *endyor*.'

[1] The last sentence (as printed) read: 'A definition is faultless, or it is nothing: and of the 45,000 entries here, I should guess that some 10,000 fall short.'
[2] This was corrected in the second American edition.
[3] Those quoted, apart from Plomer ('a revolutionary book'), were Christopher Isherwood, E. M. Forster, Julian Huxley, Elizabeth Bowen, Rosamond Lehmann and Irving Kristol. See Letter 274.
[4] A week later A. wrote to say that he thought his letter 'inadequate'. He went on: 'Excepting for the one slip on the jacket, your production of my little book is *excellent*, not a comma misplaced. I am very pleased. I was unfair about Mrs Cook's drawing too. It stares out well. It is impressive. I suppose one has an image in one's mind against which all else seems to fail. I am apologising to you.'

novels in the last par. of the review which began 'Also recommended': then, perhaps in a single sentence of two or three lines to each book, a couple or more novels would be mentioned as worth looking at, with their authors' names, and publishers and prices in brackets. I don't know why this sensible method of doing more than four books without overloading the heading was abandoned. If you like to revive it, do so;[1] I can't suppose that my successor would object.

Yes, Miss Muriel Spark should be done.[2] My notion is that all serious and intelligent writers, and all successful writers (the Spark is that, is she not?), should be done, somehow or other, even if they slip up; the object of the exercise being to give the general novel reader some idea of what to read, even if he has to be given disappointing news of his, perhaps, favourite novelists.

Yes, Roy does write well, doesn't he, almost too well. I find his novel[3] requires such concentration of thought that I wonder who, except you and I, is going to give it that. Francis King makes no such demands.

J.R.A.

[1] On 28 October Brooke began his 'New Fiction' column by reviewing Iris Murdoch's *The Red and the Green*, which he thought 'well up to competent middle-brow standards'. He then turned to *Friends in Low Places* by Simon Raven, *Games of Chance* by Thomas Hinde and *The Egyptologists* by Kingsley Amis and Robert Conquest. He ended his column: 'Other brief recommendations: *The Sioux*, a long amusing first novel by Irene Handl about a rich cosmopolitan French family (Longmans, 25s.). Also two new Simenons, *Maigret Sets a Trap* and *The Man with the Little Dog* (the first, 13s. 6d., the second 15s., both from Hamish Hamilton). If I were reviewing novels merely for pleasure, these are the two to which I should have devoted most of my space; but I have a guilty feeling that M. Simenon's novels are too purely enjoyable to be considered "significant".'
[2] Her novel *The Mandelbaum Gate* was reviewed by Brooke on 14 October, along with *The Last of the Pleasure Gardens* by Francis King, *My Child, My Sister* by Roy Fuller and *August is a Wicked Month* by Edna O'Brien.
[3] *My Child, My Sister*.

Part Fourteen
SECOND RETIREMENT

To Roy Fuller (1912–   )   17 Star & Garter Mansions, Putney, S.W.15   286
                                                                     3/10/65

Dear Roy

I was sorry to see *The Times* so irritable with you this week, but it is true, I think, that you make no concessions to the reader and that *My Child, My Sister* belongs in that sad category of novels which needs to be read twice—though you could reply to this that, on the other hand, *I* belong to that sad category of readers too blockheaded to take things in at once. At any rate, as I said earlier, the book made heavy demands upon my powers of concentration (as, for instance, Compton-Burnett does, and Francis King doesn't), and I found myself making a genealogical table of the relationships of your characters—what is more, having to correct it later, for I got it wrong. On second reading, of course, all that was plain, and I could give clearer attention to Mr Shore's reflections upon life and art, many of which previously I had had to read twice to get the hang of them. It must have been a very difficult book to write, to get the right tone and balance between detachment and involvement. The starling is of vital importance, the passages about it, pp. 72–75, 108–110, are deeply affecting and illuminating, injecting into the whole that poetry of tender feeling which, in his human relationships, your elderly novelist is unable to express. The image of the nigger-minstrel, so exact,[1] brought to my eye the tear you bestowed upon the waist of your wasp.[2] Yes, I was 'with' you the second time, and marked many other striking reflections that emerge from the pondering mind of Mr Shore—pp. 10, 18, 50, 54, 57, 63, 70 (revealing of your aim?), 86, 103, 107, 108, 138. But it *is* a difficult book, and I wonder whether you don't plague us, in your strict way, with too many adjectives, too many and too long, having a clotting effect: 'The Leafs are indubitably visible . . . One had the residual feeling . . .': perfectly proper but, after a time, they hold the reader up.

---

[1] 'A yellow edge surrounding its bill, thickset at the corners, the shape of the mouth left by nigger minstrels when they black their faces.'

[2] This is a reference to Fuller's poem 'To a Wasp', which A. had accepted during his month at *The Listener* in September—though it was not published until 25 November. Here is the last verse:

> I see your feet, that almost boast
> Boots, would be comic features, while
> Finding your negligible waist
> Bring the tear splashing down my smile.

Two other things in the writing obtrude—and are, in fact, revealing of the difficulties of your story, the use of the word 'facetious' (I think you must employ it often or it wouldn't strike upon the eye), and the number of sentences you begin with some such phrase as 'Remarkable that . . .', 'Curious to find . . .', 'Strange indeed . . .' This top-dressing of triviality, in human intercourse, of the serious, incommunicable problems below, is, I suppose, part of your tricky plan, and brings in those scenes of humdrum life, such as the Larabeiti meeting, which, excepting as triviality, seem to have no part in the 'plot'.

Love from

Joe

287   To David Sylvester (1924–   )   17 Star & Garter Mansions, Putney,
                                       S.W.15   5/10/65

Thank you, dear David, it is a letter for keeps, even for framing, like a diploma, had you not written on both sides of the paper.[1] Few such letters have come my way, none so emotional; one is awfully glad to get them. I can't feel surprised at your tears, for I summoned them, weeping myself at the points you mention as I wrote, weeping the more as I got my words and sentences more and more perfect, and weeping still whenever I re-read them. Perhaps there is something pathological shared by both of us, since you tune in to me so beautifully. But you say nothing of laughter, which it was also my purpose to summon. Did not poor Frank's futile and exasperated efforts to communicate, to make himself understood by anyone, make you giggle? The third visit to Millie is a highly successful, 'tight' piece of comedy,[2] I think, from her opening remarks about having lost her voice and her failure to get through to Tom, to Frank's fury at not being able to make himself understood by her, her failure to make herself understood by him, and Evie's failure, until Frank arrives, in gaining the understanding of anyone. When I had hammered it out and polished it up I was delighted with it. I was pleased too with Evie's ball game.[3] Though of vital importance in the book, it remained flabby when all other problems had been overcome. Then suddenly, like a gift from the gods, I saw how to electrify it. What joy![4] It *is* nice to write to someone as mentally unstable as oneself about it—and to someone who reads as slowly as one writes.

Did I tell you that I've not only at last got *My Dog Tulip* off onto the American market, but that it has been awarded alternate choice by the N[ew] Y[ork] Book of the Month Club? This after nearly ten years effort

[1] The letter had been in praise of *We Think the World of You.*
[2] Pages 37–46.
[3] Pages 74–6.
[4] On 19 January 1961 A. had written to Stephen Spender: 'The ball game was one of the last things to come right, I am so glad you selected it; it remained commonplace description for a long time, then I suddenly saw that it was the bridge across and that the magic of it already contained needed stress. It excited me very much when I got it right.' See Letter 136.

and failure to get *any* publisher there to touch it. A galaxy of famous authors recommend it on the dust-jacket, and poor William Plomer has turned into William Polmer.[1]
Love from
  Joe

To John Morris (1895–) 17 Star & Garter Mansions, Putney, S.W.15 288
  19/10/65
Dearest John
        just a little line to say that your visit on Sunday gave us great pleasure and we hope you may soon repeat it. Suggest yourself for any day you feel at a loose end, you will always be welcome. I have a housekeeper[2] and you have not, so only one-way traffic is possible. [— —] says that when you come again he would like to be asked too; we will try to catch that slippery eel if we can. Often on Sunday afternoons, if weather good, we borrow a little dog and take it for a walk on Putney Common. It is quite a pleasant walk and if you, a famous traveller,[3] cared to make a 'day' of it with us, come too and return to dine.
Your loving
  Randolph[4]

To Norah Smallwood[5]   17 Star & Garter Mansions, Putney, S.W.15 289
  25/10/65
Dear Norah
        a small matter which may well come to O. You may vaguely recall that some two years ago the Indian dancer, Ram Gopal,[6] began to scheme to make a film of *Hindoo Holiday*. I should have put him on to you, but forgetting your agency side sent him to the Higham Associates (my own agents). Nothing came of it, of course—nothing ever does come of Ram's enthusiastic projects. This morning he rings me again, more enthusiasm, he has some line on Anthony Asquith and wants to interest him in my book. But before proceeding, would I promise him a partnership in the production? I said no. I like little Ram, he is a deliberate charmer, but [. . .] how can I admit to partnership a man who admittedly wants the narrative of my book to be bi-sexual (the introduction of girls and orthodoxy); who fancies himself as the Maharajah (I don't know if he still does), who would then of course become a glamorous figure; and who desires to turn the book into a

---

[1] Cf. Letter 284.
[2] i.e. a sister.   [3] See page 163, note 1.
[4] Morris writes: 'Jokingly, I always addressed Joe as Randolph, which was actually his second name, because it seemed so ill-suited to him.'
[5] Partner and later Director of Chatto & Windus since 1945. Now Managing Director. Publishers of A.'s *The Prisoners of War* and *Hindoo Holiday*.
[6] See page 233, note 4.

glittering spectacle of wild dances, tiger-shooting expeditions and pig-stick safaris? I've told him all this, but he seems undeterred by my refusal to guarantee him anything. (He's rolling in money; I can't understand what he's after). At any rate, he asked to whom, as an agent, he could apply . . . so I named you. He took your address—perhaps he will turn up, perhaps he won't. This is just to give you the background of the story—and my own rather weary botherations. I suppose if he does turn up and could get Asquith interested (do I love Asquith? I don't know), he should have some small percentage of any result, but I won't have him script-writing the book (Henry Reed could be asked to do that), or interfering in the production: he could play a minor role if he wished—very minor. His address, if you should entice him along after my rebuffs, is 17 Draycott Avenue, S.W.3. You could say that I phoned you. Don't bother to answer.
Love from
    Joe

290 To Geoffrey Gorer (1905–)   Putney
                                                                       30/10/65

Thank you, dear G.G. I won't keep this little book, it will only become sub-merged in my small untidy room—and others should see your essay.[1] I enjoyed reading it very much, it is strong and lucid. I don't know about your solution; humility is not the most noticeable quality in homo sapiens, but I daresay that where there's a will there's a way. Fortunately you are not writing for me, or I should accuse you of malice, offering me penal servitude among the kiddiwiddies.

You don't now take *The Listener*, I think. I found the enclosed article by [Sir Geoffrey] Vickers[2] of interest, and thought you might like to see it. It seems to provide a general frame for your particular case. Another *Listener* page is also enclosed for its historic interest: a word never before seen in these chaste pages has got in.[3]

Box Office of our cinema opens tomorrow and I will try then for seats for B[uster] Keaton. Hope you managed your Wimbledon journey without loss of temper. Getting about anywhere today so often involves that.

No reply expected by
    Joe

The fourth anniversary of Queenie's death day.

---

[1] Gorer cannot remember what the book was.
[2] 'The End of Free Fall', which had been published on 28 October. The article had originally been a Third Programme talk and dealt with 'the political challenge of an overpopulated world'.
[3] This occurred in James Joll's review of *English History 1914–1945* by A. J. P. Taylor: '. . . the book contains much social and economic material, compressed with great skill from volumes of statistics or from the monographs of the official historians of both wars, as well as enlivened by Mr Taylor's own personal observations and memories. Some of it will surprise: for example, Mr Taylor uses statistics on the manufacture of contraceptives to suggest a new explanation of the decline in the birth-rate, while a footnote on changes in the vernacular speech must surely be the first time the word "fuck" has been printed by the Clarendon Press in a historical work.'

To William Plomer (1903–1973)   Putney   291
                                                 4/11/65

D.L.B.

you will observe that I have lately been in Cambridge, in fact I have only just this hour returned, having spent 2 nights in King's, and done some of Morgan's letters for him. He is both tired and sprightly, if you know what I mean; his enfeebled body tries to put him to bed (a place for which I long) on a sunny afternoon; his spirit says 'You shall not waste this charming day in sleep, let us sally forth and contemplate the beauties of nature which soon I shall no longer see'; so, stifling a yawn (I have taken to the bottle, as you know), I potter out with the old boy after lunch and we sit on a bench in the weak but lovely sunlight, which gives Gibbs' building a lilac tint, by the Cam, observing such birds as present themselves to our notice and the red and golden autumn trees. Of course the place is ravishingly beautiful and it would be wrong to miss a moment of its transmission into sleep by falling into that state oneself. Disaster can occur at any moment, let's hope that next time it will be final if otherwise it is to ruin him further. At present he is delightful company, though difficult for deaf old Joe to hear. He tripped twice this week over his multitudinous ancestral mats, but was adroitly fielded before he fell. I caught him first time, someone else the second. Moreover, I found his stick, which had been missing for some days. Where could he have left it? Perhaps it would never have been found had he not spent so long in the bathroom, which contains also the shit-house, this morning, preventing me from visiting the latter. So I went down to the Fellows' lav. near the Combination Room instead, and there was Morgan's stick hanging on a peg. Jubilation!

Yes, I read Jane Harrison's[1] book when it appeared, last year I think. What was it called? Something like *Animal Machines*.[2] To her and Rachel Carson (who prefaced it) with her *Silent Spring*[3] belongs the credit of exposing the abominations in our midst. It contained lots of these revolting photographs. Neither of these highly important books was sent for review by the wretched *Listener*.[4] We never buy veal and scour the district always for Free Range eggs, which can be got. I have just been reading the last report of the joint committee of the British Trust for Ornithology and the Royal Soc. for the Protection of Birds on Toxic Chemicals, and in spite of the government restrictions placed on the sale of some of the most dangerous chemicals which have killed off so much of the wild life in the U.S., the news is very bad. The bodies of 236 birds of various species were sent up for chemical analysis from all parts of the country and only 10 were found free from contamination by organochlorine compounds. The birds had mostly been found dead or dying in convulsions, some were shot. Nestlings, eggs, small

[1] A slip. For 'Jane Harrison' read 'Ruth Harrison'.
[2] Correct. This study of 'The New Factory Farming Industry' (as it was sub-titled) had been published in 1964.
[3] 1963.
[4] On 20 September 1968 Janet Adam Smith in a review in the *New Statesman* of A.'s *My Father and Myself* wrote: 'After I became literary editor of the NEW STATESMAN, I could occasionally bribe him to do a piece on animal books by offering him more space than he would allow himself in his own paper.' She was literary editor from 1952 to June 1960.

mammals, and insects (caterpillars, slugs, etc.) were also analysed; all contained these compounds in small or large degree. These analyses were carried out Aug. '63 to Aug. '64. I'm glad your own birds bound and bounce. What is needed, of course, is *human* illness and death indisputably traceable to these chemicals; if and when *that* starts, something will be done—though then it may be too late.

I am all right, dear William; my ear is still there, but no great trouble to its owner who today reaches the age of 69. Shall I be alive to read your new book of poems? One needs reasons for making another step forward worthwhile, and until your letter came there seemed none.
Much love to you and Charles
J

P.S. Fish-eating birds seem to come off worst—highest residues of poison. They are followed by owls, hawks and falcons. Then come farmland birds. Two blackbirds which came from orchards (Kent and Wiltshire) were highly toxic. This to complete your discomfiture.

To James Kirkup (1923–   )   King's College, Cambridge
                                                            9/11/65
Dear James
              I write to you by Joe's hand to thank you for your letter and for what used to be called a 'doyley'. You say that the latter represents your favourite pop-singer. I should have thought that it represented a 'popess', but anyhow I am delighted with it. I have been ill, so write by Joe's hand as I said, which is certainly much better, and, being Joe's, well-expresses my emotion.

With love and I am so pleased to hear from you and will write in my own illegible hand later on. Do please write again.

                              Morgan

Dearest Jim
              I *have* neglected you rather—yet I haven't. I was thinking of you all through Sept., when I did my month with *The Listener*, and published one of the Marine poems,[1] leaving the other in galley[2] behind for Derwent May.[3] Did you ever get a copy of the one I published, 'The Sea Within'? It must have been sent to you, the issue in which it appeared, but although I thought of an address for your cheque, I never thought of an address for anything else. It was only at the end of my stint that I wondered what

---

[1] September 23.
[2] 'Bitter Peace' from the sequence *Japan Marine*. But it was never published in *The Listener*. Later, Kirkup included it in his collection of poems *Paper Windows* (1967). Cf. Letter 272.
[3] New literary editor of *The Listener* whose appointment had begun on 1 October.

addresses they had for you, and looking in the book found masses of them, but not your Osaka one. That I have now supplied. I asked Rena where she thought the cheque should go, and she named your Bank in Bath (Barclays? I forget) and I took her advice. I don't think I edited your poem very cleverly. I was in rather a tizzy for some time. I gave it the title you gave it in the sequence, and a number of people found it obscure. I should have called it 'Nagasaki', then all would have been clear as crystal. I think it a very beautiful poem and carry it always in my pocket-book, together with Edwin Muir's 'The Horses'.[1] Your *Japan Industrial*[2] came this week; I have looked at the picture but have not yet read the text, but I will in time. I hope you're making lots of yen out of it. My *Tulip* book is having good reviews in the States and has gained the alternate choice in the N[ew] Y[ork] Book of the Month Club. I hope to get some dollars out of that. We are worried about Rena. She has not been at all well—vomiting and so on—and has now stopped answering our letters. That does seem to me an anxiety. She was to have gone to Paris with Roger a couple of weeks ago but couldn't make it. He phoned us on his way through, making light of it, but that is what worried people sometimes do. Morgan was pleased with your doyley or handkerchief but thought the boy was a girl—hence his joke—not as good as the one I suggested but which he rejected 'Can it be a boyley?' I am not very well today, myself, so shall proceed no further. Morgan has improved since his last September stroke, in gait at least, but he has trouble with his speech and is very forgetful. We live too long, no doubt of it, the doctors oblige us to, though to be very old must be perfect hell.

Much love, dear Jim

    Joe

To Marjorie Redman (1907–)   Putney 293
                                            20/11/65

Dear Marjorie

          thank you for telling me. I am sorry she[3] was defeated. She had courage and a zest she was able to impart, even to me. I admired her for it, that sparkle she had, her enthusiasm, especially for music. It is wretched to think of her losing what she so much enjoyed, and in pain. Death should come only to the easy yielders.

    Yes, I enjoyed being with you again,[4] the more so as the rust wore off and I saw that I was not going to bring down shame upon you all. You and Elizabeth [Arnold][5] were so sweet to me, as ever.

    Love from

    Joe

---

[1] A. had first published this poem in *The Listener* on 10 March 1955. Muir subsequently included it in his collection *One Foot in Eden* (1956).

[2] See page 258, note 4.

[3] Joan Taylor—who had died recently of cancer. She had been secretary to two Editors during A.'s period at *The Listener*.

[4] A reference to A.'s month at *The Listener* during September.

[5] A member of *The Listener* staff.

294   To William Plomer (1903–1973)   Putney

                                                               2/12/65

D.L.B.

      how delightful for you to have stirred the heart of an Eton boy. I too seem to have moved someone lately, though more a mountain than a mouse. David Sylvester, reading, rather belatedly, my novelette[1] in Paris, burst into such uncontrollable sobs at some point that not only could he not visit the Louvre—his destination that afternoon—but he became quite concerned about his health and had to return to bed. Had he not written on both sides of the paper, I would have had his letter framed.[2] Can you compete with this? Has anyone ever given up the Louvre for you, or the ghost? Come clean; I believe I am ahead of you. The tadpole of the Common Frog (*Rana temporaria*) has 640 teeth in order to rasp the slippery food on which it feeds. They are gradually shed.[3] The adult frog also has teeth, not so many but quite a lot. *Bufo bufo* has no teeth, but the palatine bone has a sharpened edge, similarly with *Morgan morgan*. He rasped or bit me by letter on Monday, before my Tuesday visit to him: 'I had never realised that you loathed Cambridge, and your outburst gave me quite a shock. It *is* so good of you to come out to the hated city and we must see whether something else can be arranged.' What on earth was he talking about? When I saw him on Tuesday I said: 'Now explain me to myself, Morgan. How came I to speak disrespectfully of Cambridge?' 'You said it was an awful place.' 'How did I come to make such a remark, so contrary to my belief?' 'You looked out of the window and said "God, how awful it all is!" ' I said 'Do *you* ever look out of your window?' The view is an immense dirty hole in the ground and a gigantic crane poised over it. Well, we got that straight, but I felt rather vexed, the more so since I had already been bitten, by a dog (*canis familiaris*), on Saturday when I was staying with Jack in Nottingham. Of this wretched creature, a large wire-haired terrier, belonging to one of Jack's stupidest working-class friends, I had predicted disaster years ago, since it was never let off its lead and lived in a perpetual state of frantic excitement. Little did I think that I, its attempted benefactor, should be its victim. On Saturday it bit me in the hand, and by the time I got bitten again by *Morgan morgan* I was aware that beneath my elastoplast all was not well. Today I took it to the doctor and am now swallowing every six hours a large penicillin capsule. I do see that no more appropriate death than rabies could be devised for me, but I would prefer not to have it nevertheless for I believe it is painful.

      What good news, the report today on the cruelty of factory farming. Let us hope that legislation will follow. What sickening news about the seals. One is kept much in the dark, but I wondered whether these intelligent creatures would return a third time to the place once trusted, where they had twice seen their female babies 'humanely' slaughtered before their eyes. As you know, they have one pup only per year: gestation period over eleven

---

[1] *We Think the World of You.*
[2] Cf. Letter 287.
[3] A. took this fact from *British Amphibians and Reptiles* by Malcolm Smith (1951), which he had just been reading.

months. The females need come ashore therefore only once a year, when they give birth and are again fertilised by the males. This autumn only a fraction of them returned to the Farne Islands. The quota for this year's killing was 650, but only 315 could be found. These were massacred.

Joe's love

To Geoffrey Gorer (1905–   )   17 Star & Garter Mansions, Putney   295
                                                                    12/12/65

Dear G.G.
            your beautiful bottles are a great pleasure and comfort. I face a featureless Christmas, which booze alone can save, booze inducing sleep. I don't think you go in for that, the afternoon siesta, such a comfort to old geezers like myself who have no future. Though to take a wider sample, in your language, Prof. Sprott, who is endlessly busy, can't do without it either, but, having sipped gin from 12 to 1.30 and cracked a ½ bottle of claret at lunch, dozes in his armchair with pussy-cat on his knee in front of a large coal fire beneath a portrait of Lytton Strachey until tea-time. Then he comes to life, with its tiresome realities once more, and threshes about among criminological and sociological problems until 7.0, when the dear gin bottle is again brought out. So sensible; the period between lunch and tea, can it be praised? I stayed with him a fortnight ago and was bitten by a dog, a large wire-haired terrier, the property of one of his working-class menials, a repulsive youth. The irony of this incident lay in the fact that 2 or 3 years ago I had warned this repellent young man that if he never let his wild, hysterical dog off the lead it would surely bite someone at last; after this attempt to help the wretched animal it seemed a little unfair that it should bite *me*. It bit my friendly hand. Blood flowed, T.C.P. was applied and an elastoplast eventually fixed. This occurred on a Saturday. All seemed well Sunday and Monday, then on Tuesday I was appointed to Cambridge to help Forster with his letters; meanwhile *he* had bitten me too. On a previous visit I had looked out of his window—demolition and derricks—and said 'God, what a ghastly place!' Soon after I got a letter from him which said 'I had never realised that you loathed Cambridge, and your outburst gave me quite a shock. It *is* so good of you to come out to the hated city and we must see whether something else can be arranged.' This senile but intentionally stinging remark did rather rile me, but we got it straight, and it was about then that I noticed that beneath my elastoplast, all was not well with my other bite. I could do nothing about it until Thursday morning when I was back in my flat, then I removed the elastoplast and found, as I suspected, pus. I took it to my doctor at once, thinking that, after all, no more suitable death than rabies could be devised for me, and he put me on a five-day course of pencillin capsules, four per day. All is now well. The wound has healed. I give you this little amusing anecdote, not seriously, though it is true, but as a possible enlivenment to your Christmas, dear G.G., and in gratitude for your welcome bottles.

Much love to you and darling Slimima,[1] both of whom I hope will pass unbored, and unbitten by God or man, through Merry Yuletide into the happiest of New Years
Joe

296 To James H. Lawrie[2] (1907–)   17 Star & Garter Mansions, Putney,
                                         S.W.15   13/12/65
Dear Mr Lawrie
                you owe me no apology, of course; I never expected an acknowledgement of my letters. On the other hand did I ever thank you for the gracious things you said about my own ancient play?[3] It pleased me very much that it should be remembered.

I had a most agreeable session with Toby [Robertson][4] and Richard [Cottrell][5] and am glad to hear that it was thought 'helpful and constructive.' I was afraid I might be regarded as an interfering old busy-body. I should like to meet you very much if I can be of any further use to you.
Yours
J. R. Ackerley

297 To Paul Cadmus (1904–) 17 Star & Garter Mansions, Putney, S.W.15
                                                              1/1/66

Thank you, dear Paul, it was good to hear from you, and a pretty little Hiroshige[6] which I don't remember to have seen before. Health seems good, spirits no higher, and no lower, than their usual low. Xmas eve was spent with a dentist, who extracted two teeth. I rather like losing bits of myself. Did you know that the tadpole of the Common Frog has 640 teeth? It is so: consult Mr Malcolm Smith *British Amphibians and Reptiles*,[7] a fascinating book I have just been reading, far more rewarding than *The History of England* (Maurois)[8] which has also formed part of my holiday literary diet.

[1] This was a private dog joke. A. had nicknamed Gorer's black labrador bitch Onyx 'Fatima', but 'she had taken umbrage' so he altered it to 'Slimima'.
[2] Managing Director of Gleneagles Productions. In 1967 Lawrie and the Earl of Harewood presented a dramatisation of Forster's *Howards End*. Before its opening in the West End on 28 February at the New Theatre (renamed Albery in January, 1973), there was a four-week tour. See Letters 303, 311, 320, 322, 329 and 331.
[3] Lawrie writes: 'When I first met Joe Ackerley [in 1965] I thought I would begin tactfully by telling him with what pleasure I still recalled his own play *The Prisoners of War*, which I had seen as a schoolboy. He seemed quite pleased, but did not go on to talk about the play as I hoped he would. Later, I got the feeling that he felt he ought to have gone on from there to greater success as a dramatist; what I had to suffer later, sometimes, was the creative urge of a dramatist *manqué*.'
[4] See page 288, note 4.
[5] See page 288, note 4.
[6] This refers to a New Year's card that Cadmus sent A. On 16 March 1961 A. had reviewed a batch of books about Japan for *The Listener*, which included Walter Exner's study of Ando Hiroshige, the nineteenth-century Japanese artist whose coloured wood-engravings were so popular then—and still are.
[7] Cf. page 280, note 3.
[8] 1927.

What fun to think that you and Jon [Anderson] have been to India with me.[1] I am hoping that dear Mr Collier, my N[ew] Y[ork] publisher, will republish that book in time.[2] He thinks the world of me, though he sends me no cash. I don't understand about your Book of the Month Club. Ours is subscribed and guarantees a sale of perhaps 5000 copies. But yours seems different. Mr Collier says he hopes to sell of *Tulip* a minimum of 7500 copies, but does not explain whether the Book of the Month Club is included in that estimate. No doubt a flood of light will be shed in time. I am pleased by the way he put it out—hardly any printing errors, except that poor William Plomer, praising me on the dust-jacket, turned into William Polmer, but that is to be corrected when there is a second printing—and although Gladys Emerson Cook's cover drawing administered rather a shock at first sight, I have got used to it now and think it rather effective in its way.[3]

Yes, I returned to *The Listener* for the month of September to help out over some staff difficulty and rather enjoyed it when I found that my brains had not entirely decayed away after seven years in the dustbin—ash can, do you call it? And they paid me £10 per day which was worth having— far more than they ever paid me when I was on the staff. And I got everything done that I intended to do, for I went as a crusader. The previous Lit. Ed. had reviewed no animal books in all his four years[4]—he thought only people important—so I did all the animal books I could lay hands on.[5] I was also determined to get in some poems by James Kirkup who is neglected here, and that too I did.[6] I even got in a poem of my own, but that was an afterthought, not part of the crusade.[7]

Morgan is up at Bob's in Coventry and stays there until the 6th. He is wonderfully better. The head of his Cambridge hospital designed a stick for him to prevent him falling about. It is made of steel, and sprouts three legs at the bottom, a tripod. This strange contraption, which would certainly support anybody, and trip up everybody else, he regards with deep distaste

[1] They had just read *Hindoo Holiday*. In a letter dated 8 September 1952, A. had written to Donald Windham: '... I'm delighted you like my Indian book ... It was published in the States, but—I was almost about to say before your time. The Viking Press did it. Could it be 20 years ago? And indeed I made more money out of your country than my own. It has just been re-issued over here ... in a slightly enlarged edition: "unexpurgated" is the inelegant word used on the dust-cover.' See page 160, note 1.

[2] Nothing came of this. A. had sent him a copy of *Hindoo Holiday* to consider in the previous April. See Letter 275.

[3] See Letter 284.

[4] Three years in fact.

[5] These included *The World of Birds* by James Fisher and R. T. Peterson, which Desmond Morris had reviewed on 30 September 1965, and *The Wood-Pigeon* by R. K. Murton, which A. himself had reviewed on 7 October. A. also had accepted two animal poems: 'Cow' by Hugh Massingham, which had appeared on 16 September, and 'To a Wasp' by Roy Fuller, which had appeared on 25 November. A.'s claim that the previous literary editor (Anthony Thwaite) sent out no animal books for review is an exaggeration.

[6] Only one poem in fact—'The Sea Within'.

[7] A. must have had a lapse of memory, because no poem of his appeared in *The Listener*. He did, though, toy with the idea of publishing 'After the Blitz, 1941'; he had spent 'twenty-five years revising the poem, on and off', and on 16 September 1965 he sent it to Francis King for his verdict. Next he sent it to Roy Fuller. Then he reported back to King on 24 September: 'I have made two of your three suggested alterations, but to change "neat as new pins" is now quite beyond me after 25 years and an intimate friendship with the gin bottle ... Roy Fuller ... passes "neat as new pins", but looks sternly at the word ... "defect".' A. left in both 'defect' and 'neat as new pins' in the final version which was found amongst his papers after his death. It was published posthumously in *Micheldever & Other Poems* (1972). Cf. page 65, note 6.

and some apprehension (will he be sent a bill for it?) and has never used. Now, Bob tells me, he is going about quite confidently without any stick at all. The dear old boy loves life (a thing I can never understand), so may 1966 be kinder to him than 1965 was—though as he says, in defence of that year, he suffered no pain. Shall I end on this cheerful note? Not to do so will mean a third sheet. Better not risk it.

So love from
  Joe

298 To James Kirkup (1923–)   Putney
                                           1/1/66

Darling Jim
        I owe you a letter, and this seems an appropriate day for turning over a new leaf as a correspondent and writing it. I wonder where you are, having a heavenly time anyway I am sure, and I hope that this time you will manage to publish your travel notes,[1] for we are badly in want of something to read. Xmas has been ever so dull. My Duchess half-sister sent us the customary turkey and Nancy said it needn't go in the frige [*sic*], so for five days it occupied the bathroom and went secretly bad there—the liver, which Nancy had searched the bird's interior for in vain, must have been there all the time. On Xmas morning the secret was out and the bathroom unenterable. Nancy tried washing out the creature's inside with boiling water and that made the stench even worse, so we had to roast the thing at once, although we had intended to cook it on Boxing Day when we had three guests for lunch, Villiers and his friend Gérard, and a young Irish novelist friend of mine, John McGahern. The bird still smelt even after cooking, but fortunately it was only the inside that was affected, and when we had dismembered it and thrown away the undercarriage, the rest, the larger part, was quite all right. Nancy then got into an ill-humour, so we scarcely spoke to each other at all on that rejoiceful day, the birthday of Our Lord; but Boxing Day was jolly and happy. Since then the days have been indistinguishable in their monotony and the weather, of course, foul. However, the shortest day is over, so we have that small pleasure, the lengthening of light to look forward to. I have read a good deal, in a rather dull desultory way—nothing new, for there seems nothing new to read, but taking old books from my shelves at random, Hester Chapman's life of Charles II, Maurois' *History of England* (to educate myself, for I suddenly realised that I never have read a history of England in my life, not even at school), Lermontov *A Hero of Our Time*, Aksakoff *A Russian Gentleman* and *Years of Childhood*, and a book of *British Amphibians and Reptiles*. This last gave me most pleasure and I started to make notes on toads and frogs, newts, lizards and snakes, hoping that by such means I might, for a change, keep a

---

[1] These 'notes' were subsequently incorporated in Kirkup's travel books—*Bangkok* (1968), *Streets of Asia* (1969), *Hong Kong and Macao* (1970) and *Japan Behind the Fan* (1970).

little knowledge in my head. Did you know that the tapdole of the Common Frog has 640 teeth? Not as large, I expect, as yours and mine, dear Jim. They enable the creature to rasp its slippery food and they are constantly and gradually shed. Two of my own teeth were extracted on Xmas eve—I had developed a palatal abscess, and my kind dentist left his golf-course to attend to me. Painless but unpleasant; a pity we do not have teeth like the adders and snakes, who do not go in for roots and sockets, but drop their teeth when they are bored with them, replacing them with new ones which push the old ones out. I have, in short, been dreadfully bored [. . .] for company and cannot take to drink as heavily as I would like, it is so bloody expensive, nearly 50/- for a bottle of gin or whisky. Even so I spend £10 per week at least on those two drinks alone. Rena seems to be improving in her health, she rang us up at Xmas, and Morgan (up in Coventry with his friends the Buckinghams) is much stronger and better, walking now without the aid of a stick. I go on Friday to stay with Jack in Norfolk for four nights. No more now. A dull letter, but you can't make a silk purse out of a sow's ear.

Much love, sweet Jim

Joe

To Idris Parry (1916–   )   17 Star & Garter Mansions, Putney, S.W.15   299
4/1/66

Dear Parry

you sent me a Christmas card, which pleased me very much. Now I have just been reading in *The Listener* (belatedly arriving today) your Third Programme talk[1] which gives me more pleasure than anything I have read for years, it is profound thought beautifully expressed. It particularly moves and excites me because it reaches down into something— man's separation from the other animals and his guilt[2]—which my own inadequate mind has been fumbling and stumbling around for a long time and which I tried to formulate lately in an article called 'I Am a Beast' for a Japanese magazine.[3] What I was insufficiently well-equipped to express, you, from a different angle, have most brilliantly done. I hope you may get many other letters of gratitude and congratulation.

Yours sincerely

Joe Ackerley

[1] 'The Druid and the Wren', which was published on 30 December 1965. It was sub-titled 'Boxing Day Traditions', and the author subsequently included it, in a revised version, in a collection of his Essays on Art, Nature and Folk-Tale called *Animals of Silence* (1972).

[2] Here is the relevant section (taken from *The Listener* text): 'All through human development runs the story of the sacrifice and resurrection of the god-king. We are told in a legend from Pembrokeshire that the druid was the judge in legal disputes. If his verdict were questioned he called upon the wren to speak the truth. As a result, a feeling of violent revulsion against the wren grew among the people of Pembrokeshire (which suggests they must have been an uncommonly guilty lot), and so began the immemorial custom of hunting the wren at Christmas . . . The assault on truth in any case seems to be a prime human obligation, the last resort of guilty men.'

[3] *Orient/West* (March–April 1964).

300* To Alan Thomas (1896–1969)

6/1/66

—good. The 26th. I suppose you can take a bus from Victoria to Hyde Park Corner, then the No. 9 or No. 73 to the Albert Hall. 15 minutes at most. The new Royal College [of Art] (Kensington Gore its address) is cheek by jowl with the Albert Hall—the College, I fear, being the jowl, for it has a hideous, grim, grey external aspect, like Scrubwood Worms. However, every cloud is said to have a silver lining, and the Coll. silver is impressive. I will be in the entrance (which faces the Albert Hall's pink cheek) at 12.30 and pleasurably await you.

    Joe

301 To Idris Parry (1916–   )   17 Star & Garter Mansions, Putney, S.W.15

15/1/66

Dear Parry
        I am late in writing to you because I have had a little travel, six nights, the longest I have had for a year. Four were spent in Norfolk and two in Cambridge, to which my Norfolk friends drove me; I took your article with me—yes, it was 'The Druid and the Wren'.[1] My Norfolk friend, Professor Sprott, read it and said 'No wonder you wrote to Professor Parry.' I told Desmond Shawe-Taylor to read it too, and he also thanked me for drawing his attention to it: 'I think the boys did kill the wren in Co. Galway when I was young. I remember them bringing it round hanging from a stick.' So you have pleased Sociology[2] and Music.[3] I meant to read it to old Forster in Cambridge—his eyes have deteriorated—but the chance did not offer. However I go to him again in a fortnight (I do a little secretarial work for him) and will take it again then. No, I didn't read your Rumpelstiltskin article[4] (do send me a copy); it was idleness, for I noticed it in the paper, but I am not well-educated, and knowing little about Rilke and not caring much for Kafka I stupidly passed it by. Worse still perhaps, I know nothing about Günter Grass, but I have enjoyed your article. I like so much the way you write, your terse sentences that nevertheless have a rhythm. And your froggy jumps from thought to thought, You make me want to read Grass, but is he translated?[5] I am sorry to expose so much ignorance. My grasp on life has slackened in the last few years. Tell me more about yourself. Have you published anything? I ought to know. Clearly you should be writing, but

---

    [1] See Letter 299.
    [2] W. J. H. Sprott was Professor of Psychology at Nottingham University from 1960 to 1964 and subsequently Emeritus Professor. But as Professor Donald G. MacRae wrote in *The Times* on 9 September 1971, in the week of Sprott's death: '. . . it is as a sociologist that he will be remembered.'
    [3] Shawe-Taylor has been music critic to the *Sunday Times* since 1958.
    [4] 'Kafka, Rilke and Rumpelstiltskin'—a Third Programme talk subsequently published in *The Listener* on 2 December 1965. Parry included it, in a revised version, in his book *Animals of Silence* (1972).
    [5] The English translators are Ralph Manheim, Ernst Kaiser and Eithne Wilkins.

to give up a position and salary for a free-lance life was something I was too nervous to do myself—too lacking in confidence. So I stayed for 30 years, getting old, tired, grey and stale in the B.B.C., clinging to my far from generous salary. I regret it rather; it is only since I left that I have seen more of the world than Europe (America, the Far East); had I seen the Far East earlier, perhaps I would have made a different life; it seems so very short as we draw to its end. So I have no suggestions for you, until I know more, perhaps not then. I think we all do what we have to do, that is to say what is dictated by our psychologies.

I send this Japanese letter of mine, which I fear is no good.[1] I think it has something to say, but I had neither the material, nor the apparatus, for saying it. James Kirkup pushed me on to provide it, he was Lit. Ed. of *Orient/West* at that time. I enjoyed writing the first teasing part of it, and I think the Zen paras. are good—at any rate they are good Zen—but afterwards it fell off and I seemed unable to retrieve it. A bit got left out by the Japanese printers, so I have stuck it back; not that it adds anything more. I would like it back, please, it is the only copy I have.

Yours sincerely

Joe Ackerley

To Idris Parry (1916–   )   17 Star & Garter Mansions, Putney, S.W.15   302
19/1/66

Dear Parry

thank you for sending back my article,[2] and for liking it, and for the gift of yours.[3] I have wondered what Rilke[4] would have said to Zen: perhaps he knew about it? His note 'Stay at your table and listen . . .' etc. would have been acceptable to that cult, I think. The Buddhists allow *six* senses; the sixth dwells in the mind, and training makes it supreme over the other five. In his inmost soul man is good. If his impulse can be directly embodied in his deed, he acts virtuously and easily (I forget from what source I took these notes: perhaps from Ruth Benedict *The Chrysanthemum and the Sword*).[5] Therefore he undergoes, in 'expertness', self-training to eliminate the self-censorship of shame (*haji*). Only then is his sixth sense free of hindrance. This is his supreme release from self-consciousness and conflict. Zen seeks only the light man can find in himself. No hindrance to this seeking can be tolerated. Every obstacle must be cleared out of the way—Buddha, Christ, the Saints, away with them all. *Nothing at second-hand.* The twelve chapters of the Buddhist canon are a scrap of paper. Some profit may

---

[1] This 'letter' reached the proof stage for *Orient/West* but never appeared there—or anywhere. The magazine died in late 1964.

[2] A.'s Japanese 'letter'. See Letter 301.

[3] 'Kafka, Rilke and Rumpelstiltskin.' See note 4 opposite.

[4] A slip. For 'Rilke' read 'Franz Kafka', who is the author of the saying quoted in the next sentence. The passage comes from his *Notebooks*—and in full reads: 'Stay at your table and listen. Don't even listen, just wait, be completely quiet and alone. The world will offer itself to you to be unmasked. It cannot do otherwise. It will writhe before you in raptures.' See *Wedding Preparations in the Country* by Kafka, translated by Ernst Kaiser and Eithne Wilkins (1954).

[5] Correct. See Chapter 2 entitled 'Self-Discipline'.

be gained by studying them, but they have nothing to do with the lightning flash in one's own soul which is all that gives enlightenment (*satori*).[1]

I don't know why I write all this, curiosity about Rilke[2] perhaps. The Buddhist ideas interested me some years ago, and I took notes; I seldom think of them now, more interested in other things, animal literature and such small facts as that the tadpole of the Common Frog has 640 teeth.[3]

Yours sincerely

Joe Ackerley

303 To James H. Lawrie (1907–)   17 Star & Garter Mansions, Putney, S.W.15   23/3/66

Dear Mr Lawrie

thank you for your letter. Forster and I *were* wondering what had happened to the play,[4] for which a February date had been tentatively suggested for West End production, and he dictated to me a note to [Richard] Cottrell only last week to ask if any progress had been made. I am glad to hear that there have been developments, even though they have developed away from the original team. Lord Harewood[5] is an old friend of Forster's, so I expect the latter will be pleased about that. Frith Banbury[6] is no more than a name to me. It will be interesting to see what ideas he has in mind; though one rather wonders how much resemblance to the novel will remain after all these birds have had a peck at it. Admittedly it is a difficult book to stage and should perhaps never have been attempted. But will you manage to interest first-class players in it until the script has been completed? However, your news is interesting and I look forward to hearing more; I am also at your service always for any help I am able to give you.

Yours sincerely

Joe Ackerley

---

[1] Buddhists believe that a man who has been 'enlightened' is already in *nirvana* (i.e. in a state of non-being); but *nirvana* is here and now, and may be seen in a pine tree or a wild bird. See page 311, note 1.

[2] Same slip. See page 287, note 4.

[3] Cf. Letter 294.

[4] A dramatisation of *Howards End*. In the previous year. Tony Robertson who was running Prospect Productions at Cambridge, and Richard Cottrell who was a director, decided that they would like to put on an adaptation of Forster's novel. Forster agreed, but mentioned in passing that he had previously given 'some kind of rights' to Lance Sieveking who had adapted the novel for radio and subsequently prepared an expanded version for the stage. Forster was often vague about the rights he gave away and he himself had been pleased with Sieveking's adaptation for radio, which had been broadcast in thirteen instalments in the Home Service between 14 June and 6 September 1964. But Robertson and Cottrell did not care greatly for Sieveking's stage adaptation as it stood, and decided that work needed to be done on it: they also came to an agreement whereby a joint credit should be printed on the programme—'by Lance Sieveking in collaboration with Richard Cottrell'—and royalties be split between the two. This version had first been produced at the Arts Theatre, Cambridge on 20 July 1965. Lawrie liked the production, but felt a good deal had gone wrong with the adaptation—though nothing that could not be set right. He took over Prospect Productions' option with a view to presenting the play later in London.

[5] Lord Harewood came in as a partner with Lawrie.

[6] Banbury was engaged to direct the play.

To William Plomer (1903–1973)   Putney   304
                                                          4/4/66

D.L.B.

I was thinking of you and wondering how you were; you did not give a very good account of yourself in the short time I had with you at the Spender party. It is excellent news that your prospects of getting out of Rustington and nearer to the centre of things (and of our retinas) have improved; whatever advantages Rustington ever possessed, they must be hard to remember now. The shifting will be a bother, of course. Yes, accumulations are a nuisance, for one's executor too, as I remember you found with [Richard] Rumbold's chaos;[1] I have them myself, but am gradually sifting and weeding (mostly they are weeds) and destroying, so that my executor[2] may find everything neat and tidy. I have at last finished that old memoir of *My Father and Myself* (as I call it) which I began in the '30s, with you beside me in Maida Vale. It has cost me much sad thought, and has, I think, some importance as an exercise in self-analysis, but I have managed to spice the disagreeable dish so that it can be swallowed with a smile. Though not thinking of Boatswain[3] (whose epitaph I knew and cherished), I have dedicated it to Queenie,[4] who has only a page of it but to whom, in the deepest psychological justice, it belongs.

What else have I to tell you? I see Morgan constantly (I go tomorrow for a night) and we viewed the boat race together from Hammersmith; I am sitting for my portrait to an old artist, very agreeable, named Adrian Daintrey[5] (a friend of Georges Duthuit, of whom the news is sad); I am trying to find accommodation for a fortnight's holiday in Brighton for Nancy and myself as soon as possible, and there is a possibility that I may return to Japan in September to stay with J. Kirkup (who comes to England in July) if I am still alive then.

Much love to you and Charles

Joe

To Norman Caney (1909–   )   17 S. & G. Mans. 305*
                                                          18/4/66

Thank you, dear Norman, that was extravagantly kind. We hope that you and Conchie and 'Cyclops'[6] will come in and help us drink it. We enjoyed having your little apple, over-fond of trees though he is, and were quite sad

---

[1] See page 221, note 2.
[2] See page 266, note 3.
[3] Byron's Newfoundland dog. See page 307, note 1.
[4] The dedication read 'To Tulip'.
[5] Daintrey held an exhibition of paintings and drawings at the Canaletto Gallery between 29 April and 29 May 1970. The card announcing the exhibition ended: 'In addition I am showing a few works, mainly in line, of friends, among them the late Joe Ackerley.'
[6] This was A.'s name for their one-eyed pekinese, which A. and his sister looked after from time to time.

to give him up at last. Had we been asked to keep him a bit longer we would have cried 'Yes' in one voice. But his delight at finding your door again silenced all our selfish feelings.

Joe

306   To Diana Petre[1] (1912–   )   Putney
                                                                      24/4/66
Dear Di
        I'm afraid this script[2] is in rather a mess, part type, part ms. But I think it is legible. If you can manage to read it without tearing the thin paper the author would be pleased, for he is bored with the book. It is the only copy and you are the only person to have read it entire.[3]

I want you to read it because, although I don't intend to publish it,[4] I would welcome your opinion of the small part you play in it. I dislike making mistakes and since my memory is undependable may have made any number. If you find yourself anywhere in disagreement or in doubt, I wish you would make notes for me—any little thing, choice of words, as well as corrections. I could then tidy it up for my executor, who, by the way, is Francis King, 42 Montpelier Road, Brighton. I had already left him instructions to get into touch with you over this in the event of my death, but it seems more sensible to talk to you about it while I still live.* Your part is necessarily small (it may be too long as I have set it down),[5] for the whole intention of the book is only to explore our father's character (of which in the end I know too little) and my own (of which I seem now to know so much) and the failure of our relationship.[6] I don't expect you to like the book, I don't enjoy it myself, but it tries to seek the truth, which is seldom palatable, and for any help you can give me I should be grateful. I am in no sort of hurry to have it back. I don't suppose you will want to show it to anyone else; if you do, I would like to be consulted. Nancy, of course, knows nothing about it and these transactions. The notes at the back are items of memory which either I could not fit into the text, or was too tired to try to fit in; I may add to them as I go on reading and destroying such notebooks and papers as I have which refer to the past. Geoffrey Gorer (no one else) has seen Chapters 12 and 13,[7] you will find his remarks at the back together with some extra family photographs. In course of time I will phone you and we will have a talk.
Much love
        Joe

        * How different from Dad!

---

[1] A.'s half-sister.
[2] *My Father and Myself.*
[3] Later Geoffrey Gorer read the 'script' in its entirety. See page 254, note 4.
[4] Cf. page 292, note 5.
[5] She writes: 'I did not get Joe to change anything in the part about me and my sisters.'
[6] See Introduction, 3.
[7] Cf. page 254, note 4.

To Oscar Collier (1924–   )   17 Star & Garter Mansions, Putney, S.W.15   307
2/5/66
Dear Mr Collier
            Sir Charles Tennyson asked me to tea today;[1] I read into
his typescript for nearly two hours and have brought it away with me. At a
word from you it shall fly to N[ew] Y[ork]. He seems to think it a bit long,
assessing it at 50,000 words—long, that is, from your point of view; but I
don't see how it could be shorter and still do the job it set out to do. It is very
untidy—scissors and paste. As you know, it is a book for students, not for the
general reader although the short preface wistfully invites him in. Its aim is
to assist research regarding the life and work of the poet, to list all material,
in book or periodical form, of substantial biographical, interpretive, or
critical value, and to indicate by brief notes the nature of each item listed.
The items are classified under such chapter headings as 'Biographical',
'Homes and Haunts', 'Religion', 'Philosophy', 'Ethics', 'Tennyson and
Science', 'Poems not included in the Collected Edition' (these, of course, are
not quoted but merely referred to), 'Tennyson and the Reviewers', 'The
Dramas' etc. Sir Charles's notes or annotations are mostly brief, a few lines,
some are more expansive; they are always scholarly, objective and readable.
I will quote a few, taken at random. 'An entertaining record by an American
admirer who visited Tennyson several times during the last years of his life
and was much liked by him.'[2] 'Tennyson's thoughts on God, freedom and
immortality, interpreted in the light of his relation to the spirit of his age.
Very good.'[3] 'A long and violent attack in rhymed couplets on the work of
Tennyson and Browning, cleverly written and interesting in view of its
date (1869).'[4] You will see that all these are sharp and pithy. Now a longer
one on W. H. Auden's book *Tennyson: an Introduction and a Selection*, London:
Phoenix House: 1945. 'A very singular volume. The selection (266 pages)
is an interesting one, and the Introduction contains some stimulating passages, but the book is very carelessly produced. There are several elementary
mistakes of fact, and one nine-line lyric is ruined by the, no doubt accidental,
omission of the last three lines. The rather jaunty introduction contains many
highly controversial statements, one at least of which has aroused universal
condemnation.'[5]
            This may be enough to tell you what the book is like; it is simply and solely
a reference book to publications about Tennyson, with critical assessments,
mostly brief, appended to each. To a researcher into the poet's life it would
be invaluable; it could scarcely interest anyone else.

[1] On 16 March A. had written to Collier, agreeing to report on a Tennyson bibliography:
'I will do what I can for you. The trouble in my mind is that I am no student of the poet Tennyson.
Some years ago I read Sir Charles's biography of him with much interest; of the poetic *oeuvre* I
know practically nothing. Can my opinion therefore of the Bibliography be of any value? I will
ask Sir Charles what he thinks . . . He was born in 1879, but seems sprightly . . .'
[2] The admirer was W. Gordon McCabe whose 'Personal Recollections of Alfred, Lord Tennyson' were printed in the *Century Magazine* (March 1902).
[3] A reference to *The Mind of Tennyson* by Elias Hershey Sneath, which came out in 1900.
[4] The attack had appeared anonymously under the title of *The Laughter of the Muses* and was
published by Thomas Murray of Glasgow.
[5] This was Auden's statement that Tennyson 'had the finest ear of any English poet; he was
also undoubtedly the stupidest'.

Finally I understand that you have a competitor, or possibly a co-operator, in its publication: The University of Georgia[1] is interested in it and Sir Charles has promised a script. There are two keen Tennysonians, friends of his, there: John O. Edison, Franklin College of Arts and Sciences, and George O. Marshall Junr., Department of English: the address of both is Athens, Georgia. I hope this earns 100 dollars, even though it is not typed. Yours sincerely

J. R. Ackerley.

308 To David Higham (1895–   ) 17 Star & Garter Mansions, Putney, S.W.15
4/5/66

Dear David

thanks for letter. Things go with me much as usual, life like time slipping away. Obolensky[2] never answered my letter. I asked Fleet[3] if they would like me to write again and was told not to do anything more, so I have done nothing more and want nothing more done.

I have completed my Memoir[4] so far as I can, except in the matter of typing. Partly in type, partly in ms., it will have to stay, for I haven't used my typewriter for a year and more, and can't face it again. I've decided not to publish it, so there's no point in showing it about.[5] I'm giving it to my executor[6] to keep for me. No one has read it in its entirety except a half-sister,[7] whose memory I needed.

With all good wishes

Joe

309 To Lady Clark   17 Star & Garter Mansions, Putney, S.W.15
8/7/66

Jane dear

I'm afraid some muddle has occurred over our visit to you, Morgan's and mine. Unless I am mistaken (and you know I have a deaf ear), you said at the Guidottis' dinner party that you wanted me to bring Morgan down to you for August Bank Holiday for the weekend. A delightful prospect which I at once inscribed in my diary. August Bank Holiday occurs at the *end* of August, the weekend of the 26th to the 30th, but when I visited Morgan today he said you were expecting us from July 29 to August 2, the *beginning* of the month, which perhaps *ought* to be Bank Holiday and isn't. This is difficult for me. I am taking my sister away to Brighton on July 16.

---

[1] They in fact published it in 1967. Sir Charles's collaborator was Christine Fall, whose name with his appeared on the title page.

[2] American publishers of *We Think the World of You*. See page 178, note 2.

[3] American publishers of *My Dog Tulip*.

[4] *My Father and Myself*.

[5] Later A. changed his mind about 'not showing it about [and began] to think vaguely about its being published—possibly posthumously'. Cf. Letter 334.

[6] See page 266, note 3.

[7] Diana Petre. See Letter 306.

We have been *given* a charming little house there by a charming young man[1] who works in the Textile Department of the Royal College of Art, in return for care of his goldfish. He has some goldfish in a small pond in his paved garden. He is attached to these goldfish and wants them fed during his absence. Am I boring you? He is off to Russia on the 16th for 'two to three weeks', his return date unknown. If you work this out, which I don't advise, you will see that 'two to three weeks', return date unknown, from July 16 leads me into Saltwood[2] before even the 'two weeks' are up. I am not, at the moment, quite sure what I can do, but I foresee no difficulty in meeting Morgan in London on the 29th, bringing him down to you by the afternoon train you indicate, and staying with you that night. Then, the following day, I may have to return to Brighton, my sister and the goldfish. A little more light on my situation and the return date of our benefactor from Russia may be cast in course of time. I do hope I shall be able to stay with you longer than one night.

Love from
    Joe

To Richard Murphy (1927–)   17 Star & Garter Mansions, Putney, 310
                                S.W.15   9/7/66

Dear Richard

I owe you a letter—high time it was written—to thank you for your hospitality and kindness to me. My restful stay with you in your beautiful landscape did me a lot of good and I enjoyed seeing you against your own poetic background.[3] It's a nuisance to be so deaf, but at any rate I heard Owen all right and took a very warm feeling towards him when he talked to me on that last day. An admirable boy, solid and serious; I hope he may be happy in his marriage. Your little hotel in Galway was very pleasant and Miss Woodham-Smith occupied my thought. What a book![4] What a story! I wish I had read it before I came; I might have regarded your tinkers with more sympathetic eyes. However, I did give them a couple of bob—whatever motive you may ascribe to that.[5] Miss W-S's book has shocked and horrified me more than any book I've read since [the] Hammonds' *The Village Labourer*[6] (about the same period), and unless it can be believed that mankind has improved in the last hundred years, which history and the events in my own life-time seem hardly to confirm, Father [Michael] Foley's hope of universal brotherhood wears a somewhat sickly look. I didn't leave behind the notes I was making on his typescript, they

---

[1] John Drummond.
[2] Saltwood Castle, Hythe, the home of Lord and Lady Clark.
[3] Cleggan, County Galway.
[4] *The Great Famine* by Cecil Woodham-Smith (1962).
[5] Murphy writes: 'He gave them 2/6 the morning they came to the house to say they were leaving. They had disturbed him annoyingly in the garden, pretending they wanted to cut the grass wherever he placed his deck-chair.'
[6] Cf. page 59, notes 3 and 4.

weren't very good. Between his thought (Christianity and salvation) and mine (unbelief and 'out of death lead no ways')[1] there is no meeting place, except in self-examination, and when he is on to that, looking himself in the face as squarely as he can with one eye still on God, he is very good indeed, respectable. Had he been even more candid about himself than he has been, his book, which I often found interesting, would have gained in strength, and he himself might have gained a larger measure of relief and release.[2] Please give him my most cordial greetings if you see him. A man trying to be honest in a world of liars.

I hope all goes well with your various plots and plans and that your beautiful new mansion is now wearing its fine green cap.[3] Nancy and I go to Brighton on the 16th for two or three weeks. We have been given a charming little house there by a friend of mine in the Royal College of Art during his absence abroad, and since there are a number of people there and there-abouts whom I know it should be a pleasant holiday.
Much love
    Joe

311 To James H. Lawrie (1907–)   17 Star & Garter Mansions, Putney,
                                       S.W.15   13/7/66
Dear Lawrie
        I'm sorry to say I don't agree with you about this final version of *Howards End*. It doesn't seem to me anything like as interesting as the Cambridge version.[4] More producible it may well be, but whatever its small gains, it has lost in character—and, of course, got further than ever from the novel.

Major points first:

1. The scene in the Basts' house is *badly* missed, indeed I don't think the play hangs without it: Helen's mimicry of Jacky falls flat; the talk about incomes that follows is too dull and academic unless we have had our introduction to the interior of Leonard's home life; and Mr Wilcox's consternation at Oniton over some 'mysterious' woman is quite enigmatic when the woman has never been seen.

2. I am still very uneasy about the Jacky disclosures—her long speech in particular (11–1–8) after her display of caution. Drunk though she may be, I doubt whether she would complete that speech from, at *most*, 'It's all forgiven and forgotten now,' confronted by Margaret's grave face, for Margaret is receiving a profound shock. In any case, even if we disagree,

---

[1] This line comes from Thomas Lovell Beddoes' poem 'Dream-Pedlary'. In the following year when A. came to write an obituary article on Forster, he attributed the line direct to Forster. Robert Buckingham wrote to Braybrooke on 1 March 1973: 'I never actually heard Morgan quote [the Beddoes line], but it would certainly fit his attitude towards religion and death.'

[2] Father Foley was dying of cancer when Murphy introduced him to A. and showed him the manuscript of his autobiography. After the priest's death, the book, which he had wanted to be published and willed to his brother with this intention, never appeared.

[3] Murphy writes: 'With antiphonal irony, other friends describe this house as a cottage.'

[4] See page 288, note 4.

do the details of that speech matter—Cyprus, and the house on the harbour, and the currant farm? They contribute nothing and seem to me quite bizarre. Should not Henry himself, when he enters, supply to Margaret's questions whatever else we need to know? What we do need to know, which has slipped out of the dialogue, is that the Jacky affair happened in Mrs Wilcox's lifetime. *Margaret*: 'Poor Mrs Wilcox!' This connects with her long speech (11.2–28): 'A man who insults his wife when she's alive . . .'

3. The death of Leonard seems to me not only feeble but almost ridiculous. Are you asking us to believe that Charles, having struck a single blow with his fist in self-defence (Leonard having been the aggressor, ll. 2–34), is sent to gaol because the blow happened to be fatal? Charles is a shit, Forster dearly hates him as he hated Gerald in *The Longest Journey*, he must *deserve* his punishment, he must be armed (the gardener's spade will do), and Leonard should not attack him first, I think. Even so, I confess to preferring the old version with the sword and Miss Avery's 'Aye, murder's enough!' It was more *interesting*, however difficult to produce. Curious, though profitless, speculation: how did Charles defend his action at the inquest? how did he explain Leonard? Not, I suppose, as Helen's seducer. As a man with a grudge against his father? Or just as a trespassing prowler? And what did the ladies say?

4. I suppose this is not a major point, but how sadly has Miss Avery diminished. I think of her as a rather grand, sibylline, dignified, forthright old woman, formidable in her outspokenness and calling Wilcox 'Henry', and Charles 'Charles'. Now, at any rate in the office scene, she has become a sort of crackpot, unnecessarily rude to everyone, and over-loquacious (ants and ant heaps). I think of her as sparing of speech and dry in humour.

Those are my main objections. I won't bother you with detail, though I think some of the dialogue needs tightening up. The opening to Act 1, Scene 2 is particularly flabby and a bit muddling to anyone who knows the story; with all the talk about Howards End between Charles, Paul and Dolly I thought at first that the cat (Mrs W.'s dying request) must already be out of the bag. Would it not be better if we understood *at once* that they had gathered to hear about Mrs W.'s will? Conversation could then pass on to queries about the fate of H[owards] E[nd]. As it is the house alone, which they all dislike, seems, for some reason, to be bothering them. And why is conversation about it hush-hush? See Charles' third remark 1–2–16? I couldn't make that out. It is quite calmly discussed by Henry when he brings it up. And would Paul be likely to say to his brother 'Why can't you and Dolly live there?' knowing that they have just bought and moved into a new and expensive house? Talking without thinking! It occurs elsewhere in the text.

Well, enough of this carping, as it may seem to you. The loss of the Basts-at-home scene seems to me the most serious matter. The other main objections are where objections have always lain: Oniton and Leonard's death. If Charles seizes a spade and savagely (he *is* a savage) smacks Leonard down

with it, that scene would be improved. Could he not still say 'I shall thrash you within an inch of your life'?[1] Such a typical remark, and a pleasure to Forster-fans filling the stalls. The rest of the play runs along all right.[2] On Friday I go to Brighton for 2–3 weeks. 92 Montpelier Road if you want to write me there. Tel. Brighton 28601. If you want to come to lunch, come.
Yours sincerely
    Joe Ackerley

312 To Geoffrey Gorer (1905–)   Putney
                                                        26/8/66

Dear G.G.
         I am glad you are taking the bull so valiantly by the horns—I refer not so much to Onyx[3] as to Life. I hope I would do so too, but until one has had the severe shock you have suffered, one can't tell how one would behave.[4] I know not what has happened to poor old Morgan—not another stroke, it is thought—but senility has crept upon him in the last month. It is not just that his faculties have deteriorated, especially his sight, but his behaviour has become so odd. Shuffling round the suburban Coventry streets with his stick, he makes, upon the side pavements, the most elaborate withdrawal from the path of anyone approaching, as though sufficient room could never be sufficient, moving sideways like a crab with outstretched arms, as if clearing space in a crowd where space is plentiful and no crowd exists, mopping and mowing like a clown with a gentle smile on his face. People must think him very peculiar. I suppose this is the end result of that consideration for humanity upon which you too have employed your life and which I, thinking the animals more interesting and even worthier, am unable to share. I am more likely to elbow people out of the way to make room for a hyena. But it must be added that, though dim, he is charming, it is a pleasure to sit quietly with him in his silences; the Buckinghams, his guardian angels, with whom he must stay until Christmas at least, for he has nowhere else to go, King's College being uninhabitable, would rattle me with their [. . .] disputations if they do not rattle him, and he gave me a hundred pounds before I left.
    How good you are about my book.[5] I am so deeply grateful for all the trouble you take, and indeed quite puffed up by your praise, for there can be

---

[1] In the novel the line reads: 'I now thrash you within an inch of your life.' See note 2 below.

[2] The dramatised version of *Howards End* that A. read this month was by no means the final one. Several of his criticisms made in this letter—such as his point that the scene in the Basts' home should be restored—were carried out. Some of his ideas, though, were considered rather old-fashioned. No one connected with the production of the play thought that Charles Wilcox would get away with the Forster line 'I now thrash you within an inch of your life', without causing laughter in the theatre—and at a moment when laughter could be ill afforded. In its place, this line was substituted: 'And as for you, you sneaking little upstart, you're going to get what you deserve.'

[3] Gorer's black labrador bitch.

[4] Gorer writes: 'I was a semi-invalid, recovering from a quite severe coronary and was unable to take my dog for her accustomed walks. J.A. would come down and see me and give Onyx a good run—but after about half a mile she would turn and run back, arriving nearly an hour before J.A.'

[5] *My Father and Myself.*

few critics harder to please than you with your sharp discerning eye. I will follow all your advice, girding up my loins, when I meet the object again. By the way, should I show it to David Higham?[1] For years now he has been enquiring about it, I have told him bluntly that it isn't for sale but his curiosity continues unabated. He just wants to read it, he says.

I *don't* make too many excuses for Onyx, only one, she wanted me to take her home. Her 'reason' was probably, not certainly, the reason you give: she wanted to return to her beloved master. Admirable girl, she adores you. To dub her 'ungrateful' is absurd, unless you believe that dogs say to themselves 'I suppose it's awfully kind of this man Ackerley to take me for a walk for which I haven't the smallest inclination; perhaps I ought to caper about and pretend to enjoy it just to please him.' No. She would not have had 'a really good race around' with *me* and been 'a different girl after', her disconsolate mind was elsewhere, and I should have granted her request. Had she been a human being who had said 'I wish I hadn't left the wife alone at home, it worries me,' I would have said 'Let's go back.'

Does a poor semi-invalid like long letters, or do they fret him? For I can easily continue my dissertation on doggery, and I can easily stop. Lacking a sure answer to that question also, let us continue. We frequently take a little bitch here for walks. How joyfully does she fly out of her shop with us! She loves us, and our walks, including swims for her in the river, are the most exciting she ever gets. But if we meet her out with her fat inactive mistress who may say 'Would you like to take Maggie with you?' the dog won't leave her side. Should I force her, 'for her own good'? You think yes and that she should be 'grateful'. But I give her a kiss for renouncing a pleasure for the sake of her mistress. Perhaps the difference between us is that you prefer obedience to character. You can't have both. I say! How vexed you are getting at my blythe [*sic*] assertions! I can see you beginning to munch your anthropological jaws. Shall I go on and risk a slap? I was going to tell you about Queenie's wilful character and how she once taught me a lesson by vomiting on the floor of the No. 30 Bus Depot to which I had irritably forced her against her clearly stated wishes to go no further. But I too had better go no further except to subscribe myself

Yours with love

Joe

To Lady Clark   17 Star & Garter Mansions, Putney, S.W.15   313
                                                                      3/9/66

My dear Jane

      if this is a bread-and-butter letter I am late in writing it, partly because I have been Cherry Orcharding in Chichester (rather good),[2] partly because I have been appointed tutor to Villiers' young German-Swiss friend who believed that Wordsworth and Good Queen Bess were

---

[1] A.'s literary agent.
[2] *The Cherry Orchard* was one of the plays in the Chichester Festival Theatre season of 1966. The producer was Lindsay Anderson.

contemporaries, and partly because I found some difficulty in telling you how much I enjoyed my visit to Saltwood when you yourself were so little upon its blissful scene. Indeed, dear Jane, your sharp and sudden illness left the delightful domestic scene sadly incomplete, but what remained of it, K., Collette, and Emma, was wonderfully consoling. You will be wholly recovered now, I trust, standing firmly upon your feet and looking prettier than ever in your new perm, which I hope to see at the Rembrandt party if only I can remember the date.

This morning I have a very muddled letter from dear old Morgan who seems to have changed his plan and is to return to Cambridge on the 10th, though whether he will be able to use his own rooms I know not. He says that as soon as he has established himself and found a place for me he will send for me.

Much love to you and K.

Joe

314 To Geoffrey Gorer (1905–   )   17 Star & Garter Mansions, Putney
4/9/66

Dear G.G.

the imperfectly progressive progress of your return to health, as reported in your last letter, displeased me, as I would have said earlier, had I not been diverted to other engagements, pleasurable all. Perhaps you had overtired yourself to please dear Fatima,[1] and although I believe high moral marks are gained by laying down one's life for one's friend or country—well, finding myself in some doubt I won't finish the sentence. I hope there have been no more set-backs and that absolute self-confidence has been restored.

I spent the bank holiday weekend in Saltwood Castle, which is an earthly paradise, for if the weather drives one indoors from the beautiful grounds and woods, one enters a sort of Aladdin's cave, packed with treasures. Nothing can seriously spoil one's pleasure, although Jane Clark was almost instantly struck down by 'flu and vanished from the domestic scene, the [——— ———]s were invited to lunch in the mistaken belief that they were interesting, and Kenneth is engaged in gassing his moles, which naturally lowered him in my estimation. Since then I have been to Chichester to see a play,[2] and have been appointed tutor to Villiers David's young German Swiss friend who was discovered to be harbouring the belief that Wordsworth and Good Queen Bess were contemporaries.

I have a book of yours[3]—Hubert Selby jun.—which I must soon return, by your recorded delivery. Some of it is very good, I think, the first short story in particular which enables him to use his taut laconic style without

---

[1] Gorer's bitch. See page 282, note 1.
[2] *The Cherry Orchard*. See Letter 313.
[3] *Last Exit to Brooklyn* (1966). In the following year, in November, the novel was found to be obscene by a jury at the Old Bailey—a verdict which was later reversed by an Appeal Court judgment in July 1968.

wastage and to bring the violent story starkly out. But it is difficult to describe monotony without becoming monotonous oneself; there is a feeling of slackness in the more elaborate pieces, and of sentimentality. The mixture of semen, vaseline and poetry is a bit sticky. 'Strike' is surely two stories rolled into one and doesn't come out as it should with Harry getting fired. He is beaten up instead for his homosexuality, which is the second story. Nevertheless I enjoyed reading it, it fits in with my own ideas about human psychology; perhaps that is why I found it slightly boring, like one's image in a mirror. What particularly struck me in the book was not Selby's own writing, but his first quotation from Ecclesiastes, which I didn't know: 'For that which befalleth the sons of men befalleth beasts; even one thing befalleth them: as the one dieth, so dieth the other; yea, they have all one breath; so that a man hath no preeminence above a beast: for all is vanity.'[1] As soon as I read this I knew it was fundamental in my own thought, therefore to me profound—though Morgan, when I quoted it to him, did not think it profound at all. Selby's use of it puzzled me; is he pitying people or reducing them, so to speak, to the level of the beasts? Even so, it doesn't seem to me to work, for his book is all about cruelty, hatred, and violence which animals don't know, they are human characteristics only. Even violence, we are told by [George B.] Schaller,[2] Konrad Lorenz and others, is avoided by the animals within their own species.

How ghastly is the world, my dear G.G., I can hardly read a paper without feeling sick; biology has nearly banished frogs from Britain, says Professor Pringle (*The Times*), they are all disappearing into laboratories, and the monkeys, according to *Oryx*[3] (and Mr Schaller), are going the same way. The U.S.A. alone, the most insatiable experimentalists, imported 115,000 to 223,000 monkeys annually between 1958 and 1964, and 'for every monkey that arrives alive it is estimated that two die in capture or transport.' And all this to keep Mr Selby's charming characters in health. And Professor Steel tells us that by the end of the century the human population of the world will be doubled. And Sir Joseph Hutchinson in the current *Listener*,[4] in his presidential address[5] to the B[ritish] A[ssociation], says 'For make no mistake, the country already carries a population as great as the environment can support without degeneration, and it will call for all the knowledge and skill it can command to prevent irreparable damage before we achieve a stable population, *even if we set about sterilization without delay*' (my italics). 'Our greatest need is to master the threat of our own numbers.' He wants birth control, and he won't get it, nor does he seem to think that he will, at any rate not in time. What is the answer to all this, my dear G.G.? You will say that it doesn't concern us, we shall be dead. It concerns me, however; firmly seated upon Ecclesiastes, it concerns me. Your myxomatosis for birds, or the addition of any other animal to the list of pests, can be only

[1] Ecclesiastes III, 19.
[2] Author of *The Mountain Gorilla* (1963) and *The Year of the Gorilla* (1965).
[3] Journal of the Fauna Preservation Society. See 'Monkeys and Medical Research' (August 1966). Cf. page 312, note 3.
[4] September 1.
[5] 'Land and Human Populations.'

a short-term solution. I have no animus against the human race, I simply want it painlessly but drastically reduced, for I don't believe it will ever reduce itself. I don't want a nuclear war, it would destroy the animals and our treasures, which I wish to preserve. I want a beautiful plague, a human scourge, which would take off in a jiffy three-quarters at least of the entire population. I'm sorry that plagues have no discrimination; I would follow you sadly to the grave as perhaps you would sadly follow me, but I can see no other solution to a doubled population (already doomed) at the end of the century and the animals all gone.

This is just another little chat from Auntie Josephine to a poor semi-invalid to cheer him up.

Love to you and Onyx—or should it be Onyx and you?

Joe

315 To Geoffrey Gorer (1905–)   Putney
18/9/66

Dear G.G.

I think I am becoming a bore; I will try to be brief. First of all my hope of myxomatosis for people is far from original, it was offered in September 1959 by Dr Harrison Matthews in his presidential address to the B[ritish] A[ssociation] (I have collected cuttings for many years) as one of three alternatives 'for avoiding an extremely unpleasant crash' (population increase). 'First, do nothing,' he said, 'and wait for the stress syndrome of some new virus like that of myxomatosis to do its work.' Now, seven years later, we have this year's presidential address from Sir Joseph Hutchinson,[1] an agriculturalist (you should read it, I will send it if you like), another Cassandra voice, advocating birth control and suggesting that even if instantly practised it may be too late. So if you regard me as a crank, there are others, I am in company. When I say that it would be a good thing if the human race were 'swept away' I don't necessarily advocate total extinction. I don't mind, but I agree with you that it would be a pity if there was no observer of the results. Myxomatosis has not killed off all the rabbits, I see a few about in all my journeyings, to you, Jack, Morgan, and especially in Norfolk. So, if you like, we will leave a few people alive, though it is danger-ous, as in Morgan's last story (unpublished),[2] in which, after the Third World War, such few people as remained could only produce female child-ren; then they managed to beget males 'and the fourth world war began.' My difficulty is in understanding what is in *your* mind; you are ready enough to pull *my* knitting to pieces, but provide none of your own, the only sock is a sock in the jaw! Perhaps you are quite uninterested, excepting, as a farmer with a kitchen garden, in the elimination of birds. Also, as a soci-ologist, I see that the human race is important to you, as to Jack: what would

---

[1] See Letter 314.

[2] This story was never quite finished. It was called 'Little Imber' and written in November 1961. 'Joe has helped me to get "Little Imber" right, or rather less wrong,' Forster noted at the time. It is to be published in a volume of Forster's 'incomplete fiction' now in preparation, edited by Oliver Stallybrass.

you both do without it? Yet it seems necessary, indeed interesting, to take a wider view. 'Psychoanalysis in the world can make the world a less unhappy place; but this is not going to happen quickly.'[1] No, it isn't, nor is birth control, nor is Lorenzo's[2] hope 'that natural selection will favour the emergence of a new type of man with greater inhibitions on his aggression than we possess'. What does seem to be about to happen pretty quickly is a doubled population, and a trebled one, and so on. And what you don't do for me, dear G.G., is that little bit of knitting which will answer my question: What do you feel about that?

I agree with you that it would be sad not to survive the sudden extinction of the human race, now, at once, and see how the animals would re-organise themselves in a world free from human domination. I suppose most of the domestic creatures would die for want of human attention. I wonder what the dear old dogs would do with no people to attach themselves to. Many would also die, no doubt, of grief or hunger; others would run wild and, with the cats, who would mind less, eat up the rats, of which, as you say, there are too many, and the lambs or whatever else offered. And perhaps the higher apes, of whose conduct you so strongly approve, would evolve in time another super-ape, a Kingly creature, happier and less aggressive than ourselves. 'Happy'—how important that word is! As you suggest, it is our unhappiness that makes us so unworthy and disgraceful. My last piece of knitting!
Love from
    Joe

To Geoffrey Gorer (1905–)   Putney 316
                                                   2/10/66

Dear G.G.
            I will endeavour to put myself with you the weekend after this, Fri., Sat. or Sunday according to the behaviour of our climate. I enjoyed seeing you this evening but sorry you felt a tiredness you did not exhibit; perhaps it was fortunate that I was a few minutes too late in securing those seats for the Whitehall Theatre yesterday. They would have meant for you a tiresome rush. Get on with your article on murderous humanity[3] and pull no punches. I shall be glad to see it, if I may, when I call . . . I meant to tell you that I have lately been asked by some do-gooder to add my opinion to those of many others—a highly distinguished group from which, incomprehensibly, you seem missing—as to what I think, in a para., about the war in Vietnam. It is a little sample or survey for publication.[4] Following [Konrad] Lorenz, and you?, I said that my chief sympathy lay with the animals, wild

---

[1] This was a quotation from Gorer's essay 'Psychoanalysis in the World', which had appeared in *Psychoanalysis Observed*, edited by Charles Rycroft (1966).
[2] i.e. Konrad Lorenz.
[3] 'The Joy of Killing'. See page 302, note 3.
[4] The survey came out in 1967 under the title of *Authors Take Sides on Vietnam*, edited by Cecil Woolf and John Bagguley, and published by Peter Owen. It includes the views of over 250 writers from some thirty countries—and A. ended his contribution: 'I believe with Dr Konrad Lorenz that we have not yet learned how to curb the intraspecific instinct for aggression which many other

or otherwise, whose more ordered and peaceable lives were being so in-
convenienced or destroyed by all the stupid activities of the human race
with their bombings and poisonings of the forests and countryside.
Love from
  Joe

317 To Geoffrey Gorer (1905–)   Putney
                                                             ?/10/66
Dear G.G.

         so pleased to see [John] Weightman's review in *The Observer*.[1]
Perhaps because, in the past, he has written pleasing things about me, I have
a regard for him as a serious critic, and though he may not have the re-
quisite knowledge for assessing *you*, I knew at once that he would be appreciative and intelligent, which I think he was.[2] Were you pleased with it, I
wonder; it seemed to me a most *interesting* review, and to interest the public
is the important thing.

    What convenient topical publicity you have got for your 'Joy of Killing'
article[3] in the behaviour of Robert E. Smith. I half suspect you of having

---

animals know how to control in order to save their own species from destruction. Hopeless therefore
of permanent solutions to uninhibited human aggression, my pity in the Vietnamese war turns
first to the inconvenience, worry, fear, pain and death caused to the lower beasts in their peaceful
pursuits by all the savage and stupid bombing and chemical poisoning of the country in which
they try to live.' On 25 April 1966 a full-page advertisement had appeared in *The Times* in which
a number of eminent Labour supporters dissociated themselves from President Lyndon B. Johnson's Vietnam policies. (The President had said on 2 April that he regarded the Labour election
victory as an endorsement by the British electorate of his Vietnam policies.) A.'s name headed the
list of signatories, and it was as a result of seeing this 'public advertised reminder' of A.'s concern
about Vietnam that Woolf decided to approach him for his views. Later, when acknowledging A.'s
statement on Vietnam, Woolf added a postscript to his letter: 'I cannot refrain from telling you
how very much I enjoyed your *Hindoo Holiday*. I read it first after coming across a reference to it in
Norman Douglas (*Late Harvest*, I think) and not one of the literally dozens of friends and acquain-
tances to whom, over the years, I have presented copies has ever failed to enthuse about it. Forgive
this uncharacteristic outburst, but, after all, there are not so many modern books worth re-reading.'
Cf. page 25, note 1.

    [1] This was of Gorer's *The Danger of Equality*, a collection of essays, drawn from over 18 years.
The review had appeared on 13 November. Cf. note 2 below and page 308, note 1.
    [2] '. . . [Mr Gorer] maintains the contemplative stance, and is content to give a clear and witty
account of changing contemporary assumptions, in their relationship to those of the past or of
different, and often primitive, societies. On adolescents, the over-sixties, the changing role of
grandparents, the Kinsey Reports, the significance of the Sade cult, etc., he writes with unfailing
penetration and human sympathy . . .'
    [3] On 6 December A. wrote to May Buckingham: 'At the invitation of the *New York Times*,
Geoffrey has written an article on "The Joy of Killing", the subject they proposed. As you know, the
Americans, what with Kennedy's assassination, the Vietnam war, and three recent mass murders,
are somewhat self-conscious on the subject. While agreeing, in a learned anthropological article,
that people *do* enjoy killing each other, he sees a glimmer of future hope in the Top of the Pops.'
The article appeared on 27 November, under the title 'Man Has No "Killer" Instinct', and ended:
'Even idiotic slogans such as "Make love, not war" (as if the two activities had ever been incom-
patible!) and the use of drugs make the same point. Mankind is safer when men seek pleasure than
when they seek the power and the glory. If the members of the youth international—the beats and
the swingers, the *provos* and the *stilyagi*—maintain the same scale of values and the same sex ideals
20 years hence when they themselves are middle-aged and parents, then they may, just possibly,
have produced a permanent change in the value systems and sex roles of their societies, which
will turn the joy of killing into an unhappy episode of man's historic past, analogous to human
sacrifice, which ascribed joy in killing to the gods also . . . It is just possible that the youth international, with its emphasis on shared sensual pleasure and its repudiation of the ideal of truculent
"manliness", may succeed where the grandiose schemes of idealists have always failed. For man
has no "killer instinct"; he merely lacks inhibitions.'

somehow turned him on. Such a handsome boy, too; he is pictured in the picture papers. Has any research been done on the correspondence between beauty and callousness? So many of the most ruthless people seem such good-lookers.

I remember you saying some time ago that the mass murders would breed more mass murders. How right you were. So interesting that the human race is getting such a bad name—to which you have added, so to speak; I should say, which you have added up.

I enjoyed my day with you and Onyx, and, if Morgan may be called a bull, I have followed your advice and taken him by the horn. A letter asking him if he could settle me in a solid way as he has settled Bob. It might have been better to say it personally, but he seems to get on without me now and I had no expectation of being asked down again: he would have to buy a bottle of gin. I fear that somehow I have fallen from grace, and hardly expect a generous reply. But it was a straightforward dignified letter and 40 years of friendship bind us, so we will see.[1] I am glad to have got it off my chest, even if it goes into the wastepaper basket.
Much love, dear G.G.
    Joe

To Donald Windham (1920–)   17 Star & Garter Mansions, Putney, 318
                               S.W.15   5/11/66

Dear Don
            sweet of you to remember [my birthday], and to write. I am now a septuagenarian. I never expected to be that. My father and *his* father broke loose in their middle sixties, and five years ago when I was with you all Gerald Heard, to comfort me, said 'I expect you'll be dead next year.' But here I still am. Two of my friends here, William Plomer and Jack Sprott, put their heads together . . . and said 'We want to give you a birthday party. Invite all your friends.' I said 'Yes, on my 80th birthday you may do that. On this occasion take me out, just the two of you my oldest friends, and Morgan also if he can come.' Morgan couldn't come, so we had our small party, Jack's sister and my sister added, in a London fish restaurant. In the same week Edmund Blunden reached 70, and a party was arranged for him too, including William Plomer. Blunden acquiesced in the large celebration I shrank from, 300 guests were invited, and on the very morning of the party he fell downstairs and broke something or other and went to hospital instead, so speeches at the party had to be made to an empty chair. I'm not sure what the moral of this story is. Ask dear Paul [Cadmus]. Fancy having supper

---

[1] In the next month A. wrote to Gorer: 'Dear Morgan has sent me £1000, with a charming letter to say that it was "both easy and pleasant" to send and that he wonders if I am in his will and must look. I know from him already that I am *not* in his will, except for £100 . . .' But A.'s memory was at fault—and his sister writes: 'Morgan left Joe £500 in his will, and the cheque was sent to me by mistake and naturally had to be returned . . .' See Introduction, 4.

with him! At the very mention of his name my ancient heart gave a little thump.

I had no idea you'd changed address. It shows how slack I am, or you are. I hope it is fun and that you are concocting something jolly in it. No *horrors*, please; life and Mr Hubert Selby junr. suffice.[1] I have finished my Memoir,[2] excepting for some dirty little notes for an appendix,[3] in itself a dirty little thing and a useless one. It is ever so sad, but rises above itself in a cackle of laughter. That is the way to look at life, I believe. Geoffrey Gorer gives it high marks; to get high marks from him is even more difficult than to get them from the angel Gabriel. I have a bit of autobiography coming out in *Encounter* some time or other, but nothing to do with my Memoir. It is called 'Robbing the Mail'.[4] It is terribly wicked, but I think quite amusing and may make you laugh. Ah to laugh, and to laugh at ourselves, if only we can do that!

Morgan is well, I believe—I haven't seen him for a month—very much himself, but getting rather senile, poor darling. We drift apart a little, I fear. I hardly dare look at a robin, he prefers to talk about human cock-stands. The other day, in Coventry, I was watching from my window the black-birds and thrushes picking the rowan-berries from a tree in the garden. Their dexterity pleased me, the red berries were visible for a moment in their beaks, then swallowed. I mentioned this to Morgan. He said, 'Yes, aren't they a nuisance.' 'What is a nuisance?' I asked. 'I like to see the berries on the tree.'[5] Well, here is another question or a moral. Ask darling Paul. He under-stands everything.

Love to you and Sandy

Joe

319 To William Plomer (1903–1973)   Putney
                                                          6/11/66

Darling William

    I keep thinking of that dinner you and Jack stood me, and the magnificent cheque you sent me, which I had barely time to thank you for. I was so touched by everything. Seldom can a septuagenarian have entered that decade more happy than I, to be fêted by my two oldest and dearest friends. I'm so glad you are comfortably settled in your new house, which one day I must see. Charles' story delighted me. I expect you are practically vegetarians now; as Bridgit [*sic*] Brophy so often says, it is the only way. I would like to return to that diet too, but Nancy, who used to preach it thirty years ago and even fed Queenie on prunes and ground-nuts, has become a carnivore again. Perhaps she thinks that meat is good for me.

[1] Author of *Last Exit to Brooklyn*. See Letter 314.
[2] *My Father and Myself*.
[3] See page 254, note 4.
[4] The article never appeared—though A. received a fee of £50 for it. Goronwy Rees wrote to Braybrooke on 10 November 1972: '. . . the difficulty was that "Robbing the Mail" was precisely about robbing the mail, and the editors were uneasy . . .'
[5] See Letter 319 in which A. retells this story of the blackbirds—but, characteristically, 'a little improved on the way'. Cf. Introduction, 2.

But I keep thinking of the death of the animals, in such vast quantities, to keep the human race going (humanely killed, we are assured, but of that we know and prefer to know nothing), and feel sick. We have a joint of lamb this evening. Charles is so right about the pheasants, but it is difficult to live up to, difficult even to be a vegetarian, without being a bother. In contrast to his story I went to buy some fish for supper last month. A woman and her small boy, about 5, were being served when I reached the shop. She wanted an eel. I hadn't noticed then that a placard outside the shop advertised 'live eels'. Two eels were brought by the fishmonger to be weighed. They were large, handsome creatures, a couple of feet long, and they didn't like what was happening to them in the least. In their efforts to escape they kept squirming off the scales and falling back into their bucket or onto the floor. Eventually they were weighed, the larger of the two was chosen and taken to the back of the shop. Then the child said: 'Can I see it killed, mummy?' She said: 'Yes' and they went to watch. Chop, chop and the eel was dead. The child then said: 'May I see the other one killed too, mummy?' And the fishmonger, who had been joking throughout, said: 'Not today, sonny, he might bite me.' What does Charles think of a story like this? I think the child was wrong to want to see the rejected eel killed, but was he wrong to want to see killed the one they were going to eat? Life constantly presents these problems. Morgan provided one the other day.[1] There is a rowan tree in Bob's front garden in Coventry, and when I was last there I was watching, with interest and pleasure, the blackbirds and thrushes eating the berries. They would pluck one, hold it visibly for a moment, like a coral bead, in their beaks, then swallow it at a gulp. I mentioned this to Morgan. He said: 'Yes, aren't they a nuisance.' Astonished I said: 'Why a nuisance?' He said: 'I like to see the berries on the tree.' I still think that selfishness could hardly go farther; the birds are in trouble enough for eating *our* food without being reproached for eating their own; yet many people would agree with Morgan in objecting to the spoliation of a pretty view, and many people—Bob, for instance—would kill for food with their own hands if no one else did it for them.

Much love to you both

  Joe

To James H. Lawrie (1907–)   17 Star & Garter Mansions, Putney, 320
                                    S.W.15   1/12/66

Dear Lawrie

      thanks for yours. I'm glad the play [of *Howards End*] is building up so satisfactorily. I shall see it in Wimbledon, our most convenient theatre[2] and one I much like visiting.

---

[1] Cf. Letter 318.
[2] In the end A. decided to see it with Forster at the Golders Green Hippodrome on 25 February 1967. See Letters 322 and 329.

I suppose you have thought of Beatrix Lehmann for Miss Avery?[1] Perhaps the part is too small for her, though she always seems accommodating. Perhaps she is already engaged. She admires Forster greatly and has often met him. If you have made the part more like the Miss Avery of the novel, something of a witch, terse, dignified, formidable, I see her in it. Only a thought, don't bother to answer.
Yours
Joe Ackerley

321 To William Plomer (1903–1973)   Putney
                                                                       7/12/66
D.L.B.
          yes, I saw the bird news. Some years ago when Morgan was asking me 'What shall I do with my money?' I said 'Give it to the animals,' but this of course did not suit him. Now I am saying 'Give it to me.' This suits him better.

I have a gull protégé (or protégée) named Dingle Dangle. It has a badly broken leg which dangles as it flies, so that it is easily identified and gets all the scraps, catching them on the wing. The moment I appear on my terrace Dingle Dangle arrives. So, I'm afraid, do countless others, but it's impossible to feed them all. I never saw such a population of gulls as we have here in winter. They roost on the grass round the reservoirs beyond what was Ranelagh; one might think that snow had fallen, the ground is so white with them. They seem not at all quarrelsome among themselves. They are mostly the black-headed sort, dark heads in summer, white with a smudge or two in winter; but we have all kinds. They fly and balance in the air most beautifully.

I have just read *Don Juan* through, from cover to cover, with great pleasure. Was there ever such a rhymer, such unflagging ingenuity and impudence! He kept me constantly on the giggle. Any word that comes into his head as an end word to his first lines, he just has a go at it and gets away with rhymes to it as effortlessly as a gull flies. I think he must have been a delightful man.[2] One of his footnotes remarks 'No angler can be a good man.' I was interested to discover, by the way, that that epitaph on Boatswain's monument in Newstead which you sent me some months ago, beginning

> Near this spot
> Are deposited the remains of one
> Who possessed Beauty without Vanity
> Strength without Insolence . . . etc.

---

[1] Lawrie replied on 7 December: 'Your idea of Beatrix Lehmann was an interesting one, but we have not pursued it, because she's playing in *The Storm* at the National Theatre, and even if they take it out of the repertoire we think she would regard Miss Avery as too small a part.' Marda Vanne was chosen for the role. Cf. Letter 322.
[2] See Letter 328.

was not written by Byron at all.[1] I suppose you knew that. I didn't. It is rather a touching story.

I hope all goes well with you, D.L.B. and with your Charles. We potter along here quite peacefully, though one day is so like another that the distinction between life and death becomes rather blurred.
Love from
  Joe

To James H. Lawrie (1907–)   Putney 322
                                             8/12/66

Dear Lawrie
          good. Marda Vanne's name is well known to me though I don't recall her appearance.[2] Stupidly I don't recall either now the other towns—besides Wimbledon—of your tour, but I'm pretty sure that Cambridge was not one of them, and it is highly unlikely that Morgan Forster himself could put in an appearance anywhere else, excepting the West End. For that possibility one can't plan, not yet anyway. It so happens that he is to be in London next week for a couple of nights and I shall be keeping him company, but it is quite six months since his last visit, and it has needed a combination of favourable circumstances and some 'staff work' to make this one feasible. Oh yes, I remember now that Golders Green is one of your places; well, he *might* manage that, if he wanted to, but it is all much too far ahead for any present planning.[3]
Yours
  Joe Ackerley

To Geoffrey Gorer (1905–)   Putney 323
                                           9/12/66
Dear G.G.
         poor darling Onyx, give her my love and don't forget that all the evidence (*my* evidence, no other is available) goes to show that dogs have

---

[1] This mistake seems to have slipped into Byronic lore, having first been perpetrated by John Galt in his *Life of Lord Byron* (1830), a book which lifts from many sources and checks none. John Hobhouse, Byron's friend and executor, when going through Galt's 'compendium of errors', wrote: 'Another fact is that the [Boatswain] epitaph was not written by Lord Byron but by himself.' Byron had shown him some verses he had written about his Newfoundland dog, which concluded:

> To mark a friend's remains these stones arise
> I never knew but one—and here he lies.

On reading these lines Hobhouse suggested an alteration, which would substitute worse grammar for better sense: it was to insert 'I' for 'he' in the final line. Byron merely laughed and exclaimed: 'Why, you are not jealous of the dog, are you?' Hobhouse replied: 'Perhaps I am a little—but I can praise him in prose and match your misanthropy.' Later, Byron ordered Hobhouse's epitaph to be engraved together with his own verses on the monument in Newstead gardens. It reads: 'Near this spot are deposited the remains of one who possessed Beauty without Vanity, Strength without Insolence, Courage without Ferocity, and all the Virtues of Man without his Vices. This praise, which would be unmeaning Flattery, if ever inscribed over human ashes, is but a just Tribute to the Memory of BOATSWAIN, a Dog.'

[2] She had been chosen to play the part of Miss Avery in *Howards End*.
[3] See Letter 329.

forgotten how to fuck, so don't get into a panic if a gentleman dog comes visiting or follows you when out.

No, I don't see the *N*[*ew*] *S*[*tatesman*]. Sorry about Bridgit [*sic*]¹ . . . She is good about the beasts.
Love
  Joe

324 To B. J. Kirkpatrick²   17 Star & Garter Mansions, Putney, S.W.15
                                           12/12/66
Dear Miss Kirkpatrick
                    no. The Secker & Warburg Edition (1956) of *My Dog Tulip* carries the following quotation: 'However much readers dislike or like this book, they will be obliged to agree that it is unlike any other book that they have read.'

                                           E. M. Forster

Mr Forster sent me this rather tepid remark for 'blurb' purposes by letter—or perhaps put it into my hand, I don't remember which. At the end of that year (I cannot give you exact date) he was asked by *The Sunday Times* to be one of the judges of 'The Best Book of the Year.'³ This, as you doubtless know, is a feature run annually by both the big Sunday papers. He gave his award to *My Dog Tulip* in a longer and less cautious statement. Last year the book was published in the States by the Fleet Publishing Corporation of New York. I was asked, as usual, to collect favourable critical opinions for the dust-cover and copied out in the offices of *The Sunday Times* Mr Forster's comment. I'm sorry that I have not a copy of it any longer, but Fleet used this quotation from it:

'Where she innovates, where she rebels, is in demanding to be treated as a creature in her own right, as a dog of dogdom, and not as an apanage of man. This Mr Ackerley accords, with a freshness and an innocence of vision that have never before been directed at the canine world.'

                                       E. M. Forster[4]

¹ Brigid Brophy had reviewed Gorer's *The Danger of Equality* in the *New Statesman* on 2 December. She had begun the notice: 'The volume in which Mr Gorer has assembled 23 essays published over the last 18 years should have come furnished with wide margins and a pencil tucked down the spine. For his gift is to bring out the scholiast—or the graffitist—in the reader. His assertions are liable to excite whole catalogues by way of refutation. It is without irony that I call this a gift. Shrapnel from exploded hypotheses is more interesting and fertile stuff than no hypotheses. Mr Gorer often seems to me to have failed to think critically about his ideas, but I praise him for *having* ideas . . .'
² Compiler of *A Bibliography of E. M. Forster* (1965). A 'second edition, revised' appeared in 1968, incorporating part of the information given in this letter. See Appendix E.
³ The feature that year was published in two parts in two successive issues, and Forster's contribution was printed in the first on 23 December 1956. See note 4 below and Introduction, 3.
⁴ The full text of Forster's comment read: 'Of the few 1956 books that I have read, J. R. Ackerley's *My Dog Tulip* (Secker & Warburg) is by far the most remarkable. It is a biography of the New Dog—a creature comparable to the New Woman who disturbed our grandparents. Tulip, the Alsatian bitch in question does not indeed demand a latch-key; if all doors and windows are left open, all traffic stopped when she crosses a road, and all Guy Fawkes celebrations banned, she is fairly content. Where she innovates, where she rebels, is in demanding to be treated as a creature in her own right, as a dog of dogdom, and not as an apanage of man. This Mr Ackerley accords, with a freshness and an innocence of vision that have never before been directed at the canine world. "Innocence" may seem an odd word for a book which describes excretion, copulation and parturi-

This year The Bodley Head re-published the book and took from Fleet the last few words of the quotation.[1]

I hope this answers your query and that you can read my writing.

Yours truly

J. R. Ackerley

To Francis King (1923–)   17 Star & Garter Mansions, Putney, S.W.15 325

3/1/67

Dear Francis

you deserved a quicker reply. I am so pleased with your news, the Arts Council grant.[2] Justice, as reward, is too seldom done. I am delighted, though we shall miss your lodgers. Now write us, with your fertile and less distracted mind, a lot of nice things to read, plays (comedies, about the lodgers perhaps), novels (not about the Moors murders), short stories (miscellaneous), you are permitted to let yourself go in some of those. I wonder what you are up to at the moment.

We had the very dullest of Xmases. One guest only, my half-sister Diana; otherwise we confronted alone, day after day, the Duchess of [——]'s annual large turkey. I must really stop that terrible gift. It is too disgusting to approach with a groan the inexhaustible flesh of an animal that has been deprived of its life for our pleasure. I kept imagining the spirit of the slaughtered creature hovering above us, complaining about the useless loss of its precious life. 'There is no wealth but life' as that bore Ruskin remarked, more profoundly than he knew.[3] Turkeys are highly aggressive birds, and rather interesting. They have no innate information as to what their chicks, which they valiantly defend, look like—or what their many predatory enemies look like. They simply attack anything that approaches the nest. They know their chicks aurally only, by their cheeping. If the mother turkey is deafened, by an operation on her inner ear, she destroys all her chicks as soon as they are hatched. On the other hand, if a mechanical loud-speaking, or rather loud-cheeping, apparatus is built into the body of a rat, a weasel, a polecat, she offers it maternal protection. All this is extracted from Konrad Lorenz's recent book *On Aggression*,[4] so I daresay I am teaching granny to suck turkey eggs.

I don't think I take your Clifford[5] *seriously*, so perhaps I should leave him

---

tion realistically; but they are part of the outlook that includes the beauty of her fur, the grace of her movements, her happiness on Wimbledon Common, her loyalty, and her exasperatingness. She is often tremendous fun. The account of the wrecking by her admirers of Mon Repos, "quite the prettiest bungalow in Witchball Lane," when she is on heat inside it is magnificent. Tulip's biography has shocked some people. Sometimes it shocks me, but much too much fuss is made over feeling shocked. And—as one of its readers has gaily remarked—it will certainly not corrupt or deprave any dog into whose paws it is likely to fall.' The reader was Fredric Warburg. See page 120, note 2.

1 'A freshness and an innocence of vision that have never before been directed at the canine world.'

2 King had been awarded a £1200 grant in December 1966.

3 See page 311, notes 4 and 6.

4 1966.

5 C. H. B. Kitchin the novelist (1895–1970).

at that. I hope he is not 'boring upon your time' as one of my characters[1] says in *Hindoo Holiday*. Invalids are liable to parasitism. [——] too is a person I found it hard to take seriously, but he has shed so many tears in my presence that I begin to wonder whether there is not something there. A well, at least. He writes from Bangkok, to apprise me of a 'tragedy'—Robin Curtis[2] found murdered in his house, in Kyoto. Did I know Robin Curtis? Did you? I suppose you did. [——] adds no further details, and I don't know why he dubs it a 'tragedy'. Let me know the answer to all this, from your own knowledge and sources.

I am busy transferring my life from a 1966 diary to a 1967 diary, a tired task about which I think each year 'Well, anyway, this will be the last.' I must pop you and Bruce[3] into my new book[4] before he goes off to Norfolk to worry the litter-baskets there. My Queenie tended to chase anything that 'ran away', especially when she was in high spirits; bicycles, horses, children, dogs, cats, birds, she thought it great fun. In Richmond Park I was always careful to put her on the lead if I saw deer or sheep ahead. If Bruce is not a general chaser like that, perhaps he won't run after sheep; I think it is more the instinct than the object.

I am beginning to think that my U.S. publisher has gone bust. A cheque was due to me in October—a fairly substantial one, perhaps £500—and hasn't come. I've written for it three times. My agent there said he hoped to get it to me in a 'few days'. That was on December 1st. Letters from me since have elicited no reply.

Much love, dear Francis

Joe

326 To David Sylvester (1924–)   17 Star & Garter Mansions, Putney,
                                             S.W.15   8/1/67

Dear David

I enclose the story from *Encounter* you asked to see. I haven't read it for some years and may have over-stated its merits. I also enclose an article by myself,[5] written for a U.S.-Japanese magazine[6] three years ago and which I don't think you could have seen. It may have something to your purpose and will show you anyway where my setting sun of thought is setting. It isn't a bad article in its teasing way; indeed I think it has something important to say, but I felt I never managed quite to say it and it has left in my mind a feeling of frustration and dissatisfaction. I haven't got the mental apparatus for large universal pronouncements. But it is pretty good,

---

[1] Abdul Haq, the tutor provided for A. by the Maharajah of Chhokrapur.
[2] An American antique dealer.
[3] King's labrador.
[4] According to reports from friends, it would seem that what A. had in mind was a collection of short pieces published over the years, to which he intended adding several new ones. *I Am a Beast & Other Pieces*, edited by Neville Braybrooke, will be published by Duckworth in 1975.
[5] 'I Am a Beast.'
[6] *Orient/West* (March–April 1964).

the Zen part in particular,[1] I was very pleased with that sudden inspiration. In its way it anticipates Lorenz's findings in his new book *On Aggression*.[2] Please let me have it back when you have read it—it is the only copy I have —and the *Encounter* story too.

Of course your subject[3] interests me, and I'm glad you are doing it. It occupies my own thought a great deal, but in a tired, desultory, hopeless way, evil without remedy. I was writing to Kenneth Clark the other day about his Ruskin book,[4] which he had given me. I didn't get on with it, the fine writing and word-paintings bore me;[5] but one of his famous aphorisms struck me: 'There is no wealth but life.' This seemed to me a profoundly important remark, profounder, perhaps, than Ruskin himself realized, for he was speaking in his capacity as an economist.[6] But simply and on its face value it seemed to me a good slogan for a new religion out of which all superstition would be drained away, life itself, for its own sake, would become the only serious and valuable thing. However, as I have said, my mind is not large enough to encompass such grand subjects. But I told K. that the phrase was knocking about in my head when I went to buy some fish for supper. A woman and her small boy, about 5, were in front of me, being served. They wanted an eel. I hadn't then noticed that a placard outside the shop advertised 'Live eels.' Two eels were brought by the fishmonger in a pail and were weighed. They were large magnificent creatures, shining with health and vitality. And they were frightened. They kept squirming off the scales and falling to the floor in their efforts to escape. With a running commentary of jokes the fishmonger picked them up and put them back. Only after a struggle were they weighed. I knew what they were saying, they were saying 'Don't! There is no wealth but life,' but only I heard them. The larger of the two was chosen and taken to the back of the shop; the other was

---

[1] '. . . By saying "yes" instead of "no" I communicated with [my alsatian bitch]. Thus was *she* able to instruct *me*. This remark, which a Westerner would smile at, will be readily understood by the Japanese. It was Zen, that enlightenment which may come to us by concentration of thought and to which no master can do more than point a way. It was through the discipline and submission she exacted with her gaze, her constant and demanding attention, that I reached a state of enlightenment . . .' Cf. Letter 302.

[2] See note 4 below.

[3] Sylvester was editing an issue of the *Sunday Times Magazine* devoted to man's treatment of animals. 'How We Use Animals' was its title, and it appeared on 3 September. A. did not contribute—though he was the first potential author that Sylvester approached.

[4] In late 1966 Sir Kenneth Clark sent A. an advance copy of the paperback edition of his Ruskin anthology *Ruskin Today* (which had first come out in 1964), and drew his attention to the aphorism: 'There is no wealth but life.' A., when thanking him, replied that, while he agreed with the saying, he might interpret it in ways which would not please Ruskin—and went on to describe, as he does here, the incident about the two eels. Earlier still, on the previous 7 November, A. had described the same incident of the eels to William Plomer, though at the time he did not know of the Ruskin saying. Lord Clark treasured A.'s letter and often read it aloud to friends. Several searches were made for it but to no effect. He wrote to Braybrooke on 27 May 1972: 'As two eel stories in the book will be enough, I will not worry too much at the disappearance of my letter.' See Letter 319. Cf. Letter 325.

[5] Ruskin wrote to Susanna Beever when she was making an anthology of descriptive passages from his *Modern Painters* under the title *Frondes Agrestes* (1875): 'It is the chief provocation of my life to be called a word painter instead of a thinker.'

[6] The remark occurs in Essay IV of *Unto This Last* (1860): 'I desire, in closing the series of introductory papers, to leave this one great fact clearly stated. THERE IS NO WEALTH BUT LIFE. Life, including all its powers of love, of joy, and of admiration. That country is the richest which nourishes the greatest number of noble and happy human beings; that man is richest, who, having perfected the functions of his own life to the utmost, has also the widest helpful influence, both personal, and by means of his possessions, over the lives of others.'

restored to its pail. The child then said 'May I see the eel killed, Mummy?' She assented and they went to watch. Chop, chop, and the eel was dead. The child then said 'May I see the other eel killed too, Mummy?' and the fishmonger laughed it off with 'Oh no, sonny, I'm afraid he might bite me.'

That story is to your purpose, I think, and it is a difficult story. All allowances have to be made, we have to be fed and can we be expected also to *feel* for the lives of the creatures we take away for our pleasure? *I* think yes; there seems to be something profoundly *wrong* with the story; it is more than the arrogance of 'There is no wealth but *human* life', it has callousness also. I could add a somewhat similar episode about Forster ('There is no wealth but *human* life'),[1] but you might put it accidentally into your horrid newspaper,[2] and that I do not want. But the feeling, under the pressure of profit and population, is widespread; Geoffrey Gorer, being a farmer, wants myxomatosis for the birds, [Michael] Pitt-Rivers wages endless war against the Wiltshire deer that destroy his plantations; my friend Villiers David often says that so far as he is concerned the animals can all be abolished—with a single exception of his beloved cat Anna; he wants only people. William Plomer says that if I am not careful I shall be taken for a misanthropist. I don't want to be careful in the least. I am *not* a misanthropist; I like people and get on well with them; I am only a *numerical* misanthropist. I think there are too many people, too dangerously many for the salvation of the beasts and even of ourselves; I want the population drastically reduced *at once*, for there is no time to be lost. Tell me how that is to be done. Better brains than mine have been staring hopelessly at the problem for the last fifteen years. And then I want the new religion—away with God—'there is no wealth but life.' But I shan't get it. Lorenz, so far as I understand him, believes that we are not the finished product of the highest creation; we are merely a link—unhappily a far from *missing* link—between early man and the noble man we shall evolve in the future. He is speaking Darwinly. He is a far more important and knowledgeable thinker than I, but, to my mind, a sad optimist; by the time that his noble man has been evolved, if he ever is, there will be no animals left in the world, and, after all, his living depends upon them as a comparative ethologist. I myself am out to save the animals, such as remain; if necessary at the expense of mankind.

Do not omit *laboratory* animals from your scheme; their story is no more appalling than the slaughter-house, and as carefully concealed. *Oryx* (August 1966), the journal of the Fauna Preservation Society (a most reliable body), tells me that between 1958 and 1965 the U.S.A. alone (the largest importers) imported *per annum* 115,000 to 223,000 monkeys for experimental purposes.[3] Even the biologist George [B.] Schaller in his marvellous book *The Gorilla Year*[4] was shocked; he said that if these charming creatures went into laboratories in such quantities, there would soon be no

---

[1] See Letters 318 and 319. [2] See page 311, note 3.

[3] This item appeared in *Oryx* under the title of 'Monkeys and Medical Research'. It consisted of a report of a medical conference, sponsored in 1966 by the New York Zoological Society and International Union for Conservation of Nature, to investigate the supplies of primates provided for medical research. The figures quoted by A. were given by W. G. Conway, Director of the New York Zoo. Cf. Letter 314.

[4] Correct title—*The Year of the Gorilla* (1965).

monkeys left. *The Times* tells me that the remarkable decline in the frog population in this country is due to the demand for them in school and other laboratories. This is all done for you and me, dear, to prevent or cure our diseases, to find out why we quarrel with our wives or sisters, and to understand and 'help', I suppose, such charming characters as throng the pages of Mr Selby's *Last Exit to Brooklyn*. Monkeys are considered highly important for studying human psychological problems; there is scarcely any situation of mental torment, of misery and frustration, into which the Harlows (American scientists) do not put them, separating husbands and wives, mothers and children, for months, for years, in order to study their grief and the deterioration of their faculties, to prove something which any bloody fool could guess for himself.[1] But, essentially, I am only repeating in this over-long letter what I said in my Japanese article 'Animals don't matter; only people matter.' Yet I protest, I am not a misanthropist, I only want the human race abolished before it can do further harm.

Much love

  Joe

To David Sylvester (1924–   )   Putney 327
                                                        16/1/67

No, dear David, I didn't send my Beastly article[2] to you for publication—no first-rate paper like yours[3] would take second-hand stuff—only for you to look at and also to realise (your kind invitation to contribute)[4] that I had already shot my bolt. It is addressed to a Japanese audience and I doubt if I could adapt it to a different one or drag anything fresh from my mind.

I was watching a Western on A.T.V. the other evening, 'The Command', the usual American nostalgia, quite exciting. Endless battles took place between Red Indians and a military convoy guarded by mounties. In the engagements and pursuits dozens of horses on both sides crashed to the ground with their riders. Much, I suppose, is trick photography, but how much? Do the horses fall, brought down by a wrench of the bit, as it looks, and do they get hurt? They certainly seem to come the most awful croppers, and in a picture I saw some months ago a horse, scrambling back to its feet, limped off the screen. Was this trickery too? I expect you will know the answers to this; if not it might be a matter to look into for your feature on the

---

[1] On 13 January there appeared in *The Times* a letter 'From Mr J. R. Ackerley and others'. Its subject was 'Moves to Ban Export of Animals'. The other signatories were Walter Allen, John Bayley, Neville Braybrooke, Brigid Brophy, Arthur Calder-Marshall, Ivy Compton-Burnett, Kay Dick, Maureen Duffy, Isobel English, Kathleen Farrell, Gillian Freeman, L. P. Hartley, Patricia Highsmith, Elizabeth Jane Howard, Pamela Hansford Johnson, Francis King, Doris Lessing, Shena Mackay, Olivia Manning, Derwent May, Iris Murdoch, Charles Osborne, Jerzy Peterkiewicz, Anthony Powell, William Sansom, Stevie Smith, Henry Williamson, Angus Wilson, Francis Wyndham and Stephen Vizinczey. Olivia Manning had been largely responsible for organising the protest.
[2] 'I Am a Beast'.
[3] *Sunday Times*.
[4] See page 311, note 3.

use of animals by human beings. I am always worried by these Westerns, just on the horses' account, and am reminded of the Charge of the Light Brigade, that much lauded and revolting story which earned a popular poem, not of course about the beautiful innocent horses that got blown to bits, but about the mindless oafs who rode them. How the human race does love itself! I daresay you know Edwin Muir's poem '[The] Horses'?[1] I will send it to you if you don't. It may be germane to your plan.
Love
   Joe

[1] Cf. Letter 292.

Part Fifteen
MORGAN

To William Roerick (1912–   ) and Thomas Coley (1913–   )

17 Star & Garter Mansions, Putney, S.W.15

4/2/67

Dear Bill and Tom

Morgan is much better. I have just returned from Coventry where I spent three days with him. It was called a 'fall', which indeed it was, but it was also one of his strokes and the misfortune of it was that it happened one evening in his King's sitting-room where he was not supposed to be, for, as you know, that staircase is under reconstruction, his rooms, though visible are not yet habitable, and he was roosting in Alex [*sic*] Vidler's rooms¹ on X staircase. Fortunately he had managed to light the electric fire in his sitting-room on A staircase before he collapsed, or he might have been dead by now, for he was not discovered, lying insensible on the floor on a very cold night, until his bedmaker arrived next morning. As it was he had a touch of pneumonia, but after a few days in Addenbrooke's [Hospital] he made one of his usual recoveries and now seems much as he was before it happened, though his sight and speech seem not quite so good, or bad, but this may just as well be caused by a further advance into old age as by his disaster. I need hardly say that his spirits are quite unimpaired; he is cheerful, jolly, and amusing as ever, and the Bucks are determined not to let him out of their hands again until March, when his own Cambridge rooms will be habitable, it is hoped, and no persuasion is likely to keep him out of those when they are ready.

So much for dear old Morgan. I never thanked you and Tom for your Xmas greetings. Is it ever too late to mend? I was interested to hear of your respective activities. I couldn't bear the de Sade play² and left in the middle of it, but I'm sure you are improving it. Indeed, yes, he was a much-maligned man, like Lord Byron, a near contemporary and to whom he bears certain

¹ From October 1956 to September 1966 the Rev. Alec. R. Vidler was Dean of King's College, Cambridge, and remained on till September 1967 as a fellow and university lecturer. From April 1966 onwards he lived out of Cambridge at Shepreth and so only needed one of his set of three rooms in College. Forster used the other two while his own were under repair.

² Roerick at this time was appearing on Broadway as de Sade in the *Marat/Sade* play by Peter Weiss, and had written to A. to put forward some of his theories about the Marquis—principally, that Krafft-Ebing had done de Sade irreparable harm by naming sadism after him, because that was at once both a simplification and a distortion. He told Braybrooke: 'I wouldn't go so far as Joe and say that de Sade settled down happily with his wife, but they did have some curious sort of understanding—despite his anger and impatience with her.'

resemblances. Both were regarded as wicked and were persecuted in their lives, monstered into posterity; both had their works destroyed as obscene or blasphemous; both were extremely honest men, despising cant and lies; both were immensely hard workers, omnivorous readers and voluminous writers; both enjoyed freedom in sexual matters, though de Sade did have a rather commonplace perversion, he liked to be whipped and, being good-natured, thought that others must like it too, a reciprocated pleasure; both were kind men and did no intentional harm to anybody; both were eccentric individuals and behaved recklessly in their warfare against convention; both had early good looks and charm, and both tended to corpulence, which de Sade eventually reached; both married rather cold, puritanical women, though I believe that if Byron could have patched matters up with his wife he would have settled down with her as happily as de Sade did with his; both drew enormous devotion from the women in their lives, and both must have been interesting, fascinating, to meet—though, on the whole, if I had to choose, I would have preferred Byron,[1] he had a sense of humour, lacking, I think, in de Sade.

Love to you both

   Joe

329 **To James H. Lawrie (1907–)**   c/o Buckingham, 11 Salisbury Avenue,
                                          Coventry   15/2/67

Dear Jimmie

        I have spoken to Morgan about your news and plans. He is so pleased to hear of your success in getting the play[2] into the West End. I have also mentioned to him your hope of a charity performance at the New Theatre[3] on the Monday. It would be too difficult for him however to alter his original plan of seeing the play on the evening of Saturday, Feb. 25 at Golders Green.[4] Could you very kindly send the four tickets to him here?

Yours ever

   Joe Ackerley

330 **To James Kirkup (1923–)**   c/o 17 Star & Garter Mansions, Putney,
                                          S.W.15   16/2/67

Darling Jim

        such gay amusing letters from you: one wonders, in England, how it is possible, *whether* it is possible, for anyone to enjoy life so much any-where, and I hope there is reality behind your beautiful nonsense. I have

---

[1] Cf. Letter 321.
[2] *Howards End.*
[3] Renamed Albery in January 1973.
[4] This was the last night of the tour before the play came into the West End—and the Golders Green Hippodrome was packed. The audience cheered enthusiastically. Afterwards, Forster told Lawrie how pleased he had been with the reception and how much more attractive a figure of Leonard Bast had been presented on the stage than in his own novel. 'That was one of my mistakes,' he added.

been reading you to old Morgan, much to his delight; though his post-bag is heavy with tributes from all over the world and concern for his health, *he* does not get, nor anyone else I am sure (except Rena? how goes she?) such joyous letters as you write to me. He has been ill again—you may not know—another stroke in Cambridge, a tiresome one because he was alone, and lay in his room all night long on the floor in his own vomit until the bedmaker arrived in the morning to find him. Fortunately the electric fire was on, for it was a perishing night and although he did have a touch of pneumonia it could have been much worse. But a fortnight in hospital recovered him and now, in Coventry, where he is more safely bestowed and I am spending a few days with him, he is as sprightly as ever and no less mobile than he was before. I keep him company to relieve the Buckinghams, trot him round these ever so boring suburbs, and answer his letters for him. We have just had one from a journalist lady in New Zealand, a fan of his work, enclosing an obituary of him which she has composed for the N.Z. press where it should come in handy, and wanting his opinion of it. He was so cross and tore it up unread. I said 'Weren't you curious to know what you are worth?' He said 'I restrained my curiosity.'[1] Actually I have been writing an obituary of him too,[2] but have a little more delicacy than to tell him so or to show it to him. Whenever he is ill and the news leaks out, as it did this last time, some newspaper always rings me up for an article on him; I always refuse, but began to wonder what I *would* say about him and our long friendship if I tried to set him down, and became interested enough to have a shot at him before gin and whisky wash all my memory and softening brains away. Also, it occurred to me, that although I am nearly 20 years his junior, that is no guarantee that I shall not pre-decease him—younger people than I tumble down and off all round me from coronary thrombosis, the new fashionable death—so I decided to put him down on paper if I could (not an easy task) and leave him perhaps behind me. He comes out, in some important respects, rather like his own creature, that grand philosopher [Stewart] Ansell in *The Longest Journey*.[3] I don't know about your 'odontoglossums'[4] to M., whatever they may be—yes, I do, May Buckingham has just told me that they arrived while he was in his hospital, but he forgets things now, you know, almost immediately and we think it best not to remind him, for then he rather fusses. So we shall thank you this time for him.

No more now, dearest Jim. I am well, our winter has been unusually good, better, it seems, than yours. More letters, please. Morgan sends greetings. I send my heart.

Joe

---

[1] Cf. Letter 333.

[2] See Letters 332, 333 and 334.

[3] 'Though neither rude nor heroic like Ansell, Morgan . . . bears many resemblances to that serious young philosopher with his questioning mind and strict regard for truth, his far-reaching listening perception of character and of consequences, and his determination to expose falsity wherever he found it . . .' (1907). This passage was 'cut' from the obituary article when it was printed in the *Observer*. See page 321, note 1.

[4] Kirkup had used the term to describe some orchids of great size which he had had sent to Forster. Ronald Firbank in Chapter 13 of *The Flower Beneath the Foot* (1923) refers to 'a basket of odontoglossums eked out with gypsophila'.

331 To E. M. Forster (1879–1970)   Putney
                                                                        1/3/67
Darling Morgan
                   just a line of love to say I hope you are well. I expect you
will have seen all the notices of your play,[1] and sadly agreed with the general
disappointment and occasional yawns they voiced. Not good box-office
notices, I fear; pretty intelligent on the whole in realising that a major novel
had made a minor play. I haven't heard from [James] Lawrie,[2] I daresay
he's feeling rather blue; but the front-page picture, in one of the more popular rags, of Lord [———]'s new woman entering the theatre in a mini-skirt
may sell a few more tickets. And the Sunday papers and weeklies are still to
come.
     All well here and nothing much to report. High tides and flooded roads
day after day, and the swans floating out of the river and holding up the
motor-cars by refusing to move off the highway. A pleasant pub lunch with
Stuart Hampshire, on leave from Princeton, and tomorrow I lunch with
Christabel Aberconway[3] 'to welcome Villiers David back from his Far
Eastern excursion.' [. . .] She has a superb cook and her house contains some
of the most beautiful French Impressionist paintings in the world [. . .]
     Much looking forward to seeing you on Monday week.
     Joe

332 To Geoffrey Gorer (1905–   )   Putney
                                                                        4/4/67

Thank you, dear G.G. Sonia is coming to dine here on Saturday and I shall
not allow Mr Rota to visit me until I have seen her.[4] I have been copying
the early letters out from idle interest and to occupy my empty time—and
to remind myself of Morgan's younger character as a check to the article
about him I have already done.[5] Stuart Hampshire, who read it, seemed to
think he came out rather too good to be true: 'Where are the defects of the
qualities?' he asked, so I thought that by raking over the ashes of the past I
might find something to charge him with—so far unsuccessfully.[6] Some of
the letters are very private and I wonder whether I should remember him
as being pretty misanthropic himself, in spite of all his toilings for the betterment of humanity. I got bullied for my views on *Last Exit to Brooklyn*[7] which

---

[1] *Howards End*. A. had been invited to the first night by Lance Sieveking, one of the adapters.
But A. had already seen it twice—once at the Cambridge Arts Theatre and once at Golders Green
Hippodrome—and he declined. Earlier, he had written to May Buckingham: 'Three goes of
Howards End would be Joe's end.'
     [2] One of the impresarios connected with the production. See Letter 296.
     [3] Christabel Lady Aberconway, youngest daughter of Sir Melville Macnaghten, and author of
A Dictionary of Cat Lovers (1949) and an autobiography, *A Wiser Woman?* (1966). She died in 1974.
     [4] See Letter 336.
     [5] 'An article . . . which takes the form of an obituary . . .' See Letter 333.
     [6] But A. did add one characteristic minor criticism—probably in the light of Hampshire's
comments. Originally he had written in his article: 'Morgan did not like dogs, he was, if anything
in the animal line, a cat man . . .' Later he revised this to: 'Morgan did not like dogs (a bad mark!),
he was, if anything in the animal line, a cat man . . .'
     [7] See Letter 314.

he hadn't read, and when I remarked that nothing would induce me to give the kiss of life to a stranger I got bullied again. I said 'What about a clergyman? Would you give the kiss of life to a R.C. priest for instance?' He *abominates* the clergy. He said 'Certainly, to save life, if I knew how to do it I should have to, though I think people are better off dead.' I knew not what to make of all this and am nursing my wounds.

Well, dear, I'm sorry about poor William's[1] fingers, very painful I'm afraid. Life has been dreary here too, but tomorrow I am lunching with Lady Diana Cooper, Lady Waverley, and a Lord whose name I have forgotten, so I don't suppose I'll be seeing you again.

Fond love to dear Onyx.[2] *She* could have the kiss of life from me if ever she needed it.

So sorry to hear about your beautiful flowers.

Love
  Joe

To David Sylvester (1924–   )   17 Star & Garter Mansions, Putney,   333
                                    S.W.15   8/4/67

Dear David
             you have asked me at times to write about Forster for *The S[unday] T[imes]* and hitherto I have refused. Others have also asked me— the B.B.C. some years ago,[3] *The Observer* last year after his recent illness. I began to wonder what I *would* say about this old friend of forty-five years if he happened to pre-decease me, and started to jot things down to interest myself. An article has emerged of about 4000–5000 words,[4] which takes the form of an obituary—or what James Kirkup, who likes playing with words, calls a 'sobituary', and indeed it contains a sob or two, Forster's not mine.[5] They *might* be mine if he knew I had done such a thing, for when I was with him last month[6] he was in a great state of vexation because a New Zealand lady journalist, a stranger but a disciple, had sent him for his opinion an obituary of him *she* had composed for her N.Z. paper. She could of course be accused of lack of tact, but I think she was inspired by the highest motives; she wished to get him right and to please him beyond the grave; but he was incensed and tore her obituary up unread.

I too was actuated by respectable motives, I wanted to know what I thought, the intellectual exercise; the motives for this letter are lower, I want to make out of it as much money as I can. I wonder whether I might send it to you to read, privately, as a friend? It would interest me to know i) if you thought it worthy and ii) how much you thought it worth, and to

---

[1] Gorer's manservant.
[2] Gorer's labrador bitch.
[3] See Letter 269 and Appendix E.
[4] 8000 words in fact. See Introduction, 4.
[5] 'He . . . wept to hear of the death of André Gide, not for personal reasons, he knew him only slightly, but because he felt that one of the few great props of his own civilization had been withdrawn.' This passage was 'cut' from the obituary article when it was printed in the *Observer*.
[6] The scene described here occurred in February, not March. See Letter 330.

whom. I wouldn't want you to take any *steps* about it, just to read and return it, if you kindly would, with advice. I am regarding my financial future with some dismay and, as you know, am rarely able to put pen to paper.
Love from
  Joe

334 To David Higham (1895–)   17 Star & Garter Mansions, Putney,
                                        S.W.15   19/4/67
Dear David
                  when you have recovered from my Memoir,[1] I wonder whether you and Miss LeRoy could sell this[2] for me, here and in America. I had qualms about sending it out—to kill an old friend before he is dead seemed so indelicate—but by holding it up I have lost the place for which I intended it, *The Sunday Times*: they have already secured an obituary article by someone else for their cold storage.[3] It seems that since Forster's last illness got into the news, the rat race has already begun, and this rat may now be too late for any of the rewarding Sunday papers. Of course Forster may easily outlast me and his other old friends; he seems quite recovered and doctors are wonderfully clever at keeping the spark of life going. However, in the event of his pre-deceasing me, I would like, as his oldest and closest friend, to say my say, and here it is. Place it, and discreetly, if you can; it is a bit long and could be shortened.

When Howard Newby of the B.B.C. spoke to me about Forster some eighteen months ago, I used the phrase which you will find at the bottom of my page 10.[4] Agreeing with it, he asked who would say it in a broadcast, but he did not actually ask me and I didn't put myself forward. Now I have said it, and he *might* be interested; on the other hand, the B.B.C. already has recorded a feature programme to put out in the event of Forster's death, a poor affair I think, sundry voices on various aspects of his life, mine included.[5] I wasn't informed until the moment of recording that the feature was an obituary, and contributed merely the cheerful short statement I had prepared on the help Forster gave me on *The Listener*.

What about America, where his fame stands high? Would, for instance, *The New Yorker* accept this for their larder? Or *The N[ew] Y[ork] Times*?

---

[1] *My Father and Myself*.
[2] The obituary article on E. M. Forster, mentioned in the previous letter (333).
[3] This was by William Plomer. J. W. Lambert, the literary editor, writes: 'But owing to an absurd muddle, involving not the Arts Section but the Leader Page, it never appeared.'
[4] Page 11 in fact, since the ts. had two pages marked 6 and 6a. The phrase which A. used to P. H. Newby was 'our greatest living novelist'—though in the obituary article itself A. added another—namely, 'perhaps the greatest living world novelist.' Newby told Braybrooke: ' "Our greatest living novelist". I have a recollection of agreeing with this. I don't remember Joe claiming E.M.F. was "perhaps the greatest living world novelist". I would not have agreed with that.' Neither phrase appeared in the obituary article when it was printed in the *Observer*.
[5] In the course of A.'s contribution to the BBC programme on E. M. Forster, he had worked in the phrase 'our greatest living novelist'. '[Forster] even wrote unsigned reviews . . . Now, that was something! Our greatest living novelist doing unsigned reviews . . .' See Letter 269 and Appendix E.

They, too, may have made other arrangements. Anyway, if this is to go about, it must be made clear that Forster is alive and well.
Yours
  Joe

P.S. When he was last ill *The Observer* asked me to write about him. I said he was recovering and declined. Whether they pursued the matter elsewhere I know not.[1]

To Paul Cadmus (1904–) 17 Star & Garter Mansions, Putney, S.W.15   335
27/5/67
Dear Paul
      I found your letter waiting for me last Sunday when I returned from a week with Morgan in Coventry. I'm not expecting to see him again now until perhaps the last week in June, so I sent that part of your letter which concerns the drawing of Morgan[2] to May and Bob, unable myself to answer your questions or take measurements. The drawing does hang in their Coventry house, but I believe they told me it was a photograph. It is all I can tell you.
      Morgan's health seems remarkably good—he is off to the Aldeburgh Festival next week for a fortnight with the Bucks. After that he intends to return to King's to resume his interrupted college life. We fear this may lead to another disaster, but he will have his way. If *you* don't remember whether you sent your photos to him, I am sure *he* doesn't; he forgets everything and lives in a constant muddle. And it is difficult to help him, for he employs as 'secretary' anyone who happens to be at hand, then forgets what he's dictated (he can no longer write a letter himself), so that the next secretary hasn't a clue about how to carry on the correspondence. In contractual matters this is often serious; he has *never* employed a literary agent, he conducts all such business himself, so that if, while *you* are the current amenuensis, he gets a letter from some Czech publisher asking permission to translate and publish *A Passage to India*, you haven't a notion, nor any way to find out, whether he's already given translation rights to some other Czech publisher—and he has no notion either! Poor old boy! We should not live so long, dear; life reaching a point when we become clowns, or positively disgusting, like Harold Nicolson.
      I am so glad you will send your photos of Jon to me instead; I will show them to Morgan when I see him; his sight may not be good, but it is *quite* good enough to see a male nude.
      I haven't much to report about myself, except that I have given up

----

[1] Higham sold them the obituary article and, when it appeared three years later on 14 June 1970, it filled nearly half a page and had to be extensively 'cut'. An 'uncut' version of it, under the title *E. M. Forster: A Portrait*, was issued separately by Ian McKelvie later in the year.
[2] This drawing had been reproduced on the dust-jacket of *Two Cheers for Democracy* (1951). Cadmus wrote to Braybrooke on 4 April 1972: 'I drew it, I remember, in Morgan's rooms in King's, sitting up in a window embrasure, while he read *Maurice* to me. Several sittings, I believe. Morgan gave the drawing to the Buckinghams some years before he died.' *Maurice* was published posthumously in 1971. See page 257, note 2.

smoking,[1] somewhat late in my day. For years I have been asking myself if I could; for years I haven't enjoyed smoking, have coughed myself sick, expending over £100 a year on a mere bad habit. The other day I brought 55 years of it to an abrupt end. It hasn't bothered me much. I've been rather restless and I drink rather more than usual; my sombre misanthropic outlook on life has not been flooded with any new transforming light,[2] but I no longer cough.

Goodbye, dear Paul. Send me the photos, write to me again, and believe that I am
Your loving
Joe

336 To Sonia Brownell Orwell   17 Star & Garter Mansions, Putney, S.W.15
                                                          27/5/67
Dear Sonia
          bidden to keep you informed of these [. . .] dealings,[3] I enclose Mr [Anthony] Rota's[4] proposition, he brought it along yesterday [. . .] I am of course entirely ignorant of the worth of these letters of mine, and am interested not so much in that as in securing for them a sum of money which will enable Nancy and me to drink ourselves carelessly into our graves— since the sum offered,[5] when added to my other resources, would give me a capital of about £12,000, I am not inclined to *sneer* at it. But that, on your instructions, I leave to you. Point 4 however dismays me; it is not primarily with Forster's reputation that I am concerned; planning indeed is already in progress (instituted by himself) for the production of a full and candid biography of him, with free use of all the unpublished material (more than is known) and access, if friends will permit it, to his personal correspondence. (An incidental point: When Nick Furbank,[6] the biographer appointed, comes to me and says 'Will you be k-kind enough to l-let' (he stutters) 'me see Morgan's letters to you . . .? 'Well, you twig the difficulties. I *may* have to reply 'T-take a t-ticket to Texas'—and I may have to add that even if he gets there they may be under seal.) Nick's real problem, the same as my own, is stated in his last letter to me: 'Outspoken? Yes I think I must

---

[1] A. had made several previous attempts to give up smoking. See Letter 281.

[2] Towards the end of his life, A. was given to exaggerating his 'gloom'. This letter is a characteristic example. Only a week before, A. had told Robert Buckingham that he had just had 'the nicest time he had had for years'. Buckingham explains: 'This referred to an invitation we had received from a friend of mine, a Dr Joe Spears who lives in Coventry with his family. His three sons all went to Rossall and all the family were very much "Ackerley fans" . . . I took Joe to the Spears home for drinks. He was immediately surrounded by the Spears boys who wanted to know what Rossall was like in Joe's day. There was much perusing over copies of the school magazine. Meanwhile, Dr Spears plied Joe with large quantities of gin, all of which pleased Joe immensely. All of Joe's books were produced for him to autograph and I had rarely seen him so animated and happy. With Christopher [Isherwood]'s arrival [that weekend] the party really lit up . . .' See Introduction, 4.

[3] These concerned the sale of A.'s letters from Forster to the University of Texas. See page 51, note 1 and Introduction, 4.

[4] Director of the booksellers Bertram Rota Ltd.

[5] His sister writes: 'It was £6000 . . . Joe only heard that the deal had gone through . . . about a week before he died.'

[6] P. N. Furbank.

be that, or it wouldn't be worth writing the book. But it's one thing to be outspoken about Morgan, and another to be so about people he knew who are still alive.' Do you see what I am driving at? Geoffrey saw it, I think. He said I could put a seal upon the letters for 10 or 12 years [. . .] Mr Rota suggests a closing date which might happen at any time, *probably* in the near future, tomorrow, next week [. . .] I do think it would be unconscionable of me to allow my letters, which give a unique and progressive account of Morgan's deeply-felt emotional affairs with people still living and still his close and constant friends as well as my own, to be open to public inspection while they live.[1] I mentioned this to Mr Rota, who wondered whether *some* of the letters might not be put under extended seal. This would be a task in selection for me; I daresay I could do it; a great many of the letters, it is true, could be read by anyone at any time. Mr Rota also intimated that the more obstacles I put in the way of perfect Texan freedom the lower the price would be.

Well, too long a letter and now enough. Come and dine with us again, dear, we would both like it. You were not, or had not been, in the best of spirits when I last saw you; I would like to imagine a reason for their improvement, but—I am not shrieking with laughter myself and have at long last given up smoking.[2]

Love from

Joe

---

[1] Earlier, the same problem had faced A. during the Second World War. In an undated letter to Herbert Read, he had written: 'Could I send you a registered parcel of letters, for you to put away in your "safe" for me until such time as I ask for their return? . . . There is nothing disgraceful in the parcel: the letters are E. M. Forster's correspondence with me over nearly 25 years . . . He does not want them to fall into the hands of officialdom. Nor do I want them in his hands, which is what he desires, for I should never get them back again, and I have both a personal and a posterity interest in them. But you could give them to him if I died.'

[2] Cf. Letter 335.

Appendix A
LITERARY POLICY OF *THE LISTENER*
BBC internal memo from
J. R. Ackerley to R. S. Lambert[1]

24 February, 1937

1. Eight pages in each issue of *The Listener* are allocated to art, poetry, books and literature. As a rule art takes from two to three of these pages, leaving the remainder to other subjects.

2. Normally, priority of consideration in the literary section of *The Listener* is given to broadcast material, i.e. book talks and short stories; but much of this material is unsuitable for *The Listener*, or else *The Listener* is not allowed to use it, for example, Desmond MacCarthy. Recently the Talks Department has abandoned broadcast reviews of new books and Book Talks have been mainly of an elementary character, dealing with out-of-date publications. Many of the broadcast short stories are either readings from old stories that have been published several years ago, or in some cases have been composed with a technique which does not lend itself to printed reproduction.

3. The literary pages of *The Listener* are therefore used to supplement to some extent the literary deficiency of the microphone. This is done by reviewing current books in three forms:

   (*a*) A fortnightly article on current novels by Edwin Muir, with a 're-commended' list for reading;
   (*b*) '*The Listener*'s Book Chronicle', ranging from two to four pages, and consisting of shortish, unsigned reviews;
   (*c*) Longer, signed reviews of specially important, or controversial, books.

4. The reviewing of books in *The Listener* is based on the following three considerations:

   (*a*) Use of specialised, as distinguished from general reviewers; i.e. books are given, wherever possible, to individual reviewers with special qualifications for reviewing the particular book in question. *The*

---

[1] R. S. Lambert, the first Editor of *The Listener* (1929–39), gave this memo his blessing. But he quarrelled with the expression of Section 6 and pencilled in the margin the comment 'Wordy'.

Listener has no general body of reviewers, nor does it entrust groups of books haphazard to individual journalists to review. The result is that the Book Chronicle reviews maintain a high critical standard;

(*b*) Reviews are kept as short as possible, but specialised reviewers of standing cannot be induced to undertake reviews of serious works, as a rule, unless they are allowed at least 500 words' space. Very short reviews, or reviewing of a large number of books by giving brief descriptive remarks about each, is ruled out. On the whole, specialised reviewing makes against topicality, since such reviewers take time to read and digest books thoroughly. A good number of books are sent out to specialised reviewers, with the request that they judge whether the book be worth review at all, or not. Going by their judgment we do not publish reviews of bad books unless some public interest is served, for example, by exposing the faults of a book which has gained a fictitious reputation by unskilful reviewing elsewhere. The policy of giving each book reviewed in *The Listener* fair space, limits the total number of books which can be included in the Book Chronicle and prevents all books being dealt with close to their date of publication. A certain inevitable time-lag occurs which could only be prevented by increasing the space allocated to the Book Chronicle.

5. *The Listener* does not publish reading lists, lists of books received, or notes on books, on the grounds that these would take up space which were better employed as above; also recommendations of books given without reasons would be invidious as part of *The Listener* editorial policy.

6. With regard to short stories, first consideration is given to any which have been broadcast, but in addition *The Listener* publishes each year some fifteen or twenty contributed short stories. It is our belief that not more than this number of good short stories are written in any one year in this country. We therefore maintain a high selective standard and have gained a reputation for publishing only really good stuff.

7. *The Listener* has not had adequate space (except in the Summer months) to publish general literary articles which would lend variety and interest to our literary pages if we could include them. (For example, in *The Listener* of February 17th, 1937, 'Nonsense as a Literary Form', by Professor Sherard Vines.) Occasionally articles do, however, appear, on current foreign books, particularly French, but sometimes also German and Italian.

J. R. Ackerley

Appendix B
A DELICATE QUESTION OF PAYMENT
An exchange between J. R. Ackerley
and John Maynard Keynes

The Listener, Broadcasting House, W.1
27 May, 36

Dear Keynes,

       I am trying to organise a series of articles for *The Listener*, for the summer months, under the title of 'Art and the State'. It will form a kind of inquiry into the condition of modern art at home and abroad in relationship to the social crisis. By art, perhaps I had better explain to start with, I mean painting, architecture, and such new forms of art as, for instance, the pageantry of ceremony and festivity. I am trying to get nationals from Italy, Germany and Russia to give an account of what art is doing under their various political régimes; what its object is under Fascism, Nazism and Communism, and what are its achievements—what, in short, is, or should be, in their view, the relationship between Art and the State. I think, and hope you will agree, that this is a fascinating subject.

       After some investigations I have asked Staatskommissar Hans Hinkel, who has been newly appointed by Goebbels to direct German cultural matters, to put the Nazi point of view (and I understand that he has consented to do so); and for the Fascist and Communist theories, I have written respectively to Ugo Ojetti and Victor Lazareff. Georges Duthuit will probably write for France; and Kenneth Clark[1] has consented to sum up the whole series. What I want now, however, is somebody to write an introductory article, and I am wondering whether I could persuade you to do this? We feel that this article should, so to speak, put the problems in connection with Art and the State as they would present themselves to the ordinary intelligent man's mind, and that it would be better, therefore, to get a layman, like yourself, with an interest in the subject to do this. I do hope you will feel inclined to accept this suggestion; and should be exceedingly grateful, also, for any advice you could give me.

Yours sincerely,
  J. R. Ackerley

[1] See page 32, note 1.

46, Gordon Square, Bloomsbury
May 28th, 1936

My dear Ackerley,
I always regret it afterwards when I get lured into taking on another job. However, the article you suggest does interest me, and I am not disinclined to try my hand at it.

May I assume that you do not mean to exclude opera, ballet and drama? The failure of the nineteenth century democracies to maintain the grandeur and dignity of the State is, in my judgment, one at least of the seeds of their decay; and what I should offer would be a development of that theme. Is that the sort of thing you have in mind?

Yours sincerely,
J. M. Keynes

The Listener, Broadcasting House, W.1
12 June, 36

Dear Keynes,
I am returning now to the subject of 'Art and the State' which, after receiving your exceedingly welcome and gratifying consent to open the series with an introduction, I put aside to await replies to my invitations abroad. These are now coming in.

Goebbels' new Director of Culture Staatskommissar Hans Hinkel is furnishing me with an explanation of the art principles of German National Socialism which, with its pictorial illustrations, is, I gather, to receive the authorisation of the leading personality in German Art matters himself; L. Cherniavsky, Acting President of the U.S.S.R. Society for Cultural Relations, has actually written to say he has the matter in hand, and Georges Duthuit has promised to turn France inside out.

Only Italy so far refuses to answer my letters of entreaty; but if [Gino] Severini, my present candidate, refuses I believe that I can always fall back on F. T. Marinetti, unless the political situation is still too strained for even an art article to pass from Italy to us. I have asked all these people to tell me what in theory and practice the relationship is, under their particular régimes, between Art and the State: what its objects are, how it works, and what are the fruits of that relationship.

I have defined art as painting, sculpture and architecture, with any new forms such as pageantry; but I am quite ready to include opera, ballet, drama and even the films too, if you think that they, besides yourself in your introduction, should treat of them. My only reason for not including them was that I was afraid of overloading comparatively short MSS. But I agree perfectly that you should not exclude them in your introductory article, and, no doubt, you will be mentioning, too, the commercial art of the poster, etc. This side of it naturally interests Sir Stephen Tallents, and I thought it might interest you to see his pamphlet on the subject,[1] which I enclose.

The point of view from which you wish to discuss the whole subject in your introduction to it is a very interesting one, I think, and I look forward

[1] *The Art of the Poster* (1936).

327

with much eagerness to reading it. I am hoping to start the series off in the issue of July 29th, and, since we like to have scripts in our hands a fortnight in advance, that takes us back to July 15th; but if it would be possible for you to send me in your article even a week earlier than that—by July 8th—it would be convenient, as I am anxious to assemble the whole series as soon as I can, so that they can all be forwarded to Kenneth Clark for his summing-up.[1] Another point is—will you be illustrating your article? My Editor always likes illustrations whenever possible, so if this is practicable and agreeable to you will you let me know what you would like, and I would set about procuring them.

Finally, we have not yet discussed a fee for your article. Would ten guineas be a satisfactory one?

Yours sincerely,

    J. R. Ackerley

> 46, Gordon Square, Bloomsbury
> June 14th, 1936

Dear Ackerley,

I will let you have the article in good time. Would you tell me the approximate number of words required? As regards illustrations, I am not very good at finding them, but possibly your pictorial department could supply some when they see the article. Will the question of illustration affect the number of words you will want?

The question of fee raises rather a delicate question and also a matter of principle. My practice has been to make a distinction between papers which are not run for profit, where I accept whatever I am offered down to nothing, and papers which are run for profit. In the case of the latter, my practice for many years past has been to vary the rate, according to circumstances from a minimum of 6d a word up to 1/- a word, and occasionally higher. As it happens, by the same post that I am writing this I am refusing a request to write a series of articles for £100 a week which does work out at 8d a word, and I have little doubt that, if I were to bargain, I could obtain a higher figure.

Now, I imagine that *The Listener* is run for profit. If not, it would make a great difference. Assuming it is run for profit, I think your rate should approach my normal minimum figure, that is to say, it should approximate to 6d a word, though I should raise no objection if you were to round the resulting figure off a bit in your own favour.

Yours sincerely,

    J. M. Keynes

> *The Listener*, Broadcasting House, W.1
> 16 June, 36

Dear Keynes,

Thank you so much for your letter. I perfectly understand your principle and practice in the matter of fees, but the position with regard

---

[1] See page 32, note 1.

to *The Listener* is that, contrary to your impression, it is not a profit making journal. In January, 1929, when it first appeared, the B.B.C. entered into a contract with the Publishers' Committee respecting the publishing and press interests of the whole country—the principal item of the contract being that *The Listener* was never to make a profit, and that if at any time its revenue exceeded its expenditure, it was to carry less advertisements, etc. You will see, therefore, that *The Listener* does not contribute to the Corporation's revenue from publications, and is not to be numbered among profit-making journals. In the light of this, therefore, will you consider it possible to accept a lower fee for the article than the one mentioned in your letter?

The number of words required for this article should not exceed 2000, which is assuming that we should be able to give it about 3 inset illustrations. If it were not to be illustrated, the article could, of course, be a little longer.

Yours sincerely,

J. R. Ackerley

46, Gordon Square, Bloomsbury
June 18th, 1936

Dear Ackerley,

I am greatly interested in what you tell me in your letter of June 16th. But the peculiar result is that I shall apparently benefit no-one whomsoever by accepting less than my usual fee. I shall not benefit *The Listener* or the B.B.C. or the public, but merely defeat some would-be advertiser of his desire to advertise. I am afraid this can hardly be considered on all fours with assisting a publication which has no great financial resources. I am extremely amused that this should be the result of a contract with the Publishers' Committee. For, obviously, it enormously increases your power to compete, since you are free to devote to the improvement and attractiveness of the paper sums which would almost certainly be diverted into the coffers of the B.B.C., if the contract had not been made. What the Publishers' Committee ought to have stipulated for, if they wished to avoid competition, is that *The Listener* should never make a profit of less than x per cent of its published price!

Having said the above, and having pointed out that a lower fee will benefit neither you, nor me, nor Sir John, nor the listener-in, nor the tax-payer, nor anyone else, I will leave myself in your hands with the suggestion that a fee of 25 guineas might be a proper compromise. I can honestly say that I am not in the least concerned from the financial point of view, and have given up writing as a means of income. But as a member, so to speak, of the Trade Union of writers, and by general habit of mind, I cannot bring myself altogether to neglect the point of principle.

Yours sincerely,

J. M. Keynes

Ackerley wrote in the margin: 'Editor—We shall have to accept this.' But on second thoughts he decided not to be so easily 'out-argued' and wrote the following letter:

The Listener, Broadcasting House, W.1

19 June, 36

Dear Keynes,

I am so highly diverted by your letter and this correspondence that I cannot forgo the pleasure of continuing it to enquire whether I am to understand that because the B.B.C. is under an obligation not to make a profit out of *The Listener* it ought therefore to be content to make a loss? The object of the B.B.C. in conducting *The Listener* is to run it as a non-profit-making service, neither involving a financial liability in the shape of a loss, which presumably must come out of the licence-holder's pocket, nor a profit. This being so, it follows that by accepting less than your usual fee you would, in fact, be benefiting the listening public, because you would bring the accounts of *The Listener* nearer to that state of exact balance between profit and loss which will free *The Listener* from dependence upon the licence-holder. On the other hand, if your argument were sound that you would apparently benefit no-one whomsoever by accepting less than your usual fee, this principle would be satisfactory if applied generally to all non-profitmaking undertakings. It would then follow that if you were writing for a charity or a public service of any kind, there would be no point in charging less than the standard fee. In fact, however, doctors and other professional people do make a considerable difference between the fees which they charge when they are working for a non-profitmaking concern, and those which they charge when they are working for an ordinary profit-making commercial undertaking. Nor would your action defeat some would-be advertiser of his desire to advertise, since it is reasonable to suppose that he would spend the same money in advertising in some other organ, which would actually be a benefit to our competitors. So may I reduce your suggestion to 20 guineas?

Yours sincerely,

J. R. Ackerley

46, Gordon Square, Bloomsbury

June 23rd, 1936

My dear Ackerley,

My letter was based on the assumption that you are already restricting your advertising revenue below its maximum. I was also assuming that the amount spent by advertisers on weekly papers is not a fixed amount, but depends on their view as to the value they are getting.

My argument only applies, of course, to a non-profit-making undertaking which is deliberately raking in smaller receipts than it could get. I know no other example of such a state of affairs except your peculiar organ.

Yours sincerely,

J. M. Keynes

Keynes sent his article in in good time—and it appeared on 26 August. Unfortunately the BBC records, which would have shown the fee that he was paid, were destroyed during an air raid on London early in the war.

Appendix C
HISTORY OF A POEM

Here is the version of Ackerley's poem which he submitted for the 1942 Christmas issue of *The Listener*, and that the Editor turned down because 'it was too personal'.

December

We never knew what became of him, that was so curious;
He embarked, it was in December, and never returned;
No chance to say Goodbye, and Christmas confronting us;
A few letters arrived, long after, and came to an end.

The weeks lagged into months, and then it was December;
We troubled the officials, of course; they were willing, no doubt,
But dreadfully busy, enquiries and names without number;
Some told us one thing, some another; they never found out.

There's a lot go like that, I suppose, without explanation;
And death is death, after all, small comfort to know how and when;
But I keep thinking, now that we've dropped the investigation,
It was more like the death of an insect than of a man.

This beetle, for instance: I lower my foot now and crush it,
And who's to connect me, correct me? Who is to know?
I do not ask whether the other beetles will miss it,
Or God will say 'Where is my beetle? Where did it go?'

The life and the tiny delight, the sublime inspiration
Of colour, mechanics and form, I care nothing for that;
I am man with his mind, the master, the lord of creation;
This beetle obstructs me, offends me; I lower my foot.

And that was the way that he went. Yes, I see the rejoinder;
He was bound with us, armed with us—man in his anger and pride.
What use then to speak of his kindness, the gentle remainder?
But he was my friend, and that was the way he died.

Ackerley next submitted the poem to the *Spectator*, where it was accepted by W. J. Turner, the literary editor, and published under the title of 'December (To F. H.)' on 25 December. Ackerley revised Verse 2:

The weeks dragged into months, and then it was December.
We troubled the officials, of course, and they cabled about;
They were patient but busy, importunities without number;
Some told us one thing, some another; they never found out.

    The only other alterations, apart from some minor changes in punctuation, were 'the sublime fabrication' for 'the sublime inspiration', in Verse 5, line 1; 'man in his violence and pride' for 'man in his anger and pride', in Verse 6, line 2; and 'now' for 'then' in Verse 6, line 3. But Ackerley was never quite happy with this printed version and felt it needed 'perfecting'. On 31 July 1958 he wrote to Richard Murphy: 'In moments of solitude [during a holiday in Herefordshire], I tried to refurbish a poem I published years ago in *The Spectator*. I was never satisfied with it, though I thought I had something to say. I've tried to improve it, and set it out below . . . It has no title yet . . .' Here is that version:

We never knew what became of him, that was so curious;
He embarked, it was late in November, and never returned;
No time for farewells, and the journey so far and precarious;
A few letters reached us long after and came to an end.

The weeks lingered on into months and again to November;
We bothered the officials, of course, and they cabled about;
They were patient and busy, importunities without number;
Some told us one thing, some another; they never found out.

There's a lot go like that, I suppose, without explanation,
And death is death, after all, small comfort to know where and when;
Yet I keep thinking, now that we've dropped the investigation,
It was more like the death of an insect than of a man.

This beetle, for instance; I lower my foot now to crush it,
And who's to accuse me, connect me? Who is to know?
I do not ask whether the other beetles will miss it,
Or God will say 'Where is my beetle? Where did it go?'

The life and the tiny delight, the sublime fabrication
Of colour, mechanics and form, I care nothing for that,
I am Man with his mind, the master, the lord of creation,
This beetle has got in my way, I lower my foot.

And that was the way that he went. Yes, I see the rejoinder,
He was bound with us, armed with us, merged in the violence and pride
Of Man in his madness, of Man the eternal contender:
But he was my friend, and that was the way that he died.

    Among Ackerley's papers two other versions were found. One entitled 'November (to F.H.)' which, judging by the faded ink and yellowing paper, would seem to pre-date the version that he sent his Editor in 1942 and may be the version that he refers to as being 'a year old' (See Letter 68). Throughout, the month is given as November, not December, and there is no mention of 'Christmas confronting us'. The other version—probably the final version—was called 'Missing' and was included in the limited edition of 350 copies of *Micheldever & Other Poems* issued by Ian McKelvie in 1972. The punctuation is more emphatic—commas on several occasions give way to semi-colons; in Verses 4 and 5, 'foot' becomes 'boot'; and the penultimate line has been changed from:

Of Man in his madness, of Man the eternal contender

to:

Of man in his militant madness, of man the contender . . .

Appendix D
A MISSING PAGE FROM *HINDOO HOLIDAY*

The passage below should be inserted on page 251 of the 1952 revised edition of *Hindoo Holiday*, beginning after the exchange:

'How would he show his shame?'
'He would turn away his face.'

Moreover, if this passage is compared with the printed text, it will be seen that although most of it is new, some of the exchanges in the dialogue remain the same as before but are presented in a different order. See Letters 4, 110 and 158.

Swish went the water against the screen, swish . . .
'I tell you secret thing, you not speak to any man?' Narayan said. I nodded.
'Sharma the father of little Raja and the girl baby.'
'You mean he has lain down with the Queen?'
'Many times. Sharma and his brother.'
'How do you know? Sharma is a great story-teller.'
'Every man know, but no man say. They have much fear. If you say any man "Is it true?" he say you "I do not know". But you are my friend, so I must speak you all things in my heart.'
'Does His Highness know?'
'Yes, Maharajah Sahib make him do this work. He take Sharma to Garha Palace and say him "Love her. I wish to see".'
'Why doesn't the Maharajah Sahib do it himself?'
'He not like. He like boys. He like Sharma.'
'Does the Queen like it?'
'She like Sharma. He young and strong and beautiful. But she not like Sharma's brother. He fat and ugly.'
'And Sharma. Does he like it?'
'I think yes. He is a fool boy.'
'Well then they all seem suited,' I said, pleased to know that the Queen's life was not quite so lonely and monotonous as Miss Trend had led me to believe. 'But how can you be sure that the children are Sharma's? May they not equally well be Sharma's brother's?'
'Sharma say me they his.'

'Ah, Sharma!' I said smiling. 'And he gives pleasure also to His Highness himself?'

'Yes, many times.'

'Does he like that?'

'No, he does not like.'

'Then why does he do it?'

'I do not know. He is half-made.'

'You don't approve either, do you?'

'No, I do not like. It is bad, wrong. But what can I do?'

I closed my eyes drowsily.

'*You* get much love Sharma one time,' said Narayan, after a pause, smiling at me.

'What did he tell you?' I asked.

'He tell me "The Sahib try to kiss me".'

'And what did you say?'

'I say he must kiss you if you want.'

Appendix E
'THE SUPREME REVIEWER'
Transcript of a tape-recording between
J. R. Ackerley and Frederick Laws
about E. M. Forster

The tape-recording was made on 29 March 1965. Parts of the transcript—those in italics—were incorporated in the obituary programme on E. M. Forster, which was broadcast in the Third Programme on 29 June 1970. The producer was Robert Pocock, and the programme was compiled and narrated by Frederick Laws. Others who took part in it were (in order of speaking): William Plomer, Leonard Woolf, Sir Dennis Proctor, W. J. H. Sprott, Patrick Wilkinson and Benjamin Britten. See Letters 269 and 334.

ACKERLEY: *Morgan Forster was the greatest journalistic 'catch' during my twenty-five years as literary editor of* The Listener, *and became increasingly so during that period.* If you could 'land' him for an article, or a book review, you landed the 'whale' and were the envy of every other literary editor in London. *The Listener* was fortunate . . . fortunate enough to get a double lot of him, for we got his broadcasts to publish—he was a good broadcaster—and he also contributed to my independent literary side of the paper. Those two books of his, *Abinger Harvest* and *Two Cheers for Democracy*, collect the best of his journalism. They are excellent bedside books. Morgan did a lot for me during my literary-editorship. He always helped his friends—and I was one of his oldest. Also he had a certain, if intermittent respect for the paper. Sometimes he'd say to me 'How dreadfully dull your paper's getting.' This often occurred when Sir Stephen Tallents was crouching over it with his busy 'blue pencil' in the war years and afterwards. And I was then in a good position to say to Morgan 'In that case why not write something for me to cheer the paper up?'

He even wrote unsigned reviews—at the time when the Book Chronicle was unsigned, that is to say before the advent of the present Editor—Maurice Ashley. *Now, that was something! Our greatest living English novelist doing unsigned reviews. Moreover he disapproved of anonymity—as readers of his essay[1] on that subject will know.* He thought that information should always be

---

[1] *Anonymity: An Inquiry* by E. M. Forster appeared as No. 12 in the Hogarth Essays, edited by Leonard and Virginia Woolf (1925). Subsequently the author included it in *Two Cheers for Democracy* (1951).

signed, but that creative literature didn't want to be signed. And reviewing, of course, is information. It tells you—or ought to—what a book is about and what it is worth. I believe I am right in saying that *he thought anonymous reviewing 'sheer funk'*. A way of 'taking the mickey' out of someone without risking the loss of a friend, or the addition of an enemy. Incidentally, these anonymous pieces of his aren't lost. A painstaking and exhaustive bibliography of his writings has been compiled[1] ... Yes, he was very good to me. He always did for *The Listener* whatever I asked him to do, if he was interested. 'Send the book along' he'd say and 'I'll see if I like it.' Even when he could have got better paid elsewhere. For there was a time—a rather early time in my stewardship when *The Listener* seemed to think that contributors ought to feel privileged to be asked to write for it, and that only tiresome, ill-mannered people noticed how puny the fee was. Morgan was very good at standing up for his pocket, which is unfortunately a rather un-English characteristic.

LAWS: Was there any special category of book which you used to send him?

ACKERLEY: Well you know, *he had his particular likes and dislikes. He got awfully bored repeating himself. I mean if you wanted him to go on writing about Virginia Woolf—or D. H. and T. E. Lawrence—or something like that, he would be bored.[2] But certain things attracted him. You could always get him on Voltaire for instance, and on civil liberties* he would usually come in. *You had to know what he was interested in at the moment, and then he would say 'Yes'. But mostly he said 'Send the things along and if I like them I'll do them.'*

---

[1] By B. J. Kirkpatrick. See Letter 324.

[2] On 4 October 1940, in answer to a request from A. to review *Two Generations [of Sitwells]*, edited by Osbert Sitwell, Virginia Woolf wrote: '. . . the Sitwells, as a family, bore me.' But she did review the book, which concerns Georgiana Sitwell who was born in 1824 and Florence Sitwell who was born in 1858, and her notice appeared in *The Listener* on 31 October 1940. It was the last review but one that she was to write. Talking of reviewers in general, A. once said to Braybrooke: 'I have been lucky with my team—in particular with Morgan and Virginia Woolf. What they said really did matter. You could feel their impact.'

Appendix F
RESTORING THE TEXT OF A NOVEL

Ackerley hoped that at some future date 'a final revised edition' of *We Think the World of You* (1960) would appear. With this in mind, he therefore specially annotated a copy of the first edition of his novel for Colin Haycraft. His corrections, deletions and substitutions are given below. See Letter 218.

Page 11, line 6.   Close inverted commas after 'I got' and add—*I kissed him.* Then open inverted commas again

Page 32, line 5.   *forecast* not 'forecasts' [1]

Page 32, line 21.   Full-stop not comma after 'reprovingly'. Capital N for *Nothing* (These corrections already made by The Bodley Head in the second impression of 1962.)

Page 47, line 27.   Insert *on the lead* after 'every day'

Page 74, line 20.   Insert comma after Barnes Common, and delete 'and'

Page 74, line 21.   Comma not full-stop after 'on the move', and add the phrase—*and to have me entirely to herself.*

Page 75, line 33.   Comma not full-stop after 'of course'

Page 78, line 12.   Substitute after 'on my bed'—*It was a double bed, bought to contain Johnny as well as myself, and sometimes she would curl up at my feet, but mostly against the pillow, laying down her head where his head used to lie. She was quite odourless* . . . Remainder of page stays as before

Page 86, line 24.   Delete dots after 'Of me' (This correction already made by The Bodley Head in the second impression.)

Page 96, line 5.   Delete rest of paragraph after 'any clothes on?' and substitute—*The very sight of her bare legs chilled me.* [2]

Page 99, line 9.   Paragraph to begin—*This remark, as coming from her, stunned me* . . . Remainder as before.

Page 102, line 3.   Substitute after 'silently'—*with that wide-eyed, baffling look she had doubtless learnt to bestow upon detectives and other unwelcome callers.* Remainder of paragraph as before.

[1] See page 169, notes 1 and 2.   [2] See page 171, note 4.

Page 134, line 8. Delete from after 'anything' to end of paragraph end-ing ' "You and you" ' Substitute—*that could help to bind him to me. Happiness had to be paid for. But the four hours—I managed to extend them to four—that he spent with me were so delightful, making up as they did, it seemed to me, for all the frustrations and sorrows of the past and whatever frustrations and sorrows were to come, that he could have had the very shirt off my back, which, indeed, soon joined his upon the floor. It was now, as the rest of our garments followed, that Evie began to exhibit an increasing perturbation as though whatever was happening before her eyes was having, upon the confidence she had hitherto shown in the distinctness of our identities, a confusing effect. Uttering little quavering cries of doubt and concern, she sat first upon our mingled clothes, gazing at us with a wild surmise, then upon our mingled bodies, excitedly licking our faces as though she would solve her perplexing problem either by cementing them together with her saliva or by forcing them apart. She lay with us throughout the afternoon, her fur against our flesh, and we talked of her most of the time.*

Page 135, line 20. Substitute *clothes* for his 'coat'

Page 141, line 23. After 'him enough,' substitute *as though she, too, knew how delicious was the taste of his flesh* . . .

Page 141, line 32. Correct 'here' to *her*, and substitute after 'He knew—*it was what he was good at, the conferring of physical pleasure—exactly where and how to touch her* . . .[1]

---

[1] See page 168, note 4.

INDEX OF RECIPIENTS

[References are to Letters. An asterisk above a number indicates a postcard.]

Index of Recipients

INDEX OF WRITINGS BY J.R.A.

[References are to pages. Where a reference occurs *only* in the footnote, the page number is followed by an n]

GENERAL INDEX

[References are to pages. Where a reference occurs *only* in the footnote, the page number is followed by an n]